Edexcel

GCSE Mathematics

higher

book 2

Keith Pledger

Gareth Cole

Peter Jolly

Graham Newman

Joe Petran

Sue Bright

www.heinemann.co.uk

✓ Free online support
✓ Useful weblinks
✓ 24 hour online ordering

01865 888058

Heinemann Educational Publishers
Halley Court, Jordan Hill, Oxford OX2 8EJ
Part of Harcourt Education Limited

Heinemann is the registered trademark of
Harcourt Education Limited

First published 2006

10 09 08 07 06
10 9 8 7 6 5 4 3 2 1

British Library Cataloguing in Publication Data is available from the British Library on request.

10-digit ISBN: 0 435 53366 5
13-digit ISBN: 978 0 435533 66 3

Typeset by Tech-Set Ltd, Gateshead, Tyne and Wear
Original illustrations © Harcourt Education Limited, 2006
Illustrated by Adrian Barclay and Mark Ruffle
Cover design by mccdesign
Printed by CPI Bath Press
Cover photo: Digital Vision ©

Acknowledgements
Harcourt Education Ltd would like to thank those schools who helped in the development and trialling of this course.

This high quality material is endorsed by Edexcel and has been through a rigorous quality assurance programme to ensure that it is a suitable companion to the specification for both learners and teachers. This does not mean that its contents will be used verbatim when setting examinations nor is it to be read as being the official specification – a copy of which is available at www.edexcel.org.uk

The publisher's and authors' thanks are due to Edexcel Limited for permission to reproduce questions from past examination papers. These are marked with an [E]. The answers have been provided by the authors and are not the responsibility of Edexcel Limited.

The authors and publisher would like to thank the following individuals and organisations for permission to reproduce photographs:

Corbis pp**320**, **343**, **385**, **458**; Alamy Images p**464**; Empics pp**380**, **440**; Science Photo Library p**340**; iStockPhoto.com / Gisele Wright p**291**; Photos.com pp**338**, **371**, **376**, **388**; Alamy Images / Elmtree Images p**337**; Action+ Images p**346**; Brand X Photos p**403**; Lonely Planet Images p**429**

Every effort has been made to contact copyright holders of material reproduced in this book. Any omissions will be rectified in subsequent printings if notice is given to the publishers.

Publishing team

Editorial	James Orr, Lindsey Besley, Evan Curnow, Katherine Pate, Nick Sample, Alex Sharpe, Laurice Suess, Elizabeth Bowden, Ian Crane
Design	Phil Leafe
Production	Siobhan Snowden
Picture research	Chrissie Martin

Websites
There are links to relevant websites in this book. In order to ensure that the links are up-to-date, that the links work, and that the sites aren't inadvertently linked to sites that could be considered offensive, we have made the links available on the Heinemann website at www.heinemann.co.uk/hotlinks. When you access the site, the express code is **4092P**.

Tel: 01865 888058 www.heinemann.co.uk

Quick reference to chapters

Introduction

Introduction

These revised and updated editions have been carefully matched to the new two-tier specification for GCSE Maths. Books 1 and 2 cover everything you need to know to achieve success in your exam, up to and including Grade A*. The author team is made up of Senior Examiners, a Chair of Examiners and Senior Moderators, all experienced teachers with an excellent understanding of the requirements of the Edexcel specification.

Key features

- **Chapters** are divided into **sections**, each with a simple explanation followed by clear examples or a worked exam question. These show you how to tackle questions. Each section also contains practice exercises to develop your understanding and help you consolidate your learning.
- **Key points** are highlighted throughout, like this:

  If $x \times x = A$, then x is the **square root** of A, written $\sqrt{A}$

  Each chapter ends with a summary of key points you need to remember.
- **Hint boxes** are used to make explanations clearer. They may also remind you of previously learned facts or tell you where in the book to find more information.

  Remember:
  $(x + 3)^2 = (x + 3)(x + 3)$
- **Mixed exercises** are designed to test your understanding across each chapter. They include past exam questions which are marked with an [E]. You will find a mixed exercise at the end of almost every chapter.
- **Examination practice papers** are included to help you prepare for the exam at the end of your course.
- **Answers** are provided at the back of the book to use as your teacher directs.

Quick reference and detailed Contents pages

- Use the thumb spots on the edge of the **Quick reference** page to help you turn to the right chapter quickly. Note that Book 1 contains Chapters 1–15 and Book 2 contains Chapter 16–29.
- Use the detailed **Contents** to help you find a section on a particular topic. The summary and reference codes on the right show your teacher the part(s) of the specification covered by each section in the book. (For example, NA 3h refers to Number and Algebra, section 3 Calculations, subsection h.)

Use of a calculator or a computer

These symbols show you where you must, or must not, use a calculator. Sometimes you may wish to use a spreadsheet package on a computer. There are also links to websites and suggested activities that require an internet search.

Coursework

A Coursework Guide is available online at www.zebramaths.co.uk

18.3	**Using ratios to find proportionality rules**	331–333	Finding the rule connecting quantities, using ratio	NA5h
18.4	**Writing proportionality formulae**	333–334	Connecting variables in direct proportion with a formula	NA3l/5h
18.5	**Square and cubic proportionality**	335–338	Extending to square and cubic relationships	NA3l/5h
18.6	**Inverse proportion**	339–342	Solving problems involving inverse proportion	NA3l/4a/5h
Summary of key points		344–345		

19 Quadratic equations

19.1	**Solving quadratic equations by factorising**	346–348	Rearranging and then factorising	NA5k
19.2	**Completing the square**	349	Completing the square for a quadratic expression	NA5k
19.3	**Solving quadratic equations by completing the square**	350	Using the method of completing the square	NA5k
19.4	**Solving quadratic equations by using a formula**	351–353	Using the quadratic formula to solve quadratic equations	NA5k
19.5	**Equations involving algebraic fractions**	354–355	Rearranging into quadratic equations and then solving	NA5b/k
19.6	**Problems leading to quadratic equations**	355–358	Setting up and solving quadratic equations	NA5k
19.7	**Solving linear and quadratic equations simultaneously**	358–360	Using algebraic methods and geometric interpretation	NA5l
19.8	**The intersection of a line and a circle**	361–362	Using algebraic methods and geometric interpretation; includes tangents to a circle	NA5l/6e/h
19.9	**Solving equations graphically**	363–366	Rearranging equations and solving graphically	NA6e/f
Summary of key points		368		

20 Presenting and analysing data 2

20.1	**Upper class boundaries**	369–370	Upper boundaries for class intervals	SSM4a/HD2d
20.2	**Cumulative frequency**	370–372	Calculating cumulative frequencies	HD4a
20.3	**Cumulative frequency graphs**	372–373	Drawing cumulative frequency graphs	HD4a
20.4	**Using cumulative frequency graphs**	374–377	Estimating the median and quartiles	HD4a/e
20.5	**Using cumulative frequency graphs to solve problems**	377–379	Estimating percentages from cumulative frequency graphs	HD4e
20.6	**Box plots**	379–381	Drawing box plots	HD4a/e
20.7	**Comparing sets of data with box plots**	382–383	Comparing distributions	HD4a/4e/5d
20.8	**Plotting data in a histogram**	383–388	Understanding frequency density	HD4a/5d
20.9	**Interpreting histograms**	389–393	Interpreting histograms	HD5b/d
Summary of key points		398		

Contents

16 Basic trigonometry

16.1	Right-angled triangles and the trigonometric ratios	291–294	Opposite, adjacent, hypotenuse and the sin, cos and tan formulae	SSM2g
16.2	Using a calculator	294–295	Obtaining sin, cos and tan, and their inverses	NA3o
16.3	Using trigonometric ratios to find angles	295–296	With any two sides given	SSM2g
16.4	Using trigonometric ratios to find the lengths of sides	296–298	With one angle and any side	SSM2g
16.5	More about trigonometric functions	298–299	For angles greater than 90°	SSM2g
16.6	The graph of sin x	300	For 0°–360° and then extended	SSM2g
16.7	The graph of cos x	301	For 0°–360° and then extended	SSM2g
16.8	The graph of tan x	302–304	For 0°–90° and 90°–270°, and then extended	SSM2g
16.9	Solving a trigonometric equation	304–306	Finding one solution algebraically and others from the symmetries of the graph	SSM2g
Summary of key points		308–309		

17 Graphs and equations

17.1	Graphs of quadratic functions	310–311	Drawing graphs of quadratic functions	NA6e
17.2	Graphs of cubic functions	311–312	Drawing graphs of cubic functions	NA6f
17.3	Graphs of reciprocal functions	312–314	Drawing graphs of reciprocal functions	NA6f
17.4	Graphs of the form $y = ax^3 + bx^2 + cx + d + \frac{e}{x}$	314–315	Drawing graphs of cubic functions with up to three terms	NA6f
17.5	Using graphs to solve equations	315–316	Finding solutions to a quadratic equation from its graph	NA6e/f
17.6	Trial and improvement methods for solving equations	317–318	Using trial and improvement to solve equations	NA5m
17.7	Solving problems by trial and improvement	318–319	Using trial and improvement to solve problems	NA5m
17.8	Graphs that describe real-life situations	320–325	Drawing and interpreting graphs, both accurate and sketched	NA6d
Summary of key points		327		

18 Proportion

18.1	Direct proportion	328	Direct proportion and the $\propto$ symbol	NA5h
18.2	Graphs that show direct proportion	329–331	Straight line graphs showing direct proportion	NA5h

21 Advanced trigonometry

21.1	The area of a triangle	399–401	Calculating area of a triangle using $A = \frac{1}{2}ab \sin C$	SSM2g
21.2	The sine rule	402–405	The sine rule	SSM2g
21.3	The cosine rule	405–407	The cosine rule	SSM2g
21.4	Trigonometry and Pythagoras' theorem in three dimensions	407–409	Finding lengths and angles in 3-D problems	SSM2g
	Summary of key points	411		

22 Advanced mensuration

22.1	Finding the length of an arc of a circle	412–414	Calculating arcs given the angle and vice versa	SSM4d
22.2	Finding the area of a sector of a circle	414–415	Calculating areas of sectors	SSM4d
22.3	Finding the area of a segment of a circle	416–418	Calculating areas of segments	SSM2i
22.4	Finding volumes and surface areas	418–421	Volume and surface area of prisms, including cylinders	SSM2i
22.5	The volume of a pyramid	421–423	Volume of pyramids, including cones	SSM2i
22.6	The surface area and volume of a sphere	423–424	Surface area and volume of spheres	SSM2i
22.7	Areas and volumes of similar shapes	424–427	Using area and volume scale factors	SSM3d
22.8	Compound solids	427–429	Volume of combined shapes; includes truncated solids	SSM2i
	Summary of key points	431		

23 Exploring numbers 2

23.1	Terminating and recurring decimals	432–434	Converting fractions into decimals that terminate or recur	NA2d/3c
23.2	Finding a fraction equivalent to a recurring decimal	434–435	Converting recurring decimals to fractions	NA2d/3c
23.3	Surds	435–438	Manipulating expressions with surds	NA3n
23.4	Rounding	438	Rounding measurements	NA2a
23.5	Upper bounds and lower bounds	439–440	Finding bounds of numbers expressed to a given degree of accuracy	NA3q
23.6	Calculations involving upper and lower bounds – addition and multiplication	440–441	Calculating the bounds in problems involving addition or multiplication	NA3q
23.7	Calculations involving upper and lower bounds – subtraction and division	441–443	Calculating the bounds in problems involving subtraction or division	NA3q
	Summary of key points	444–445		

24 Probability

24.1	Finding probabilities	446–448	Calculating theoretical probabilities	HD4b
24.2	Mutually exclusive events	448–449	Calculating probabilities of mutually exclusive events	HD4d/g

24.3	**Lists and tables**	**449–452**	Listing outcomes systematically	HD4c
24.4	**Relative frequency**	**452–453**	Estimating probability using relative frequency	HD4b/5h/i
24.5	**Estimating from experience**	**453**	Estimating and justifying probabilities	HD4b
24.6	**Independent events**	**453–454**	Calculating probabilities of independent events	HD4g
24.7	**Probability trees**	**455–456**	Using probability trees to calculate probabilities	HD4g/h
Summary of key points		**459**		

25 Transformations of graphs

25.1	**Function notation**	**460–462**	Using f(x) notation	NA6a/e
25.2	**Applying vertical translations to graphs**	**463–466**	Using transformations of the form $y = f(x) + a$	NA6g
25.3	**Applying horizontal translations to graphs**	**467–470**	Using transformations of the form $y = f(x + a)$	NA6g
25.4	**Applying double translations to graphs**	**470–472**	Combining horizontal and vertical translations	NA6g
25.5	**Applying reflections to graphs**	**472–474**	Reflections in the x and y axes	NA6g
25.6	**Applying combined transformations**	**474–475**	Combining reflections and translations	NA6g
25.7	**Applying stretches to graphs**	**475–479**	Stretches parallel to the axes, $y = af(x)$ and $y = f(ax)$	NA6g
25.8	**Applying transformations to trigonometric functions**	**479–480**	Transformations applied to the sine and cosine functions	NA6g
Summary of key points		**483–484**		

26 Circle theorems

26.1	**Circle theorems**	**485–487**	Tangents from a point to a circle; angle between radius and tangent; perpendicular from centre to chord	SSM2h
26.2	**More circle theorems**	**487–492**	All the recognised circle theorems	SSM2h
26.3	**Proving circle and geometrical theorems**	**492–496**	Proofs of key circle theorems	SSM2h
Summary of key points		**500**		

27 Vectors

27.1	**Translations**	**501–503**	Using column vectors to describe translations	SSM3f
27.2	**Vectors**	**503–506**	Vector addition and subtraction by calculation and graphically	SSM3f
27.3	**Vector algebra**	**506–508**	Applying rules of algebra to vectors	SSM3f
27.4	**Finding the magnitude of a vector**	**508–509**	Using Pythagoras' theorem	SSM3f
27.5	**Linear combinations of vectors**	**509–511**	Combinations of vectors of the form $p\mathbf{a} + q\mathbf{b}$	SSM3f
27.6	**Position vectors**	**511–513**	Vectors related to the origin	SSM3f

27.7	Proving geometrical results	514–515	Using properties of parallel vectors	SSM3f
Summary of key points		518		

28 Introducing modelling

28.1	Modelling using exponential functions	519–521	Using the exponential function	NA3t/6f
28.2	Modelling using trigonometric functions	522–525	Using trigonometric functions	NA6f/SSM2g
28.3	Using a line of best fit to obtain a relationship	525–527	Using lines of best fit	NA6c/HD1g/4i
28.4	Reducing equations to linear form	527–531	Rewriting relationships in linear form and reading values from the graph	NA6c/e
28.5	Finding the constants in an exponential relationship	531–533	Matching a graph or coordinates to $y = pq^x$	NA6f
Summary of key points		533		

29 Conditional probability

29.1	Dependent and independent events	534–536	Extending ideas of probability	HD4g
29.2	Paths through tree diagrams	536–538	Calculating conditional probabilities	HD4h
29.3	Probability and human behaviour	538–540	Conditional probabilities	HD4h/5g
Summary of key points		541		

16 Basic trigonometry

This chapter introduces the trigonometric functions sine, cosine and tangent, often shortened to sin, cos and tan.

Trigonometry (or 'trig' for short) looks at how the sides and angles of a triangle are related to each other.

Trigonometry was first used in astronomy and navigation. How to tell the time from the position of the Sun was just one of the many practical problems that contributed to its development. Sundials work because shadows move and change length as the height of the Sun changes in the sky. But without trigonometry, sundials wouldn't have been possible.

Today, trigonometry is used by engineers, surveyors, architects and others who need to work out relationships connecting distances and angles. Trigonometry is always tested in GCSE exams.

16.1 Right-angled triangles and the trigonometric ratios

In any right-angled triangle you can name the sides in relation to the angles:

- side a is **opposite** to angle x
- side b is **adjacent** to angle x
- side c is the **hypotenuse** (opposite the right angle).

(hypotenuse) c

a (opposite)

x

b (adjacent)

Sin x

Consider a right-angled triangle OAM with hypotenuse 1 unit in length.

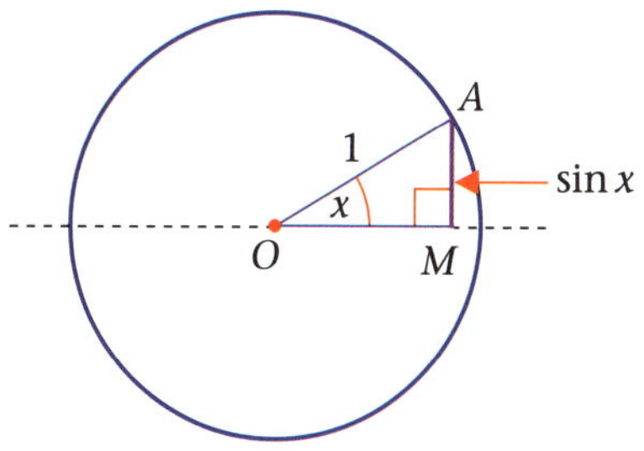

When you apply the function **sine** to the angle x in the triangle you get the length of the side opposite x, AM.

The vertical height of the triangle OAM is $\sin x$.

Using similar triangles, when the length of the hypotenuse is doubled, the vertical height is also doubled.

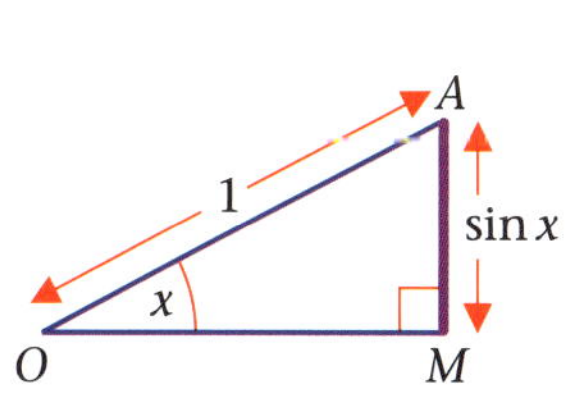

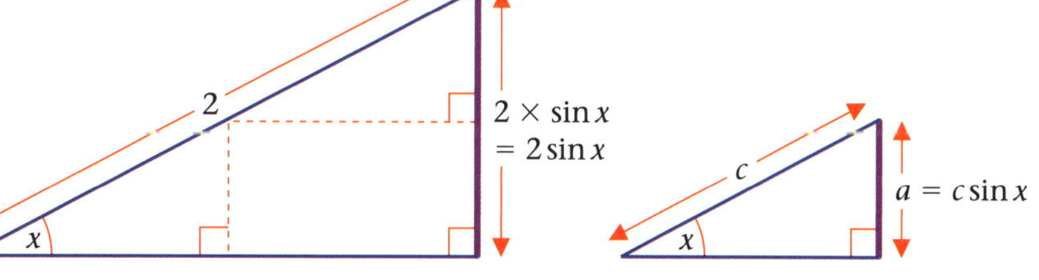

In the general case, when the length of the hypotenuse is c units and the vertical height is a units, then the length of a is given by

$$a = c \sin x$$

Making $\sin x$ the subject of the formula gives:

$$\sin x = \frac{a}{c}$$

$$\sin x = \frac{\text{length of side opposite } x}{\text{length of hypotenuse}} \quad \text{or} \quad \sin x = \frac{\text{opposite}}{\text{hypotenuse}}$$

$$\sin x = \frac{\text{opp}}{\text{hyp}}$$

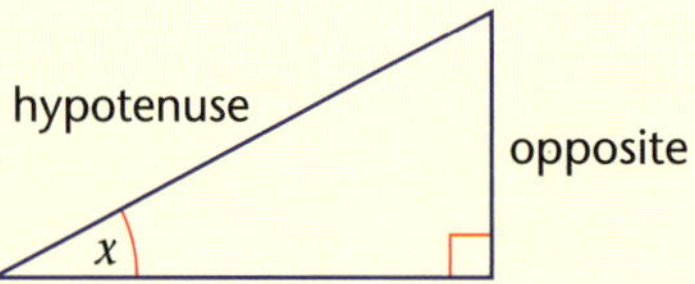

Cos x

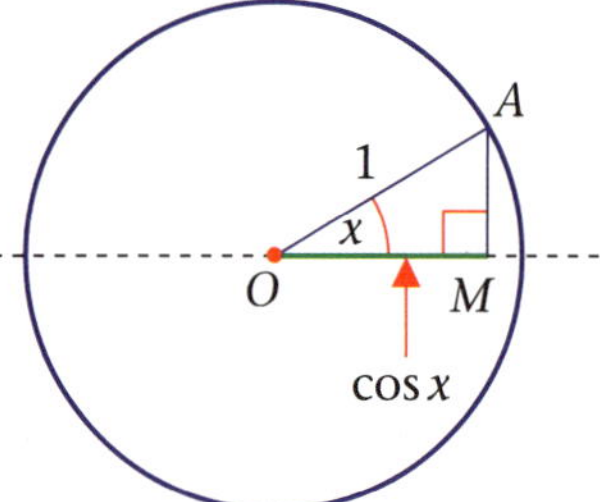

Consider again the triangle OAM

When you apply the function **cosine** to the angle x in the triangle you get the length of the side adjacent to x, OM.

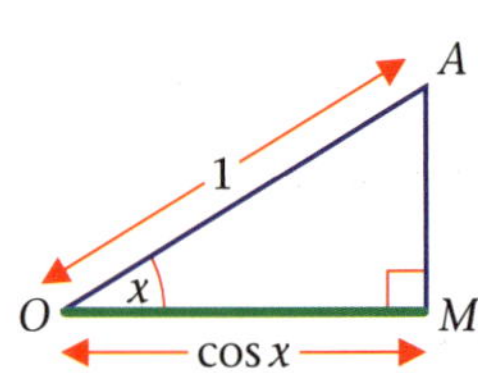

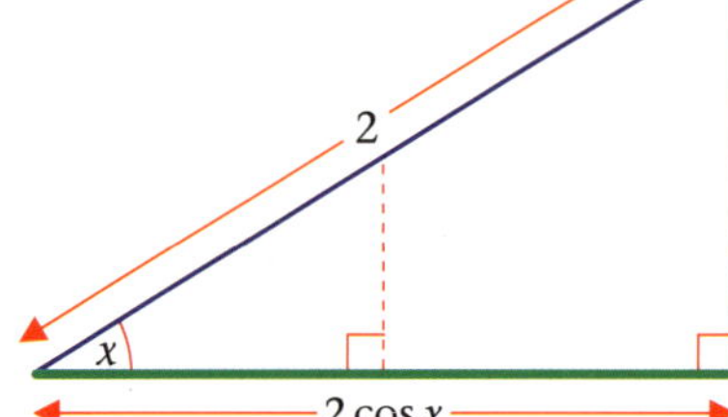

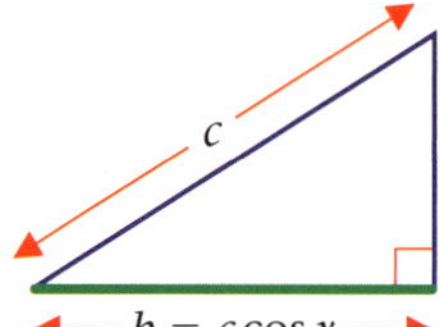

Making $\cos x$ the subject of the formula $b = c \cos x$ gives

$$\cos x = \frac{b}{c}$$

$$\cos x = \frac{\text{length of side adjacent to } x}{\text{length of hypotenuse}} \quad \text{or} \quad \cos x = \frac{\text{adjacent}}{\text{hypotenuse}}$$

$$\cos x = \frac{\text{adj}}{\text{hyp}}$$

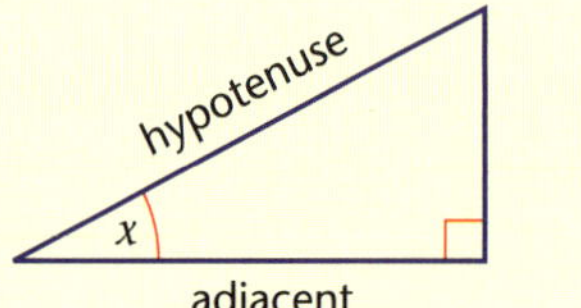

Tan x

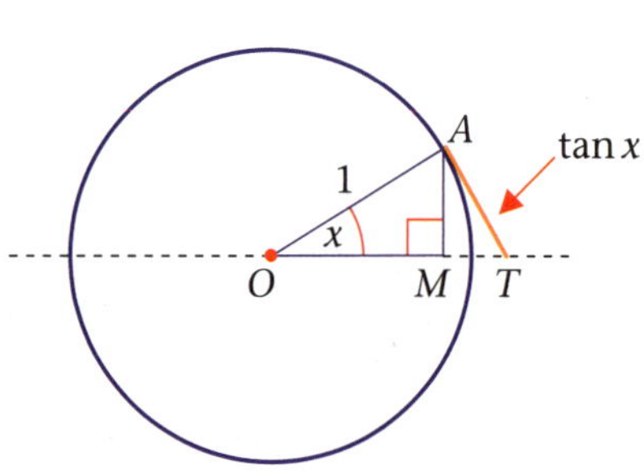

The tangent ratio is a little different.

When you apply the function **tangent** to the angle x in the triangle OAM you get the length of the tangent, AT.

Imagine the triangle OAT turned over, so OA is the base.

Consider this sequence of diagrams:

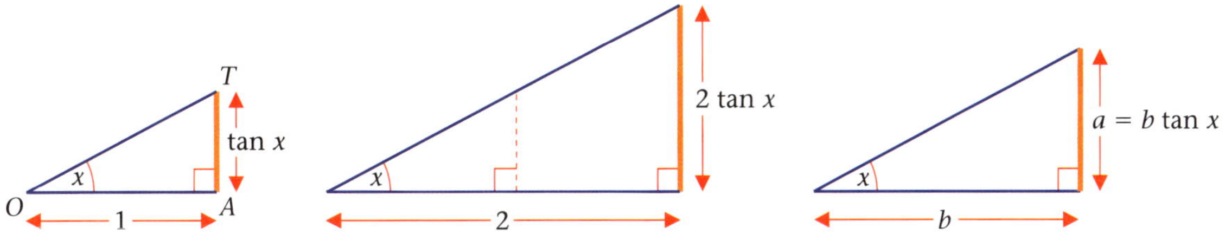

Making $\tan x$ the subject of the formula $a = b \tan x$ gives

$$\tan x = \frac{a}{b}$$

$$\tan x = \frac{\text{length of side opposite angle } x}{\text{length of side adjacent to angle } x} \quad \text{or} \quad \tan x = \frac{\text{opposite}}{\text{adjacent}}$$

$$\tan x = \frac{\text{opp}}{\text{adj}}$$

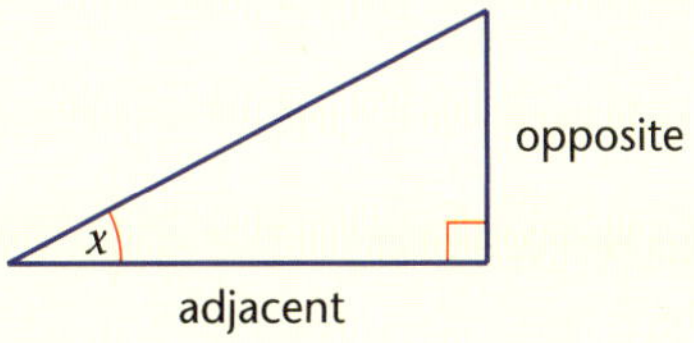

You need to understand how to use the three trigonometric ratios for your GCSE exam.

Example 1

Write down which trigonometric ratio is needed to calculate the angle θ in each of these triangles:

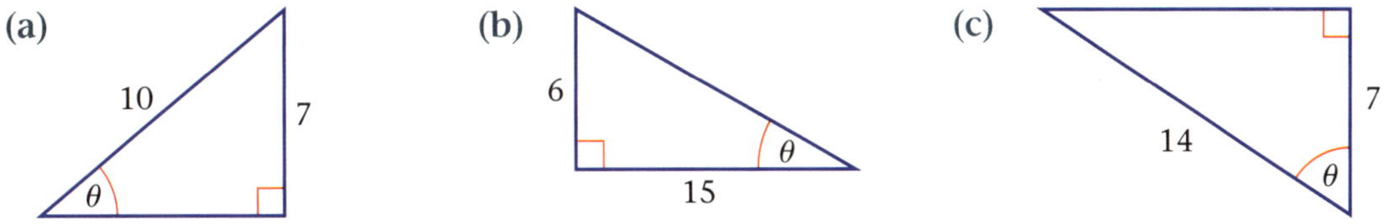

(a) The given sides are opposite to angle θ and hypotenuse so **sine** is needed.

(b) The given sides are opposite and adjacent to angle θ so **tangent** is needed.

(c) The given sides are adjacent to angle θ and hypotenuse so **cosine** is needed.

Example 2

Write down which trigonometric ratio is needed to calculate the side AB.

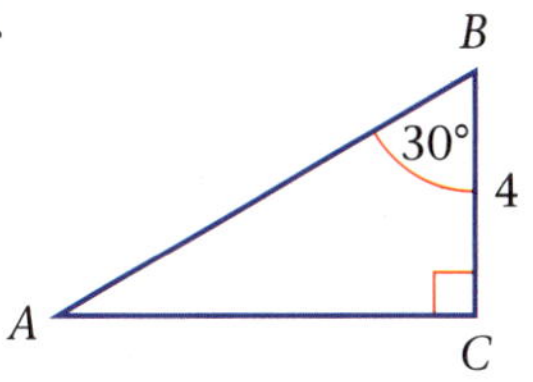

Side BC is adjacent to the given angle. Side AB is the hypotenuse.

$\cos \theta = \dfrac{\text{adj}}{\text{hyp}}$, so the ratio needed is **cosine**.

Exercise 16A

Write down which trigonometric ratio is needed to calculate the side or angle marked x in each of these triangles.

1 (a)

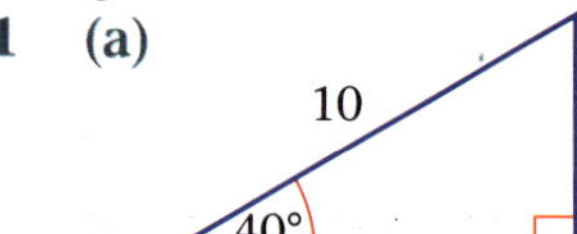

(b)

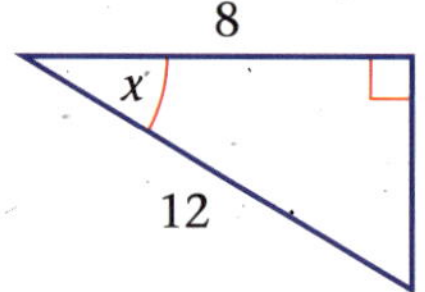

(c)

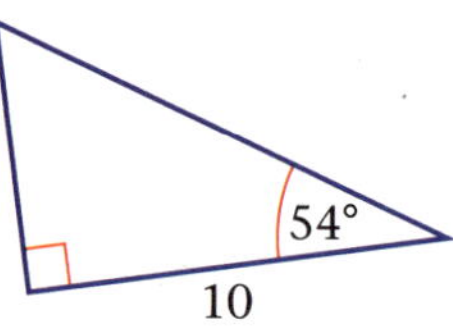

(d)

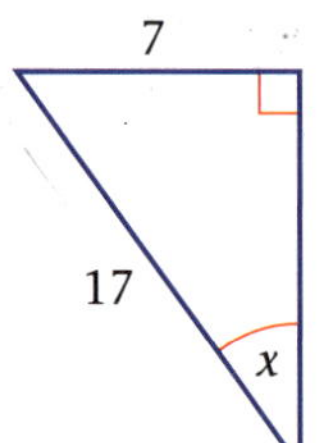

(e)

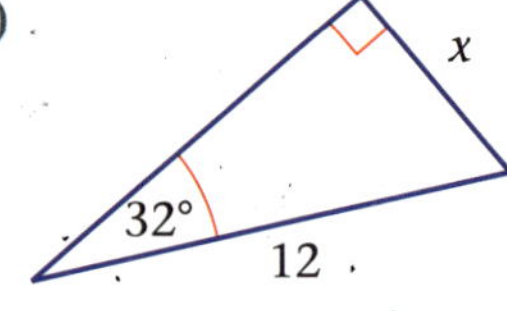

(f)

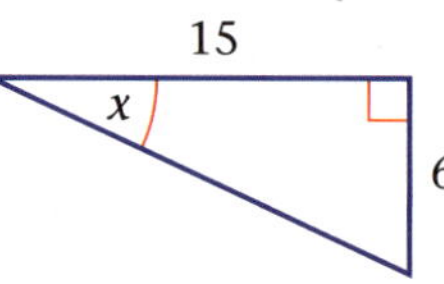

(g)

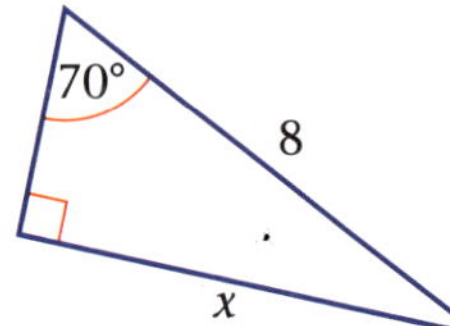

(h)

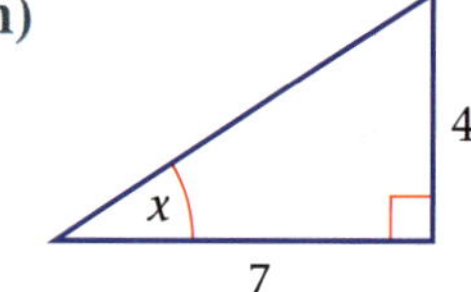

(i)

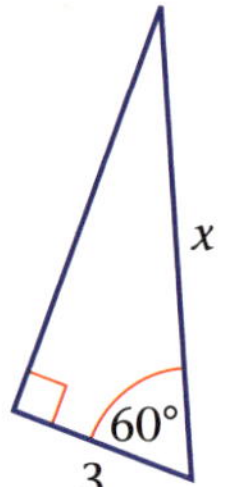

2 Shaun stands 25 m away from his house, which is built on flat ground. He uses a clinometer to measure the angle between the ground and the top of his house. The angle is 20°.

Estimate the height of Shaun's house.

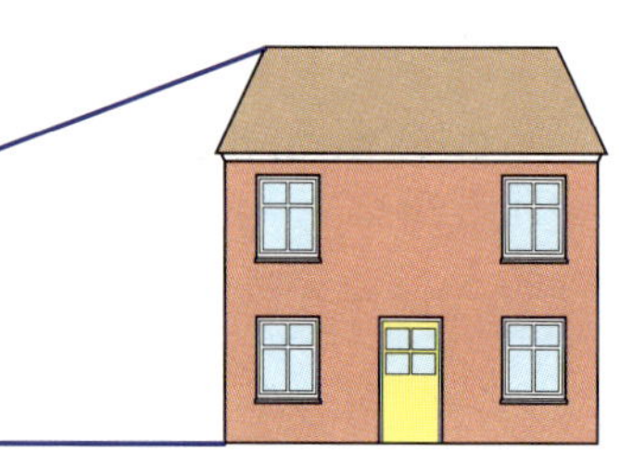

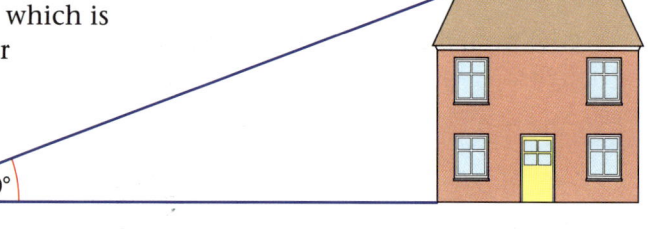

16.2 Using a calculator

You can use a calculator to find the values of sin x, cos x and tan x for different values of x.

Example 3

Find cos 43°.

The calculator display is 0.731 353 701

so cos 43° = 0.731 353 701

In most cases there is no need to give results to more than four decimal places,

so cos 43° = 0.7314

Check that you know how to use the trig functions on your calculator.

When given the value of any trigonometric function, you can use the inverse function to find the value of the angle.

The inverses of sin, cos and tan are $\sin^{-1}$, $\cos^{-1}$ and $\tan^{-1}$. If you are given $\sin x$, for example, use $\sin^{-1}(\sin x)$ to find x.

Example 4

Given that $\tan x = 1.2411$, find the value of x.

$x = \tan^{-1} 1.2411$

The calculator display is 51.140 326 82.
So, correct to two decimal places:

$x = 51.14°$

Your calculator may have INV, $\sin^{-1}$ or arc buttons for finding inverse trig functions.

Exercise 16B

1 Find these:

(a) $\sin 47°$ (b) $\cos 58°$

(c) $\tan 21°$ (d) $\tan 83°$

(e) $\cos 25°$ (f) $\sin 60°$

(g) $\tan 106°$ (h) $\cos 93°$

(i) $\sin 132°$

Give your answers correct to 4 d.p.

2 Find each angle x (correct to 0.1°) when

(a) $\sin x = 0.3524$ (b) $\cos x = 0.1364$

(c) $\tan x = 1.4142$ (d) $\tan x = 0.4365$

(e) $\cos x = 0.9854$ (f) $\sin x = 0.8856$

16.3 Using trigonometric ratios to find angles

Example 5

Calculate the size of the angle at A.

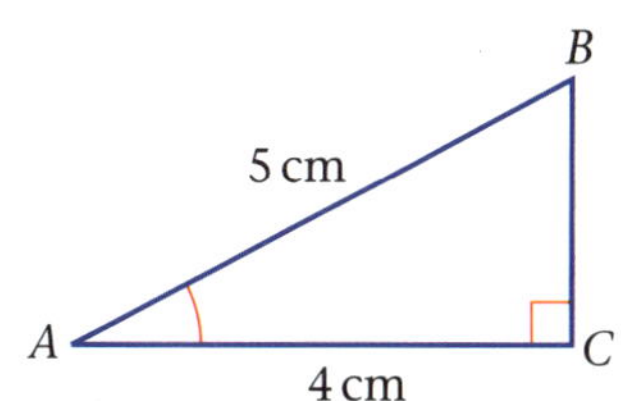

Since 4 is adjacent to A and 5 is the hypotenuse we use the cosine ratio:

$$\cos A = \frac{\text{adj}}{\text{hyp}} = \frac{4}{5} = 0.8$$

$A = \cos^{-1} 0.8$

So $A = 36.87°$ (correct to 2 d.p.)

Exercise 16C

In this exercise all of the lengths are in cm. Calculate each of the angles marked with a letter, correct to 0.1°.

1
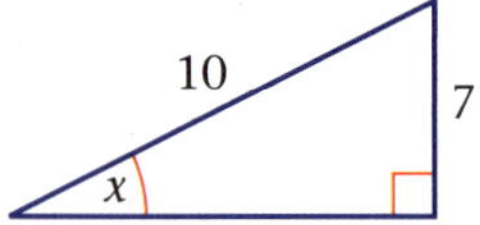

2
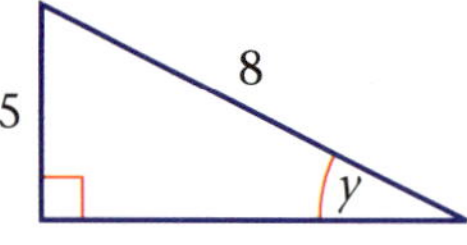

3
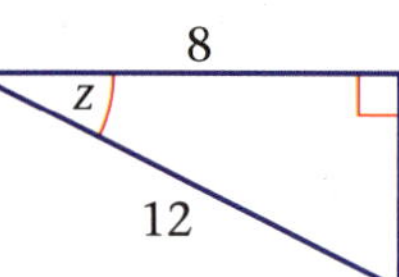

4
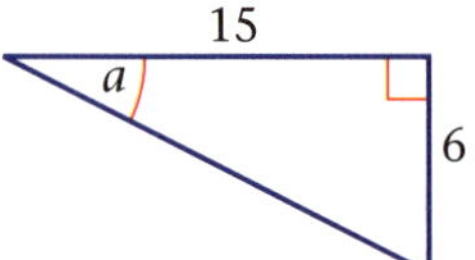

5
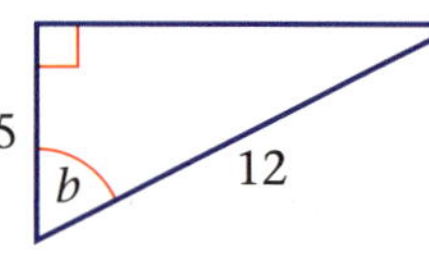

6
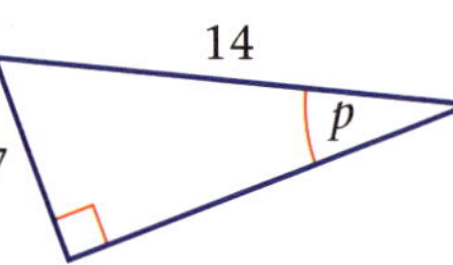

7
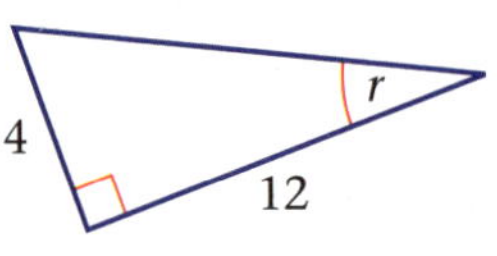

8
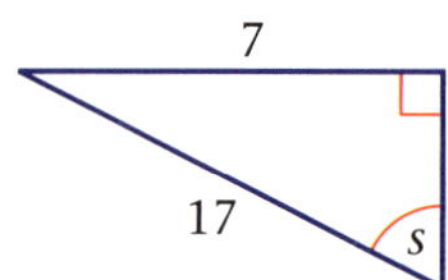

9
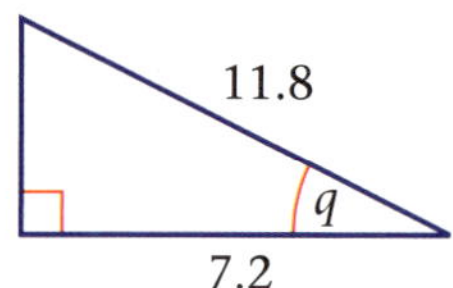

16.4 Using trigonometric ratios to find the lengths of sides

Example 6

Calculate the length of the side marked y.

For the given angle, y is opposite and 12 is adjacent.
So we use the tangent ratio:

$$\tan 72° = \frac{\text{opp}}{\text{adj}} = \frac{y}{12}$$

So $\quad y = 12 \times \tan 72°$
$\quad = 12 \times 3.0777$
$\quad = 36.93$ cm (correct to 2 d.p.)

Worked examination question 1

The distance from Alton, A, to Burton, B, is 10 km.
The bearing of B from A is 030°. A transmitter, T, is due North of A and due West of B.

(a) (i) Calculate the distance of T from B.
(ii) Calculate the distance of T from A.
Give your answer to the nearest kilometre.

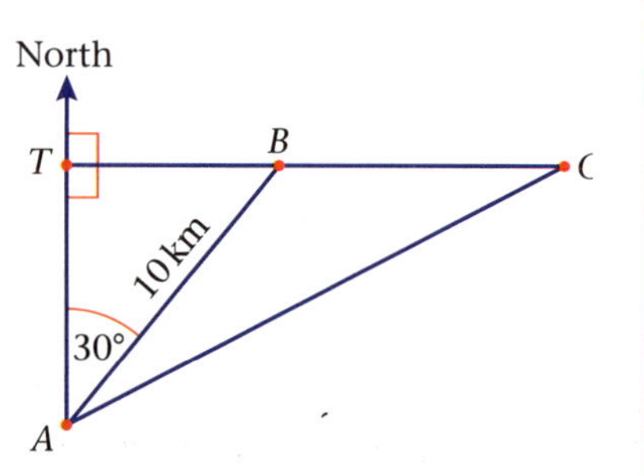

Clowne, C, is 8 km due east of Burton.

(b) Use your answers to **(a)** to calculate angle $T\hat{A}C$.
Hence give the three-figure bearing of C from A, correct to the nearest degree.

(c) A helicopter flies at the same height from A to B to C. If the average speed for the journey is 160 km/h, calculate the time taken. Give your answer correct to the nearest minute.

(a) **(i)** TB is opposite 30° and the AB is hypotenuse so we use the sine ratio:

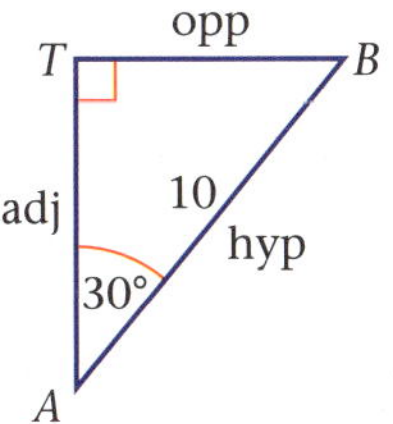

$$\frac{TB}{10} = \sin 30°$$

$$TB = 10 \times \sin 30°$$

So $TB = 5$ km

(ii) TA is adjacent to 30° and AB is the hypotenuse, so we use the cosine ratio:

$$\frac{TA}{10} = \cos 30°$$

$$TA = 10 \times \cos 30°$$

$$= 8.66 \text{ km}$$

So $TA = 9$ km, correct to the nearest km.

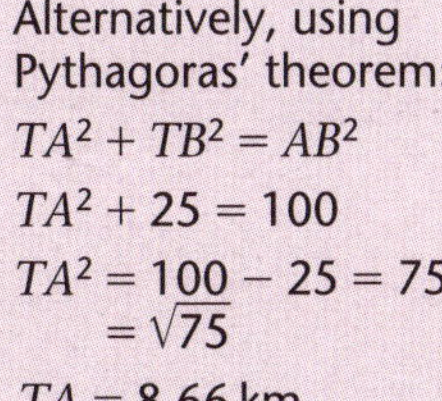

Alternatively, using Pythagoras' theorem:
$TA^2 + TB^2 = AB^2$
$TA^2 + 25 = 100$
$TA^2 = 100 - 25 = 75$
$= \sqrt{75}$
$TA = 8.66$ km

(b) Consider the diagram:

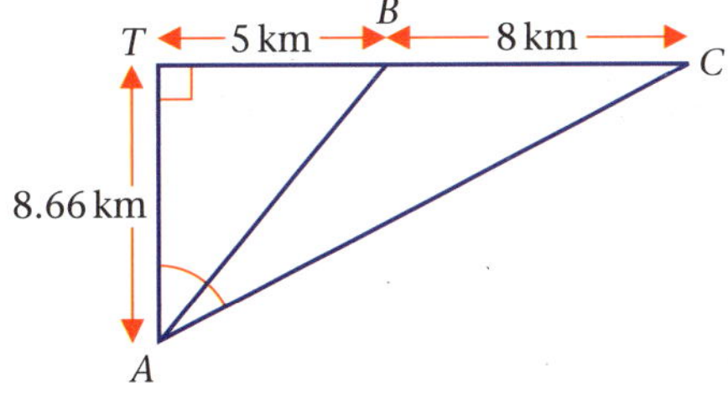

Then, for angle $T\hat{A}C$

$TC = 13 = \text{opp}$ and $TA = 8.66 = \text{adj}$

So use the tangent ratio:

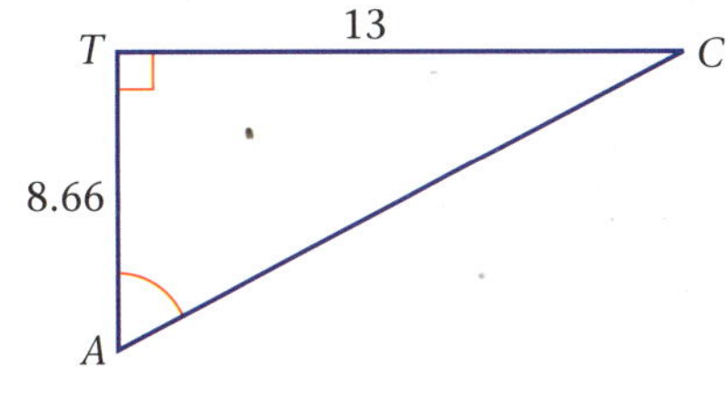

$$\tan T\hat{A}C = \frac{\text{opp}}{\text{adj}} = \frac{13}{8.66} = 1.501\,15$$

$$T\hat{A}C = \tan^{-1} 1.501\,15$$

$$= 56.33°$$

So, correct to the nearest degree, the bearing of C from A is 056°.

(c) The total distance from A to B to C is

$$10 + 8 = 18 \text{ km}$$

Distance = speed × time

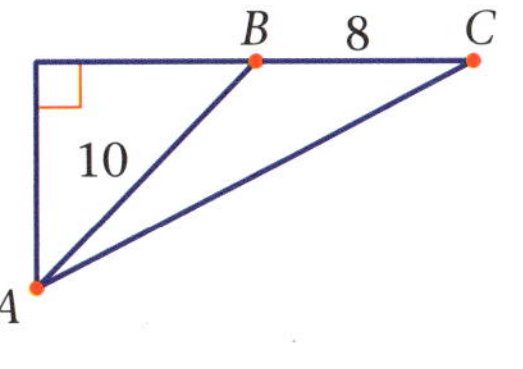

This is not trigonometry but is an example of how trigonometry can be combined with another topic in exam questions.

So $$\text{time} = \frac{\text{distance}}{\text{speed}}$$

$$= \frac{18}{160} = 0.1125 \text{ hours}$$

and 0.1125 hours = 0.1125 × 60 = 6.75 minutes

So time = 7 minutes, correct to the nearest minute.

Exercise 16D

1 All lengths are in centimetres. Calculate each length marked with a letter, correct to 2 d.p.

(a) 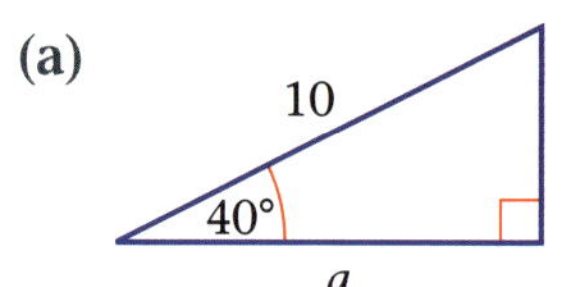

(b) 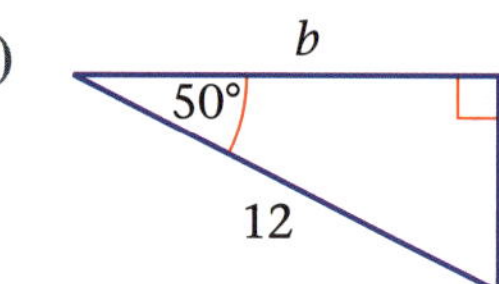

(c) 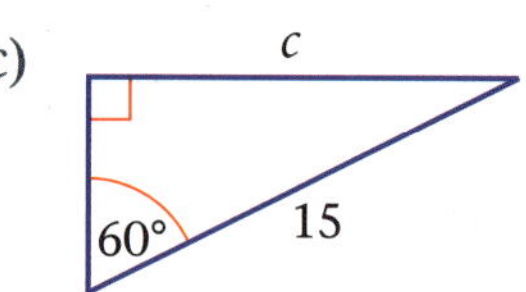

(d) 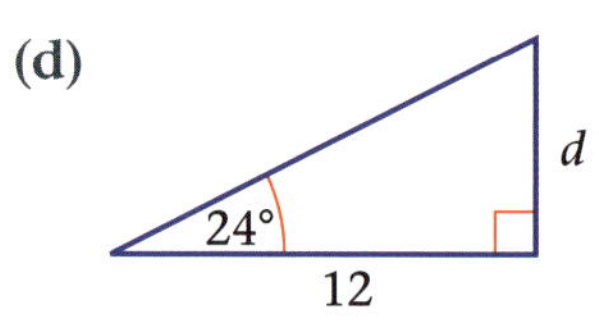

(e) 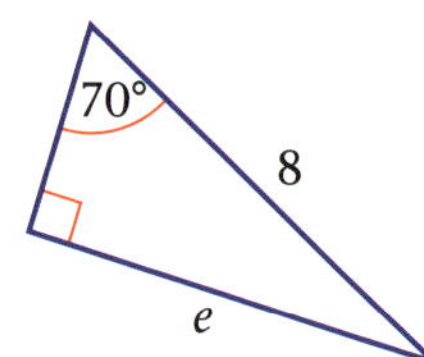

(f) 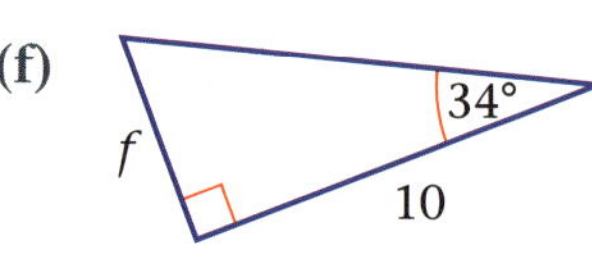

(g) 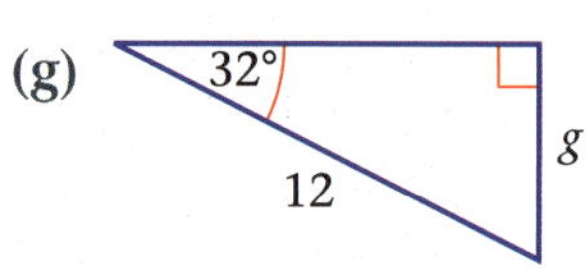

(h) 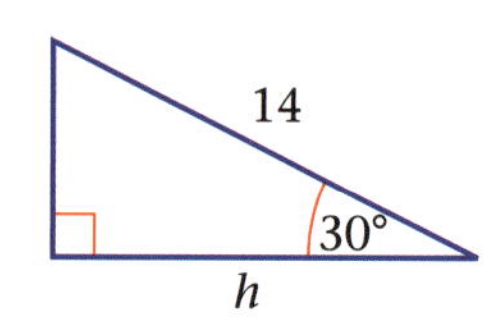

(i) 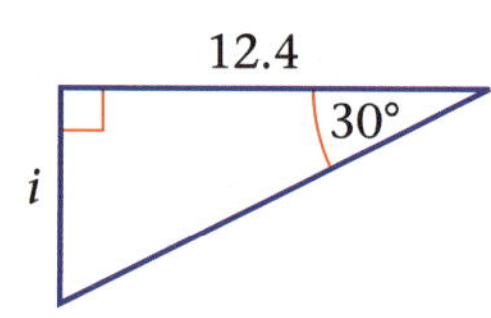

2 A lighthouse, L, is 34 km due North of a helicopter base, B.
A helicopter, H, is 21 km due West of L.
Calculate the bearing of H from B.

16.5 More about trigonometric functions

You have seen how useful the trig functions are for calculating lengths and angles in right-angled triangles. You have worked with angles between 0 and 90°, but you can apply sin, cos and tan to angles outside this range.

The three trig functions are shown on this unit circle, where $0 \leqslant x < 90°$.

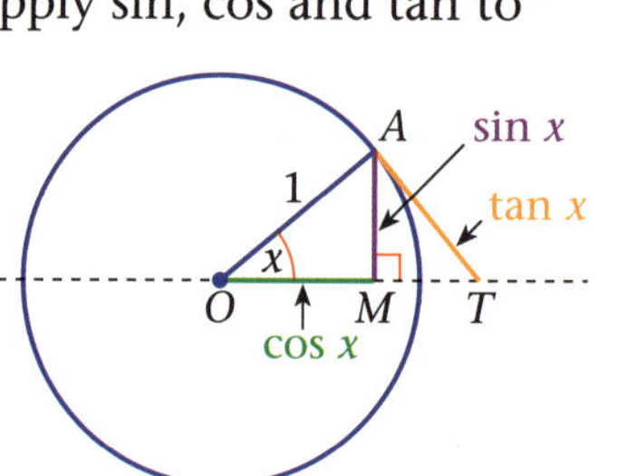

Note

$\cos x = \sin (90° - x)$

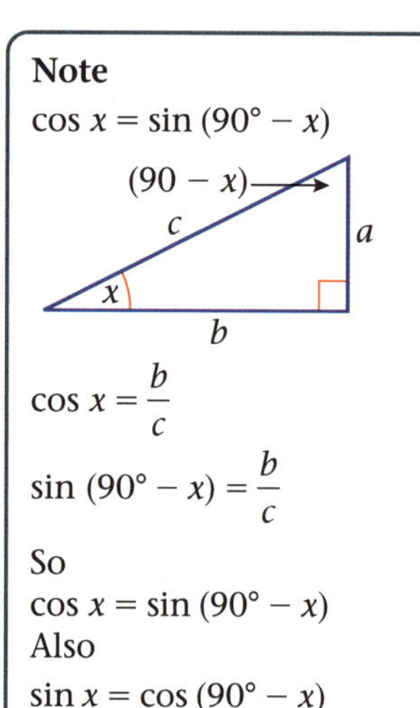

$\cos x = \frac{b}{c}$

$\sin (90° - x) = \frac{b}{c}$

So

$\cos x = \sin (90° - x)$

Also

$\sin x = \cos (90° - x)$

From the diagram you can look at sine, cosine and tangent in all 4 quandrants. That is:

1st quadrant: angles between 0° and 90°

2nd quadrant: angles between 90° and 180°

3rd quadrant: angles between 180° and 270°

4th quadrant: angles between 270° and 360°

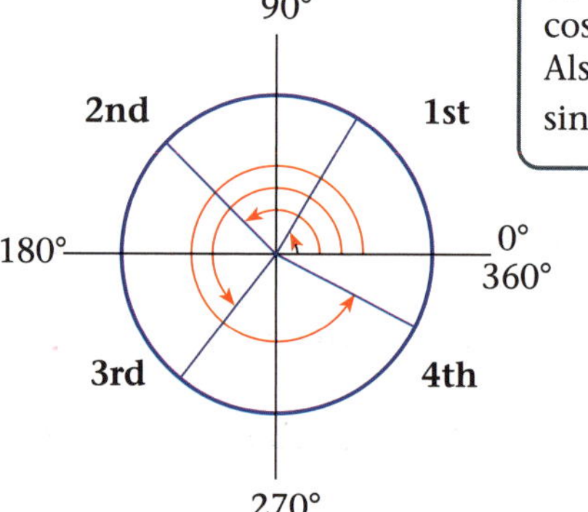

You can even consider other angles outside the range 0° to 360°, such as −50° and 410°.

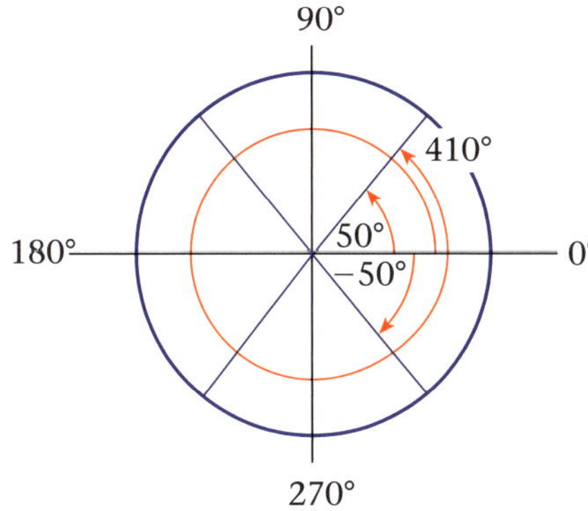

Consider the sine of these angles:

Correct to 4 d.p., your calculator gives:

$$\sin(-50°) = -0.7660$$
$$\sin 130° = 0.7660$$
$$\sin 410° = 0.7660$$

Compare these with:

$$\sin 50° = 0.7660$$

You can see that:

$$\sin(-50°) = -\sin 50°$$
$$\sin 130° = \sin 50°$$
$$\sin 410° = \sin 50°$$

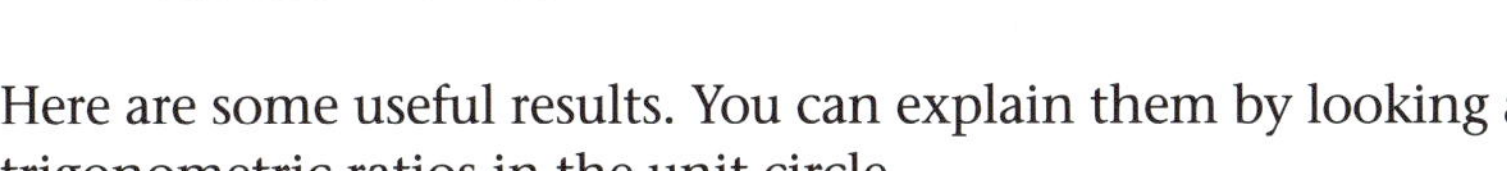
Here are some useful results. You can explain them by looking at the trigonometric ratios in the unit circle.

$\sin(-x) = -\sin x$	$\cos(-x) = \cos x$	$\tan(-x) = -\tan x$
$\sin(180° - x) = \sin x$	$\cos(180° - x) = -\cos x$	$\tan(180° - x) = -\tan x$
$\sin(360° + x) = \sin x$	$\cos(360° + x) = \cos x$	$\tan(360° + x) = \tan x$

Exercise 16E

Write an equivalent trig ratio for each of the following. The first is done for you.

1 (a) $\sin(-60°) = -\sin 60°$ (b) $\sin 410°$ (c) $\sin 50°$

2 (a) $\cos 110°$ (b) $\cos(-85°)$ (c) $\cos 405°$

3 (a) $\tan(-45°)$ (b) $\tan 130°$ (c) $\tan 390°$

16.6 The graph of sin *x*

You can draw the graph of $y = \sin x$ for values of x from 0° to 360°.

First make a table of values:

x	$\sin x$
0°	0
30°	0.5
45°	0.7071
60°	0.8660
90°	1
120°	0.8660
135°	0.7071
150°	0.5
180°	0
210°	−0.5
225°	−0.7071
240°	−0.8660
270°	−1
300°	−0.8660
315°	−0.7071
330°	−0.5
360°	0

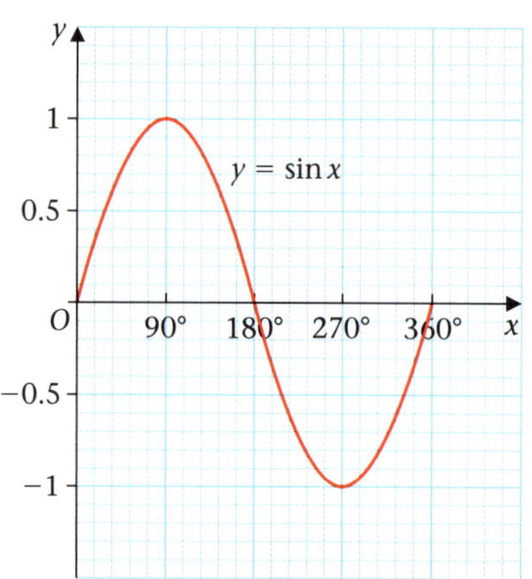

Graphical calculators are really helpful for plotting graphs of trig functions.

Key values of sin *x*

From this diagram:

1, $\sqrt{2}$, 45°, 1

hypotenuse = $\sqrt{2}$ (Pythagoras)

so $\sin 45° = \frac{1}{\sqrt{2}} = 0.707$

From this diagram:

2, 30°, 2, $\sqrt{3}$, 60°, 1, 1

height = $\sqrt{3}$ (Pythagoras)

so $\sin 60° = \frac{\sqrt{3}}{2} = 0.866$

and $\sin 30° = \frac{1}{2} = 0.5$

The extended graph of $y = \sin x$ is

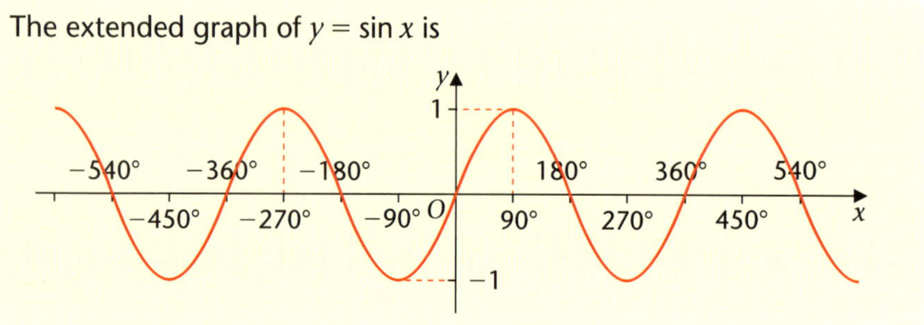

$y = 0$, i.e. $\sin x = 0$ when $x = 0$, 180°, −180°, …

The important features of the graph are:

- it repeats itself every 360°; we say that it has a **period** of 360°
- it has maximum values (the largest values of y) of 1, which occur when $x = 90°, 450°, −270°, \ldots$
- it has minimum values (the smallest values of y) of −1, which occur when $x = −90°, 270°, −450°, \ldots$

$\sin(-x) = -\sin x$ $\sin(180° - x) = \sin x$ $\sin(180° + x) = -\sin x$ $\sin(360° + x) = \sin x$

16.7 The graph of cos x

You can draw the graph of $y = \cos x$ for values of x from 0° to 360°.

x	cos x
0°	0
30°	0.8660
45°	0.7071
60°	0.5
90°	0
120°	−0.5
135°	−0.7071
150°	−0.8660
180°	−1
210°	−0.8660
225°	−0.7071
240°	−0.5
270°	0
300°	0.5
315°	0.7071
330°	0.8660
360°	1

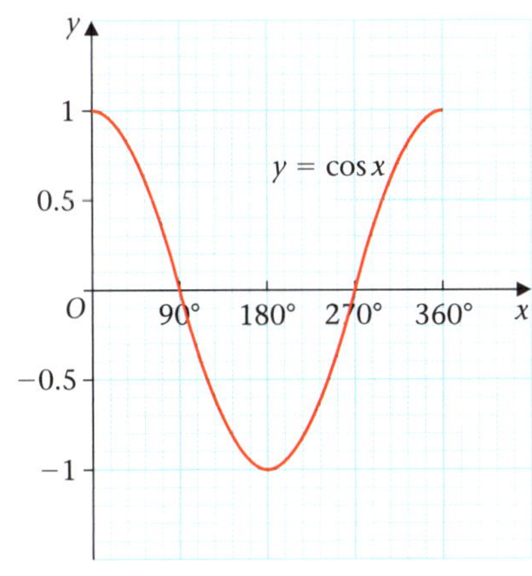

You can confirm this on a graphical calculator.

Key values of cos x

From this diagram:

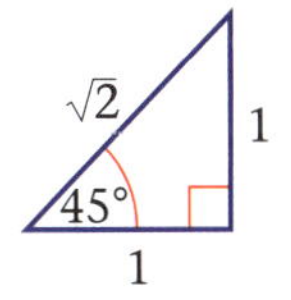

$$\cos 45° = \frac{1}{\sqrt{2}} = 0.707$$

From this diagram:

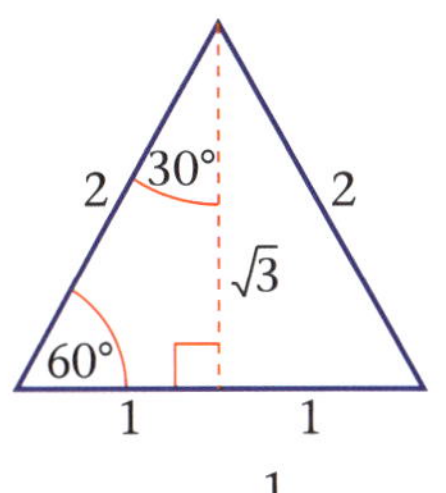

$$\cos 60° = \frac{1}{2} = 0.5$$

$$\cos 30° = \frac{\sqrt{3}}{2} = 0.866$$

The extended graph of $y = \cos x$ is

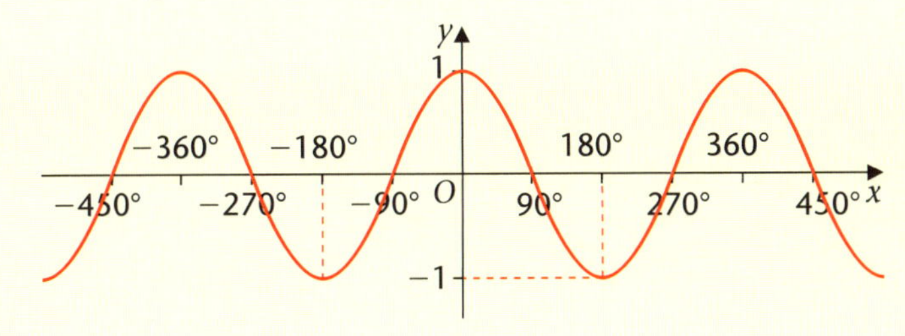

$y = 0$, i.e. $\cos x = 0$ when $x = 90°, 270°, -90°, \ldots$

The important features of this graph are:

- it repeats itself every 360°, so it has a period of 360°
- it has a maximum value of 1, which occurs when $x = 0°, 360°, -360°, \ldots$
- it has a minimum value of −1, which occurs when $x = 180°, -180°, 540°, \ldots$

The graph confirms
$\cos(90° - x) = \sin x$
$\cos x = \sin(90° - x)$

$\cos(-x) = \cos x$ $\quad \cos(180° - x) = -\cos x$ $\quad \cos(180° + x) = -\cos x$ $\quad \cos(360° + x) = \cos x$

16.8 The graph of tan x

You can draw the graph of $y = \tan x$ for values of x from 0° to 90°.

Choosing some key values:

x	$\tan x$
0°	0
30°	0.5774
45°	1
60°	1.7320
90°	infinite

Key values of tan x

From this diagram:

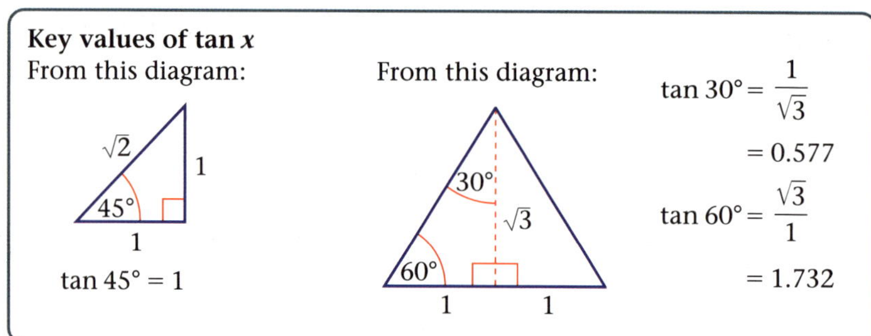

$\tan 45° = 1$

From this diagram:

$\tan 30° = \frac{1}{\sqrt{3}}$

$= 0.577$

$\tan 60° = \frac{\sqrt{3}}{1}$

$= 1.732$

The fact that tan 90° is infinite causes a problem.

In the range from 0° to 90°, the graph of $y = \tan x$ is like this:

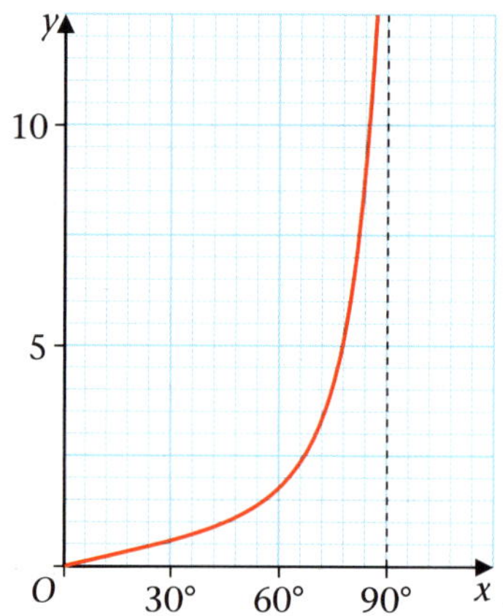

Angles between 90° and 270°

Taking an angle just greater than 90°, say 95°, you can get an idea of what happens to the tangent graph when x is just over 90° and look at some important values for x.

tan 95° is negative and large

x	$\tan x$
95°	−11.43
135°	−1
180°	0
225°	1
270°	infinite
290°	−2.75
315°	−1
360°	0

In the range from 90° to 270° the graph of $y = \tan x$ is like this:

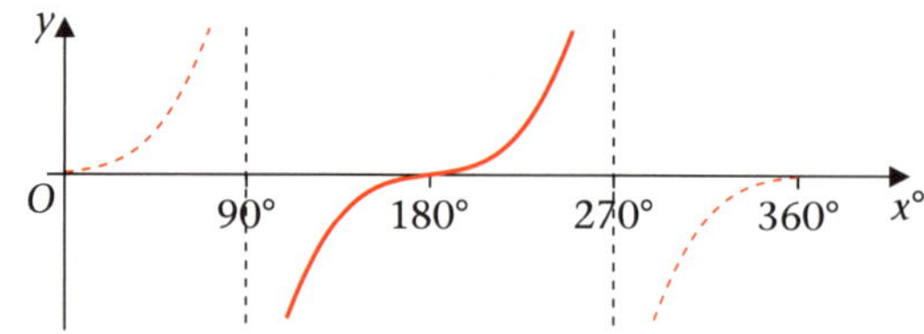

The extended graph of $y = \tan x$ is

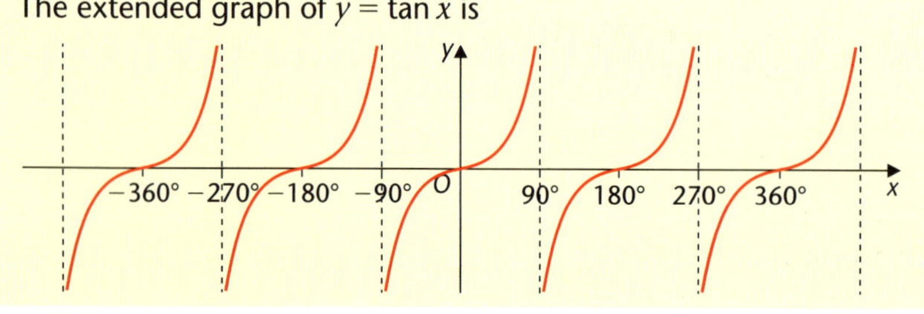

The important features of this graph are:

- it repeats itself every 180°, so it has a period of 180°
- it is infinite at $x = \pm 90°, \pm 270°, \ldots$

$\tan(-x) = -\tan x$ $\quad$ $\tan(180° - x) = -\tan x$ $\quad$ $\tan(180° + x) = \tan x$ $\quad$ $\tan(360° + x) = \tan x$

Worked examination question 2

(a) Draw the graph of $y = 3 \sin 2x$ for values of x from $-180°$ to 180°.

(b) State the period of the graph.

(c) State the maximum and minimum values of $3 \sin 2x$ and the values of x at which these occur.

(a) Start with a table of values or use a graphical calculator.

x	$2x$	$3 \sin 2x$
−180°	−360°	0
−135°	−270°	3
−90°	−180°	0
−45°	−90°	−3
0°	0°	0
45°	90°	3
90°	180°	0
135°	270°	−3
180°	360°	0

For simplicity intervals of 45° have been chosen.

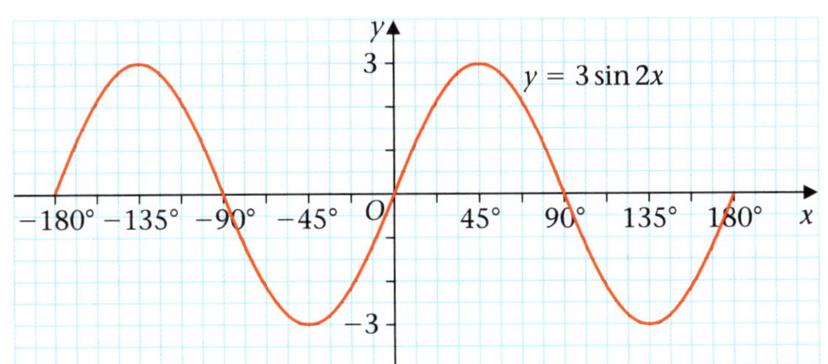

(b) From the drawing you can see that the graph repeats itself every 180°, so the period of the graph is 180°.

(c) The maximum value of $3 \sin 2x$ is 3.
This occurs when $x = -135°$ and 45°.

The minimum value of $3 \sin 2x$ is -3.
This occurs when $x = -45°$ and 135°.

Exercise 16F

1 Using a table of values or a graphical calculator, show that for the range 270° to 360° the graph of $y = \tan x$ is like this:

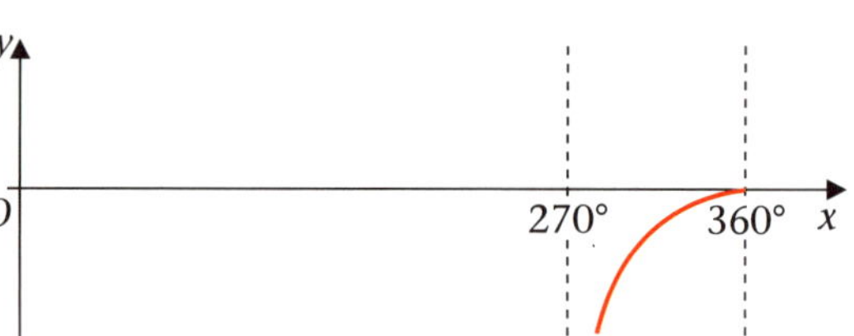

2 Using a table of values or a graphical calculator, show that the graph of $y = \tan x$ for the range $-90°$ to $0°$ is like this:

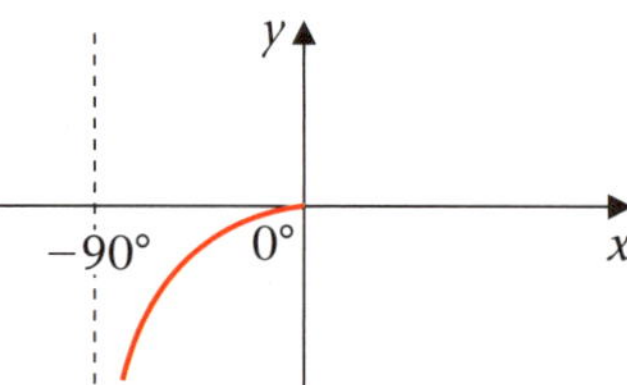

3 (a) For values of x from $-180°$ to $180°$, plot the graph of $y = 5\cos 3x$.
(b) State the period of the graph.
(c) Find the maximum and minimum values of $5\cos 3x$ and state the values of x at which these occur.

4 (a) Plot the graph of $y = 2\tan x$ for values of x from 0° to 360°.
(b) Find the period of the graph.

5 For values of x from 0° to 360°, plot the graphs of
(a) $y = \sin 4x$ (b) $y = \sin \frac{1}{2}x$
Comment on the periods of each of the two graphs.

6 Investigate graphs in the form $y = A\sin Bx$, where A and B are positive integers. Comment on the period of each graph and the maximum and minimum values in connection to A and B.

7 Investigate graphs in the form $y = A$ (trig function) Bx, where A and B can also take fractional values. Comment on your findings.

16.9 Solving a trigonometric equation

Example 7

Solve the equation $2\sin x = 1$

giving all values of x in the range $-360°$ to $360°$.

$2\sin x = 1$

so $\sin x = \frac{1}{2}$

From the calculator:

$x = 30°$

This is the first solution and you can use a sketch of the graph of $\sin x$ to find any others.

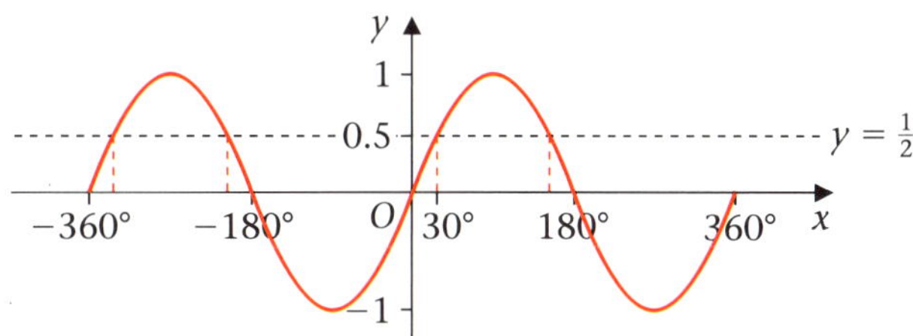

The sketch shows that there are three other solutions to the equation in the range $-360°$ to $360°$.

By examining the symmetries of the graph, you can see that the four solutions are

$$x = 30°,\ 180° - 30°,\ -180° - 30°,\ -360° + 30°$$

So the full set of solutions is

$$x = 30°,\ 150°,\ -210°,\ -330°$$

In the range 0° to 180° we have:

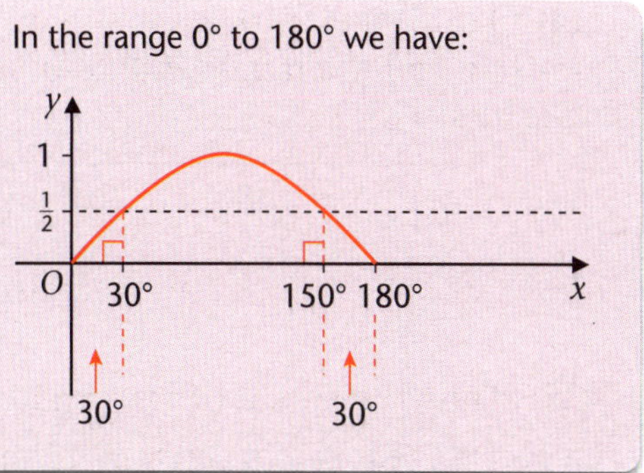

A trigonometric equation may have several solutions in any given range.

Exercise 16G

1 For values of x in the range $-360°$ to $360°$, solve the equation

$$2 \cos x = 1$$

2 (a) Show that one solution of the equation

$$5 \sin x = 2$$

is $x = 23.6°$ correct to 1 d.p.

(b) Hence find all solutions to the equation

$$5 \sin x = 2$$

which are in the range 0° to 720°, giving your answers correct to 1 d.p.

3 Find all solutions to the equation

$$\tan x = 2$$

which are in the range $-180°$ to $180°$.

4 (a) Sketch the graph of

$$y = 3 \cos x$$

for values of x from 0° to 360°.

(b) Hence, or otherwise, obtain all the solutions to the equation

$$3 \cos x = 1$$

which are between 0° and 360°.

5 (a) Show that the equation

$$5 \sin 3x = 4$$

has a solution $x = 17.71°$ correct to 2 decimal places.

(b) Hence or otherwise, obtain all solutions to the equation

$$5 \sin 3x = 4$$

which are in the range $-180°$ to $180°$.

6 Suggest suitable equations for the following graphs.
Check your answers with a graphical calculator or computer.

(a)

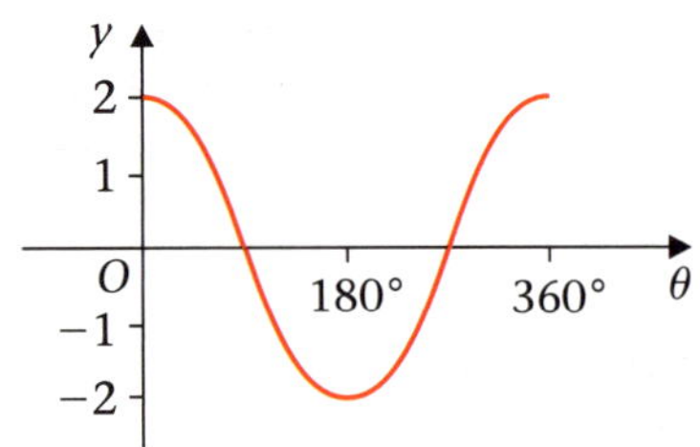

(b)

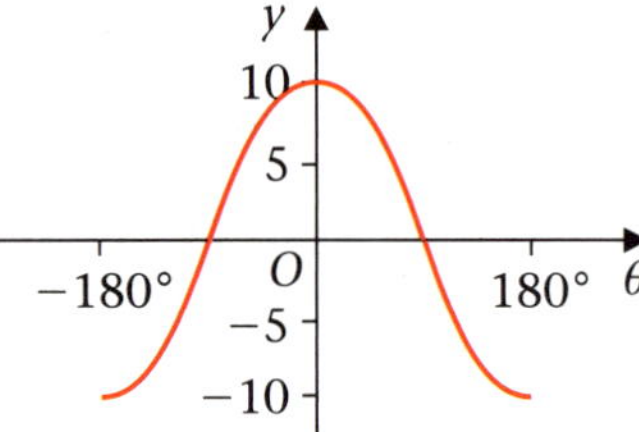

(c)

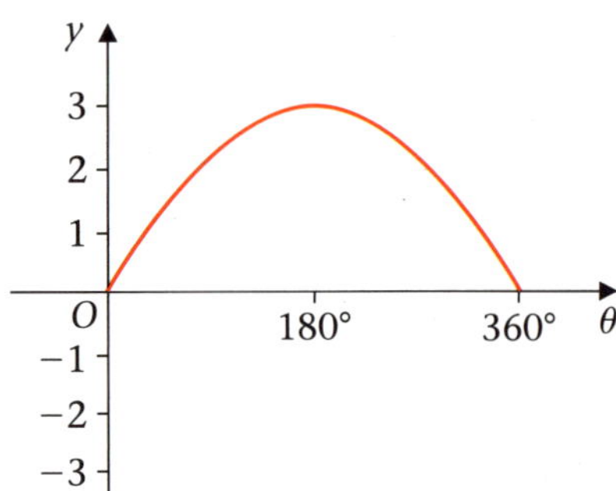

(d)

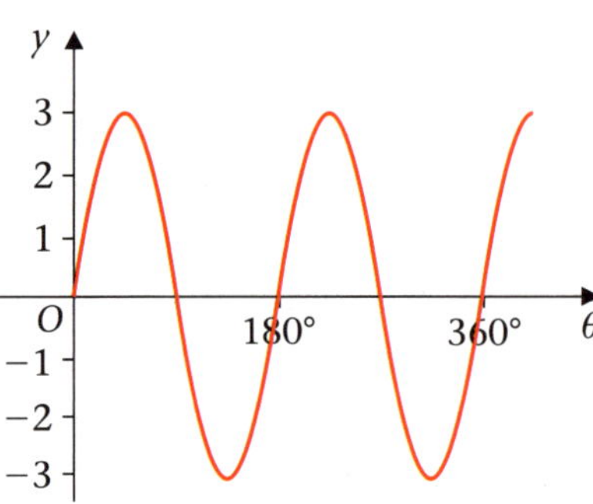

Mixed exercise 16

1 *ABC* is a right-angled triangle.
AB is of length 4 m and *BC* is of length 13 m.

(a) Calculate the length of *AC*.

(b) Calculate the size of angle $A\hat{B}C$.

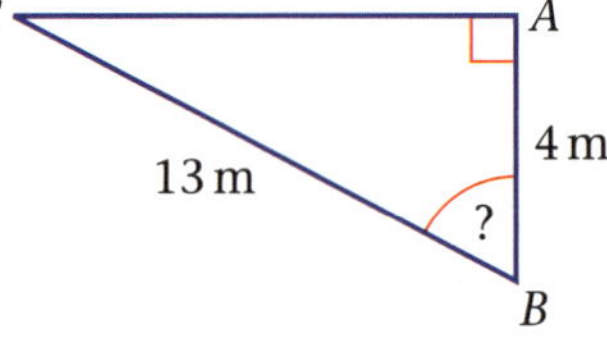

2 The diagram represents the frame, *PQRS*, of a roof.

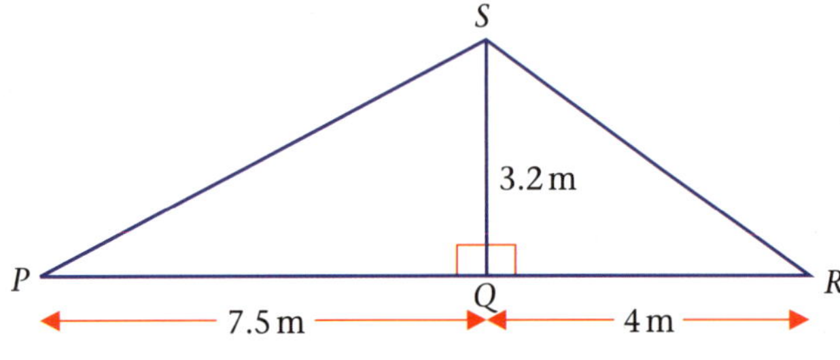

$PQ = 7.5$ m $\quad QR = 4$ m $\quad SQ = 3.2$ m

(a) Calculate the length of *PS*.

(b) Calculate the size of the angle $S\hat{R}Q$.

3 The diagram shows a ladder LD of length 12 m resting against a vertical wall. The ladder makes an angle of 40° with the horizontal.
Calculate the distance BD from the base of the wall to the top of the ladder.

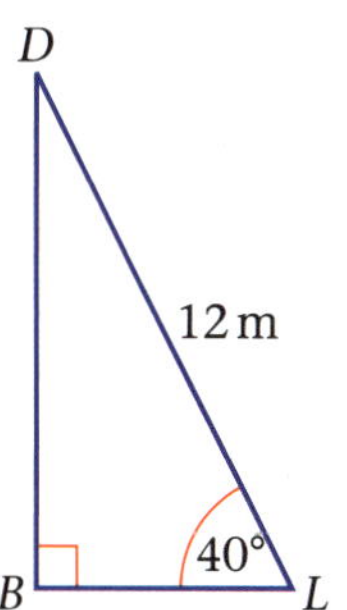

4 A lighthouse, L, is 43 km due North of a harbour, H.
A marker buoy, B, is 17 km due East of L.
Calculate the bearing of B from H.

You may find it helpful to draw a sketch.

5 Explain why it would be impossible to draw the triangle ABC.

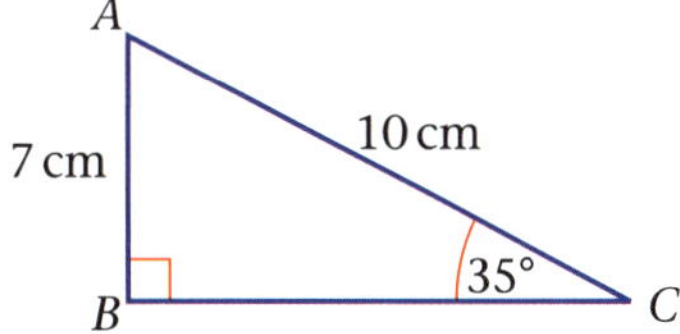

6 Coming in to land, a small aeroplane starts its descent at a vertical height of h metres above the horizontal land.
The aeroplane descends along a straight line at a constant angle of depression of 12°.
From starting its descent to touching down, the aeroplane travels through a distance of 6000 m.

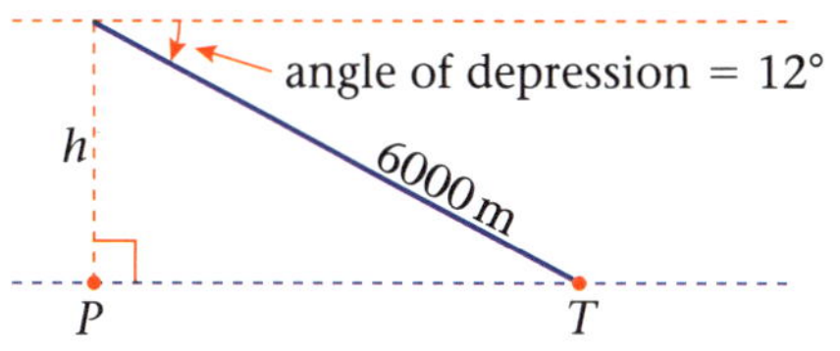

(a) Calculate the vertical height, h, at which the aeroplane starts its descent.

At the start of its descent, the aeroplane is vertically above a point P on the ground. It touches down at a point T.

(b) Calculate the distance PT.

7 This is the cross-section, $ABCD$, of a valley.

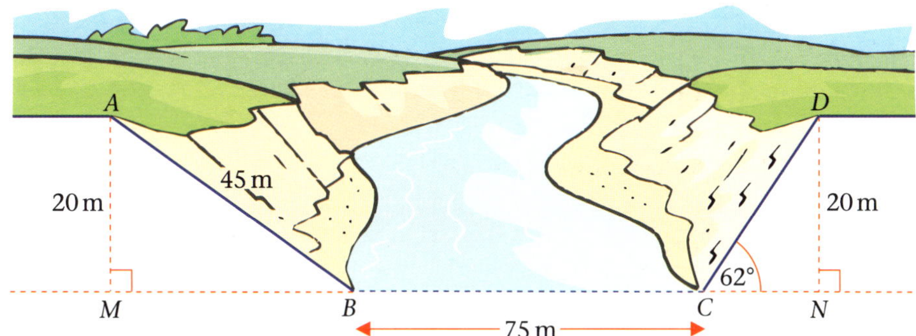

The vertical heights AM and DN above the horizontal base BC of the valley are both equal to 20 metres.

$AB = 45$ m   angle $NCD = 62°$ $BC = 75$ m

Calculate

(a) the size of the angle MBA

(b) the distance from A to D across the top of the valley.

8 **(a)** Sketch the graph of $y = 2\cos x$ for values of x from 0° to 360°.

(b) Hence find all solutions of the equation

$$2\cos x = -1$$

which are in the range 0° to 360°.

9 The height of the tide, h metres, in a river estuary is modelled by the function

$$h = 3\sin 20t + 10$$

where t is the number of hours after midnight.

(a) What is the greatest depth of the water?

(b For how long is the water over 8 metres in depth for the first time, starting from midnight?

10 Find all the solutions between 0° and 360° for the following functions:

(a) $3\sin\theta = 2$ **(b)** $5\cos\theta + 2 = 0$ **(c)** $3\cos\theta - 1 = 0$

Summary of key points

1 The three basic **trigonometric functions** are $\sin x$, $\cos x$ and $\tan x$.

2 $\sin x = \dfrac{\text{opp}}{\text{hyp}}$

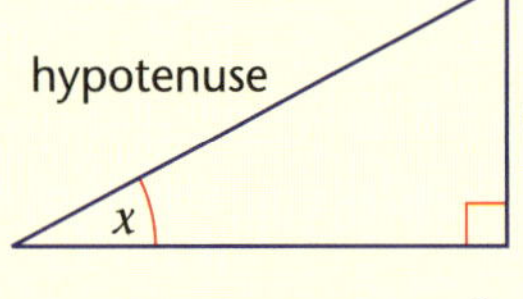

3 $\cos x = \dfrac{\text{adj}}{\text{hyp}}$

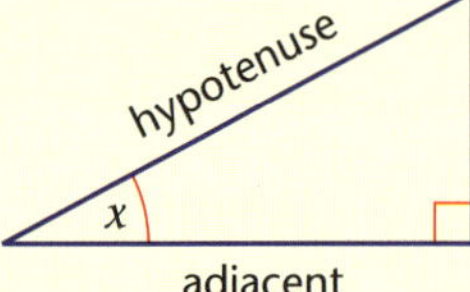

4 $\tan x = \dfrac{\text{opp}}{\text{adj}}$

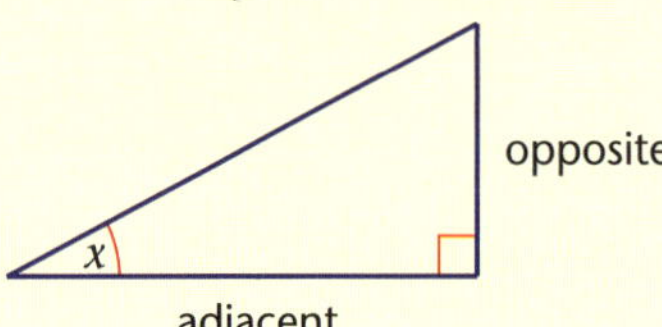

5 The extended graph of $y = \sin x$ is

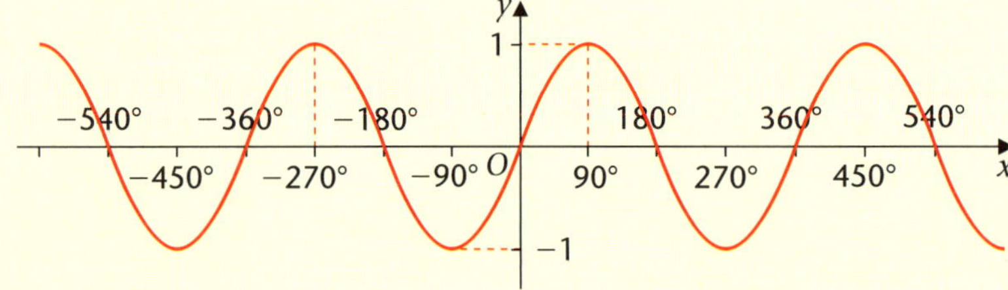

6 $\sin(-x) = -\sin x$ $\sin(180° - x) = \sin x$ $\sin(180° + x) = -\sin x$ $\sin(360° + x) = \sin x$

7 The extended graph of $y = \cos x$ is

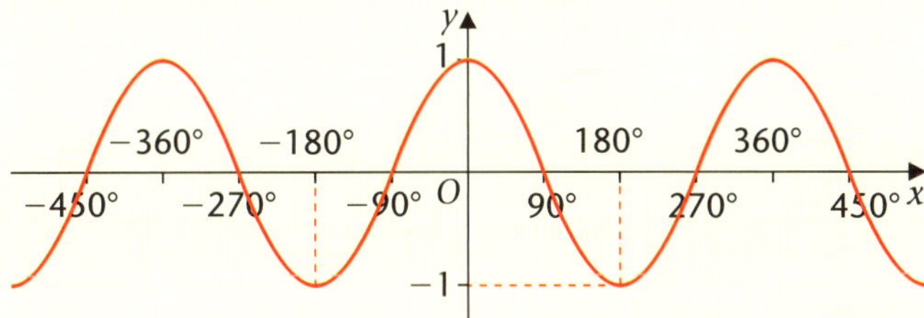

8 $\cos(-x) = \cos x$ $\cos(180° - x) = -\cos x$ $\cos(180° + x) = -\cos x$ $\cos(360° + x) = \cos x$

9 The extended graph of $y = \tan x$ is

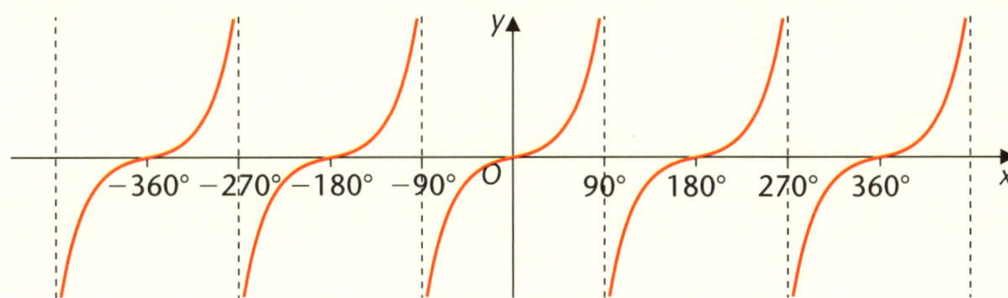

10 $\tan(-x) = -\tan x$ $\tan(180° - x) = -\tan x$ $\tan(180° + x) = \tan x$ $\tan(360° + x) = \tan x$

11 A trigonometric equation may have several solutions in any given range.

17 Graphs and equations

In this chapter you will draw graphs of equations involving powers of x, and for real-life situations. You will also use trial and improvement methods to solve equations involving powers.

17.1 Graphs of quadratic functions

A **quadratic function** is one in which the highest power of x is x^2. For example $x^2 - 7$, $2x^2 - 3x + 2$ and $3x^2 + 4x$ are quadratic functions.

The graph of a quadratic function is a U-shaped curve called a **parabola**.

The simplest parabola has the equation $y = x^2$.

Here is a **table of values** for $y = x^2$:

When $x = -4$:
$y = (-4)^2$
$= -4 \times -4$
$= 16$

x	−4	−3	−2	−1	0	1	2	3	4
y	16	9	4	1	0	1	4	9	16

You need to draw a smooth curve through the set of points. Here is the parabola. Its line of symmetry is the y-axis.

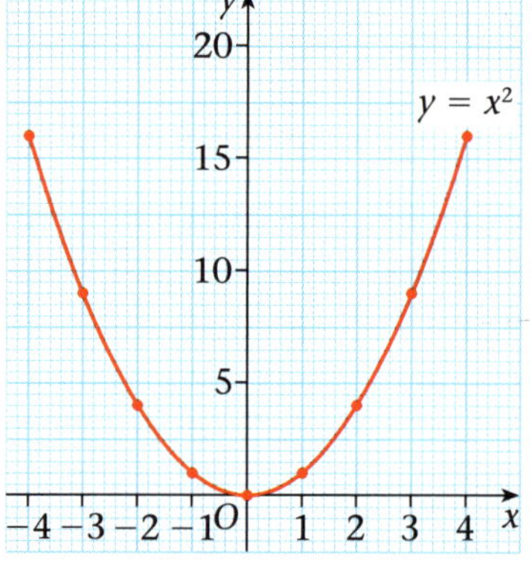

Example 1

(a) Draw the graph of $y = 2x^2 - 4x - 3$, taking values of x from −2 to 4.
(b) Draw in the line of symmetry.
(c) Label the minimum point M with a cross.
(d) Write down the minimum value of y.

(a) Here is a table of values:

x	−2	−1	0	1	2	3	4
$2x^2$	8	2	0	2	8	18	32
$-4x$	+8	+4	0	−4	−8	−12	−16
-3	−3	−3	−3	−3	−3	−3	−3
y	13	3	−3	−5	−3	3	13

Here is the graph:

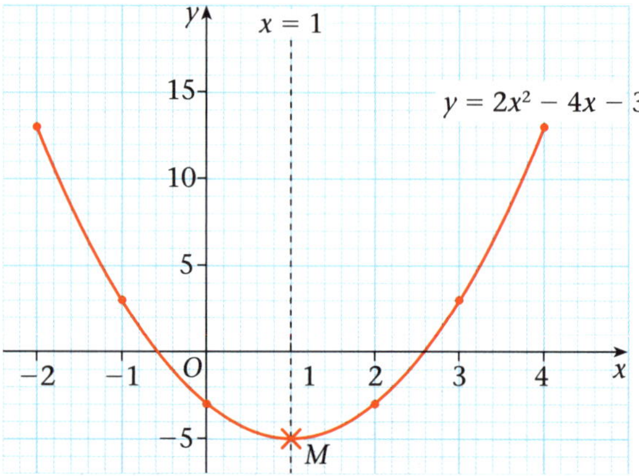

(b) The line of symmetry is $x = 1$. (c) See graph. (d) $y = -5$

Exercise 17A

(a) Draw graphs with the following equations, taking values of x from -4 to 4.

(b) In each case draw the line of symmetry and write down its equation.

(c) Label each minimum point M with a cross.

(d) Write down the minimum or maximum value of y.

1 $y = x^2 + 5$

2 $y = x^2 - 10$

3 $y = 3x^2$

4 $y = \frac{1}{2}x^2$

5 $y = -x^2$

6 $y = -2x^2$

7 $y = x^2 + 2x$

8 $y = x^2 + 3x$

9 $y = (x + 1)^2$

10 $y = (x - 2)^2$

11 $y = x^2 - 4x - 1$

12 $y = x^2 - 3x - 5$

13 $y = x^2 - x + 4$

14 $y = 2x^2 + 3x - 5$

15 $y = 3x^2 - 4x + 2$

17.2 Graphs of cubic functions

A **cubic function** is one in which the highest power of x is x^3.
For example $x^3 - 3x + 2$, $5x^3$ and $2x^3 + 5x^2 + 4x - 7$ are all cubic functions.

The simplest cubic function has the equation $y = x^3$.

x	-3	-2	-1	0	1	2	3
y	-27	-8	-1	0	1	8	27

When $x = -3$:

$$y = (-3)^3 = (-3) \times (-3) \times (-3) = -27$$

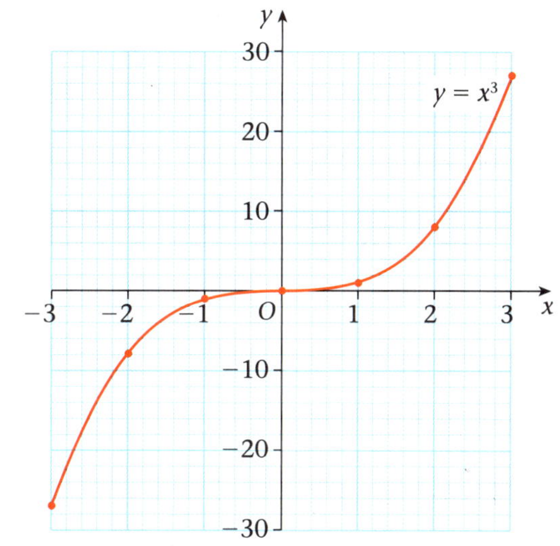

A tracing of this graph will fit on top of itself if you rotate it through 180° about the origin (0, 0).
The graph has **rotational symmetry** of order 2 about the origin.

All graphs of cubic functions have this S-shape.

Example 2

Draw the graph of $y = x^3 - 2x^2 - 4x$, taking values of x from -2 to 4.

Here is a table of values for $y = x^3 - 2x^2 - 4x$:

x	-2	-1	0	1	2	3	4
y	-8	1	0	-5	-8	-3	16

When $x = -2$:

$y = (-2)^3 - 2 \times (-2)^2 - (4 \times -2)$
$= -8 - 8 + 8$
$= -8$

When $x = 3$:

$y = 3^3 - 2 \times 3^2 - (4 \times 3)$
$= 27 - 18 - 12$
$= -3$

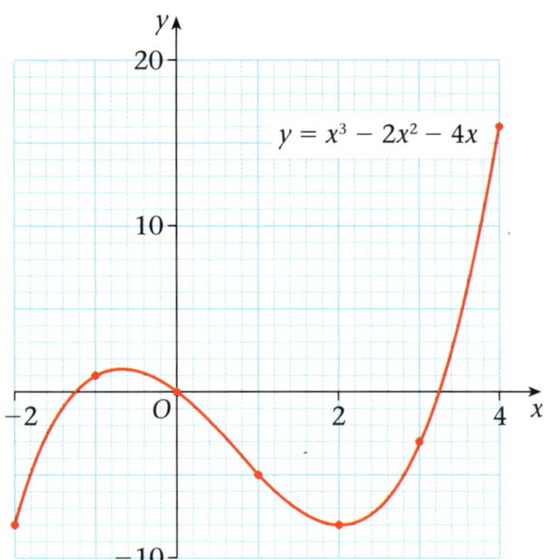

Exercise 17B

Draw graphs with the following equations, taking values of x from -3 to 3.

1 $y = x^3 + 5$

2 $y = x^3 - 10$

3 $y = 2x^3$

4 $y = \frac{1}{2}x^3$

5 $y = -x^3$

6 $y = -2x^3$

7 $y = (x - 2)^3$

8 $y = (x + 1)^3$

9 $y = x^3 - 2x^2$

10 $y = x^3 + x^2$

11 $y = x^3 + 5x$

12 $y = x^3 - 5x$

13 $y = x^3 + x^2 - 8x$

14 $y = x^3 + 3x - 2$

15 $y = x^3 - 2x^2 + 2$

17.3 Graphs of reciprocal functions

To find the **reciprocal** of a number or expression divide it into 1.

For example:

- the reciprocal of 2 is $1 \div 2 = \frac{1}{2}$
- the reciprocal of x is $1 \div x = \dfrac{1}{x}$

Example 3

(a) Make a table of values for $y = \frac{1}{x}$ and draw the graph.

(b) Is y undefined for any value of x?

When x is very small and +ve y is $\frac{1}{\text{very small}}$ and +ve so y is very big and +ve.

(a) Here is a table of values for $y = \frac{1}{x}$:

x	−3	−2	−1	−0.5	−0.2	0.2	0.5	1	2	3
y	−0.3	−0.5	−1	−2	−5	5	2	1	0.5	0.3

When $x = -3$:

$y = \frac{1}{-3} = -\frac{1}{3}$

$= -0.3$ to 1 d.p.

There is a **discontinuity** (break) in the graph at $x = 0$.

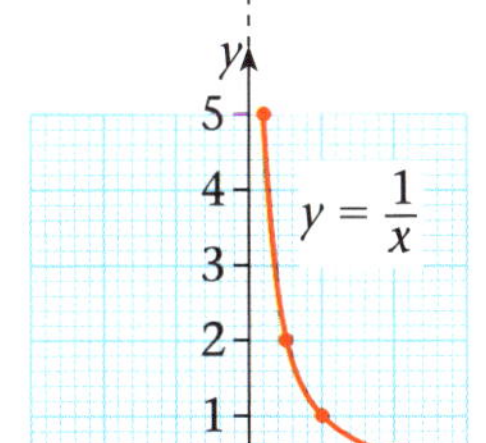

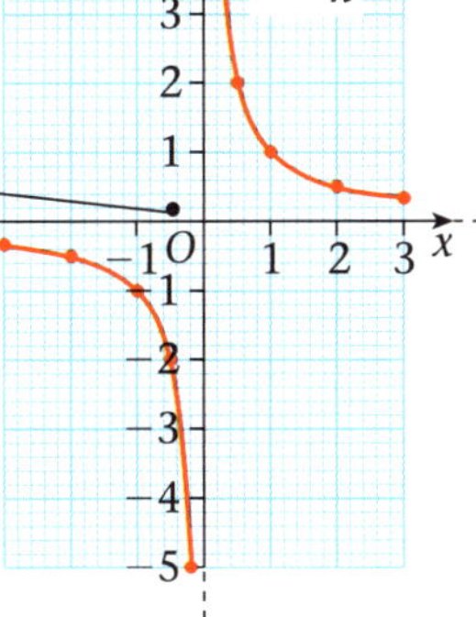

(b) y is undefined when $x = 0$ as division by 0 is undefined.

The lines $y = x$ and $y = -x$ are lines of symmetry of the graph $y = \frac{1}{x}$.

The graph approaches the axes but does not touch them. The axes are **asymptotes**.

A line which a graph approaches without touching is called an **asymptote**.

Example 4

(a) Make a table of values for $y = 3 - \frac{2}{x}$ and draw the graph.

(b) Draw in the asymptotes on the graph.

(c) Write down their equations

Asymptotes are usually drawn with dotted lines.

(a)

x	−3	−2	−1	−0.5	−0.2	0.2	0.5	1	2	3
y	3.7	4	5	7	13	−7	−1	1	2	2.3

When $x = -3$:

$y = 3 - \frac{2}{-3}$

$= 3 + \frac{2}{3}$

$= 3.7$ to 1 d.p.

When $x = -0.5$:

$y = 3 - \frac{2}{-0.5}$

$= 3 + 4$

$= 7$

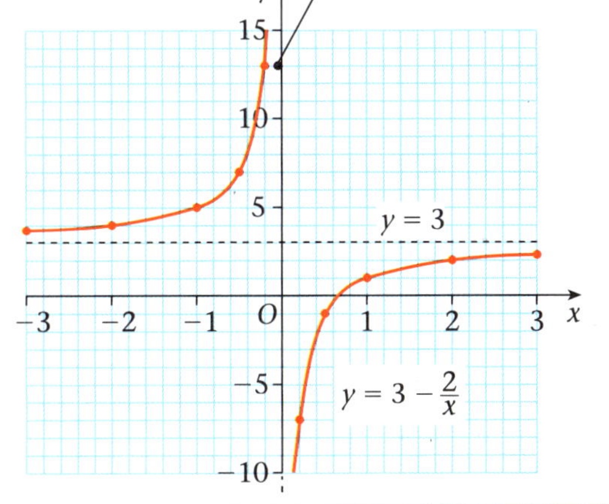

(b) See graph.

(c) The asymptotes are $x = 0$ and $y = 3$.

Exercise 17C

Draw graphs for the following equations. Use the same x-values as in Example 4. Draw in the asymptotes and write down their equations.

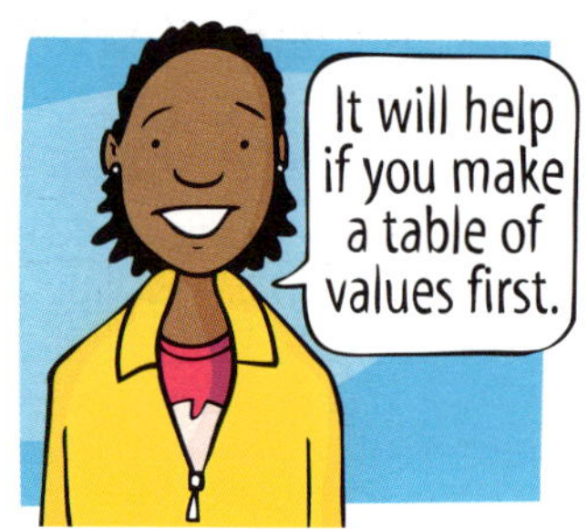

It will help if you make a table of values first.

1 $y = \frac{2}{x}$

2 $y = \frac{-1}{x}$

3 $y = \frac{-3}{x}$

4 $y = 4 + \frac{1}{x}$

5 $y = 5 - \frac{4}{x}$

6 $y = \frac{4}{x} - 3$

17.4 Graphs of the form $y = ax^3 + bx^2 + cx + d + \frac{e}{x}$

Sometimes you will need to plot graphs of equations that have a combination of cubic, quadratic, linear and reciprocal terms.

For example: $y = ax^3 + bx^2 + cx + d + \frac{e}{x}$

Here a, b, c, d, e are numbers (also called coefficients).

At GCSE level, if you are asked to plot graphs of this form, at least two of the coefficients will be zero.

Example 5

Make a table of values for $y = x + \frac{1}{x}$ and draw the graph.

Here is a table of values:

x	0.1	0.2	0.5	1	2	3	4	5
y	10.1	5.2	2.5	2	2.5	3.3	4.3	5.2

You could check this using a graphical calculator, computer or graph plotter.

When $x = 0.1$:
$y = 0.1 + \frac{1}{0.1}$
$= 0.1 + 10$
$= 10.1$

When $x = 0.2$:
$y = 0.2 + \frac{1}{0.2}$
$= 0.2 + 5$
$= 5.2$

When $x = 2$:
$y = 2 + \frac{1}{2}$
$= 2.5$

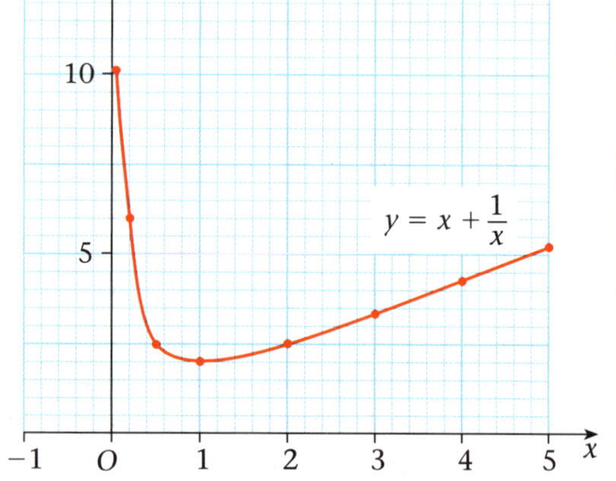

Example 6

Make a table of values for $y = x^2 + 3 + \frac{2}{x}$ and draw the graph.

Here is a table of values:

x	−3	−2	−1	−0.5	−0.2	0.2	0.5	1	2	3
y	11.3	6	2	−0.8	−7.0	13.0	7.3	6	8	12.7

When $x = -3$:

$$y = (-3)^2 + 3 + \frac{2}{-3}$$
$$= 9 + 3 - \frac{2}{3}$$
$$= 11\tfrac{1}{3}$$
$$= 11.3 \text{ to 1 d.p.}$$

When $x = 0.2$:

$$y = 0.2^2 + 3 + \frac{2}{0.2}$$
$$= 0.04 + 3 + 10$$
$$= 13.0 \text{ to 1 d.p.}$$

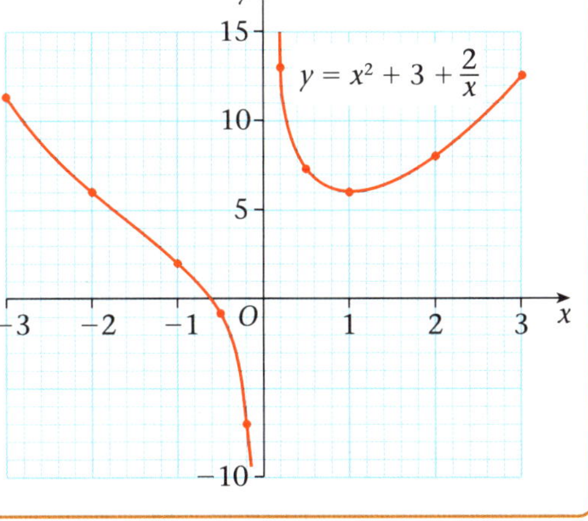

Exercise 17D

Draw graphs with the following equations. Use the values of x given in brackets to make a table of values.

1 $y = x^2 - 4x + 1$ (integers from −1 to 4)

2 $y = x^3 + 2x^2 - 3$ (integers from −3 to 2)

3 $y = x^3 - x^2 - 2x$ (integers from −2 to 3)

4 $y = x^3 - 5x + 2$ (integers from −3 to 3)

5 $y = 1 + 2x - x^2$ (integers from −2 to 4)

6 $y = 2x + \frac{1}{x}$ (values as in Example 6)

7 $y = x^2 - \frac{1}{x}$ (values as in Example 6)

8 $y = x + 2 + \frac{2}{x}$ (values as in Example 5)

9 $y = x^3 - \frac{1}{x}$ (0.2, 0.5, 1, 2, 3)

10 $y = x^2 - x + \frac{2}{x}$ (values as in Example 6)

17.5 Using graphs to solve equations

The solutions to the quadratic equation $x^2 - 4 = 0$ are $x = 2$ and $x = -2$. Notice that these are the values of x where the graph of $y = x^2 - 4$ cuts the x-axis.

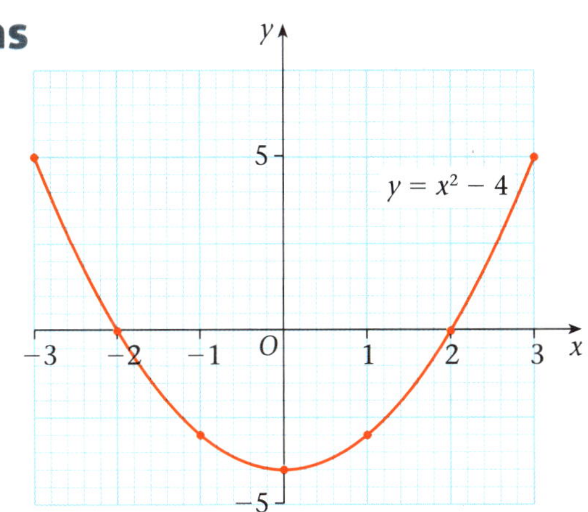

The **solutions** of a quadratic equation are the values of x where the graph cuts the x-axis.

A similar method can be used to find approximate solutions to higher order equations. There is more about this in Chapter 19.

Worked examination question 1

(a) Make a table of values for $y = x^2 - 2x - 2$.

(b) Plot the points represented by the values in your table on a grid and join them with a smooth curve.

(c) Use your graph to solve the equation $x^2 - 2x - 2 = 0$. Give your answers correct to 1 d.p.

(a) Here is a table of values:

x	-2	-1	0	1	2	3	4
x^2	4	1	0	1	4	9	16
$-2x$	4	2	0	-2	-4	-6	-8
-2	-2	-2	-2	-2	-2	-2	-2
y	6	1	-2	-3	-2	1	6

(c) The solutions to the equation $x^2 - 2x - 2 = 0$ are the values of x where the graph cuts the x-axis.
These are $x = -0.7$ and $x = 2.7$

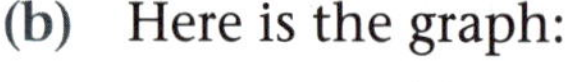
(b) Here is the graph:

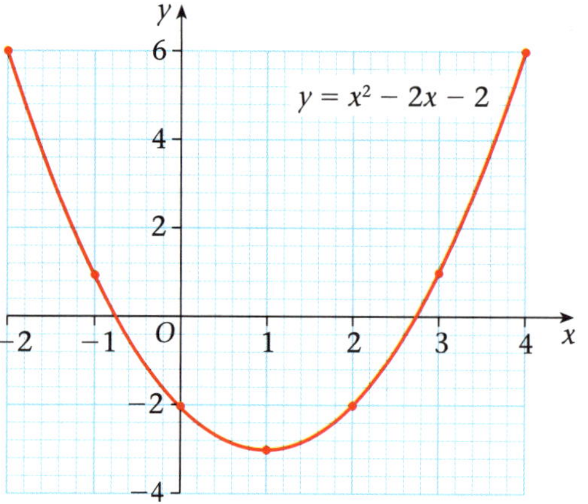

Exercise 17E

Solve the following equations correct to 1 d.p. by drawing appropriate graphs. Use the values of x given in brackets to make a table of values.

1 $x^2 - 7x + 8 = 0$ (integers from 0 to 8)

2 $x^2 - x - 3 = 0$ (integers from −3 to 4)

3 $2x^2 - 3x - 7 = 0$ (integers from −3 to 4)

4 $5x^2 - 8x + 2 = 0$ (integers from −1 to 3)

5 $x^3 - 4x + 1 = 0$ (integers from −3 to 3) — There are 3 solutions.

6 $x^3 + x^2 - 3x = 0$ (integers from −3 to 2)

7 $x^3 - 2x^2 - 1 = 0$ (integers from −2 to 3) — There is only 1 solution.

8 $x^3 - 4x^2 + 4x = 0$ (integers from −1 to 4)

9 $x - \frac{5}{x} = 0$ (0.2, 0.5, 1, 2, 3, 4)

10 $x^2 - 3x + \frac{1}{x} = 0$ (0.2, 0.5, 1, 2, 3, 4)

17.6 Trial and improvement methods for solving equations

You can use trial and improvement methods to solve an equation to any degree of accuracy.

You would normally use a calculator for your calculations.

Example 7

Find the positive solution to $x^3 - 3x - 1 = 0$.
Give your answer correct to 1 d.p.

x	0	1	2
$x^3 - 3x - 1$	−1	−3	1

There is a solution to $x^3 - 3x - 1 = 0$ between $x = 1$ and $x = 2$.

It is not obvious whether the solution is nearer to 1 or to 2.

1 2

You could try 1.1, 1.2, … until you find the first value that gives $x^3 - 3x - 1 > 0$.
It often saves time to try the middle value of an interval to establish in which half of the interval the solution lies:

x	1.5
$x^3 - 3x - 1$	−2.125 (too small)

So there is a solution to $x^3 - 3x - 1 = 0$ between $x = 1.5$ and $x = 2$

x	1.6	1.7	1.8	1.9
$x^3 - 3x - 1$	−1.704	−1.187	−0.568 (too small)	0.159 (too large)

So the solution is between $x = 1.8$ and $x = 1.9$

0.159 is nearer to 0 than −0.568 is. This suggests that the solution is nearer to 1.9 than it is to 1.8, but you must confirm this by trying $x = 1.85$:

You must always go to the next decimal place to confirm the solution, so here try 1.85

x	1.85
$x^3 - 3x - 1$	−0.218 38

There is a solution to $x^3 - 3x - 1 = 0$ between $x = 1.85$ and $x = 1.9$

So the solution is $x = 1.9$ (to 1 d.p.)

You can use a **trial and improvement method** to solve an equation. Try a value in the equation and use your result to improve your estimate. Repeat, getting closer and closer to the correct value.

Worked examination question 2

Using the method of trial and improvement, or otherwise, find the positive solution of $x^3 + x = 187$.
Give your answer correct to 1 d.p.

x	$x^3 + x$	
5	130	too small
6	222	too large
5.5	171.875	too small
5.6	181.216	too small
5.7	190.893	
5.65	186.012	

The soltion lies between 5.65 and 5.7

$x = 5.7$ (to 1 d.p.)

Exercise 17F

Find the positive solutions to these equations by trial and improvement.
Give your answers to the level of accuracy stated.

1 $x^3 - x - 1 = 0$ (1 d.p.)

2 $x^3 - x - 7 = 0$ (1 d.p.)

3 $x^3 - 4x - 1 = 0$ (1 d.p.)

4 $x^3 + 2x - 20 = 0$ (2 d.p.)

5 $x^3 + x = 300$ (1 d.p.)

6 $x^3 + x^2 = 700$ (2 d.p.)

7 $x^3 + 5x - 200 = 0$ (2 s.f.)

8 $x^3 - 4x = 300$ (3 s.f.)

9 $x^3 + 2x^2 = 120$ (2 d.p.)

10 $x^2 - \frac{2}{x} = 5$ (2 s.f.)

17.7 Solving problems by trial and improvement

Look at this problem:

Find the radius of a circle whose area is 100 cm².

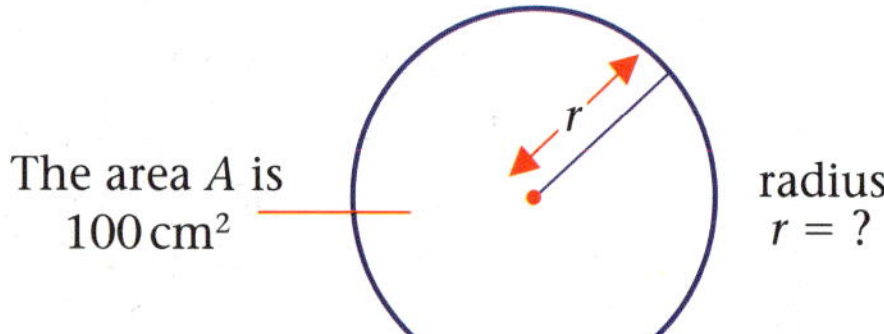

You can find the radius by guessing it and trying it in the formula
$A = \pi r^2$

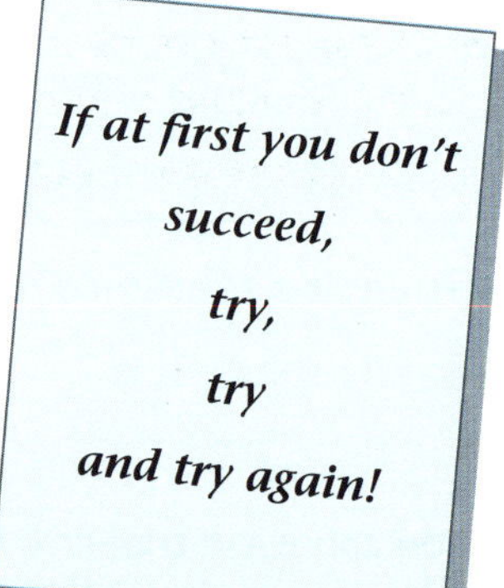

If at first you don't succeed,
try,
try
and try again!

Sometimes you can solve problems like this using trial and improvement.

Example 8

Use a trial and improvement method to find the radius r of a circle whose area is 100 cm^2.
Your answer should be accurate to 2 d.p.

r	πr^2	
5	78.539...	too small
7	153.938...	too big
6	113.097...	too big
5.5	95.033...	too small
5.75	103.868...	too big
5.65	100.287...	too big
5.64	99.932...	too small
5.645	100.110...	too big

You can now see that the radius r lies between 5.64 cm and 5.645 cm. Therefore $r = 5.64$ cm to 2 d.p.

Method:
Guess a value for r.
Calculate πr^2.
Compare your answer with 100.

Exercise 17G

1 Use a trial and improvement method to find the length l of the side of a cube whose volume V is 100 cm^3.

The formula is $V = l^3$

Your answer should be accurate to 2 d.p.

2 Use a trial and improvement method to find the length l of the side of a cube whose total surface area A is 50 cm^2.

The formula is $A = 6l^2$

Your answer should be accurate to 2 d.p.

3 Convert a temperature of 22 °C to Fahrenheit (°F) by trial and improvement.

Your answer should be accurate to 1 d.p.

The formula to convert from °F to °C is (F–32)×5÷9
22°C
18°C

17.8 Graphs that describe real-life situations

Graphs can be used to describe a wide variety of real-life situations. You may have to interpret or sketch graphs of this type.

Two important real-life graphs are distance–time graphs and speed–time graphs.

Distance–time graphs

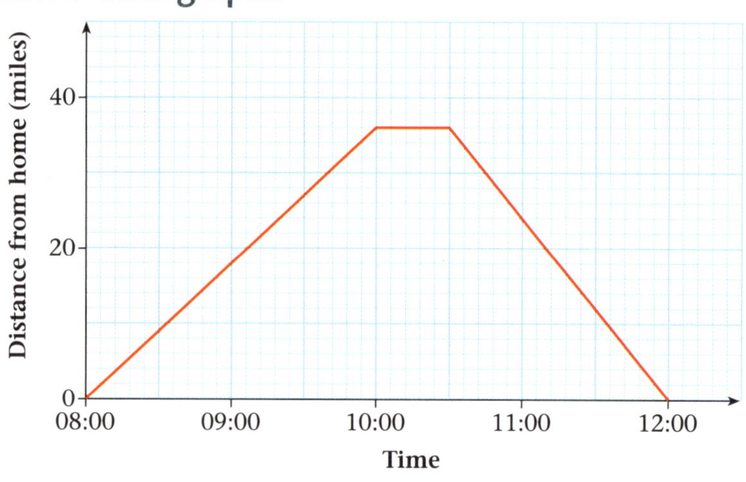

The diagram shows the distance–time graph for a cycle ride. Between 08:00 and 10:00 the cyclist travels 36 miles. This part of the graph is a straight line because she travels at a constant speed.

Her constant speed is 36 miles ÷ 2 hours = 18 mph, which is the gradient of the line.

Between 10:00 and 10:30 (the horizontal part of the graph) the cyclist is stationary, having a rest perhaps.

Between 10:30 and 12:00 she travels back home at a constant speed of 36 miles ÷ 1.5 hours = 24 mph.

On a **distance–time graph**, the gradient gives the speed.

Speed–time graphs

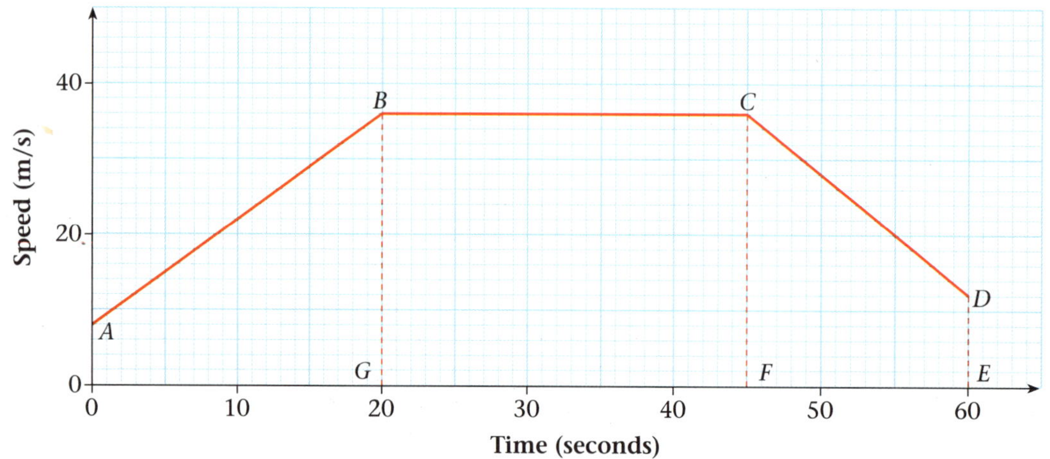

The diagram shows the speed–time graph for one minute of a car's journey.

In the first 20 seconds, its speed increases from 8 m/s to 36 m/s.
The car's speed increases steadily, so AB is a sraight line.
The gradient of the line AB gives the rate of increase of speed:

$$\frac{36 - 8}{20} = 1.4 \text{ m/s per second}$$

Rate of increase of speed is called **acceleration** and the units in this case are m/s per second or m/s^2.

In the first 20 seconds the car has a constant acceleration of 1.4 m/s^2.

Between $t = 20$ and $t = 45$, the car travels at a constant speed of 36 m/s.
Between $t = 45$ and $t = 60$, its speed decreases steadily.
The gradient of the line CD gives the constant acceleration as -1.6 m/s^2.

Negative acceleration is called **deceleration** and you could say that the deceleration between $t = 45$ and $t = 60$ is 1.6 m/s^2.

When the car is travelling at a constant speed of 36 m/s for 25 seconds, between $t = 20$ and $t = 45$, it travels a distance of $36 \times 25 = 900$ m. The area of rectangle $BCFG$ represents this distance.

Similarly, the area of trapezium $ABGO$ represents the distance travelled between $t = 0$ and $t = 20$:

$$\tfrac{1}{2}(8 + 36) \times 20 = 440 \text{ m}$$

The area of trapezium $CDEF$ represents the distance travelled between $t = 45$ and $t = 60$:

$$\tfrac{1}{2}(36 + 12) \times 15 = 360 \text{ m}$$

So you can work out the total distance travelled by the car in the whole minute:

$$900 + 440 + 360 = 1700 \text{ m}$$

On a **speed–time graph**, the gradient gives the acceleration.
When the graph is a curve, draw a tangent and find its gradient.

The area under a speed–time graph gives the distance travelled.

Sometimes 'velocity' is used instead of 'speed'.

Drawing graphs to show water levels

The vases A, B, C and D have circular cross-sections and they contain water.

They all start off with the same depth of water. The water is pumped out of the vases at the same steady rate.

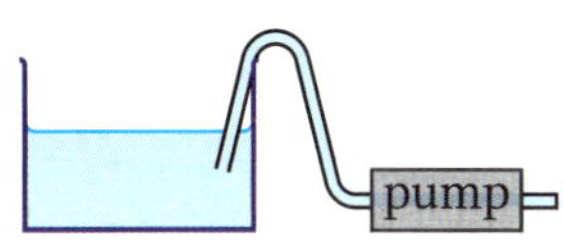

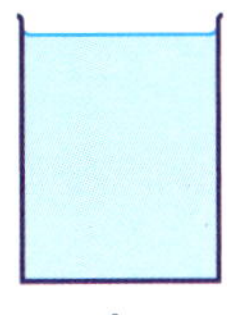

A

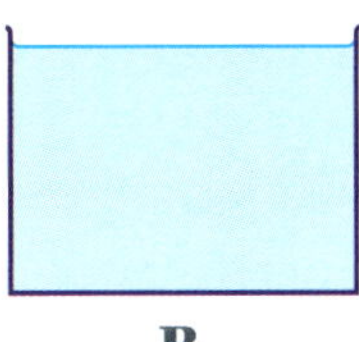

B

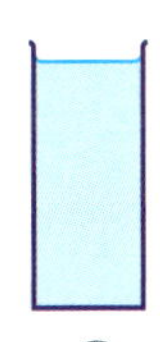

C

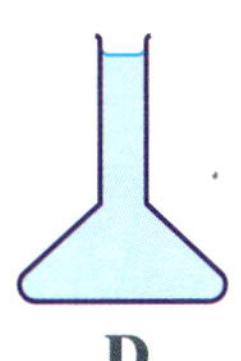

D

The graph shows the relationship between the water level in each vase and the volume of water pumped out of it.

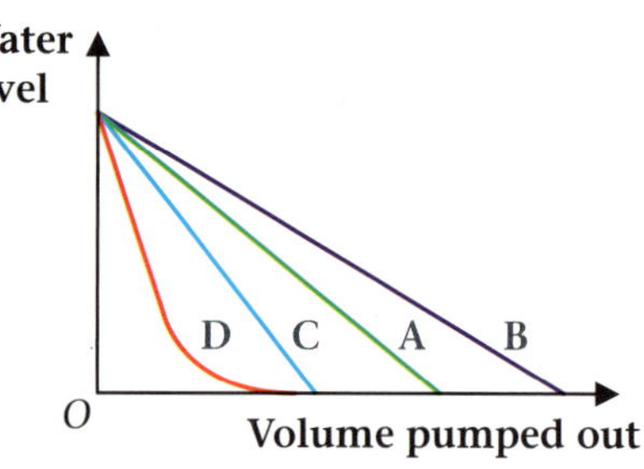

- Vase B has a bigger area of cross-section than A. When the same volume has flowed out of each vase the water level in B remains higher than in A. So the graph for B is less steep than the graph for A.
- The water level in vase C drops even more quickly than in A, so the graph for C is steeper.
- In vase D the level drops more quickly and steadily at first, then it gradually drops more slowly. The graph is straight to begin with (steeper than for C), but then it is curved to show the changing speed.

Worked examination question 3

A DJ can control the sound level of the records he plays at a club.
The sketch graph is a graph of sound level against time while one record was being played.

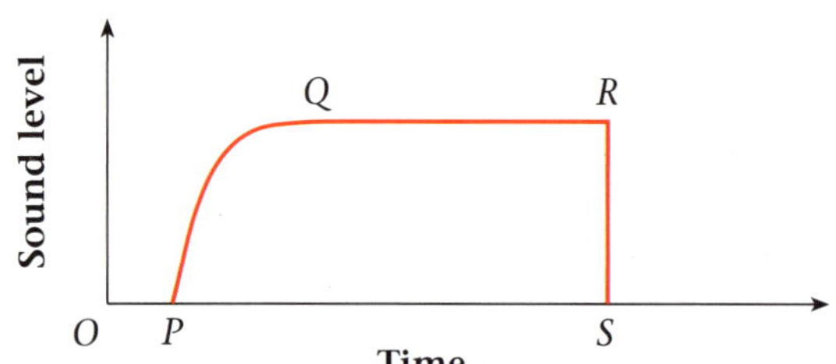

(a) Describe how the sound level changed between P and Q on the graph while the record was being played.

(b) Give one possible reason for the third part, RS, of the sketch graph.

(a) The sound level increases quickly at first and then more slowly. It then levels out.

(b) The sound level suddenly drops to zero. Possible reasons for this are the end of the record or a power cut.

Exercise 17H

1 Sharon and Tracey cycle from Sinton to Coseley and back again. The graph shows their journeys.

(a) Who sets off first?

(b) Describe what happens at A.

(c) Describe what happens at B.

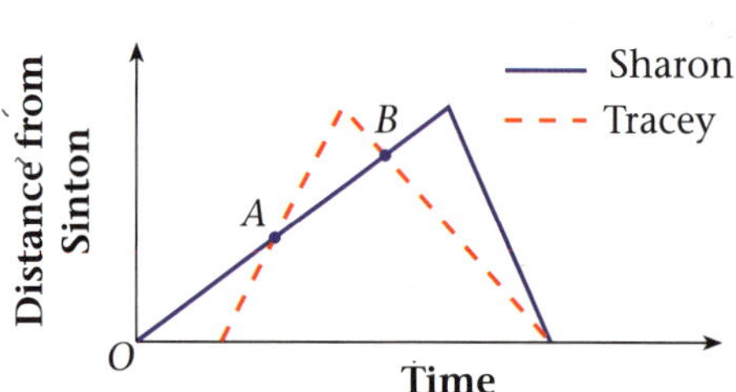

2 Heather walks home from school at a steady speed. Halfway home, she has a rest before continuing her journey at the same speed. Sketch a distance–time graph to show her journey.

3 The diagram shows a distance–time graph for a coach trip from Birmingham to Bristol and back again.

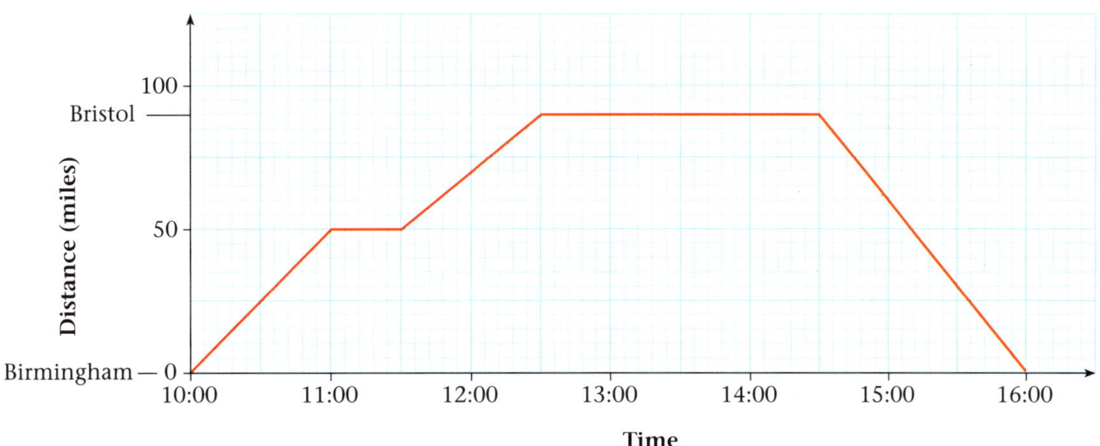

(a) At what time did the coach first stop?

(b) At what time did the coach reach Bristol?

(c) For how long did the coach stay in Bristol?

(d) Calculate the speed of the coach on the return journey.

4 A car in traffic travelled for 20 seconds at 15 m/s, stopped for 15 seconds and then travelled for 25 seconds at 10 m/s.
Draw a distance–time graph for this 60-second period.

5 The diagram shows a speed–time graph for 10 seconds of a train's journey

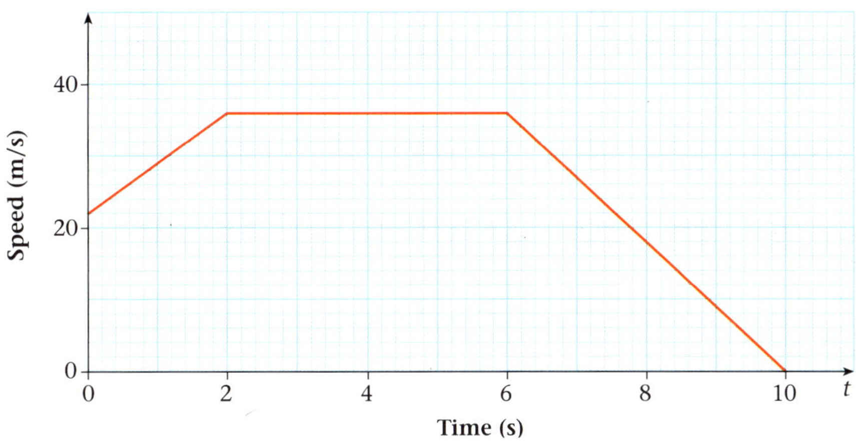

(a) Find the acceleration between $t = 0$ and $t = 2$.

(b) Describe the train's motion between $t = 2$ and $t = 6$.

(c) Find the acceleration between $t = 6$ and $t = 10$.

(d) Find the distance travelled by the train in the 10 seconds.

6 A car accelerates from rest at 5 m/s^2 for 6 seconds, travels with constant speed for 10 seconds and decelerates at 3 m/s^2 for 4 seconds.

(a) Draw a speed–time graph for this 20-second period.

(b) Find the total distance travelled by the car in the 20 seconds.

7 Here are some graphs:

A 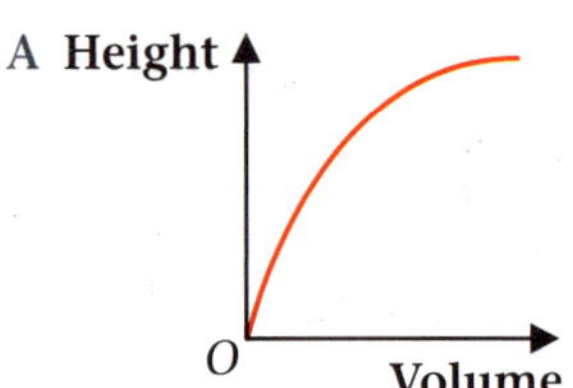

B 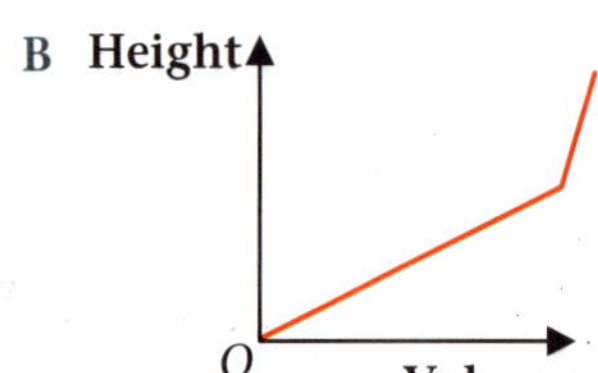

C 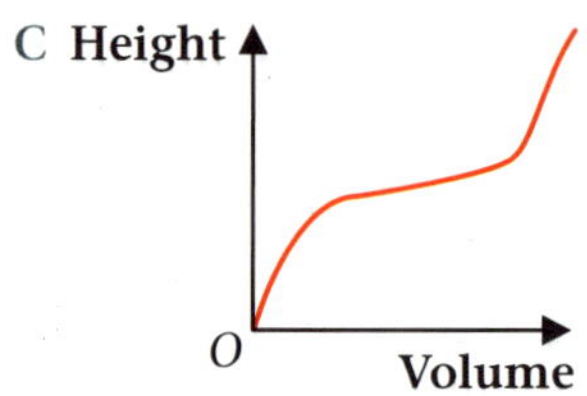

D 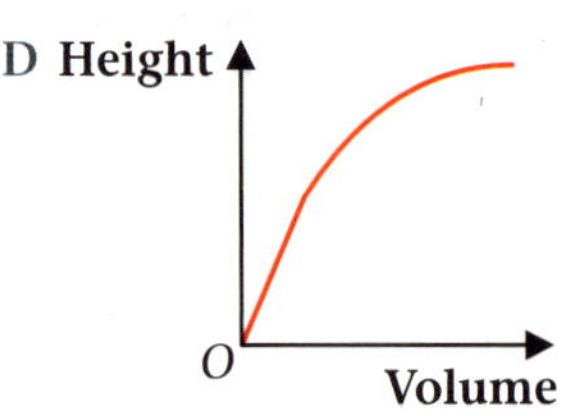

E 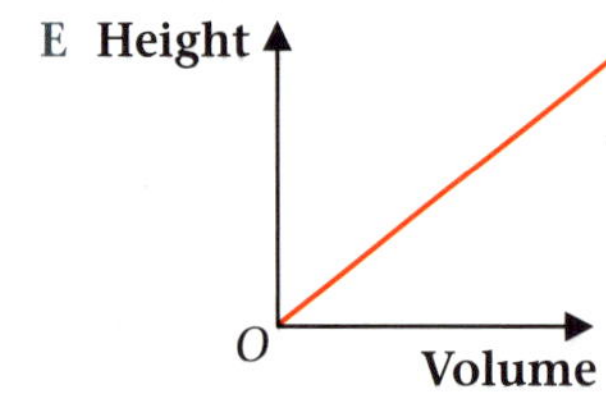

F 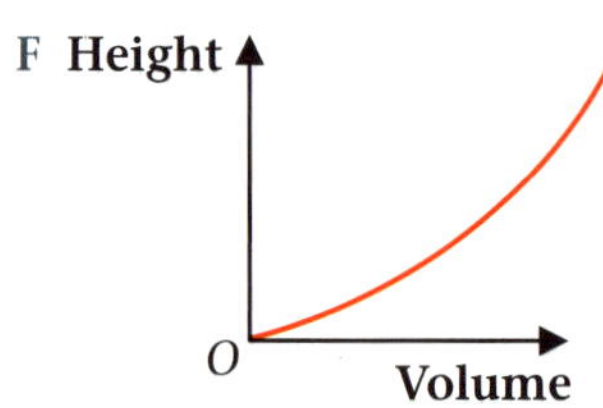

Coloured liquid is poured into the containers below. For each one write down the letter of the graph which best illustrates the relationship between the height of the liquid and the volume in the container.

(a) 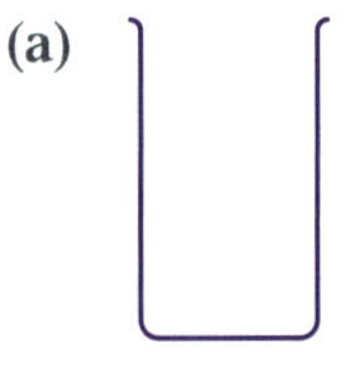
Flower vase

(b) 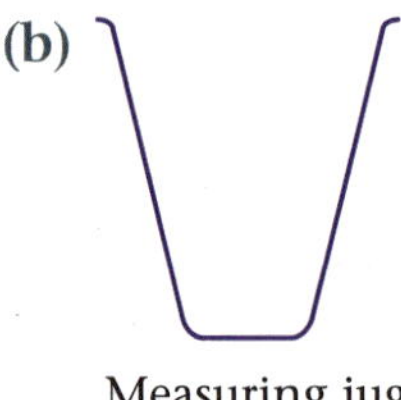
Measuring jug

(c) 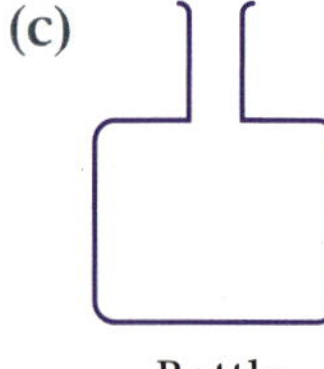
Bottle

(d) 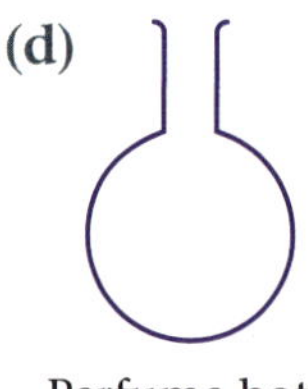
Perfume bottle

8 Water is poured into each of these containers. Sketch a graph to show the relationships between the water level and the volume of water in each container.

(a) 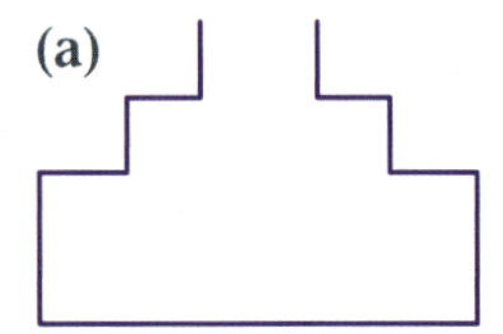

(b) 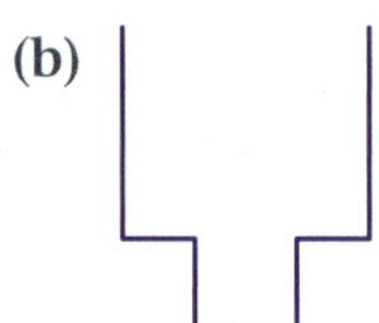

(c) 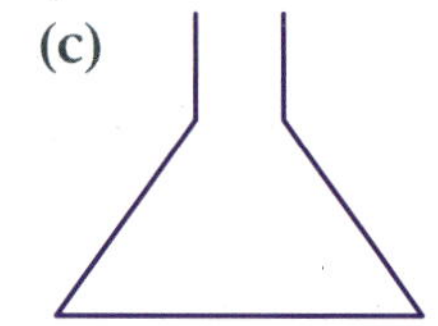

(d) 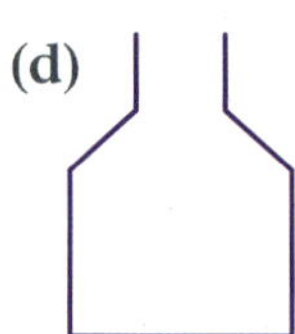

9 Nigel drives 100 miles. Sketch a graph to show the relationship between his average speed and the time he takes.

10 Sketch a graph to show how the value of a new car changes over a number of years.

11 (a) One evening Mr Fish marks a set of maths exam papers. From Graph A describe the three parts of his evening.

(b) Graph B shows the number of customers in a Post Office during one day.

(i) What was the busiest part of the day?

(ii) What happened in the time between P and Q?

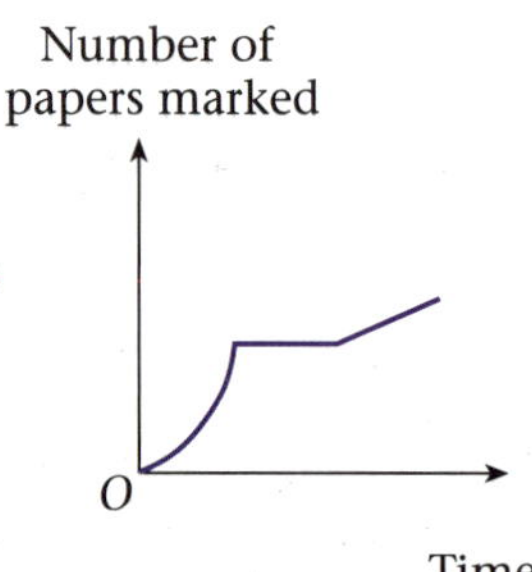

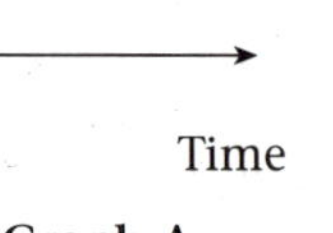

Graph A

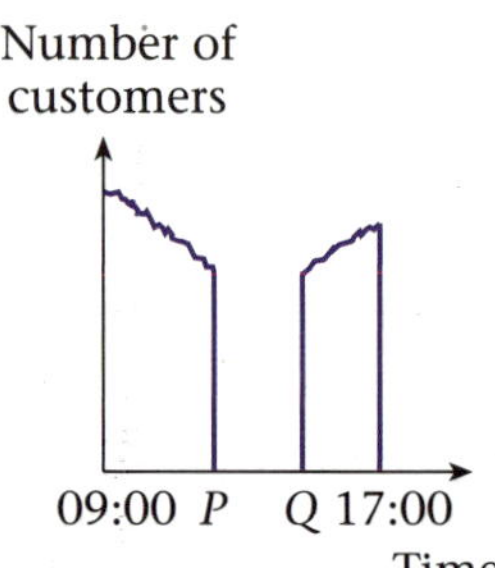

Graph B

12 The diagrams show the shapes of five graphs, A, B, C, D and E.

A

0 80
Speed in miles per hour

B

0 80
Speed in miles per hour

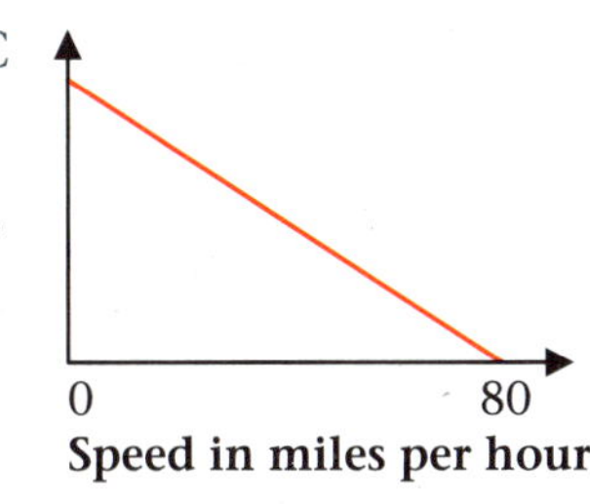

D

0 80
Speed in miles per hour

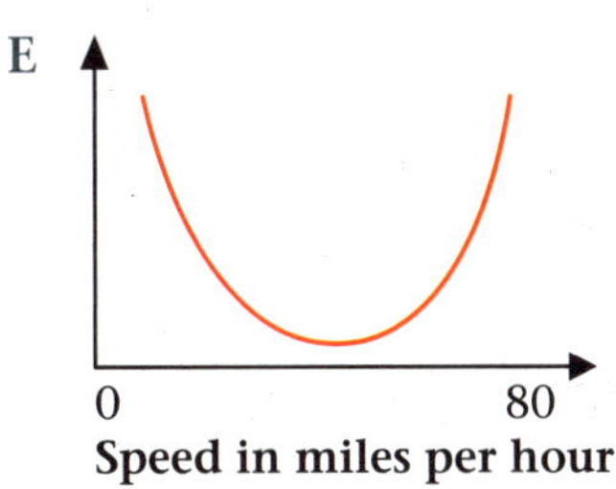

The vertical axes have not been labelled.
On one of the graphs, the missing label is 'Speed in km per hour'.

(a) Write down the letter of this graph.

On one of the graphs the missing label is 'Petrol consumption in miles per gallon'. It shows that the car travels furthest on 1 gallon of petrol when it is travelling at 56 miles per hour.

(b) Write down the letter of this graph. [E]

Mixed exercise 17

1 The equation $x^3 + 4x = 100$ has one solution which is a positive number. Use the method of trial and improvement to find this solution.

Give your answer to 1 decimal place.
You must show all your working. [E]

2 The equation $x^3 - 2x = 67$ has a solution between 4 and 5. Use the method of trial and improvement to find this solution.

Give your answer to 1 decimal place.
You must show all your working. [E]

3 Draw the graph of $y = 2 - \frac{3}{x}$ for values of x from -3 to $+3$.

Draw in the asymptotes and label them with their equations.

4 Plot the graph of $x^3 - 3x^2 + 14$ for values of x from -2 to $+3$.
Use your graph to find the solutions of

(a) $x^3 - 3x^2 + 14 = 0$

(b) $x^3 - 3x^2 + 4 = 0$

(c) $x^3 - 3x^2 + 14 = 3x$

(d) $2x^3 - 6x^2 = 9x - 12$

Draw $y = 3x$.

Divide by 2, then add 14 to both sides.

5 **(a)** Copy and complete the table of values for $y = x^2 - 6x + 10$.

x	0	1	2	3	4	5	6
y	10						10

(b) Hence draw the graph of $y = x^2 - 6x + 10$.

(c) Use your graph to find an estimate for the minimum value of y.

(d) Use a graphical method to find estimates of the solutions to the equation $x^2 - 3x + 1 = 2x - 4$.

6 Jim invests a sum of money for 30 years at 4% per annum compound interest.

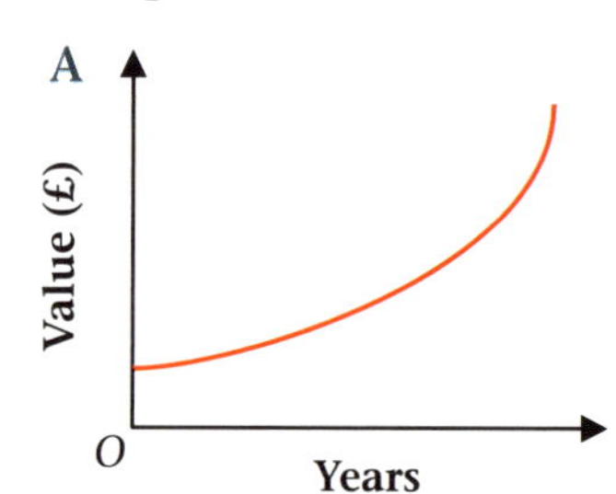

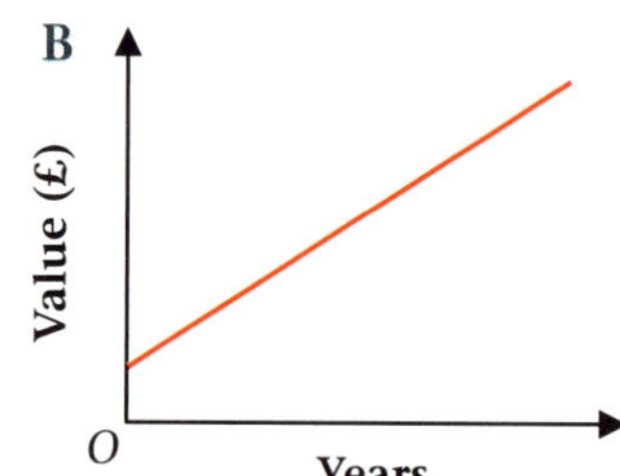

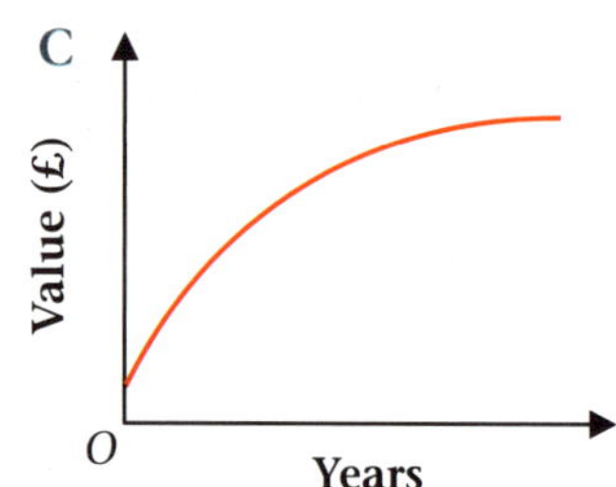

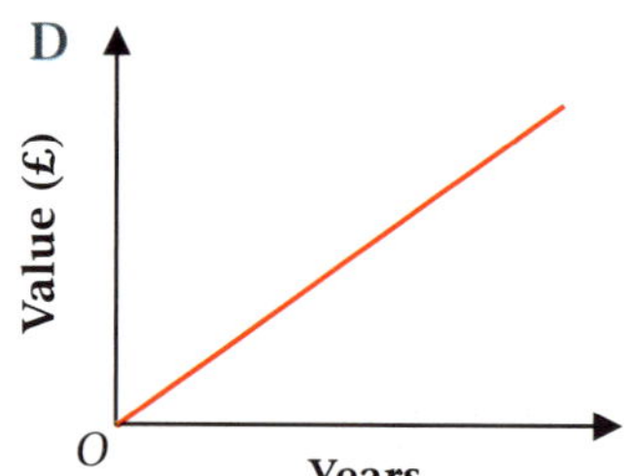

Write down the letter of the graph which best shows how the value of Jim's investment changes over the 30 years.

7 **(a)** Copy and complete the table of values for $y = x^3 - 3x^2 + 2$.

x	−2	−1	0	1	2	3	4
y		−2					

(b) Hence draw the graph of $y = x^3 - 3x^2 + 2$.

(c) Use your graph to find estimates, correct to 1 decimal place where appropriate, for the solutions of

(i) $x^3 - 3x^2 + 2 = 0$

(ii) $x^3 - 3x^2 - 4 = 0$ [E]

8 Here is a velocity–time graph for the first 6 seconds of the movement of an object:

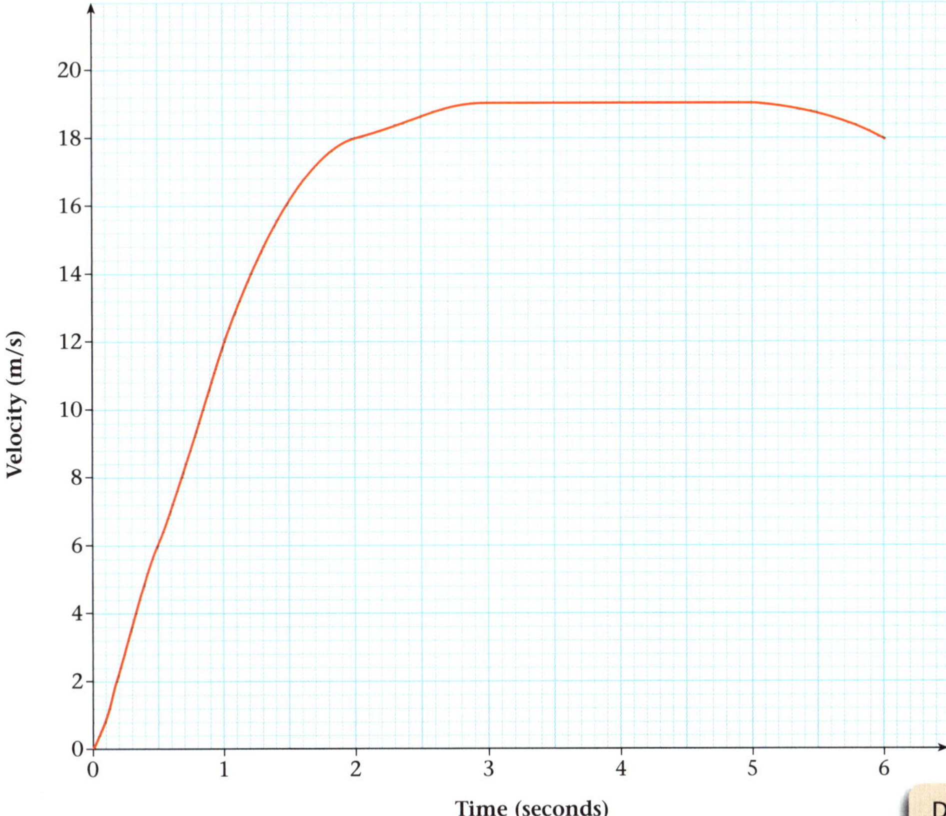

(a) Calculate an estimate for the object's acceleration at $1\frac{1}{2}$ seconds. Give your answer in m/s^2.

Draw a tangent (a straight line that touches the curve) at $(1\frac{1}{2}, 16)$.

(b) Calculate an estimate for the distance the object travelled in the first 6 seconds. [E]

Summary of key points

1. A **quadratic function** is one in which the highest power of x is x^2. For example $x^2 - 7$.
2. The graph of a quadratic function is a U-shaped curve called a **parabola**.
3. A **cubic function** is one in which the highest power of x is x^3. For example $x^3 - 3x + 2$.
4. To find the **reciprocal** of a number or expression divide it into 1.
   For example, the reciprocal of x is $1 \div x = \frac{1}{x}$.
5. A line which a graph approaches without touching is called an **asymptote**.
6. The **solutions** of a quadratic equation are the values of x where the graph cuts the x-axis.
7. You can use a **trial and improvement method** to solve an equation. Try a value in the equation and use your result to improve your estimate. Repeat, getting closer and closer to the correct value.
8. On a **distance–time graph**, the gradient gives the speed.
9. On a **speed–time graph**, the gradient gives the acceleration.
   When the graph is a curve, draw a tangent and find its gradient.
10. The area under a speed–time graph gives the distance travelled.

18 Proportion

The GCSE exam regularly contains questions involving proportion. In this chapter you will solve a variety of problems using proportion.

18.1 Direct proportion

Joan volunteers to take part in a charity fund raising walk. She is given 50 pence for each kilometre she walks.

The further she walks the more money she raises. If she doubles the distance she walks then she doubles the money she raises. But if she only walks half the distance then she raises only half the money.

This is an example of direct proportionality. The money collected, y, is **directly proportional** to the distance walked, x.

The symbol $\propto$ means **'is proportional to'**.

$y \propto x$ means 'y is **directly proportional** to x'.

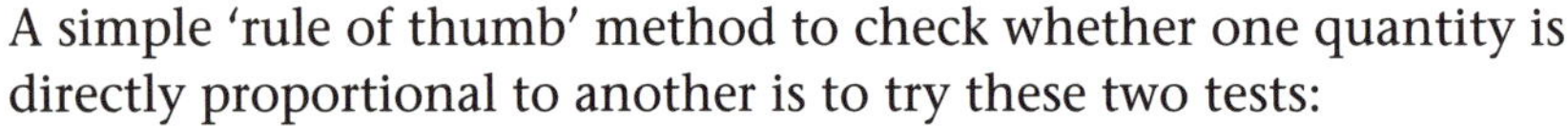

A simple 'rule of thumb' method to check whether one quantity is directly proportional to another is to try these two tests:

- If one quantity is zero, is the other also zero?
- If one quantity doubles, does the other quantity also double?

Exercise 18A

1 Which of the following could be examples of direct proportionality?

(a) profit made by selling goods

(b) final examination results and effort put into work

(c) area of a square and the length of one side

(d) the area of a rectangle with one side of constant length and the length of the other side

(e) time and distance travelled at a constant speed

(f) the height and weight of a student

2 Given that $w \propto t$ and $w = 8$ when $t = 6$, find

(a) t when w doubles in value (b) w when t halves in value.

3 Given that $a \propto b$ and $a = 10$ when $b = 8$, find

(a) b when a increases to 30 (b) a when b decreases to 2.

4 Given that $d \propto s$ and $d = 36$ when $s = 16$, find

(a) s if d decreases by 9 (b) d if s increases to 24.

18.2 Graphs that show direct proportion

In a science experiment the time it takes a small pump to fill a water cylinder is recorded. The height of the water in the cylinder is measured at regular time intervals.

Here are the results:

Height of water (cm)	2.1	4.2	6.3	8.4
Time taken (s)	5	10	15	20

The graph on the right shows the result of plotting height against time and joining the points.

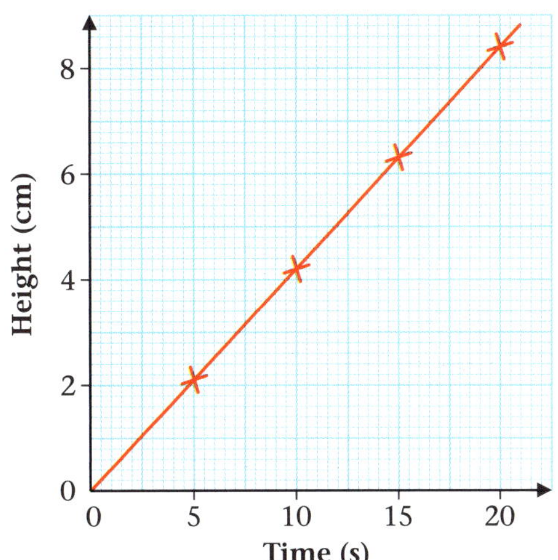

A straight line connects the points. This indicates that the two quantities, height and time taken to reach that height, are in direct proportion.

When a graph of two quantities is a straight line through the origin, one quantity is **directly proportional** to the other.

This means that if one quantity changes then the other changes in the same ratio.

Notice that this is consistent with the 'rule of thumb' in the previous section:

- If one quantity is zero, the other is also zero.
- If one quantity doubles, the other quantity also doubles.

You can use a graph to help find the rule connecting quantities that are in direct proportion to one another.

Example 1

In which of these graphs is s directly proportional to r?

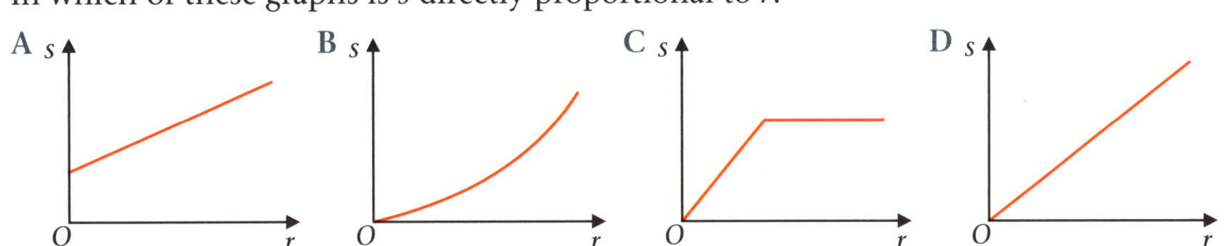

Graph D is a straight line through the origin, showing that s is directly proportional to r.

Example 2

The length of a shadow cast by a tree at midday is directly proportional to the height of the tree. At midday a tree 8 metres tall casts a shadow 10 metres long.

(a) Find a relationship connecting the height of the tree and the length of its shadow at midday.

(b) The shadow of another tree at midday is 8 metres long. How tall is the tree?

(c) Calculate the length of the shadow at midday of a tree 10 metres tall.

(a) The height and the shadow length are directly proportional to one another. The relationship can be shown on a straight line graph like this:

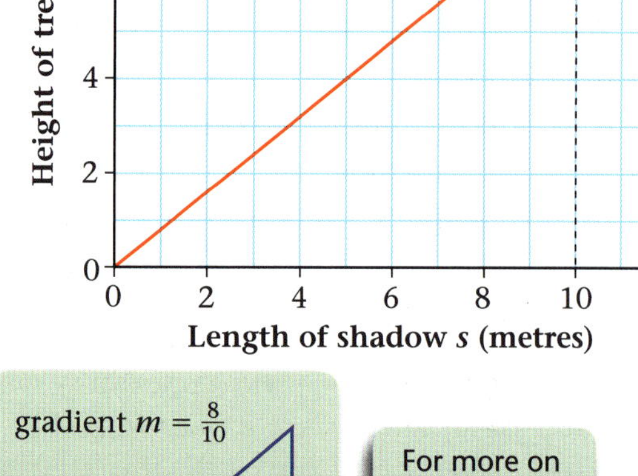

The equation of a straight line is

$$y = mx + c$$

For direct proportion the straight line passes through the origin so

$$c = 0 \quad \text{and} \quad y = mx$$

The gradient m of the line can be used to find the rule connecting h and s. Replacing y with h, and x with s, gives

$$h = ms$$

From the graph, the gradient $m = \frac{8}{10} = 0.8$.

So the relationship connecting the height of the tree and the length of the shadow is

$$h = 0.8s$$

For more on gradients see Chapter 9 (in Book 1).

(b) The relationship $h = 0.8s$ can be used to find the height h of a tree whose shadow is $s = 8$ metres long:

$$h = 0.8 \times 8 = 6.4 \text{ metres}$$

The height of the tree is 6.4 metres when the shadow is 8 metres long.

(c) The relationship can also be used to find the length of shadow for a tree of height $h = 10$ metres:

$$h = 0.8s$$

So $10 = 0.8s$

$$\frac{10}{0.8} = s \quad \text{Divide both sides by 0.8}$$

$$12.5 = s$$

For a tree height of 10 metres, the shadow is 12.5 metres long.

Exercise 18B

1 At 10 am a tree 10 metres high casts a shadow 8 metres long. The length of the shadow (l metres) is directly proportional to the height (h metres) of the tree.

(a) Sketch a graph to show this information.

(b) Find a rule connecting h and l.

(c) Find h when $l = 12.5$.

(d) Find l when $h = 15$.

2 In which of these graphs is x directly proportional to y?

A
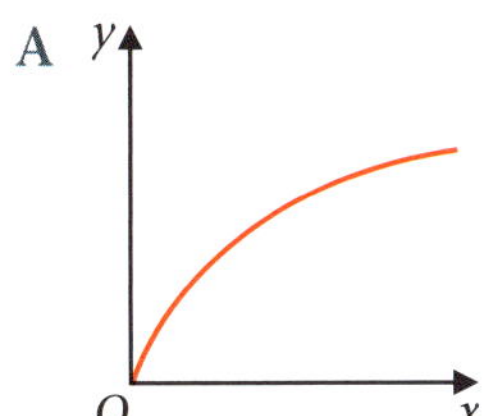

B
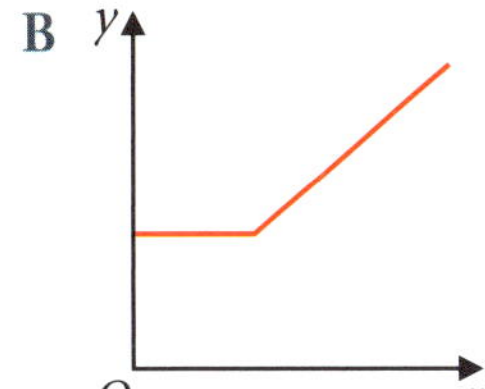

C
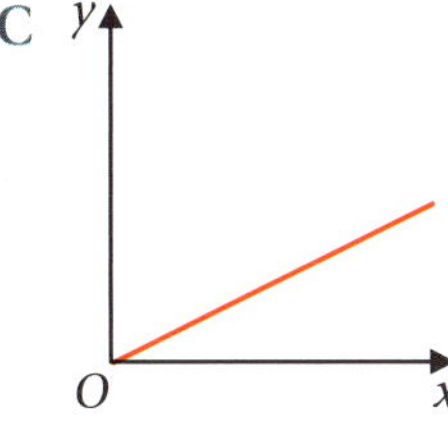

3 The area (A cm^2) of a shape is directly proportional to the length (l cm) of one of its sides. When $l = 14$, $A = 42$.

(a) Sketch a graph to show this information, with area on the vertical axis.

(b) Work out a rule connecting A and l.

(c) What is the area of a similar shape with a side length of 32.4 cm?

(d) Find l when $A = 24.6$.

4 In the recipe for Yorkshire puddings, 2 eggs (e) are required to make 24 small Yorkshire puddings (Y).

(a) Sketch the graph of $Y = 12e$ for $e = 0$ up to 10.

(b) Explain why the equation $Y = 12e$ represents the number of eggs to make a certain number of small Yorkshire puddings.

(c) How many eggs would be needed to make 84 small Yorkshire puddings?

18.3 Using ratios to find proportionality rules

You can use ratios to help find the rule connecting quantities that are in direct proportion to one another.

Example 3

The mass of a silver trophy is directly proportional to its height.

A trophy of height 8.2 cm has a mass of 1.148 kg.

(a) Find a rule connecting the mass m and height h of a trophy.

(b) Find the mass of a similar trophy with a height of 15.5 cm. Give your answer correct to 2 d.p.

(a) Instead of drawing a graph you can present this information in a table:

Mass m (kg)	1.148	?
Height h (cm)	8.2	15.5

The mass to height ratio is

$$1.148 : 8.2 \quad \text{or} \quad \frac{1.148}{8.2} = 0.14$$

The rule connecting the mass m and height h is

$$m = 0.14h$$

(b) Using the rule, when $h = 15.5$ then $m = 0.14 \times 15.5 = 2.17$

The mass of the second trophy is 2.17 kg.

Exercise 18C

1 These tables each show two variables which are directly proportional to each other.

For each of these tables find

(i) a rule connecting the two variables

(ii) the missing values correct to 1 d.p.

(a)

w	8.4	?
h	8	12

(b)

h	12.0	16.8
s	20.5	?

(c)

p	7.8	?
l	6.8	27.6

(d)

a	110.4	10.4
p	?	23.4

2 The voltage V across a resistor (in volts) is directly proportional to the current I flowing through it (in amps).

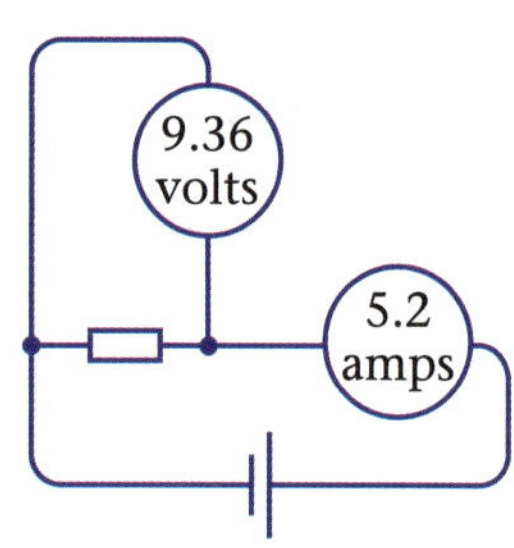

(a) Write down the readings of the two meters.

(b) Find a rule connecting the voltage and current.

(c) Calculate the current when the voltage increases to 11.52 volts.

(d) Calculate the voltage when the current is 2.46 amps.

3 Kirstine obtains these readings during an experiment, where V is proportional to I:

Voltage, V	2.8	4.6	8.4	12.6	22.4	28
Current, I	1	2	3	4.5	8	10

Unfortunately there is an error in her table.

(a) Plot the points and draw a graph of voltage V against current I.

(b) Which reading is wrong, and what should it be?

(c) Find the rule connecting V and I.

(d) Find V when $I = 3.5$

(e) Calculate I when $V = 20.5$, giving your answer correct to 3 d.p.

4 Given that $r \propto t$ and $r = 2.4$ when $t = 12.8$, find correct to 2 decimal places
(a) r when $t = 8.9$ (b) t when $r = 3.1$

5 The cost of a bottle of white correction fluid is directly proportional to the amount of fluid in the bottle. A bottle containing 20 ml of fluid costs 72p. Find
(a) a rule connecting the cost and the amount
(b) the cost of a bottle containing 100 ml of fluid.

6 On a car journey the distance travelled, d, is directly proportional to the time taken, t. In 2 hours a car travels 76 miles. Find
(a) a rule connecting d and t
(b) the distance travelled in 5 hours
(c) the time taken to travel a distance of 418 miles.

18.4 Writing proportionality formulae

When y is directly proportional to x, you can write a **proportionality statement** and a **formula** connecting y and x:

- $y \propto x$ is the proportionality statement
- $y = kx$ is the proportionality formula, where k is the constant of proportionality.

Example 4

The extension E of a spring is directly proportional to the force F pulling the spring. The extension is 8 cm when a force of 30 N is pulling it. Calculate the extension when the force is 9 N.

Force is measured in newtons (N).

As $E \propto F$ the proportionality formula can be written as:

$$E = kF$$

To find the value of the constant of proportionality k, substitute $E = 8$ and $F = 30$ in the formula:

$$8 = k \times 30$$

$$\frac{8}{30} = k$$ Divide both sides by 30

So the proportionality formula is

$$E = \frac{8}{30}F$$

When the force F is 9 N, the extension E is

$$E = \frac{8}{30} \times 9 = 2.4 \text{ cm}$$

To find the value of k, the constant of proportionality, substitute known values of y and x into $y = kx$.

Exercise 18D

1 y is proportional to x so that $y = kx$.
Given that $y = 148$ when $x = 12$, find the value of k.
Calculate the value of y when $x = 7$.

2 p is proportional to q so that $p = kq$.
Given that $p = 34$ when $q = 51$, find the value of k.
Calculate the value of p when $q = 7$.

3 z varies in direct proportion to x.
Write a formula for z in terms of x.
Given that $z = 3\frac{3}{5}$ when $x = 6$, find the value of z when $x = 14$.

4 z varies in direct proportion to w.
Write a formula for z in terms of w.
Given that $z = 315$ when $w = 7$, find the value of z when $w = 105$.

5 y is proportional to x. Given that $y = 12$ when $x = 4$, calculate the value of

(a) y when $x = 5$ (b) y when $x = 13$ (c) x when $y = 10$.

6 F varies directly as E. Given that $F = 300$ when $E = 120$, calculate the value of

(a) F when $E = 90$ (b) F when $E = 500$ (c) E when $F = 180$.

7 Given that $y \propto p$, calculate the values missing from this table:

p	1		10
y		4	28

8 The volume V of liquid in a tube is proportional to the height h of the tube. When the height of the liquid in the tube is 7 cm, the volume of liquid is 10 cm^3. Calculate the volume of liquid when the height of liquid is 4 cm.

9 The distance travelled by the tip of the second hand on a clock is proportional to the time elapsed. Calculate the increase in the distance travelled by the tip of the second hand when the time elapsed increases by 40%, giving your answer as a percentage.

10 The height h of an elephant is directly proportional to the diameter d of its footprint. A baby elephant has a height of 150 cm and the diameter of its footprint is 20 cm.

(a) Find an equation connecting h and d.

(b) Calculate the height of an elephant with a footprint of diameter 25 cm.

(c) Calculate the diameter of the footprint of an elephant whose height is 3.2 m.

18.5 Square and cubic proportionality

Sets of Russian dolls are made to fit inside each other. They are exactly the same shape as each other and are mathematically **similar**.

One of the dolls is 8 cm high and has a surface area of $115.2\,\text{cm}^2$.

The surface area S of each doll is proportional to the square of its height h. This can be written as the proportionality statement

$$S \propto h^2$$

The proportionality formula can be written as

$$S = kh^2$$

Reminder:
When two shapes are **similar**, corresponding lengths on the two shapes are in proportion.

The constant of proportionality k can be found by substituting information about the 8 cm high doll into the formula:

$$115.2 = k \times 8^2$$
$$64k = 115.2$$
$$k = \frac{115.2}{64}$$
$$k = 1.8$$

So the proportionality formula is

$$S = 1.8h^2$$

The formula can be used to find the surface area of a doll of height 10 cm:

$$S = 1.8 \times 10^2$$
$$= 1800\,\text{cm}^2$$

In this example one quantity (the surface area) is proportional to the **square** of the other quantity (the height).

When y is directly proportional to the **square** of x:

- $\boldsymbol{y \propto x^2}$ is the proportionality statement
- $\boldsymbol{y = kx^2}$ is the proportionality formula, where k is the constant of proportionality.

Example 5

The volume of a Russian doll is proportional to the cube of its height. The volume of the 8 cm high doll is $64\,\text{cm}^3$.
Find the volume of the 10 cm high doll.

The proportionality statement is

$$V \propto h^3$$

The proportionality formula can be written as

$$V = kh^3$$

The value of the constant k can be found using the information about the 8 cm high doll:

$$64 = k \times 8^3$$
$$64 = 512k$$
$$k = \frac{64}{512} = \frac{1}{8}$$
$$k = 0.125$$

So the proportionality formula is

$$V = 0.125 \times h^3$$

The formula can be used to find the volume of the 10 cm high doll:

$$V = 0.125 \times 10^3$$
$$= 125 \text{ cm}^3$$

In this example one variable is proportional to the **cube** of the other.

When y is directly proportional to the **cube** of x:

- $y \propto x^3$ is the proportionality statement
- $y = kx^3$ is the proportionality formula, where k is the constant of proportionality.

Worked examination question 1

The distance D moved by an object is proportional to the square of the time t for which it is moving.

(a) Express D in terms of t and a constant of proportionality k.

(b) When $t = 10$ seconds, $D = 500$ metres.
Calculate:

(i) the value of D when $t = 4$ seconds

(ii) the value of t when $D = 720$ metres.

(a) $D \propto t^2$

So $D = kt^2$

(b) (i) Substitute $t = 10$ seconds and $D = 500$ metres into the formula $D = kt^2$:

$$500 = k \times 10^2$$
$$500 = 100k$$
$$5 = k$$

Divide both sides by 100.

So the formula is

$$D = 5t^2$$

When $t = 4$ seconds:

$$D = 5 \times 4^2$$
$$= 5 \times 16$$
$$= 80 \text{ metres}$$

When $t = 4$ seconds, $D = 80$ metres.

(ii) When $D = 720$ metres:

$$720 = 5t^2$$
$$\frac{720}{5} = t^2 \quad \text{Divide by 5.}$$
$$144 = t^2$$
$$\sqrt{144} = t \quad \text{Take the square root.}$$
$$t = 12 \text{ seconds}$$

When $D = 720$ metres, $t = 12$ seconds.

Exercise 18E

1 y is directly proportional to the square of x so that $y = kx^2$.
Given that $y = 20$ when $x = 2$, calculate the value of k.
Calculate the value of y when $x = 4$.

2 z varies in direct proportion to the square of x so that $z = kx^2$.
Given that $z = 100$ when $x = 4$, calculate the value of

(a) the proportionality constant k

(b) z when $x = 5$

(c) x when $z = 10$.

3 s varies in direct proportion to the cube of t, so that $s = kt^3$.
Given that $s = 54$ when $t = 3$, calculate the value of

(a) the proportionality constant k

(b) s when $t = 4$

(c) t when $s = 128$.

4 l is directly proportional to the cube of m.

(a) Write a formula for l in terms of m.

(b) Given that the value of l when $m = 0.4$ is 3.2,

(i) calculate the value of l when $m = 0.8$

(ii) calculate the value of m when $l = 43.2$

5 The resistance R to the motion of a train varies directly as the square of the speed v of the train. The resistance to motion is 100 000 N when the speed is 20 metres per second. Calculate the resistance to motion when the speed of the train is 10 metres per second.

6 A stone is dropped down a well a distance d metres. The value of d is directly proportional to the square of the time of travel t seconds.

When $t = 2$, $d = 20$. Calculate the value of d when

(a) $t = 3$

(b) $t = 4.5$

7 The variables p and q are related so that p is directly proportional to the square of q. Complete this table for values of p and q:

q	0.5	2	
p		12	27

8 z varies in direct proportion to the cube of t. When $t = 5$ the value of z is 0.25.

Calculate the value of z when $t = 1$.

9 The length of a pendulum l is directly proportional to the square of the period T of the pendulum.
Given that a pendulum which has a period of 3 seconds is 2.25 metres long, calculate the length of a pendulum which has a period of

(a) 2 seconds

(b) 2.5 seconds.

The period of a pendulum is the time it takes to swing away from its starting position and back again.

10 A varies in direct proportion to the square of l. When the value of l is multiplied by 2, by what amount is A multiplied?

11 The variable z is directly proportional to the cube of the variable w. Complete the table for these variables:

w	2	1	
z	16		6.75

12 A set of models of a road bridge is made.
The surface area of the road is directly proportional to the square of the height h of the model.
The height of Model A is 50% greater than the height of Model B. By what percentage is the area of road surface in Model A greater than the area of road surface in Model B?

13 The pressure on a diver under water is directly proportional to the square of her depth below the surface of the water.
The diver has reached a depth of 10 metres.
How much further must she descend for the pressure to double?

18.6 Inverse proportion

When one quantity increases while the other decreases proportionally, the quantities are in **inverse proportion** to one another. (When one quantity decreases, the other will increase proportionally.)

$y \propto \frac{1}{x}$ means 'y is **inversely proportional** to x'.

When y is inversely proportional to x:

- $y \propto \frac{1}{x}$ is the proportionality statement
- $y = k \times \frac{1}{x}$ or $y = \frac{k}{x}$ are ways of writing the proportionality formula, where k is the constant of inverse proportionality.

Another way of describing such a relationship is to say that y is directly proportional to $\frac{1}{x}$.

Example 6

In a physics experiment the pressure P and volume V of a quantity of gas are measured at constant temperature.

The pressure is inversely proportional to the volume. When the pressure is 2 bar, the volume of the gas is 150 cm^3.

Calculate the pressure of the gas when the volume is decreased to 100 cm^3.

The bar is a unit of pressure. 1 bar = 10^5 pascals

P is inversely proportional to V so

$$P \propto \frac{1}{V}$$

The formula is

$$P = \frac{k}{V}$$

The constant k is found by substituting the pressure $P = 2$ and the volume $V = 150$:

$$2 = \frac{k}{150}$$

so $\quad k = 300$

This gives the formula

$$P = \frac{300}{V}$$

When $V = 100$:

$$P = \frac{300}{100}$$

$$= 3 \text{ bar}$$

Example 7

In Newtonian physics the force of attraction F between two bodies is inversely proportional to the **square** of the distance r between their centres.

When the distance between their centres is 1 unit, the force of attraction is 16 units.
Calculate the force of attraction when the distance between their centres is 2 units.

The planet Jupiter has over 30 moons, four of which are visible with binoculars. The moon shown here is called Ganymede.

F is inversely proportional to r^2, so the proportionality statement is

$$F \propto \frac{1}{r^2}$$

The formula is

$$F = \frac{k}{r^2}$$

where k is constant for these two bodies only. (The force between the bodies also depends on their masses.)

The constant k is found by using the fact that when $r = 1$ unit, the force $F = 16$ units:

$$16 = \frac{k}{1^2}$$

so $16 = k$

The formula is

$$F = \frac{16}{r^2}$$

When the distance between the centres of the two bodies is 2 units the force is

$$F = \frac{16}{2^2}$$

$$= 4 \text{ units}$$

In Newtonian physics the Moon orbits the Earth because there is a force of attraction across space given by the formula

$$F = \frac{G M_E M_M}{r^2}$$

In Einsteinian physics each mass is in free fall through space–time, which is curved by their presence. This curvature gives rise to the orbit.

Worked examination question 2

The resistance R of 1 metre of cable of a certain material is inversely proportional to the square of the radius r of the cable.
When the radius is 5 mm, the resistance of 1 metre of the cable is 0.06 ohms.

(a) Find a formula connecting R and r.

(b) Calculate the value of R when r is 4 mm.

(a) $$R \propto \frac{1}{r^2}$$

So $$R = \frac{k}{r^2}$$

where k is a constant.

Substitute $R = 0.06$ and $r = 5$ into the formula:

$$0.06 = \frac{k}{5^2}$$

so $$k = 1.5$$

So the formula is

$$R = \frac{1.5}{r^2}$$

(b) When $r = 4$:

$$R = \frac{1.5}{4^2}$$

$= 0.094$ ohms (correct to 2 significant figures).

Exercise 18F

1 y is inversely proportional to x so that $y = \dfrac{k}{x}$
When $x = 6$ the value of y is 12.

(a) Find the value of k.

(b) Calculate the value of y when $x = 10$.

2 z is inversely proportional to t so that $z = \dfrac{k}{t}$
When $t = 0.3$ the value of z is 16.

(a) Find the value of k.

(b) Calculate the value of z when $t = 0.5$

3 z is inversely proportional to the square of w so that $z = \dfrac{k}{w^2}$
When $w = 4$, $z = 32$.

(a) Find the value of k.

(b) Calculate the value of z when $w = 2$.

4 p is inversely proportional to the square of q so that $p = \dfrac{k}{q^2}$
When $q = 0.5$, $p = 10$.

(a) Find the value of k.

(b) Calculate the value of p when $q = 0.25$

5 An essay typed at 50 characters to the line is 372 lines long. The number of lines in the essay is inversely proportional to the number of characters to the line. Calculate the number of lines that the essay will have when it is typed with

(a) 80 characters to the line

(b) 64 characters to the line.

6 In a mathematics investigation, students draw a series of rectangles which all have the same area. The length l of each rectangle is inversely proportional to its width w.

(a) Write the proportionality statement and the formula for this situation.

(b) What does the constant of proportionality represent?

7 The light intensity I at a distance d from a light source varies inversely as the square of the distance from the source. At a distance 1 cm from the light source the light intensity is 64 units. Calculate the light intensity at a distance 4 cm from the light source.

8 The frequency f of sound varies inversely as the wavelength w. The frequency of middle C is 256 hertz and the wavelength of this note is 129 cm.

(a) Find the equation connecting frequency f and the wavelength w.

(b) Calculate the frequency of the note with a wavelength of 86 cm.

(c) Calculate the wavelength of a note whose frequency is 344 Hz.

The unit of frequency is the hertz (Hz) (cycles per second).

Mixed exercise 18

1 An electrical heater uses 16 units of electricity in 5 hours. The amount of electricity used is directly proportional to the time. How much electricity will the heater use in 3 hours?

2 A builder makes concrete paving slabs. All the slabs are the same thickness. The cross-sections of all the slabs are equilateral triangles. The mass of concrete is proportional to the square of the length of one of the sides. A slab with side 60 cm has mass 50 kg.
Calculate the mass of a slab with side 20 cm.

3 A spaceship covers a distance of 18 000 kilometres in 3 hours 20 minutes. The distance travelled is directly proportional to the time taken.
Calculate the distance that the spaceship will travel in 5 hours 20 minutes.

4 A hang-glider pilot, at a height of h metres above the sea, can see up to a distance of s kilometres.
It is known that h is proportional to the square of s.

(a) Given that $h = 140$ when $s = 16$, find the formula for h in terms of s.

(b) Calculate the height of the hang-glider when the pilot can just see a lighthouse which is 24 kilometres away.

5 The variables y and x are related by

$$y \propto \frac{1}{x}$$

When $x = 3$, $y = 30$. Calculate the value of y when $x = 5$.

6 The height h reached by a ball thrown up into the air varies in direct proportion to the square of the speed v at which the ball is thrown. A ball thrown at a speed of 20 metres per second reaches a height of 20 metres.
Calculate the height reached by a ball thrown at a speed of

(a) 25 metres per second

(b) 30 metres per second.

7 The time taken for a journey on a motorway is inversely proportional to the average speed for the journey. The journey takes 1 hour 30 minutes when the average speed is 54 miles per hour.
Calculate the time taken, in hours and minutes, for this journey when the average speed is 45 miles per hour.

8 The energy stored in a battery is proportional to the square of the diameter of the battery, for batteries of the same height. One battery has a diameter of 2.5 cm and stores 1.6 units of energy. Another battery of the same height has a diameter of 1.5 cm.
Calculate the energy stored in the second battery.

9 In a factory, chemical reactions are carried out in spherical containers.

The time, T minutes, that the chemical reaction takes is directly proportional to the square of the radius, R cm, of the spherical container.

When $R = 120$, $T = 32$. Find the value of T when $R = 150$.

10 The shutter speed, S, of a camera varies inversely as the square of the aperture setting, f. When $f = 8$, $S = 125$.

(a) Find a formula for S in terms of f.

(b) Hence, or otherwise, calculate the value of S when $f = 4$.

11 The graphs of y against x represent four different types of proportionality.

A

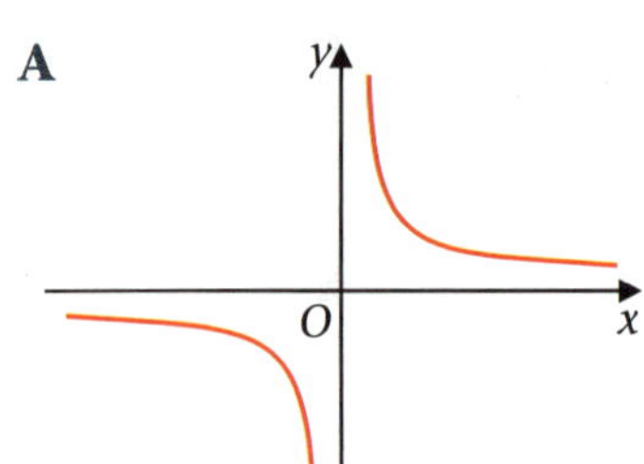

B

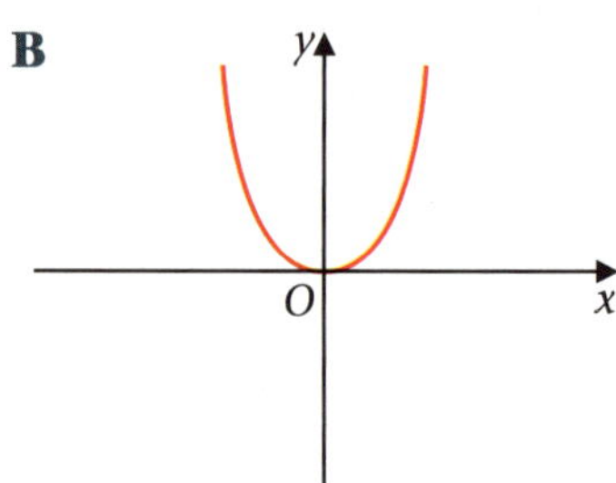

C

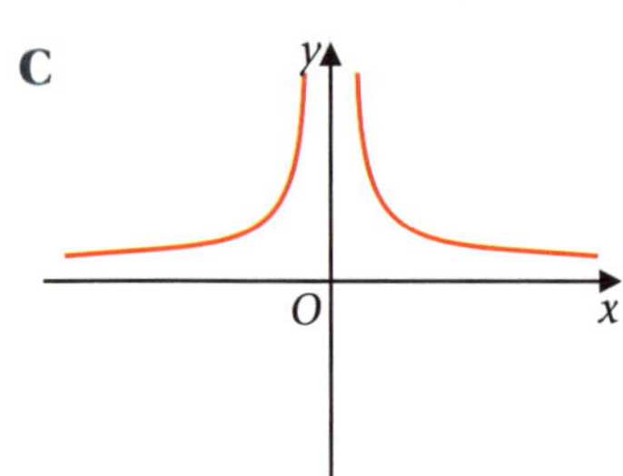

D

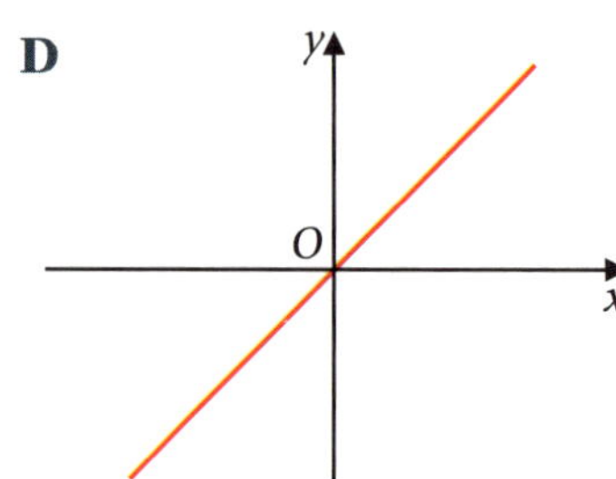

Write down the letter of the graph which represents each of these statements:

(a) y is directly proportional to x

(b) y is inversely proportional to x

(c) y is proportional to the square of x

(d) y is inversely proportional to the square of x.

Summary of key points

1 The symbol $\propto$ means '**is proportional to**'.

2 $y \propto x$ means 'y is **directly proportional** to x'.

3 When a graph of two quantities is a straight line through the origin, one quantity is **directly proportional** to the other.

4 When y is directly proportional to x, you can write a **proportionality statement** and a **formula** connecting y and x:

- $y \propto x$ is the proportionality statement
- $y = kx$ is the proportionality formula, where k is the constant of proportionality.

5 To find the value of k, the constant of proportionality, substitute known values of y and x into $y = kx$.

6 When y is directly proportional to the **square** of x:

- $y \propto x^2$ is the proportionality statement
- $y = kx^2$ is the proportionality formula, where k is the constant of proportionality.

7 When y is directly proportional to the **cube** of x:

- $y \propto x^3$ is the proportionality statement
- $y = kx^3$ is the proportionality formula, where k is the constant of proportionality.

8 $y \propto \frac{1}{x}$ means 'y is **inversely proportional** to x'.

9 When y is inversely proportional to x:

- $y \propto \frac{1}{x}$ is the proportionality statement
- $y = k \times \frac{1}{x}$ or $y = \frac{k}{x}$ are ways of writing the proportionality formula, where k is the constant of inverse proportionality.

19 Quadratic equations

In this chapter you will solve quadratic equations and equations involving algebraic fractions.

Equations of the form $ax^2 + bx + c = 0$, where $a \neq 0$ are called quadratic equations. Graphs of quadratic equations were introduced in Chapter 17.

Quadratic equations can be used to represent a wide variety of situations, for example the diving shown on the right.

The solution of $7t^2 - t - 4 = 0$ gives the time in seconds to dive into the pool.

The quadratic equation $ax^2 + bx + c = 0$, with $a \neq 0$, has two solutions (or roots), which may be equal.

When solving quadratic equations it is helpful to remember that multiplying two numbers to get the answer 0 is only possible if one of the numbers is itself 0. For example:

- if $7 \times y = 0$ then y must be 0
- if $x \times 3 = 0$ then x must be 0.

In general, if $xy = 0$ then either $x = 0$ or $y = 0$ (or both).

There are three algebraic methods for solving quadratic equations: by factorising, by completing the square, and by using a formula.

In each method the first step is to rearrange the quadratic equation into the form $ax^2 + bx + c = 0$.

19.1 Solving quadratic equations by factorising

Example 1

Solve the equation $x^2 = 8x$.

$$x^2 = 8x$$

$$x^2 - 8x = 0$$ — Rearrange into the form $ax^2 + bx + c = 0$

$$x(x - 8) = 0$$ — Factorise

So either $x = 0$ or $x - 8 = 0$

So $x = 0$, $x = 8$ are the two solutions or roots of the equation $x^2 = 8x$.

A common error is to divide both sides by x. This loses the $x = 0$ solution. Never divide by any term which can take value 0.

Example 2

Solve the equation $(3x + 2)(2x - 1) = 3$.

$(3x + 2)(2x - 1) = 3$

$6x^2 + x - 2 = 3$ — Expand the brackets

$6x^2 + x - 5 = 0$ — Rearrange into the form $ax^2 + bx + c = 0$

$(6x - 5)(x + 1) = 0$ — Factorise

So either $6x - 5 = 0$ or $x + 1 = 0$

$6x = 5$ or $x = -1$

The two solutions are $x = \frac{5}{6}$ and $x = -1$

For a reminder on how to factorise quadratic expressions see Chapter 14 (in Book 1).

Example 3

Solve the equation $y^2 - 5y + 18 = 2 + 3y$.

$y^2 - 5y + 18 = 2 + 3y$

$y^2 - 8y + 16 = 0$ — Rearrange into the form $ay^2 + by + c = 0$

$(y - 4)(y - 4) = 0$ — Factorise

So either $y - 4 = 0$ or $y - 4 = 0$

$y = 4$ or $y = 4$

$y = 4$ is the only solution. In this example the two roots of the quadratic equation are equal. This parabola touches the y-axis (horizontal axis) only once.

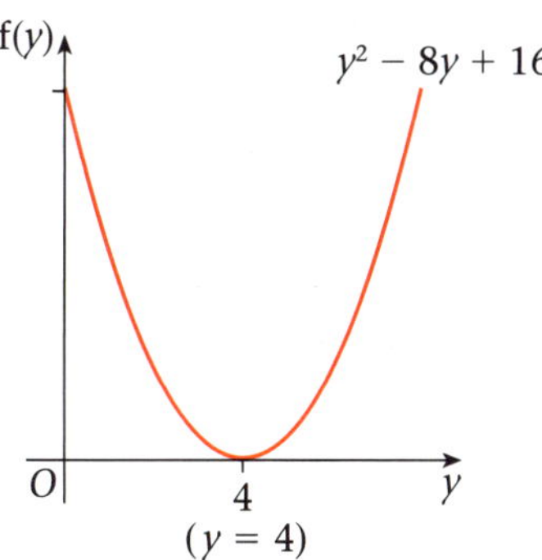

Example 4

Solve the equation $2a^2 - 162 = 0$.

$2a^2 - 162 = 0$

$2(a^2 - 81) = 0$ — Take out the common factor 2

$2(a - 9)(a + 9) = 0$ — Using the difference of two squares

For this equation to be 0, either

$a - 9 = 0$ or $a + 9 = 0$

$a = 9$ or $a = -9$

Write these roots as $a = \pm 9$.

This is read as 'a equals positive or negative 9'.

Solving equations of the type $y^2 = k$

You can solve equations of the type $y^2 = k$ by taking the square root of both sides, but you must remember to write the $\pm$ sign.

If $y^2 = k$ then $y = \pm\sqrt{k}$

Example 5

Solve the equation $(3x - 1)^2 = 64$.

$(3x - 1)^2 = 64$

$(3x - 1) = \pm 8$ —— Take the square root of both sides

$3x = 1 \pm 8$ —— Add 1 to both sides

So either $3x = 1 + 8$ or $3x = 1 - 8$

$3x = 9$ or $3x = -7$

The solutions are $x = 3$ and $x = -\frac{7}{3}$

Exercise 19A

1 Solve these equations.

(a) $(x - 1)(x + 2) = 0$ (b) $x(x - 3) = 0$

(c) $(x - 4)(2x + 1) = 0$ (d) $2x(2x - 3) = 0$

(e) $(2x - 1)(3x - 4) = 0$ (f) $2(x - 5)(x - 2) = 0$

2 Solve these quadratic equations in y.

(a) $y^2 - 3y = 0$ (b) $y^2 - 16 = 0$

(c) $y^2 - 3y - 4 = 0$ (d) $y^2 + 11y + 28 = 0$

(e) $2y^2 + 5y - 3 = 0$ (f) $12y^2 - 7y - 12 = 0$

(g) $4y^2 - 11y + 6 = 0$ (h) $2y^2 - 18y = 0$

(i) $6y^2 - 11y - 7 = 0$

3 Solve these equations.

(a) $y^2 = 25$ (b) $3x^2 = x$

(c) $3y^2 + 5y = 2$ (d) $2x^2 = 8$

(e) $5x = 2x^2$ (f) $y^2 + 2y = 35$

(g) $(a - 2)(a + 1) = 10$ (h) $(2x - 1)^2 = 3x^2 - 2$

(i) $6a^2 = 7 - 11a$ (j) $(3x - 2)^2 = x^2$

4 Explain what is wrong with Julie's method to solve the equation $6y^2 = 12y$. Write out a correct solution.

$6y^2 = 12y$

$\frac{6y^2}{6y} = \frac{12y}{6y}$

$y = 2$

19.2 Completing the square

To help solve quadratic equations you can complete the square.

Here is the diagram for $x^2 + 10x$:

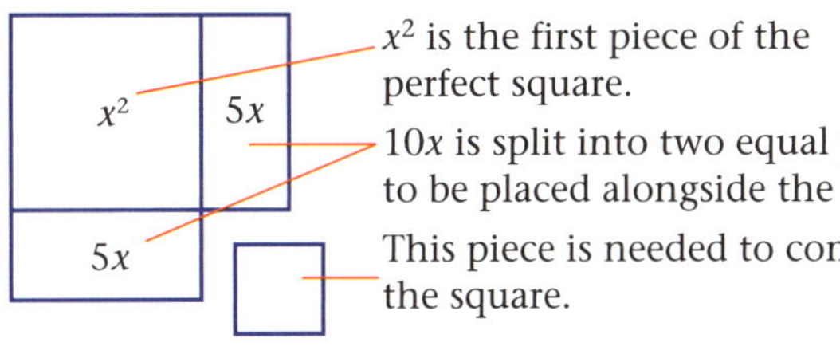

x^2
$5x$
$5x$
x^2 is the first piece of the perfect square.
$10x$ is split into two equal pieces to be placed alongside the x^2.
This piece is needed to complete the square.

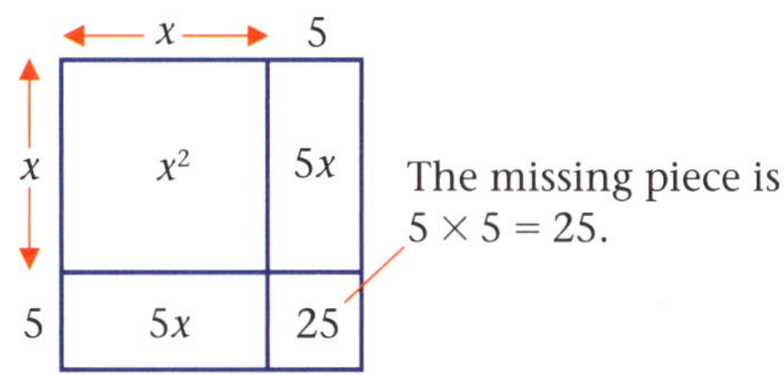

You can see that $x^2 + 10x + 5^2 = (x + 5)^2$, which is a perfect square.

So to complete the square for $x^2 + 10x$, you need to subtract 5^2 from the perfect square $(x + 5)^2$.

So $x^2 + 10x = (x + 5)^2 - 5^2$.

In general:

Completing the square: $x^2 + bx = \left(x + \frac{b}{2}\right)^2 - \left(\frac{b}{2}\right)^2$

You can use this formula when the coefficient of x^2 is 1.

The next example shows you what to do if the coefficient of x^2 is not 1.

Example 6

Write $2x^2 - 12x$ in the form $p(x + q)^2 + r$, where p, q and r are constants to be determined.

$2x^2 - 12x = 2[x^2 - 6x]$ — Take out the coefficient of x^2 as a common factor

$2[x^2 - 6x] = 2[(x - 3)^2 - 9]$ — Complete the square for $x^2 - 6x$ by using $b = -6$ in the formula

$= 2(x - 3)^2 - 18$

So $p = 2$, $q = -3$ and $r = -18$.

It is possible to write all quadratic expressions in the form $p(x + q)^2 + r$.

Exercise 19B

1 Write the following in the form $(x + q)^2 + r$.

(a) $x^2 + 4x$ (b) $x^2 - 14x$ (c) $x^2 + 3x$ (d) $x^2 + x$

(e) $x^2 - x$ (f) $x^2 - 4x$ (g) $x^2 + 7x$ (h) $x^2 - 10x$

2 Write the following in the form $p(x + q)^2 + r$.

(a) $2x^2 + 16x$ (b) $3x^2 - 12x$ (c) $2x^2 + x$ (d) $5x^2 - 15x$

(e) $2x^2 + 2x$ (f) $4x^2 - 8x$ (g) $3x^2 - 15x$ (h) $7x^2 - 28x$

19.3 Solving quadratic equations by completing the square

At first glance it *looks* as though $x^2 + 10x + 18 = 0$ cannot easily be solved by factorising. However, this quadratic can be solved by completing the square. The next example shows you how.

> You would need to find two numbers with a product of 18 and a sum of 10.

Example 7

Solve the equation $x^2 + 10x + 18 = 0$. Leave your answer in **surd** form.

$x^2 + 10x + 18 = 0$ — Check that the coefficient of x^2 is 1

$x^2 + 10x = -18$ — Subtract 18 to get constant term on RHS

$(x + 5)^2 - 25 = -18$ — Complete the square for $x^2 + 10x$

$(x + 5)^2 = 7$ — Add 25 to both sides

$x + 5 = \pm\sqrt{7}$ — Square root both sides

$x = -5 \pm\sqrt{7}$ — Subtract 5 from both sides

The solutions (roots) of $x^2 + 10x + 18 = 0$ are $x = -5 + \sqrt{7}$ and $x = -5 - \sqrt{7}$.

> **Surds** are numbers that are left in square root form. They cannot be written as a fraction. $\sqrt{2}$, $\sqrt{3}$ and $\sqrt{7}$ are examples of surds.

Example 8

Solve the equation $2y^2 - 3y - 8 = 0$. Give your answers correct to 2 d.p.

$2y^2 - 3y - 8 = 0$

$2(y^2 - \frac{3}{2}y - 4) = 0$ — Take out the coefficient of y^2

$y^2 - \frac{3}{2}y - 4 = 0$ — Divide by 2

$y^2 - \frac{3}{2}y = 4$ — Add 4 to get constant term on RHS

$\left(y - \frac{3}{4}\right)^2 - \left(\frac{3}{4}\right)^2 = 4$ — Complete the square

$\left(y - \frac{3}{4}\right)^2 = 4 + \left(\frac{3}{4}\right)^2$

$y - \frac{3}{4} = \pm\sqrt{\frac{73}{16}}$ — Take the square root of both sides

$y = \frac{3}{4} \pm \sqrt{\frac{73}{16}}$ — Add $\frac{3}{4}$ to both sides

$= 0.75 \pm 2.136\ldots$

$y = 0.75 + 2.136\ldots$ or $y = 0.75 - 2.136\ldots$

So $y = 2.89$ or $y = -1.39$ correct to 2 d.p.

Exercise 19C

1 Solve these equations. Leave your answers in surd form.

(a) $x^2 + 10x + 3 = 0$ (b) $x^2 - 8x = 2$ (c) $2x^2 + 18x + 6 = 0$
(d) $3x^2 - 6x + 1 = 0$ (e) $2y^2 - 3y - 4 = 0$ (f) $2y^2 = 4y + 7$
(g) $3x^2 = -5x + 3$ (h) $2x^2 - 7x = 2$ (i) $3x^2 = 8x + 1$

2 Solve these equations. Give your answers correct to 2 d.p.

(a) $x^2 - 4x = 3$ (b) $x^2 - 6x + 2 = 0$ (c) $2y^2 + 4y = 7$
(d) $2x^2 - 3x - 3 = 0$ (e) $3y^2 - 6y = 1$ (f) $4y^2 - y = 8$
(g) $x^2 - 4x - 3 = 0$ (h) $5x^2 + 3x - 1 = 0$ (i) $3y^2 - 5y = 3$

19.4 Solving quadratic equations by using a formula

The steps shown in the previous section can be applied to the general quadratic equation $ax^2 + bx + c = 0$. This gives a formula which can be used to solve **all quadratic equations**. This section shows a proof of the formula and how to apply it.

Here are two quadratic equations – one with number coefficients, the other a 'general' form of a quadratic with letter coefficients. The same steps are followed to solve both quadratics. Work your way down to the solutions, comparing the effect of the steps at each stage.

Number coefficients	Step	General form
$2x^2 - 6x + 1 = 0$		$ax^2 + bx + c = 0$, where $a \neq 0$
$2[x^2 - 3x + \frac{1}{2}] = 0$	Take out the coefficient of x^2	$a\left[x^2 + \frac{b}{a}x + \frac{c}{a}\right] = 0$
$x^2 - 3x + \frac{1}{2} = 0$	Divide by the coefficient of x^2	$x^2 + \frac{b}{a}x + \frac{c}{a} = 0$
$x^2 - 3x = -\frac{1}{2}$	Rearrange so constant term is on RHS	$x^2 + \frac{b}{a}x = -\frac{c}{a}$
$[x - \frac{3}{2}]^2 - (-\frac{3}{2})^2 = -\frac{1}{2}$	Complete the square	$\left[x + \frac{b}{2a}\right]^2 - \left(\frac{b}{2a}\right)^2 = -\frac{c}{a}$
$[x - \frac{3}{2}]^2 = (-\frac{3}{2})^2 - \frac{1}{2}$	Rearrange so constant term is on RHS	$\left[x + \frac{b}{2a}\right]^2 = \left(\frac{b}{2a}\right)^2 - \frac{c}{a}$
$= \frac{9}{4} - \frac{1}{2}$	Simplify RHS to a single fraction	$= \frac{b^2}{4a^2} - \frac{c}{a}$
$= \frac{9 - 2}{4} = \frac{7}{4}$		$= \frac{b^2 - 4ac}{4a^2}$
$x - \frac{3}{2} = \pm\sqrt{\frac{7}{4}}$	Square root both sides, remembering the $\pm$	$x + \frac{b}{2a} = \pm\sqrt{\frac{b^2 - 4ac}{4a^2}}$
$= \pm\frac{\sqrt{7}}{\sqrt{4}}$		$= \pm\frac{\sqrt{b^2 - 4ac}}{\sqrt{4a^2}}$
$x = \frac{3}{2} \pm \frac{\sqrt{7}}{2}$	Get x on its own	$x = -\frac{b}{2a} \pm \frac{\sqrt{b^2 - 4ac}}{2a}$
$= \frac{3 \pm \sqrt{7}}{2}$	Write as a single fraction	$= \frac{-b \pm \sqrt{b^2 - 4ac}}{2a}$

For a reminder on how to simplify algebraic fractions see Chapter 14 (in Book 1).

Note that $\sqrt{\frac{p}{q}} = \frac{\sqrt{p}}{\sqrt{q}}$

There is more on manipulating surds in Section 23.3.

The roots of the quadratic equation $ax^2 + bx + c = 0$, where $a \neq 0$, are given by the formula

$$x = \frac{-b \pm \sqrt{b^2 - 4ac}}{2a}$$

This formula will be on your GCSE exam formulae sheet. You do not have to remember it but you *must* know how to use it.

Example 9

Solve the equation $x(x + 3) = 2$. Give your answers correct to 2 d.p.

$$x(x + 3) = 2$$
$$x^2 + 3x = 2$$
$$1x^2 + 3x - 2 = 0$$

A common error is to think that x^2 is $0x^2$ and put $a = 0$. To avoid this error write x^2 as $1x^2$.

Comparing with $ax^2 + bx + c = 0$ gives $a = 1$, $b = 3$, $c = -2$.

Using the formula

$$x = \frac{-b \pm \sqrt{b^2 - 4ac}}{2a}$$

gives the solutions

$$x = \frac{-3 \pm \sqrt{3^2 - 4(1)(-2)}}{2(1)}$$
$$= \frac{-3 \pm \sqrt{9 + 8}}{2}$$
$$= \frac{-3 \pm \sqrt{17}}{2}$$

So $x = \frac{-3 + 4.123\ldots}{2}$ or $x = \frac{-3 - 4.123\ldots}{2}$

$x = 0.5615\ldots$ or $x = -3.5615\ldots$

The two solutions (roots) are $x = 0.56$ and $x = -3.56$ correct to 2 d.p.

Example 10

Solve the equation $2y^2 - y - 4 = 0$. Leave your answers in surd form.

$2y^2 - 1y - 4 = 0$ is a quadratic in y. Comparing with $ay^2 + by + c = 0$ gives $a = 2$, $b = -1$, $c = -4$.

Using the formula

$$y = \frac{-b \pm \sqrt{b^2 - 4ac}}{2a}$$

gives the solutions

$$y = \frac{-(-1) \pm \sqrt{(-1)^2 - 4(2)(-4)}}{2(2)}$$
$$= \frac{1 \pm \sqrt{1 + 32}}{4}$$
$$= \frac{1 \pm \sqrt{33}}{4}$$

In surd form, the roots are $y = \frac{1 + \sqrt{33}}{4}$ and $y = \frac{1 - \sqrt{33}}{4}$

The quadratic $x^2 + 10x + 18 = 0$ was introduced in Section 19.3. We said that at first glance it could not easily be solved by factorising because two numbers with product 18 and sum 10 would need to be found. In fact two such numbers can be found. The next example shows you how.

Example 11

Find two numbers whose sum is 10 and whose product is 18.

Half the sum is 5.

Let one number be $5 - x$. Then the other must be $5 + x$ (so that they add up to 10).

The product of the numbers is 18 so

$$(5 - x)(5 + x) = 18$$

$$25 - x^2 = 18$$ — Difference of two squares

This gives $x^2 = 7$ so $x = \sqrt{7}$ or $x = -\sqrt{7}$

The two numbers are $5 - \sqrt{7}$ and $5 + \sqrt{7}$.

Exercise 19D

In this exercise use the formula $x = \dfrac{-b \pm \sqrt{b^2 - 4ac}}{2a}$

1 Write down the values of $b^2 - 4ac$ in these equations:

(a) $x^2 + 3x + 1 = 0$ (b) $x^2 - 2x - 1 = 0$

(c) $2x^2 + 6x - 1 = 0$ (d) $8x^2 - 9 = 0$

(e) $4 - 3x - 2x^2 = 0$ (f) $2x^2 = 2x + 3$

2 Solve the equations in question **1**.
Give your answers correct to 2 d.p.

3 Solve the following equations.
Give your answers correct to 2 d.p.

(a) $x^2 - 4x + 1 = 0$ (b) $x^2 - 5x + 1 = 0$

(c) $4x^2 + 9x + 1 = 0$ (d) $4x^2 - 2x = 3$

(e) $1 = x^2 - 8x + 2$ (f) $(x + 4)^2 = 2(x + 7)$

4 Find two numbers whose sum is 18 and whose product is 21.

5 Find two numbers whose difference is 6 and whose product is 15.

19.5 Equations involving algebraic fractions

You simplified algebraic fractions in Chapter 14 (in Book 1). This section shows you how to apply this skill to algebraic equations. For example:

if $\frac{x}{4} = \frac{3}{4}$ then $x = 3$.

In general, if $\frac{p}{r} = \frac{q}{r}$ then $p = q$.

To solve equations involving algebraic fractions:

Step 1 Write both sides of the equation with the same denominator.

Step 2 Use the numerators to write an equation.

Step 3 Solve the resulting equation.

Example 12

Solve the equation $\frac{2}{y+1} - \frac{3}{2y+3} = \frac{1}{2}$

Give your answer correct to 3 d.p.

$$\frac{2}{y+1} - \frac{3}{2y+3} = \frac{1}{2}$$

The LCM of the three denominators is $2(y + 1)(2y + 3)$.

Write each fraction with the LCM as denominator:

$$\frac{2 \times 2(2y+3)}{2(y+1)(2y+3)} - \frac{3 \times 2(y+1)}{2(y+1)(2y+3)} = \frac{(y+1)(2y+3)}{2(y+1)(2y+3)}$$

Remember: when the denominators have no common factor, the LCM is the product of the denominators.

If $\frac{p}{r} = \frac{q}{r}$, then $p = q$, so ignore the denominators.

$$4(2y + 3) - 6(y + 1) = (y + 1)(2y + 3)$$
$$8y + 12 - 6y - 6 = 2y^2 + 5y + 3$$
$$2y + 6 = 2y^2 + 5y + 3$$
$$0 = 2y^2 + 3y - 3$$

Comparing this equation with the general quadratic $0 = ay^2 + by + c$ gives $a = 2, b = 3, c = -3$.

Using the formula:

$$y = \frac{-3 \pm \sqrt{3^2 - 4(2)(-3)}}{2(2)}$$
$$= \frac{-3 \pm \sqrt{33}}{4}$$
$$= \frac{-3 \pm 5.744...}{4}$$

So $y = 0.686$ or $y = -2.186$ correct to 3 d.p.

Exercise 19E

Solve the following equations. Give fractional answers exactly. In all other cases give your answers correct to 2 d.p.

1 $\dfrac{1}{x} + \dfrac{1}{x+1} = \dfrac{7}{12}$

2 $2x + \dfrac{1}{x} = 5$

3 $\dfrac{5}{2x+1} + \dfrac{6}{x+1} = 3$

4 $\dfrac{1}{x-1} - \dfrac{1}{x} = 8$

5 $\dfrac{1}{x-3} - \dfrac{3}{x+2} = \dfrac{1}{2}$

6 $\dfrac{2}{y+1} + \dfrac{3}{2y+3} = 1$

19.6 Problems leading to quadratic equations

The equation for question **1** in Exercise 19E would be the correct one to use to solve the following problem:

Find consecutive integers whose reciprocals add up to $\frac{7}{12}$.

When answering questions in the GCSE exam, candidates often find it harder to obtain the quadratic equation to represent a problem than to solve it. You will find these steps useful.

Finding the equation to represent a problem

Step 1 Where relevant, draw a diagram and put all the information on it.

Step 2 Use x to represent the unknown which you have been asked to find.

Step 3 Use other letters to identify any other relevant unknowns.

Step 4 Look for information given in the question which links these letters to x and write them down.

Step 5 Try simple numbers for the unknowns and see if this helps you to find a method.

Step 6 Make sure that the units on both sides of your equation are the same.

When applied to problem solving, one of the roots of the quadratic equation is often not a solution to the problem and must be abandoned (with an explanation).

Example 13

In a right-angled triangle, the hypotenuse is 6 cm longer than the shortest side. The third side is 2 cm shorter than the hypotenuse. Find a quadratic equation in the form $ax^2 + bx + c = 0$ which when solved leads to the length of the shortest side.

Let the shortest side be x cm.

Mark the other sides y cm and z cm like this:

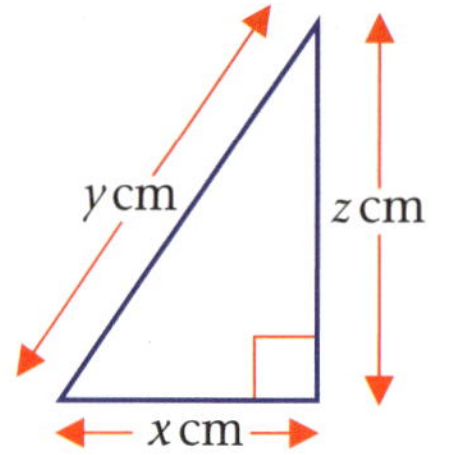

The hypotenuse is 6 cm longer than x so $y = x + 6$.

The third side is 2 cm shorter than y so $z = y - 2$ or $z = x + 6 - 2 = x + 4$.

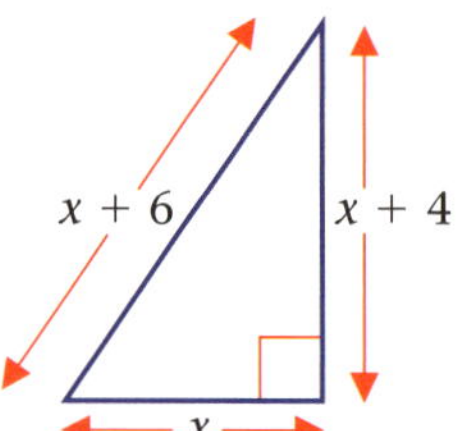

The units of length are the same.

Test:
If $x = 1$ then
$y = 1 + 6 = 7$ and
$z = 1 + 4 = 5$.
This confirms the relative size of each side.

Using Pythagoras' theorem:

$$x^2 + (x + 4)^2 = (x + 6)^2$$
$$x^2 + x^2 + 8x + 16 = x^2 + 12x + 36$$
$$x^2 - 4x - 20 = 0$$

Solving this quadratic equation gives $x = 6.899$ or -2.899.
As length is positive the only answer is 6.9 cm to 2 s.f.

Example 14

Lisa cycled from Norton to Sufton, a distance of 34 km, and then cycled the same distance back.

Lisa's average speed on the outward journey was x km/h.

On the return journey the wind was behind her so she cycled 2 km/h faster and completed the return journey 16 minutes quicker than the outward journey.

(a) Write down, in terms of x, the time (in hours) taken for
  (i) the outward journey
  (ii) the return journey.

(b) Show that $x^2 + 2x - 255 = 0$.

(c) Calculate Lisa's average speed on the return journey.

(a) (i) Using time taken $= \dfrac{\text{distance}}{\text{average speed}}$

the time for the outward journey is $\dfrac{34}{x}$ hours.

(ii) Let Lisa's average speed on the return journey be y km/h.
y is 2 more than x so $y = x + 2$.

The time for the return journey is $\dfrac{34}{y} = \dfrac{34}{x + 2}$ hours.

(b) The time taken for the outward journey is 16 minutes more than for the return journey.

Time for outward journey − time for return journey = 16 minutes.

$$\frac{34}{x} - \frac{34}{x+2} = \frac{4}{15}$$

The units must be the same.
16 min = $\frac{16}{60} = \frac{4}{15}$ hours

$$\frac{34 \times 15(x+2) - 34 \times 15(x)}{15x(x+2)} = \frac{4x(x+2)}{15x(x+2)}$$

$$510x + 1020 - 510x = 4x^2 + 8x$$

$$0 = 4x^2 + 8x - 1020$$

$$0 = 4(x^2 + 2x - 255)$$

So $x^2 + 2x - 255 = 0$.

(c) You need to find the value of y, which equals $x + 2$.

From part (b): $x^2 + 2x - 255 = 0$

$$(x + 17)(x - 15) = 0$$

You can solve this equation by using the formula, but factorising is quicker if you can spot it.

So $x + 17 = 0$ or $x - 15 = 0$

$x = -17$ or $x = 15$

Lisa's speed cannot be negative, so $x = 15$.

Lisa's average speed on the return journey is $x + 2 = 15 + 2 = 17$ km/h

Exercise 19F

Use quadratic equations to solve these problems.

1 Find two consecutive integers whose reciprocals add up to $\frac{9}{20}$.

2 The hypotenuse of a right-angled triangle is $2x$ cm.
The lengths of the other two sides are $(x + 1)$ cm and $(x + 3)$ cm.
Calculate the value of x.

3 The sum of the square of a number and 5 times the number itself is 24. Find the two possible values of the number.

4 The length of a rectangular piece of carpet is 4 m longer than its width. The area of the carpet is 16 m². Calculate the width of the carpet. Give your answer correct to the nearest centimetre.

5 One week a syndicate of x people won £400 in the National Lottery.

(a) Write down, in terms of x, how much each person should receive, if each gets an equal share.

(b) If the prize had been won the previous week when there were $(x + 2)$ people in the syndicate, each person would have received £10 less.

Show that $x^2 + 2x - 80 = 0$.

(c) Calculate the amount of money won by each person in the syndicate.

6 A right-angled triangle is cut from the corner of a rectangular piece of card 15 cm by 8 cm.

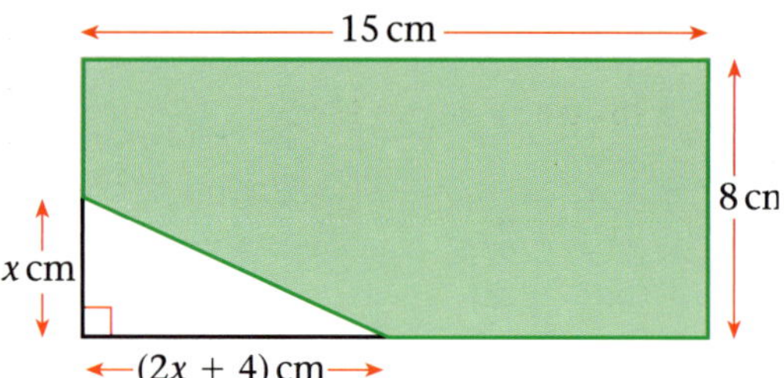

The base of the triangle is $(2x + 4)$ cm and its height is x cm.

The remaining piece of card (green) has an area of 89 cm^2. Calculate the value of x, giving your answer correct to 2 s.f.

7 Joe is training for a long-distance cycle race. One day he cycles for x hours in the morning and travels a distance of 84 km.

(a) Write down, in terms of x, Joe's average speed in km/h.

(b) In the afternoon he cycles for 1 hour more to travel the same distance and his average speed is 2 km/h slower than in the morning.

Show that $x^2 + x - 42 = 0$.

(c) Calculate the number of hours Joe cycles in the afternoon.

19.7 Solving linear and quadratic equations simultaneously

In Chapter 9 (in Book 1) you found the coordinates of the point of intersection of two straight lines by solving the equations of the lines simultaneously.

In this section you will find the coordinates of the points of intersection of a straight line and a quadratic curve.

Let us consider the curve $y = x^2$ and three different lines.

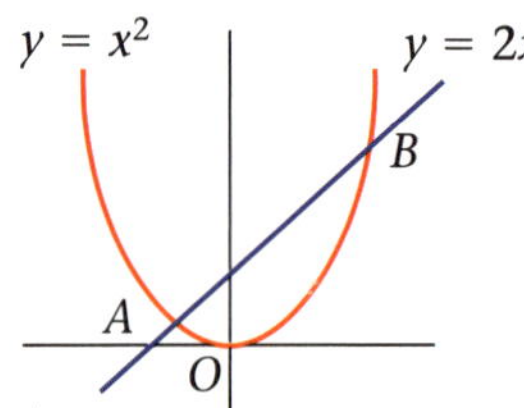

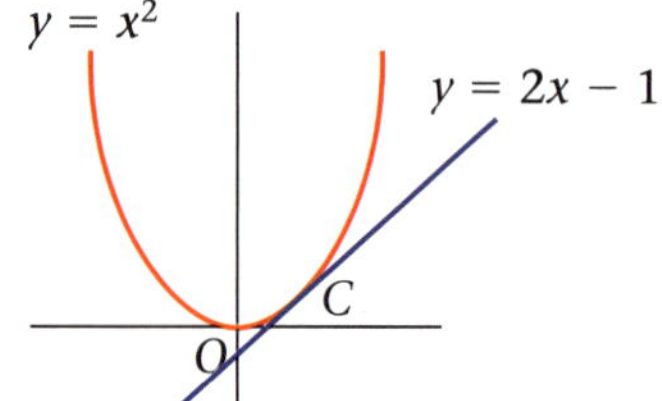

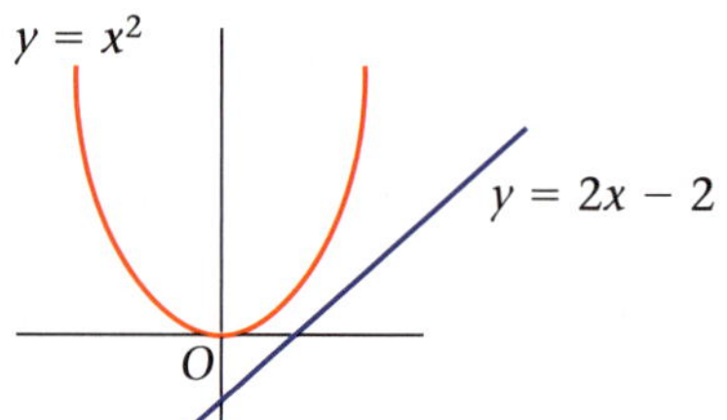

Diagram 1 The line $y = 2x + 3$ cuts the curve at two points, A and B.

Diagram 2 The line $y = 2x - 1$ just touches at the curve at the point C.

Diagram 3 The line $y = 2x - 2$ misses the curve completely.

The following three examples correspond to the three cases above.

Example 15

Find the coordinates of the points of intersection A and B of the line $y = 2x + 3$ and the curve $y = x^2$.

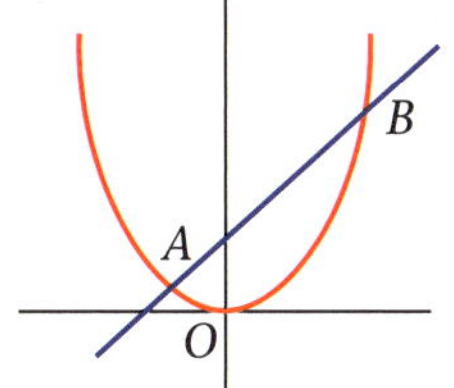

The points A and B both lie on the curve and on the line, so their coordinates must satisfy both equations:

$y = x^2$ (1)

and $y = 2x + 3$ (2)

Eliminating y by substituting (1) into (2) gives

$$x^2 = 2x + 3$$

$$x^2 - 2x - 3 = 0$$ ——— Rearrange

$$(x + 1)(x - 3) = 0$$ ——— Factorise

So $x + 1 = 0$ or $x - 3 = 0$

which gives $x = -1$ or $x = 3$

The linear equation is the equation of the straight line.

Substitute these values of x in the linear equation (2):

When $x = -1$, $y = 2(-1) + 3 = 1$

When $x = 3$, $y = 2(3) + 3 = 9$

From the sketch the x-coordinate of A is negative.

So the line $y = 2x + 3$ intersects the curve $y = x^2$ at the points $A(-1, 1)$ and $B(3, 9)$.

Example 16

(a) Solve the simultaneous equations $y = x^2$ and $y = 2x - 1$.

(b) Interpret your solution to part (a) geometrically.

(a) $y = x^2$ (1)

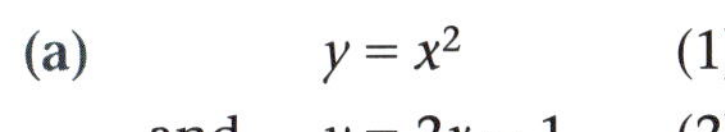

and $y = 2x - 1$ (2)

Eliminating y by substituting (1) into (2) gives:

$$x^2 = 2x - 1$$

$$x^2 - 2x + 1 = 0$$ ——— Rearrange

$$(x - 1)(x - 1) = 0$$ ——— Factorise

So $x - 1 = 0$ (repeated root)

which gives the single value $x = 1$

Substitute this value of x in the linear equation (2):

When $x = 1$, $y = 2(1) - 1 = 1$

(b) The line $y = 2x - 1$ meets the curve $y = x^2$ in just one point, (1, 1).

The line $y = 2x - 1$ is a tangent to the curve $y = x^2$ at the point (1, 1).

Example 17

(a) Show that the x-coordinate of any point of intersection of the line $y = 2x - 2$ and the curve $y = x^2$ would need to satisfy the equation $(x - 1)^2 = -1$.

(b) Interpret the result in part (a) geometrically.

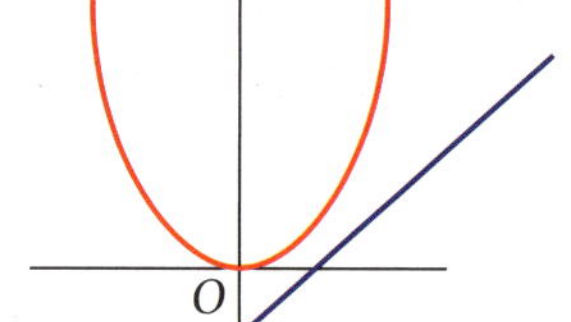

(a) $y = x^2$ (1)

$y = 2x - 2$ (2)

Eliminating y by substituting (1) into (2) gives:

$x^2 = 2x - 2$

$x^2 - 2x + 2 = 0$ —— Rearrange

$x^2 - 2x + 1 = -2 + 1$ —— Complete the square

$(x - 1)^2 = -1$ —— Factorise

The x-coordinate would need to satisfy this equation.

(b) For real numbers, $(x - 1)^2$ is always $\geqslant 0$. So there are no real number solutions to the equation, and the line $y = 2x - 2$ never intersects the curve $y = x^2$.

You can use **complex numbers** to solve this type of equation. You can learn about complex numbers at A-level.

Solving a linear equation ($y = px + q$) and a quadratic equation ($y = ax^2 + bx + c$) simultaneously:

- Find y in terms of x from the linear equation (or x in terms of y).
- Substitute for y (or x) in the quadratic equation.
- Solve the resulting quadratic equation for x (or y).
- Substitute the values of x (or y) into the linear equation to find y (or x).

If the roots of the quadratic equation are equal, the line will be a tangent to the curve.

Exercise 19G

1 Solve these pairs of simultaneous equations.

(a) $y = x^2$ and $y = 16$ (b) $y = x^2$ and $y = 12x - 36$

(c) $y = x^2$ and $y = 2x + 35$ (d) $y = x^2$ and $7x + 18$

(e) $y = 2x^2$ and $y = x + 3$ (f) $y = 3x^2$ and $y = 7x + 6$

(g) $y = 2 - x^2$ and $y = x - 4$ (h) $y = 12x^2 - 5$ and $y = 7 - 7x$

2 Find the coordinates of the points of intersection of these lines and curves.

(a) $y = 3 - 2x$ and $y = x^2$ (b) $y = 3x + 10$ and $y = 4x^2$

(c) $y = x + 5$ and $y = x^2 - 2x - 5$ (d) $y = 3x + 7$ and $y = 7 - 6x^2$

3 In each part determine the number of points of intersection of the line and the curve, and find the coordinates of any points of intersection.

(a) $y = x^2 + 3$ and $y = 2$ (b) $y = x^2$ and $y = 10x - 25$

(c) $y = 2x^2$ and $y = 5x + 7$ (d) $y = x^2 + 3x + 6$ and $y = 1 - x$

(e) $y = 5x^2$ and $y = 14x + 3$ (f) $y = 4x^2$ and $y = 10x + 6$

(g) $y = 3x - x^2$ and $y = 4 - x$ (h) $y = 12x^2 - 5x$ and $y = 6x + 5$

19.8 The intersection of a line and a circle

In Chapter 15 (in Book 1) you saw that the equation of a circle with centre (0, 0) and radius r is $x^2 + y^2 = r^2$.

Example 18

(a) Show that the x-coordinate of each point of intersection of the line $y = 2x + 2$ and the circle $x^2 + y^2 = 8$ must satisfy the equation $5x^2 + 8x - 4 = 0$.

(b) Hence find the coordinates of the points where the line $y = 2x + 2$ cuts the circle $x^2 + y^2 = 8$.

(a) The points of intersection lie on both the circle and the line, so their coordinates must satisfy both equations:

$$x^2 + y^2 = 8 \qquad (1)$$

and

$$y = 2x + 2 \qquad (2)$$

Eliminating y by substituting (2) into (1) gives

$$x^2 + (2x + 2)^2 = 8$$

$$x^2 + 4x^2 + 8x + 4 = 8$$ — Expand the brackets

$$5x^2 + 8x - 4 = 0$$ — Rearrange as required

(b) Factorise: $(5x - 2)(x + 2) = 0$

So $5x - 2 = 0$ or $x + 2 = 0$

which gives $x = \frac{2}{5}$ or $x = -2$

Substitute these values of x in the linear equation (2):

When $x = \frac{2}{5}$, $y = 2(\frac{2}{5}) + 2 = 2\frac{4}{5}$

When $x = -2$, $y = 2(-2) + 2 = -2$

The line $y = 2x + 2$ cuts the circle $x^2 + y^2 = 8$ at the points $(\frac{2}{5}, 2\frac{4}{5})$ and $(-2, -2)$.

Example 19

(a) Solve the simultaneous equations $4y + 3x = 25$ and $x^2 + y^2 = 25$.

(b) Interpret your solution to part (a) geometrically.

(a)

$$4y + 3x = 25 \qquad (1)$$

$$x^2 + y^2 = 25 \qquad (2)$$

From (1): $y = \dfrac{25 - 3x}{4} \qquad (3)$

Eliminating y by substituting (3) into (2) gives

$$x^2 + \frac{(25 - 3x)^2}{16} = 25$$

$$16x^2 + (25 - 3x)^2 = 400$$ — Multiply each term by 16

$$16x^2 + 625 - 150x + 9x^2 = 400$$ — Expand the brackets

$$25x^2 - 150x + 225 = 0$$ — Rearrange

$$25(x^2 - 6x + 9) = 0$$ — Factorise

$$25(x - 3)^2 = 0$$

So $\quad x - 3 = 0$ (repeated root)

which gives $\quad x = 3$

Substitute in (3): $\quad$ When $x = 3$, $y = \dfrac{25 - 9}{4} = 4$

$x = 3$, $y = 4$ is the only solution of the simultaneous equations.

(b) The line $4y + 3x = 25$ is a tangent to the circle $x^2 + y^2 = 25$ at the point (3, 4).

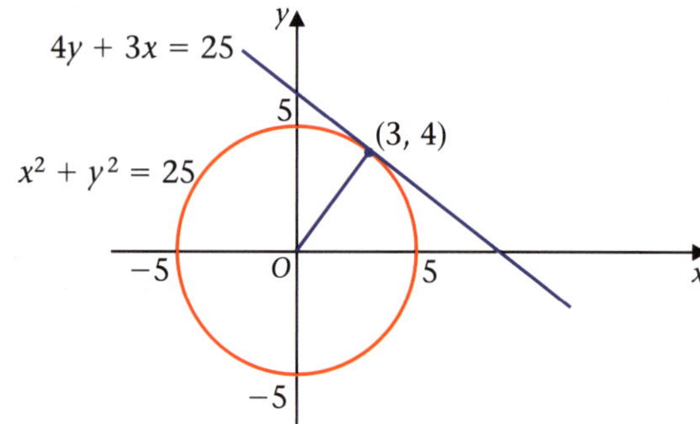

The gradient of the radius from (0, 0) to (3, 4) is $\frac{4}{3}$.

The gradient of the line $4y + 3x = 25$, or $y = -\frac{3}{4}x + \frac{25}{4}$, is $-\frac{3}{4}$.

From Section 9.6 (in Book 1), since $\frac{4}{3} \times -\frac{3}{4} = -1$, the radius and the line $4y + 3x = 25$ are perpendicular. A radius is always perpendicular to a tangent.

Exercise 19H

1 In each part solve the simultaneous equations and interpret your solution geometrically.

(a) $y = 3$ and $x^2 + y^2 = 25$

(b) $y = x + 5$ and $x^2 + y^2 = 25$

(c) $x^2 + y^2 = 25$ and $y = 3x + 13$

(d) $x^2 + y^2 = 25$ and $y + x + 1 = 0$

(e) $x^2 + y^2 = 50$ and $y = x - 10$

(f) $x^2 + y^2 = 50$ and $y + 8x = 1$

(g) $y = 3x - 10$ and $x^2 + y^2 = 10$

(h) $y + 2x = 5$ and $x^2 + y^2 = 5$

(i) $x^2 + y^2 = 2$ and $y + 7x + 10 = 0$

(j) $3y + 4x = 6$ and $x^2 + y^2 = 4$

2 The line $y = x - 3$ intersects the circle $x^2 + y^2 = 25$ at the points A and B.

(a) Show that the x-coordinates of A and B satisfy the equation $x^2 - 3x - 8 = 0$.

(b) Hence show that the coordinates of A and B are

$$\left(\frac{3 + \sqrt{41}}{2}, \frac{-3 + \sqrt{41}}{2}\right) \text{ and } \left(\frac{3 - \sqrt{41}}{2}, \frac{-3 - \sqrt{41}}{2}\right)$$

3 (a) Show that the line $y = x + 4$ is a tangent to the circle $x^2 + y^2 = 8$.

(b) (i) Find the equation of the tangent to the circle $x^2 + y^2 = 8$ that is parallel to $y = x + 4$ and write down the coordinates of the point where it touches the circle.

(ii) Find the distance between these two parallel tangents.

(c) Give a general result for the distance between two parallel tangents to any circle of the form $x^2 + y^2 = r^2$.

19.9 Solving equations graphically

Finding graphical solutions to quadratic equations was introduced in Chapter 17.

Unless graphs have been drawn for you, you could use a lot of valuable time in an exam drawing a graph accurate enough to solve an equation. Also, graphical solutions are less accurate. So you should only use a graphical approach to solve a quadratic equation if a question asks you to.

Although most cubic and higher power equations have to be solved graphically rather than algebraically at GCSE level, you should still consider an algebraic approach if x is a common factor.

Example 20

Solve the equation $x^3 - 4x^2 + 4x = 0$.

$$x^3 - 4x^2 + 4x = 0$$
$$x(x^2 - 4x + 4) = 0$$
$$x(x - 2)(x - 2) = 0$$

This leads to the solutions $x = 0$ or $x = 2$ (repeated).

Notice that the 'double solution' at $x = 2$ indicates that the graph of $y = x^3 - 4x^2 + 4x$ just touches the x-axis at $x = 2$. The x-axis is a tangent to this curve at $x = 2$.

Here is a graph of $y = x^3 - 4x^2 + 4x$:

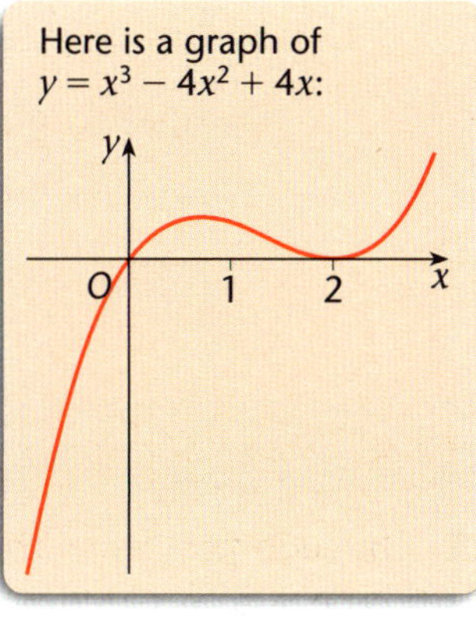

Using a given graph to solve equations

Sometimes you will need to rearrange the equation to be solved to make use of a given graph.

Example 21

The graph of $y = 2 + x - x^2$, for $-3 \leqslant x \leqslant 3$, is shown.

(a) By drawing lines on the graph, solve the following equations, giving your answers to (i) correct to 1 d.p.

(i) $1 + x - x^2 = 0$

(ii) $2 - x - x^2 = 0$

(b) Find the equation of the line you would draw on the graph to solve the equation $2x^2 - x = 6$.

(c) Explain how the graph can be used to show that the equation $x^2 - x + 3 = 0$ has no real solutions.

(d) By drawing a suitable curve on the graph, solve the equation $x^3 - x^2 - 2x + 6 = 0$.

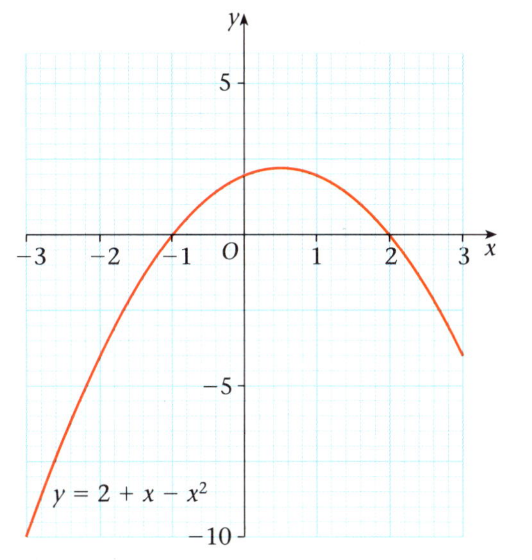

(a) **(i)** To solve $1 + x - x^2 = 0$ using the graph:

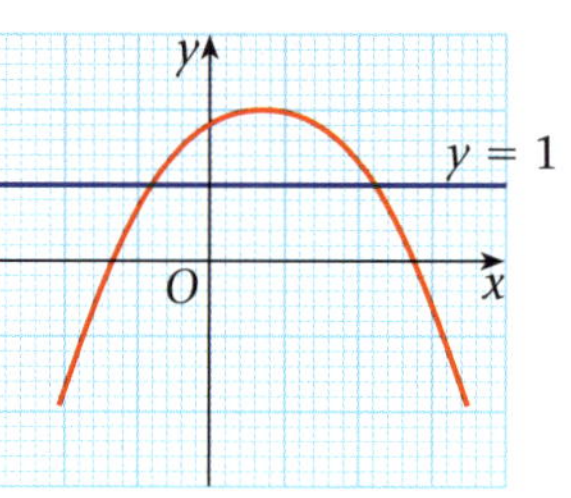

$$2 + x - x^2 = 1$$ — Add 1 to each side

The graph shows $2 + x - x^2 = y$

Comparing gives $y = 1$

So draw the horizontal line $y = 1$

This line meets the parabola at $x = -0.6$ and $x = 1.6$, so the solutions of $1 + x - x^2 = 0$ are $x = -0.6$ and $x = 1.6$ to 1 d.p.

(ii) To solve $2 - x - x^2 = 0$ using the graph:

$$2 + x - x^2 = 2x$$ — Add $2x$ to each side

The graph shows $2 + x - x^2 = y$

Comparing gives $y = 2x$

So draw the line $y = 2x$

This line meets the parabola at $x = -2$ and $x = 1$ so the solutions of $2 - x - x^2 = 0$ are $x = -2$ and $x = 1$.

(b) To solve $2x^2 - x = 6$ using the graph:

$$0 = 6 + x - 2x^2$$ — Rearrange

$$0 = 3 + \tfrac{1}{2}x - x^2$$ — Divide each side by 2

$$\tfrac{1}{2}x = 3 + x - x^2$$ — Add $\tfrac{1}{2}x$ to each side

$$\tfrac{1}{2}x - 1 = 2 + x - x^2$$ — Subtract 1 from each side

The graph shows $y = 2 + x - x^2$

Comparing gives $y = \tfrac{1}{2}x - 1$

So you would need to draw the line $y = \tfrac{1}{2}x - 1$ and find where it meets the parabola. The x-coordinates of the points of intersection give the solutions of the equation $2x^2 - x = 6$.

(c) To solve $x^2 - x + 3 = 0$ using the graph:

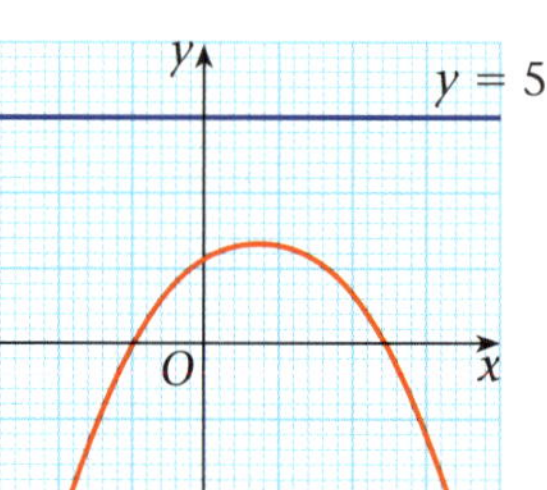

$$0 = -3 + x - x^2$$ — Rearrange

$$5 = 2 + x - x^2$$ — Add 5 to each side

The graph shows $y = 2 + x - x^2$

Comparing gives $y = 5$

The horizontal line $y = 5$ does not meet the parabola so you can deduce that $x^2 - x + 3 = 0$ has no real solutions.

(d) To solve $x^3 - x^2 - 2x + 6 = 0$ using the graph:

$6 = 2x + x^2 - x^3$ —— Rearrange

$6 = x(2 + x - x^2)$ —— Factorise

$\frac{6}{x} = 2 + x - x^2$ — Divide both sides by x

The graph shows $y = 2 + x - x^2$

Comparing gives $y = \frac{6}{x}$

Draw the graph of the reciprocal function $y = \frac{6}{x}$.

Notice that it only meets the parabola at one point. This means that there is only one real solution of the equation $x^3 - x^2 - 2x + 6 = 0$.

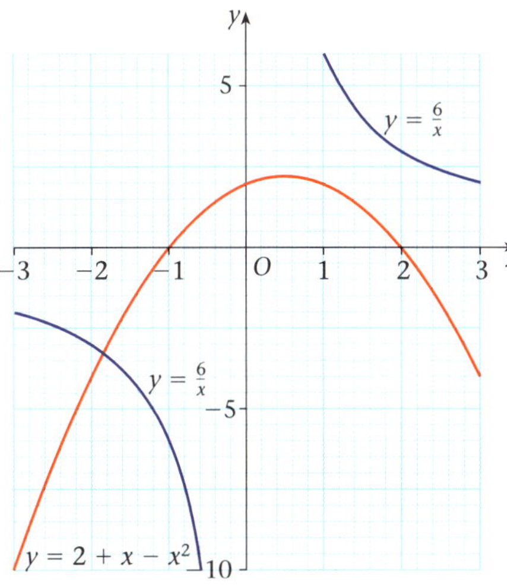

The x-coordinate of this point of intersection gives the solution. So the one real solution of $x^3 - x^2 - 2x + 6 = 0$ is $x = -1.8$ to 1 d.p.

Alternative method:
You could rearrange $x^3 - x^2 - 2x + 6 = 0$ to get $2 + x - x^2 = 3x - x^3 - 4$.

Then draw the curve $y = 3x - x^3 - 4$ and find its point of intersection with the parabola. Although this is valid, the aim is to rearrange so that the easiest graph to draw is obtained, preferably a straight line.

Solving equations from a given graph (or one to be drawn):

- Rearrange the equation to be solved to match the equation of the graph. Try to keep the rearrangement simple.
- Compare to find y. Note that y may be of the form $\frac{k}{x}$ if the equation to be solved has a higher power of x than the given graph function.
- Draw the line (or curve) from the previous step on the given axes.
- Read off the values of x at the points of intersection.

Exercise 19I

1 (a) On graph paper draw the graph of $y = x^2 - 4$ for $-3 \leqslant x \leqslant 3$.

(b) On the same axes, draw the graph of $y = 2 + \frac{1}{x}$ for $-3 \leqslant x \leqslant -\frac{1}{2}$ and $\frac{1}{2} \leqslant x \leqslant 3$.

(c) Use your graphs to find approximate solutions for

(i) $x^2 = 2$ (ii) $2 + \frac{1}{x} = 0.8$ (iii) $2 + \frac{1}{x} = x^2 - 4$

2 Part of the graph of the cubic function $y = x^3 - 4x$ is shown.

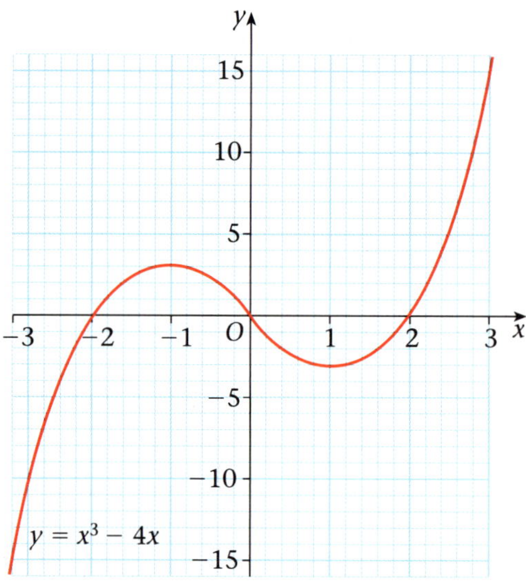

(a) Find the equation of the line which needs to be drawn on the graph to solve

(i) $x^3 - 4x = 1$ (ii) $x^3 - 4x + 2 = 0$

(iii) $x^3 - 6x = 1$ (iv) $x^3 - 2x = 4$

(b) Which one of the equations in (a) does not have three real solutions?
Explain your answer.

(c) The graph of $y = \frac{1}{x}$ (not drawn) intersects the given cubic curve $y = x^3 - 4x$ at points A and B. Find, in a form which includes an x^4 term, the equation which has the x-coordinates of A and B as two of its solutions.

3 (a) On graph paper, draw the graph of the parabola $y = (6 - x)(2 + x)$ for $-2 \leqslant x \leqslant 6$.

(b) A container is in the shape of a cuboid of height x m.
The area of the base of the container is $(6 - x)(2 + x)$ m^2.
The volume of the container is 24 m^3.

By drawing the graph of an appropriate curve on your axes in (a) find, correct to the nearest tenth of a metre, the possible values for the height of the container.

4 (a) Copy and complete this table of values for $y = x^3 - 6x + 1$.

x	−3	−2	−1	0	1	2
y	−8					

(b) On graph paper, draw and label appropriate axes.
Plot the points represented by the values in your table. Join them with a smooth curve.

(c) (i) On the same axes, draw the line with equation $y = 2x + 5$.

(ii) Write down the x-coordinates of the two points of intersection of this line and the curve you have drawn in (b).

(d) Find the equation, expressed as simply as possible, which may be solved to give the x-coordinate of each point of intersection of the curve and the line.

(e) A line L is drawn parallel to the line $y = 2x + 5$ so that L intersects the curve $y = x^3 - 6x + 1$ at the point on the y-axis.
Write down the equation of line L.

(f) By forming and solving an algebraic equation, find the x-coordinates of the three points of intersection of L and the curve $y = x^3 - 6x + 1$.

Mixed exercise 19

1 The area of this rectangle is 9 cm^2.
Find the value of x.

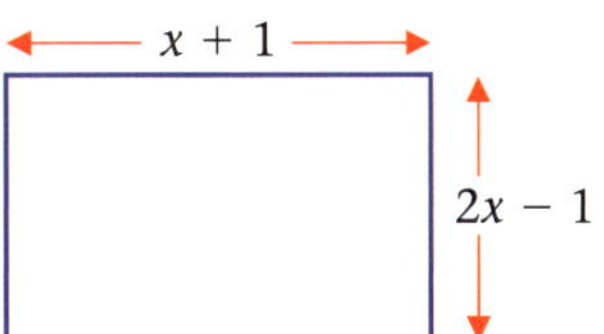

2 A rectangle measuring $(x + 3)$ cm by $(2x + 1)$ cm has a rectangle measuring 2 cm by 4 cm cut from it.
The area left is 67 cm^2.
Work out the value of x.

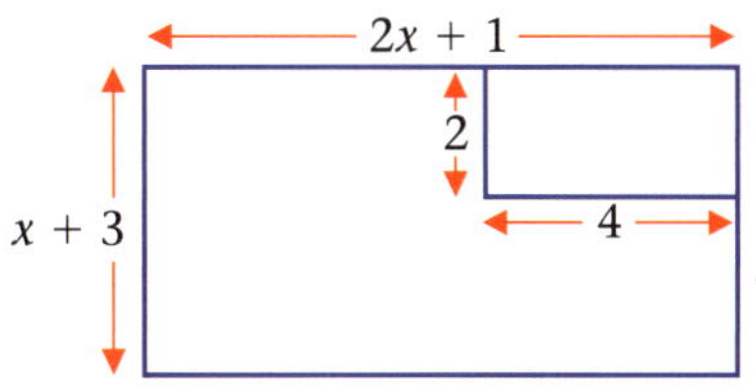

3 The length of the line joining (2, 5) to $(x, -1)$ is 7 centimetres.
Work out the value of x.
Give your answer in the form $a + \sqrt{b}$.

4 Solve $x^2 + 6x = 4$.
Give your answer in the form $p + \sqrt{q}$, where p and q are integers.

5 (a) Factorise $2x^2 - 35x + 98$.

(b) Solve the equation $2x^2 - 35x + 98 = 0$. [E]

6 Solve these simultaneous equations:

$$x^2 + y^2 = 29$$
$$y - x = 3$$ [E]

7 (a) Solve $x^2 + x + 11 = 14$.
Give your solutions correct to 3 significant figures.

(b) $y = x^2 + x + 11$

The value of y is a prime number when $x = 0$, 1, 2 and 3.

The following statement is **not** true:

'$y = x^2 + x + 11$ is **always** a prime number when x is an integer'.

Show that the statement is not true. [E]

8 AT is a tangent at T to a circle, centre O.
$OT = x$ cm, $AT = (x + 5)$ cm, $OA = (x + 8)$ cm.

(a) Show that $x^2 - 6x - 39 = 0$.

(b) Solve the equation $x^2 - 6x - 39 = 0$ to find the radius of the circle. Give your answer correct to 3 significant figures.

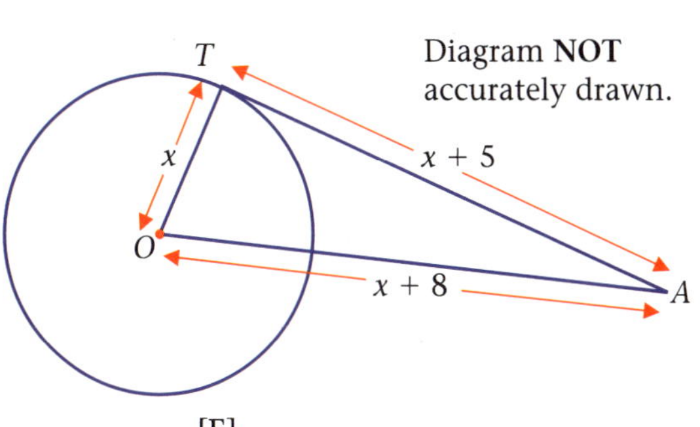

[E]

9 (a) On a grid, with $-12 \leqslant x \leqslant 12$ and $-12 \leqslant y \leqslant 12$, draw the graphs of $x^2 + y^2 = 100$ and $2y = 3x - 4$.

(b) Use the graphs to estimate the solutions of the simultaneous equations

$$x^2 + y^2 = 100$$

and $$2y = 3x - 4$$

(c) For all the values of x, $x^2 + 6x = (x + 3)^2 - q$.

Find the value of q.

(d) One pair of integer values which satisfy the equation $x^2 + y^2 = 100$ is $x = 6$ and $y = 8$.

Find one pair of integer values which satisfy

$$x^2 + 6x + y^2 - 4y - 87 = 0.$$ [E]

Summary of key points

1 The quadratic equation $ax^2 + bx + c = 0$, with $a \neq 0$, has two solutions (or roots), which may be equal.

2 If $xy = 0$ then either $x = 0$ or $y = 0$.

3 If $y^2 = k$ then $y = \pm\sqrt{k}$

4 Completing the square: $x^2 + bx = \left(x + \frac{b}{2}\right)^2 - \left(\frac{b}{2}\right)^2$

5 The roots of the quadratic equation $ax^2 + bx + c = 0$, where $a \neq 0$, are given by the formula

$$x = \frac{\sqrt{-b \pm b^2 - 4ac}}{2a}$$

6 If $\frac{p}{r} = \frac{q}{r}$ then $p = q$.

7 When applied to problem solving, one of the roots of the quadratic equation is often not a solution to the problem and must be abandoned (with an explanation).

8 Solving a linear equation ($y = px + q$) and a quadratic equation ($y = ax^2 + bx + c$) simultaneously:

- Find y in terms of x from the linear equation (or x in terms of y).
- Substitute for y (or x) in the quadratic equation.
- Solve the resulting quadratic equation for x (or y).
- Substitute the values of x (or y) into the linear equation to find y (or x).

If the roots of the quadratic equation are equal, the line will be a tangent to the curve.

9 Solving equations from a given graph (or one to be drawn):

- Rearrange the equation to be solved to match the equation of the graph. Try to keep the rearrangement simple.
- Compare to find y. Note that y may be of the form $\frac{k}{x}$ if the equation to be solved has a higher power of x than the given graph function.
- Draw the line (or curve) from the previous step on the given axes.
- Read off the values of x at the points of intersection.

20 Presenting and analysing data 2

This chapter shows you how to use and interpret cumulative frequency diagrams, box plots and histograms.

20.1 Upper class boundaries

When you form a frequency distribution you usually group the information into 'classes' or 'intervals'.

In this frequency distribution, the values 10, 20, 30, 40 and 50 are the largest possible values in each of the intervals.

Marks in test	Frequency
$0 < b \leqslant 10$	5
$10 < b \leqslant 20$	8
$20 < b \leqslant 30$	12
$30 < b \leqslant 40$	7
$40 < b \leqslant 50$	4

The largest possible value in an interval is called the **upper class boundary**.

The upper class boundary for an interval may depend upon whether the data is discrete or continuous.

Here are some examples for **discrete data**:

Number of bids in auction	Upper class boundary
5–9	9
10–14	14
15–19	19
20–25	25

Number of bids in auction	Upper class boundary
$5 < m \leqslant 9$	9
$9 < m \leqslant 14$	14
$14 < m \leqslant 19$	19
$19 < m \leqslant 25$	25

Number of bids in auction	Upper class boundary
$5 \leqslant m < 9$	8
$9 \leqslant m < 14$	13
$14 \leqslant m < 19$	18
$19 \leqslant m < 25$	24

$5 \leqslant m < 9$ means 5, 6, 7 and 8. So 8 is the largest possible value in the interval.

Here are some examples for **continuous data**:

Weight of letter (g)	Upper class boundary
$20.5 < m \leqslant 30.5$	30.5
$30.5 < m \leqslant 40.5$	40.5
$40.5 < m \leqslant 50.5$	50.5
$50.5 < m \leqslant 60.5$	60.5

Weight of letter (g)	Upper class boundary
$20.5 \leqslant m < 30.5$	30.5
$30.5 \leqslant m < 40.5$	40.5
$40.5 \leqslant m < 50.5$	50.5
$50.5 \leqslant m < 60.5$	60.5

Weight of letter (g)	Upper class boundary
21–30	30.5
31–40	40.5
41–50	50.5
51–60	60.5

If continuous data is grouped as 21–30, 31–40 and so on, then assume that the 21–30 interval goes from 20.5 to 30.5 with a midpoint of 25.5.

20.2 Cumulative frequency

The **cumulative frequency** is the total frequency up to a particular upper class boundary.

Here is an example for discrete data.

Example 1

The number of points scored in each of 40 rugby games was recorded. The results are summarised in the table.

Draw up a cumulative frequency table for this information.

Number of points	Frequency
0–10	2
11–20	5
21–30	9
31–40	12
41–50	8
51–60	4

The number of points scored in a game is discrete data, so the upper class boundaries are 10, 20, 30, …
The cumulative frequency table is:

Number of points	Cumulative frequency
0–10	2
0–20	$2 + 5 = 7$
0–30	$2 + 5 + 9 = 16$
0–40	$2 + 5 + 9 + 12 = 28$
0–50	$2 + 5 + 9 + 12 + 8 = 36$
0–60	$2 + 5 + 9 + 12 + 8 + 4 = 40$

Here is an example for continuous data.

Example 2

The table gives information about the lengths of 50 fossils.
Draw up a cumulative frequency table for this information.

Length (cm)	0–8	9–13	14–18	19–23	24–28	29–33
Frequency	5	10	16	9	7	3

The length of a fossil is continuous data, so the upper class boundaries are 8.5, 13.5, 18.5, …
The cumulative frequency table is:

Length of fossil (cm)	Cumulative frequency
$0 \leqslant l < 8.5$	5
$0 \leqslant l < 13.5$	15
$0 \leqslant l < 18.5$	31
$0 \leqslant l < 23.5$	40
$0 \leqslant l < 28.5$	47
$0 \leqslant l < 33.5$	50

Fossil ammonites range from under 2 cm to 300 cm in diameter. These marine creatures became extinct 65 million years ago.

Exercise 20A

1 Draw up a cumulative frequency table for each of the following sets of data.

(a)

Time watching TV (hours)	Frequency
0–3	3
4–7	5
8–11	8
12–15	3
16–18	1

(b)

Number of people on bus	Frequency
0–5	8
6–10	7
11–15	9
16–20	7
21–25	9

(c)

Age of mother at birth of baby (years)	Frequency
16–20	3
21–25	6
26–30	17
31–35	26
36–40	11
41–50	2

(d)

Daily temperature (°C)	Frequency
$-10 \leqslant t < 0$	12
$0 \leqslant t < 10$	86
$10 \leqslant t < 20$	185
$20 \leqslant t < 30$	79
$30 \leqslant t < 40$	3

2 Draw up a frequency table for this cumulative frequency table:

Weight of baby (kg)	Cumulative frequency
$1 \leqslant w < 2$	5
$1 \leqslant w < 3$	17
$1 \leqslant w < 4$	41
$1 \leqslant w < 5$	49
$1 \leqslant w < 6$	50

20.3 Cumulative frequency graphs

You can display data in a **cumulative frequency graph** by plotting the cumulative frequency against the upper class boundary for each class interval.

Example 3

The number of people queuing at a supermarket checkout was recorded at 10-minute intervals during one day. The table shows the frequency distribution.

Number in queue	0–9	10–19	20–29	30–39	40–49	50–59
Frequency	8	14	26	16	12	4

To draw the cumulative graph you must first draw up a cumulative frequency table. The numbers of people are discrete data, so the upper class boundaries are 9, 19, 29, 39, 49 and 59. The cumulative frequency table is:

Number in queue	Cumulative frequency
$0 \leqslant m \leqslant 9$	8
$0 \leqslant m \leqslant 19$	22
$0 \leqslant m \leqslant 29$	48
$0 \leqslant m \leqslant 39$	64
$0 \leqslant m \leqslant 49$	76
$0 \leqslant m \leqslant 59$	80

Draw the cumulative frequency graph by plotting (9, 8), (19, 22), (29, 48), …

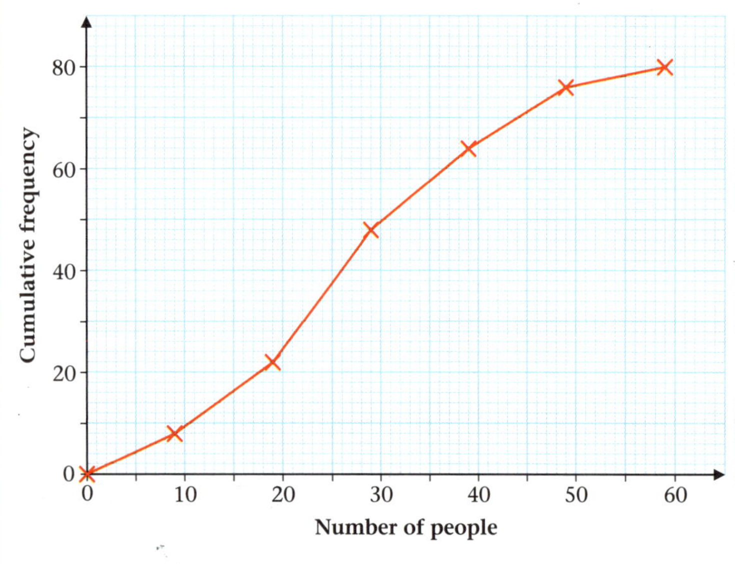

Cumulative frequency is always plotted on the vertical axis.

Here the points are joined by straight lines, giving a **cumulative frequency polygon**.

Plot the starting point (0, 0) even though it is not a value in the table.

A cumulative frequency polygon is used if the data is discrete. A cumulative frequency curve is used if the data is continuous.

Cumulative frequency diagrams may have different shapes. Here are some examples:

1 In this table of data the values increase at a steady rate, giving a straight line in the cumulative frequency diagram.

Class interval	Frequency
0–10	10
11–20	10
21–30	10
31–40	10
41–50	10

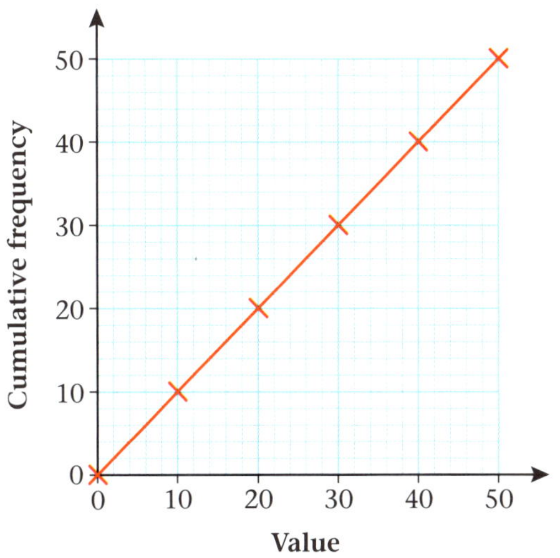

2 In this table the values are concentrated in the middle. This is shown by the steepness of the curve in the cumulative frequency diagram as it passes through the class interval 21–30.

Class interval	Frequency
0–10	6
11–20	8
21–30	22
31–40	8
41–50	6

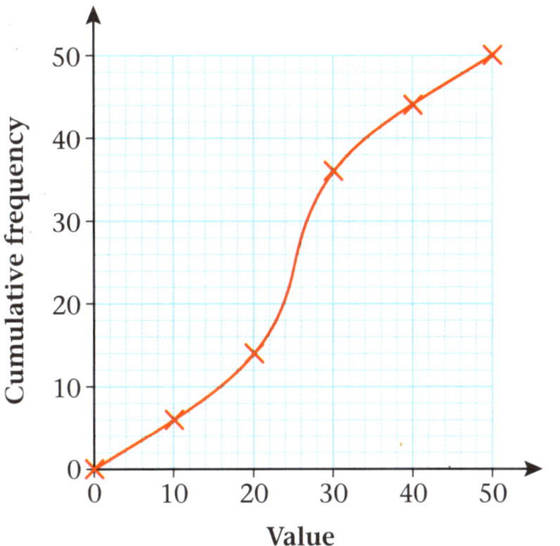

3 In this table there are few values in the class interval 21–30. This is shown in the cumulative frequency diagram by the less steep slope.

Class interval	Frequency
0–10	16
11–20	6
21–30	4
31–40	6
41–50	18

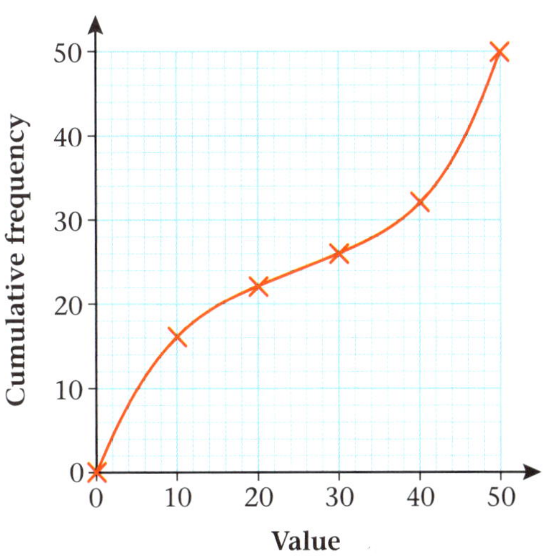

20.4 Using cumulative frequency graphs

A cumulative frequency graph can be used to *estimate* the median, the upper quartile and the lower quartile of a distribution.

Estimating the median

The **median** is the value half way into the distribution.

To estimate the median from a cumulative frequency graph, find the $\frac{n}{2}$th value in the distribution.

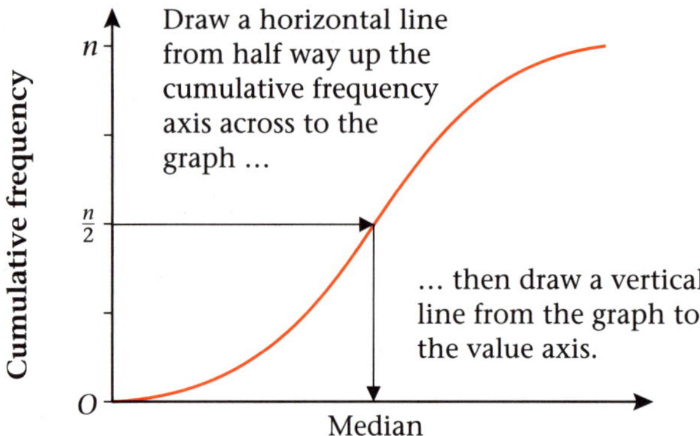
Cumulative frequency
n
$\frac{n}{2}$
O
Draw a horizontal line from half way up the cumulative frequency axis across to the graph ...
... then draw a vertical line from the graph to the value axis.
Median

Estimating the quartiles

The **lower quartile** is the value one quarter of the way into the distribution.

Here you find the $\frac{n}{4}$th value in the distribution.

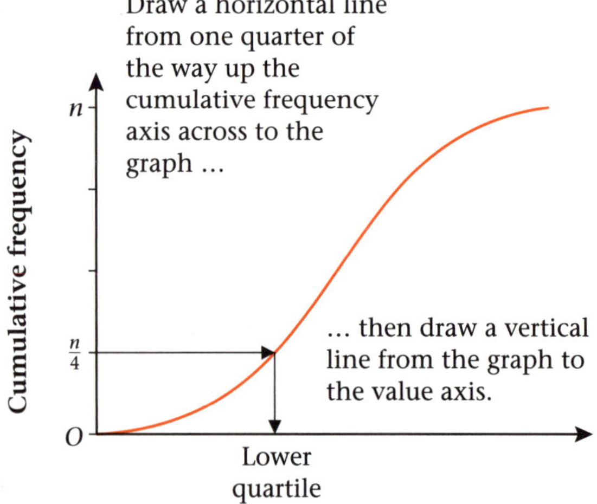
Cumulative frequency
n
$\frac{n}{4}$
O
Draw a horizontal line from one quarter of the way up the cumulative frequency axis across to the graph ...
... then draw a vertical line from the graph to the value axis.
Lower quartile

The **upper quartile** is the value three quarters of the way into the distribution.

Here you find the $\frac{3n}{4}$th value in the distribution.

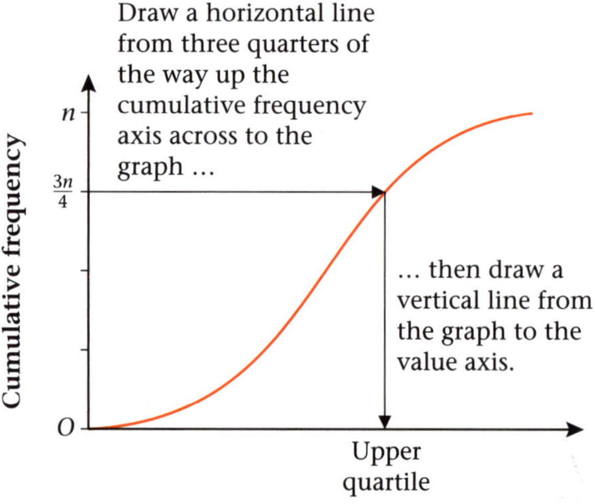
Cumulative frequency
n
$\frac{3n}{4}$
O
Draw a horizontal line from three quarters of the way up the cumulative frequency axis across to the graph ...
... then draw a vertical line from the graph to the value axis.
Upper quartile

The interquartile range

To estimate the interquartile range from a cumulative frequency graph, first estimate the upper and lower quartiles, then find:

interquartile range = upper quartile − lower quartile

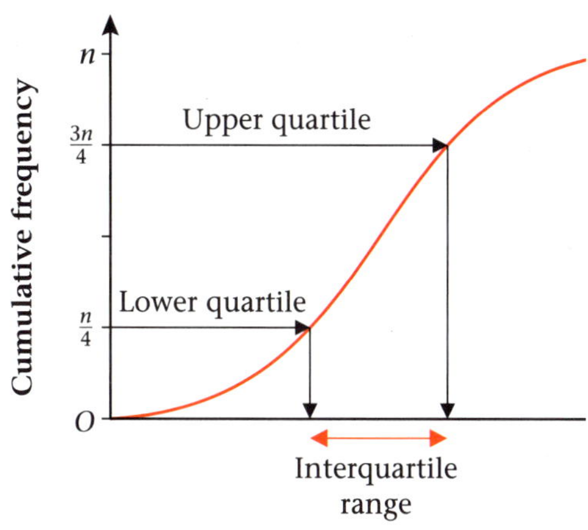

Example 4

The table gives information about the times (in seconds) between planes landing at an airport.

Find an estimate for

(a) the median

(b) (i) the lower quartile

(ii) the upper quartile

(iii) the interquartile range.

Time between planes (s)	Frequency
$60 \leqslant t < 100$	5
$100 \leqslant t < 140$	14
$140 \leqslant t < 180$	10
$180 \leqslant t < 220$	9
$220 \leqslant t < 260$	7
$260 \leqslant t < 300$	3

(a) The cumulative frequency table is on the right.

From this table the cumulative frequency graph can be drawn.

Time between planes (s)	Cumulative frequency
$60 \leqslant t < 100$	5
$60 \leqslant t < 140$	19
$60 \leqslant t < 180$	29
$60 \leqslant t < 220$	38
$60 \leqslant t < 260$	45
$60 \leqslant t < 300$	48

Remember to plot the starting point (60, 0).

Read the required estimates from the graph:

Median $= \frac{48}{2}$th value = 24th value = 160 seconds

(b) (i) Lower quartile $= \frac{48}{4}$th value = 12th value = 120 seconds

(ii) Upper quartile $= \frac{3(48)}{4}$th value = 36th value = 212 seconds

(iii) Interquartile range = upper quartile − lower quartile
= 212 − 120 = 92 seconds

Exercise 20B

1 The numbers of particles emitted each minute by a sample of uranium are summarised in the table.

Number of particles	Frequency
0–50	10
51–100	16
101–150	13
151–200	11
201–250	7
251–300	3

(a) Draw a cumulative frequency graph for this data.

(b) Use your graph to find an estimate for

(i) the median (ii) the lower quartile

(iii) the upper quartile (iv) the interquartile range.

2 A software company has a record of the age, at their last birthday, of each of its workers. This table shows the age distribution.

Age (years)	Frequency
$16 < a \leqslant 20$	6
$21 < a \leqslant 25$	9
$26 < a \leqslant 30$	14
$31 < a \leqslant 35$	4
$36 < a \leqslant 40$	2
$41 < a \leqslant 45$	1

(a) Draw a cumulative frequency graph for this data.

(b) Find an estimate for

(i) the median (ii) the interquartile range.

3 The table gives information about the body temperatures of a random sample of people.

Use this data to find an estimate for

(a) the median body temperature

(b) the interquartile range

(c) the number of people with a body temperature less than 37 °C.

Body temperature (°C)	Cumulative frequency
<36.0	8
<36.3	23
<36.6	44
<36.9	78
<37.2	101
<37.5	115
<37.8	120

Activity – World temperatures

(a) From a newspaper, collect the highest temperatures (°C) recorded in cities around the world.

(b) Using suitable class intervals (e.g. 0–5, 6–10...), draw a cumulative frequency graph and find an estimate for the median temperature.

(c) How good is your answer as an estimate for the average temperature of the Earth? Explain your answer.

20.5 Using cumulative frequency graphs to solve problems

Cumulative frequency graphs can be used to solve a variety of problems.

Worked examination question

The speeds in miles per hour (mph) of 120 cars travelling on the A4 road were measured. The results are shown in the table.

(a) Draw a cumulative frequency graph to show these figures.

(b) Use your graph to find an estimate for the percentage of cars travelling at less than 42 miles per hour.

Speed (mph)	Cumulative frequency
$5 < s \leqslant 20$	2
$5 < s \leqslant 25$	10
$5 < s \leqslant 30$	28
$5 < s \leqslant 35$	50
$5 < s \leqslant 40$	84
$5 < s \leqslant 45$	106
$5 < s \leqslant 50$	116
$5 < s \leqslant 55$	120
$5 < s \leqslant 60$	120

(a) Here is the cumulative frequency graph.

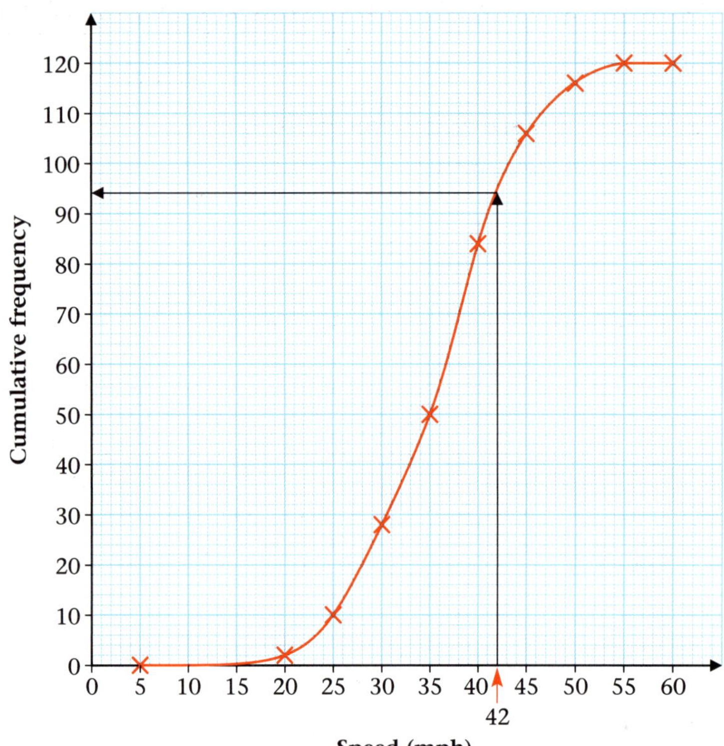

The starting point is (5, 0).

(b) The graph shows that 94 out of 120 cars are travelling at less than 42 mph.

$$\frac{94}{120} = 78.3\%$$

So 78.3% of the cars are travelling at less than 42 mph.

Exercise 20C

1 The marks in an examination are shown in the table. The maximum mark obtainable was 100.

(a) Draw a cumulative frequency polygon.

(b) Use your graph to estimate the number of people who scored more than 67 marks.

(c) Work out an estimate for the mark that was exceeded by 60% of the people.

Mark range	Frequency
0–10	4
11–20	8
21–30	13
31–40	28
41–50	45
51–60	58
61–70	53
71–80	33
81–90	17
91–100	4

2 The table shows the frequency distribution of the masses of 50 students at a college.

Mass (kg)	$40 < m \leqslant 45$	$45 < m \leqslant 50$	$50 < m \leqslant 55$	$55 < m \leqslant 60$	$60 < m \leqslant 70$	$70 < m \leqslant 80$
Frequency	2	8	15	16	6	3

(a) Draw a cumulative frequency curve. Start your graph at (40, 0).

(b) Work out an estimate for the percentage of these students with a mass less than 53 kg.

(c) Find an estimate for the mass exceeded by 20% of the students.

3 The table gives information about the ages of people at a birthday party.

Age (years)	$0 \leqslant a < 5$	$5 \leqslant a < 10$	$10 \leqslant a < 15$	$15 \leqslant a < 25$	$25 \leqslant a < 35$
Frequency	3	9	7	3	5

Age (years)	$35 \leqslant a < 40$	$40 \leqslant a < 50$	$50 \leqslant a < 55$	$55 \leqslant a < 60$
Frequency	12	10	4	1

(a) Draw a cumulative frequency graph.

(b) Find an estimate for the age exceeded by the majority of the people.

(c) Find an estimate for the number of teenagers at the party.

20.6 Box plots

Here is the cumulative frequency graph from Example 4, for times between planes landing at an airport.

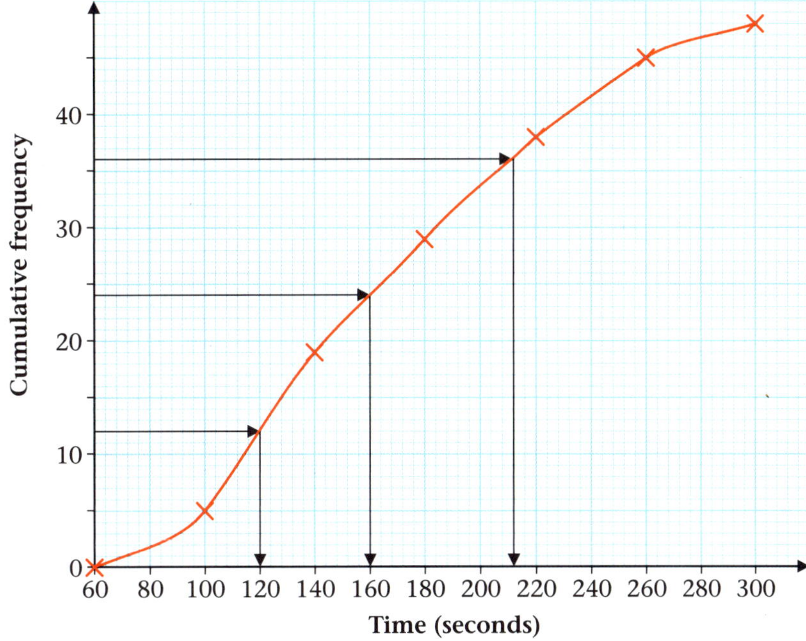

You can represent some of the important features of a cumulative frequency graph by drawing a **box plot** (or **box-and-whisker diagram**).

A box plot needs a horizontal scale.

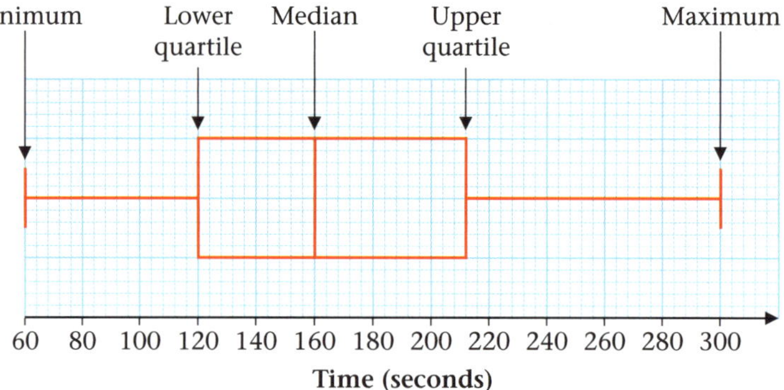

To draw a **box plot** you need five pieces of information:

- the lowest value
- the lower quartile
- the median
- the upper quartile
- the highest value.

From the box plot above, the actual lowest and highest values of the data are not known because the data is grouped. In this case you use the lowest and highest possible values for the data. The **lowest possible time** between planes is 60 seconds, and the **highest possible time** between planes is 300 seconds.

You can use a box plot to represent data given as a list or in a stem-and-leaf diagram.

Time between planes (s)	Frequency
$60 \leqslant t < 100$	5
$100 \leqslant t < 140$	14
$140 \leqslant t < 180$	10
$180 \leqslant t < 220$	9
$220 \leqslant t < 260$	7
$260 \leqslant t < 300$	3

Example 5

This stem and leaf diagram shows the age of each of the last 23 British prime ministers when taking office.

Draw a box plot to represent this information.

Age of prime minister (years)

4	3, 7, 8
5	3, 3, 3, 3, 5, 7, 7, 7, 7
6	0, 2, 2, 3, 4, 4, 5, 7, 8, 9
7	6

Key: 4 | 3 means 43.

The lowest value is 43

The lower quartile $\left(\text{the } \frac{23+1}{4} = \text{6th value}\right) = 53$

The median $\left(\text{the } \frac{23+1}{2} = \text{12th value}\right) = 57$

The upper quartile $\left(\text{the } \frac{3(23+1)}{4} = \text{18th value}\right) = 64$

The highest value is 76

So the box plot is:

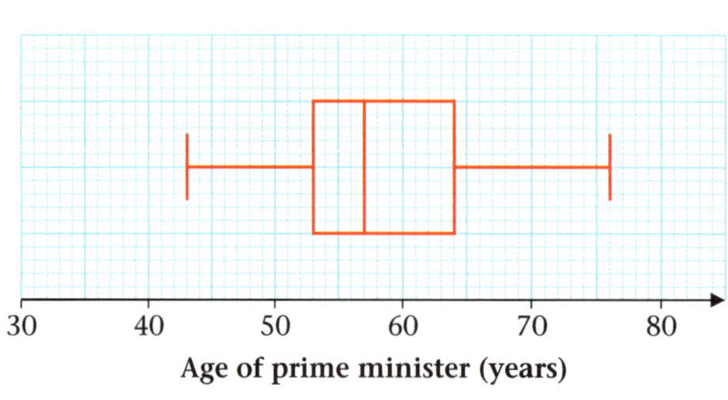

Exercise 20D

1 This cumulative frequency diagram gives information about the weights of 100 babies born at Bundledale Hospital.

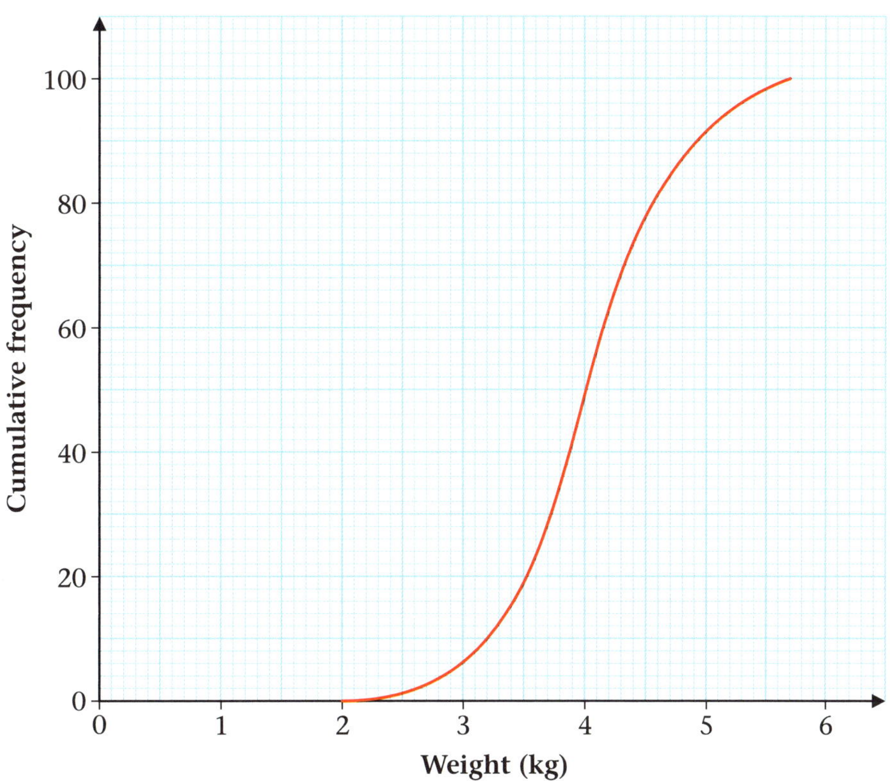

Draw a box plot to represent this information.

2 The number of consecutive press-ups by each of 27 members of a sports club are summarised in this stem and leaf diagram:

Number of press-ups

0	5, 8
1	1, 1, 2, 3, 3, 3, 5, 7, 8, 8, 9, 9
2	0, 0, 2, 4, 4, 5, 5, 7, 7
3	0, 5, 7
4	8

Key: 4 | 8 means 48.

Draw a box plot to represent this information.

20.7 Comparing sets of data with box plots

Box plots can be very useful when comparing sets of data.

When you compare the information in two or more box plots, always draw the diagrams lined up, one above the other.

Example 6

Deenita and Zac are writing party invitations. The table gives information about the times, in seconds, they take to write an invitation.

	Deenita	Zac
Lowest	20	11
Highest	58	72
Median	35	28
Lower quartile	26	20
Upper quartile	50	55

(a) Draw two box plots on the same scale to represent this information.

(b) Compare Deenita's and Zac's results.

(a)

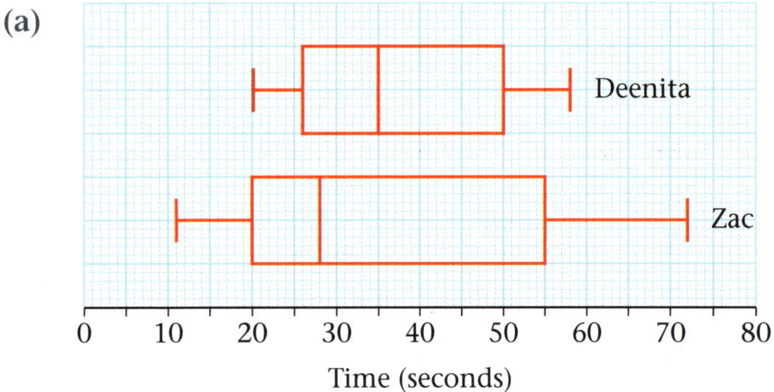

Look at the maximum and minimum values to choose a suitable scale.

(b) Zac had a lower median value but his values are spread over a much wider range overall, and the interquartile range is greater than for Deenita. Deenita was much more consistent because both the range and the interquartile range are smaller.

Exercise 20E

1 These box plots give information about the results of two different classes for the same test.
Use the diagrams to compare the performance of the two classes.

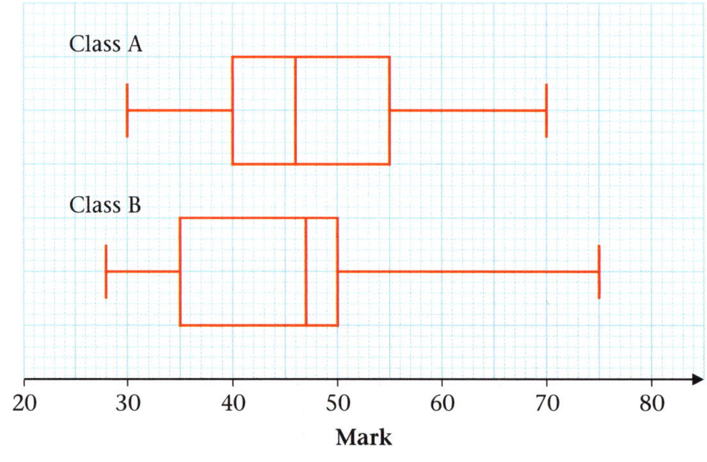

2 The cumulative frequency curves show the times taken by students to run 200 metres.

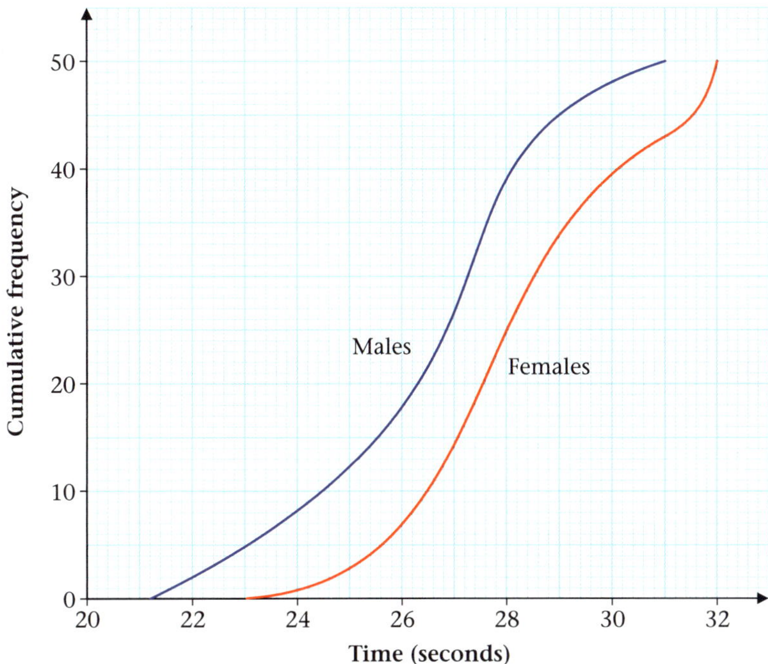

(a) Draw box plots to compare the times for males and females.

(b) Comment on the times for males and females.

Activity – The age of power

Find out the age of each of the last 23 US presidents when taking office.

Compare your results to those for the British prime ministers in Example 5.

20.8 Plotting data in a histogram

Equal-sized class intervals

The table shows how long an audience's laughter lasted, in seconds, for 54 jokes told by a stand-up comedian.

The data can be displayed in a histogram like this:

Duration of applause (s)	Frequency
$0 < t \leqslant 5$	8
$5 < t \leqslant 10$	12
$10 < t \leqslant 15$	15
$15 < t \leqslant 20$	10
$20 < t \leqslant 25$	9

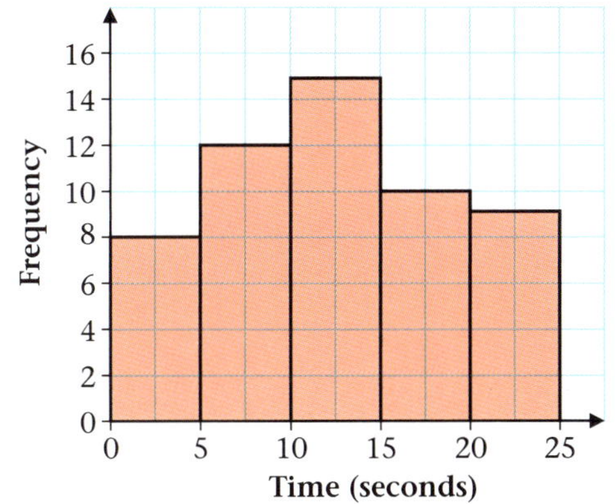

In a **histogram** the areas of the rectangles are proportional to the frequencies they represent.

In this case all the class intervals are the same (5 seconds) so the rectangles all have the same width, and the height of each rectangle is proportional to its area and to the frequency.

Unequal class intervals

When the class intervals are unequal it is incorrect to use the bar heights to represent frequencies.

If the stop-watch used to time the applause is not accurate for times of less than 5 seconds, the data can be recorded using different class intervals like this:

Duration of applause (s)	Frequency
$0 < t \leqslant 10$	20
$10 < t \leqslant 15$	15
$15 < t \leqslant 20$	10
$20 < t \leqslant 25$	9

To draw the histogram you now construct a table with a column for **frequency density**, calculated by dividing the frequency by class width:

frequency density $= \dfrac{\text{frequency}}{\text{class width}}$

Duration of applause (s)	Frequency	Frequency density
$0 < t \leqslant 10$	20	$20 \div 10 = 2$
$10 < t \leqslant 15$	15	$15 \div 5 = 3$
$15 < t \leqslant 20$	10	$10 \div 5 = 2$
$20 < t \leqslant 25$	9	$9 \div 5 = 1.8$

This histogram displays the data:

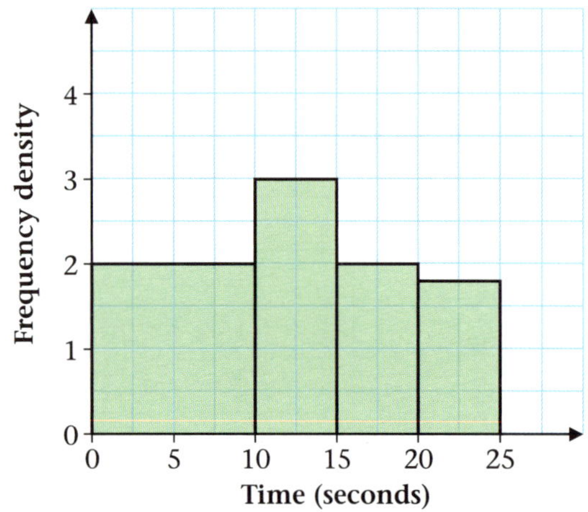

The vertical axis shows frequency density.

The areas of the rectangles are 20, 15, 10 and 9 respectively. They are in the correct proportion to the numbers of rounds of applause (frequencies).

Standard class intervals

The lengths of reign of the kings and queens of England are summarised in this table:

Length of reign (years)	Frequency
$0 < r \leqslant 10$	24
$10 < r \leqslant 20$	14
$20 < r \leqslant 30$	10
$30 < r \leqslant 40$	7
$40 < r \leqslant 50$	2
$50 < r \leqslant 60$	2
$60 < r \leqslant 70$	1

Windsor Castle is the oldest and largest inhabited castle in the world. It has been a royal home and fortress for over 900 years.

The last three class intervals ($40 < r \leqslant 50$, $50 < r \leqslant 60$ and $60 < r \leqslant 70$) have low frequencies compared to the others and will not show up so clearly on a histogram with class intervals of equal width. They will show up more clearly if the last four class intervals are combined:

Length of reign (years)	Frequency
$0 < r \leqslant 10$	24
$10 < r \leqslant 20$	14
$20 < r \leqslant 30$	10
$30 < r \leqslant 70$	12

You could now simply calculate frequency densities by using

$$\text{frequency density} = \frac{\text{frequency}}{\text{class width}}$$

but it is more convenient to use a **standard class interval**.

A standard class interval can be anything you wish, but in this case 10 years is sensible. So the class $30 < r \leqslant 70$ years is 4×10 years or 4 standard intervals.

The table is now:

Length of reign (years)	Class width in standard class intervals	Frequency	Frequency density
$0 < r \leqslant 10$	1	24	$24 \div 1 = 24$
$10 < r \leqslant 20$	1	14	$14 \div 1 = 14$
$20 < r \leqslant 30$	1	10	$10 \div 1 = 10$
$30 < r \leqslant 70$	4	12	$12 \div 4 = 3$

Here the frequency density column has been calculated using standard class intervals:

$$\textbf{frequency density} = \frac{\text{frequency}}{\text{class width in standard class intervals}}$$

This histogram shows the frequency density plotted against length of reign:

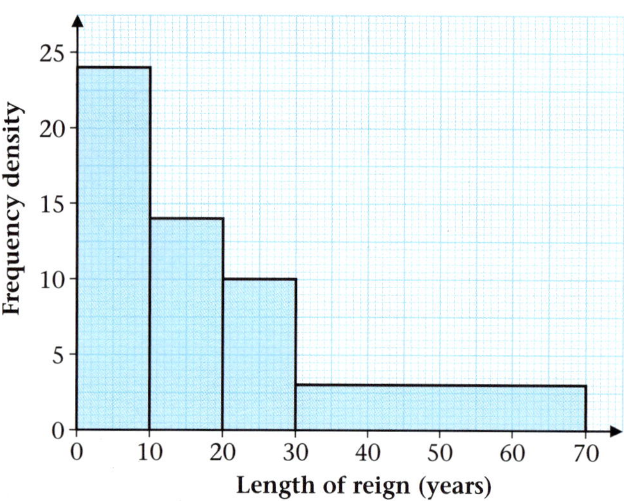

Handling continuous data

Sometimes data which is continuous is recorded as if it were discrete.

Example 7

Agnes drives a van making deliveries for mail order catalogues. She records the distance travelled for each delivery correct to the nearest mile:

3	12	18	13	16	18	19	15	17	16
15	7	20	22	15	18	14	19	17	6
14	17	21	25	18	14	12	17	8	19
13	25	15	14	5	16	16	12	11	7
19	12	26	18	19	10	11	26	7	16
33	13	8	22	16	18	11	38	31	21

(a) Produce a frequency table using intervals 0–9, 10–14, 15–19, 20–24 and 25–39.

(b) Use your completed frequency table to draw a histogram.

(a) As the distances are recorded to the nearest mile the class widths are 9.5, 5, 5, 5 and 15 respectively.

There is no advantage here in defining a standard class interval, so we will use:

$$\text{frequency density} = \frac{\text{frequency}}{\text{class width}}$$

This gives the following table:

Distance travelled miles	Tally	Frequency	Frequency density
0–9	~~IIII~~ III	8	$8 \div 9.5 = 0.84$
10–14	~~IIII~~ ~~IIII~~ ~~IIII~~	15	$15 \div 5 = 3$
15–19	~~IIII~~ ~~IIII~~ ~~IIII~~ ~~IIII~~ ~~IIII~~	25	$25 \div 5 = 5$
20–24	~~IIII~~	5	$5 \div 5 = 1$
25–39	~~IIII~~ II	7	$7 \div 15 = 0.47$

The data is continuous so the 0–9 class is actually 0–9.5, which has a width 9.5. The 10–14 class is actually 9.5–14.5, which has a width 5; and so on.

(b) Using the frequency density, you can draw the histogram.

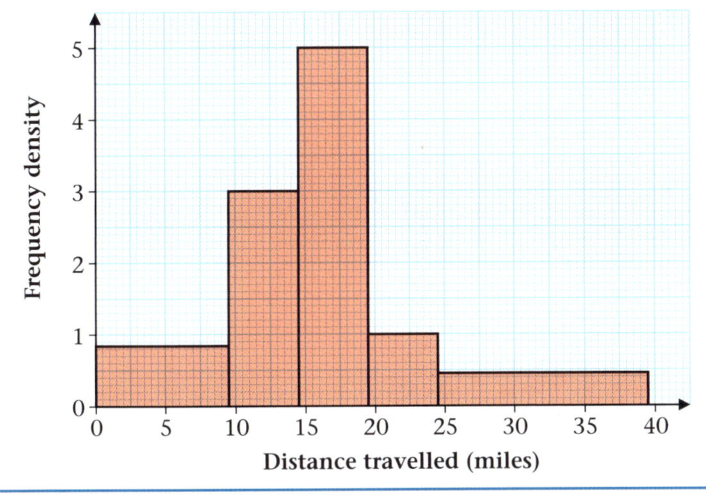

Note that the histogram is drawn to the upper class boundaries: 9.5, 14.5, 19.5, 24.5 and 39.5.

Exercise 20F

1 This table shows the distribution of times, in seconds, required for students to memorise a list of 10 words.

Draw a histogram to display this data.

Time to memorise (s)	Frequency
$0 < t \leqslant 30$	3
$30 < t \leqslant 60$	9
$60 < t \leqslant 80$	10
$80 < t \leqslant 90$	8
$90 < t \leqslant 100$	6
$100 < t \leqslant 150$	12

2 This table shows the distribution of weights, in grams, of 40 portions of rice served in a restaurant.

Weight (g)	Frequency
$0 \leqslant w < 30$	5
$30 \leqslant w < 45$	7
$45 \leqslant w < 60$	11
$60 \leqslant w < 75$	8
$75 \leqslant w < 105$	9

Draw a histogram to represent this information.

3 A group of people were asked to throw a tennis ball. The distances thrown, in metres, were recorded in a table:

Distance thrown (m)	Frequency
0–9	18
10–14	14
15–19	16
20–24	15
25–34	17
35–50	10

Draw a histogram to show this data.

4 In a survey of hand-lengths in centimetres these results were obtained:

20.1	13.8	17.9	14.6	20.3	16.3	21.5
21.6	17.9	18.3	17.7	21.8	18.4	22.1
22.1	20.3	18.7	18.7	23.1	19.1	19.9
21.7	21.0	21.8	18.4	19.7	18.7	24.7
21.5	22.3	20.9	17.1	18.8	19.6	21.6
20.2	23.1	15.8	18.2	22.0	20.8	22.0

Remember:
The interval 18–19 goes from 17.5 to 19.5, but does not include 19.5.

(a) Produce a frequency table with class intervals of 13–17, 18–19, 20–21 and 22–25.

(b) Draw a histogram to show this data.

Activity – Distances travelled to school

(Go to www.heinemann.co.uk/hotlinks, insert the express code 4092P and click on this activity.)

Use the information in the Mayfield High School database to draw a histogram for the distances between home and school of female KS4 students.

20.9 Interpreting histograms

Frequency = frequency density × class width

or

Frequency = frequency density × class width in standard class intervals

Example 8

The histogram below shows the distribution of the lifetimes of bees in a small colony.
Use the information to complete the frequency table.
One of the frequencies has already been entered in the table.

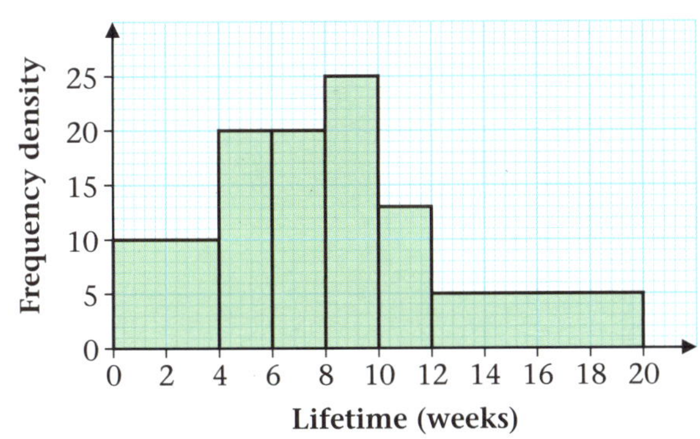

Lifetime (weeks)	Frequency density	Frequency
$0 \leq t < 4$	10	40
$4 \leq t < 6$	20	
$6 \leq t < 8$	20	
$8 \leq t < 10$		
$10 \leq t < 12$		
$12 \leq t < 20$		

The frequency densities can be read straight from the histogram.

The frequencies are obtained by multiplying the frequency density by the class width.

For the $0 \leq t < 4$ class interval:

frequency = frequency density × 4
= 10 × 4 = 40 bees

For the class intervals in the middle:

frequency = frequency density × 2

For the $12 \leq t < 20$ class interval:

frequency = frequency density × 8
= 5 × 8 = 40 bees

Here is the completed table of frequencies:

Lifetime (weeks)	Frequency density	Frequency
$0 \leq t < 4$	10	10 × 4 = 40
$4 \leq t < 6$	20	20 × 2 = 40
$6 \leq t < 8$	20	20 × 2 = 40
$8 \leq t < 10$	25	25 × 2 = 50
$10 \leq t < 12$	13	13 × 2 = 26
$12 \leq t < 20$	5	5 × 8 = 40

Example 9

This histogram has been drawn using a standard class interval of 5 units.
Complete the frequency table.

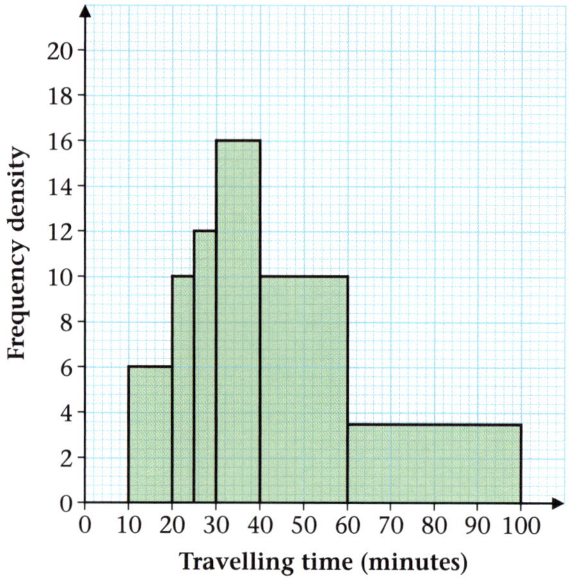

Class interval	Frequency density	Frequency
$10 < t \leqslant 20$	6	
$20 < t \leqslant 25$	10	
$25 < t \leqslant 30$	12	
$30 < t \leqslant 40$	16	
$40 < t \leqslant 60$	10	
$60 < t \leqslant 100$	3.5	

The frequencies can be obtained by multiplying the frequency density by the class width in standard class intervals.

For the $10 < t \leqslant 20$ class interval:

width = 10 units = 2 standard class intervals

So

$$\begin{aligned} \text{frequency} &= \text{frequency density} \times 2 \\ &= 6 \times 2 = 12 \text{ journeys} \end{aligned}$$

For the $20 < t \leqslant 25$ class interval:

width = 5 units = 1 standard class interval

So

$$\begin{aligned} \text{frequency} &= \text{frequency density} \times 1 \\ &= 10 \times 1 = 10 \text{ journeys} \end{aligned}$$

and so on for the remaining class intervals.

Here is the completed table of frequencies:

Class interval	Frequency density	Frequency
$10 < t \leqslant 20$	6	$6 \times 2 = 12$
$20 < t \leqslant 25$	10	$10 \times 1 = 10$
$25 < t \leqslant 30$	12	$12 \times 1 = 12$
$30 < t \leqslant 40$	16	$16 \times 2 = 32$
$40 < t \leqslant 60$	10	$10 \times 4 = 40$
$60 < t \leqslant 100$	3.5	$3.5 \times 8 = 28$

A simpler method of showing frequencies is to draw a key to show what a standard area represents.

In this histogram the key shows the size of the area that represents 4 people.

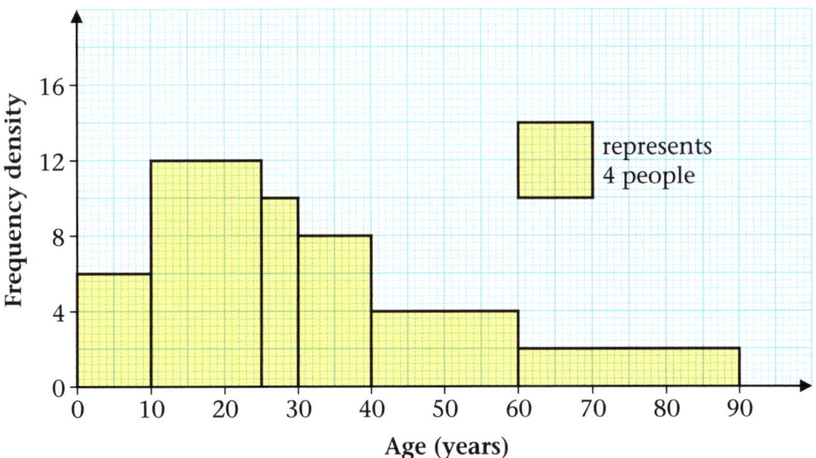

The histogram shows that there are

- 6 people aged between 0 and 10
- 18 people aged between 10 and 25
- 5 people aged between 25 and 30, and so on.

This method can be used with all histograms.

Exercise 20G

1 Students were asked to estimate the length of a line. Their responses are summarised in this histogram:

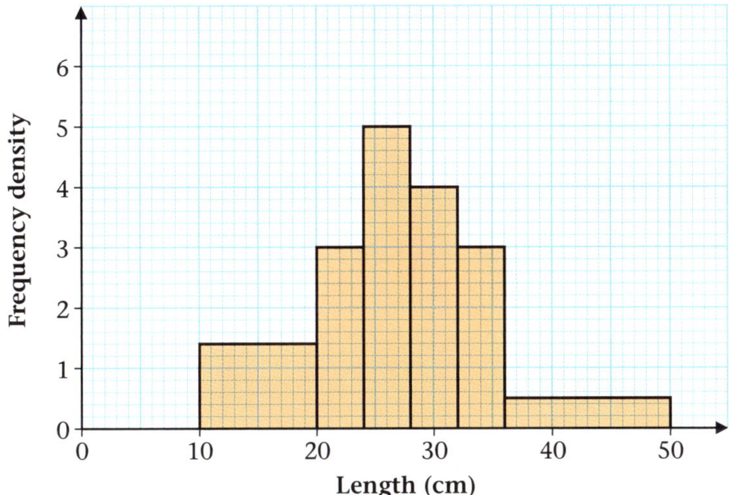

Estimate of length (cm)	Frequency
$10 < l \leqslant 20$	14
$20 < l \leqslant 24$	
$24 < l \leqslant 28$	
$28 < l \leqslant 32$	
$32 < l \leqslant 36$	
$36 < l \leqslant 50$	

Copy and complete the table.

2 The lifetimes of bulbs in an advertising hoarding were recorded. The information is summarised in this histogram:

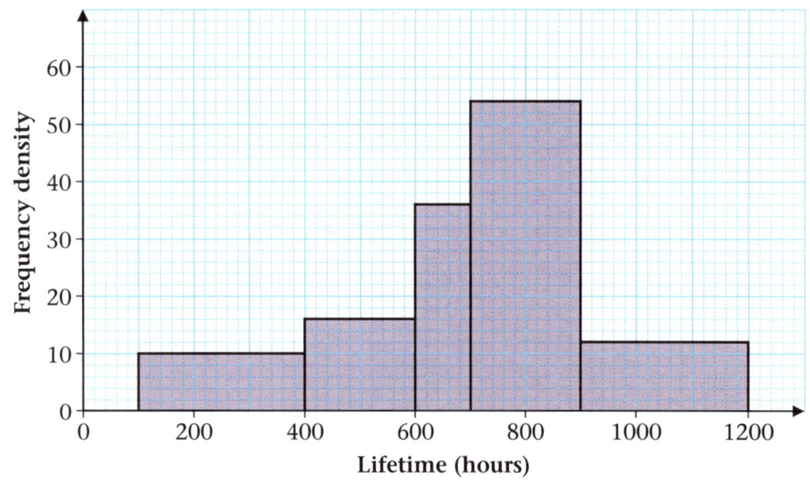

Lifetime (hours)	Frequency
$100 \leqslant t < 400$	
$400 \leqslant t < 600$	
$600 \leqslant t < 700$	
$700 \leqslant t < 900$	
$900 \leqslant t < 1200$	

The histogram was drawn using a standard class interval of 100 hours. Copy and complete the table.

3 The histogram shows the distribution of the weights of the letters in a mail bag. The histogram has been drawn using a standard class interval of 8 units.

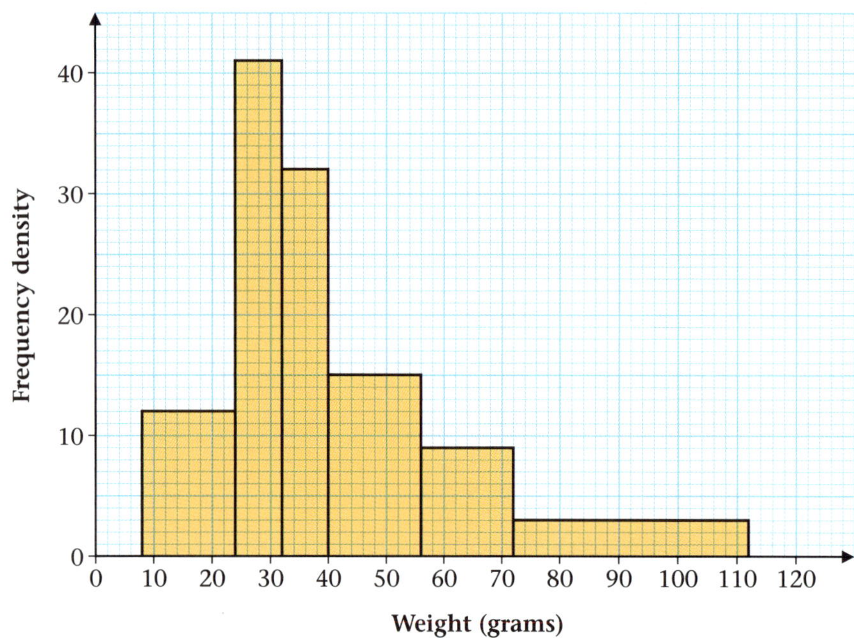

(a) Draw a frequency table.

(b) How many letters were in the mail bag?

(c) Find the percentage of letters that weighed 40 grams or more. [E]

4 The histogram shows the distribution of the times taken to perform 180 operations in a hospital.

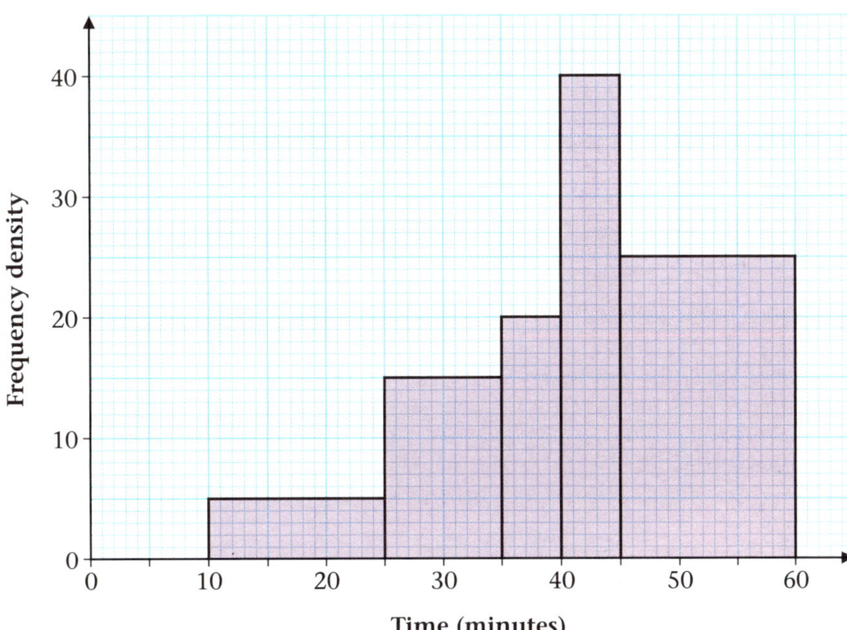

(a) Copy and complete the table.

Time (minutes)	Frequency
$10 \leqslant t < 25$	
$25 \leqslant t < 35$	
$35 \leqslant t < 40$	
$40 \leqslant t < 45$	
$45 \leqslant t < 60$	

Find the number of operations represented by 1 large square.

(b) How many operations took less than 35 minutes? [E]

Mixed exercise 20

1 This ordered stem and leaf diagram shows the times taken for each of 29 students to complete their maths homework.

Time to complete homework (minutes)

1	6, 7, 8, 8, 9
2	0, 1, 1, 1, 1, 3, 5, 5, 5, 6, 7, 8, 9
3	3, 5, 5, 5, 5, 7, 7, 8, 8
4	1, 2

Key: 4 | 1 means 41 minutes.

Draw a box plot to represent this information.

2 A supermarket manager wants to compare the performance of two checkout assistants. She gathers the information in the table for the time taken, in seconds, to serve each customer.

	Assistant A	Assistant B
Lowest	50	42
Highest	110	144
Median	80	76
Lower quartile	62	60
Upper quartile	90	84

(a) Choose an appropriate scale and draw two box plots for these results.

(b) The manager concluded that because Assistant B had a maximum of 144 seconds she was not performing as well as Assistant A.

Explain why the manager's conclusion might have been wrong.

3 The table shows information about the heights of 40 bushes.

Height (h cm)	Frequency
$170 \leqslant h < 175$	5
$175 \leqslant h < 180$	18
$180 \leqslant h < 185$	12
$185 \leqslant h < 190$	4
$190 \leqslant h < 195$	1

(a) Complete the cumulative frequency table.

Height (h cm)	Cumulative frequency
$170 \leqslant h < 175$	
$170 \leqslant h < 180$	
$170 \leqslant h < 185$	
$170 \leqslant h < 190$	
$170 \leqslant h < 195$	

(b) Draw a cumulative frequency graph for your table, using a scale of 2 cm for every 5 cm height.

(c) Use your graph to find an estimate for the median height of the bushes. [E]

4 40 boys each completed a puzzle. This cumulative frequency graph gives information about the times it took them to complete the puzzle.

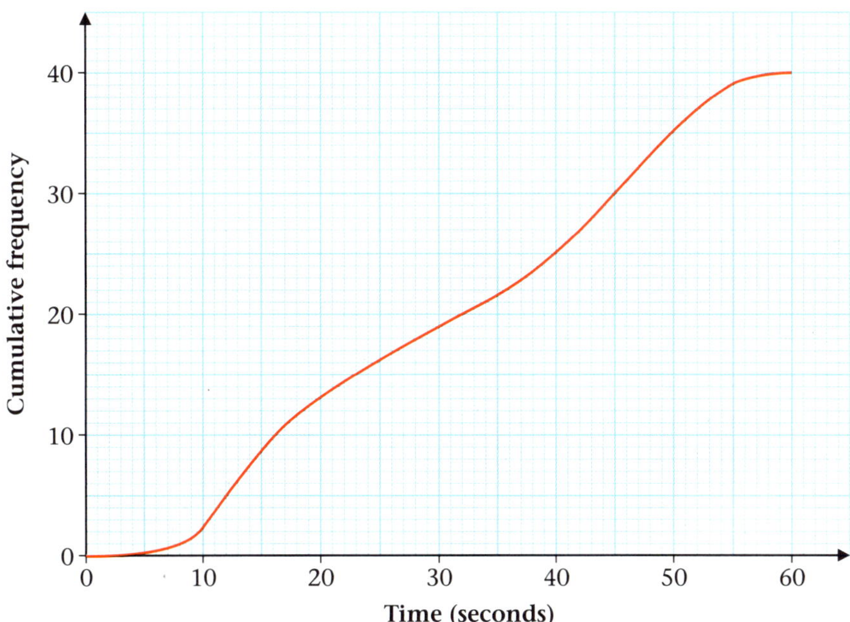

(a) Use the graph to find an estimate for the median time.

For the boys, the minimum time to complete the puzzle was 9 seconds, and the maximum time to complete the puzzle was 57 seconds.

(b) Use this information and the cumulative frequency graph to draw a box plot showing information about the boys' times. (Use graph paper and the same scale as in the diagram below.)

This box plot shows information about the times taken by 40 girls to complete the same puzzle.

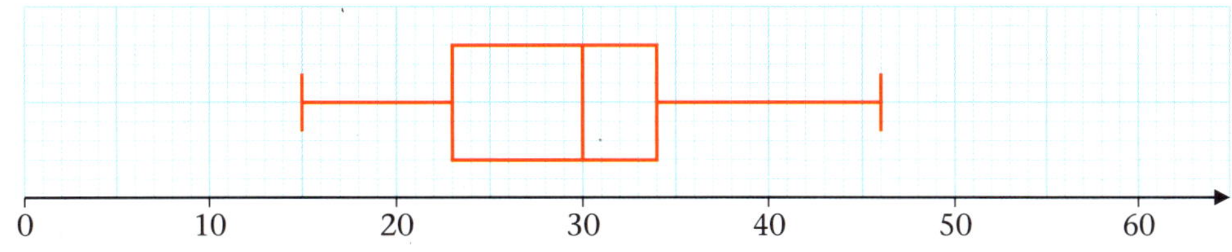

(c) Make two comparisons between the boys' times and the girls' times. [E]

5 The incomplete table and histogram give some information about the ages of the people who live in a village.

Age (x) in years	Frequency
$0 < x \leq 10$	160
$10 < x \leq 25$	
$25 < x \leq 30$	
$30 < x \leq 40$	100
$40 < x \leq 70$	120

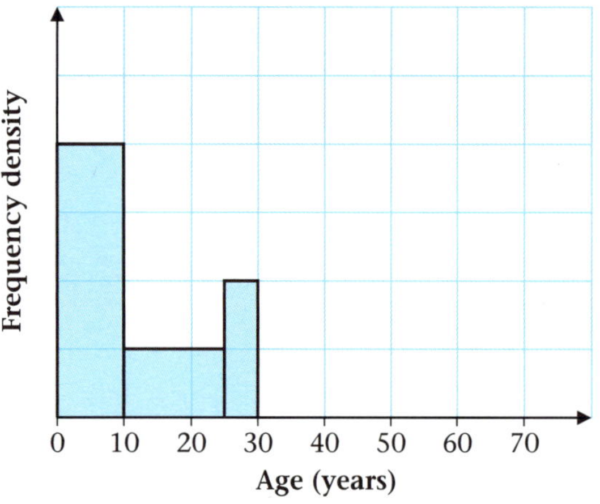

(a) Copy and complete the frequency table, using the information in the histogram.

(b) Copy and complete the histogram. [E]

6 The histogram gives information about the times, in minutes, 135 students spent on the internet last night.

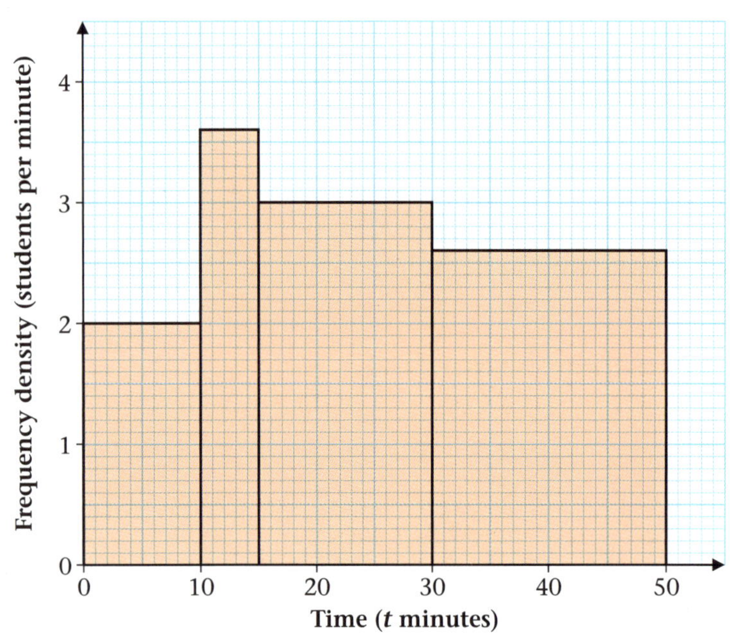

Time (t minutes)	Frequency
$0 < t \leq 10$	
$10 < t \leq 15$	
$15 < t \leq 30$	
$30 < t \leq 50$	
Total	135

Copy and complete the table, using the information in the histogram. [E]

7 One Monday, Tessa measured the times, in seconds, that individual birds spent on her bird table. She used this information to complete a frequency table.

Time (t seconds)	Frequency
$0 < t \leqslant 10$	8
$10 < t \leqslant 20$	16
$20 < t \leqslant 25$	15
$25 < t \leqslant 30$	12
$30 < t \leqslant 50$	6

(a) Use the table to draw a complete histogram.

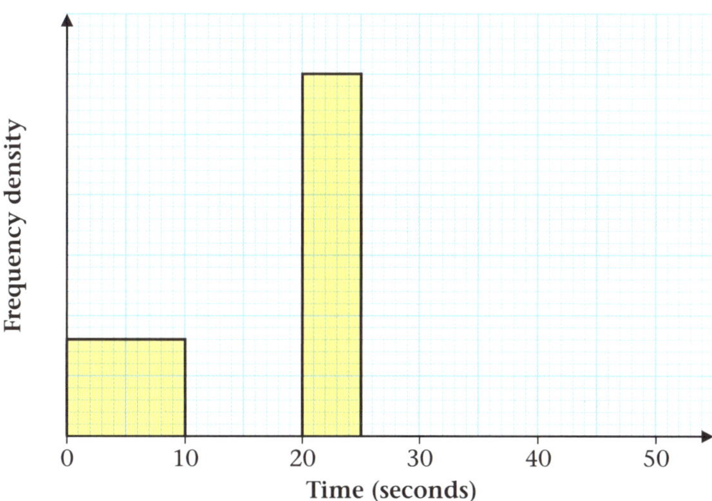

On Tuesday she conducted a similar survey and drew the following histogram from her results.

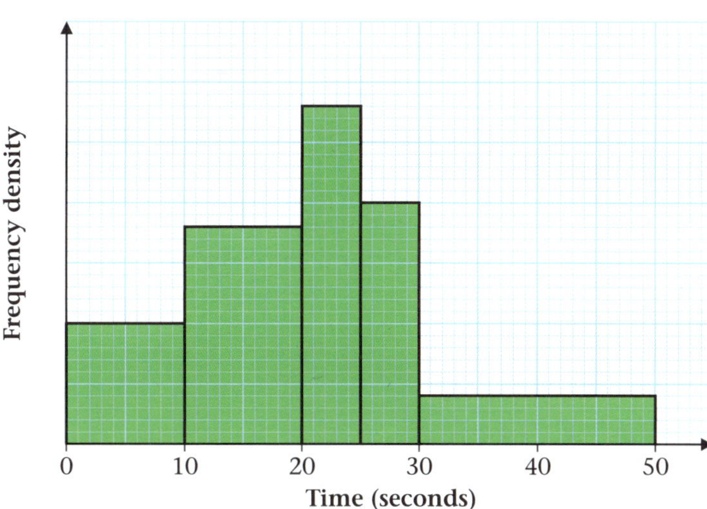

(b) Use the histogram for Tuesday to complete a frequency table.

Time (t seconds)	Frequency
$0 < t \leqslant 10$	
$10 < t \leqslant 20$	
$20 < t \leqslant 25$	
$25 < t \leqslant 30$	
$30 < t \leqslant 50$	

[E]

8 This back-to-back stem and leaf diagram gives information about the ages of oak trees in two forests:

Forest A Age in years		Forest B Age in years
	1	5
6, 4, 2	2	1, 9
7, 7, 2, 0	3	5, 6
6, 5, 5, 3, 1	4	1, 2, 2, 4, 8
8, 8, 5, 2, 2, 0	5	3, 6, 6, 7, 7, 9
9	6	1, 1, 2, 2, 3, 4, 5

Key: 9 | 6 | 1 means 69 years and 61 years.

(a) Draw box plots to compare this information.

(b) Comment on the ages of the oak trees in the two forests.

Summary of key points

1 The largest possible value in an interval is called the **upper class boundary**.

2 The **cumulative frequency** is the total frequency up to a particular upper class boundary.

3 You can display data in a **cumulative frequency graph** by plotting the cumulative frequency against the upper class boundary for each interval.

4 The **median** is the value half way into the distribution.

5 The **lower quartile** is the value one quarter of the way into the distribution.
The **upper quartile** is the value three quarters of the way into the distribution.

6 **Interquartile range** = upper quartile − lower quartile

7 To draw a **box plot** you need five pieces of information:
- the lowest value
- the lower quartile
- the median
- the upper quartile
- the highest value.

8 In a **histogram** the areas of the rectangles are proportional to the frequencies they represent.

9 **Frequency density** $= \dfrac{\text{frequency}}{\text{class width}}$

or

Frequency density $= \dfrac{\text{frequency}}{\text{class width in standard class intervals}}$

10 **Frequency** = frequency density × class width

or

Frequency = frequency density × class width in standard class intervals

21 Advanced trigonometry

This chapter extends the work on Pythagoras' theorem (Chapter 15, in Book 1) and basic trigonometry (Chapter 16) to finding areas, lengths and angles in triangles which do not contain a right angle. You will also learn to apply Pythagoras' theorem and trigonometry in three dimensions.

21.1 The area of a triangle

The diagram opposite shows a general triangle ABC. The lengths of its sides are a, b and c units.

The perpendicular from B to AC is drawn. It meets AC at X. Its length is h.

a is opposite angle A

The area of a triangle is $\frac{1}{2} \times$ base $\times$ height. So the area of triangle ABC is $\frac{1}{2}bh$.

Using the **sine ratio**:

$$\sin C = \frac{h}{a} \quad \text{or} \quad h = a \sin C$$

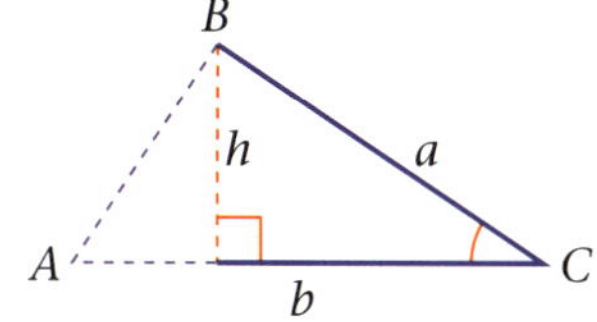

Substituting $h = a \sin C$ into area $ABC = \frac{1}{2}bh$ gives

area $ABC = \frac{1}{2} \times b \times a \sin C$, which you can write as

area $ABC = \frac{1}{2}ab \sin C$

Similarly, it can be shown that

area $ABC = \frac{1}{2}ac \sin B$

and

area $ABC = \frac{1}{2}bc \sin A$

Notice that, in all cases, to find the area of a triangle you need the **lengths of two sides** of the triangle and the **size of the angle between these sides**. Then the area is

area of triangle = length of first side × length of second side × sine of angle between these sides

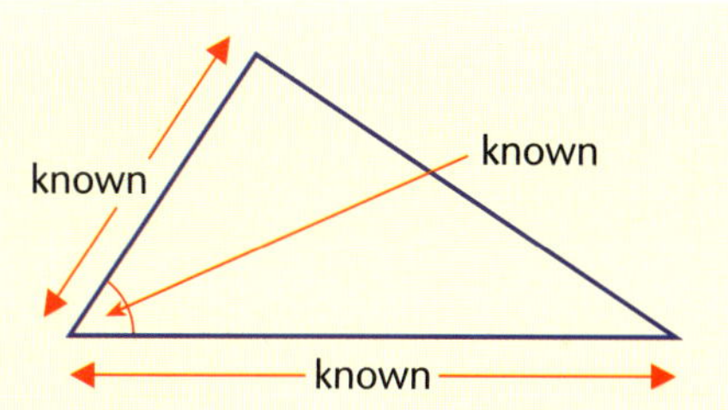

Example 1

Find the area of the triangle PQR.

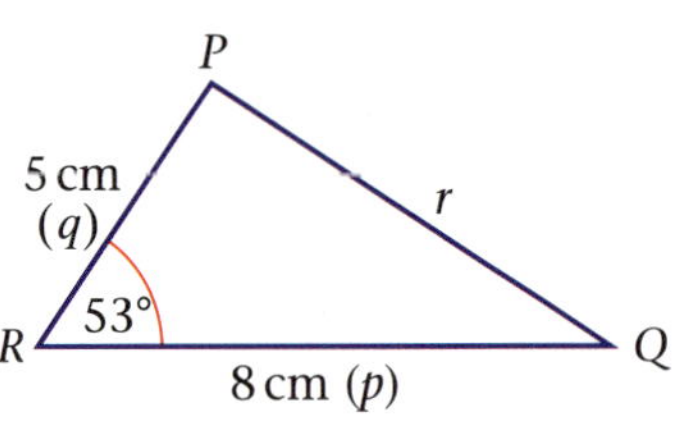

Using area $PQR = \frac{1}{2}pq \sin R$:

$$\text{area } PQR = \tfrac{1}{2} \times 5 \times 8 \times \sin 53°$$
$$= 20 \times 0.7986\ldots$$
$$= 15.97 \text{ cm}^2 \text{ (to 2 d.p.)}$$

Example 2

A builder fences off a triangular plot of land XYZ.

$XY = 43$ m $\quad XZ = 58$ m $\quad Y\hat{X}Z = 125°$

Calculate the area of the plot.

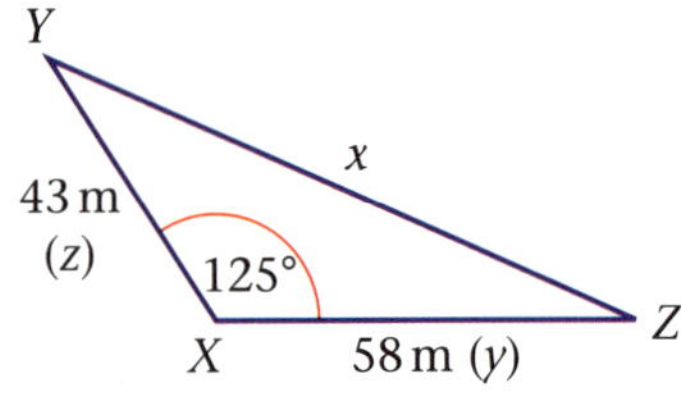

Using area $XYZ = \frac{1}{2}zy \sin X$:

$$\text{area } XYZ = \tfrac{1}{2} \times 43 \times 58 \times \sin 125°$$
$$= \tfrac{1}{2} \times 43 \times 58 \times 0.8192\ldots$$
$$= 1021.5 \text{ m}^2 \text{ (to 1 d.p.)}$$

Example 3

The area of a triangle ABC is 52 cm^2.
All three angles of this triangle are acute.

$AB = 14$ cm $\quad AC = 12$ cm

Calculate the angle A.

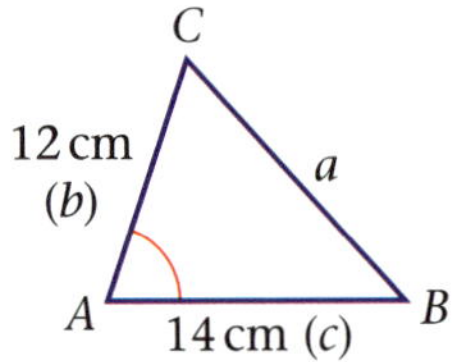

$$\text{Area} = \tfrac{1}{2} \times 14 \times 12 \times \sin A$$
$$52 = 84 \times \sin A$$

So, dividing both sides by 84:

$$\sin A = \tfrac{52}{84}$$
$$\sin A = 0.6190\ldots$$

So $\quad A = 42.5°$ (to 3 s.f.)

$A = \sin^{-1} 0.6190\ldots$

Exercise 21A

1 Calculate the area of each of the triangles.
All lengths are in centimetres.

(a)

5
60°
8

(b)

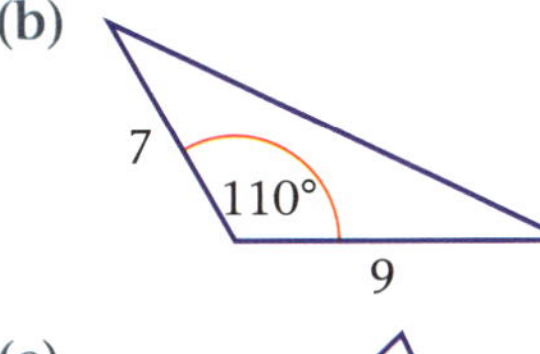

(c)

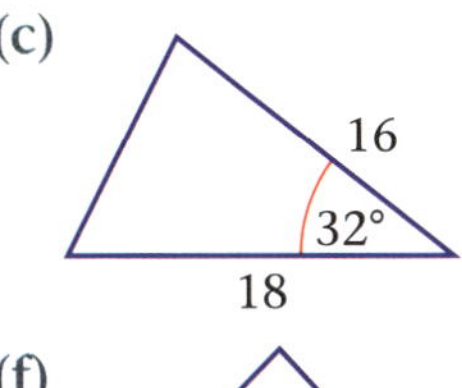

(d)

10
40°
10

(e)

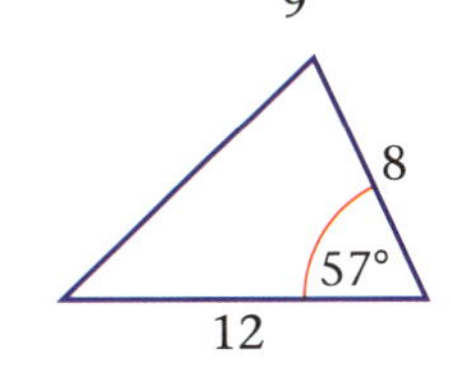

(f)

19
123°
14

2 A farmer fences off a triangular field PQR.
$PQ = 30$ metres, $PR = 34$ metres and the angle at P is 75°.
Calculate the area of the field.

3 Calculate the area of this parallelogram:

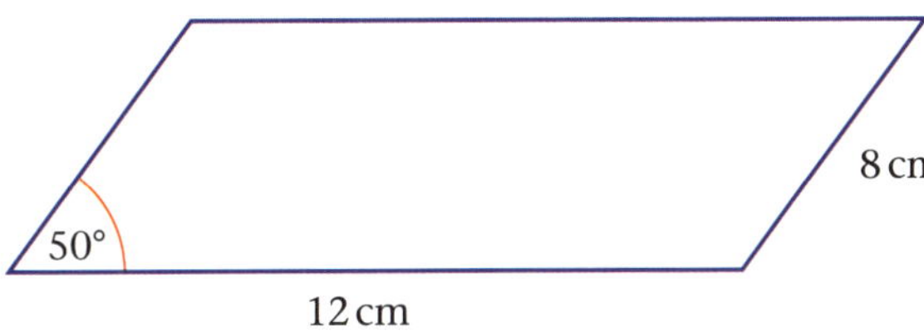

The parallelogram can be treated as two triangles:

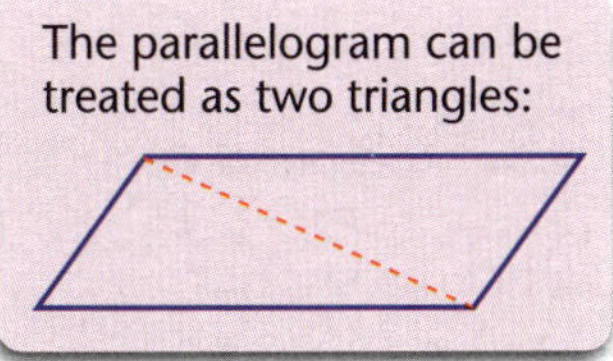

4 A triangle ABC has an area of 60 cm^2, $AB = 15$ cm and $AC = 10$ cm.

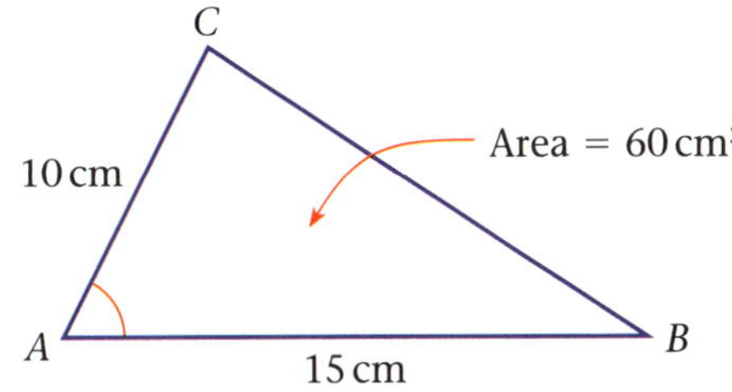

Calculate the size of the acute angle at A.

5 The area of triangle PQR is 40 cm^2.

R
8 cm
Area = 40 cm²
P
12 cm
Q

$PQ = 12$ cm $\quad PR = 8$ cm

The angle at P is obtuse.

Calculate the angle at P.

The $\sin^{-1}$ function on a calculator gives the value of P between 0 and 90°. Remember that $\sin(180° - x) = \sin x$

21.2 The sine rule

The diagram shows a general triangle ABC. The lengths of its sides are a, b and c. The perpendicular from C to AB is drawn and its length is labelled h. It meets AB at X.

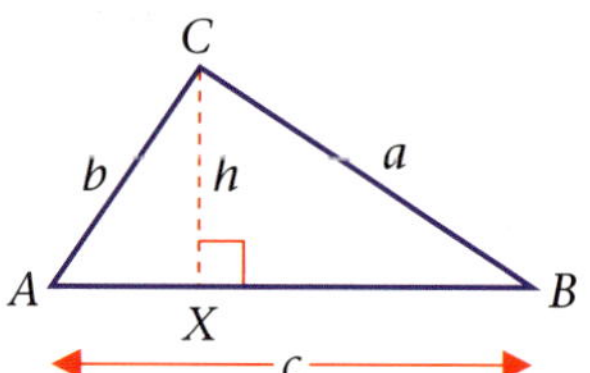

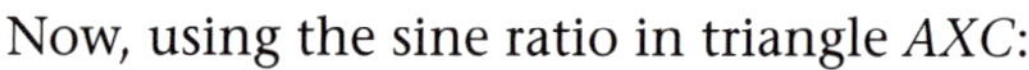

Now, using the sine ratio in triangle AXC:

$$\sin A = \frac{h}{b} \quad \text{or} \quad h = b \sin A$$

Also

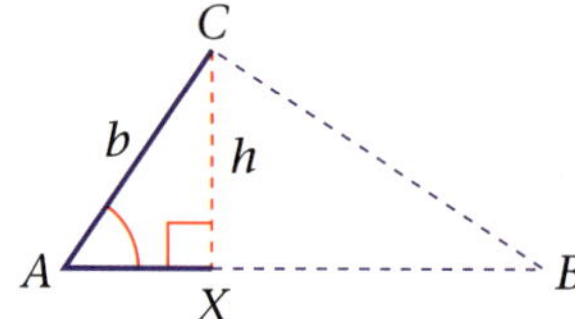

$$\sin B = \frac{h}{a} \quad \text{or} \quad h = a \sin B$$

so $a \sin B = b \sin A$

So $\dfrac{a}{\sin A} = \dfrac{b}{\sin B}$ or $\dfrac{\sin A}{a} = \dfrac{\sin B}{b}$

This result is known as the **sine rule**.

Exercise 21B

Draw a triangle ABC.

Draw a perpendicular from B to AC.

Hence show that $\dfrac{a}{\sin A} = \dfrac{c}{\sin C}$.

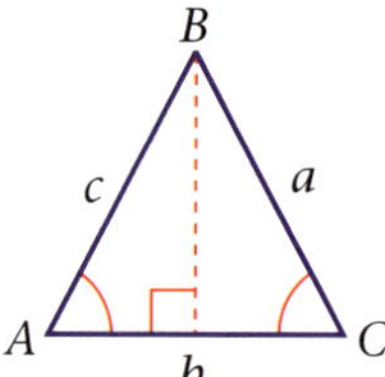

Using the sine rule

The full version of the **sine rule** is

$$\frac{a}{\sin A} = \frac{b}{\sin B} = \frac{c}{\sin C}$$

or

$$\frac{\sin A}{a} = \frac{\sin B}{b} = \frac{\sin C}{c}$$

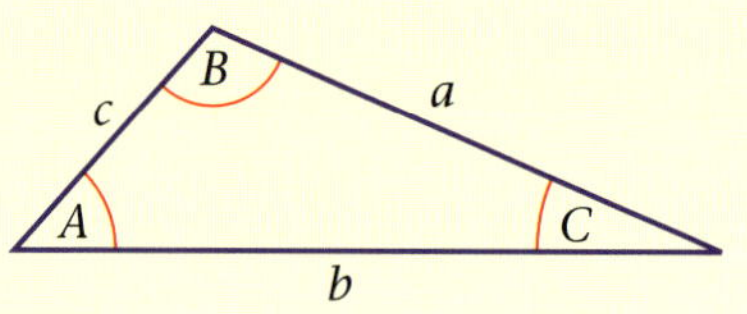

Example 4

Calculate the length of the side marked p.

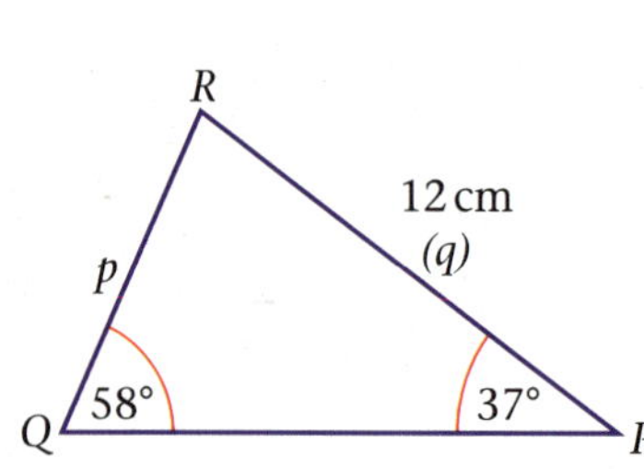

By the sine rule:

$$\frac{p}{\sin P} = \frac{q}{\sin Q}$$

$$\frac{p}{\sin 37°} = \frac{12}{\sin 58°}$$

$$p = \frac{12 \times \sin 37°}{\sin 58°}$$

$$= \frac{12 \times 0.6018\ldots}{0.8480\ldots}$$

$= 8.52$ cm (correct to 3 s.f.)

Example 5

The angles in the triangle ABC are all acute.

Calculate the size of the angle at A.

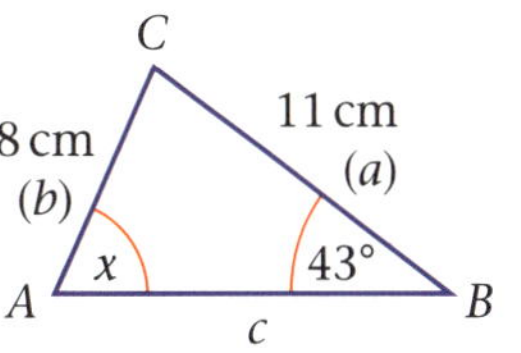

Using the sine rule:

$$\frac{\sin A}{a} = \frac{\sin B}{b}$$

$$\frac{\sin x}{11} = \frac{\sin 43°}{8}$$

So $\sin x = \dfrac{11 \times \sin 43°}{8}$

$$= \frac{11 \times 0.6820\ldots}{8}$$

$$= 0.9377\ldots$$

$x = 69.7°$ (correct to 3 s.f.)

Example 6

A lighthouse, L, is 40 km due North of a harbour, H.

A speedboat leaves H and travels on a bearing of 053° from H until it reaches a point P.

The point, P, lies on a bearing of 075° from L.

Calculate the distance travelled by the speedboat.

First make a sketch:

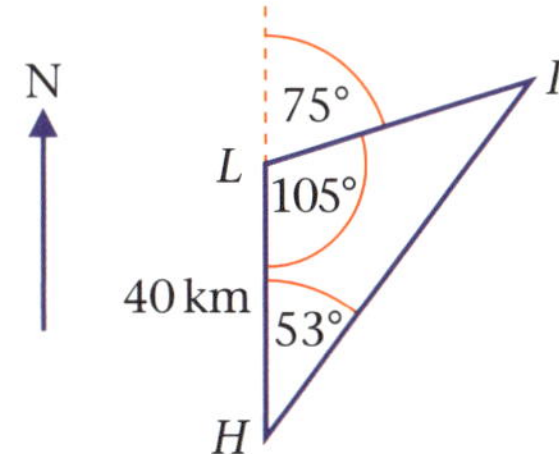

So the angle at P is $180° - (105° + 53°) = 22°$.

Now you can use the sine rule:

$$\frac{HP}{\sin 105°} = \frac{40}{\sin 22°}$$

So $HP = \dfrac{40 \times \sin 105°}{\sin 22°}$

$$= \frac{40 \times 0.9659\ldots}{0.3746\ldots}$$

$= 103.14$ km (to 2 d.p.)

Exercise 21C

1 Calculate the lengths of the sides marked with letters.
All lengths are in centimetres.

(a)
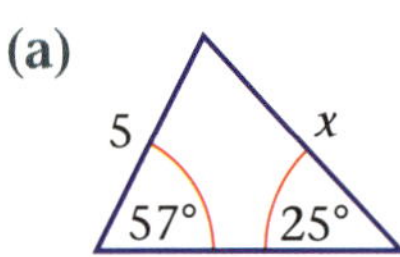

(b)
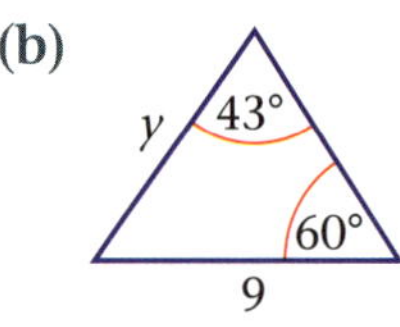

(c)
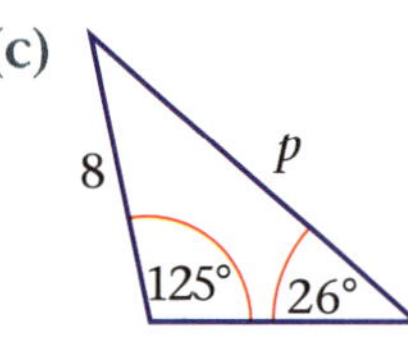

(d)
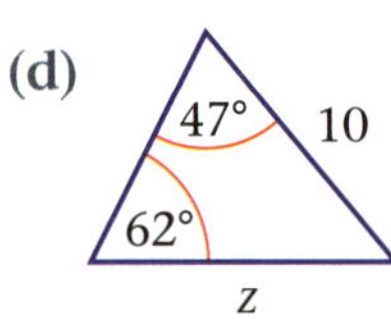

(e)
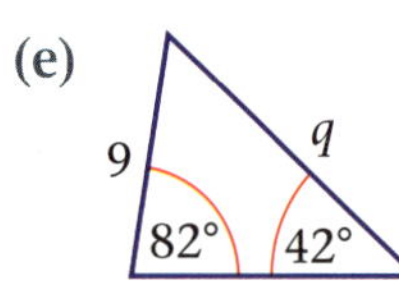

(f)
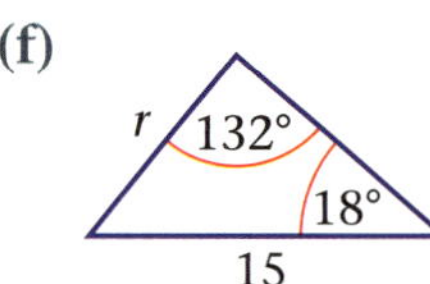

2 Calculate the sizes of the angles marked with letters.
All of these angles are acute.

(a)
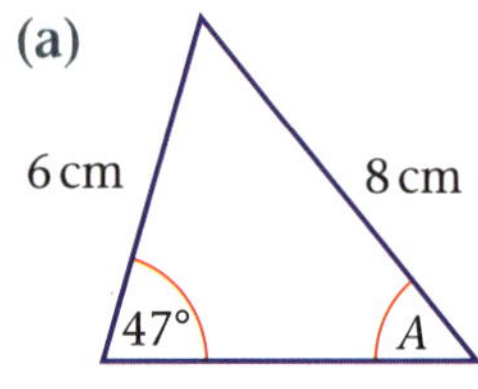

(b)
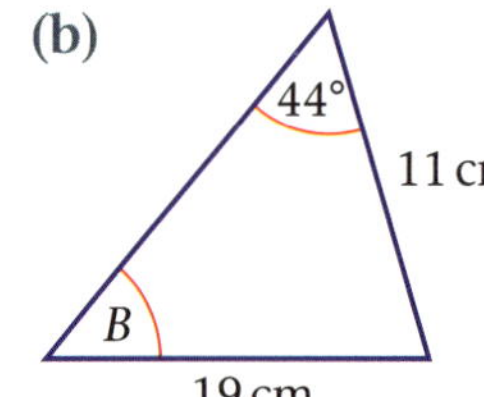

(c)
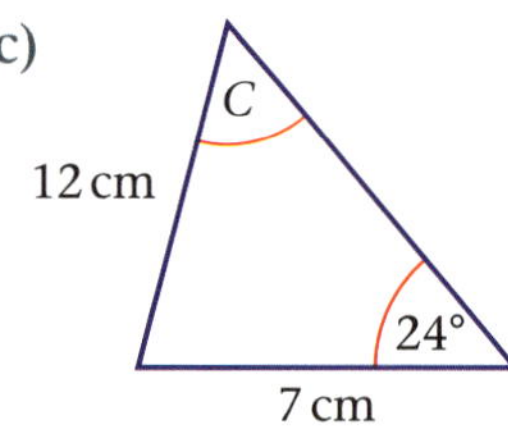

3 The diagram shows the relative positions of a port, P, a marker buoy, B, and a lighthouse, L.
The bearing of L from P is 110°.
The distance PL is 56 km.
The bearing of B from P is 147°.
The bearing of L from B is 030°.
Calculate

(a) the distance PB

(b) the distance BL.

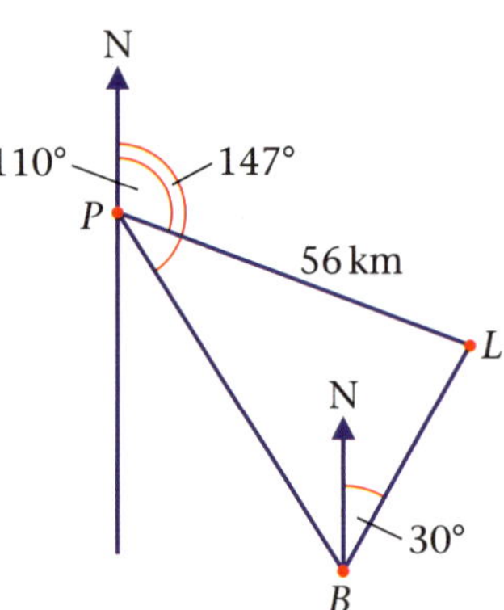

The ambiguous case (for an unknown angle)

In a triangle ABC, $AB = 9$ cm, $BC = 5$ cm and the angle at $A = 24°$.

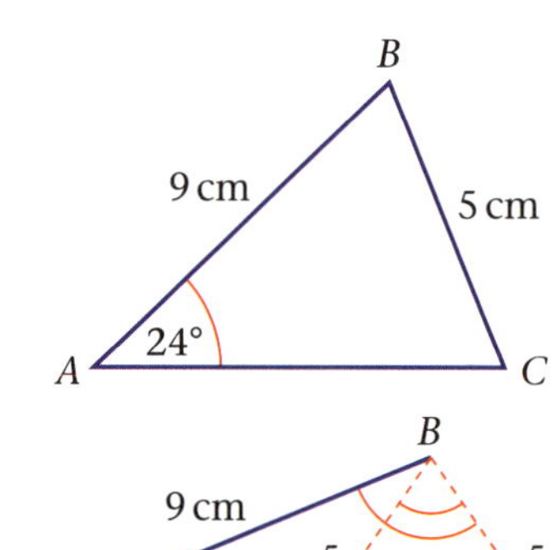

Draw the base line AC, and $AB = 9$ cm, with the angle at A as 24°:

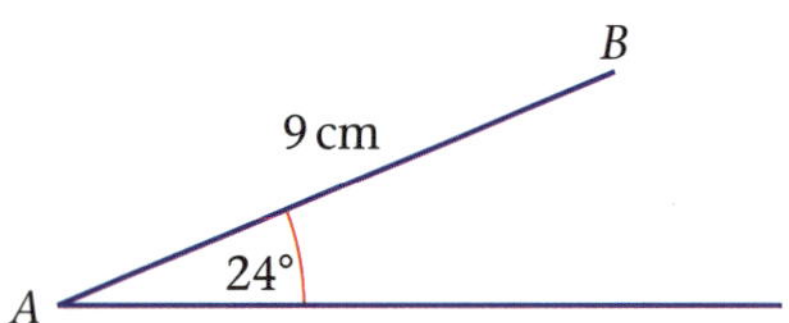

Imagine putting a compass point at B, then drawing a circle centre B of radius 5 cm. This circle will intersect AC at two possible points, marked as C and C'.
This shows that there are two possible angles at B, $A\hat{B}C$ or $A\hat{B}C'$.

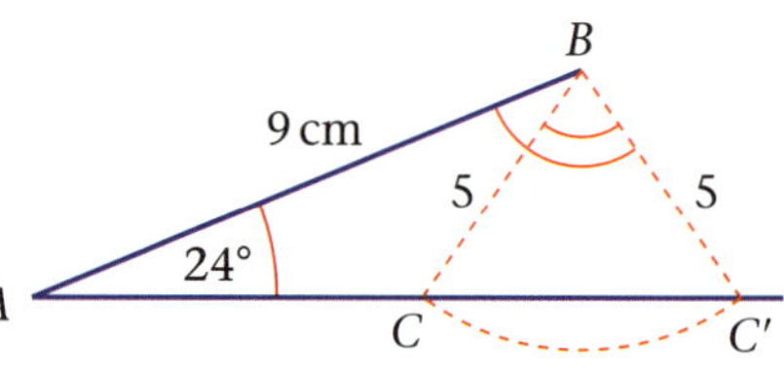

You can compare the triangle to the general triangle ABC:

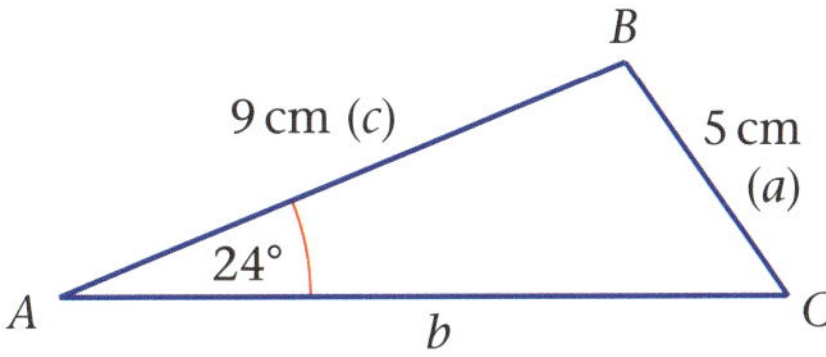

So, by the sine rule: $\frac{\sin C}{c} = \frac{\sin A}{a}$

You have $A = 24°, a = 5, c = 9$

So $\frac{\sin C}{9} = \frac{\sin 24°}{5}$

$$\sin C = \frac{9 \times \sin 24°}{5}$$

$$= 0.7321...$$

$$C = 47.06°$$

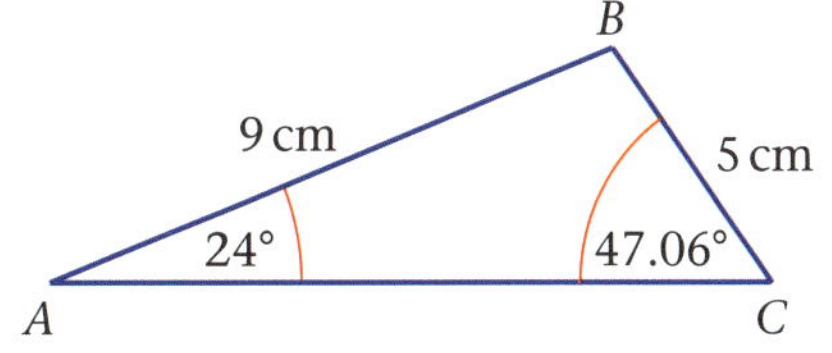

But $\sin(180° - x) = \sin x$, so we could also have

$C = 180° - 47.06°$

$C = 132.94°$

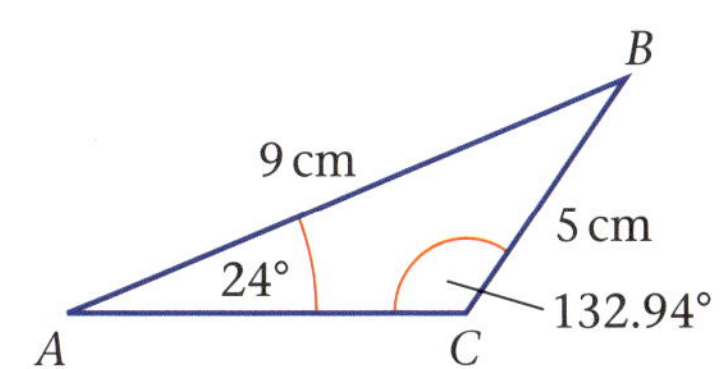

Exercise 21D

In a triangle PQR, $PQ = 10$ cm, $QR = 8$ cm and the angle $QPR = 48°$.

Calculate the two possible values for the angle PQR.

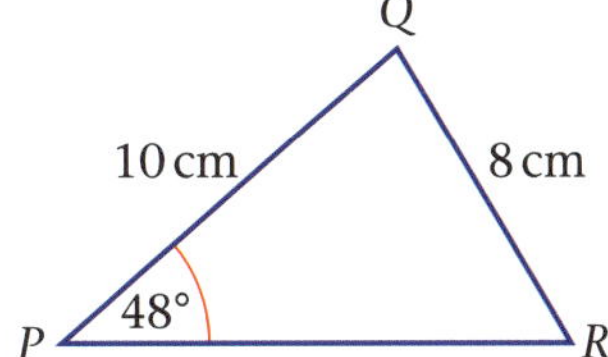

21.3 The cosine rule

ABC is a general triangle with sides a, b and c.
Side a is opposite angle A, and so on.
The perpendicular from B to AC meets AC at P.
This perpendicular has length h units.
Let $CP = x$ units, so $PA = (b - x)$ units.

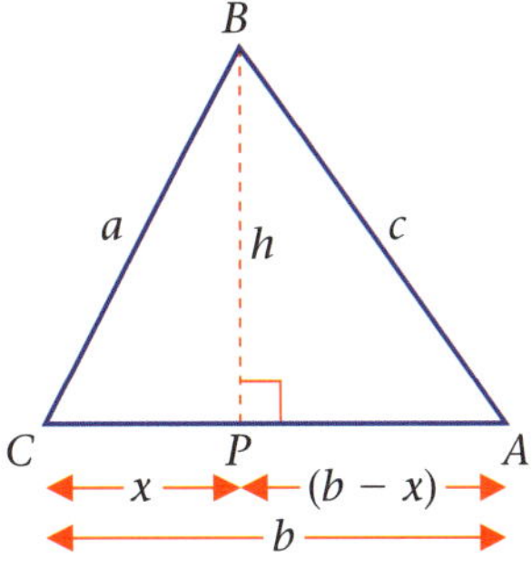

In triangle BPA, Pythagoras' theorem gives

$$c^2 = h^2 + (b - x)^2$$

$$= h^2 + b^2 - 2xb + x^2$$

$$c^2 = h^2 + x^2 + b^2 - 2xb \qquad (1)$$

But using Pythagoras' theorem again in triangle BPC gives

$$a^2 = h^2 + x^2 \qquad (2)$$

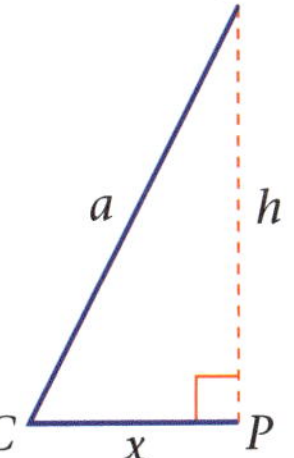

Substituting a^2 for $h^2 + x^2$ in (1):

$$c^2 = a^2 + b^2 - 2xb \qquad (3)$$

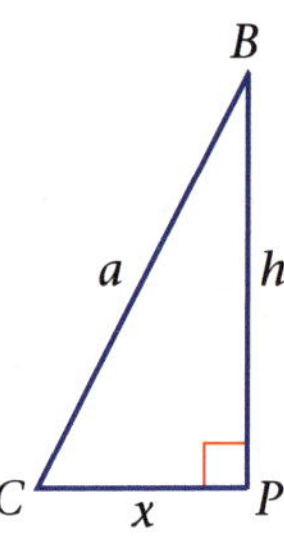

But using the cosine ratio on triangle BPC gives

$$\cos C = \frac{x}{a} \quad \text{or} \quad x = a\cos C$$

Substituting $a\cos C$ for x in (3) gives

$$c^2 = a^2 + b^2 - 2ab\cos C$$

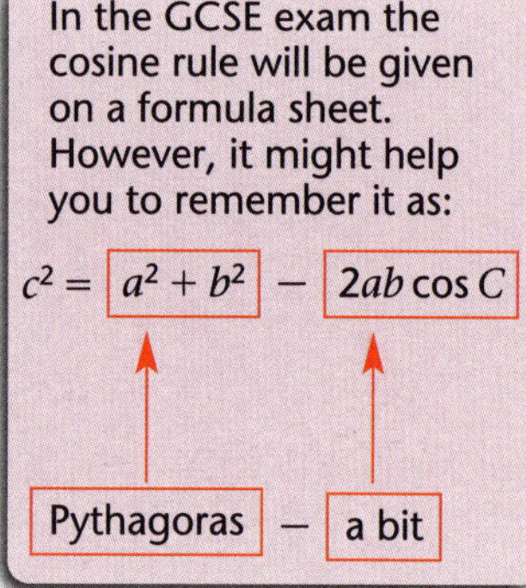

In the GCSE exam the cosine rule will be given on a formula sheet. However, it might help you to remember it as:
c² = a² + b² − 2ab cos C
Pythagoras − a bit

This is the **cosine rule**.

You can rearrange this to give

$$2ab\cos C = a^2 + b^2 - c^2 \quad \text{or}$$

$$\cos C = \frac{a^2 + b^2 - c^2}{2ab}$$

Example 7

Calculate the length of the side marked y.

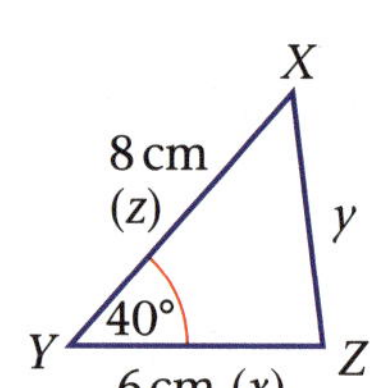

Using the cosine rule:

$$\begin{aligned} y^2 &= x^2 + z^2 - 2xz\cos Y \\ &= 6^2 + 8^2 - 2 \times 6 \times 8 \times \cos 40^\circ \\ &= 36 + 64 - 96 \times \cos 40^\circ \\ &= 100 - 96 \times 0.766\ldots \end{aligned}$$

$$y^2 = 100 - 73.54\ldots \quad \text{or} \quad y^2 = 26.46\ldots$$

$$y = \sqrt{26.46\ldots} = 5.14\text{ cm (to 3 s.f.)}$$

Example 8

Calculate the angle at A.

B, 3 cm (c), 5 cm (a), A, 7 cm (b), C

Using the cosine rule:

$$\begin{aligned} \cos A &= \frac{c^2 + b^2 - a^2}{2cb} \\ &= \frac{3^2 + 7^2 - 5^2}{2 \times 3 \times 7} \\ &= \frac{9 + 49 - 25}{42} = \frac{33}{42} = 0.7857\ldots \end{aligned}$$

So $\quad A = 38.2^\circ$ (to 1 d.p.)

Exercise 21E

1 Calculate the lengths marked with letters. All lengths are in centimetres.

(a)

(b)

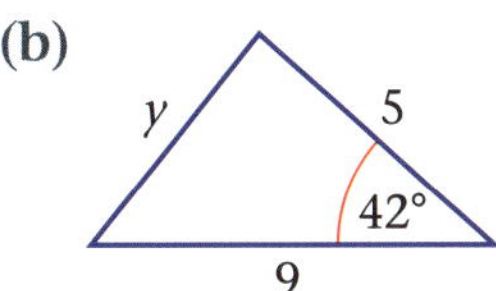

(c)

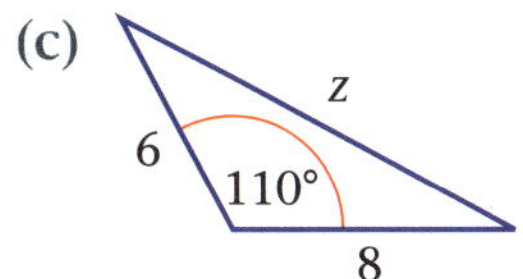

(d)

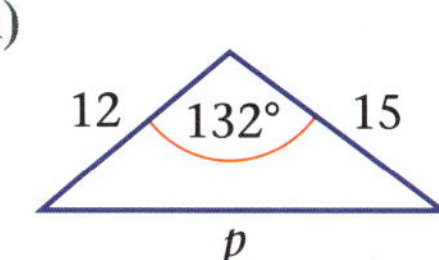

2 Calculate the angles marked with letters. All lengths are in centimetres.

(a)

(b)

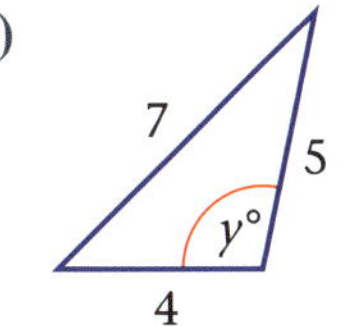

(c)

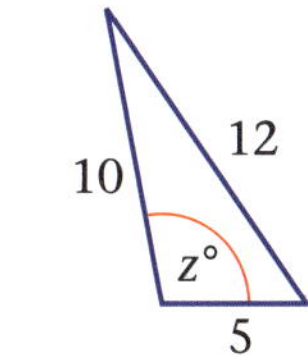

(d)

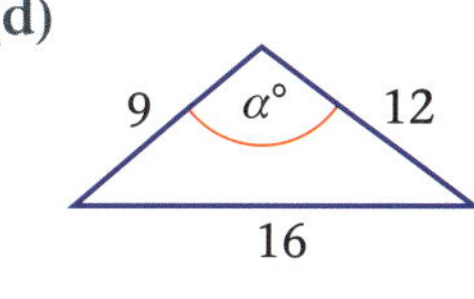

3 A builder ropes off a triangular plot of ground, *PQR*.
The length of $PQ = 42$ m and the length of $PR = 50$ m.
The angle $QPR = 72°$.

Calculate the length of rope needed by the builder.

4 A lifeboat leaves its base, *S*, and travels 32 km due North to a lighthouse *L*. At *L* the lifeboat turns onto a bearing of 056° from *L* and travels for a further 45 km until it reaches a marker buoy, *B*. At *B* the lifeboat turns again and travels back in a straight line to *S*.

Calculate the total distance travelled by the lifeboat.

21.4 Trigonometry and Pythagoras' theorem in three dimensions

You need to be able to use Pythagoras' theorem and trigonometry in three dimensions.

For finding the longest diagonal in a cuboid see Section 15.8 (in Book 1).

Example 9

The diagram shows a triangle-based pyramid *VABC* with *V* vertically above *A*. The base *ABC* has a right angle at *A*.

$AB = 8$ cm $\quad AC = 6$ cm $\quad VA = 15$ cm

Calculate

(a) the length *BC*
(b) the length *VB*
(c) the length *VC*
(d) angle *VBA*
(e) angle *AVC*
(f) angle *BVC*

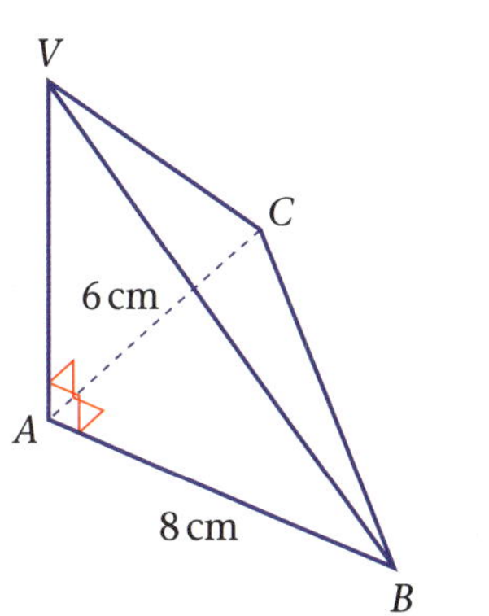

(a) Using $BC^2 = AB^2 + AC^2$ by Pythagoras' theorem:

$$BC^2 = 8^2 + 6^2$$
$$= 64 + 36$$
$$= 100$$
$$BC = \sqrt{100}$$
$$= 10\text{ cm}$$

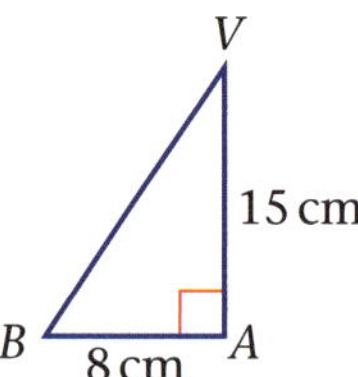

(b) Using $VB^2 = VA^2 + AB^2$:

$$VB^2 = 15^2 + 8^2$$
$$= 225 + 64$$
$$= 289$$
$$= \sqrt{289}$$
$$= 17\text{ cm}$$

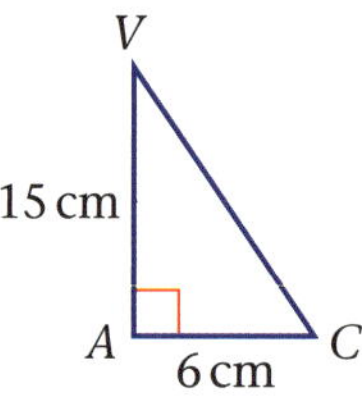

(c) Using $VC^2 = VA^2 + AC^2$:

$$VC^2 = 15^2 + 6^2$$
$$= 225 + 36$$
$$= 261$$
$$VC = \sqrt{261}$$
$$= 16.16\ldots\text{ cm}$$

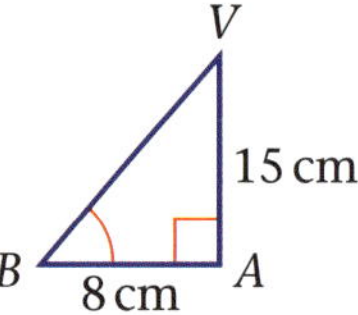

(d) Using the tangent ratio:

$$\tan V\hat{B}A = \frac{15}{8}$$
$$= 1.875$$
$$V\hat{B}A = 61.92°$$

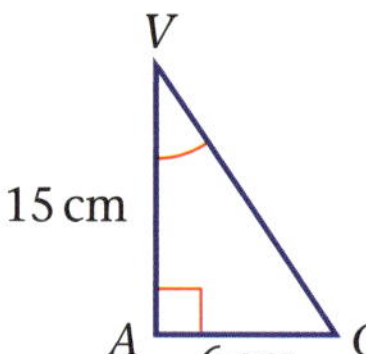

$\tan V\hat{B}A = \dfrac{\text{opp}}{\text{adj}} = \dfrac{AV}{AB}$

(e) Using the tangent ratio:

$$\tan A\hat{V}C = \frac{6}{15}$$
$$= 0.4$$
$$A\hat{V}C = 21.80°$$

V

15 cm

A

6 cm

C

$\tan A\hat{V}C = \dfrac{\text{opp}}{\text{adj}} = \dfrac{AC}{AV}$

(f) Using the cosine rule:

$$\cos V = \frac{17^2 + 261 - 10^2}{2 \times 17 \times \sqrt{261}}$$
$$= \frac{450}{549.3\ldots}$$
$$= 0.8192\ldots$$
$$V = 35°$$

$VC^2 = 261$ (from part (c))

$\cos V = \dfrac{c^2 + b^2 - v^2}{2cb}$

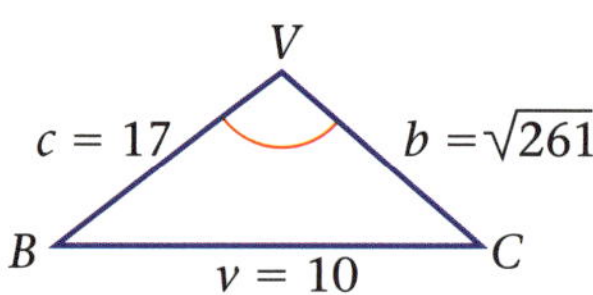

Exercise 21F

1 Here is a wedge *ABCDEF*. The base, *BCDE*, is a rectangle. The back face, *ABEF*, is also a rectangle. The angle between these two rectangles is 90°. *M* is the mid-point of *CD*.

Calculate

(a) the length *AC* (b) the length *FC*

(c) the length *EC* (d) angle *ACB*

(e) angle *ECF* (f) angle *EMF*.

2 *VABCD* is a square-based pyramid. The vertex *V* is vertically above the mid-point, *M*, of the square base.

$AB = 10$ cm $VA = 16$ cm

Calculate

(a) the length of *BD*

(b) the length of *VM*

(c) the angle *VAM*

(d) the angle *AVM*.

3 *ABCV* is a pyramid with base *ABC*, right-angled at *A*.

$AB = 24$ cm $AC = 7$ cm

The vertex *V* is vertically above *A* with $AV = 30$ cm. The point *M* lies on *BC* with angle $AMB = 90°$.

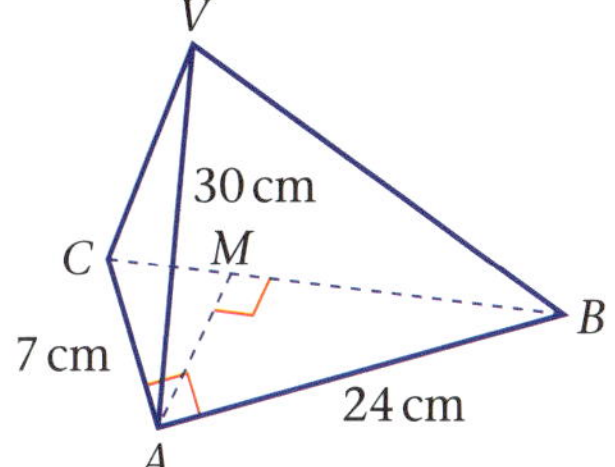

(a) Show that $BC = 25$ cm.

(b) Calculate the length of
(i) *VB* **(ii)** *VC*.

(c) Calculate the length *AM*.

(d) Calculate the angle *VMA*.

Mixed exercise 21

1 Calculate

(a) the area of triangle *ABC*

(b) the length of *BC*

(c) the angle *BCA*.

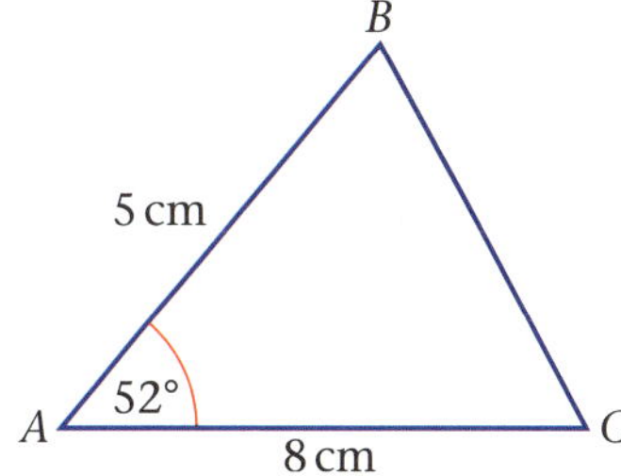

2 In triangle ABC, $AC = 8$ cm, $CB = 15$ cm and angle $ACB = 70°$.

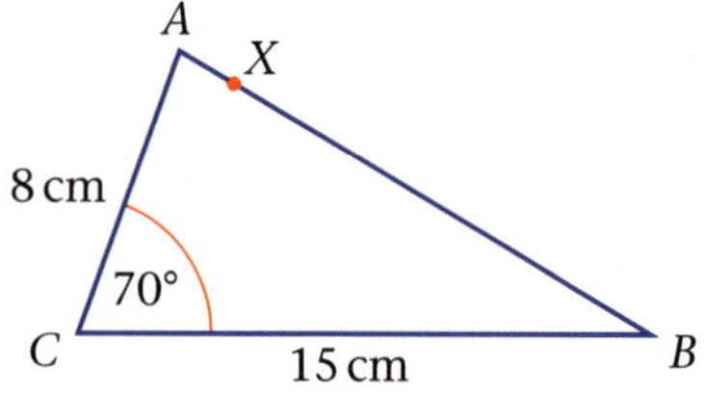

(a) Calculate the area of triangle ABC. Give your answer correct to three significant figures.

(b) X is the point on AB such that angle $CXB = 90°$.

Calculate the length of CX.
Give your answer correct to three significant figures.

3 $AB = 3.2$ cm, $BC = 8.4$ cm.

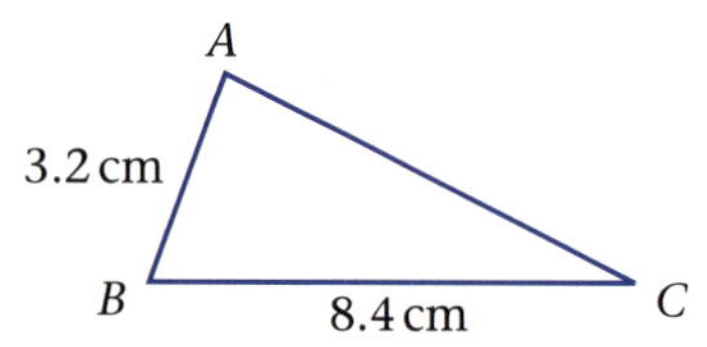

The area of triangle ABC is 10 cm^2.

Calculate the perimeter of triangle ABC. Give your answer correct to three significant figures.

4 A yacht, Y, leaves a harbour, H, and travels 45 km due North until it reaches a marker buoy, B. At B the yacht turns onto a bearing of 290° from B and travels for a further 56 km until it reaches a lighthouse, L. At L it turns again and travels in a straight line back to H.

Calculate

(a) the total distance travelled by the yacht

(b) the bearing of L from H

(c) the shortest distance between Y and B on the yacht's return journey from L to H.

5 A man walks from his home H on a bearing of 060° for 3.2 miles until he reaches his friend's house, F. At F he turns onto a bearing of 280° from F and travels a further 4.1 miles to his sister's house, S. At S he turns again and walks in a straight line back home.

Calculate

(a) the distance he walks

(b) the bearing of H from S

(c) the shortest distance between the man and F on the man's return journey from S to H.

6 $VPQR$ is a triangle-based pyramid. The vertex V is vertically above P with $VP = 16$ cm.

In the triangular base, $Q\hat{P}R = 120°$.

Calculate

(a) the length QR

(b) the length VQ

(c) the angle QVR.

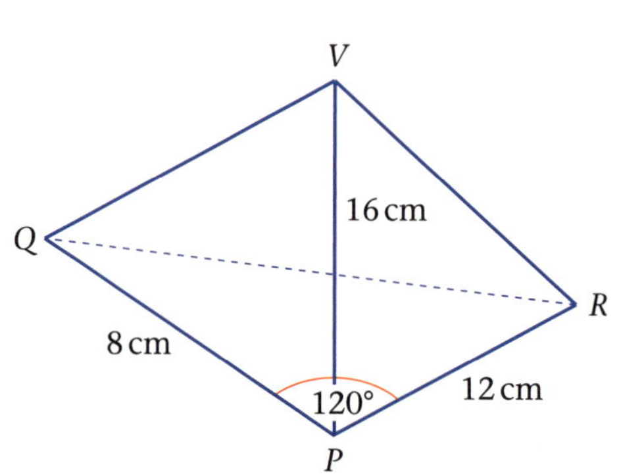

Summary of key points

1 For any triangle ABC, the **area of the triangle** is

$$\tfrac{1}{2}ab\sin C = \tfrac{1}{2}ac\sin B = \tfrac{1}{2}bc\sin A$$

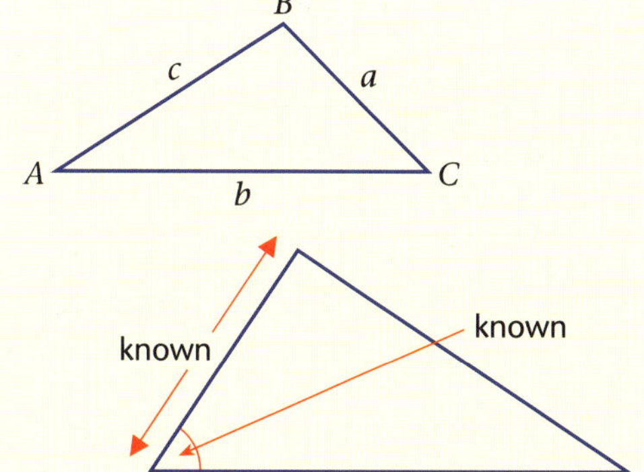

2 area of triangle = length of first side × length of second side × sine of angle between these sides

3 The **sine rule** is

$$\frac{a}{\sin A} = \frac{b}{\sin B} = \frac{c}{\sin C} \quad \text{or} \quad \frac{\sin A}{a} = \frac{\sin B}{b} = \frac{\sin C}{c}$$

4 The **cosine rule** is

$$c^2 = a^2 + b^2 - 2ab\cos C \quad \text{or} \quad \cos C = \frac{a^2 + b^2 - c^2}{2ab}$$

These formulae appear on the formula sheet which you will be given in the GCSE exam.

Remember also that

$$\sin x = \sin(180° - x)$$

This fact is not given on the sheet. You may need it for ambiguous cases related to the sine rule or for the area of a triangle.

22 Advanced mensuration

One of the problems involved in the development of trigonometry was finding the relationship between the angle a cannon could pivot through, the distance a cannon ball could travel, and the width of a passage into a harbour.

A natural extension of this work was to look at how to find:

- the length of an arc of a circle for an angle θ
- the area of a sector
- the area of a segment

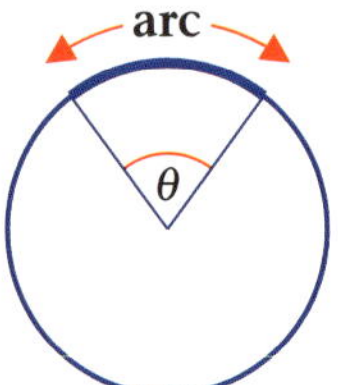

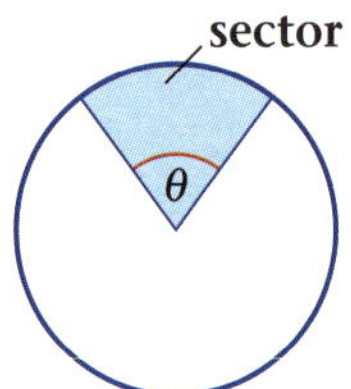

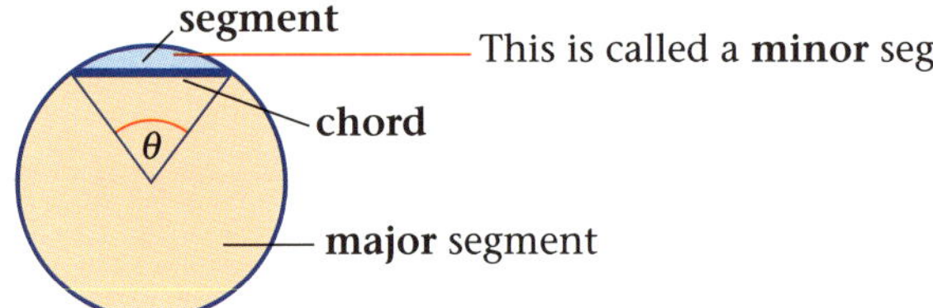

To do this you need these formulae:

Circumference of a circle $= 2\pi r$

Area of a circle $= \pi r^2$

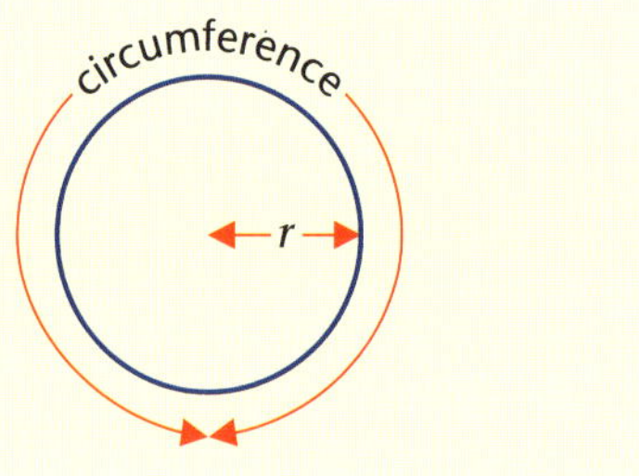

For more on circumference and area of a circle see Section 13.4 (in Book 1).

22.1 Finding the length of an arc of a circle

In this diagram the arc length is $\frac{1}{4}$ of the circumference because the angle at the centre is 90°, which is $\frac{90}{360} = \frac{1}{4}$ of a whole turn.

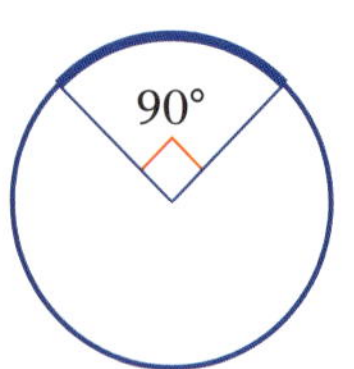

In this diagram the angle at the centre is 60°. This is $\frac{60}{360} = \frac{1}{6}$ of a whole turn. So the arc length is $\frac{1}{6}$ of the circumference of the circle.

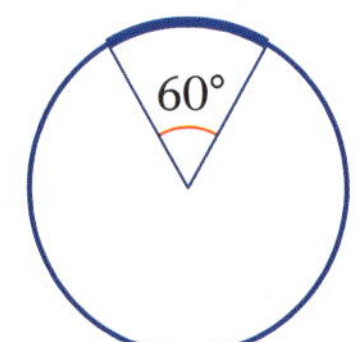

In this diagram the angle at the centre is 240°. This is $\frac{240}{360} = \frac{2}{3}$ of a whole turn. So the arc length is $\frac{2}{3}$ of the circumference of the circle.

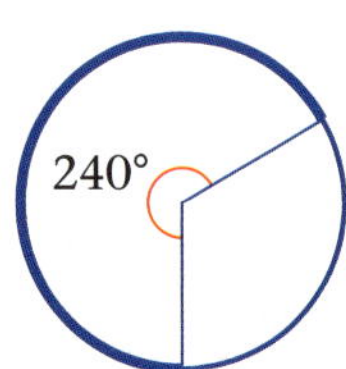

If the angle at the centre of a circle is θ then

$$\text{arc length} = \frac{\theta}{360} \text{ of the circumference}$$
$$= \frac{\theta}{360} \times 2\pi r$$

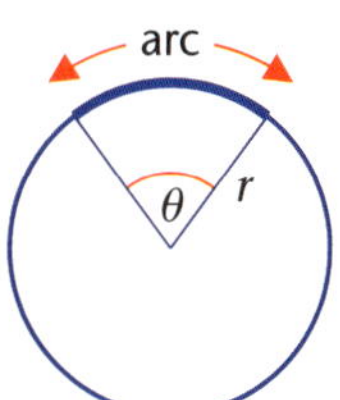

This gives the formula:

Arc length $= \dfrac{2\pi r\theta}{360} = \dfrac{\pi r\theta}{180}$

Example 1

Calculate the length of the arc AB.

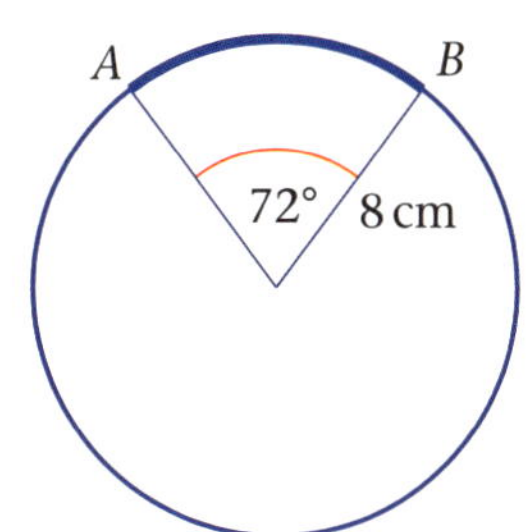

$$\text{Arc length} = \frac{\pi \times 8 \times 72}{180}$$
$$= 10.05 \text{ cm (correct to 2 d.p.)}$$

Example 2

The length of the arc PQ is 12 cm. Calculate the angle θ.

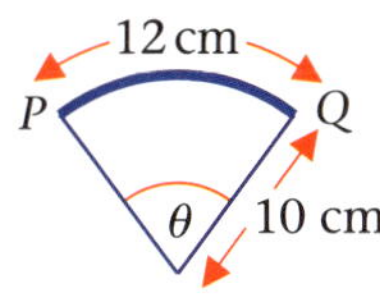

$$\text{Arc length} = \frac{\pi r\theta}{180}$$

so $\dfrac{\pi \times \overset{1}{\cancel{10}} \times \theta}{\underset{18}{\cancel{180}}°} = 12$

Multiply each side by 18 and divide each side by π:

$$\theta = \frac{18 \times 12}{\pi}$$

so $\theta = 68.75°$ (correct to 2 d.p.)

Exercise 22A

1 Calculate each of these arc lengths:

(a) 

(b) 

(c) 

(d) 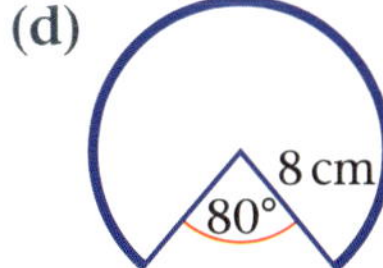

(e) 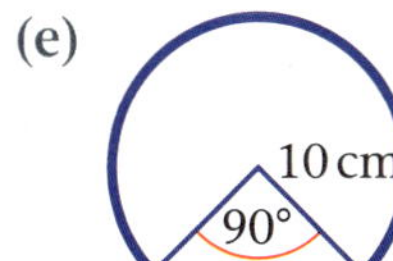

(f) 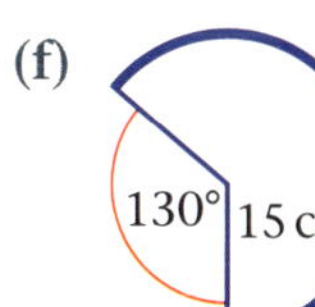

2 Calculate each of the angles marked θ.

(a)

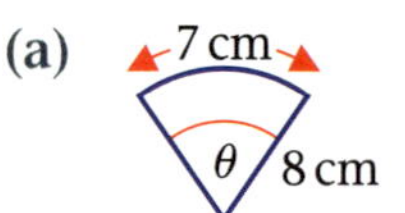

(b)

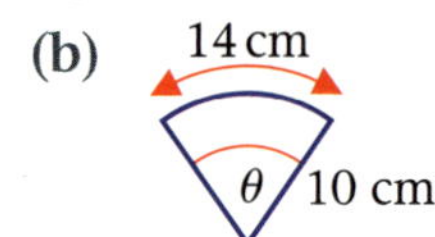

(c)

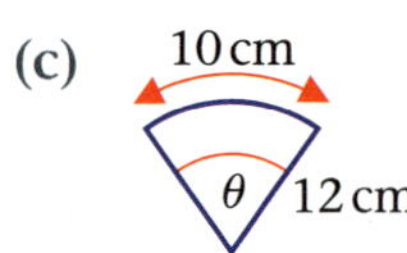

(d)

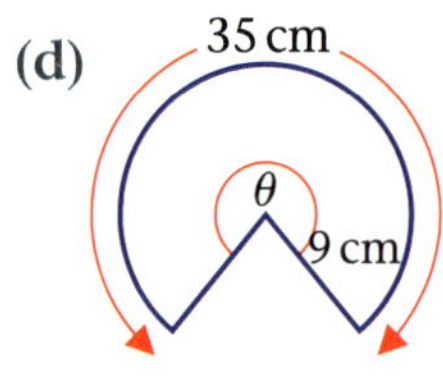

(e)

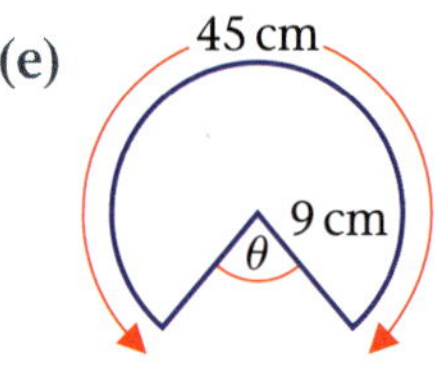

(f) 28 cm, 5 cm, θ

22.2 Finding the area of a sector of a circle

In this diagram the sector is $\frac{1}{4}$ of the whole circle, because the angle at the centre is 90°. This is $\frac{1}{4}$ of a whole turn or 360°. So the area of this sector is $\frac{1}{4}$ of the area of the circle.

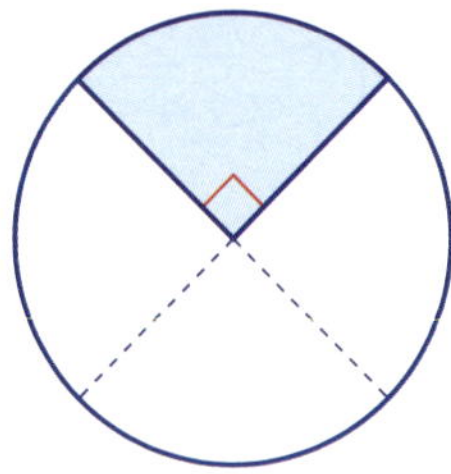

In this diagram the angle at the centre is 60°. So the sector is $\frac{60}{360}$ or $\frac{1}{6}$ of the area of the whole circle. The area of this sector is $\frac{1}{6}$ of the area of the circle.

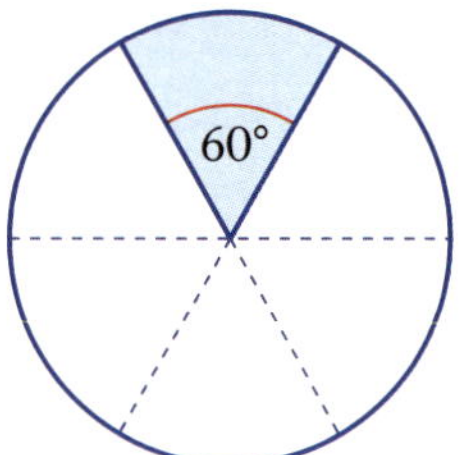

If the angle at the centre of a circle is θ then

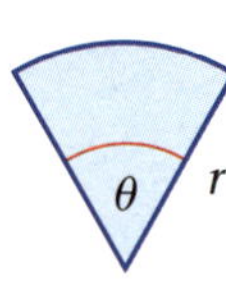

$$\textbf{area of a sector} = \frac{\theta}{360} \text{ of area of circle}$$

$$= \frac{\theta}{360} \times \pi r^2$$

$$= \frac{\theta \times \pi \times r^2}{360}$$

This gives the formula:

Area of a sector $= \dfrac{\pi r^2 \theta}{360}$

Example 3

Calculate the area of this sector:

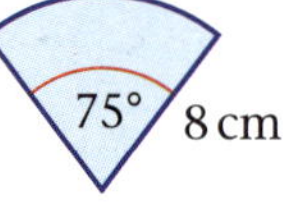

$$\text{Area} = \frac{\pi r^2 \theta}{360}$$

$r = 8$, so $r^2 = 64$

So $\quad \text{area} = \dfrac{\pi \times 64 \times 75}{360}$

$= 41.89\text{ cm}^2$ (correct to 2 d.p.)

Example 4

AOB is a sector of a circle.
Angle $AOB = 130°$
Area of the sector $AOB = 200\,\text{cm}^2$.

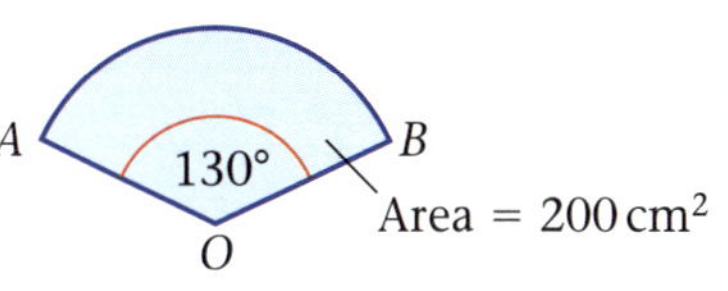

Calculate the radius *OA* of the circle of which *AOB* is a sector.

$$\text{Area of sector} = \frac{\pi r^2 \theta}{360} = 200$$

Multiply each side by 360 and divide each side by $\pi\theta$:

$$r^2 = \frac{200 \times 360}{\pi \times \theta} = \frac{200 \times 360}{\pi \times 130}$$

$$= 176.2947$$

So $\quad r = \sqrt{176.2947}$

$$= 13.28\,\text{cm (correct to 2 d.p.)}$$

Exercise 22B

1 Calculate the area of each of these sectors of circles:

(a) 40°, 8 cm

(b)

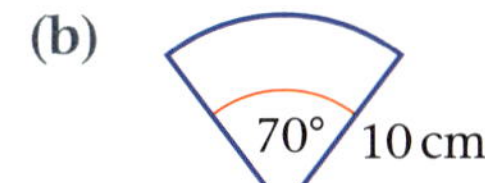

(c) 140°, 5 cm

(d)

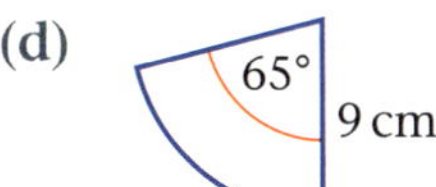

(e) 250°, 8 cm

(f)

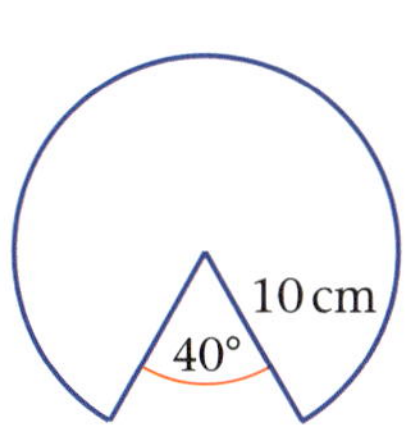

2 *OPQ* is a sector of a circle centre *O* of radius 9 cm.
The area of the sector *OPQ* is $51\,\text{cm}^2$.
Calculate the size of the angle *POQ*.

P, Q, Area = 51 cm², 9 cm, O

3 *OXY* is a sector of a circle centre *O*.
The area of the sector *OXY* is $60\,\text{cm}^2$.
The angle $XOY = 68°$.
Calculate the length of the radius *OX* of the circle.

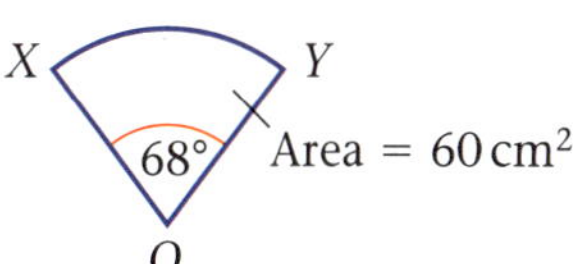

22.3 Finding the area of a segment of a circle

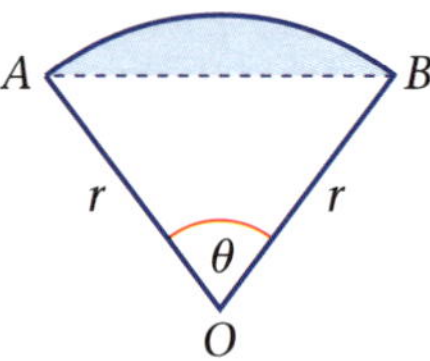

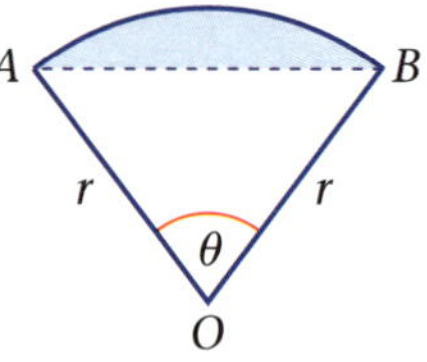

The area of the sector $OAB = \dfrac{\pi r^2\theta}{360}$

In triangle OAB: area of triangle $OAB = \frac{1}{2}r \times r \sin\theta$
$= \frac{1}{2}r^2 \sin\theta$

So the area of the shaded segment is the difference between these two areas:

Area of a segment $= \dfrac{\pi r^2\theta}{360} - \frac{1}{2}r^2 \sin\theta$

For any triangle:
Area $= \frac{1}{2}ab\sin C$

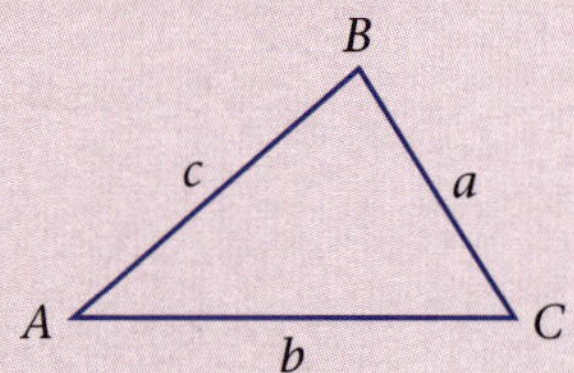

For more on this see Section 21.1.

Example 5

Calculate the area of the shaded segment of the circle.

$$\text{Area of segment} = \frac{\pi r^2\theta}{360} - \frac{1}{2}r^2\sin\theta$$
$$= \frac{\pi \times 6^2 \times 75}{360} - \frac{1}{2} \times 6^2 \times \sin 75^\circ$$
$$= 23.562 - 17.387$$
$$= 6.18\ \text{cm}^2\ \text{(correct to 2 d.p.)}$$

Exercise 22C

1 Calculate the area of each shaded segment.

(a)
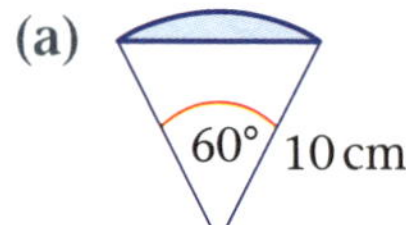

(b)
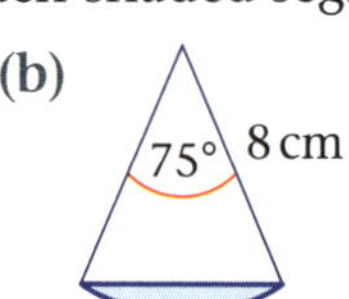

(c)
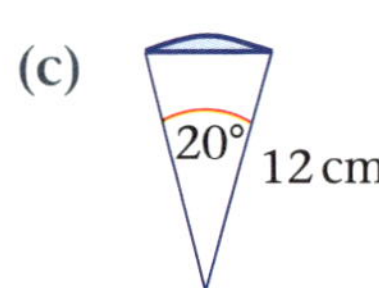

(d)
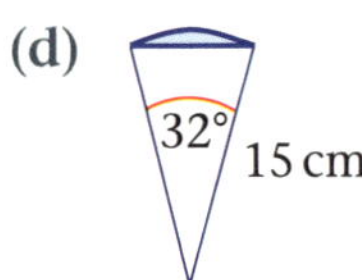

(e)
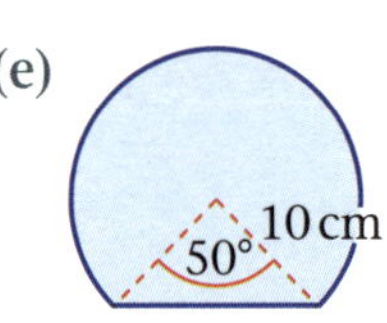

(f)
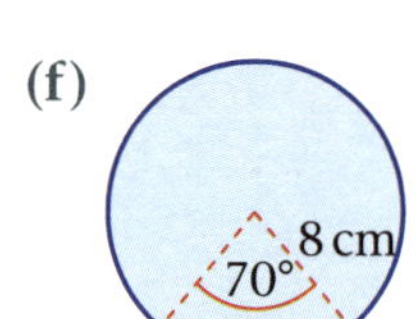

Worked examination question 1

O is the centre of a circle, radius 8 cm.
P and Q are points on the circumference.
Angle $POQ = 108^\circ$.

(a) Calculate the area of the sector POQ.

(b) Calculate the difference between the arc length PQ and the length of the chord PQ.

(c) Calculate the area of the shaded segment PQ.

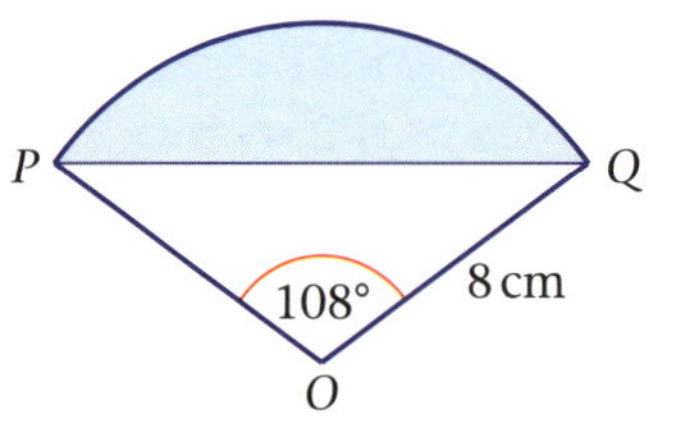

Give your answers correct to three significant figures.

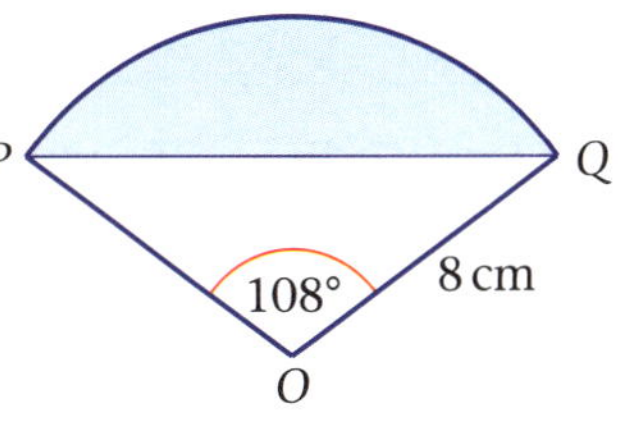

(a) Area of sector $= \dfrac{\pi r^2 \theta}{360}$

$r = 8$, so $r^2 = 64$, and $\theta = 108°$

So area of sector $= \dfrac{\pi \times 64 \times 108}{180} = 60.318\,578\,95$ (by calculator)

$= 60.3$ cm^2 (correct to 3 s.f.)

(b) Length of arc $PQ = \dfrac{\pi r \theta}{180} = \dfrac{\pi \times 8 \times 108}{180} = 15.0796\ldots$ cm

To find the length of the chord PQ mark the mid-point of PQ as M:

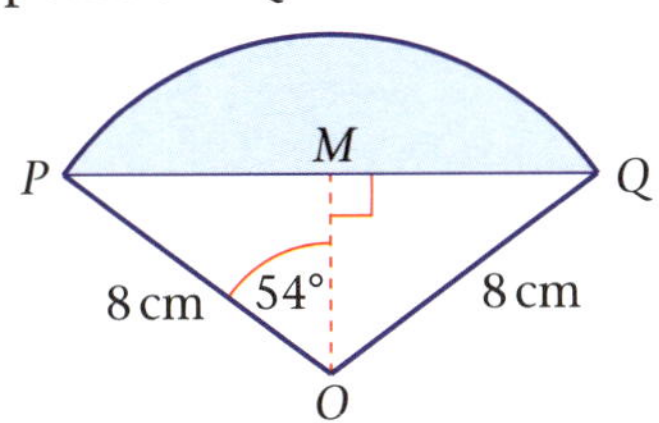

You could also use the sine rule.

$O\hat{P}Q = O\hat{Q}P = 36°$ (isosceles triangle)

So $\dfrac{8}{\sin 36°} = \dfrac{PQ}{\sin 108°}$

$PQ = \dfrac{8 \sin 108°}{\sin 36°}$

$= 12.9442\ldots$

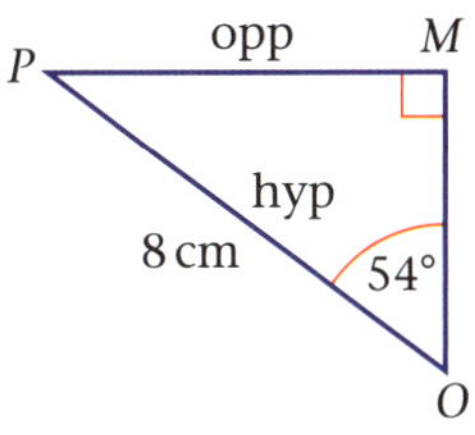

$\dfrac{PM}{8} = \sin 54°$, so $PM = 8 \times \sin 54° = 6.4721\ldots$ cm

$PQ = 2 \times PM$, so $PQ = 2 \times 6.4721\ldots = 12.9442\ldots$ cm

The difference between the arc length PQ and the chord PQ is

$15.0796\ldots - 12.9442\ldots = 2.1354\ldots$

$= 2.14$ cm (correct to 3 s.f.)

(c) The area of the shaded segment $PQ = \dfrac{\pi r^2 \theta}{360} - \tfrac{1}{2} r^2 \sin \theta$

$= 60.3185\ldots - \tfrac{1}{2} \times 64 \times \sin 108°$

$= 60.3185\ldots - 30.4338\ldots$

$= 29.8848\ldots$

$= 29.9$ cm^2 (correct to 3 s.f.)

Exercise 22D

1 An arc of a circle of radius 15 cm has a length of 18 cm. Calculate (a) the angle θ (b) the area of the sector.

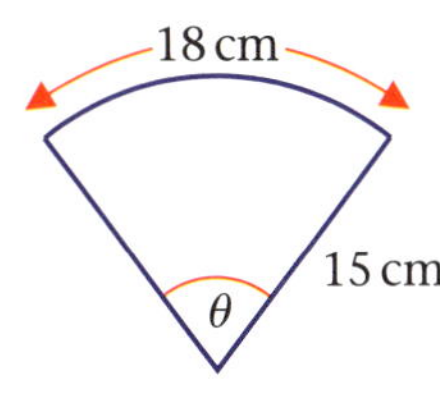

2 The diagram shows the landing area for a javelin competition. $OPQR$ is a sector of a circle, centre O, of radius 120 metres. Calculate

(a) the length of the chord PR

(b) the length of the arc PQR

(c) the area of the sector $OPQR$

(d) the area of the segment PQR.

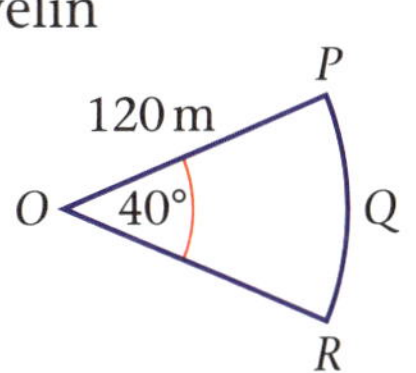

3 A door is in the shape of a rectangle $ABCD$ with a sector OAD of a circle.

$DC = AB = 2.3$ m, $BC = AD = 1.2$ m and the radius of the circle is OA where $OA = OD = 0.8$ m.
Calculate

(a) the perimeter of the door

(b) the area of the door.

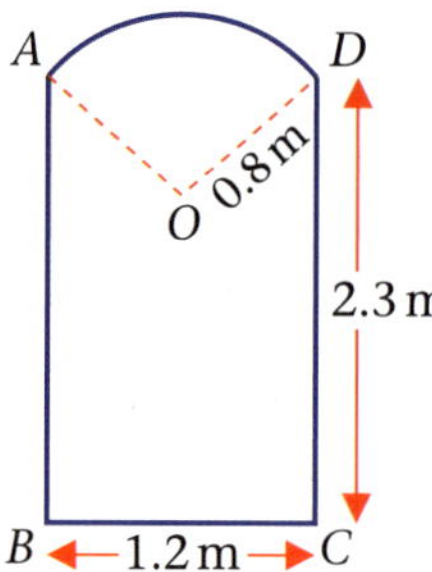

22.4 Finding volumes and surface areas

You need to know how to find the volumes and surface areas of a variety of 3-D objects.

The surface area of a cylinder

This cylinder has a circular base of radius r cm and a height of h cm.

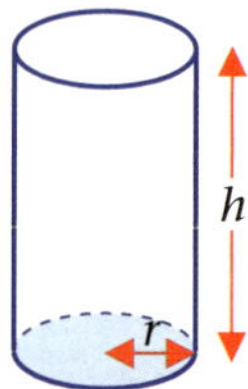

Its surface area is made up of the area of the curved surface plus the areas of the circular top and base.

The area of the circular base and top are both equal to πr^2. So the combined area of the top and base is $2\pi r^2$.

For the area of the curved surface, imagine unwrapping the cylinder. This creates a rectangle with length equal to the circumference of the circular base $2\pi r$ and width equal to the height h:

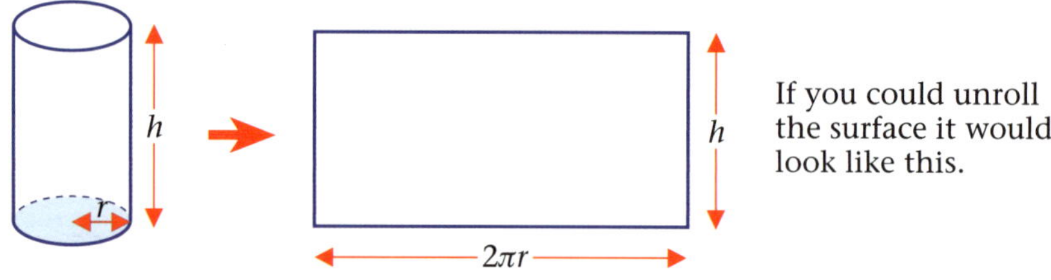

The area of the curved surface is $2\pi rh$.

So the total surface area of the cylinder in cm^2 is $2\pi rh + 2\pi r^2$.

For a **cylinder** of height h with a circular base of radius r,

surface area $= 2\pi rh + 2\pi r^2$

The volume of a cylinder

The **volume** of a cylinder is $\pi r^2 h$.

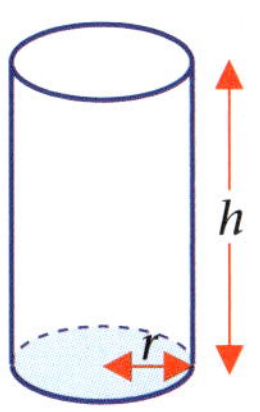

Example 6

Calculate the surface area and volume of a cylinder with circular base of radius 12 cm and height 30 cm.

$$
\begin{aligned}
\text{Surface area} &= 2\pi rh + 2\pi r^2 \\
&= 2 \times \pi \times 12 \times 30 + 2 \times \pi \times 12^2 \\
&= 2261.947 + 904.778 \\
&= 3166.725 = 3167\ \text{cm}^2 \text{ (to 4 s.f.)}
\end{aligned}
$$

$$
\begin{aligned}
\text{volume} &= \pi r^2 h \\
&= \pi \times 12^2 \times 30 \\
&= 13\,572\ \text{cm}^3 \text{ (to 5 s.f.)}
\end{aligned}
$$

Volume and surface area of prisms

A prism is a 3-D shape which has the same cross-section throughout its height.

These are prisms: cuboid, triangular prism, pentagonal prism

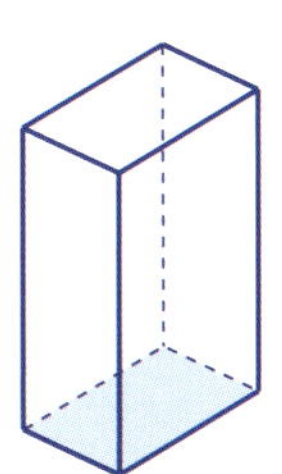
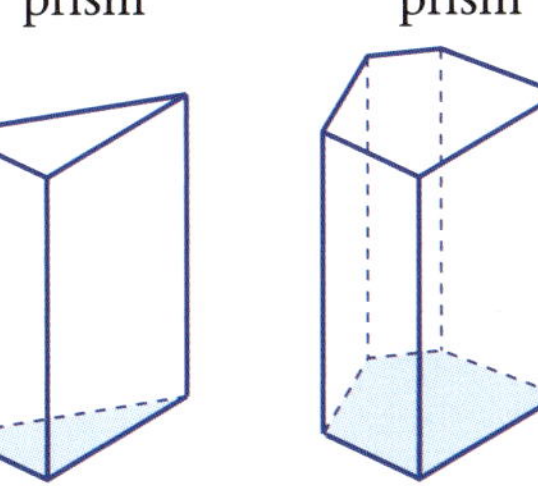
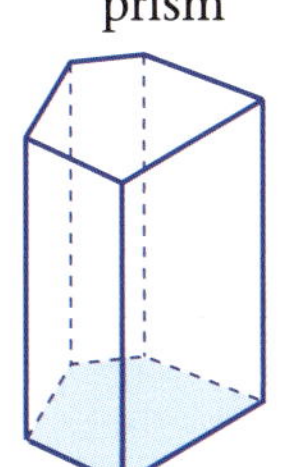

The **volume of any prism** is

area of base × vertical height

or

area of cross-section × vertical height

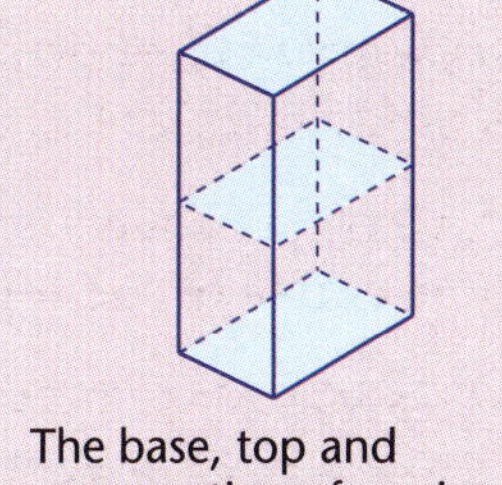

The base, top and cross-section of a prism are all identical.

The **surface area of any prism** is

2 × area of base + total area of vertical faces

Example 7

Here is a pentagonal prism.
The base *ABCDE* is a regular pentagon of side length 8 cm.
The height of the prism is 15 cm.

Calculate the volume of the prism.

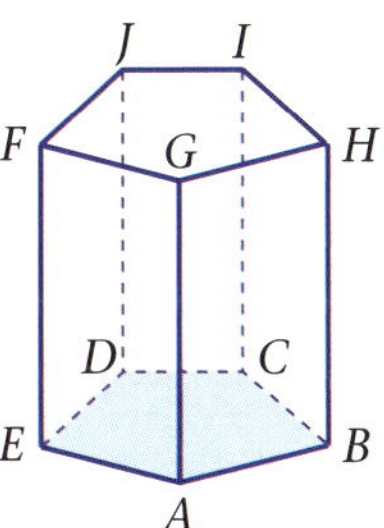

First calculate the area of the base *ABCDE*.

To do this split it into five congruent triangles and look at the area of one of these triangles, *AOB*.

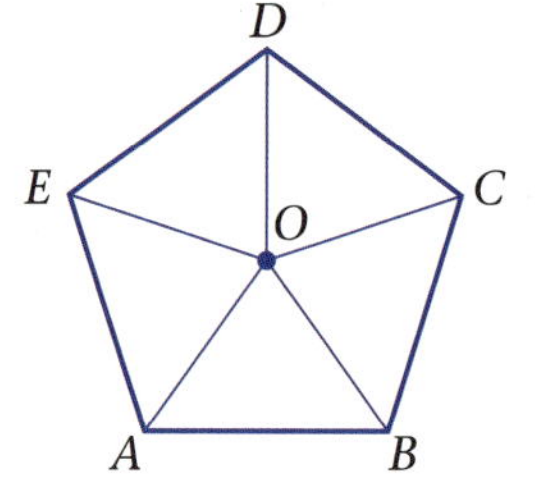

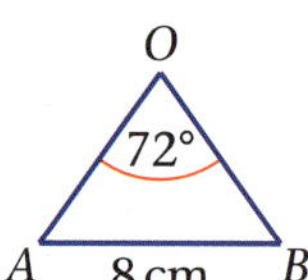

Angle $AOB = \dfrac{360°}{5} = 72°$

The area of *AOB* is $\frac{1}{2}AB \times p$ where p is the perpendicular distance *OM* from *O* to *AB*.

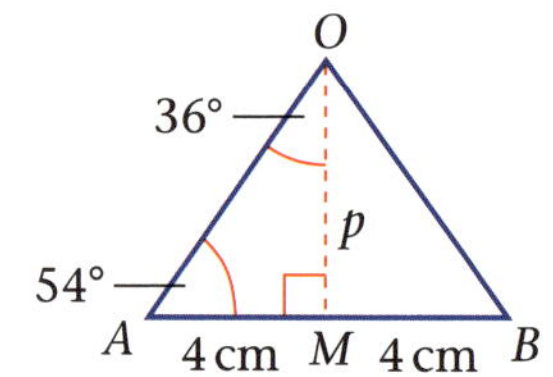

Angle *AOB* is 72°

so angle AOM is $\frac{1}{2} \times 72° = 36°$

and angle OAM is $90° - 36° = 54°$

Using the tangent ratio: $\dfrac{p}{AM} = \tan 54°$, so $p = AM \times \tan 54°$

So $p = 4 \times \tan 54°$

$= 5.5055\ldots \text{ cm}$

For more about the tangent ratio see Section 16.1.

So the area of triangle *AOB* is

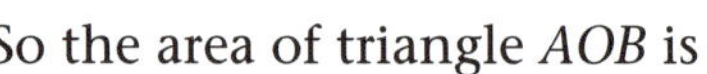

$\frac{1}{2}AB \times p = AM \times p = 4 \times 5.5055\ldots = 22.022\ldots \text{ cm}^2$

As *ABCDE* is made up of five identical triangles:

area $ABCDE = 5 \times 22.022\ldots = 110.1105\ldots$

$= 110.11 \text{ cm}^2$ (to 2 d.p.)

The volume of the prism is area of base × vertical height

so volume of prism $= 110.11\ldots \times 15$

$= 1651.65\ldots \text{ cm}^3$

$= 1652 \text{ cm}^3$ (to 4 s.f.)

Exercise 22E

1 Find the volume and surface area of a cylinder of height 4 cm and circular base of radius 5 cm (to 3 s.f.).

2 A prism of height 10 cm has the cross-sectional shape of an equilateral triangle of side 6 cm. Find the volume and surface area of the prism (to 3 s.f.).

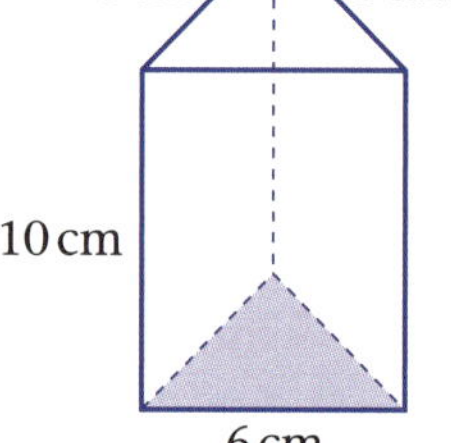

3 A waste bin is the shape of a cylinder. Its base has radius 0.5 m and its height is 1.2 m. Find its volume (to 3 s.f.).

4 A hexagonal prism has a vertical height of 32 cm. The base of the prism is a regular hexagon of side length 12 cm. Calculate the volume of the prism.

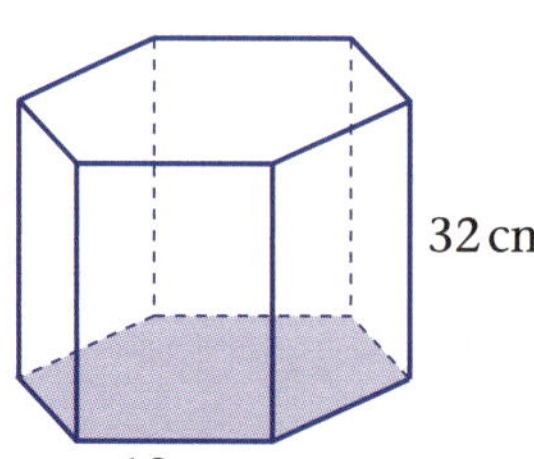

5 A prism has a vertical height of 30 cm.
The base of the prism is a regular polygon with 10 sides.
Each side is of length 6 cm.

(a) Calculate the volume of the prism.

(b) Calculate the surface area.

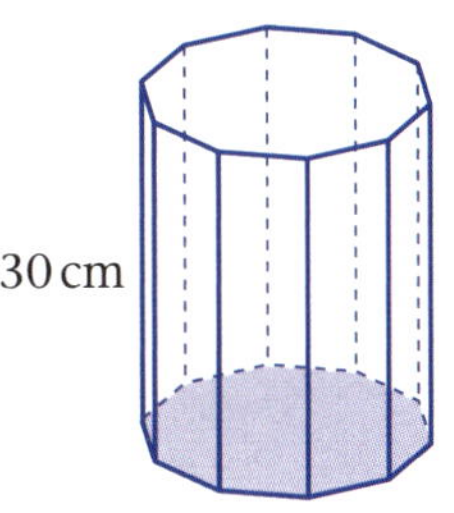

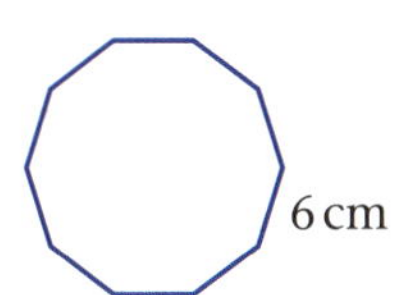

22.5 The volume of a pyramid

These shapes are all **pyramids**:

triangle-based pyramid

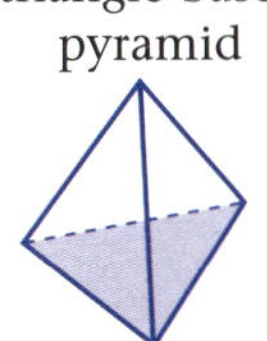

square-based pyramid

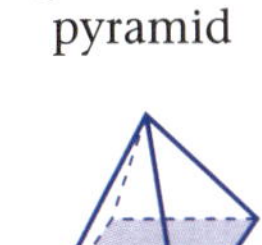

hexagonal pyramid

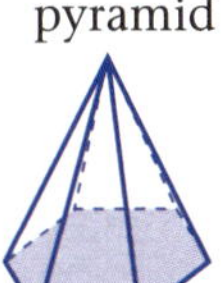

The base of any pyramid is a **polygon**.
The other edges are all straight lines which meet at a point, usually called the vertex.

The area of a triangle is $\frac{1}{2}$ the area of its smallest surrounding rectangle.

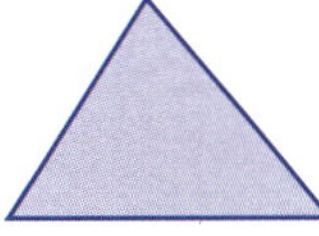

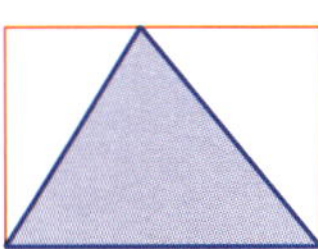

In a similar way the volume of a pyramid is $\frac{1}{3}$ the volume of its smallest surrounding prism.

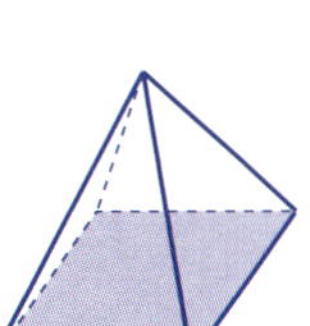

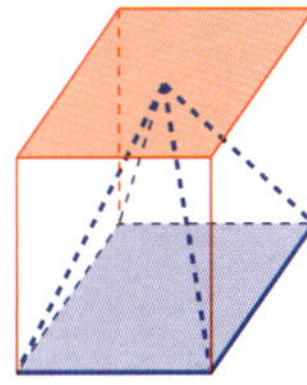

As the volume of a prism is area of base × vertical height:

Volume of a pyramid $= \frac{1}{3} \times$ area of base $\times$ vertical height

A cylinder is a 'special prism'.

A **cone** is a special pyramid with a circular base.
Its smallest surrounding prism is a cylinder, so:

Volume of a cone $= \frac{1}{3} \times$ area of base $\times$ height

$= \frac{1}{3}\pi r^2 h$

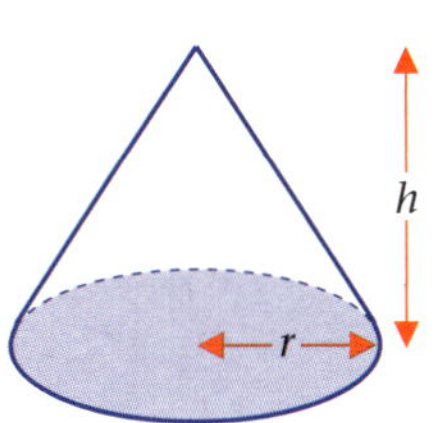

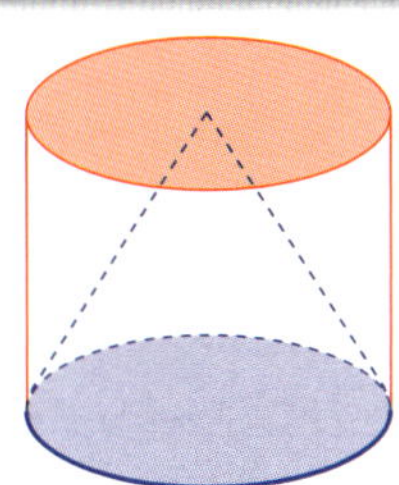

Example 8

A pyramid *VABCD* has a rectangular base *ABCD*.
The vertex *V* is 15 cm vertically above the mid-point *M* of the base. $AB = 4$ cm and $BC = 9$ cm.

Calculate the volume of the pyramid.

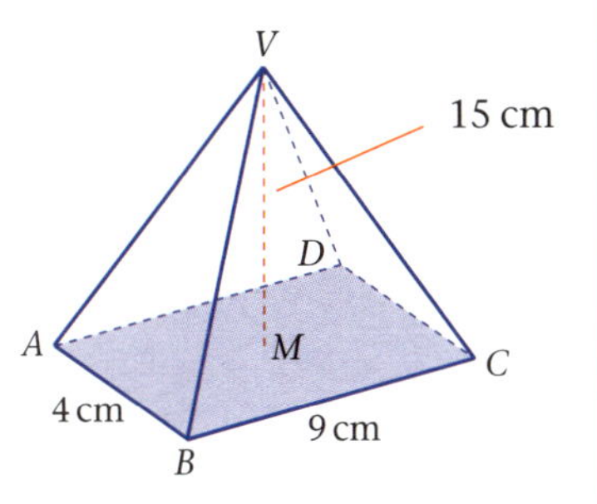

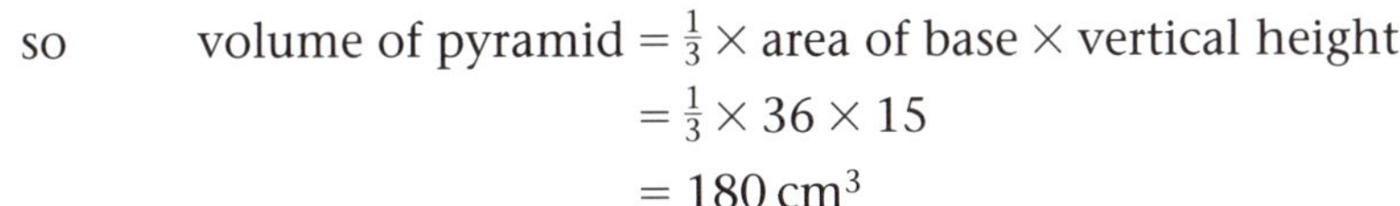

The area of the base is $4 \times 9 = 36\text{ cm}^2$

so volume of pyramid $= \frac{1}{3} \times$ area of base $\times$ vertical height

$= \frac{1}{3} \times 36 \times 15$

$= 180\text{ cm}^3$

Example 9

Here is a cone. The circular base has a diameter AB of length 10 cm. The **slant height** AV is of length 13 cm.

Calculate the volume of the cone.

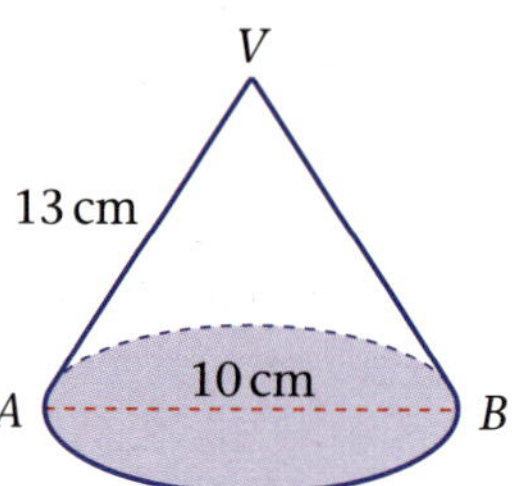

Before you can work out the volume, you need to work out the vertical height from the mid-point of AB to V.

Do this by applying Pythagoras' theorem to the triangular section ABV:

$$AV^2 = h^2 + MA^2$$
$$h^2 = AV^2 - MA^2$$
$$= 13^2 - 5^2$$
$$= 169 - 25 = 144$$
$$h = 12\text{ cm}$$

So volume of cone $= \frac{1}{3}\pi r^2 h$

$$= \frac{1}{3} \times \pi \times 5^2 \times 12$$
$$= \frac{1}{3} \times \pi \times 25 \times 12$$
$$= 314.2\text{ cm}^3 \text{ (correct to 1 d.p.)}$$

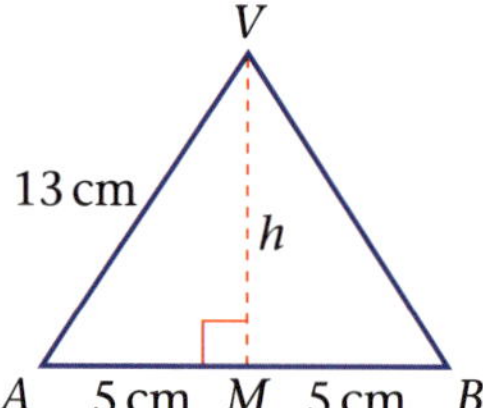

Example 10

A pyramid has a square base of side x cm and a vertical height 24 cm. The volume of the pyramid is 392 cm^3.

Calculate the value of x.

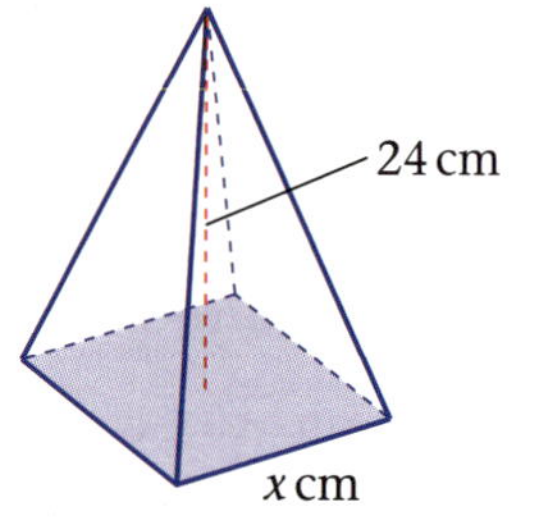

$$\text{Volume} = \frac{1}{3} \times \text{area of base} \times \text{height}$$
$$= \frac{1}{3} \times x^2 \times h$$

so

$$392 = \frac{1}{3} \times x^2 \times 24$$
$$x^2 = \frac{3 \times 392}{24} = 49$$
$$x = 7$$

Exercise 22F

1 $VABCD$ is a square-based pyramid. The vertex V is 20 cm vertically above the mid-point of the horizontal square base $ABCD$, and $AB = 12$ cm.

Calculate the volume of the pyramid.

2 $VABC$ is a triangle-based pyramid.
The vertex V is vertically above the point B.
The base, ABC, is a triangle with a right angle at B.
$AB = 5$ cm, $BC = 7$ cm and $VC = 25$ cm.

Calculate the volume of the pyramid $VABC$.

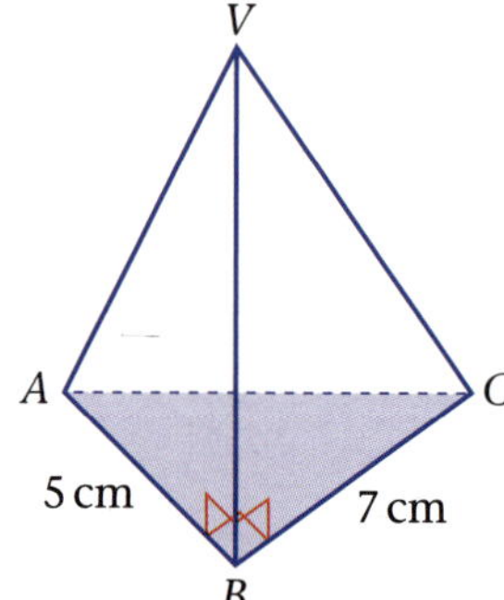

3 A cone has a circular base of radius r cm. The vertical height of the cone is 15 cm. The volume of the cone is 600 cm^3. Calculate the value of r.

4 A solid metal cube of side length x cm is melted down and re-cast to make a cone. During this process none of the metal is lost and all of the metal is used to make the cone. The cone has a circular base of diameter 12 cm and a slant height of length 10 cm. Calculate

(a) the volume of the cone **(b)** the value of x.

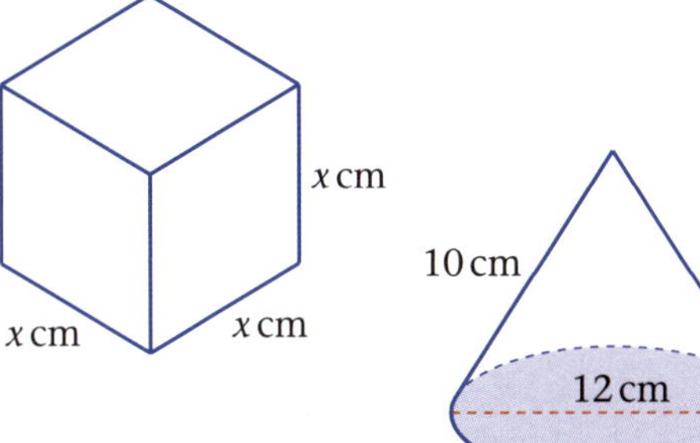

5 A solid pyramid has a square base of side length 8 cm. The vertical height of the pyramid is 15 cm. The pyramid is made by melting down and re-casting a metal cube of side length y cm. During the melting and re-casting process 10% of the metal is lost but all of the remainder is used to make the cone. Calculate the value of y.

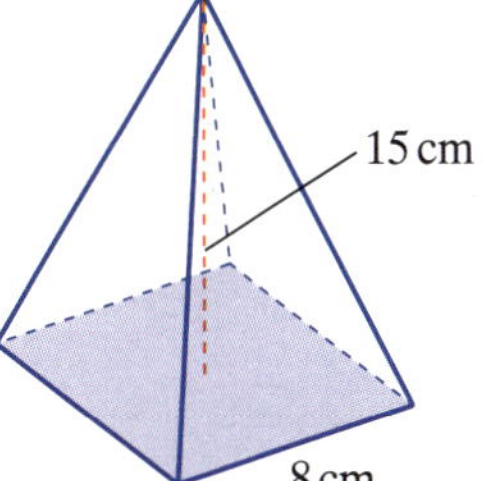

22.6 The surface area and volume of a sphere

For a sphere of radius r: **volume of sphere** $= \dfrac{4\pi r^3}{3}$

surface area $= 4\pi r^2$

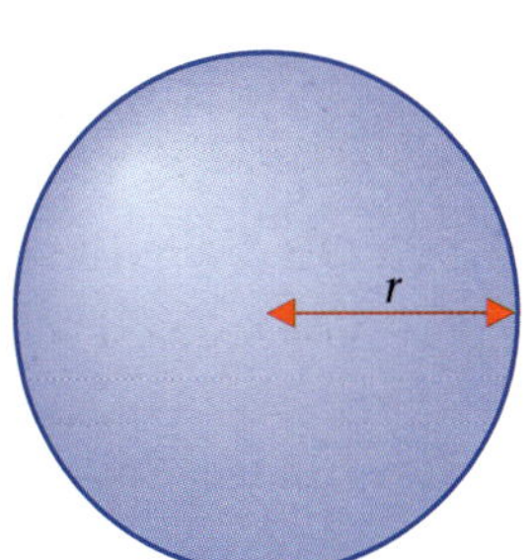

Example 11

Calculate the volume of a sphere of radius 5 cm.

$$\text{Volume of sphere} = \frac{4 \times \pi \times 5^3}{3}$$
$$= \frac{4 \times \pi \times 125}{3}$$
$$= 523.6 \text{ cm}^3 \text{ (correct to 1 d.p.)}$$

Example 12

The surface area of a sphere is 2000 cm^2.
Calculate the radius of the sphere.

Using surface area $= 4\pi r^2$:

$$4\pi r^2 = 2000$$

so
$$r^2 = \frac{2000}{4\pi}$$
$$r^2 = \frac{500}{\pi}$$
$$r^2 = 159.15\ldots$$

So
$$r = 12.62 \text{ cm (correct to 2 d.p.)}$$

Exercise 22G

1 Calculate the volume and surface area of a sphere
 (a) of radius 8 cm (b) of radius 7.2 cm
 (c) of diameter 19 cm (d) of diameter x cm.

2 A sphere has a volume of 5000 cm^3.
 Calculate the radius of the sphere.

3 A cube of side x cm and a sphere of radius 6 cm have equal volumes.
 Calculate the value of x.

22.7 Areas and volumes of similar shapes

This rectangle measures 1 unit by 2 units:

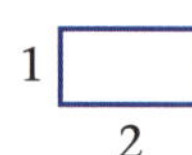

Enlarge it by scale factor 2:

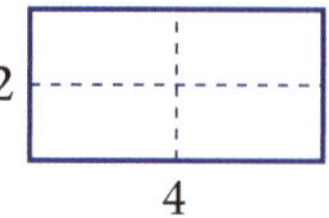

It takes four of the smaller rectangles to fill the enlarged one:

area of enlarged rectangle = 4 × area of first rectangle

Here is the 1 by 2 rectangle again:

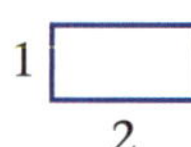

Enlarge it by scale factor 3:

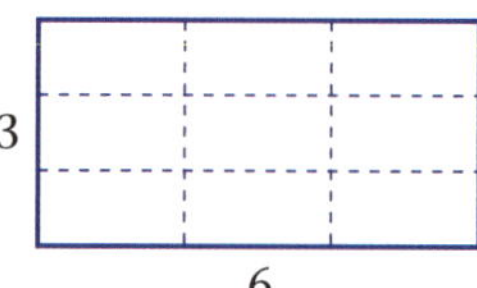

This time it takes nine (or 3^2) of the smaller rectangle to fill the larger one

area of enlarged rectangle = 9 × area of first rectangle

This relationship can be generalised for any enlargement:

When a shape is enlarged by scale factor k, the area of the enlarged shape is k^2 × area of the original shape.

For example, if the scale factor is 5, the new area will be 5^2 (or 25) times the original area.

A similar result holds for 3-D shapes:

Here is a 1 by 1 by 2 cuboid:

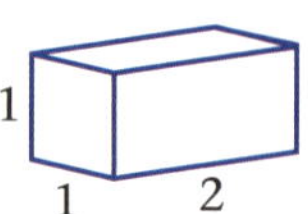

Enlarge it by scale factor 2:

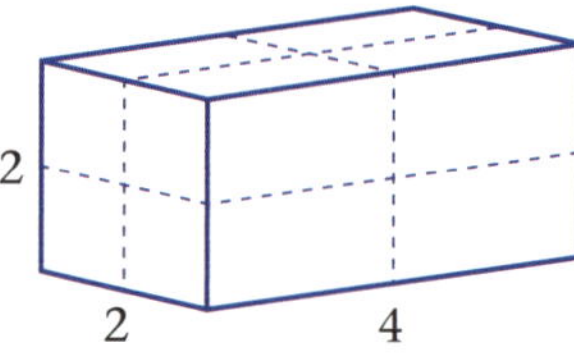

Eight (or 2^3) of the smaller cuboids are needed to fill the enlarged shape:

volume of enlarged cuboid = 8 × volume of first cuboid

This result generalises to:

When a 3-D shape is enlarged by scale factor k, the volume of the enlarged shape is k^3 × volume of the original shape.

For example, if the scale factor is 5, the new volume will be 5^3 (or 125) times the original volume.

Example 13

A soft drinks company manufactures two **similar** bottles called *Standard* and *Super*.

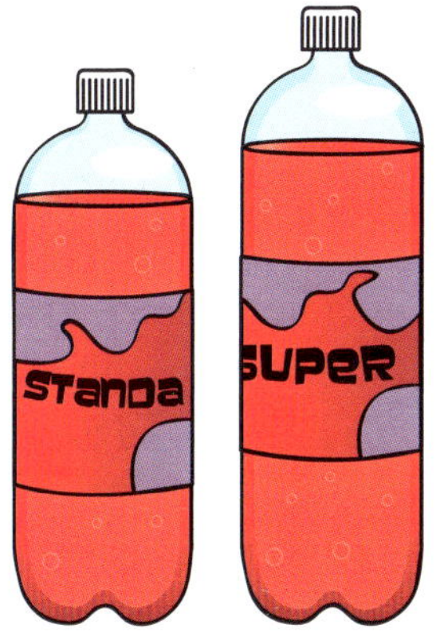

The *Standard* bottle has volume 1000 cm^3. The *Super* bottle has volume 1500 cm^3. The height of the *Standard* bottle is 30 cm. Calculate the height of the *Super* bottle.

Because the two bottles are similar, *Super* is an enlargement of *Standard*.

To find the height of *Super* you need to calculate the scale factor of the enlargement. Let this scale factor be k.

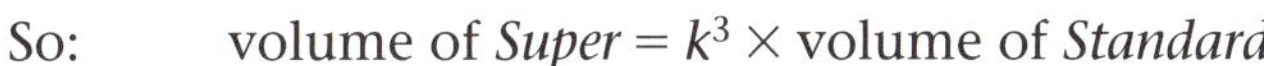

So: volume of *Super* = $k^3 \times$ volume of *Standard*

$$k^3 = \frac{\text{volume of } \textit{Super}}{\text{volume of } \textit{Standard}}$$

$$= \frac{1500}{1000}$$

$$= 1.5$$

$$k = \sqrt[3]{1.5}$$

$$= 1.1447\ldots$$

Then the height of *Super* is scale factor ($k = 1.1447\ldots$) $\times$ height of *Standard*.

The height of *Super* is $1.1447\ldots \times 30 = 34.34$ cm (correct to 2 d.p.)

Example 14

The ratio of the radii of two spheres is 1 : 3.
Calculate the ratio of:

(a) the surface areas of the spheres

(b) the volumes of the spheres.

Radius of larger sphere = 3 $\times$ radius of smaller sphere

(a) The large sphere is an enlargement of the small sphere, scale factor 3.

So surface area of larger sphere

= $3^2 \times$ surface area of smaller sphere

The ratio of the surface areas is 1 : 9.

(b) Volume of larger sphere

= $3^3 \times$ volume of smaller sphere.

The ratio of the volumes is 1 : 27.

Worked examination question 2

The diagram represents a box of chocolates.
This is a *Standard* size box.

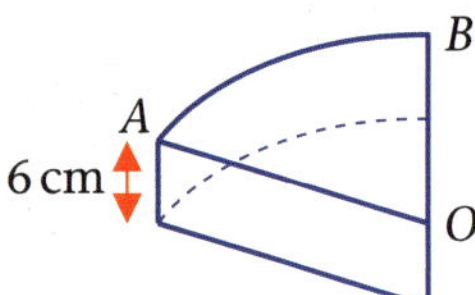

The lid and base of the box are sectors of a circle centre O.
The radius OA of the circle is 18 cm.
The angle $AOB = 75°$.
The box is 6 cm deep.

Calculate

(a) the area of the face of the top of the box

(b) the volume of the box.

The company manufacturing these boxes decides to manufacture a *Large* size box which will be similar in shape to the *Standard* size box.
The volume of the *Large* size box is to be twice the volume of the *Standard* size box.

(c) Calculate the depth of the *Large* size box.

(a) Area of the face of the top $= \dfrac{\pi \times 18^2 \times 75}{360}$

$$= \frac{\pi \times 324 \times 75}{360}$$

$$= 212.0575\ldots$$

$$= 212 \text{ cm}^2 \text{ (correct to 3 s.f.)}$$

(b) Volume of box = area of top (or area of base) × height (or depth)

so volume of the box $= 212.0575\ldots \times 6$

$= 1272 \text{ cm}^3$ (to the nearest whole number)

(c) Let the scale factor for the lengths be k.

The volume of *Large* box $= k^3 \times$ volume of *Standard* box

So $k^3 = \dfrac{\text{volume of } \textit{Large} \text{ box}}{\text{volume of } \textit{Standard} \text{ box}} = 2$

$k = \sqrt[3]{2} = 1.2599\ldots$

As the scale factor k is 1.2599…

depth of the *Large* box = 1.2599… × depth of *Standard* box

$= 1.2599\ldots \times 6 = 7.56$ cm (correct to 2 d.p.)

Exercise 22H

1 Washing liquid is sold in two sizes of similar bottles called *Basic* and *Extra*. The volume of a *Basic* bottle is $\frac{1}{2}$ litre and its height is 20 cm. The volume of an *Extra* bottle is 0.8 litres.
Calculate the height of an *Extra* bottle.

2 A ball is a sphere of radius 12 cm.
The ball is inflated to increase its radius to 12.5 cm.
Show that the volume of air in the ball increases by approximately 13%.

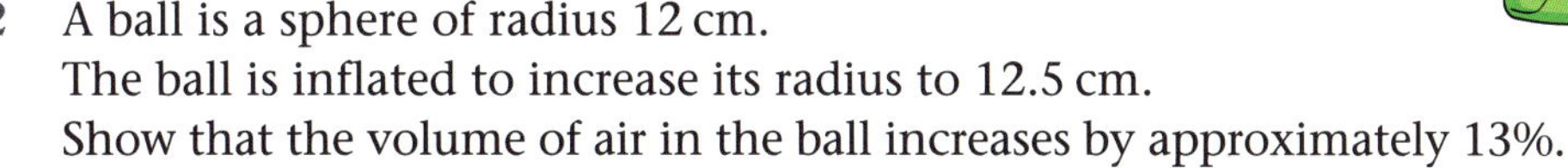

3 The heights of two similar cylinders are in the ratio 2 : 3.
Calculate the ratio of

(a) the surface area of the cylinders

(b) the volumes of the cylinders.

4 A model car is a scale replica of the real car.
The length of the model car is $\frac{1}{50}$ of the length of the real car.

Calculate the fraction $\dfrac{\text{volume of the model car}}{\text{volume of the real car}}$

5 Beans are sold in two similar cylindrical cans called *Standard* and *Large*. The *Standard* can holds 500 grams of beans. The *Large* can holds 750 grams of beans. The height of a *Standard* can is 11 cm.
Calculate

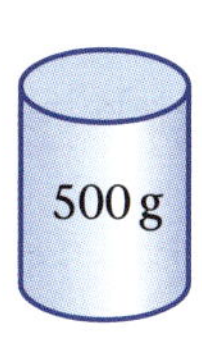

Standard

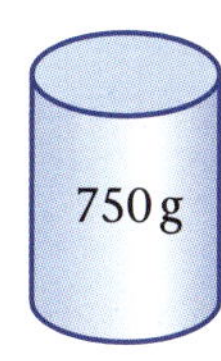

Large

(a) the height of a *Large* can

(b) the ratio of the areas of the circular bases of the cans.

22.8 Compound solids

You need to be able to find the volume of solids made from combining shapes you already know.

Example 15

This spinning top is made from a hemisphere and a cone.
Find its volume. Give your answer to 2 d.p.

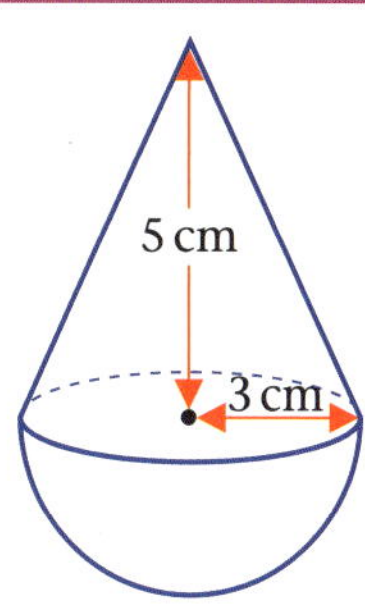

Imagine splitting the shape into two sections.

A sphere of radius 3 cm has volume

$$\frac{4\pi(3)^3}{3} = 36\pi\,\text{cm}^3$$

The hemisphere is half a sphere so it has volume $18\pi\,\text{cm}^3$.

The volume of the cone is $\frac{1}{3}\pi r^2 h$

$$\frac{1}{3}\pi \times 3^2 \times 5 = 15\pi\,\text{cm}^3$$

So the volume of the entire spinning top is

$$18\pi + 15\pi = 33\pi = 103.67\,\text{cm}^3 \text{ (correct to 2 d.p.)}$$

You can leave your answers in terms of π until you have finished your working out.

Example 16

This hat is made from a cone with the top chopped off.
Find its volume correct to 2 d.p.

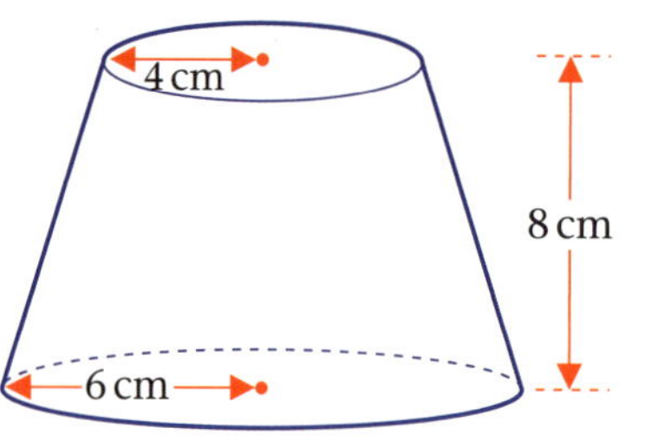

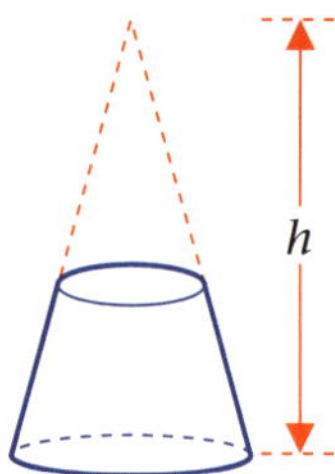

Imagine the hat was continued up to make a complete cone of vertical height h. If you know the value of h you can find the volume of the hat by subtracting the volume of the smaller cone from the volume of the larger one.

This is known as a **truncated cone** or a **frustum**.

You can find h using similar triangles.

See Section 3.6 (in Book 1) for more about similar triangles.

The shape $ABCD$ is a section from the hat.

Triangle ABE and triangle APD are similar, so

$$\frac{h}{6} = \frac{8}{2}$$

$$h = 24\text{ cm}$$

So volume of larger cone $= \frac{1}{3}\pi r^2 h$

$= \frac{1}{3}\pi \times 6^2 \times 24$

$= 288\pi$

volume of smaller cone $= \frac{1}{3}\pi \times 4^2 \times (h - 8)$

$= \frac{1}{3}\pi \times 4^2 \times 16$

$= \dfrac{256\pi}{3}$

So the volume of the hat is

$$288\pi - \frac{256\pi}{3} = \frac{608\pi}{3} = 636.70\text{ cm}^3 \text{ (correct to 2 d.p.)}$$

Exercise 22I

1 This spinning top is made from a cube, a cylinder and a cone.

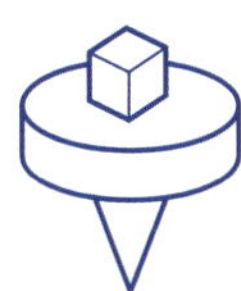

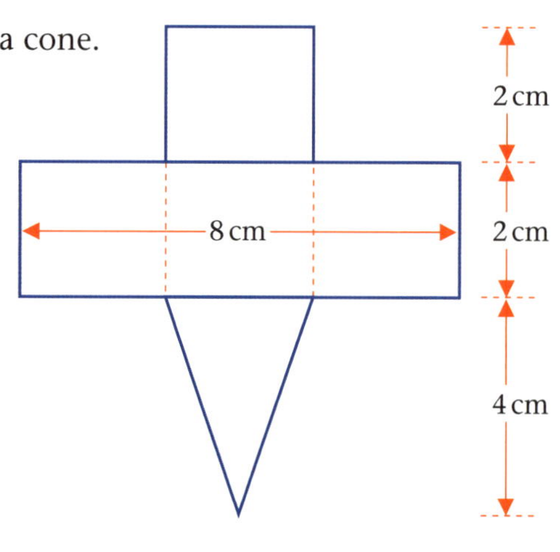

Find its volume, giving your answer to 2 d.p.

2 This box is made from a cube of side 8 cm and a pyramid of height 5 cm.
Find its volume.

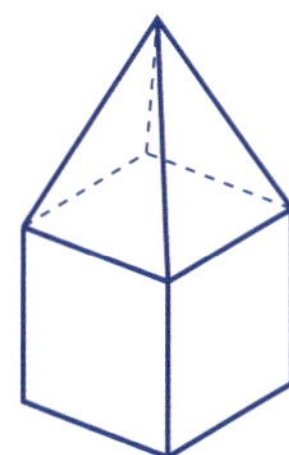

3 Find the volume of this truncated cone.
Give your answer to 2 d.p.

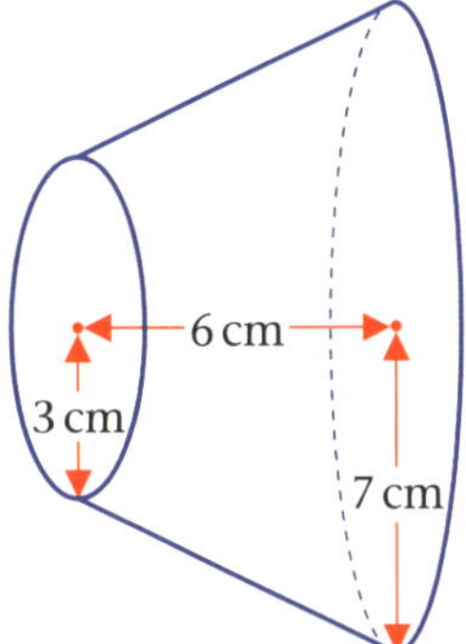

4 The diagram represents a model of Cleopatra's Needle.
It is made from a truncated square-based pyramid and a smaller square-based pyramid.

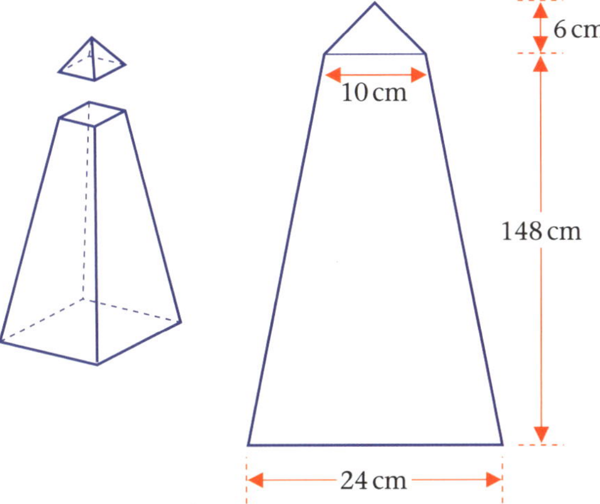

Cleopatra's Needle on the Thames Embankment in London is an original Egyptian obelisk.

Find its volume, giving your answer to 2 d.p.

Mixed exercise 22

1 Here is a sector of a circle, *OAPB*, with centre *O*.
Calculate
(a) the length of the chord *AB*
(b) the length of the arc *APB*
(c) the area of the sector *OAPB*
(d) the area of the segment *APB*.

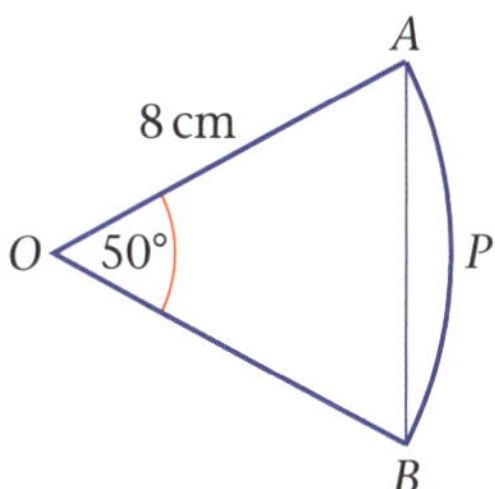

2 Calculate the volume and surface area of a cylinder with circular base of radius 12 cm and with vertical height 20 cm.

3 Calculate the volume of a sphere of diameter 8 cm.

4 The volume of a sphere of radius r cm is numerically equal to the radius of that sphere.

Show that $r = \sqrt{\dfrac{3}{4\pi}}$.

5 $VABCD$ is a pyramid with a rectangular base $ABCD$.

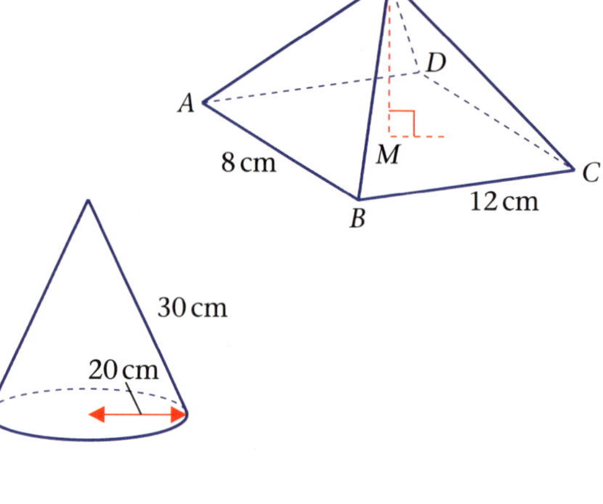

$AB = 8$ cm $BC = 12$ cm
M is at the centre of $ABCD$ and $VM = 35$ cm.
V is vertically above M.

Calculate the volume of $VABCD$.

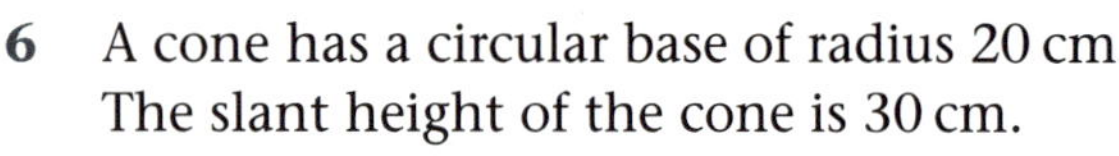

6 A cone has a circular base of radius 20 cm.
The slant height of the cone is 30 cm.

Calculate the volume of the cone.

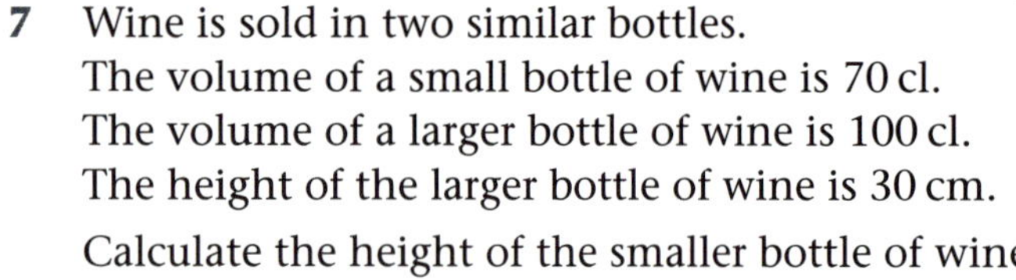

7 Wine is sold in two similar bottles.
The volume of a small bottle of wine is 70 cl.
The volume of a larger bottle of wine is 100 cl.
The height of the larger bottle of wine is 30 cm.
Calculate the height of the smaller bottle of wine.

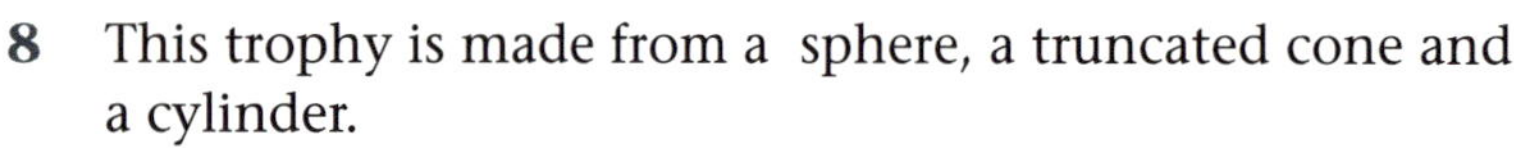

8 This trophy is made from a sphere, a truncated cone and a cylinder.
Find its volume correct to 2 d.p.

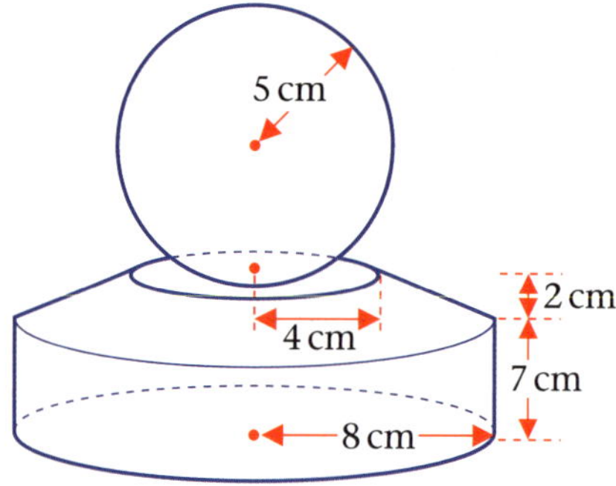

9 X and Y are two geometrically similar solid shapes.
The total surface area of shape X is 450 cm^2.
The total surface area of shape Y is 800 cm^2.
The volume of shape X is 1350 cm^3.
Calculate the volume of shape Y. [E]

10 Cylinder A and cylinder B are mathematically similar.

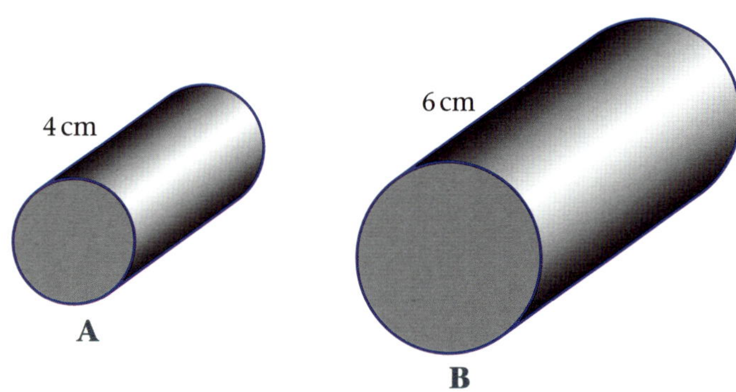

The length of cylinder A is 4 cm and the length of cylinder B is 6 cm. The volume of cylinder A is 80 cm^3.
Calculate the volume of cylinder B. [E]

Summary of key points

1. **Circumference** of a circle $= 2\pi r$
   Area of a circle $= \pi r^2$

2. **Arc length** of a circle $= \dfrac{\pi r\theta}{180}$

3. **Area of a sector** of a circle $= \dfrac{\pi r^2\theta}{360}$

4. **Area of a segment** $= \dfrac{\pi r^2\theta}{360} - \frac{1}{2}r^2 \sin\theta$

arc
sector
segment

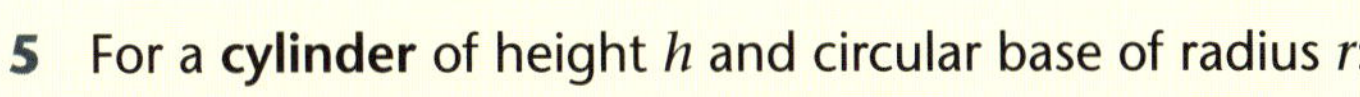

5. For a **cylinder** of height h and circular base of radius r:

   surface area $= 2\pi rh + 2\pi r^2$

   volume $= \pi r^2 h$

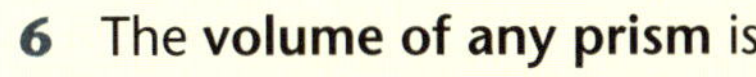

6. The **volume of any prism** is

   area of base × vertical height or area of cross-section × vertical height

7. **Volume of a pyramid** $= \frac{1}{3} \times$ area of base × vertical height

8. **Volume of a cone** $= \frac{1}{3} \times$ area of base × height $= \frac{1}{3}\pi r^2 h$

9. Cylinders and cones are special types of prisms and pyramids, respectively.

10. **Volume of a sphere** $= \dfrac{4\pi r^3}{3}$

    Surface area of a sphere $= 4\pi r^2$

11. When a shape is enlarged by a scale factor k to produce a similar shape:
    - area of enlarged shape $= k^2 \times$ area of original shape
    - volume of enlarged shape $= k^3 \times$ volume of original shape.

23 Exploring numbers 2

In this chapter you will investigate decimals and their fraction equivalents, and extend your knowledge of surds and upper and lower bounds.

23.1 Terminating and recurring decimals

When a fraction of the type $\frac{a}{b}$ is converted into a decimal, there are two different types of answer. The result will either be a **terminating decimal** such as 0.75 or 0.174 or a **recurring decimal** such as 0.3333… or 0.34343434… .

For more on recurring decimals see Section 4.6 (in Book 1).

Terminating decimals

When the denominator, b, of the fraction $\frac{a}{b}$ is a factor of 10^n for some integer n (e.g. b is a factor of 10 or 100 or 1000 and so on), the division to evaluate the decimal will always finish at some stage. There will be an exact answer.

The only prime factors of 10 are 2 and 5. So the only prime factors of 10^n are 2 and 5, for any value of n.
So $\frac{a}{b}$ is equivalent to a terminating decimal if b has prime factors of 2 and 5 only.

A fraction is equivalent to a **terminating decimal** if the denominator is a factor of 10^n for some integer n.

Example 1

Decide whether these fractions convert into terminating or recurring decimals.

(a) $\frac{1}{4}$ (b) $\frac{13}{64}$

Work out their decimal equivalents.

(a) 4 is a factor of $10^2 = 100$, so $\frac{1}{4}$ is a terminating decimal.
$\frac{1}{4} = 0.25$

(b) Try dividing 64 into powers of 10.
64 is a factor of $10^6 = 1\,000\,000$, so $\frac{13}{64}$ is a terminating decimal.
$\frac{13}{64} = 0.203\,125$

```
      0.203 125
64)13.000 000
    12 8
       200
       192
         80
         64
         160
         128
          320
          320
```

To convert 0.25 to a fraction you multiply 0.25 by 100 and then divide this result by 100:

$$0.25 = \frac{0.25 \times 100}{100} = \frac{25}{100} = \frac{1}{4}$$ — Cancel by 25

To convert a decimal which terminates after 2 places into a fraction you multiply the decimal by 10^2 and then divide this result by 10^2.

For a decimal which terminates after 3 decimal places, do the same but multiply and divide by 10^3. For example:

$$0.125 = \frac{0.125 \times 1000}{1000} = \frac{125}{1000} = \frac{1}{8}$$ — Cancel by 125

Any terminating decimal with n decimal places can be converted into a fraction by multiplying the decimal by 10^n and dividing the result by 10^n.

Cancel and write the fraction in its simplest form.

Recurring decimals

As a decimal, $\frac{1}{7}$ is

$\frac{1}{7} = 0.142857142857\ldots$ or $0.\dot{1}4285\dot{7}$

A **recurring decimal** has a repeating pattern in its digits.

Example 2

Write these fractions as decimals.

(a) $\frac{1}{3}$ (b) $\frac{1}{9}$ (c) $\frac{1}{6}$ (d) $\frac{1}{11}$ (e) $\frac{10}{21}$

(a) $\frac{1}{3} = 0.33333\ldots$ or $0.\dot{3}$

(b) $\frac{1}{9} = 0.11111\ldots$ or $0.\dot{1}$

(c) $\frac{1}{6} = 0.16666\ldots$ or $0.1\dot{6}$

(d) $\frac{1}{11} = 0.090909\ldots$ or $0.\dot{0}\dot{9}$ (a pattern every 2 decimal places)

(e) $\frac{10}{21} = 0.476190476190\ldots$ or $0.\dot{4}7619\dot{0}$ (a pattern every 6 decimal places)

Exercise 23A

1 Convert the following fractions into decimals. Indicate which of the decimals are terminating and which are recurring.

(a) $\frac{3}{4}$ (b) $\frac{3}{5}$ (c) $\frac{3}{7}$ (d) $\frac{3}{8}$ (e) $\frac{3}{10}$ (f) $\frac{3}{11}$

2 State, with a reason, whether the equivalent decimals for these fractions are terminating or recurring.

(a) $\frac{5}{6}$ (b) $\frac{5}{7}$ (c) $\frac{5}{8}$ (d) $\frac{5}{9}$ (e) $\frac{5}{12}$ (f) $\frac{5}{13}$ (g) $\frac{5}{16}$

3 Write out the recurring decimals equivalent to these fractions:

$\frac{1}{7}$, $\frac{2}{7}$, $\frac{3}{7}$, $\frac{4}{7}$, $\frac{5}{7}$, $\frac{6}{7}$

Explain the relationship between the pattern of the recurring digits.

4 How many digits are there in the recurring pattern of digits in the decimal equivalent of the fraction $\frac{3}{17}$?

5 Find the recurring decimals which are equivalent to the fractions

$\frac{1}{13}, \frac{2}{13}, \frac{3}{13}, \ldots, \frac{10}{13}, \frac{11}{13}, \frac{12}{13}$

Separate the recurring decimals into two distinct sets of numbers. Explain the connection between them.

6 By considering the process of long division to find a recurring decimal equivalent to a fraction $\frac{1}{m}$, such as $\frac{1}{17}$, explain

(a) why the decimal will recur

(b) why the number of digits in the recurring pattern is less than m.

23.2 Finding a fraction equivalent to a recurring decimal

The method is best illustrated with three examples.

Example 3

Find a fraction equivalent to 0.55555...

Let $x = 0.55555\ldots$ (1)

Multiply equation (1) by 10:

$10x = 5.55555\ldots$ (2)

Subtract equation (1) from equation (2):

$10x - x = 5$

So $9x = 5$

$x = \frac{5}{9}$

The fraction equivalent to 0.55555... is $\frac{5}{9}$

Pattern recurs every 1 decimal place, so multiply by 10^1.

Example 4

Find a fraction equivalent to 0.636363...

Let $x = 0.636363\ldots$

Multiply by 100:

$100x = 63.6363\ldots$

Subtract:

$100x - x = 63$

So $99x = 63$

$x = \frac{63}{99} = \frac{7}{11}$

The fraction equivalent to 0.636363... is $\frac{7}{11}$

Pattern recurs every 2 decimal places, so multiply by 10^2.

Example 5

Find a fraction equivalent to 0.103103103…

Let $x = 0.103103103\ldots$

Multiply by 1000: $1000x = 103.103103103\ldots$

Subtract: $999x = 103$

So $x = \frac{103}{999}$

The fraction equivalent to 0.103103103… is $\frac{103}{999}$

Pattern recurs every 3 decimal places, so multiply by 10^3.

Example 6

Write $1.1\dot{2}\dot{3}$ as a fraction in its simplest form.

Let $x = 1.1\dot{2}\dot{3}$

Multiply by 100: $100x = 112.3\dot{2}\dot{3}$

Subtract: $99x = 111.2$

Multiply by 10: $990x = 1112$

So $x = \frac{1112}{990} = 1\frac{122}{990} = 1\frac{61}{495}$

Exercise 23B

1 Find the fractions which are equivalent to the recurring decimals:

(a) 0.666666… (b) 0.777777…
(c) 0.34343434… (d) 0.91919191…
(e) 0.181818… (f) 0.125125125…
(g) 0.513513513… (h) 0.100110011001…
(i) 0.127912791279… (j) 0.089108910891…
(k) 1.4133333… (l) 4.72121212…
(m) $2.3\dot{4}\dot{5}$ (n) $5.6\dot{2}\dot{7}$

2 Find the fraction which is equivalent to the recurring decimal 0.9999999… Explain the significance of your result.

23.3 Surds

The area of this square lawn is 20 m^2. The length of each side is x m.

$$x^2 = 20$$
$$x = \sqrt{20}$$

x metres
x metres
20 m^2
x metres
x metres

Using a calculator, you could write x as 4.47. This is correct to 2 decimal places but it is not an exact answer. If you wanted to say exactly what the number was you could just write $\sqrt{20}$.

A number written exactly using square roots is called a **surd**.
For example, $\sqrt{3}$ and $2 - \sqrt{5}$ are in surd form.

Unless you are told otherwise in a question, you can leave your answer as a surd.

Example 7

Solve the equation $x^2 - 8x + 11 = 0$, leaving your answer in surd form.

Complete the square:

$$(x - 4)^2 - 16 + 11 = 0$$
$$(x - 4)^2 - 5 = 0$$
$$(x - 4)^2 = 5$$
$$x - 4 = \pm\sqrt{5}$$

So $x = 4 + \sqrt{5}$ or $x = 4 - \sqrt{5}$

For more about completing a square see Sections 19.2 and 19.3.

$\sqrt{5}$ is the positive square root of 5. You have to use a $\pm$ sign to show both possible values.

Manipulating surds

Surds can be added, subtracted, multiplied and divided.

$$\sqrt{a \times b} = \sqrt{a} \times \sqrt{b}$$

$$\sqrt{\frac{a}{b}} = \frac{\sqrt{a}}{\sqrt{b}}$$

You can work these rules out using the rules of indices. For example:

$(ab)^n = a^n b^n$

When $n = \frac{1}{2}$, $(ab)^{\frac{1}{2}} = a^{\frac{1}{2}} b^{\frac{1}{2}}$

$\sqrt{ab} = \sqrt{a}\sqrt{b}$

Example 8

Simplify $\sqrt{12}$

$$\sqrt{12} = \sqrt{4 \times 3}$$
$$= \sqrt{4} \times \sqrt{3}$$
$$= 2\sqrt{3}$$

Sometimes you will be asked to simplify a fraction with a surd as the denominator.

Example 9

Simplify $\frac{1}{\sqrt{2}}$

Multiply the top and bottom by $\sqrt{2}$:

$$\frac{1}{\sqrt{2}} = \frac{1}{\sqrt{2}} \times \frac{\sqrt{2}}{\sqrt{2}} = \frac{\sqrt{2}}{2}$$

Simplified surds should never have a square root in the denominator.

Example 10

Rationalise $\frac{1}{3\sqrt{5}}$

Multiply the top and bottom by $\sqrt{5}$:

$$\frac{1}{3\sqrt{5}} = \frac{1}{3\sqrt{5}} \times \frac{\sqrt{5}}{\sqrt{5}}$$

$$= \frac{\sqrt{5}}{3 \times 5} = \frac{\sqrt{5}}{15}$$

Simplifying an expression to remove the square root in the denominator is called 'rationalising'.

Example 11

Rationalise the denominator of $\frac{\sqrt{2}}{5 + \sqrt{2}}$

Multiply the top and bottom by $(5 - \sqrt{2})$:

$$\frac{\sqrt{2}}{5 + \sqrt{2}} = \frac{\sqrt{2}(5 - \sqrt{2})}{(5 + \sqrt{2})(5 - \sqrt{2})}$$

$$= \frac{5\sqrt{2} - 2}{23}$$

$(5 + \sqrt{2})(5 - \sqrt{2})$
$= 5 \times 5 - 5\sqrt{2} + 5\sqrt{2} - \sqrt{2}\sqrt{2}$
$= 25 - 2$
$= 23$

Exercise 23C

1 Solve the equation $x^2 = 30$, leaving your answer in surd form.

2 The area of a square is 40 cm². Find the length of one side of the square. Give your answer as a surd in its simplest form.

3 The lengths of the sides of a rectangle are

$3 + \sqrt{5}$ and $3 - \sqrt{5}$ units

Work out, in their most simplified forms,

(a) the perimeter of the rectangle

(b) the area of the rectangle.

4 Rationalise each of the following:

(a) $\frac{1}{\sqrt{7}}$ (b) $\frac{3}{\sqrt{5}}$ (c) $\frac{1}{\sqrt{17}}$

(d) $\frac{1}{\sqrt{11}}$ (e) $\frac{\sqrt{32}}{\sqrt{2}}$ (f) $\frac{\sqrt{5}}{3 + \sqrt{5}}$

(g) $\frac{\sqrt{7}}{2 - \sqrt{7}}$ (h) $\frac{\sqrt{3}}{2 - \sqrt{3}}$ (i) $\frac{\sqrt{11}}{\sqrt{11} - 7}$

5 Solve these equations, leaving your answers in surd form.

(a) $x^2 - 6x + 2 = 0$ (b) $x^2 + 10x + 14 = 0$

6 Show that $\frac{1}{2\sqrt{17}} = \frac{\sqrt{17}}{34}$

7 *ABCD* is a rectangle.

$AB = 2\sqrt{2}$ units $\quad BC = \sqrt{3}$ units

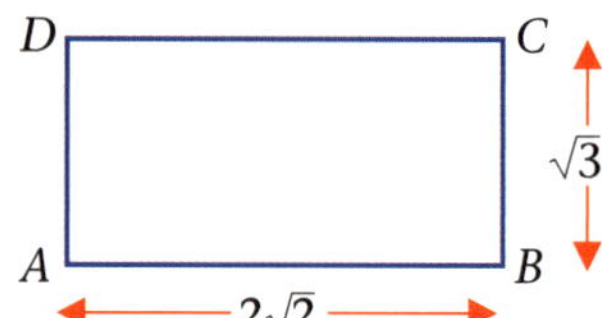

Work out the length of the diagonal *AC*.
Give your answer in surd form.

8 The diagram represents a right-angled triangle *ABC*.

$AB = \sqrt{7} + 2$ units $\quad AC = \sqrt{7} - 2$ units

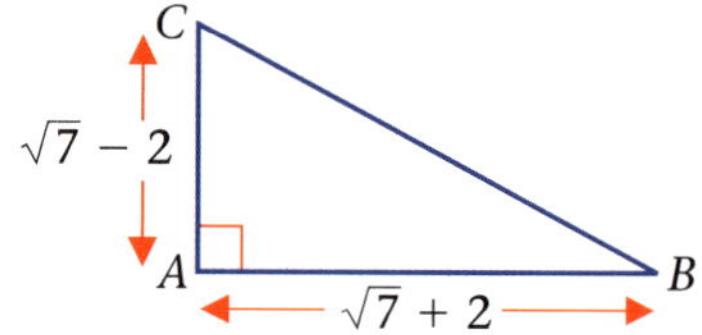

Work out, leaving any appropriate answers in surd form,

(a) the area of triangle *ABC* **(b)** the length of *BC*.

9 Simplify $\frac{\sqrt{3}}{\sqrt{2}}$

23.4 Rounding

When you round the measurements 2.14 cm, 2.15 cm and 2.16 cm to 1 decimal place

- 2.14 cm **rounds down** to 2.1 cm
- 2.16 cm **rounds up** to 2.2 cm.
- By convention, 2.15 cm **rounds up** to 2.2 cm.

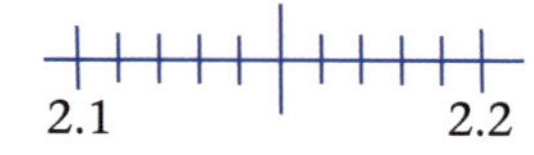

However, you know that 2.15 cm is really exactly the same distance from both 2.1 cm and 2.2 cm.

The largest measurement that rounds down to 2.1 cm is 2.1499999... (recurring).

What is the value of $2.14\dot{9}$?

Let $x = 2.149999...$ (1)

Then using the method of Section 23.2:

$10x = 21.49999...$ (2)

Subtract equation (1) from equation (2):

$$\begin{aligned} 10x &= 21.49999... \\ x &= 2.14999... \\ \hline 9x &= 19.35 \end{aligned}$$

So $x = \frac{19.35}{9} = 2.15$

So 2.1499... (recurring) is the same as 2.15

23.5 Upper bounds and lower bounds

All these numbers round down to 3.1 cm correct to 1 decimal place:

3.11 cm, 3.136 cm, 3.1475 cm, 3.14 cm, 3.149 cm

A number is an upper bound of 3.1 cm if it is greater than or equal to all the numbers which round down to 3.1 cm. So upper bounds of 3.1 cm include the measurements

3.2 cm, 3.16 cm, 3.155 cm, 3.152 cm, 3.151 cm and 3.15 cm

They are all greater than any number that rounds down to 3.1 cm.

Because 3.15 cm is the **smallest** measurement in this list, it is called the **least upper bound** of 3.1 cm.

Using similar arguments, the measurement 3.05 cm is the **greatest lower bound** of 3.1 cm.

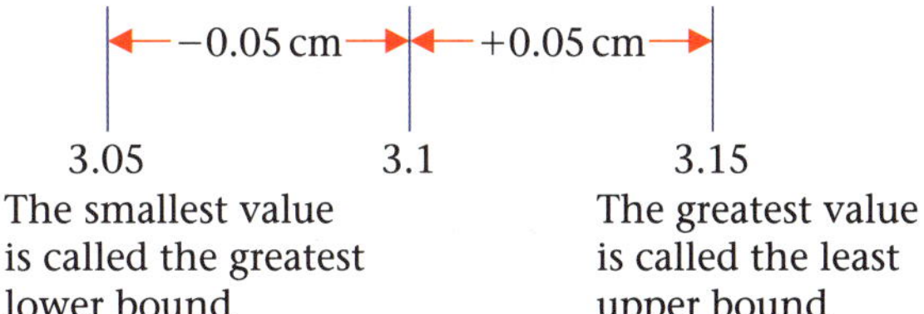
−0.05 cm
+0.05 cm
3.05
3.1
3.15
The smallest value is called the greatest lower bound
The greatest value is called the least upper bound

The **greatest lower bound** and the **least upper bound** are the minimum and maximum possible values of a measurement or calculation.

Sometimes these are called simply the **upper bound** and the **lower bound**.

Exercise 23D

In questions **1–7** write down the lower bound and the upper bound for each measurement, to the given degree of accuracy.

1 To the nearest unit: 4, 14, 104, 10, 100

2 To the nearest 10: 30, 50, 180, 3020, 10, 100

3 To 1 decimal place: 4.7, 2.9, 13.6, 0.3, 157.5, 10.0, 100.0

4 To 2 significant figures: 37, 50, 180, 3.2, 9.5, 9400, 10, 100

5 To the nearest 0.5 unit: 4.5, 7.5, 16.5, 3.0, 15.5, 10, 100

6 To the nearest 0.2 unit: 3.4, 3.2, 4.0, 9.4, 12.2, 24.6, 10.0, 100.0

7 To the nearest quarter unit: 3.75, 3.5, 4.25, 6.0, 15.5, 10.0, 100.0

8 Three students, James, Sunita and Sara, all try to find the size of their classroom.

(a) James estimates the lengths of the walls to be 7 m and 6 m to the nearest metre. Write the least upper bound and the greatest lower bound for the lengths of the classroom walls.

(b) Sunita measures the lengths of the classroom walls with her ruler. She writes '730 cm and 590 cm correct to 2 significant figures'. Write the least upper bound and the greatest lower bound for the lengths of the classroom walls.

(c) Sara measures the walls with a tape measure and obtains the lengths 7.32 m and 5.94 m correct to 2 decimal places. Write the least upper bound and the greatest lower bound for the lengths of the classroom walls.

(d) Explain whether the students' measurements are consistent.

9 The lap record for a racing circuit is 74.36 seconds correct to the nearest $\frac{1}{100}$ of a second.

(a) Write down the upper bound and the lower bound for the lap record.

(b) A racing driver has a recorded lap time of 74.357 seconds. Explain whether this is a new record.

23.6 Calculations involving upper and lower bounds – addition and multiplication

When two (or more) measurements are used in a calculation, the degree of accuracy of the measurements affects the degree of accuracy of the calculated result.

Example 12

Mr Robinson's garden is a rectangle with sides measured as 3.2 m and 5.9 m, both correct to 1 d.p. Calculate the greatest lower bound and the least upper bound for the area of the rectangle.

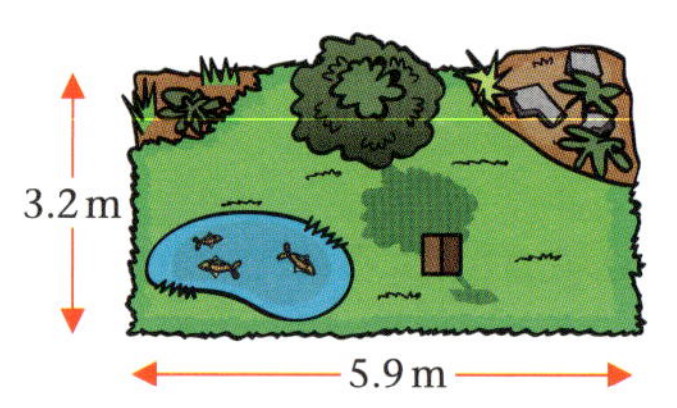

The largest area is found from the longest possible sides:

$$3.25 \times 5.95 = 19.3375\ \text{m}^2$$

The smallest area is found from the shortest possible sides:

$$3.15 \times 5.85 = 18.4275\ \text{m}^2$$

In addition and multiplication calculations use

- the two lower bounds to obtain the lower bound of the result
- the two upper bounds to obtain the upper bound of the result.

Exercise 23E

Using the upper and lower bounds for these measurements, find the upper and lower bounds for these quantities. The degree of accuracy of each measurement is given.

1 The area of a rectangle with sides 6 cm and 8 cm, both measured to the nearest centimetre.

2 The perimeter of a rectangle with sides 6 cm and 8 cm, both measured to the nearest centimetre.

3 The area of a square with side 7.5 cm measured to 2 s.f.

4 The perimeter of a square with side 7.5 cm measured to 2 s.f.

5 The area of a circle with radius 3 cm measured to 1 s.f.

6 The circumference of a circle with radius 0.34 m measured to 2 d.p.

7 The area of a circle with radius 41 mm measured to 2 s.f.

8 The area of a triangle with base length 8 cm and perpendicular height 6 cm, both measured to the nearest centimetre.

9 The area of a triangle with base length 8.0 cm and perpendicular height 6.0 cm, both measured to 2 s.f.

10 The area of a triangle with base length 18 cm and perpendicular height 16 cm, both measured to the nearest 2 cm.

11 The area of a rectangle with sides 3.75 cm and 1.5 cm, both measured to the nearest 0.25 cm.

12 The circumference of a circle with radius 3.5 cm measured to the nearest 0.5 cm.

13 The volume of a sphere with radius

(a) 15 cm measured to the nearest 5 cm

(b) 15 cm measured to 2 s.f.

(c) 15.0 cm measured to 1 d.p.

23.7 Calculations involving upper and lower bounds – subtraction and division

The upper bound of the calculation results from a calculation using one upper bound and one lower bound.

Example 13

A piece of metal 32 cm long is cut from a 100 cm length. Both the measurements are correct to the nearest centimetre.
Find the least upper and greatest lower bounds of the length of the remaining piece.

100 cm lies between 99.5 cm and 100.5 cm
32 cm lies between 31.5 cm and 32.5 cm

The least upper bound for the remaining piece
$= 100.5 - 31.5 = 69$ cm

The greatest lower bound for the remaining piece
$= 99.5 - 32.5 = 67$ cm

If in doubt, do these four calculations:
$100.5 - 31.5 = 69$ (circled)
$100.5 - 32.5 = 68$
$99.5 - 31.5 = 68$
$99.5 - 32.5 = 67$ (circled)

Example 14

The maximum and minimum temperatures, to the nearest °C, at Atlanta one day in 1993 were 27 °C and 8 °C, respectively. Calculate the range of temperatures.

27 °C represents a temperature between 26.5 °C and 27.5 °C
8 °C represents a temperature between 7.5 °C and 8.5 °C

Least upper bound of the range = 27.5 − 7.5 = 20 °C

Greatest lower bound of the range = 26.5 − 8.5 = 18 °C

So the range of temperatures could be any value between 18 °C and 20 °C.

You need to think carefully how to combine the correct pair of initial bounds to find the upper and lower bounds of the result.

If you are in any doubt, do the calculation with the four different pairs of upper and lower bounds. Then choose the largest and the smallest values for the bounds.

Exercise 23F

1 A bar measures 44.8 cm long to 3 s.f. It is heated and expands to 45.7 cm. Calculate the upper bound and the lower bound of the expansion.

2 Two recordings of the same piece of music are measured, correct to the nearest minute, to be 34 minutes and 37 minutes. Calculate the least upper bound and the greatest lower bound for the difference in the times of the two recordings.

3 Calculate the least upper bound and the greatest lower bound for the difference in length of two pieces of paper. One measures 110 cm and the other 95 cm, both correct to 2 s.f.

4 Jeremy's time for a 100 m race is 14.7 seconds to the nearest 0.1 second. Calculate the upper bound and the lower bound of Jeremy's average speed in metres per second for the race

(a) assuming that the distance was accurately measured

(b) assuming that the distance was measured correct to the nearest metre.

5 Jennifer starts the day with a full tank of petrol. At the end of the day she has travelled 165 miles (correct to the nearest 5 miles). She fills the tank with 18 litres of petrol (correct to the nearest litre). Calculate the upper bound and the lower bound of the petrol consumption of Jennifer's car in

(a) miles per litre

(b) miles per gallon.

4.54 litres = 1 gallon

6 In a triangle ABC, angles A and B have been measured to be 35° and 72°, respectively. Length BC is 15 cm. All the measurements are correct to 2 s.f. Use the sine rule to calculate the upper bound and the lower bound of the length AC.

For more about the sine rule see Section 21.2.

7 A ball has mass 130 g and volume 40 cm^3, both correct to the nearest 10 units. Calculate the least upper bound and the greatest lower bound of the density of the ball.

$$\text{Density} = \frac{\text{mass}}{\text{volume}}$$

8 Triangle DEF has sides of length 6 cm, 7 cm and 8 cm, all correct to the nearest centimetre. Use the cosine rule to calculate the upper bound and the lower bound of the smallest angle in the triangle.

For more about the cosine rule see Section 21.3.

Mixed exercise 23

1 Convert the following fractions to decimals and indicate which of the decimals are terminating and which are recurring.

(a) $\frac{7}{8}$ (b) $\frac{7}{9}$ (c) $\frac{7}{10}$ (d) $\frac{7}{11}$ (e) $\frac{7}{12}$ (f) $\frac{7}{13}$

2 Find a fraction equivalent to these decimal numbers:

(a) 13.747474... (b) 6.753213213 21...

3 Simplify each of the following:

(a) $\frac{1}{\sqrt{5}}$ (b) $\frac{5}{\sqrt{7}}$ (c) $\frac{1}{\sqrt{29}}$

(d) $\frac{\sqrt{81}}{\sqrt{9}}$ (e) $\frac{\sqrt{48}}{\sqrt{2}}$ (f) $\frac{\sqrt{64}}{\sqrt{8}}$

4 Write the least upper bound and the greatest lower bound for

(a) 250 000 miles (correct to 2 s.f.)

(b) 6×10^6 cm (correct to 1 s.f.).

5 Explain the difference between these three lengths:

4 cm, 4.0 cm and 4.00 cm

6 Find the least upper bound and the greatest lower bound of the shaded area. The two circles have radii of 5 cm and 3 cm, both correct to 1 s.f.

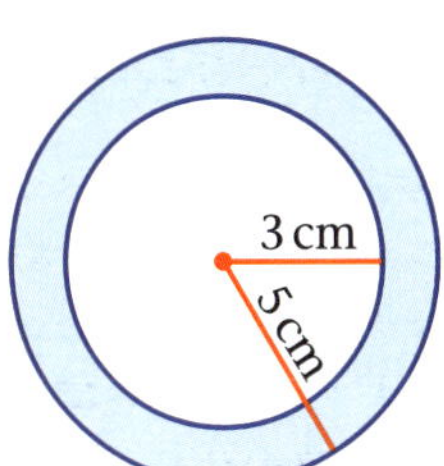

7 A cube has volume 55 mm^3 correct to the nearest mm^3. Calculate the least upper bound and the greatest lower bound of the length of a side of the cube.

8 (a) Find the value of $16^{\frac{1}{2}}$

(b) Given that $40 = k\sqrt{10}$, find the value of k.

(c) A large rectangular piece of card is $(\sqrt{5} + \sqrt{20})$ cm long and $\sqrt{8}$ cm wide.

A small rectangle $\sqrt{2}$ cm long and $\sqrt{5}$ cm wide is cut out of the piece of card.

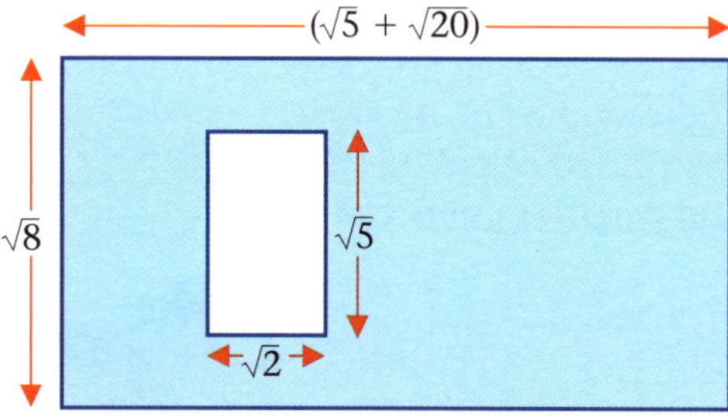

Express the area of the card that is left as a percentage of the area of the large rectangle. [E]

9 Elliot did an experiment to find the value of g m/s^2, the acceleration due to gravity.
He measured the time, T seconds, that a block took to slide L m down a smooth slope of angle $x°$.

He then used the formula $g = \dfrac{2L}{T^2 \sin x°}$ to calculate an estimate for g.

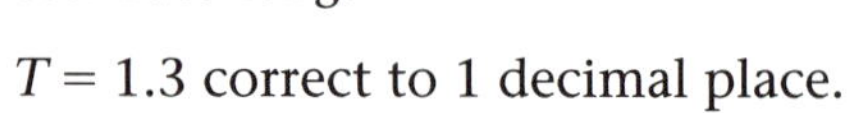

$T = 1.3$ correct to 1 decimal place.
$L = 4.50$ correct to 2 decimal places.
$x = 30$ correct to the nearest integer.

(a) Calculate the lower bound and the upper bound for the value of g. Give your answers correct to 3 decimal places.

(b) Use your answers to part (a) to write down the value of g to a suitable degree of accuracy. Explain your reasoning.

Summary of key points

1 A fraction is equivalent to a **terminating decimal** if the denominator is a factor of 10^n for some integer n.

2 Any terminating decimal with n decimal places can be converted into a fraction by multiplying the decimal by 10^n and dividing the result by 10^n.

3 A **recurring decimal** has a repeating pattern in its digits.

4 A number written exactly using square roots is called a **surd**.
For example, $\sqrt{3}$ and $2 - \sqrt{5}$ are in surd form.

5 $\sqrt{a \times b} = \sqrt{a} \times \sqrt{b}$

6 $\sqrt{\frac{a}{b}} = \frac{\sqrt{a}}{\sqrt{b}}$

7 Simplified surds should never have a square root in the denominator.

8 The **greatest lower bound** and the **least upper bound** are the minimum and maximum possible values of a measurement or calculation.

9 In addition and multiplication calculations use

- the two lower bounds to obtain the lower bound of the result
- the two upper bounds to obtain the upper bound of the result.

24 Probability

Probability is about calculating or estimating what might happen in the future.

In this chapter you will find probabilities by considering all possible outcomes of an event, and estimate probabilities from experimental data.

24.1 Finding probabilities

The **probability** of an event is expressed as a number from 0 to 1 inclusive.

That number can be expressed as a fraction, a decimal or a percentage. The larger the number, the greater the *likelihood* of the event happening.

If an event is **impossible** its probability is 0.

If an event is **certain** its probability is 1.

You can calculate the probability of events for simple activities such as tossing coins and rolling dice.

When there are n equally likely possible outcomes, the probability of each outcome $\frac{1}{n}$

Example 1

The numbers 1 to 10 are written on pieces of card which are then placed face downwards on a table. Ian picks up one of the cards at random. Calculate the probability that Ian's card will be

(a) a multiple of 3 (b) an even number (c) a prime number.

The key word **random** indicates that each of the possible outcomes is equally likely.

Number	1	2	3	4	5	6	7	8	9	10
Multiple of 3	✗	✗	✓	✗	✗	✓	✗	✗	✓	✗
Even	✗	✓	✗	✓	✗	✓	✗	✓	✗	✓
Prime	✗	✓	✓	✗	✓	✗	✓	✗	✗	✗

(a) Three of the 10 numbers are multiples of 3. The probability of Ian selecting one of these is $\frac{3}{10}$ (or 0.3 or 30%).

(b) Five of the 10 numbers are even, so the probability of Ian choosing one of these is $\frac{5}{10}$ (or $\frac{1}{2}$ or 0.5 or 50%).

(c) Four of the 10 numbers are prime, so the probability of Ian choosing one of these is $\frac{4}{10}$ (or $\frac{2}{5}$ or 0.4 or 40%).

It is often worth drawing a rough diagram of all the possible outcomes.

If all the outcomes are equally likely, the probability of an event can be calculated using the formula:

It may help your understanding if you read a probability like $\frac{3}{4}$ (three quarters) as 'three out of four possibilities'.

$$\text{P(event)} = \frac{\text{the number of ways the event can occur}}{\text{the total number of possible outcomes}}$$

Example 2

Trevor and Kevin both answer this question:

There are eight snooker balls in a bag. Six of them are red, one is green and the other is yellow. Calculate the probability that a ball taken at random from the bag will be red.

Trevor's answer

There are 3 possible outcomes:
red, green and yellow
$P(\text{red}) = \frac{6}{3} = 2$

Kevin's answer

There are $6 + 1 + 1 = 8$ outcomes
$P(\text{red}) = \frac{6}{8} = \frac{3}{4}$

P(red) means 'the probability of selecting a red ball'. You should use this shorthand for expressing probabilities.

Who is correct? Explain your reasoning.

Kevin is correct. He realised that each of the snooker balls is a possible outcome and that altogether there are 8 balls and hence 8 possible outcomes. He could have left his answer as $\frac{6}{8}$ because the question did not ask him to cancel his answer. Equally correct answers are $\frac{3}{4}$, 0.75 and 75%.

Trevor made the common mistake of just counting the three possible colours. He was correct when he used the fact that there are 6 red balls as *the number of ways the event can occur*. He should have realised from his answer greater than 1 that he had made a mistake, because a probability is always between 0 and 1.

Exercise 24A

1 Nine playing cards are numbered 2 to 10. A card is selected from them at random. Calculate the probability that the card will be

(a) an odd number

(b) a multiple of 4.

2 Five strawberry, two orange and three blackcurrant flavoured sweets are placed in a box. One sweet is taken at random from the box. Calculate the probability that the sweet will be

(a) blackcurrant flavoured

(b) not orange flavoured.

3 A normal dice is rolled. Calculate the probability that the number on the uppermost face when it stops rolling will be

(a) 5 (b) odd (c) prime (d) not 6

A normal dice is a cube. It is unbiased and has the numbers 1 to 6 on it. The numbers on opposite faces add up to 7.

4 A spinner is made from a regular octagon. It is labelled with three As, two Bs and three Cs. Each of the sides is equally likely to be resting on the table when it stops spinning. Calculate

(a) P(A resting on the table)

(b) P(B resting on the table)

(c) P(not C resting on the table).

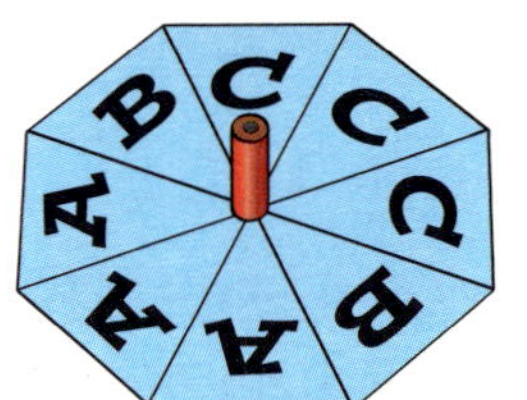

5 A company is trying to prove that most cats prefer chicken flavoured cat food. Unfortunately, Alfred the cat doesn't know this and selects his food at random. The company puts out 10 saucers of rabbit, 6 saucers of sardine and only 4 saucers of chicken flavoured food. Calculate

(a) P(Alfred selects sardine flavoured food)

(b) P(Alfred selects rabbit flavoured flood)

(c) P(Alfred selects sardine or rabbit flavoured food)

(d) P(Alfred does not select chicken flavoured food).

(e) The answer to part (c) can be calculated from the answers to parts (a) and (b). Explain how.

(f) Explain how the answer to part (d) can be calculated if you are given that:
P(Alfred selects chicken flavoured food) = p

24.2 Mutually exclusive events

If two events cannot occur at the same time they are **mutually exclusive**.

Events A and B are mutually exclusive when
- if A happens then B does not
- if B happens then A does not.

Example 3

A card is selected from a pack of 52 cards. What is the probability that the chosen card is either a 'king' or a '10'?

Choosing a 'king' and choosing a '10' are mutually exclusive events.

$$P(K) = \frac{4}{52}$$

$$P(10) = \frac{4}{52}$$

$$P(K \text{ or } 10) = \frac{4}{52} + \frac{4}{52} = \frac{8}{52}$$

When events A and B are mutually exclusive

$$P(A \text{ or } B) = P(A) + P(B)$$

Example 4

There are five red, three green and two yellow counters in a bag.
A counter is taken at random from the bag.
Calculate the probability that the counter will be

(a) red (b) green (c) yellow (d) red or green (e) not yellow.

(a) P(red) = $\frac{5}{10}$ = 0.5 (b) P(green) = $\frac{3}{10}$ = 0.3 (c) P(yellow) = $\frac{2}{10}$ = 0.2

(d) A counter cannot be both red and green. So the events 'selecting a red' and 'selecting a green' are **mutually exclusive**.

So P(red or green) = P(red) + P(green) = 0.5 + 0.3 = 0.8

(e) The only possible colours which can occur are red, green and yellow. The sum of their probabilities is 1. You are *certain* to get a red, a green or a yellow counter.

P(red) + P(green) + P(yellow) = 1

so P(red) + P(green) = 1 − P(yellow)

so P(red or green) = 1 − P(yellow)

If a counter selected is not yellow, it must be red or green.

So P(not yellow) = 1 − P(yellow)
= 1 − 0.2
= 0.8

An obvious case of mutually exclusive events is 'selecting A' and 'not selecting A'. In this situation there is a general statement that is often a useful short cut:

Event A and event 'not A' are mutually exclusive and cover all possibilities and so P(not A) = 1 − P(A)

24.3 Lists and tables

You can make lists or tables to work out all the possibilities in experiments where two or more objects are used to generate outcomes.

Example 5

Three coins are tossed. Calculate the probability of getting

(a) two heads and one tail (b) at least one head.

Consider the three coins separately. Think of them as the first, second and third coins even if they are tossed simultaneously. Draw up a list of possible outcomes:

First coin	H	H	H	H	T	T	T	T
Second coin	H	H	T	T	H	H	T	T
Third coin	H	T	H	T	H	T	H	T

Each of the 3 coins can land in 2 different ways – head or tail. So to check that you have found all the possible outcomes use the fact that there should be 2^3 outcomes, which is 8. Write down the 8 different possibilities systematically. This helps to avoid missing any or repeating some of them.

(a) Three of the eight possible outcomes have 2 heads and 1 tail.

So P(2H and 1T) = $\frac{3}{8}$

(b) P(at least one head) = 1 − P(no heads)
= 1 − $\frac{1}{8}$ = $\frac{7}{8}$

You can see from the list that 7 of the 8 possible outcomes have at least one head.

When there are many outcomes, it may be more efficient to draw a table.

Example 6

Two normal dice are rolled and the numbers on the tops are added together. Calculate the probability that the sum will be

(a) 10 (b) a multiple of 5 (c) not 7

There are 2 dice and 6 ways each can land. The total number of possibilities is $6^2 = 36$.

Draw a sample space diagram for the sums.
There are 36 different ways that the two dice can land.

(a) 10 can occur in 3 ways so $P(10) = \frac{3}{36}$

(b) 5 can occur in 4 ways so $P(5) = \frac{4}{36}$

$P(\text{multiple of } 5) = P(10) + P(5)$

$= \frac{4}{36} + \frac{3}{36} = \frac{7}{36}$

(c) 7 can occur in 6 ways so $P(7) = \frac{6}{36}$

$P(\text{not } 7) = 1 - P(7)$

$= 1 - \frac{6}{36} = \frac{30}{36}$

Number on the first dice

Number on the second dice

+	1	2	3	4	5	6
1	2	3	4	5	6	7
2	3	4	5	6	7	8
3	4	5	6	7	8	9
4	5	6	7	8	9	10
5	6	7	8	9	10	11
6	7	8	9	10	11	12

Example 7

Arif and Moira are working together. Arif has a spinner which has an equal chance of landing on 1, 2, 3, 4 or 5. Moira has a normal dice. Arif spins his spinner and Moira rolls her dice. Calculate the probability that the two numbers they generate will:

(a) have an odd sum

(b) have a product which is a multiple of 3

(c) be consecutive numbers.

The total number of possibilities is the product of the possibilities on each piece of equipment. So the total number of possibilities is $5 \times 6 = 30$.

Draw a sample space diagram and

- put 'o' in every square where the sum of the two scores is an odd number
- put 't' in every square where the product of the two scores is a multiple of 3
- put 'c' in every square where the two scores are consecutive numbers.

Dice score

Spinner score

	1	2	3	4	5	6
1		o c	t	o		o t
2	o c		otc		o	t
3	t	otc	t	otc	t	o t
4	o		otc		o c	t
5		o	t	o c		otc

(a) There are 15 squares on the sample space diagram labelled 'o'.

$P(\text{odd sum}) = \frac{15}{30}$

(b) There are 14 squares labelled 't'.

$P(\text{product is a multiple of } 3) = \frac{14}{30}$

(c) There are 9 squares labelled 'c'.

$P(\text{consecutive numbers}) = \frac{9}{30}$

Do not cancel fractions in probability questions unless you are asked to. Adding or subtracting probabilities is easier with uncancelled fractions which have the same denominator.

Exercise 24B

1 A game is played using these two boards. In one 'go' a player spins both arrows. The sum of the numbers where the two arrows point is the score for the 'go'. In the diagram the score is 9.

(a) Copy and complete the table showing all the possible scores for one 'go'.

+	1	3	5	7
2				
4				
6				
8	9			

(b) Write the probability that a player will score 11 in one 'go'. [E]

2 In a game, two normal dice, one red and the other blue, are thrown simultaneously. A score is found by adding together the numbers on the faces which finish uppermost.
Four players, Adam, Bethan, Christos and Dean, decide that Adam will win if the red dice shows 6, Bethan will win if the score is 5 or 6, Christos will win if the score is 2 or 3 or 4, and that Dean will win otherwise.
Find the probability, expressed as a fraction, that the game will be won by

(a) Adam (b) Bethan (c) Christos (d) Dean. [E]

3 Four coins are tossed simultaneously. List all the possible ways in which the coins can land with heads or tails uppermost.
Calculate the probability that

(a) four heads will occur

(b) an equal number of heads and tails will occur

(c) at least one coin will land tail uppermost.

4 A bag contains one red and one white snooker ball. A second bag contains one brown, one green and one yellow ball. A third bag contains one blue, one pink and one black ball.
List all the possible sets of three balls which can arise when one ball is selected from each bag at random.
Calculate the probability that the three balls selected will include the red and the black ball.

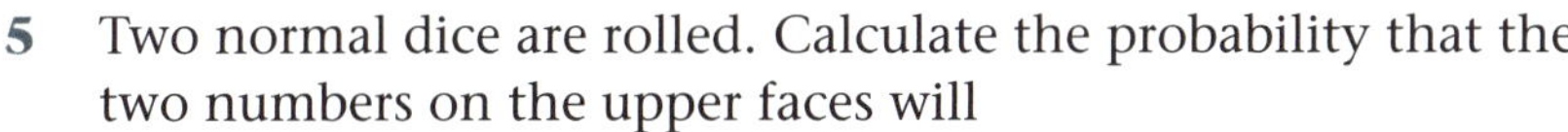

5 Two normal dice are rolled. Calculate the probability that the two numbers on the upper faces will

(a) sum to a prime number

(b) have an odd difference

(c) have an even product

(d) have one which is a factor of the other.

6 A fair octahedral dice with the numbers 1 to 8 on its faces is rolled at the same time as a normal dice. The number on the upper face of the normal dice is used as the x-coordinate and the number from the upper face of the octahedral dice is used as the y-coordinate of a point on a grid. Calculate the probability that when the two dice are rolled the point generated will lie on the line:

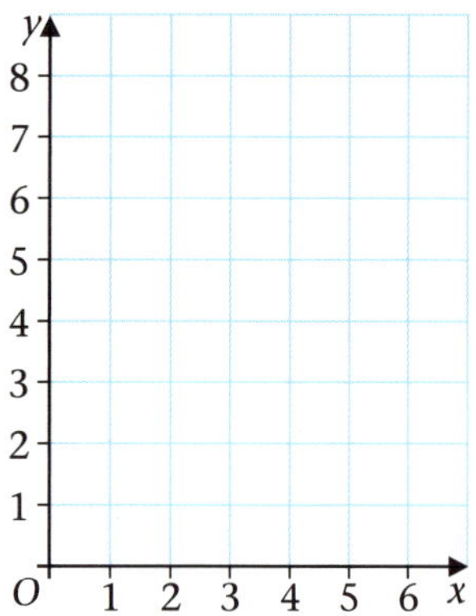

(a) $x = 3$ (b) $y = 5$ (c) $y = 2x$

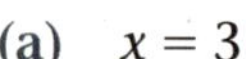

(d) $x + y = 8$ (e) $y = x + 2$ (f) $y + 2x = 7$

24.4 Relative frequency

So far you have calculated probabilities when all possible outcomes are equally likely. Sometimes you can only estimate probabilities based on experimental results.

Hannah and Ruth want to estimate the probability of a drawing pin landing point up.

They carry out an experiment which consists of throwing the drawing pin into the air 50 times.

Result	Tally	Frequency
Point up	𝍸 𝍸 𝍸 |||	18
Point not up	𝍸 𝍸 𝍸 𝍸 𝍸 𝍸 ||	32

They calculate an estimate for the probability using

$$\text{relative frequency} = \frac{\text{number of times event occurs}}{\text{total number of trials}}$$

The pin lands point up 18 times out of 50. The **relative frequency** of the pin landing point up is $\frac{18}{50}$.

To impove the estimate they should carry out more trials or combine their results with those of their classmates who have also done the experiment.

To estimate a probability:

- carry out a large number of trials
- calculate the relative frequency.

The larger the number of trials, the closer the relative frequency is to the probability.

Sometimes you can estimate probability by experiment and then compare with the theoretical probability.

Activity – Playing cards

Select a card from a normal pack. Record whether it is odd, even, picture card or ace. Replace the card in the pack.

Repeat 99 times (100 times in total).

From your experimental data estimate the probability of picking each type of card. Compare these estimates with the theoretical probabilities.

Example 8

Some plastic trapezia like the one on the right are turned into spinners. Ten pairs of students each spin their spinner 20 times. They find that the relative frequencies of the 6 cm side stopping on the table are

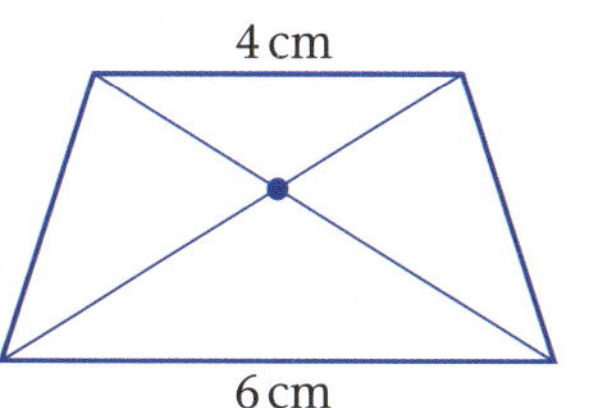

$\frac{7}{20}$ $\frac{4}{20}$ $\frac{11}{20}$ $\frac{8}{20}$ $\frac{5}{20}$ $\frac{8}{20}$ $\frac{9}{20}$ $\frac{7}{20}$ $\frac{10}{20}$ $\frac{9}{20}$

Calculate the relative frequency when the trials are combined.

Total number of trials = $10 \times 20 = 200$

Number of trials where event occurs = sum of numerators

= 78

Relative frequency = $\frac{78}{200} = \frac{39}{100} \approx \frac{8}{20}$

Two pairs actually got this result but some other pairs got results that were quite different from this. In real experiments, this does happen.

Exercise 24C

1 Roll an eraser and work out the relative frequency of it finishing in each of its possible positions after 100 trials.

2 Roll an object like a shoe or a small toy and work out the relative frequencies of it ending up in different positions. Estimate the probability of each of the possibilities and combine your results with other students' results to refine your estimates.

24.5 Estimating from experience

In some cases, even carrying out trials is impossible and so probabilities have to be estimated and justified using a reasonable argument.

Example 9

Hamwick rugby team have won each of their last six home games by at least 20 points.
St Debes have lost their last four away games quite heavily.
If St Debes play at Hamwick it is much more likely that Hamwick will win than that St Debes will. An estimate of Hamwick's probability of winning of 80% or more would be reasonable.

Challenge
Think of some more examples like this one.

24.6 Independent events

James tosses a coin and Sarah rolls a dice. James knows that the probability of his coin landing 'heads' is $\frac{1}{2}$.

The probability of Sarah's dice showing a 6 is $\frac{1}{6}$.

What is the probability of getting a head and a 6?

The sample space diagram shows that there are 12 possible outcomes.

$P(\text{H and } 6) = \frac{1}{12}$

		Dice					
		1	2	3	4	5	6
Coin	H						✓
	T						

Whether or not the coin lands 'heads' has no effect on whether the dice shows a 6 or any other score. The two events, getting a head and scoring a 6, are **independent**.

$P(\text{H and } 6) = P(\text{H}) \times P(6)$

Notice that
$P(\text{H}) = \frac{1}{2}$, $P(6) = \frac{1}{6}$ $P(\text{H and } 6) = \frac{1}{2} \times \frac{1}{6} = \frac{1}{12}$

Two events are **independent** when one does not affect the outcome of the other.

If events A and B are independent
$P(\text{A and B}) = P(\text{A}) \times P(\text{B})$

Worked examination question

Some college students have to take three examination papers, one in English, one in maths and one in science.
P(passing English) = 0.7, P(passing maths) = 0.5 and P(passing science) = 0.8
Assume these events are independent. Calculate the probability that a student will

(a) pass all three papers (b) fail all three papers.

(a) P(passing all 3) = $0.7 \times 0.5 \times 0.8 = 0.28$

(b) P(failing all 3) = $0.3 \times 0.5 \times 0.2 = 0.03$

A, B and C are independent events, so P(A and B and C) = P(A) × P(B) × P(C)

Exercise 24D

1 When Nina and Zoe go to the shop the probability of Nina choosing a chocolate bar is $\frac{1}{3}$ and of choosing a toffee bar is $\frac{1}{5}$. The probability of Zoe choosing a chocolate bar is $\frac{1}{4}$ and of choosing a toffee bar is $\frac{1}{2}$. The girls choose independently of each other. Calculate the probability of

(a) both choosing chocolate bars
(b) both choosing toffee bars
(c) one choosing a chocolate and the other choosing a toffee bar.

2 There are three tame mice, Roger, Susan and Timmy. They can choose to eat at five troughs (A, B, C, D and E) independently and at random.

(a) What is the probability that Roger will eat from trough A?
(b) Find the probability that Susan and Timmy will both eat (i) at trough A (ii) at the same trough. [E]

24.7 Probability trees

Tree diagrams can be used to illustrate possible outcomes for two or more independent events.

Example 10

Newton High School students can choose to wear or not wear a sweatshirt as part of the uniform. The probability that Ali will choose to wear a sweatshirt is $\frac{1}{3}$. The probability that Bethan will wear one is $\frac{2}{5}$ and the probability that Chris will wear one is $\frac{1}{2}$. Calculate the probability that:

(a) all three wear a sweatshirt
(b) exactly two of them wear a sweatshirt
(c) at least two of them wear a sweatshirt.

Each student has 2 choices: to wear or not to wear a sweatshirt. So there are $2^3 = 2 \times 2 \times 2$ or 8 paths.

(a) The path to A includes the probabilities of each student wearing a sweatshirt.

$$\text{P(all wear sweatshirt)} = \frac{1}{3} \times \frac{2}{5} \times \frac{1}{2}$$
$$= \frac{2}{30}$$

Their choices are independent so multiply the probabilities along the branches.

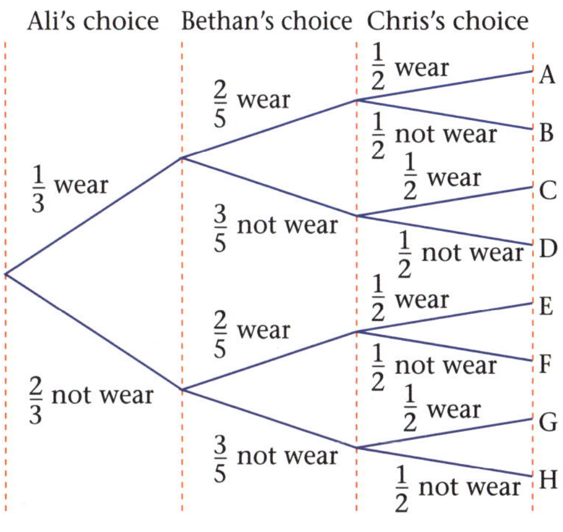

(b) Paths B, C and E all involve exactly two wearing sweatshirts.

P(exactly 2 wear sweatshirts)

$$= (\tfrac{1}{3} \times \tfrac{2}{5} \times \tfrac{1}{2}) + (\tfrac{1}{3} \times \tfrac{3}{5} \times \tfrac{1}{2}) + (\tfrac{2}{3} \times \tfrac{2}{5} \times \tfrac{1}{2})$$
$$= \frac{2}{30} + \frac{3}{30} + \frac{4}{30}$$
$$= \frac{9}{30}$$

The events A to H are mutually exclusive and add to 1.
So P(B or C or E)
= P(B) + P(C) + P(E)

(c) P(at least 2) = P(all 3 or exactly 2)

$$= \frac{2}{30} + \frac{9}{30}$$
$$= \frac{11}{30}$$

It does not matter which choice is put first in the tree because the probabilities are multiplied by each other and multiplication is a commutative operation.

Exercise 24E

1 Rick, Sher and Tessa always wear a coloured T-shirt when they go to the Youth Club. Amongst other colours they each have one, and only one, red T-shirt. They each pick a T-shirt at random from the pile in their drawer. Including the red one, there are three T-shirts in Rick's drawer, four in Sher's and five in Tessa's. Calculate the probability that:

(a) they will all go to the Youth Club in a red T-shirt
(b) none of them will go in a red T-shirt
(c) exactly two of them will go in a red T-shirt
(d) at least two of them will go in a red T-shirt.

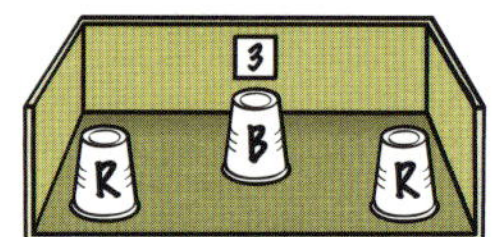

2 A game at a school fair involves choosing a plastic cup from each of three boxes. The plastic cups each cover a coloured cube which the player cannot see. The first box contains 5 cups, covering 3 red and 2 blue cubes. The second box contains 4 cups, covering 3 red and 1 blue cube. The third box contains 3 cups, covering 2 red and 1 blue cube.

Vicky pays 20p for a go. If she selects 3 reds she loses her money. If she gets exactly 1 blue she gets 10p back. If she uncovers exactly 2 blue cubes she gets 30p back, and if all three of her choices cover blue cubes she receives 50p back.

Calculate the probability that Vicky will

(a) receive 50p

(b) receive 30p

(c) have less money at the end of the game than she had before paying her 20p.

Mixed exercise 24

1 A 50p, a 20p, a 10p and a 2p coin are tossed at the same time. List all the possible outcomes. Find the probability of obtaining

(a) exactly two heads (b) more than two heads.

2 One letter is selected at random from the word 'PARALLELOGRAM'. Write down the probability of selecting

(a) a P (b) an L (c) an A or an R.

3 The spinner shown has five equal sectors. How many 3s would you expect in 600 spins?

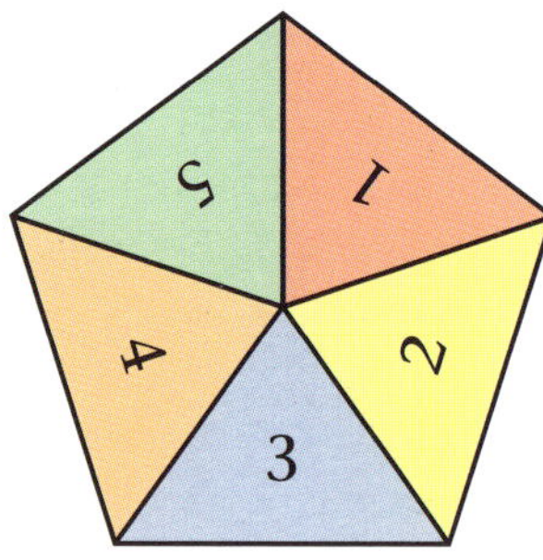

4 One ball is selected from a bag containing eight balls, of which x are black.

(a) Write down, in term of x, the probability of selecting a black ball.

(b) Write down, in terms of x, the probability of not selecting a black ball.

(c) When a further four black balls are added to the bag, the probability of selecting a black ball is doubled. Find x.

5 In an opinion poll some people were asked to state their favourite football team. The results are summarised in the pie chart.

If one person is chosen at random from the sample, find an estimate of the probability that their favourite football team is either Chelsea or Liverpool.

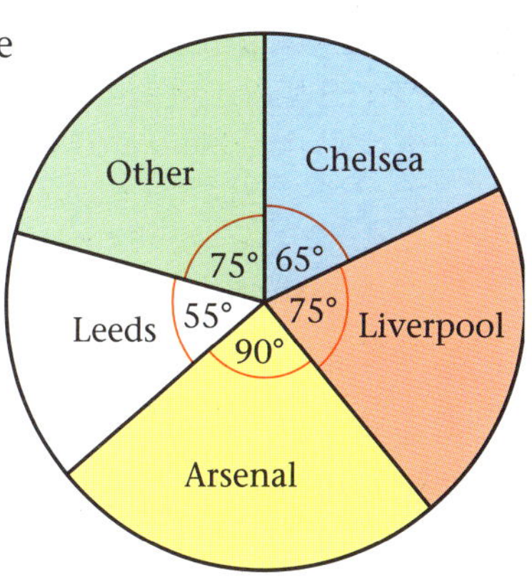

6 These spinners are spun together.

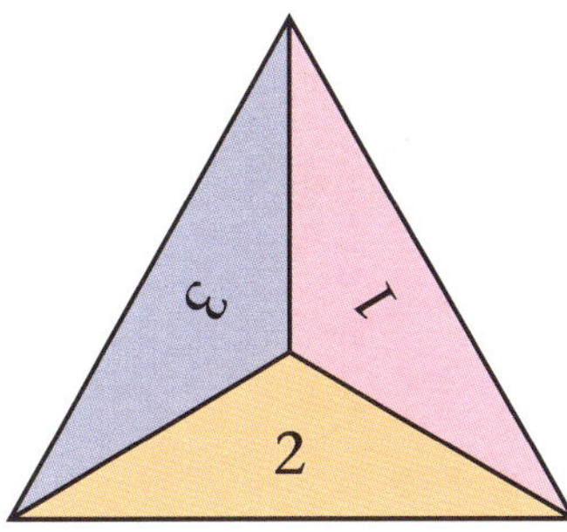

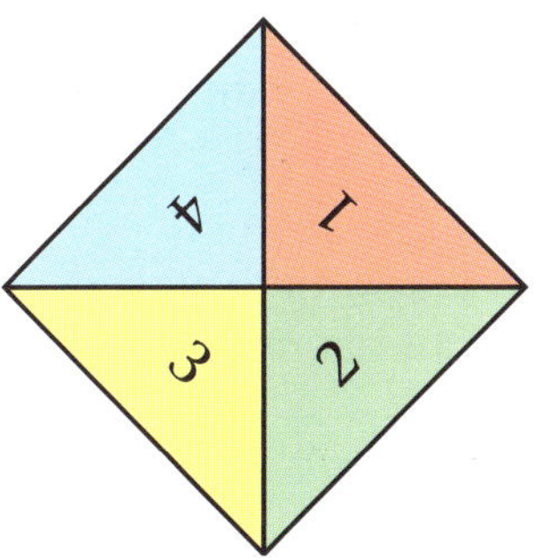

The numbers shown on the spinners are added. Display all the possible outcomes in a suitable way.
Find the probability of obtaining

(a) a total of 5

(b) the same number on both spinners

(c) an even number on one spinner and an odd number on the other spinner.

7 A tetrahedral dice (4 sides, numbered 1 to 4) and a normal dice (6 sides) are thrown at the same time. A 'win' occurs when the number on the tetrahedral dice is greater than or equal to the number on the normal dice. What is the probability of a 'win'?

8 Box A contains three blue and four red balls.
Box B contains two blue and seven red balls.
One ball is selected at random from box A and one ball is selected at random from box B. Find the probability that

(a) both balls are red

(b) both balls are the same colour.

9 A fruit machine has three independent reels and pays out a Jackpot of £50 when three raspberries are obtained. Each reel has 12 pictures. The first reel has four raspberries, the second has three raspberries and the third has two raspberries.
Find the probability of winning the Jackpot.

10 A biased dice is thrown 100 times. The results are shown in the table.

Number on dice	1	2	3	4	5	6
Frequency	14	16	15	12	11	32

Write down an estimate of the probability of throwing a 6 with this dice.

11 Jim is practising his golf. He drives a number of balls at a green. If he hits the green he records 'H', and if he misses the green he records 'M'. Here are his results for the first 17 drives:

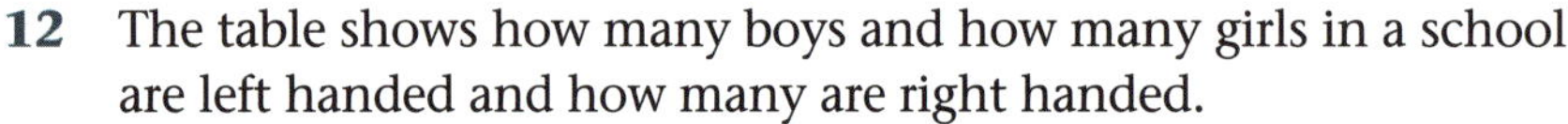
H M M H M H H M M M H H H H H H H

(a) Assuming that his drives are independent, write down an estimate of the probability that the next time he drives a ball he will hit the green.

(b) Is it reasonable to assume that his drives are independent? Give a reason for your answer.

12 The table shows how many boys and how many girls in a school are left handed and how many are right handed.

	Girls	Boys
Left handed	32	28
Right handed	143	137

(a) A student is selected at random from the school.
Find the probability that the student is
(i) a boy
(ii) a left-handed girl

(b) A boy is selected at random from the school.
Find the probability that he is right handed.

13 There are two parts to a driving test, the theory test and the practical test. You must pass the theory test before you take the practical test.
Sethina plans to take her driving test.
The probability that she will pass her theory test is 0.8
The probability that she will pass her practical test is 0.75

(a) Draw a tree diagram to represent this information.

(b) Calculate the probability that Sethina will pass her driving test.

14 The diagram shows a circle drawn inside a square.
A point is chosen at random from inside the square.

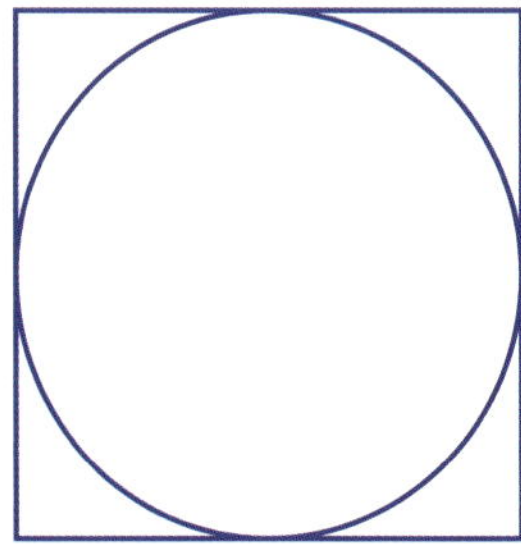

What is the probability that the point lies inside the circle?

Summary of key points

1 The **probability** of an event is expressed as a number from 0 to 1 inclusive.
- If an event is **impossible** its probability is 0.
- If an event is **certain** its probability is 1.

2 When there are n equally likely possible outcomes, the probability of each outcome is $\frac{1}{n}$

3 $\text{P(event)} = \dfrac{\text{the number of ways the event can occur}}{\text{the total number of possible outcomes}}$

4 If two events cannot occur at the same time they are **mutually exclusive**.

5 When events A and B are mutually exclusive

P(A or B) = P(A) + P(B)

6 Event A and event 'not A' are mutually exclusive and cover all possibilities and so

P(not A) = 1 − P(A)

7 $\text{Relative frequency} = \dfrac{\text{number of times event occurs}}{\text{total number of trials}}$

8 Two events are **independent** if one does not affect the outcome of the other.

9 If events A and B are independent

P(A and B) = P(A) × P(B)

25 Transformations of graphs

To draw a graph, you can draw up a table for values of x, plot the points and join them using a smooth curve. The range of values for x is chosen so as to include the main features of the graph.

You will now consider examples where this is not the case. For example, the graph on the right shows five points plotted for the equation $y = x^2 - 9x + 10$ for $-2 \leqslant x \leqslant 2$.

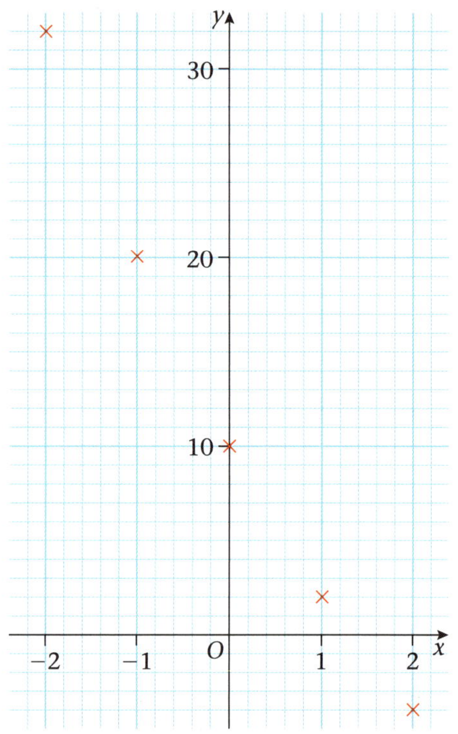

Without plotting any more points, consider what the graph looks like for values of x up to 10.

This chapter shows you how to use your knowledge of the graphs of some basic functions, and to apply suitable transformations (translations, reflections and stretches) to sketch the main features of more complicated graphs without the need to find and plot lots of points.

In previous chapters you have been using graphs with equations:

$$y = x^2,\ y = x^3,\ y = \frac{1}{x}$$

You will be using the graphs of these three equations along with the straight line $y = x$ in many examples during this chapter. For reference these four equations are called 'the basic functions'.

You will need tracing paper for many of the exercises in this chapter.

25.1 Function notation

A **function** is a rule which shows how one set of numbers relates to another set.

You can think of a function, f, as a machine which changes an input x into an output.

input x → f → output $\mathrm{f}(x)$

When the function f is 'square' then, for an input x, the output is x^2 so $\mathrm{f}(x) = x^2$.

$\mathrm{f}(x)$, which denotes the output, is read as 'f of x'.

In this case, for an input of 3 the output is 9. You write $\mathrm{f}(3) = 3^2 = 9$.

input x → square → output x^2

Similarly $\mathrm{f}(-4) = 16$, and $\mathrm{f}(k + 1) = (k + 1)^2 = k^2 + 2k + 1$.

A function f can also be equivalent to a sequence of operations (rules).

For example, $\mathrm{f}(x) = 2x^2 + 1$ is the output from this flow diagram:

input x → square → $\times 2$ → $+ 1$ → $2x^2 + 1$

Example 1

When $f(x) = 2x^2 + 1$, find

(a) $f(3)$ (b) $f(-4)$ (c) $f(0)$ (d) $f(-k)$

(a) Replacing x by 3: $f(3) = 2(3)^2 + 1 = 19$

(b) Replacing x by -4: $f(-4) = 2(-4)^2 + 1 = 33$

(c) Replacing x by 0: $f(0) = 2(0)^2 + 1 = 1$

(d) Replacing x by $-k$: $f(-k) = 2(-k)^2 + 1 = 2k^2 + 1$

Example 2

When $f(x) = x^2$, find

(a) $f(x + 1)$ (b) $f(2x)$ (c) $1 - f(-x)$ (d) $f(-\frac{1}{2}x) + 4$

(a) Replacing x by $x + 1$: $f(x + 1) = (x + 1)^2 = x^2 + 2x + 1$

(b) Replacing x by $2x$: $f(2x) = (2x)^2 = 4x^2$

(c) Replacing x by $-x$: $1 - f(-x) = 1 - (-x)^2 = 1 - x^2$

(d) Replacing x by $(-\frac{1}{2}x)$: $f(-\frac{1}{2}x) + 4 = (-\frac{1}{2}x)^2 + 4 = \frac{x^2}{4} + 4$

Example 3

Given that $f(x) = x^2 + 2$, find the values of x when $f(x) = 11$.

When $f(x) = 11$:

$11 = x^2 + 2$

$9 = x^2$ —— Subtract 2 from both sides

$\pm 3 = x$ —— Take the square root of both sides

The plotted points for the graph of $y = x^2 - 9x + 10$ shown on page 460 came from the table:

x	-2	-1	0	1	2
y	32	20	10	2	-4

$f(-2) = (-2)^2 - 9(-2) + 10$
$= 4 + 18 + 10$
$= 32$

Using function notation, this is the same as the graph $y = f(x)$, where $f(x) = x^2 - 9x + 10$, $f(-2) = 32$, $f(-1) = 20$ and so on.

Example 4

Here is part of the graph of $y = f(x)$, where $f(x) = x^2 + 1$

From the graph, find

(a) the value of (i) $f(0)$ (ii) $f(2)$

(b) the values of x when $f(x) = 2$.

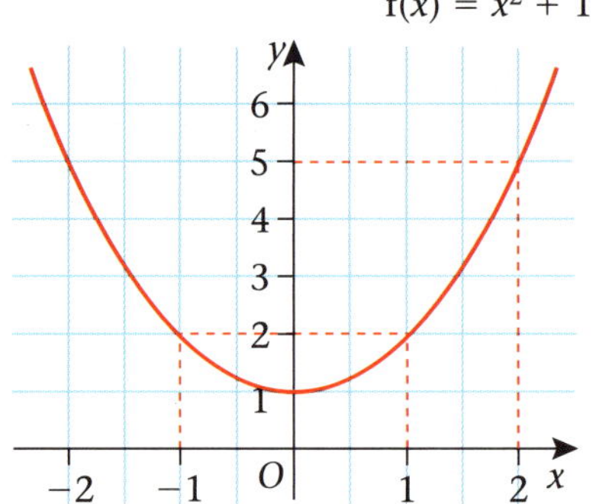

(a) (i) $f(0)$ is the output (y) when $x = 0$.
From the graph, $f(0) = 1$.

(ii) From the graph, $f(2) = 5$.

(b) $f(x) = 2$; we need x when $y = 2$.
From the graph, when $y = 2$, $x = -1$ or $x = 1$.
So when $f(x) = 2$, $x = \pm 1$.

If $f(x)$ is a function then $y = f(x)$ is the equation of the graph of the function.

Exercise 25A

1 When $f(x) = x^2 - 2$, find

(a) $f(2)$ (b) $f(4)$ (c) $f(0)$

(d) $f(-1)$ (e) $f(-3)$ (f) $f(\frac{1}{4})$

2 When $f(x) = x^2$, find

(a) $f(-x)$ (b) $f(3x)$ (c) $f(x + 2)$

(d) $f(x + 1) + 3$ (e) $f\left(-\frac{x}{2} + 1\right) - 4$ (f) $5 - f(2x)$

(g) $f(kx + a) + b$

3 Paul accidentally spilled some ink on his text book. His teacher says that he should have been able to answer the questions without using the equation for $f(x)$. Explain why Paul did not need the equation for $f(x)$. Then answer the question.

Part of the graph of $y = f(x)$,

where $f(x) = x^2 -$ [ink blot] is drawn.

Find

(a) the value of
(i) $f(3)$ (ii) $f(1)$ (iii) $f(0)$ (iv) $f(-1)$

(b) the values of x when $f(x) = 0$.

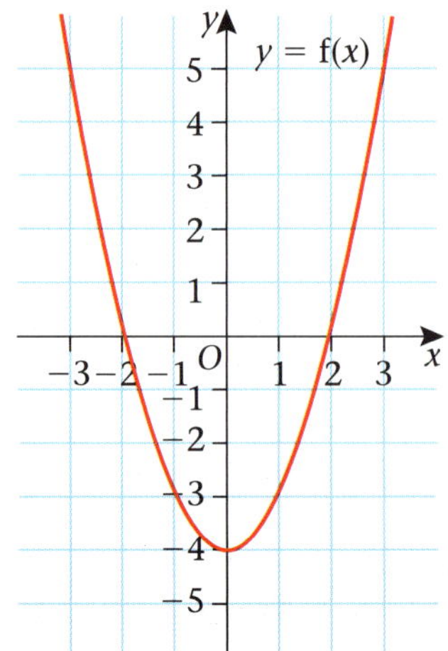

25.2 Applying vertical translations to graphs

Parabolas

The graphs of the parabolas $y = x^2$, $y = x^2 + 8$ and $y = x^2 - 15$ are shown below. Another parabola is also shown.

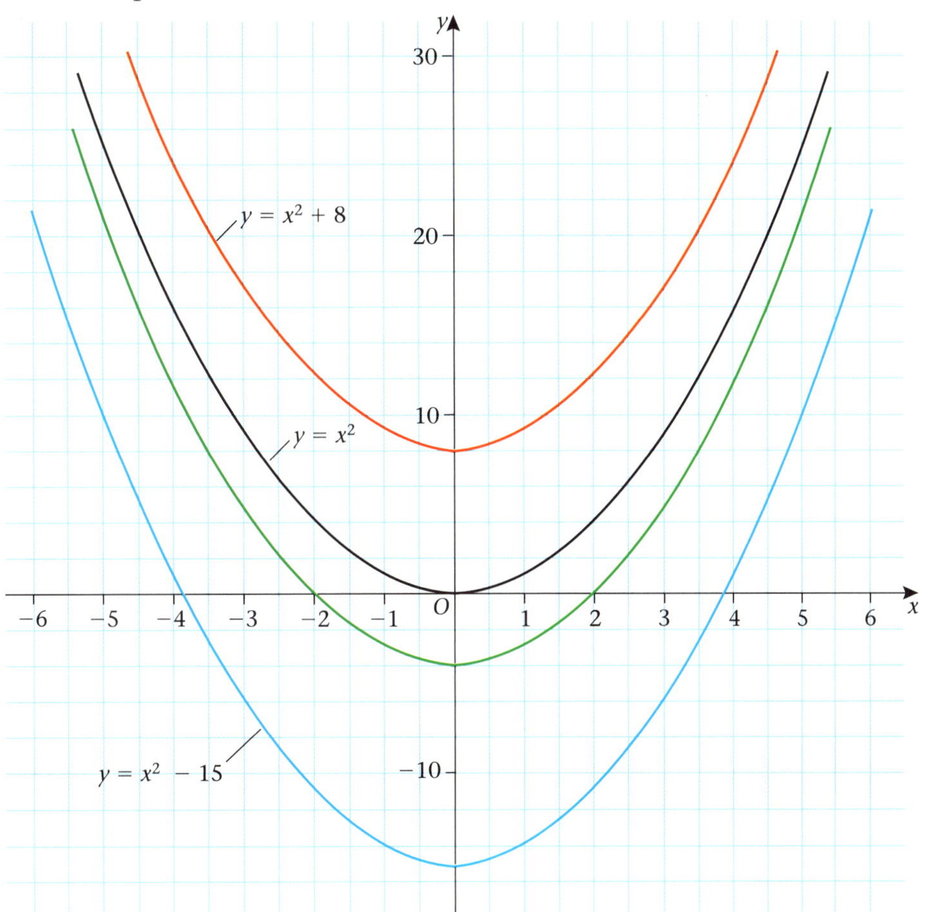

These are all graphs of functions.

Step 1 Trace the graph of $y = x^2$.

Step 2 Slide your tracing paper vertically upwards along the y-axis so that your trace of $y = x^2$ coincides with the parabola $y = x^2 + 8$.

The tracing paper has moved *up* 8 units.

The graph of $y = x^2 + 8$ is the graph of $y = x^2$ **translated 8 units vertically** in the *positive* y-direction.

Step 3 Now put your tracing paper back on the parabola $y = x^2$.

This time slide your tracing paper vertically downwards so that it coincides with the parabola $y = x^2 - 15$.

The tracing paper has moved *down* 15 units.

The graph of $y = x^2 - 15$ is the graph of $y = x^2$ **translated 15 units vertically** in the *negative* y-direction.

The graph of $y = x^2 + a$ is the graph of $y = x^2$ translated a units vertically (in the *positive* y-direction if $a > 0$, in the *negative* y-direction if $a < 0$).

Exercise 25B

1 Using the graphs on the previous page, place your tracing paper on the parabola $y = x^2$ and slide it so that it coincides with the unlabelled parabola. What is the equation of this parabola?

2 Write down the equations of three different parabolas that always lie between the parabolas $y = x^2$ and $y = x^2 + 8$.

3 The parabola $y = x^2 + k$ always lies between the parabolas $y = x^2$ and $y = x^2 - 15$. Write down an inequality for k.

The Millennium Bridge in Gateshead is a parabola.

Other basic functions

The graphs below show how curves related to the basic functions $y = x$, $y = x^3$ and $y = \frac{1}{x}$ can be drawn by applying a vertical translation.

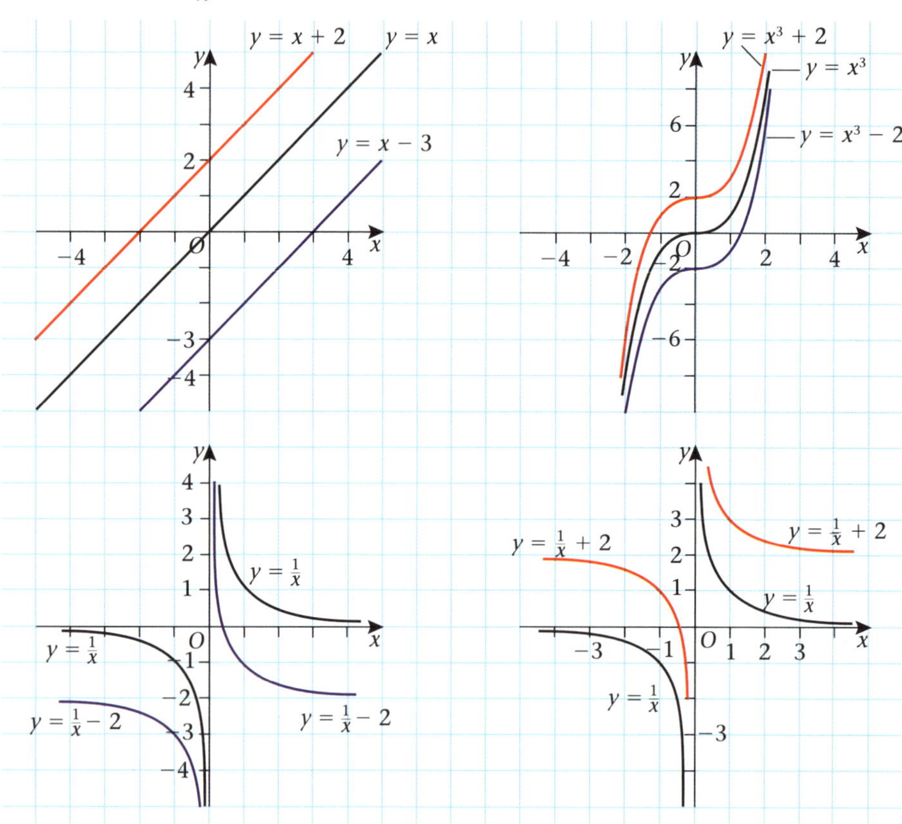

Example 5

Copy and complete these sentences:

(a) The graph of $y = x + 2$ is the graph of $y = x$ translated ________.

(b) The graph of $y = x^3 - 2$ is the graph of $y = x^3$ translated ________.

(c) The graph of $y = \frac{1}{x} + 2$ is the graph of $y = \frac{1}{x}$ ________.

(d) The graph of $y = x^3 + 2$ is the graph of $y = x^3$ ________.

(e) The graph of $y = \frac{1}{x} - 2$ is the graph of $y = \frac{1}{x}$ ________.

(a) The graph of $y = x + 2$ is the graph of $y = x$ translated 2 units vertically in the positive y-direction.
(b) The graph of $y = x^3 - 2$ is the graph of $y = x^3$ translated 2 units vertically in the negative y-direction.
(c) The graph of $y = \frac{1}{x} + 2$ is the graph of $y = \frac{1}{x}$ translated 2 units vertically in the positive y-direction.
(d) The graph of $y = x^3 + 2$ is the graph of $y = x^3$ translated 2 units vertically in the positive y-direction.
(e) The graph of $y = \frac{1}{x} - 2$ is the graph of $y = \frac{1}{x}$ translated 2 units vertically in the negative y-direction.

The graph of $y = x + a$ is the graph of $y = x$ translated a units vertically (in the *positive* y-direction if $a > 0$, in the *negative* y-direction if $a < 0$).

The graph of $y = x^3 + a$ is the graph of $y = x^3$ translated a units vertically (in the *positive* y-direction if $a > 0$, in the *negative* y-direction if $a < 0$).

The graph of $y = \frac{1}{x} + a$ is the graph of $y = \frac{1}{x}$ translated a units vertically (in the *positive* y-direction if $a > 0$, in the *negative* y-direction if $a < 0$).

Using function notation we can generalise all the results obtained so far:

For any function f, the graph of $y = f(x) + a$ is the graph of $y = f(x)$ translated a units vertically (in the *positive* y-direction if $a > 0$, in the *negative* y-direction if $a < 0$).

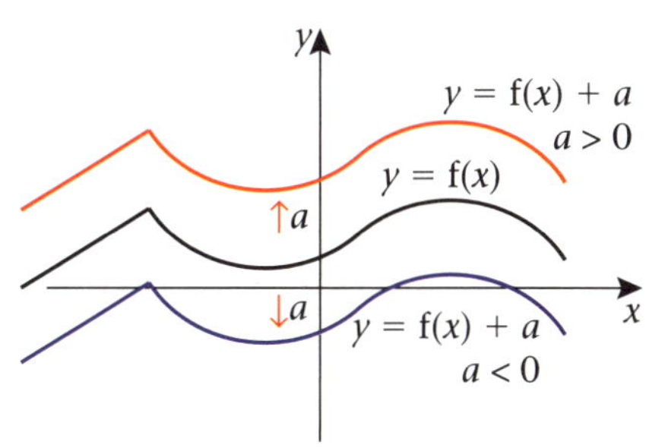

Example 6

Here is the graph of $y = f(x)$, where $f(x) = x^3 - x$, (in black).
(a) Sketch, on the same axes, the graph of $y = x^3 - x + 10$.
(b) Describe the transformation that gives $y = x^3 - x + 10$ from $y = x^3 - x$.

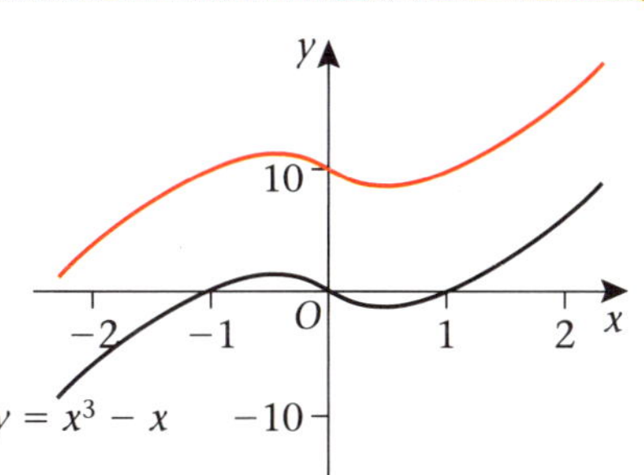

(a) $x^3 - x + 10 = f(x) + 10$
The graph of $y = x^3 - x + 10$ is shown in red.
(b) A vertical translation of 10 units in the positive y-direction.

Exercise 25C

1 In diagrams (a) to (e) the graphs of 'basic functions' are in black. In each part, write down the translations which have to be applied to these basic functions in order to obtain the graphs labelled A, B, C.

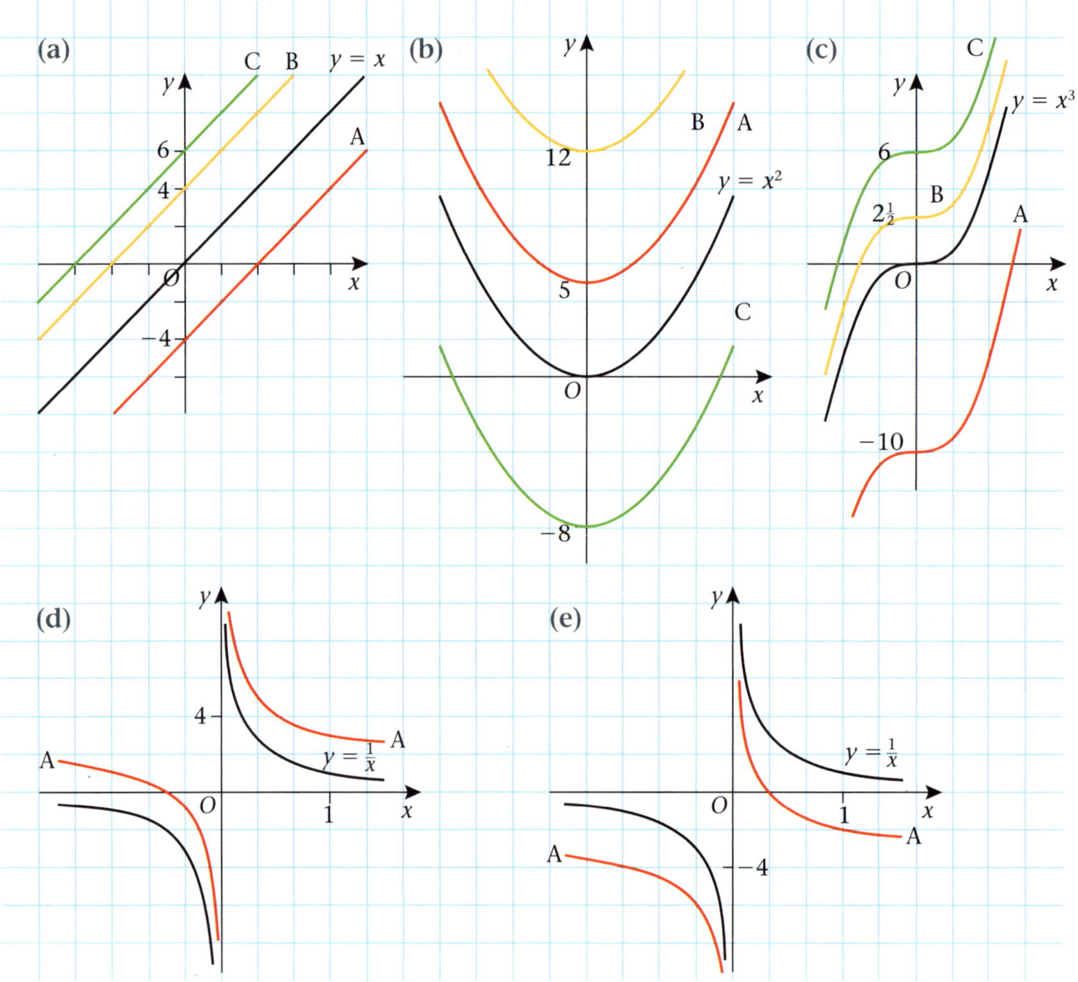

(a) C B $y = x$ A; y, x, O, 6, 4, −4

(b) y, 12, B A, $y = x^2$, 5, C, O, x, −8

(c) C, y, $y = x^3$, 6, $2\frac{1}{2}$, B, A, O, x, −10

(d) y, 4, A, $y = \frac{1}{x}$, A, O, 1, x

(e) y, $y = \frac{1}{x}$, O, 1, x, A, A, −4

2 (a) Trace the axes and sketch of the graph of $y = f(x)$ below.

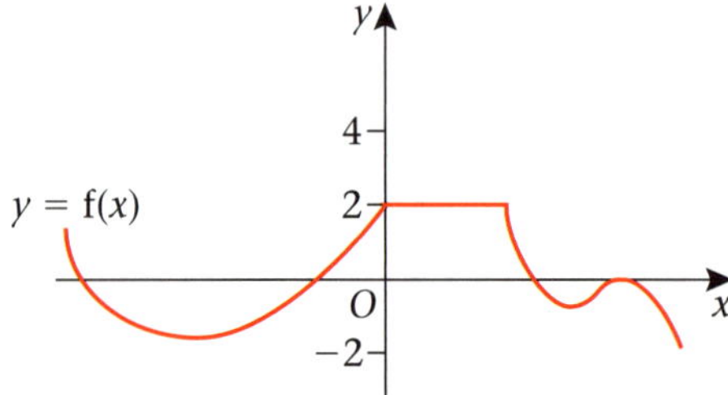

(b) On the same axes, sketch the graph of $y = f(x) + 2$.

(c) Describe the transformation which gives $y = f(x) + 2$ from $y = f(x)$.

25.3 Applying horizontal translations to graphs

Parabolas

The graphs of the parabolas $y = x^2$, $y = (x + 2)^2$ and $y = (x - 4)^2$ are shown below. One other parabola is also shown.

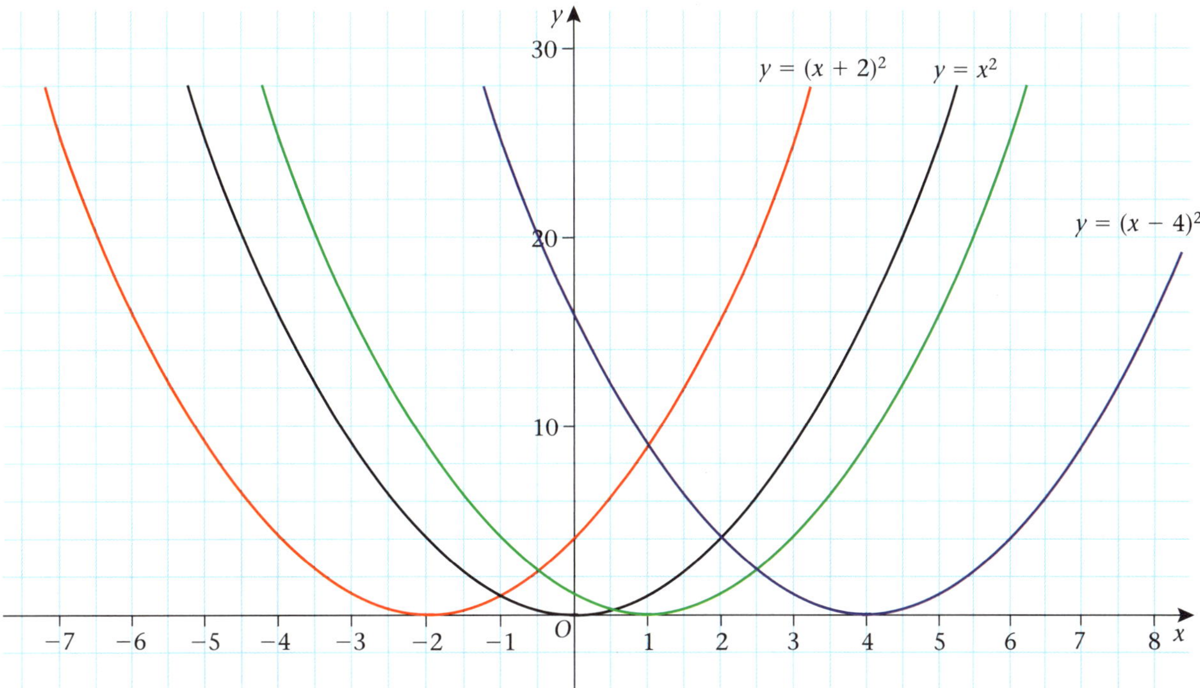

Use your tracing of the graph of $y = x^2$ (or trace a new one).

Put your tracing paper on the parabola $y = x^2$.

Slide your tracing paper horizontally along the x-axis so that your trace of $y = x^2$ coincides with the parabola $y = (x + 2)^2$.

You should have slid the tracing paper along 2 units in the *negative* x-direction.

The graph of $y = (x + 2)^2$ is the graph of $y = x^2$ **translated 2 units horizontally** in the *negative* x-direction.

Similarly, the graph of $y = (x - 4)^2$ is the graph of $y = x^2$ **translated 4 units horizontally** in the *positive* x-direction.

The graph of $y = (x + a)^2$ is the graph of $y = x^2$ translated a units horizontally (in the *negative* x-direction if $a > 0$, in the *positive* x-direction if $a < 0$).

The **vertex** of the parabola $y = (x + a)^2$ is at the point $(-a, 0)$.

Example 7

Sketch the graph of $y = x^2 + 6x + 9$. State the coordinates of the points where the graph crosses the axes.

Factorising $x^2 + 6x + 9$ gives $(x + 3)^2$
so $y = (x + 3)^2$.

The graph of $y = (x + 3)^2$ is the graph of $y = x^2$ translated 3 units horizontally in the *negative* x-direction.

The graph of $y = (x + 3)^2$ is a parabola with vertex (–3, 0).
When $x = 0$, $y = (x + 3)^2$.
The parabola crosses the y-axis at the point (0, 9) and touches the x-axis at the point (–3, 0).

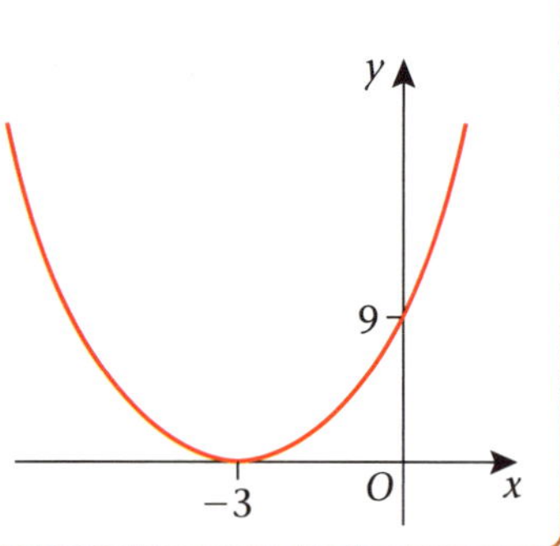

Exercise 25D

1 Using the graphs on the previous page, place your tracing paper on the parabola $y = x^2$ and slide it so that it coincides with the unlabelled parabola. What is the equation of this parabola?

2 Sketch the graph of (a) $y = (x + 1)^2$ (b) $y = (x + 5)^2$.

3 Sketch the graph of $y = x^2 - 4x + 4$.

Mark the coordinates where the graph crosses the axes.

Lines, cubics and reciprocals

Look back at the sketches of the lines on page 464.

The graph of the straight line $y = x - 3$ is the graph of $y = x$ translated *either* 3 units vertically down *or* 3 units horizontally in the positive x-direction.

The cubic and reciprocal graphs below have undergone transformations. You should examine these sketches carefully to understand the horizontal translations that have been applied.

Use tracing paper if necessary to help you.

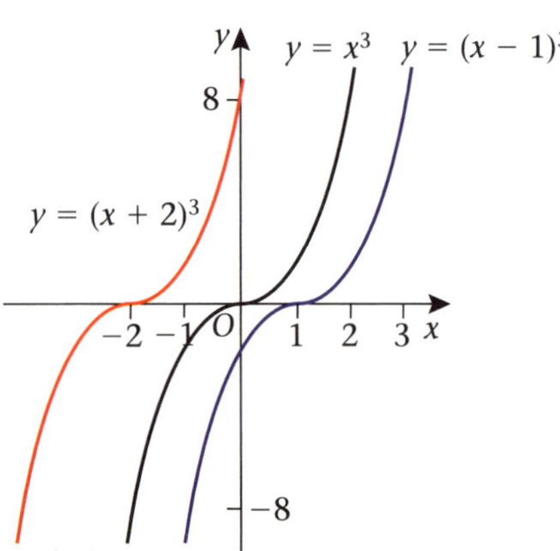

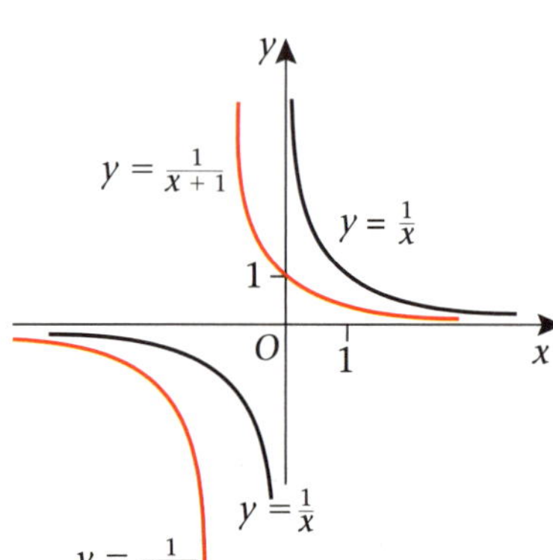

Example 8

Copy and complete these sentences:

(a) The graph of $y = \dfrac{1}{x+1}$ is the graph of $y = \dfrac{1}{x}$ ________.

(b) The graph of $y = (x+2)^3$ is the graph of $y = x^3$ ________.

(a) The graph of $y = \dfrac{1}{x+1}$ is the graph of $y = \dfrac{1}{x}$ translated 1 unit horizontally in the negative x-direction.

(b) The graph of $y = (x+2)^3$ is the graph of $y = x^3$ translated 2 units horizontally in the negative x-direction.

In general, for any function f, the graph of $y = \mathrm{f}(x + a)$ is the graph of $y = \mathrm{f}(x)$ translated a units horizontally (in the *negative* x-direction if $a > 0$, in the *positive* x-direction if $a < 0$).

Example 9

The graph of $y = \mathrm{f}(x)$, where $\mathrm{f}(x) = x(x + 2)$, is sketched below (in black).

(a) On the same axes sketch the graph of $y = x^2 + 4x + 3$.

(b) Describe the transformation which gives $y = x^2 + 4x + 3$ from $y = x(x + 2)$.

(a) Factorising $x^2 + 4x + 3$ gives $(x + 1)(x + 3)$ so we need to sketch the graph of $y = (x + 1)(x + 3)$.

Comparing $x(x + 2)$ with $(x + 1)(x + 3)$, we see that the x in the first expression has been replaced by $(x + 1)$ to get the second.

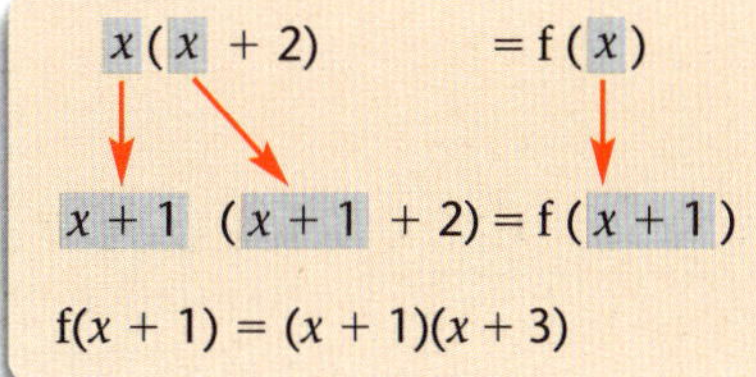

But $\quad \mathrm{f}(x) = x(x + 2)$

so $\quad \mathrm{f}(x + 1) = (x + 1)(x + 1 + 2) = (x + 1)(x + 3)$.

So sketching the graph of $y = (x + 1)(x + 3)$ is the same as sketching $y = \mathrm{f}(x + 1)$.

The graph of $y = \mathrm{f}(x + 1)$ is the graph of $y = \mathrm{f}(x)$ translated 1 unit in the negative x-direction.

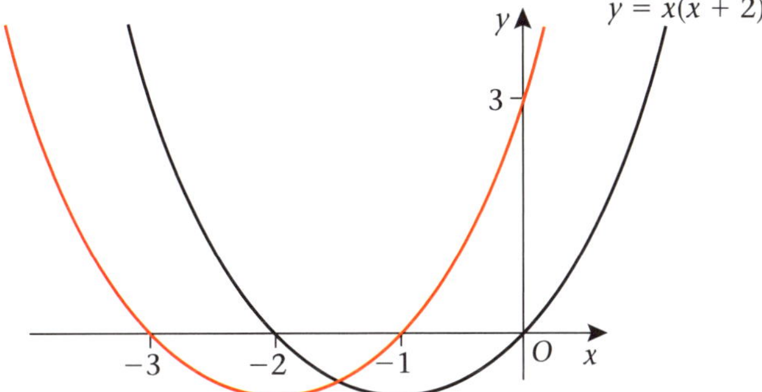

The graph of $y = x^2 + 4x + 3$ is sketched above (shown in red).

(b) A horizontal translation of 1 unit in the negative x-direction.

Exercise 25E

1 The graph of $y = x^3$ is transformed to $y = (x - 1)^3$.
Write down the translation which has taken place.

2 The graph of $y = x(x + 2)$ is transformed to $y = (x - 1)(x + 1)$.
Write down the transformation which has taken place.

3 The graph of $y = \dfrac{1}{x+3} - 3$ is transformed to $y = \dfrac{1}{x+3} + 4$.
Write down the transformation which has taken place.

4 Graph A becomes $y = x^3 - 1$ following a vertical translation by 3 units downwards. Write the equation of Graph A.

5 The graph of $y = x(x - 1)(x + 5)$ is translated by 4 units horizontally in the positive x-direction. Write down its new equation.

25.4 Applying double translations to graphs

This section shows you how to apply two translations and to sketch the graphs of various functions.

Example 10

Sketch the graph of $y = (x - 2)^3 + 1$.

This graph can be built up from the basic curve $y = x^3$ like this:

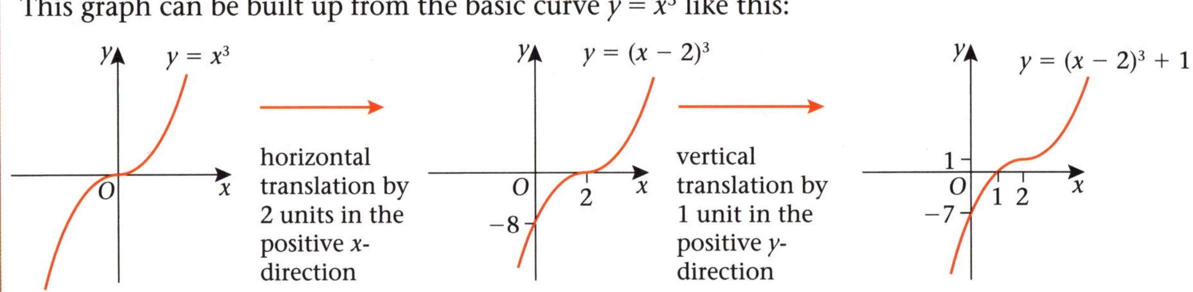

For **double translations**, the order does not matter. You should convince yourself by sketching $y = x^3 + 1$ then applying the horizontal translation to get the final result.

However, when combining **a translation with a different type of transformation**, the order of the transformations becomes critical.

To sketch a quadratic function whose coefficient of x^2 is 1

Example 11

Sketch the graph of $y = x^2 + 4x - 1$.
State the coordinates of the vertex and the points at which the curve crosses the x-axis.

$y = x^2 + 4x - 1$
$= (x + 2)^2 - 4 - 1$ — Complete the square
$= (x + 2)^2 - 5$

Check:
$(x + 2)^2 - 5$
$= x^2 + 4x + 4 - 5$
$= x^2 + 4x - 1$

Start with the basic curve $y = x^2$:

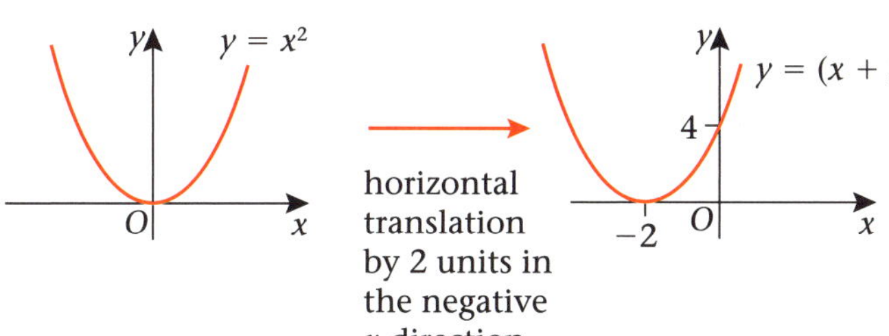

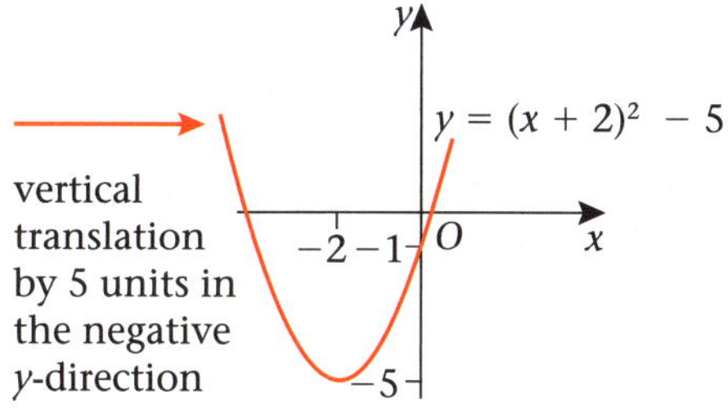

The coordinates of the vertex are $(-2, -5)$.

To find where the graph crosses the x-axis solve the equation:

$$(x + 2)^2 - 5 = 0$$

$$(x + 2)^2 = 5$$

$$(x + 2) = \pm\sqrt{5}$$

$$x = -2 - \sqrt{5} \text{ or } -2 + \sqrt{5}$$

To sketch the graph of $y = x^2 + bx + c$, complete the square and apply a double translation to the parabola $y = x^2$.

In general, for any function f, the graph of $y = \mathrm{f}(x + a) + b$ is the graph of $y = \mathrm{f}(x)$ translated a units horizontally (in the *negative* x-direction if $a > 0$, in the *positive* x-direction if $a < 0$) followed by a translation of b units vertically (*upwards* if $b > 0$, *downwards* if $b < 0$).

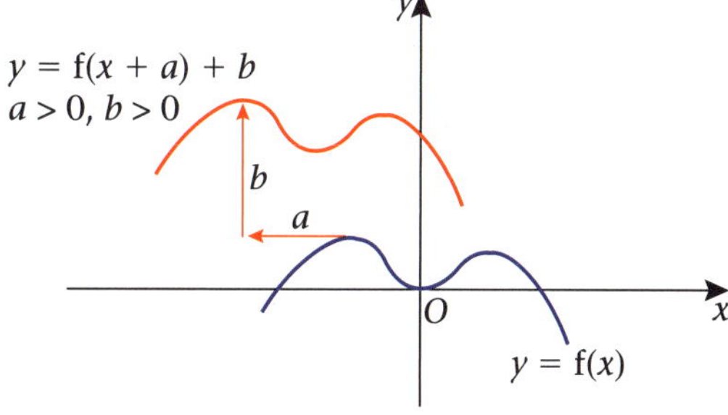

Exercise 25F

1 Sketch the graphs of the following quadratic functions. In each case give the coordinates of the vertex.

(a) $y = x^2 + 2x + 4$ (b) $y = x^2 - 6x + 4$

(c) $y = x^2 + 3x - 1$ (d) $y = x^2 - 4x - \frac{1}{2}$

2 Describe the transformations which transform the graph of $y = (x + 1)^2$ to the graph of:

(a) $y = (x + 7)^2$ (b) $y = (x - 3)^2 - 4$

3 Sketch the graphs of these quadratic functions:

(a) $y = x^2 - 6x + 2$ (b) $y = x^2 + 2x - 4$

Describe the transformations which give the graph in (b) from the graph in (a).

4 What is the equation of the graph obtained by applying these transformations to the graph of $y = x^2 - 16x$?

a horizontal translation of 1 unit in the positive x-direction followed by a vertical translation of 3 units down

5 Sketch the graph of $y = 3 + \dfrac{1}{x + 2}$

Give the coordinates of the points where the graph and the asymptotes cross the axes.

25.5 Applying reflections to graphs

In the x-axis

The sketch graphs show $y = \text{f}(x)$ (in black) and $y = -\text{f}(x)$ (in red) for each of the four basic functions.

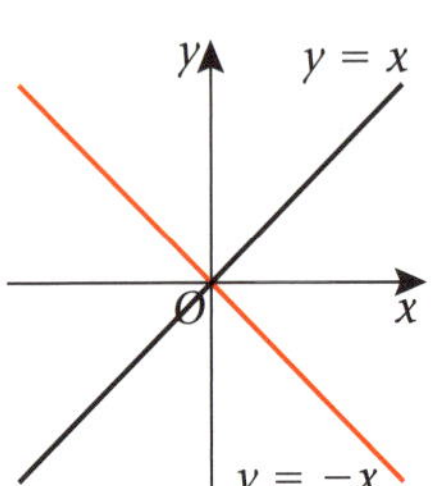

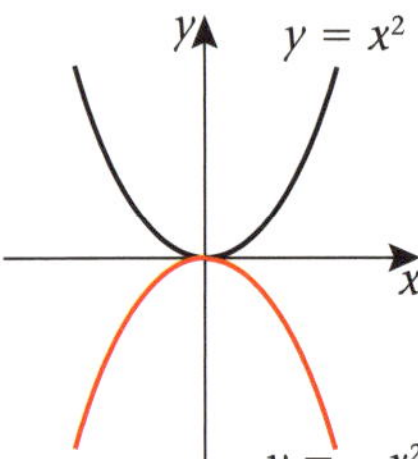

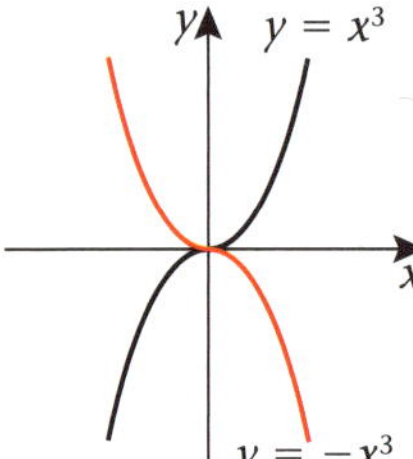

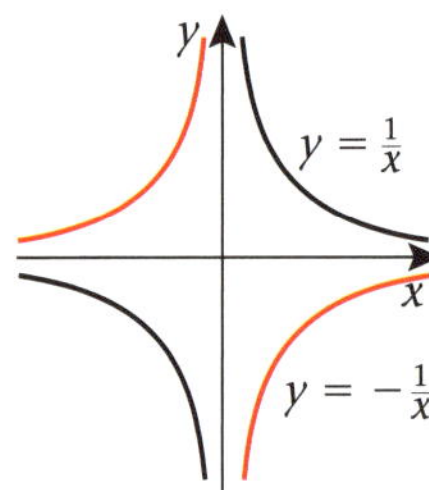

The graph of $y = -\text{f}(x)$ is obtained by changing the sign of y in $y = \text{f}(x)$.

Each red graph is obtained by reflecting each black graph in the x-axis.

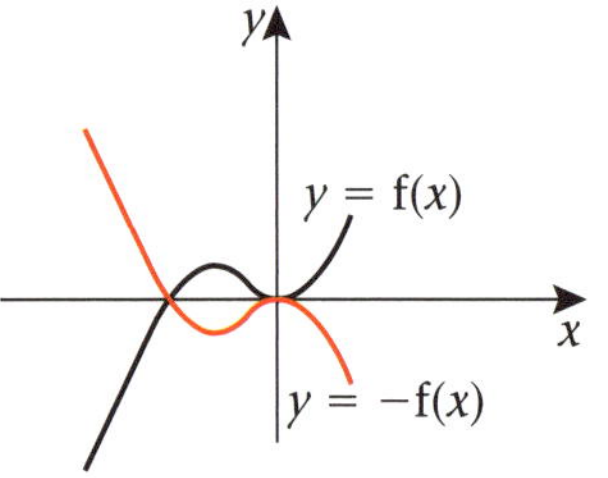

For any function f, the graph of $y = -\text{f}(x)$ is obtained by reflecting $y = \text{f}(x)$ in the x-axis.

You can use tracing paper to help you reflect graphs in the x-axis:

- trace the function and the x-axis and mark the origin
- turn over the tracing paper and match up the origin and the x-axis. The trace now shows the reflection of the original function in the x-axis.

Example 12

A sketch of the parabola $y = \text{f}(x)$, where $\text{f}(x) = -x^2 + 4x$, is shown in black. Its vertex has coordinates (2, 4).

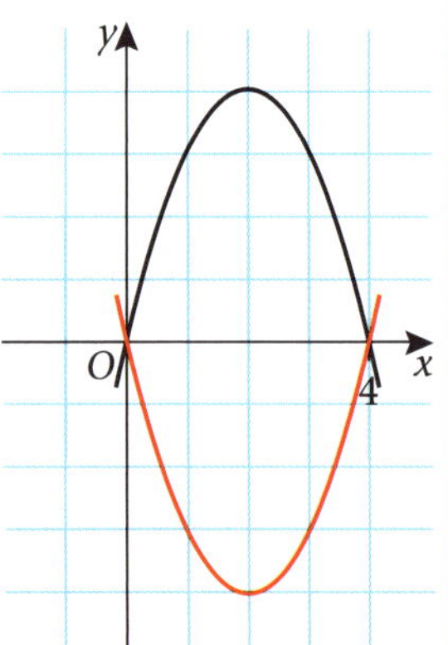

(a) Find the equation of $y = -\text{f}(x)$. (b) Sketch the graph of $y = -\text{f}(x)$.

(c) Describe the transformation which is applied to $y = \text{f}(x)$ to obtain $y = -\text{f}(x)$.

(d) Write the coordinates of the vertex of $y = -\text{f}(x)$.

(a) $\text{f}(x) = -x^2 + 4x$

$y = -\text{f}(x) = -(-x^2 + 4x)$

So the equation of $y = -\text{f}(x)$ is $y = x^2 - 4x$.

(b) The graph of $y = -\text{f}(x)$ is shown in red.

(c) Reflection in the x-axis. (d) Vertex is $(2, -4)$.

In the y-axis

The sketch graphs show $y = f(x)$ (in black) and $y = f(-x)$ (in red) for $f(x) = x + 1$ and $f(x) = x^3 + 8$.

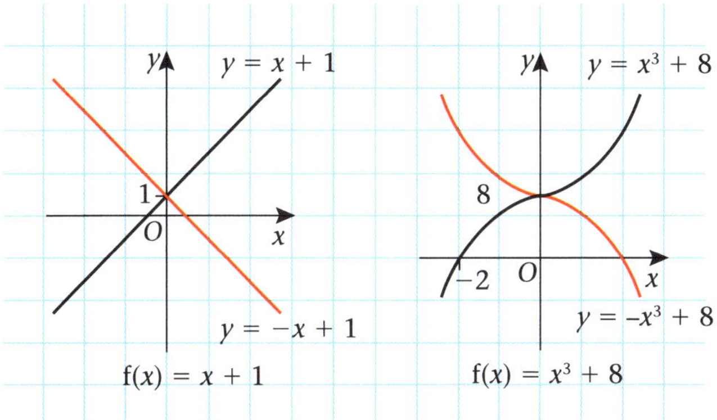

The graph of $y = f(-x)$ is obtained by changing the sign of x in $y = f(x)$.

Each red graph is obtained by reflecting each black graph in the y-axis.

For any function f, the graph of $y = f(-x)$ is obtained by reflecting $y = f(x)$ in the y-axis.

Example 13

This is a sketch of the parabola $y = f(x)$, where $f(x) = -x^2 + 6x$.

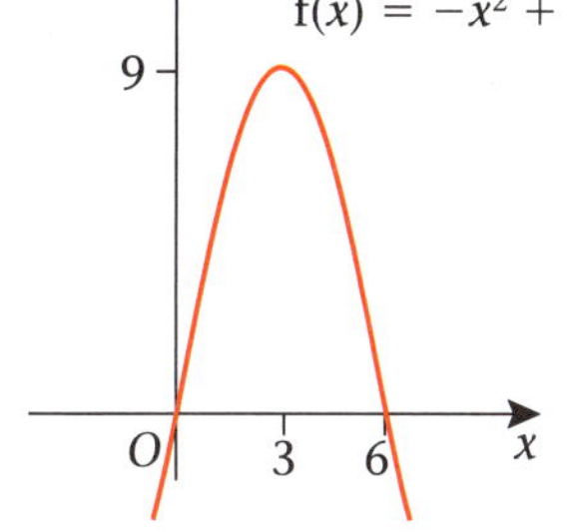

Its vertex has coordinates (3, 9).

(a) Find the equation of $y = f(-x)$.

(b) Sketch the graph of $y = f(-x)$.

(c) Describe the transformation which is applied to $y = f(x)$ to obtain $y = f(-x)$.

(d) Write the coordinates of the vertex of $y = f(-x)$.

(a) $f(x) = -x^2 + 6x$

$y = f(-x) = -[(-x)^2] + 6(-x) = -[x^2] - 6x$

So the equation of $y = f(-x)$ is $y = -x^2 - 6x$.

(b)

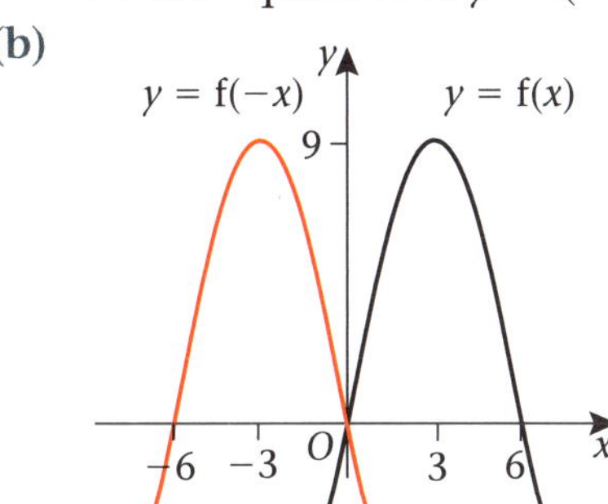

(c) Reflection in the y-axis.

(d) Vertex is (−3, 9).

Exercise 25G

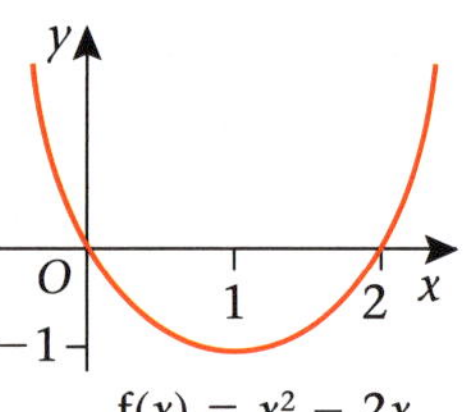

1 This is a sketch of $y = f(x)$, where $f(x) = x^2 - 2x$. The vertex of this parabola is $(1, -1)$.

(a) Find the equation of $f(-x)$.

(b) Sketch the graph of $y = f(-x)$.

(c) Sketch the graph of $y = -x^2 + 2x$.

(d) Write the coordinates of the vertex of $y = -x^2 + 2x$.

2 A reflection is applied to the graph of $y = f(x)$, where $f(x) = x^3 + 2x^2$.

Find the equation of the new graph if

(a) the reflection is in the x-axis

(b) the reflection is in the y-axis.

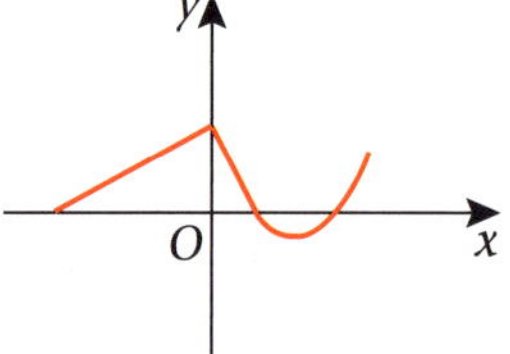

3 (a) Copy this sketch of the graph of $y = f(x)$.

(b) On the same axes, sketch the graph of $y = -f(x)$.

(c) Describe fully the single transformation which when applied to the graph of $y = f(x)$ gives the graph of $y = -f(x)$.

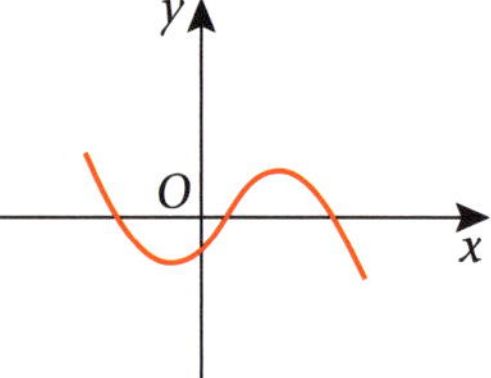

4 (a) Copy this sketch of the graph of $y = f(x)$.

(b) On the same axes, sketch the graph of $y = f(-x)$.

(c) Describe fully the single transformation which when applied to the graph of $y = f(x)$ gives the graph of $y = f(-x)$.

25.6 Applying combined transformations

You can use a combination of transformations to sketch a function.

Example 14

Explain how to sketch the graph of $y = -x^2 + 6x + 3$ by applying transformations to the graph of $y = x^2$.
Illustrate your answer by sketches and state the coordinates of the vertex of $y = -x^2 + 6x + 3$.

> Check:
> $-(x - 3)^2 + 12$
> $= -(x^2 - 6x + 9) + 12$
> $= -x^2 + 6x - 9 + 12$
> $= -x^2 + 6x + 3$

$$-x^2 + 6x + 3 = -(x^2 - 6x) + 3$$
$$= -[(x - 3)^2 - 9] + 3 \quad \text{Complete the square}$$
$$= -(x - 3)^2 + 12$$

Let $f(x) = x^2$ so $y = x^2$ becomes $y = f(x)$

1 $y = (x - 3)^2$ becomes $y = f(x - 3)$

2 $y = -(x - 3)^2$ becomes $y = -f(x - 3)$

3 $y = -(x - 3)^2 + 12$ becomes $y = -f(x - 3) + 12$.

> For a combination of transformations, the order of the transformations is critical.

To transform the graph of $y = x^2$ to the graph of $y = -x^2 + 6x + 3$, apply the following transformations in this order:

1 horizontal translation of 3 units in the positive x-direction
2 reflection in the x-axis
3 vertical translation of 12 units in the positive y-direction.

The transformations are in the order given on the previous page.

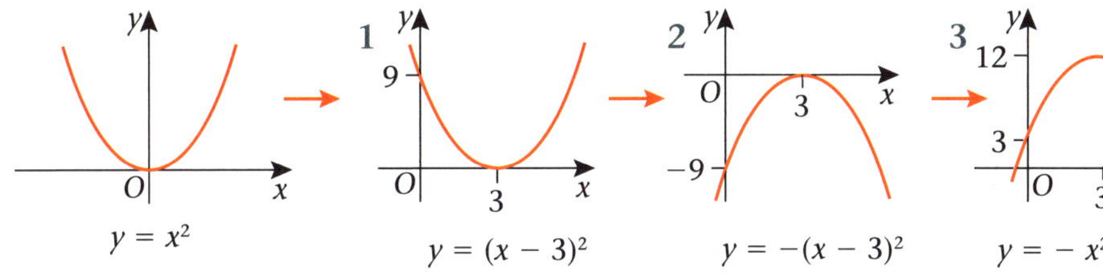

The coordinates of the vertex of $y = -x^2 + 6x + 3$ are (3, 12).

Exercise 25H

1 List the transformations, in the correct order, which when applied to $y = x^2$ give the graphs of the following functions.

(a) $y = -x^2 + 6$ (b) $y = (x - 4)^2 + 2$ (c) $y = -x^2 + 4x - 3$

Sketch each graph.

25.7 Applying stretches to graphs

Stretch in the y-direction

The graphs show

$y = \text{f}(x)$ (in black) $y = 2\text{f}(x)$ (in red) $y = \frac{1}{2}\text{f}(x)$ (in green)

for the two functions $\text{f}(x) = x$ and $\text{f}(x) = x^2$.

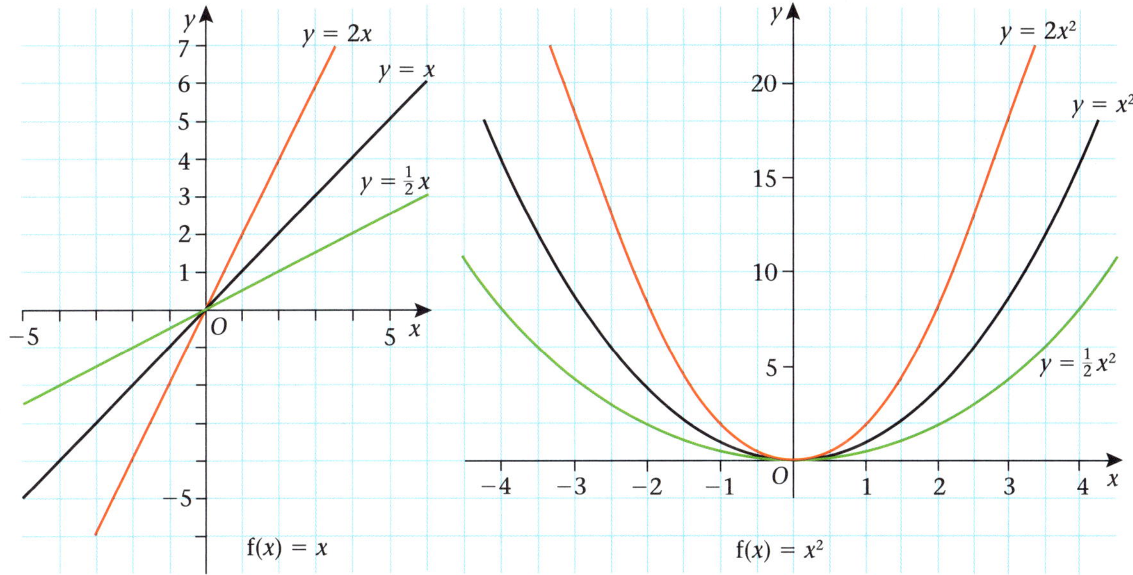

To obtain the graph of $y = 2f(x)$ from the graph of $y = f(x)$, multiply the y-coordinate of each point on the graph of $y = f(x)$ by 2 but leave the x-coordinate unaltered. For example, the point (1, 1) becomes (1, 2) and so on.

This has the effect of stretching the curve out in the direction of the y-axis by a scale factor 2. Points of the graph on the x-axis remain fixed.

> A stretch is similar to an enlargement but in one direction only.

Similarly, by comparing the curves $y = x^2$ and $y = \frac{1}{2}x^2$ we can see that the stretch required to get $y = \frac{1}{2}f(x)$ from $y = f(x)$ is again in the direction of the y-axis but with scale factor $\frac{1}{2}$.

> For any function f, the graph of $y = af(x)$, where a is a positive constant, is obtained from $y = f(x)$ by applying a stretch of scale factor a parallel to the y-axis.

Example 15

The graph of $y = f(x)$, where $f(x) = -x^2 + 6x - 5$, is shown below (in black) and labelled.

(a) Sketch the graphs of

(i) $y = -2x^2 + 12x - 10$ (ii) $y = -\frac{1}{2}x^2 + 3x - \frac{5}{2}$ on the same axes.

(b) Describe the transformation which is applied to $y = -\frac{1}{2}x^2 + 3x - \frac{5}{2}$ to get $y = -2x^2 + 12x - 10$.

(a) (i) $y = -2x^2 + 12x - 10 = 2(-x^2 + 6x - 5) = 2f(x)$

Apply a stretch of scale factor 2 parallel to the y-axis.

The graph of $y = -2x^2 + 12x - 10$ is shown in red.

> $(0, -5) \to (0, -10)$
> $(3, 4) \to (3, 8)$
> $(5, 0) \to (5, 0)$

(ii) $y = -\frac{1}{2}x^2 + 3x - \frac{5}{2} = \frac{1}{2}(-x^2 + 6x - 5) = \frac{1}{2}f(x)$

Apply a stretch of scale factor $\frac{1}{2}$ parallel to the y-axis.

The graph of $y = -\frac{1}{2}x^2 + 3x - \frac{5}{2}$ is shown in green.

> $(0, -5) \to (0, -\frac{5}{2})$
> $(3, 4) \to (3, 2)$
> $(5, 0) \to (5, 0)$

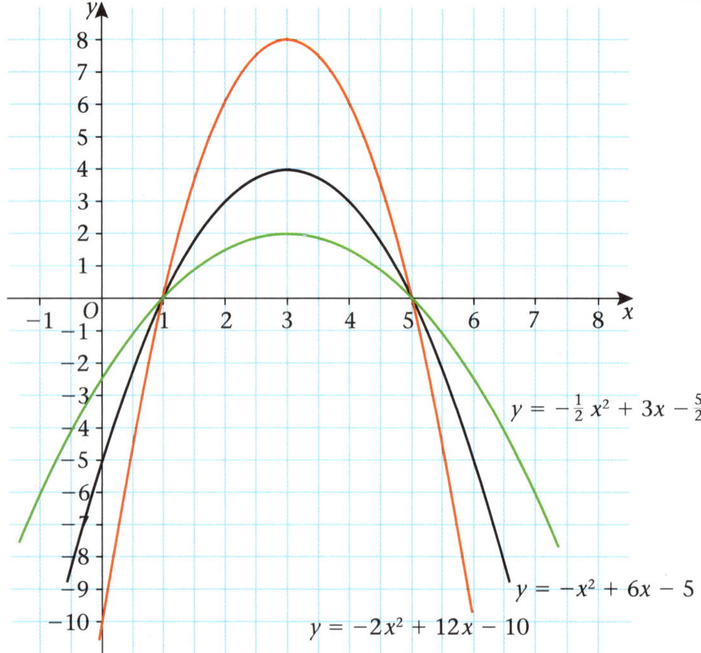

(b) The transformation applied to $y = \frac{1}{2}f(x)$ to get $y = 2f(x)$ is a stretch of scale factor 4 parallel to the y-axis.

Stretch in the x-direction

The graphs show

$y = f(x)$ (in black) $y = f(2x)$ (in red) $y = f(\frac{1}{2}x)$ (in green)

for the two functions $f(x) = x + 1$ and $f(x) = x^2 - 9$.

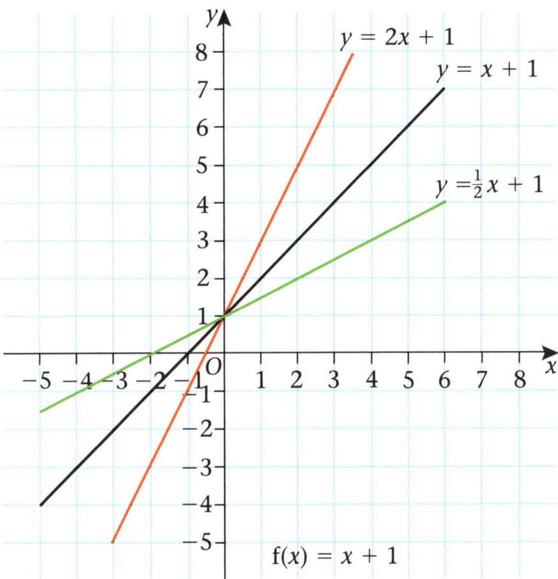

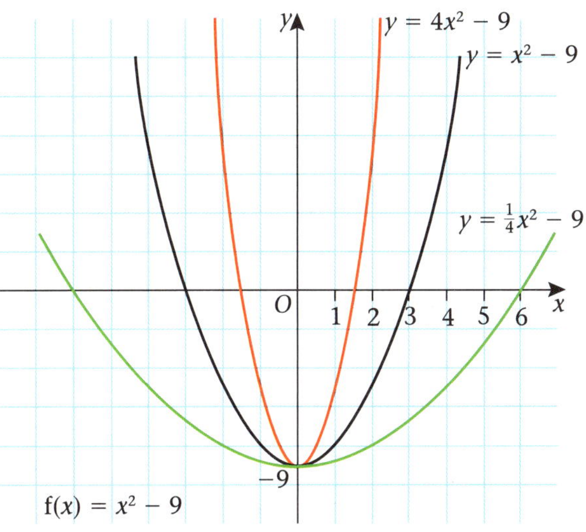

To get the graph of $y = f(2x)$ from the graph of $y = f(x)$, multiply the x-coordinate of each point on the graph of $y = f(x)$ by $\frac{1}{2}$ but leave the y-coordinate unaltered. For example, for the parabolas (4, 7) becomes (2, 7), (2, −5) becomes (1, −5) and so on.

This has the effect of stretching the curve out (in fact it is 'squashed') in the direction of the x-axis by scale factor $\frac{1}{2}$. Points on the graph on the y-axis remain fixed.

Similarly, by comparing the black and green curves you can see that the stretch required to get $y = f(\frac{1}{2}x)$ from $y = f(x)$ is again in the direction of the x-axis with scale factor 2.

For any function f, the graph of $y = f(ax)$, where a is a positive constant, is obtained from $y = f(x)$ by applying a stretch of scale factor $\dfrac{1}{a}$ parallel to the x-axis.

Example 16

This is a sketch of $y = f(x)$, where $f(x) = 6x - x^2$.

The vertex of the parabola is (3, 9).

(a) Write the equation of $y = f(2x)$.

(b) Sketch the graph of $y = f(2x)$. Give the coordinates of the vertex and the points where the graph crosses the axes.

(c) Sketch the graph of $y = 4f(x)$. Give the coordinates of the vertex and the points where the graph crosses the axes.

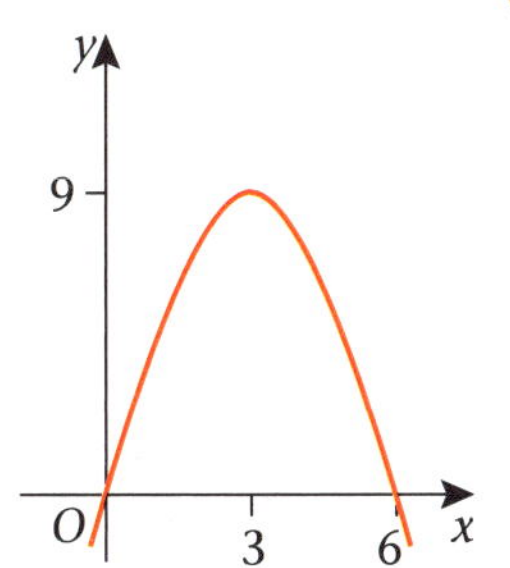

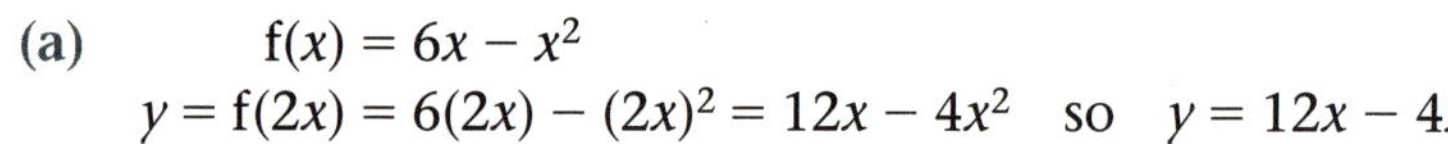

(a) $f(x) = 6x - x^2$

$y = f(2x) = 6(2x) - (2x)^2 = 12x - 4x^2$ so $y = 12x - 4x^2$

(b)

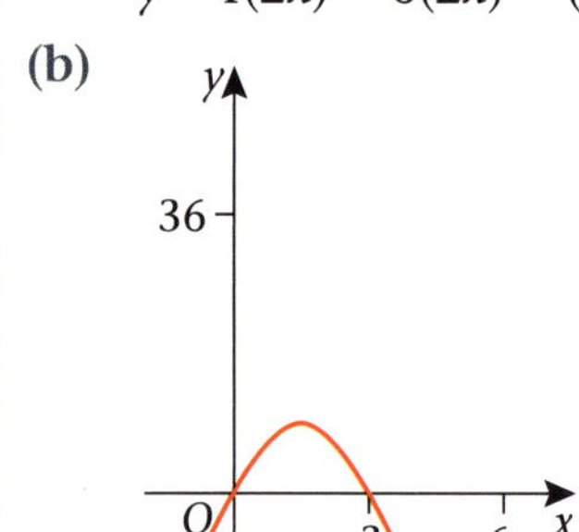

The vertex is $(\frac{3}{2}, 9)$. The graph crosses the axes at (0, 0) and (3, 0).

(c)

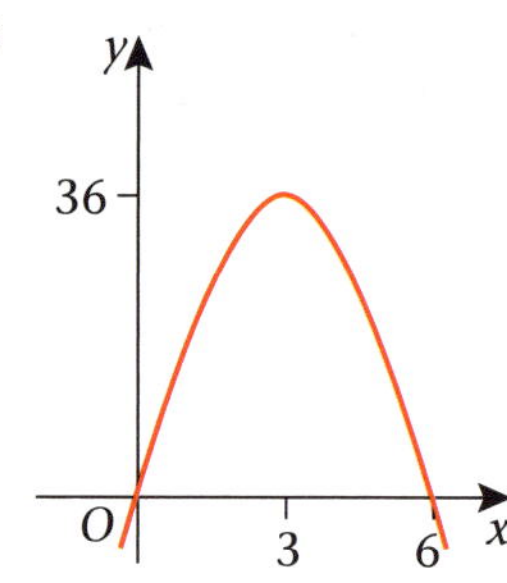

The vertex is (3, 36). The graph crosses the axes at (0, 0) and (6, 0).

Example 17

Explain how to sketch the graph of $y = -4x^2 + 8x + 3$ by applying transformations to the graph of $y = x^2$. Illustrate your answer by sketches and state the coordinates of the vertex of $y = -4x^2 + 8x + 3$.

$$-4x^2 + 8x + 3 = -4(x^2 - 2x) + 3$$
$$= -4[(x-1)^2 - 1] + 3 \quad \text{—— Complete the square}$$
$$= -4(x-1)^2 + 7$$

Check:
$-4(x-1)^2 + 7$
$= -4(x^2 - 2x + 1) + 7$
$= -4x^2 + 8x - 4 + 7$
$= -4x^2 + 8x + 3$

Let $f(x) = x^2$ so $y = x^2$ becomes $y = f(x)$

1 $y = (x-1)^2$ becomes $y = f(x-1)$

2 $y = 4(x-1)^2$ becomes $y = 4f(x-1)$

3 $y = -4(x-1)^2$ becomes $y = -4f(x-1)$

4 $y = -4(x-1)^2 + 7$ becomes $y = -4f(x-1) + 7$.

To transform the graph of $y = x^2$ to the graph of $y = -4x^2 + 8x + 3$, apply the following transformations in this order:

1 horizontal translation of 1 unit in the positive x-direction
2 stretch of scale factor 4 parallel to the y-axis
3 reflection in the x-axis
4 vertical translation of 7 units in the positive y-direction.

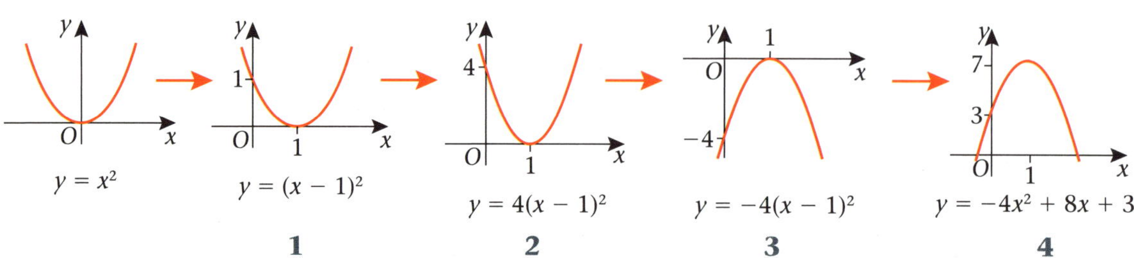

The vertex of $y = -4x^2 + 8x + 3$ is (1, 7).

$\frac{120}{4} = 30$

0.9

$101 + 78 = \frac{174}{2} \approx 90 \approx 37.05$

$23 < 30 < 44$

$36.3 < x < 36.6$

$36.45 \approx 33.5$

$36.4 \approx 30$

$$\begin{array}{r} 37.05 \\ -\ 36.4 \\ \hline 0.65 \end{array}$$ ✓

c) 86 ✓

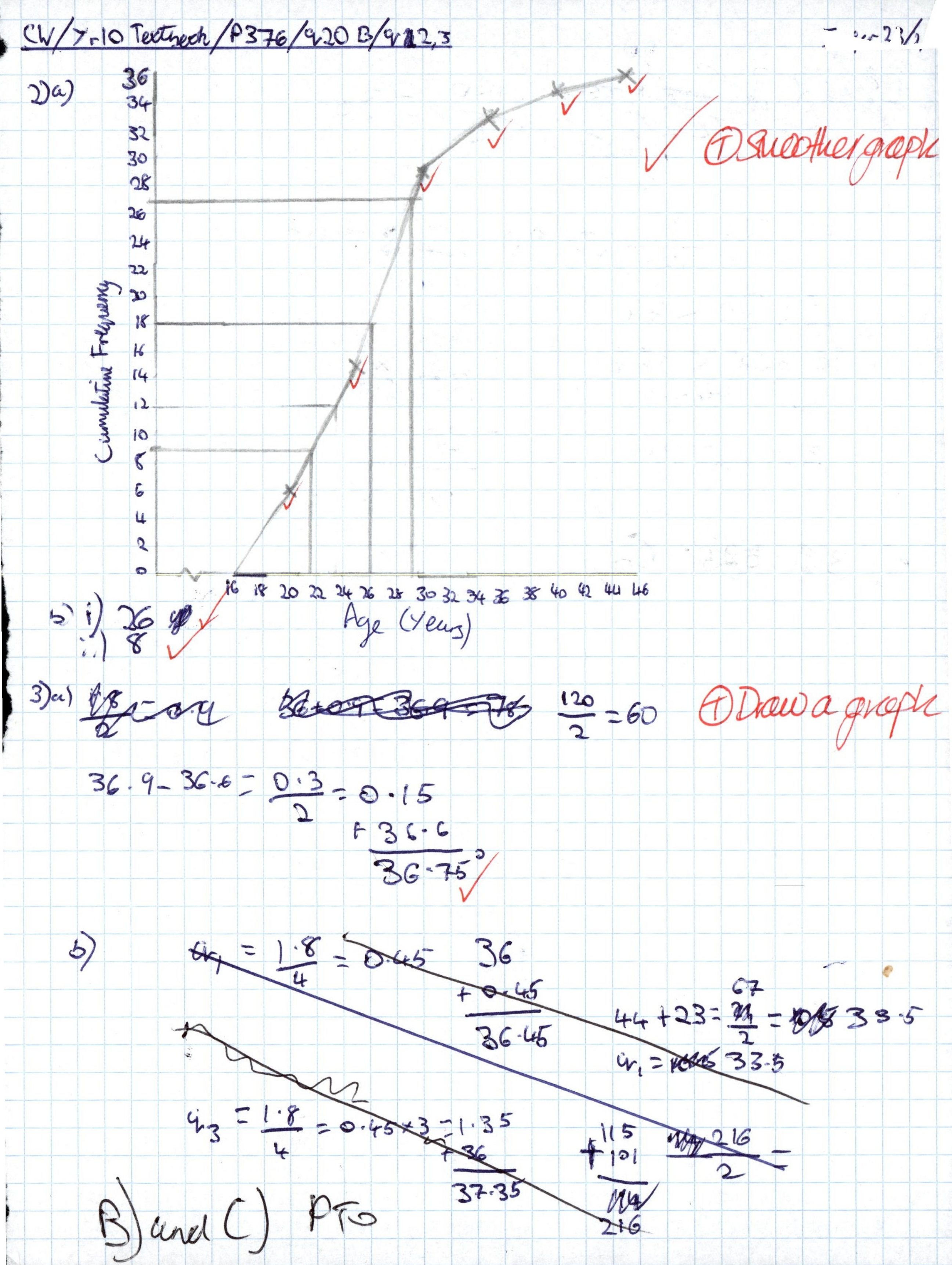

CW / Yr10 Textbook / P376 / 9.20 B / Q1,2,3
2) a)
Cumulative Frequency
36
34
32
30
28
26
24
22
20
18
16
14
12
10
8
6
4
2
0
16 18 20 22 24 26 28 30 32 34 36 38 40 42 44 46
Age (Years)
① Smoother graph
b) i) 26
ii) 8
3) a)
120/2 = 60
① Draw a graph
36.9 − 36.6 = 0.3/2 = 0.15
+ 36.6
36.75
b)
= 1.8/4 = 0.45
36
+ 0.45
36.45
44 + 23 = 67/2 = 33.5
q_1 = 33.5
q_3 = 1.8/4 = 0.45 × 3 = 1.35
+ 36
37.35
115
+ 101
216
216/2 =
B) and C) PTO

Exercise 25I

1 List the transformations, in the correct order, which when applied to $y = x^2$ give the graphs of the following functions.

(a) $y = 2x^2 + 4x - 1$

(b) $y = 3x^2 - 12x + 2$

(c) $y = x^2 - 4x + 2$

Sketch each graph.

2 List the transformations, in the correct order, which when applied to $y = x^3$ give the graphs of the following functions.

(a) $y = 4(x + 2)^3$

(b) $y = 8 - x^3$

(c) $y = 5 + (x - 1)^3$

(d) $y = (2x)^3 - 8$

Sketch each graph.

3 Explain how you would use your graph for question **1**(c) to sketch the graphs of these functions:

(a) $y = (x + 1)^2 - 4(x + 1) + 2$

(b) $y = x^2 + 4x + 2$

(c) $y = -x^2 + 4x$

25.8 Applying transformations to trigonometric functions

For more on graphs of trigonometric functions see Chapter 16.

These are the graphs of $y = \sin x$ and $y = \cos x$ for $-360° \leqslant x \leqslant 360°$:

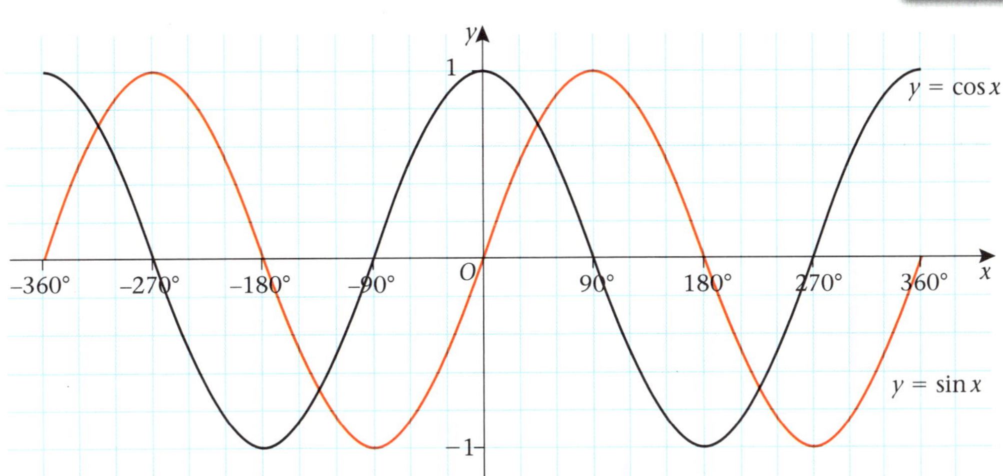

Example 18

Starting with $y = f(x)$, where $f(x) = \cos x$, apply a translation of 90° horizontally in the positive x-direction.

This leads to a trigonometrical identity. What is the identity?

$y = f(x)$ translated 90° in the positive x-direction becomes $y = f(x - 90°)$.

Applying this translation to $f(x) = \cos x$ you obtain $y = \cos(x - 90°)$.

But from the graphs, a translation of 90° horizontally in the positive x-direction on $y = \cos x$ gives the graph of $y = \sin x$.

Since $y = \cos(x - 90°)$ is the same graph as $y = \sin x$, we can deduce the trigonometrical identity:

$$\cos(x - 90°) = \sin x$$

Exercise 25J

1 Starting with $y = f(x)$, where $f(x) = \sin x$, apply a translation of 90° horizontally in the negative x-direction. This leads to a trigonometrical identity. What is the identity?

2 (a) What is the transformation which needs to be applied to $y = f(x)$, where $f(x) = \cos x$, to obtain $y = \cos 2x$?

(b) Sketch the graph of $y = \cos 2x$ for $-360° \leqslant x \leqslant 360°$.

(c) How many solutions of the equation $\cos 2x = \frac{1}{2}$ lie within the range $-360° \leqslant x \leqslant 360°$?

3 (a) What is the transformation which needs to be applied to $y = f(x)$, where $f(x) = \sin x$, to obtain $y = 2 \sin x$?

(b) Sketch the graph of $y = 2 \sin x$ for $-360° \leqslant x \leqslant 360°$.

(c) How many solutions of the equation $2 \sin x = 1$ lie within the range $-360° \leqslant x \leqslant 360°$?

(d) Without any further sketches, state how many solutions of the equation $2 \sin 2x = 1$ lie within the range $-360° \leqslant x \leqslant 360°$. Explain your answer.

4 For $f(x) = \sin x$, sketch the graph of (a) $y = f(-x)$ (b) $y = -f(x)$.

5 The greatest value which $\cos x$ can have is $+1$.
The lowest value that $\cos x$ can have is -1.
Write down the greatest and lowest values for

(a) $5 \cos x$ (b) $\cos 3x$ (c) $\cos(x + 60°)$

(d) $-2 \cos x$ (e) $6 + 3 \cos 4x$

Mixed exercise 25

1 A sketch of the curve $y = \sin x$ for $0 \leqslant x \leqslant 360°$ is shown below.

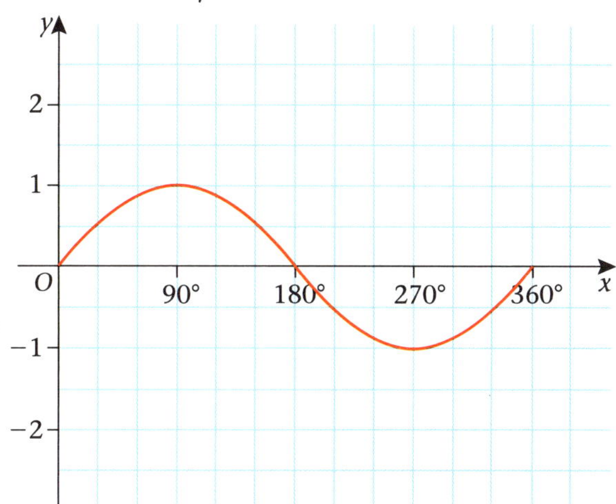

(a) Using the sketch above, or otherwise, find the equation of each of the following curves.

(i)

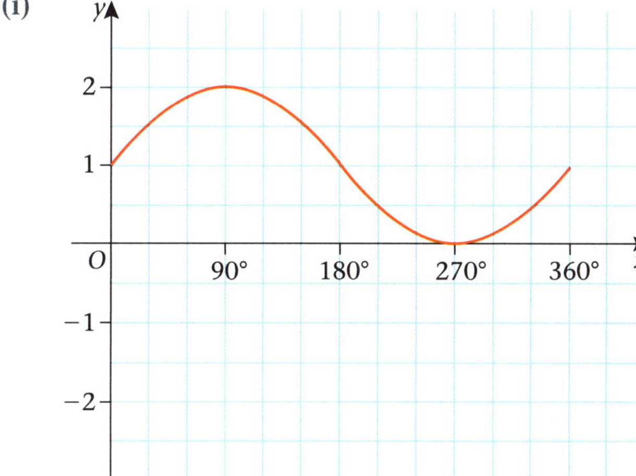

(ii)

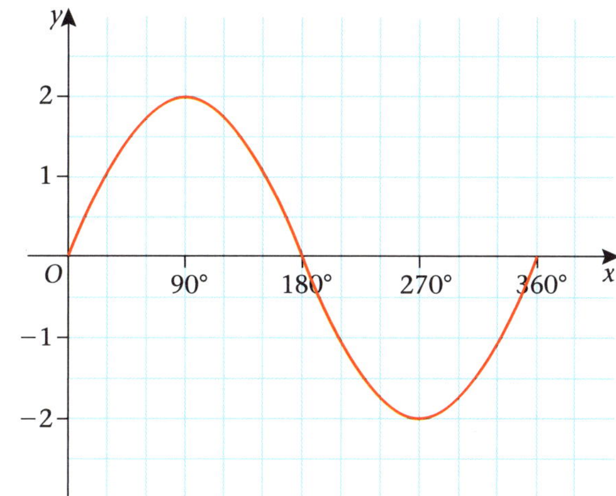

(b) Describe fully the sequence of two transformations that maps the graph of $y = \sin x$ on to the graph of $y = 3 \sin 2x$.

2

$y = a \sin x$

$y = \cos x + b$

Diagram **NOT** accurately drawn

The diagram shows part of two graphs.

The equation of one graph is $y = a \sin x$
The equation of the other graph is $y = \cos x + b$

(a) Use the graphs to find the value of a and the value of b.

(b) Use the graphs to find the values of x in the range $0° \leqslant x \leqslant 720°$ for which $a \sin x = \cos x + b$

(c) Use the graphs to find the value of $a \sin x - (\cos x + b)$ when $x = 450°$.

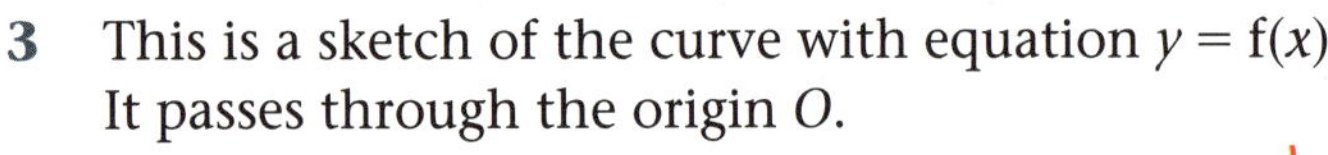

3 This is a sketch of the curve with equation $y = \text{f}(x)$.
It passes through the origin O.

The only vertex of the curve is at $A(2, -4)$.

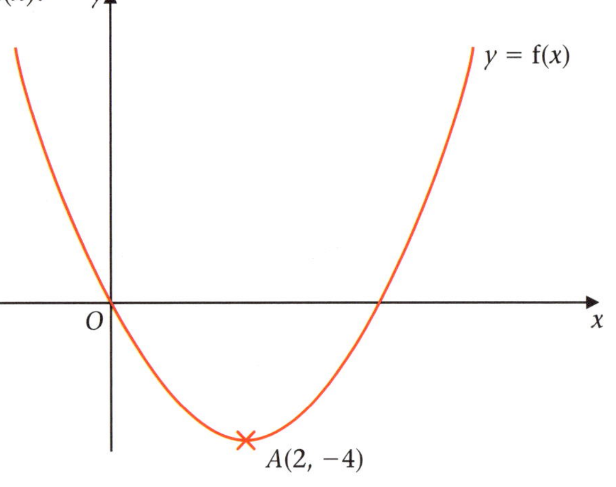

(a) Write down the coordinates of the vertex of the curve with equation

  (i) $y = \text{f}(x - 3)$

  (ii) $y = \text{f}(x) - 5$

  (iii) $y = -\text{f}(x)$

  (iv) $y = \text{f}(2x)$.

(b) The curve with equation $y = x^2$ has been translated to give the curve $y = \text{f}(x)$.
Find $\text{f}(x)$ in terms of x.

4 This is a sketch of the curve with equation $y = \text{f}(x)$.

The only maximum point of the curve $y = \text{f}(x)$ is $A(3, 6)$.

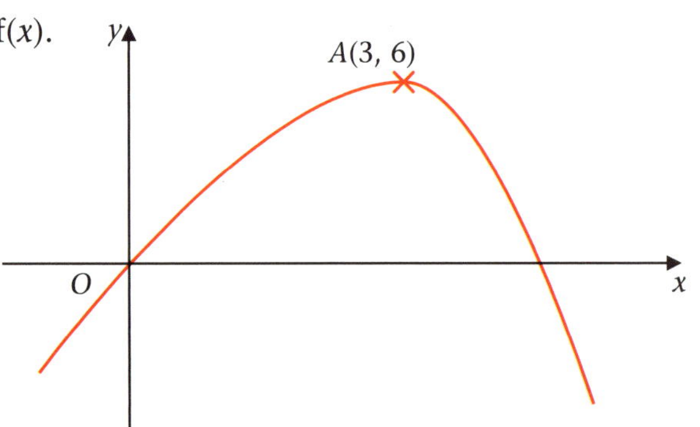

Write down the coordinates of the maximum point for curves with each of the following equations.

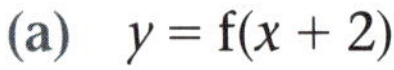

(a) $y = \text{f}(x + 2)$

(b) $y = \text{f}(x) + 4$

(c) $y = \text{f}(-x)$

5 This is a sketch of the curve with equation $y = f(x)$.
The only vertex of the curve is at $P(2, -25)$.

(a) Write down the coordinates of the vertex for curves with each of the following equations.

(i) $y = f(x - 2)$

(ii) $y = f(x) + 22$

(iii) $y = f(2x)$

(b) $f(x) = (2x + a)(2x - b)$, where a and b are positive integers.
The curve $y = f(x)$ passes through the point $(2, -25)$.
The curve $y = f(x + 4.5)$ passes through the point $(0, 0)$.

Find the value of a and the value of b.

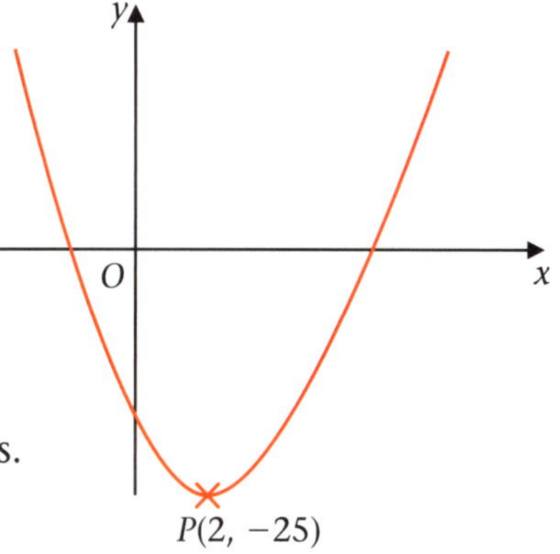

Summary of key points

1 A **function** is a rule which shows how one set of numbers relates to another set.

2 The graph of $y = x^2 + a$ is the graph of $y = x^2$ translated a units vertically (in the *positive* y-direction if $a > 0$, in the *negative* y-direction if $a < 0$).

3 The graph of $y = x + a$ is the graph of $y = x$ translated a units vertically (in the *positive* y-direction if $a > 0$, in the *negative* y-direction if $a < 0$).

4 The graph of $y = x^3 + a$ is the graph of $y = x^3$ translated a units vertically (in the *positive* y-direction if $a > 0$, in the *negative* y-direction if $a < 0$).

5 The graph of $y = \frac{1}{x} + a$ is the graph of $y = \frac{1}{x}$ translated a units vertically (in the *positive* y-direction if $a > 0$, in the *negative* y-direction if $a < 0$).

6 For any function f, the graph of $y = f(x) + a$ is the graph of $y = f(x)$ translated a units vertically (in the *positive* y-direction if $a > 0$, in the *negative* y-direction if $a < 0$).

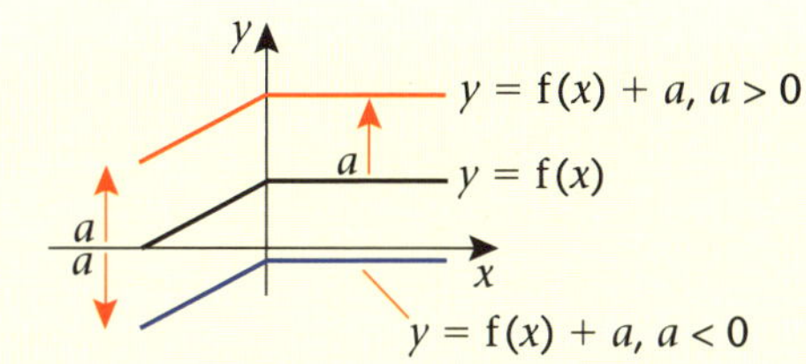

7 The graph of $y = (x + a)^2$ is the graph of $y = x^2$ translated a units horizontally (in the *negative* x-direction if $a > 0$, in the *positive* x-direction if $a < 0$).

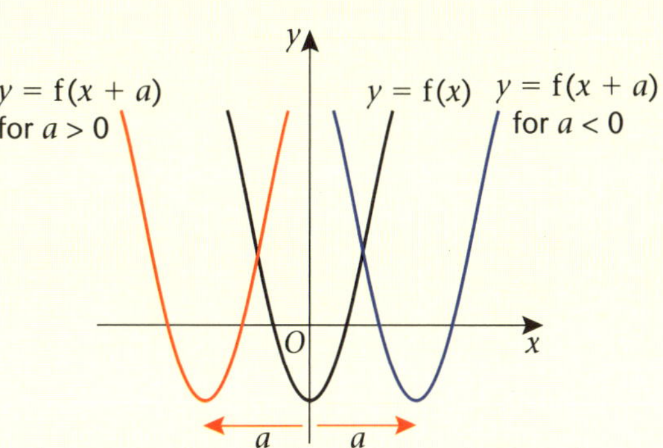

8 The **vertex** of the parabola $y = (x + a)^2$ is at the point $(-a, 0)$.

9 For any function f, the graph of $y = \mathrm{f}(x + a)$ is the graph of $y = \mathrm{f}(x)$ translated a units horizontally (in the *negative* x-direction if $a > 0$, in tthe *positive* x-direction if $a < 0$).

10 To sketch the graph of $y = x^2 + bx + c$, complete the square and apply a double translation to the parabola $y = x^2$.

11 For any function f, the graph of $y = \mathrm{f}(x + a) + b$ is the graph of $y = \mathrm{f}(x)$ translated a units horizontally (in the *negative* x-direction if $a > 0$, in the *positive* x-direction if $a < 0$) followed by a translation of b units vertically (*upwards* if $b > 0$, *downwards* if $b < 0$).

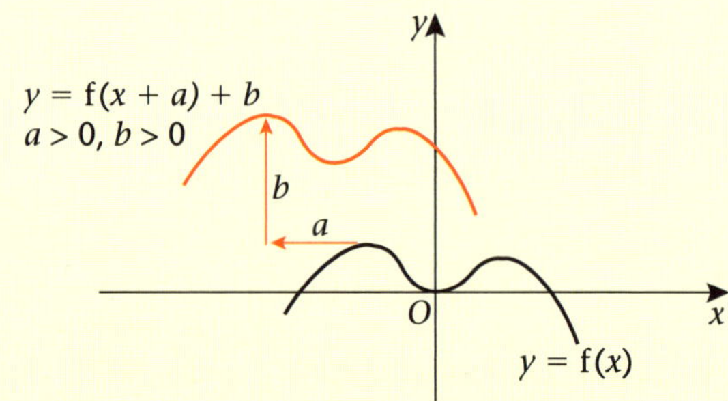

12 For any function f, the graph of $y = -\mathrm{f}(x)$ is obtained by reflecting $y = \mathrm{f}(x)$ in the x-axis.

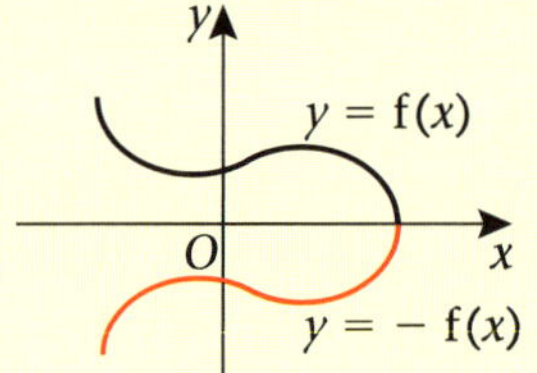

13 For any function f, the graph of $y = \mathrm{f}(-x)$ is obtained by reflecting $y = \mathrm{f}(x)$ in the y-axis.

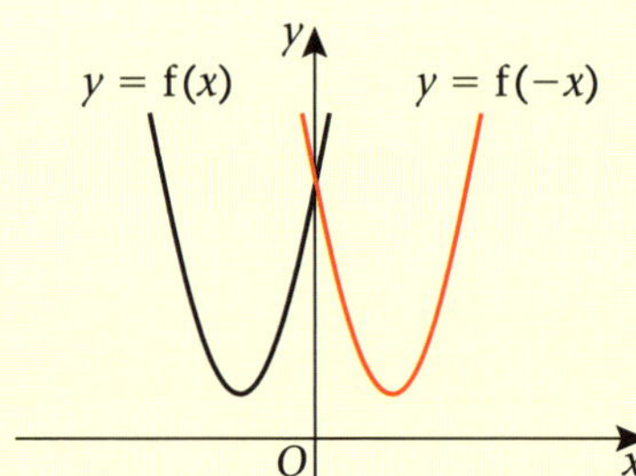

14 For any function f, the graph of $y = a\mathrm{f}(x)$, where a is a positive constant, is obtained from $y = \mathrm{f}(x)$ by applying a stretch of scale factor a parallel to the y-axis.

15 For any function f, the graph of $y = \mathrm{f}(ax)$, where a is a positive constant, is obtained from $y = \mathrm{f}(x)$ by applying a stretch of scale factor $\frac{1}{a}$ parallel to the x-axis.

26 Circle theorems

In this chapter you will learn about calculating angles and using angle properties related to circles, and about proof.

We shall start by looking at a collection of important mathematical results known as **circle theorems**.

Proofs that may be required in the GCSE exam are given in Section 26.3.

26.1 Circle theorems

Axiom

An axiom is a given fact that can be used to prove a theorem.

The angle between a tangent and a radius is 90°.

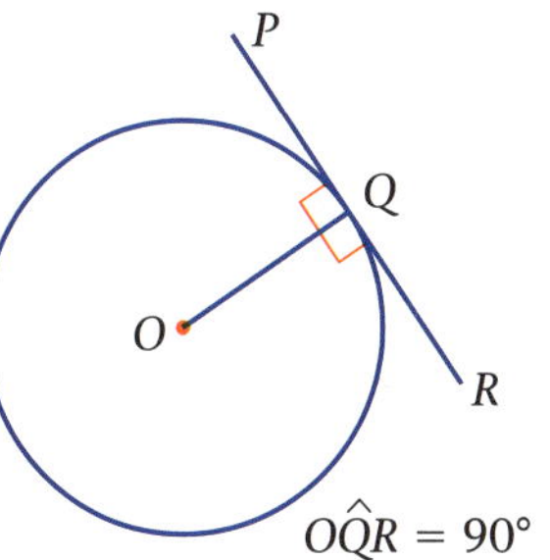

Example 1

In the diagram on the right, given that PT is a tangent to the circle, find angle PTQ (x).

$OT = OQ =$ radius

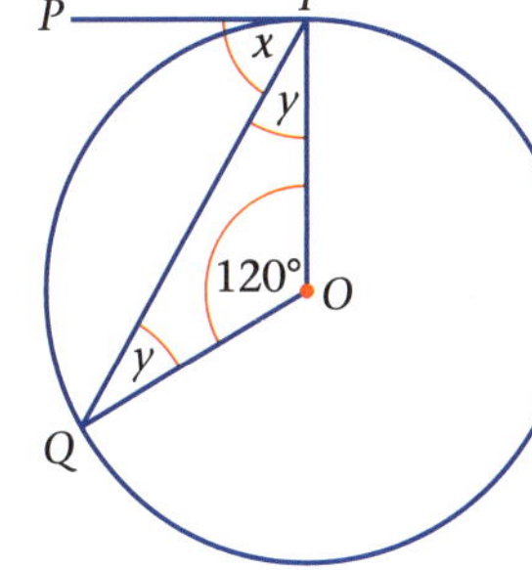

So triangle QOT is isosceles.

So angle OQT = angle OTQ (call each y)

Then $y + y + 120° = 180°$ (angles in a triangle)

$2y + 120° = 180°$

$2y = 60°$

$y = 30°$

But $x + y = 90°$ (PT is a tangent, OT a radius)

So $x = 90° - y$

$= 90° - 30°$

$= 60°$

Theorem 1

The lengths of the two tangents from a point to a circle are equal.

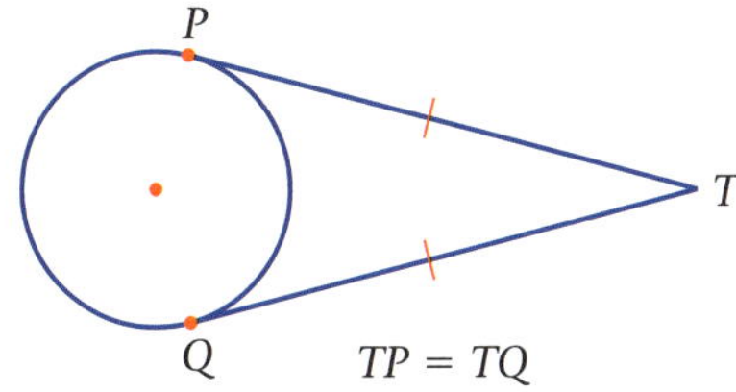

For a proof of Theorem 1 see Section 26.3.

Example 2

O is the centre of the circle.
TA and TB are the tangents from T to the circle.
Angle $ATB = 64°$
Calculate the size of

(a) angle BAT (b) angle OAB.

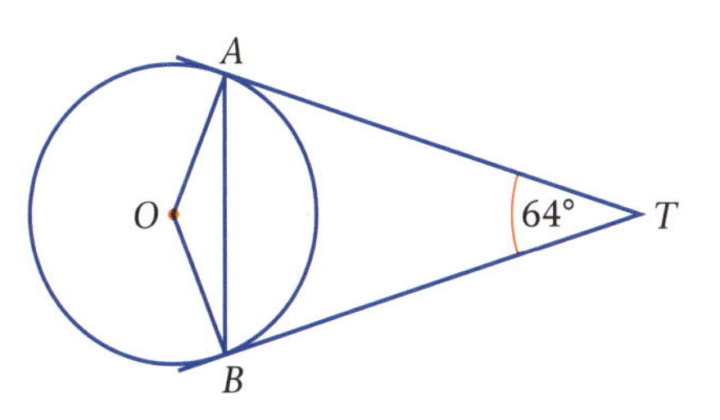

(a) The tangents TA and TB are equal, so ATB is isosceles.

$B\hat{A}T + T\hat{B}A = 180° - 64° = 116°$
(sum of angles of triangles)

$B\hat{A}T = T\hat{B}A = 116° \div 2 = 58°$
(base angles of isosceles triangle)

(b) $O\hat{A}T = 90°$ (radius perpendicular to tangent)

So $O\hat{A}B = 90° - 58° = 32°$

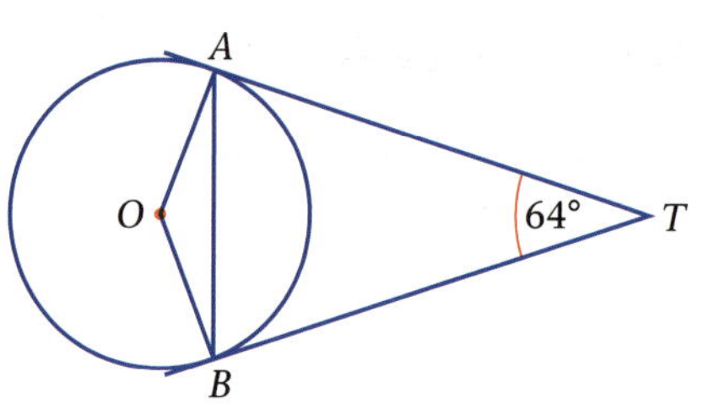

Theorem 2

The perpendicular from the centre of a circle to a chord bisects the chord.

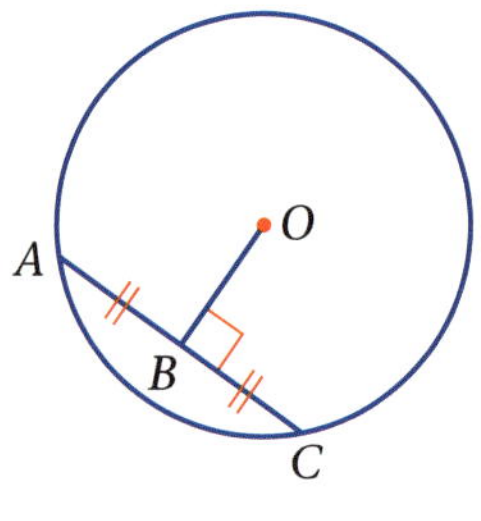

$AB = AC$

For a proof of Theorem 2 see Section 26.3.

Example 3

Find the values of a and b.

$A\hat{O}B = 360° - 230° = 130°$

$a = \frac{1}{2}$ of $A\hat{O}B$ (by symmetry)

so $a = \frac{1}{2}$ of $130°$

$= 65°$

In the triangle AMO:

$b + a + 90° = 180°$

$b = 180° - 90° - a$

$= 90° - 65°$

$= 25°$

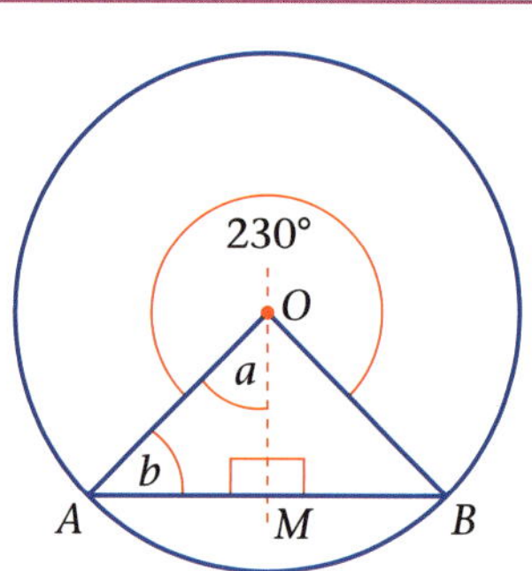

Example 4

The distance of the chord AB from the centre O is 5 cm. $AB = 12$ cm.

Calculate the radius of the circle.

$AM = \frac{1}{2}AB = \frac{1}{2} \times 12 = 6$ cm

Using Pythagoras' theorem in triangle OAM:

$OA^2 = 25 + 36$

$OA = \sqrt{61}$

$= 7.81$ cm

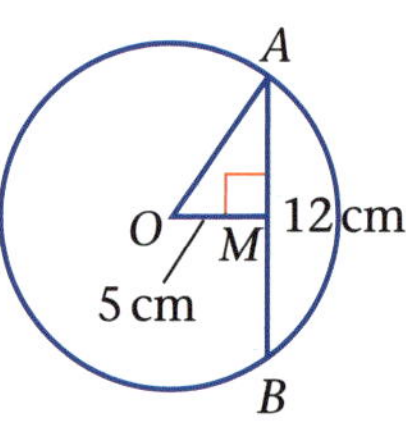

Exercise 26A

1 N is the middle point of the chord PQ.

$Q\hat{O}N$ is 52°

Calculate angle NQO.

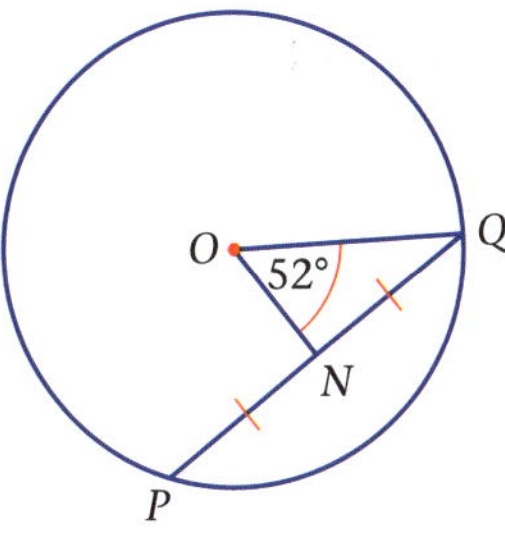

2 BC is the tangent at B to the circle.

$O\hat{B}A = 24°$

Calculate

(a) $A\hat{B}C$

(b) $O\hat{A}B$

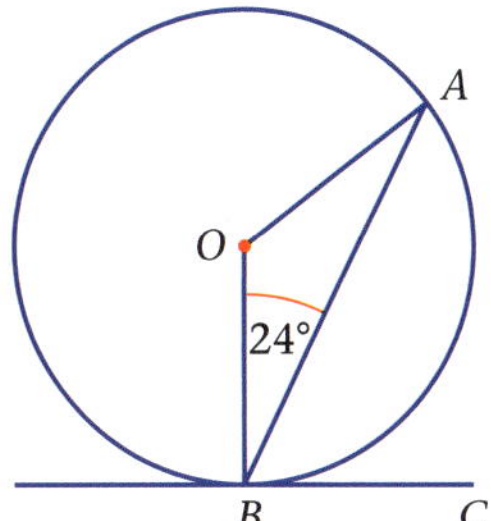

3 QP and QR are the tangents from Q to the circle.

$Q\hat{P}R = 73°$

Calculate

(a) $P\hat{Q}R$

(b) $O\hat{P}R$

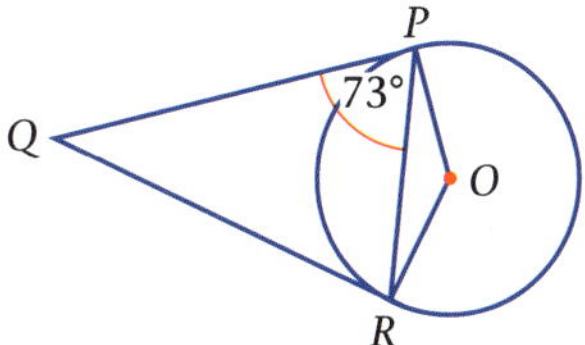

26.2 More circle theorems

Theorem 3

The angle subtended at the centre of a circle is twice the angle at the circumference.

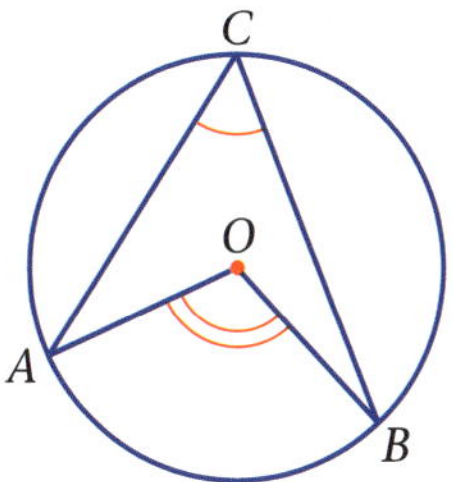

$A\hat{O}B = 2 \times A\hat{C}B$

For a proof of Theorem 3 see Section 26.3.

The subtended angle is the angle formed at O by the straight lines AO and BO.

Example 5

Calculate the size of angles ACB and ADB.

Angle ACB $= \frac{1}{2}$ angle AOB

$= 40°$

Reflex angle AOB $= 360° - 80°$

$= 280°$

Angle ADB $= \frac{1}{2}$ reflex angle AOB

$= 140°$

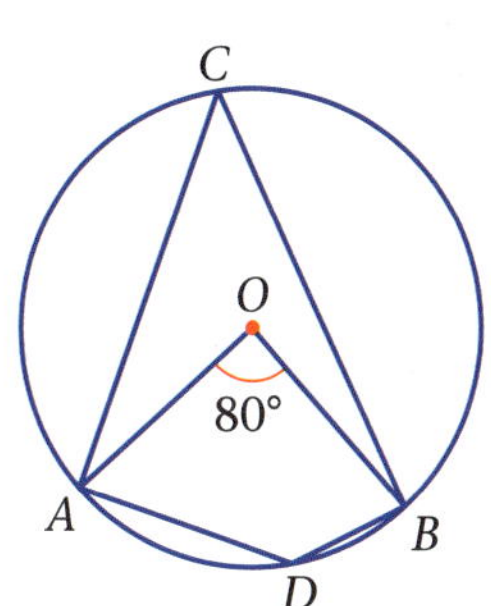

From Theorem 3 it follows that:

Theorem 4

The angle in a semicircle is a right angle.

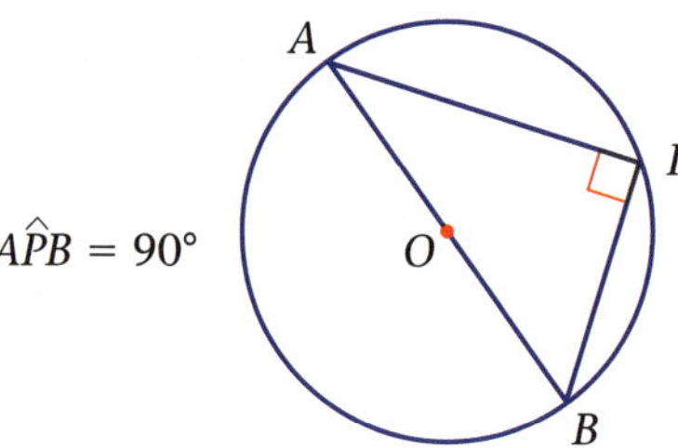

For a proof of Theorem 4 see Section 26.3.

Example 6

In the diagram, calculate the size of angle AOX.

Angle $BDA = 90°$ (angle in semicircle)

Angle $BAD = 32°$ (third angle of triangle)

Angle $AOX = 32°$ (alternate angles)

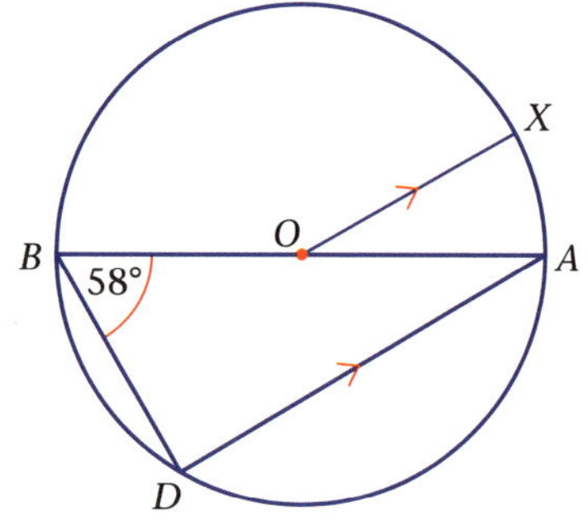

Theorem 5

Angles in the same segment are equal.

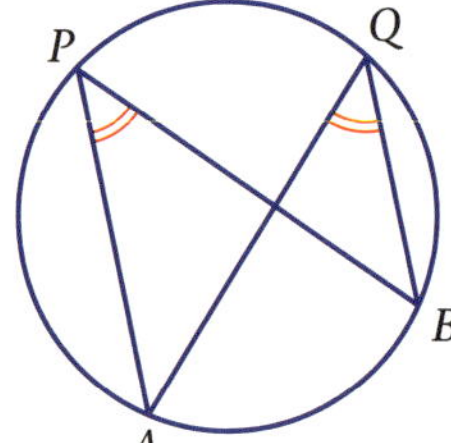

For a proof of Theorem 5 see Section 26.3.

Example 7

Calculate the angle a.

$a = 54°$ (angles in the same segment are equal)

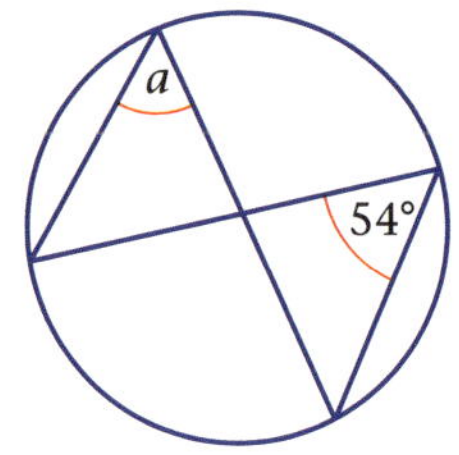

Theorem 6

Opposite angles of a cyclic quadrilateral are supplementary.

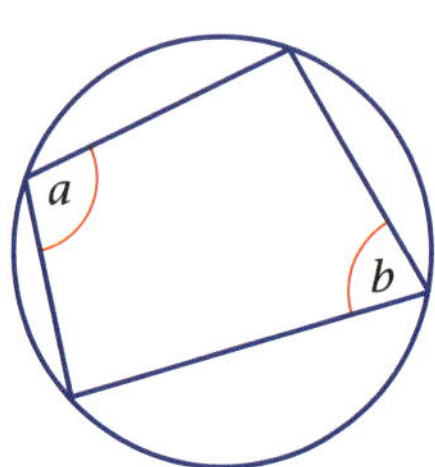

For a proof of Theorem 6 see Section 26.3.

Points which lie on the circumference of the same circle are called **concyclic**. If a circle can be drawn through all four corners of a quadrilateral, then the quadrilateral is known as **cyclic**.

Two angles are **supplementary** if their sum is 180°.

Example 8

Find the sizes of angles ABC and BAC.

Angle $ABC = 146°$ (opposite angles of a cyclic quadrilateral)

Angle $BAC = \frac{1}{2}(180° - 146°)$ (triangle ABC is isosceles)

$= \frac{1}{2} \times 34°$

$= 17°$

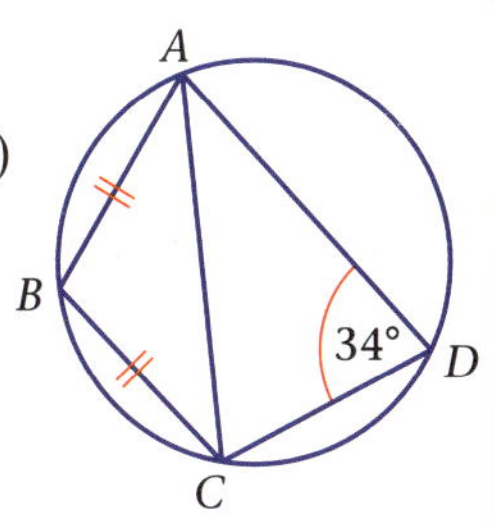

Theorem 7

The angle between a tangent and a chord is equal to the angle in the alternate segment.

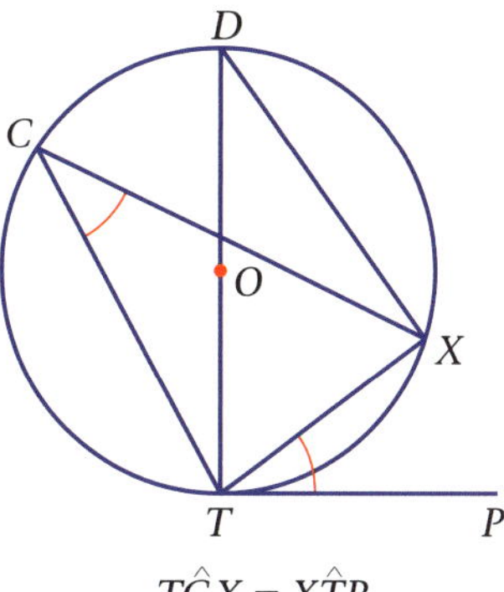

$T\hat{C}X = X\hat{T}P$

For a proof of Theorem 7 see Section 26.3.

This theorem is called the **alternate segment theorem** because the angle a chord makes with a tangent is equal to the angle subtended by the chord at the circumference in the alternate segment to the tangent.

Example 9

Calculate the sizes of angles TQX and TXQ.

Angle $TQX = 36°$ (alternate segment)

Angle $TXQ = \frac{1}{2}(180° - 36°)$ (triangle TXQ is isosceles)

$= \frac{1}{2} \times 144°$

$= 72°$

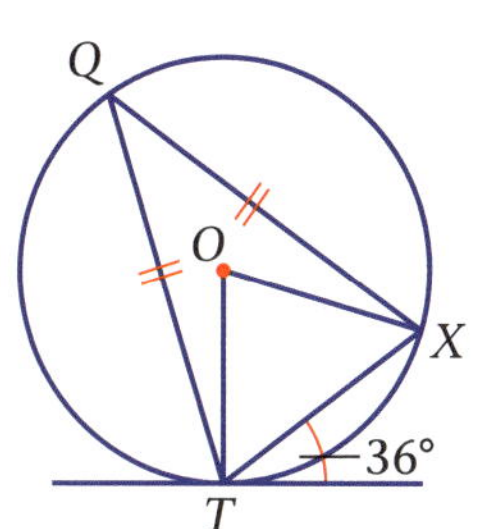

Exercise 26B

1 PQ is a diameter of the circle. TS is the tangent at P.
$P\hat{R}Q = 90°$ and $P\hat{Q}R = 34°$.
Calculate

(a) $R\hat{P}Q$ (b) $R\hat{P}T$

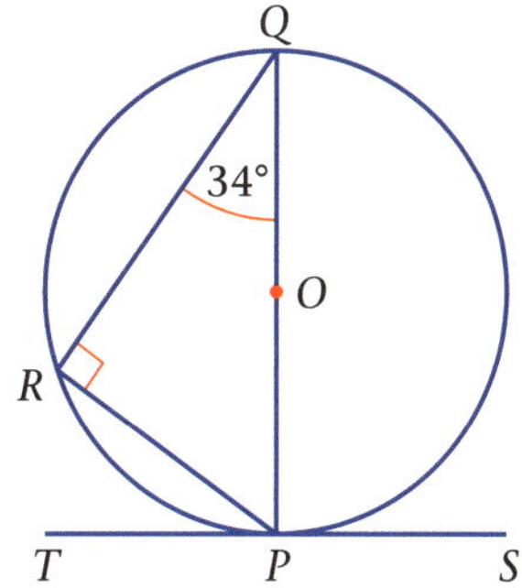

2 DE is the tangent at B to the circle.
AO is parallel to BC. $O\hat{B}A = 56°$.
Calculate

(a) $A\hat{B}D$ (b) $O\hat{A}B$ (c) $A\hat{O}B$
(d) $O\hat{B}C$ (e) $C\hat{B}E$

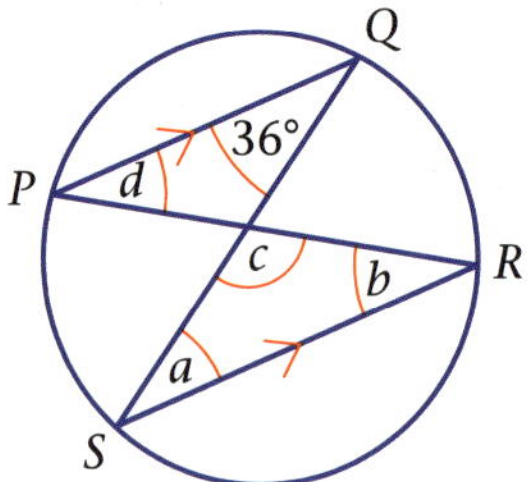

3 PQ is parallel to SR.
Calculate a, b, c and d.

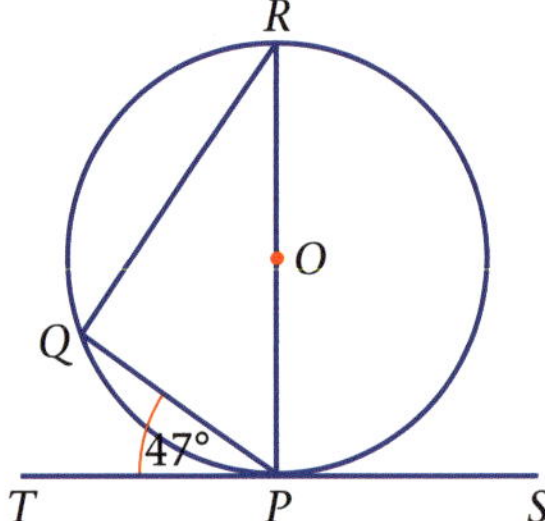

4 TPS is the tangent to the circle at P.
$T\hat{P}Q = 47°$.
Calculate the size of

(a) $P\hat{Q}R$
(b) $Q\hat{R}P$

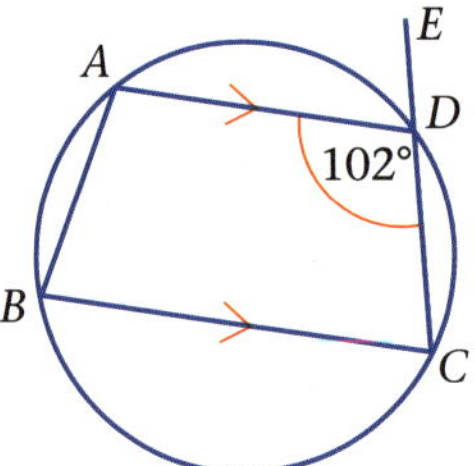

5 AD is parallel to BC. $A\hat{D}C = 102°$.
Calculate the size of

(a) $A\hat{D}E$ (b) $A\hat{B}C$
(c) $D\hat{C}B$ (d) $B\hat{A}D$

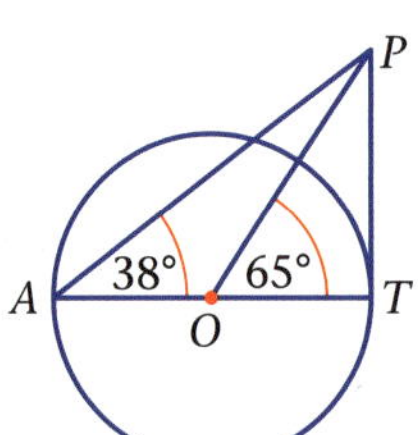

6 PT is a tangent to the circle.
Find the angles OPT and OPA.

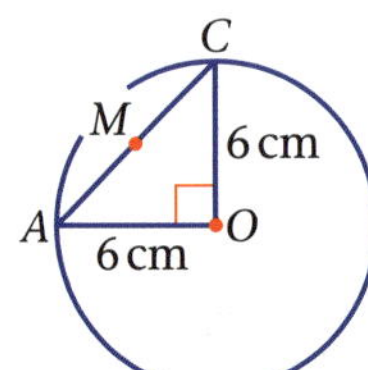

7 M is the mid-point of AC.
Calculate the lengths of AC and OM.

8 *M* is the mid-point of *PQ*.
Calculate angle *POM* and angle *OPM*.

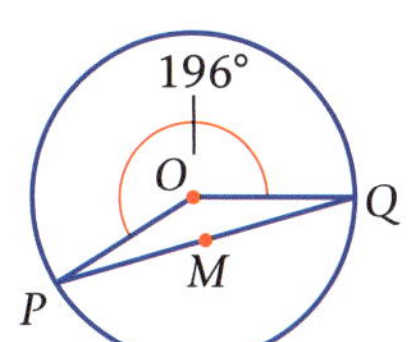

9 Calculate *SO* and the area of *OSPT*.

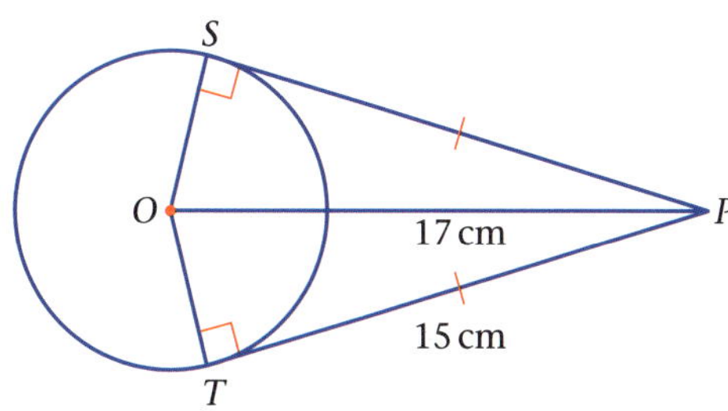

10 *M* is the mid-point of *AC*.
Calculate the size of angle *MOC*.

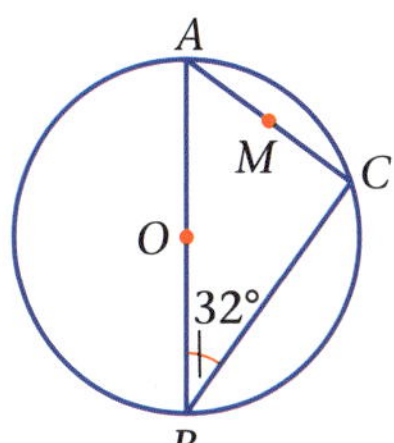

11 *AB* is a diameter.
Angle $ABC = 54°$ and angle $ABD = 32°$.
Calculate the sizes of angles *CXD* and *CAD*.

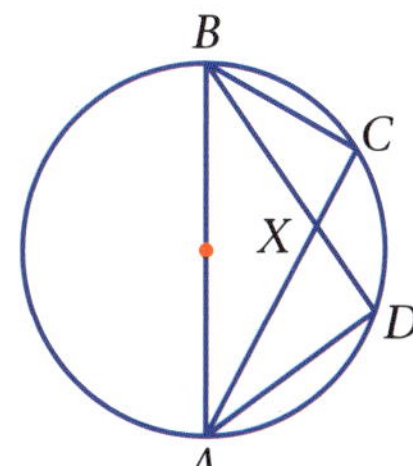

12 *TQ* is a diameter. *PT* is a tangent.
Find, in terms of *x*,

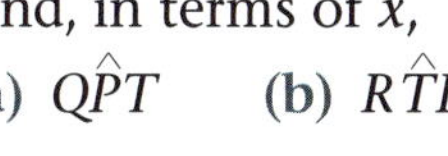
(a) $Q\hat{P}T$ (b) $R\hat{T}P$

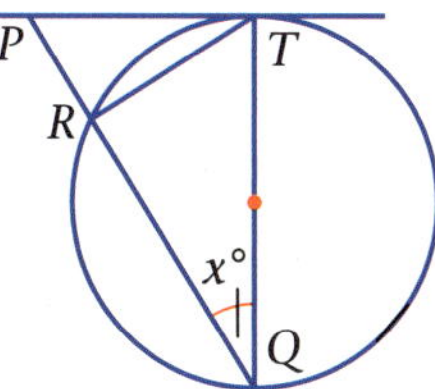

13 *AB* is a diameter.
Calculate the area of triangle *ABD*.

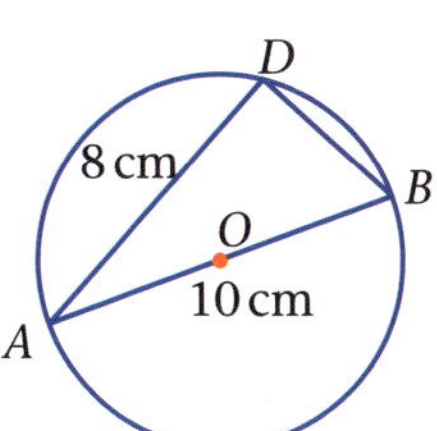

14 Calculate angles *d*, *e* and *f*.

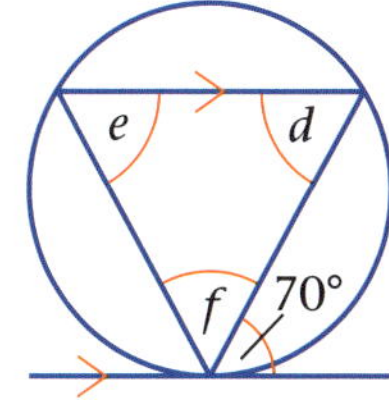

15 Calculate the sizes of angles TBA and TCA.

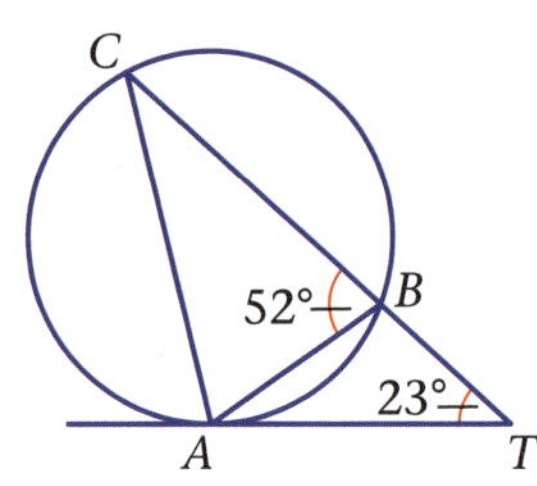

16 Calculate the length of AB.

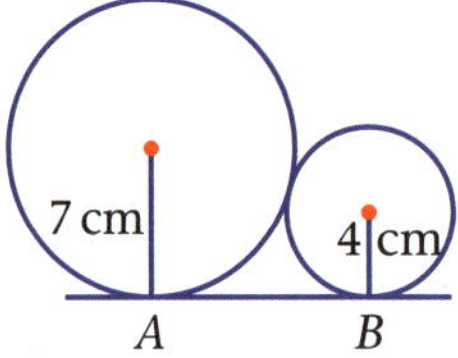

17 PT is a tangent to the circle at T.
Calculate the size of angle TXS.

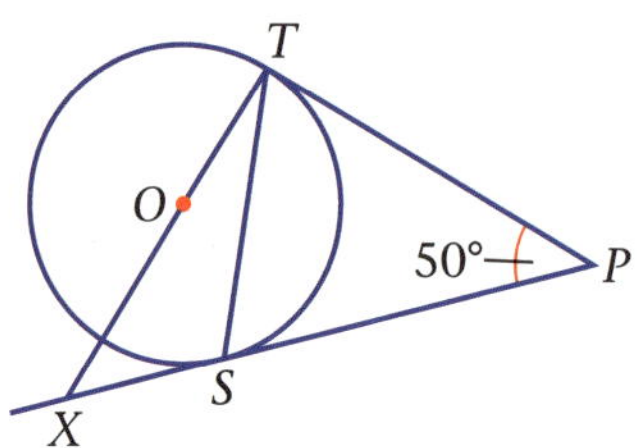

18 A bridge is built in the shape of the arc of a circle, centre O. The width, AB, is 12 m and the height is 4 m. Calculate the distance AO.

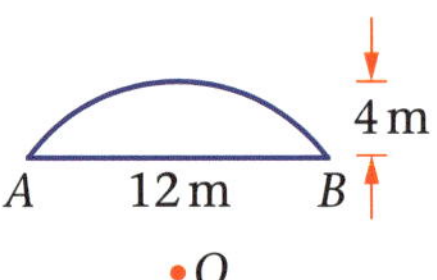

19 Draw accurately a triangle ABC which has all its angles acute. Draw the perpendicular bisectors of the sides AC and AB. These meet at the point O. Explain why O is the centre of the circle which passes through the three corners of the triangle.

26.3 Proving circle and geometrical theorems

This section shows the proofs you may need for your GCSE exam.

When writing geometrical proofs you need to give reasons for the steps that you take. This usually means stating reasons or theorems that justify the steps in your proof.

Proof of Theorem 1

The lengths of the two tangents from a point to a circle are equal.

In triangles OPS and OPT:

$OS = OT$ (radii)

OP is common to both

angle OSP = angle $OTP = 90°$ (tangent and radius)

So triangles OPS and OPT are congruent. (RHS)

So $PS = PT$

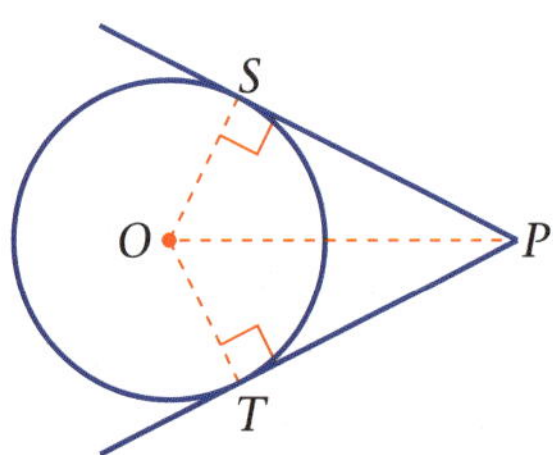

Proof of Theorem 2

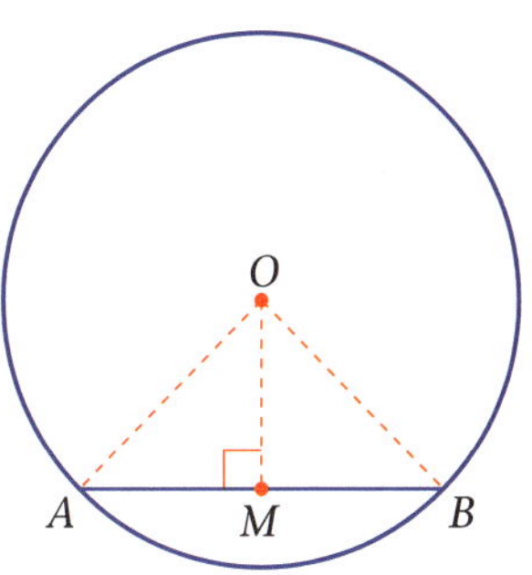

The perpendicular from the centre of a circle to a chord bisects the chord.

M is the point where the perpendicular from O meets the chord AB.
In triangles OAM and OBM:

$OA = OB$ (radii)

OM is common to both

angle OMA = angle $OMB = 90°$

So triangles OAM and OBM are congruent. (RHS)

So $AM = MB$

Proof of Theorem 3

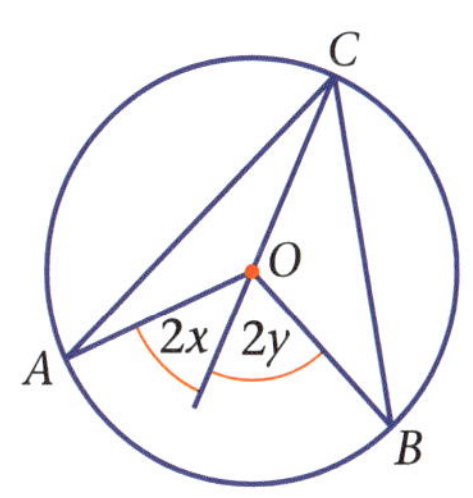

The angle subtended at the centre of a circle is twice the angle at the circumference.

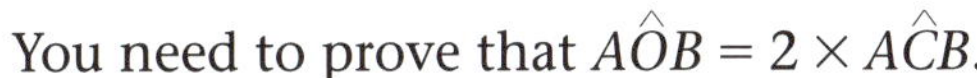

You need to prove that $A\hat{O}B = 2 \times A\hat{C}B$.
Call the two parts of $A\hat{O}B$ $2x$ and $2y$, as shown.
So $A\hat{O}B = 2x + 2y$

Now $A\hat{O}C = 180° - 2x$ (straight line)

$O\hat{A}C + O\hat{C}A = 2x$ (exterior angle of triangle = sum of two interior opposite angles)

$O\hat{A}C = O\hat{C}A = x$ (triangle AOC is isosceles)

Similarly, $O\hat{B}C = O\hat{C}B = y$

So $A\hat{C}B = x + y$

That is, $A\hat{O}B = 2 \times A\hat{C}B$

Since nothing has been assumed about the values of x and y, this result must be generally true for all diagrams like the one above.

The theorem is also true if C is on the minor arc, as shown on the right.

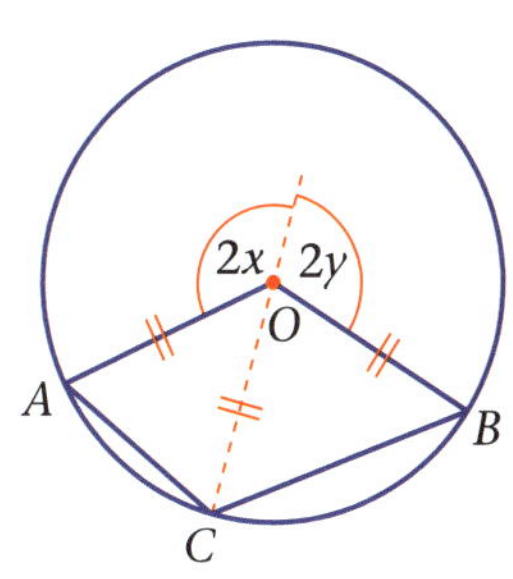

To prove, call the two parts of the the reflex angle AOB $2x$ and $2y$, as before.

$A\hat{O}C = 180° - 2x$ (straight line)

So $O\hat{A}C = O\hat{C}A = x$ (triangle OAC is isosceles)

Similarly $O\hat{C}B = O\hat{B}C = y$

So $A\hat{C}B = x + y$

That is, reflex angle $AOB = 2 \times A\hat{C}B$

There is another case to consider. Here C is on the major arc but relatively close to B. The theorem is still true but the proof is not demonstrated here.

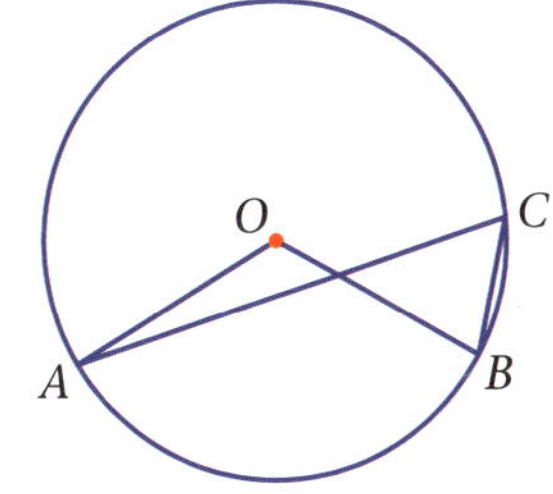

Proof of Theorem 4

The angle in a semicircle is a right angle.

In triangle ABC:

angle $AOB = 180°$ (straight line)

So angle $ACB = \frac{1}{2} \times 180°$ (angle at centre is twice angle at circumference)

$= 90°$

Proof of Theorem 5

Angles in the same segment are equal.

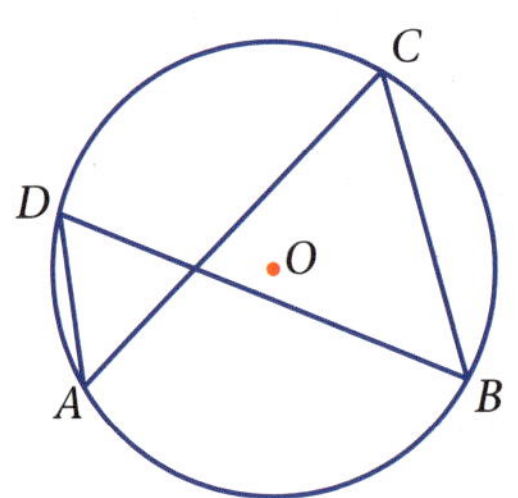

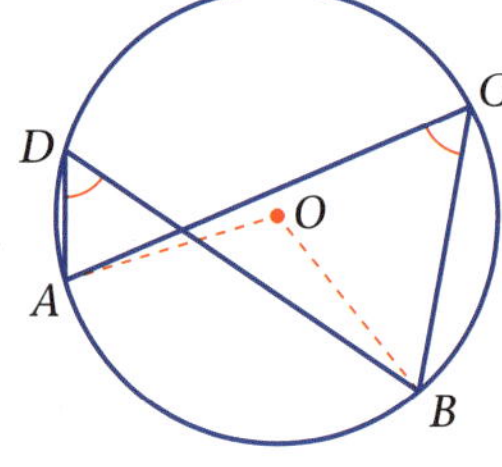

Join AO and OB.

angle $ACB = \frac{1}{2}$ angle AOB (angle at centre is twice angle at circumference)

and angle $ADB = \frac{1}{2}$ angle AOB

So angle ACB = angle ADB

Proof of Theorem 6

Opposite angles of a cyclic quadrilateral are supplementary.

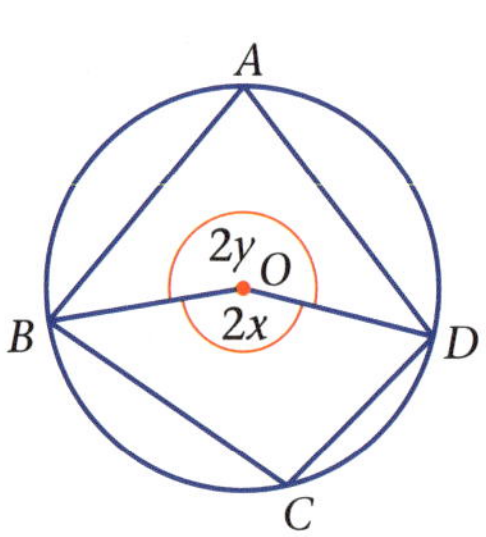

$2x + 2y = 360°$

So $x + y = 180°$

angle $BAD = x$ (angle at centre is twice angle at circumference)

angle $BCD = y$ (angle at centre is twice angle at circumference)

angle BAD + angle $BCD = x + y = 180°$

You can show that $A\hat{B}C + C\hat{D}A = 180°$ by drawing AO and CO.

Proof of Theorem 7

The angle between a tangent and a chord is equal to the angle in the alternate segment.

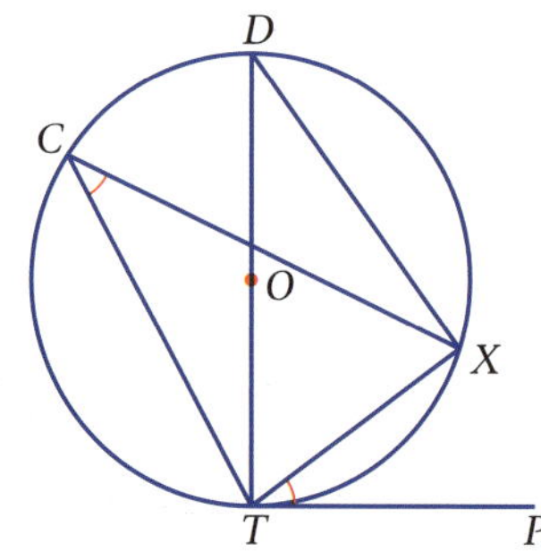

TD is the diameter of the circle, so $T\hat{X}D = 90°$.

(angle in a semicircle is a right angle)

$T\hat{D}X + D\hat{T}X = 90°$ **(1)** (angle sum of triangle is 180°)

PT is a tangent so $P\hat{T}D$ is 90°.

Thus $P\hat{T}X + D\hat{T}X = 90°$ **(2)**

From **(1)** and **(2)**:

$T\hat{D}X + D\hat{T}X = P\hat{T}X + D\hat{T}X = 90°$

So $T\hat{D}X = P\hat{T}X$

C is any other point on the circumference.

Now $T\hat{C}X = T\hat{D}X$ (angles in the same segment)

Thus $P\hat{T}X = T\hat{C}X$

Example 10

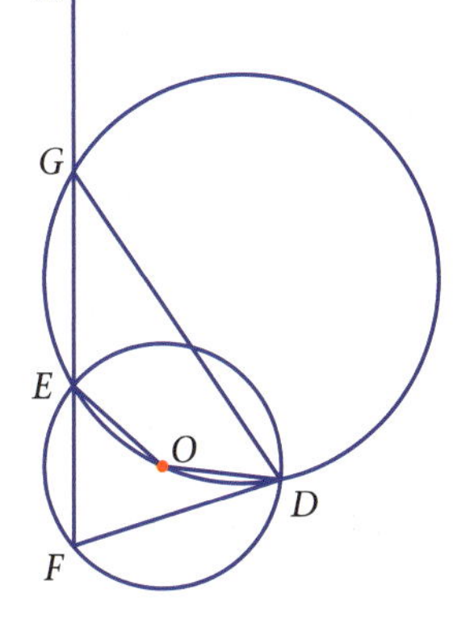

O is the centre of the smaller circle. $FEGH$ is a straight line.
Prove that:

(a) angle $DGH = 2 \times$ angle DFE (b) $FG = DG$

(a) In the small circle, angle $DOE = 2 \times$ angle DFE
(angle at centre is twice angle at circumference)

In the large circle, angle $DOE = 180° -$ angle DGE
(opposite angles of a cyclic quadrilateral)

Thus $180° -$ angle $DGE = 2 \times$ angle DFE

But $180° -$ angle $DGE =$ angle DGH ($FEGH$ is a straight line)

So angle $DGH = 2 \times$ angle DFE

(b) Let angle $DFE = x$.

Then from **(a)** angle $DGE = 180° - 2x$

Thus angle $FDG = x$ (angle sum of triangle is 180°)
and $FG = DG$ (DFG is an isosceles triangle)

Exercise 26C

1 O is the centre of the circle. AOC is a straight line.
TB and TC are tangents.
Prove that the triangles AOB and BTC are similar.

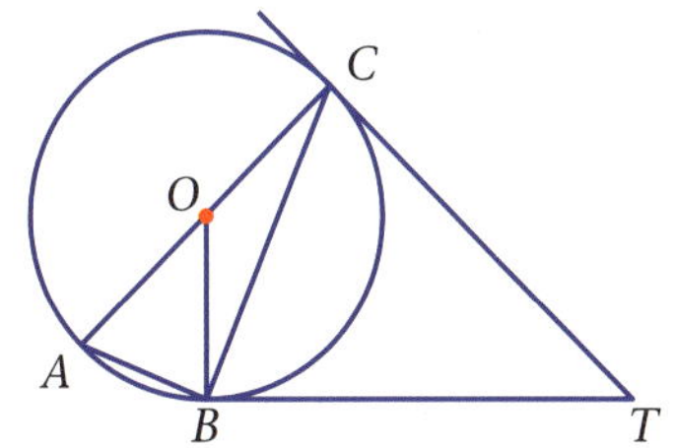

2 PQ and RS intersect at right angles. PY is a tangent.
$RXSY$ is a straight line so that $YX = XR$. QSZ is a straight line.
Prove that:

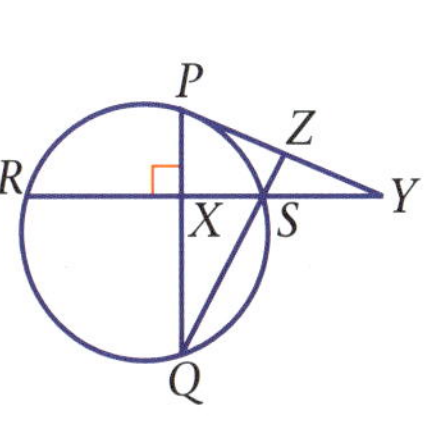

(a) angle $YPX =$ angle XSQ

(b) angle $PZQ = 90°$

3 AB is parallel to CD. Prove that

(a) angle $AEC = 2 \times$ angle ABC

(b) $AE = BE$

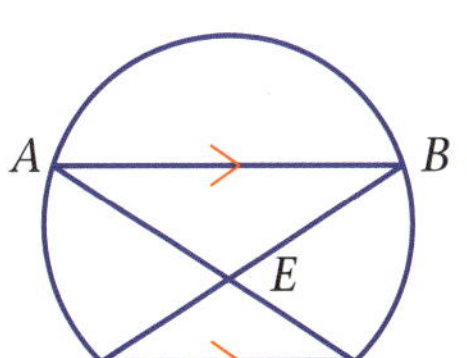

4 ADX and BCX are straight lines.
The straight line XFE bisects angle AXB.
Prove that angle $DFE =$ angle FEA.

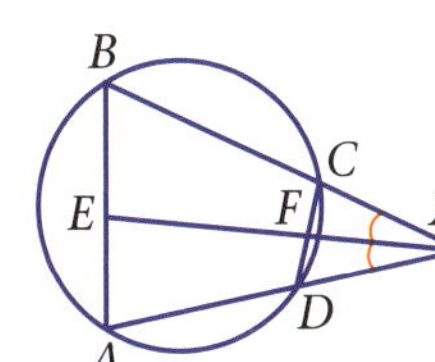

5 Prove that angle ADC = angle BCD.

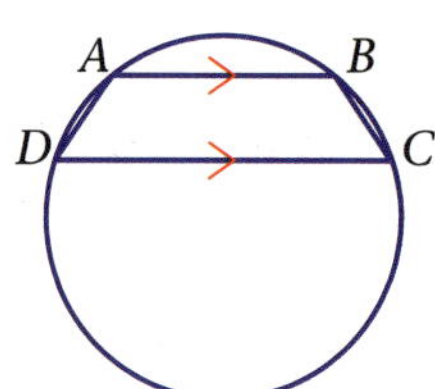

6 $ABCD$ is a cyclic quadrilateral with $AB = AD$. Prove that the line AC bisects the angle DCB.

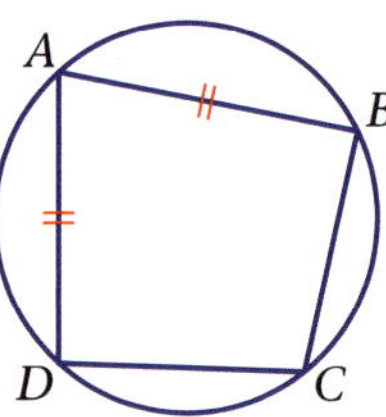

7 $ABCD$ is a parallelogram. Prove that $AE = AD$.

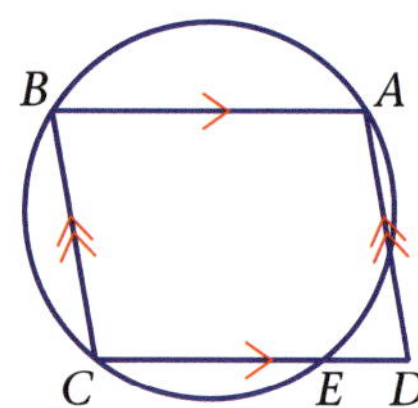

8 ADE is a straight line. FD bisects angle EDC. Prove that FB bisects angle ABC.

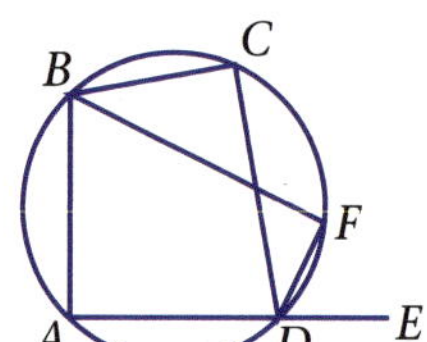

9 AB is parallel to the straight line CDE. AF bisects angle DAG. Show that $AF = FE$.

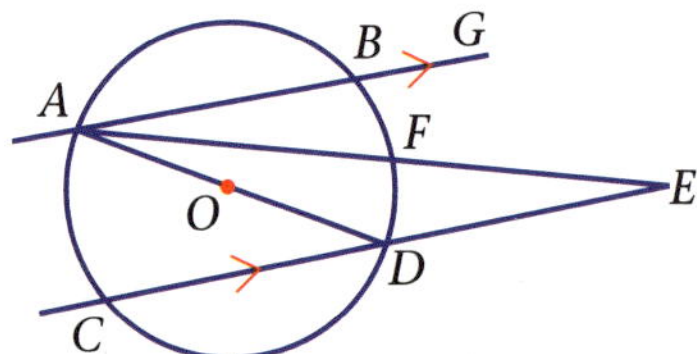

10 C is the point on the circumference such that BT bisects angle CBA. Prove that angle $COA = 4 \times$ angle ATP.

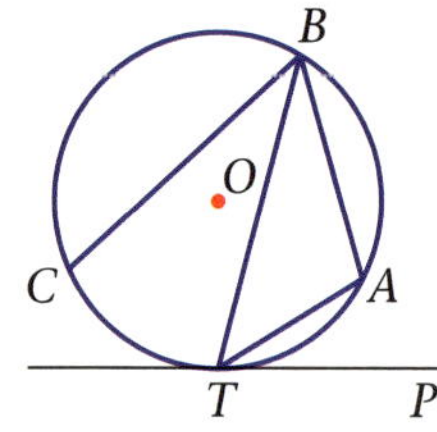

Mixed exercise 26

1 For each of the diagrams below, calculate the length of the chord AB.

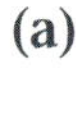

(a)

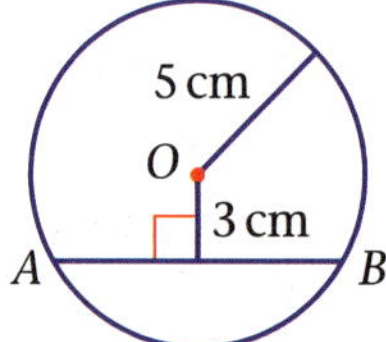

(b)

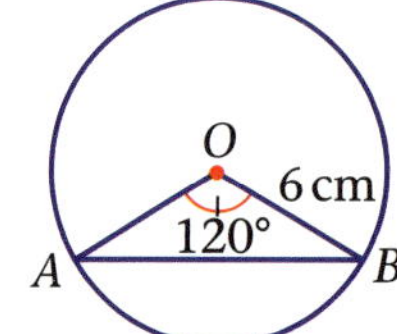

2 Angle $ABC = 42°$.
Name two other angles in the diagram with size 42°.

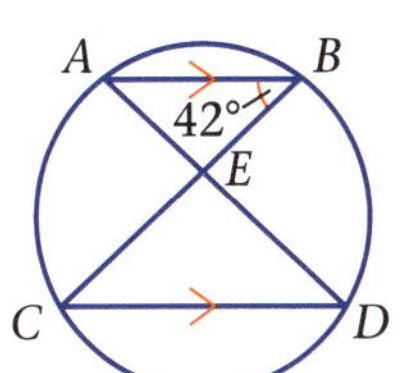

3 QS is a diameter. Triangle PQS is isosceles.
Calculate the size of angle PQR.

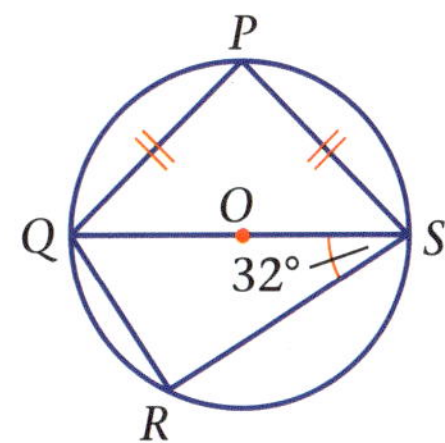

4 PR is a diameter of the semicircle.
PRY is a straight line.
Find the sizes of these angles:

(a) $P\hat{Q}R$ (b) $Q\hat{R}P$ (c) $Q\hat{R}X$

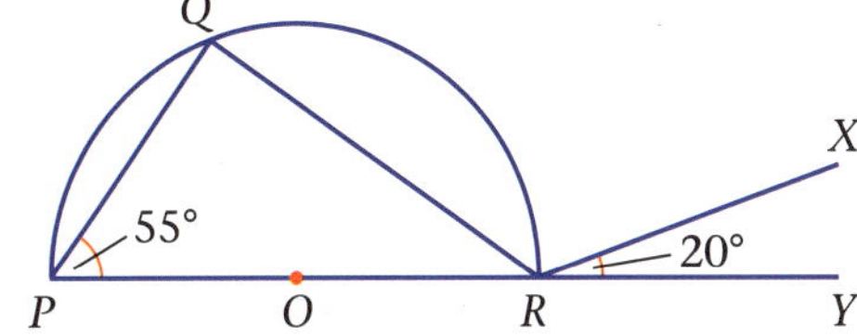

5 Calculate the sizes of these angles:

(a) $C\hat{A}D$ (b) $A\hat{D}B$ (c) $A\hat{C}D$

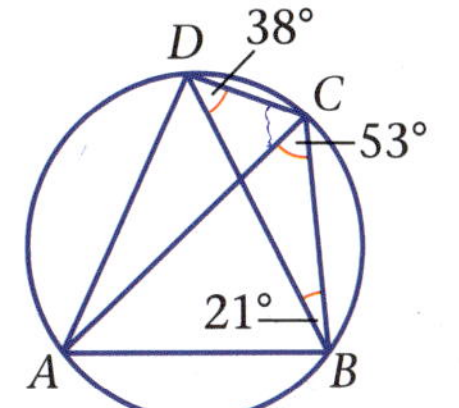

6 AOB is a diameter.
Calculate the size of angle ADC.

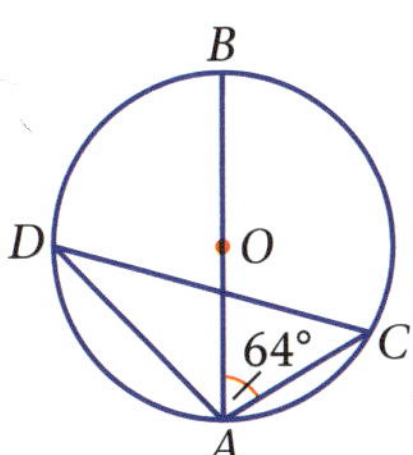

7 AOB is a diameter. Calculate the sizes of angles OBC and OCA.

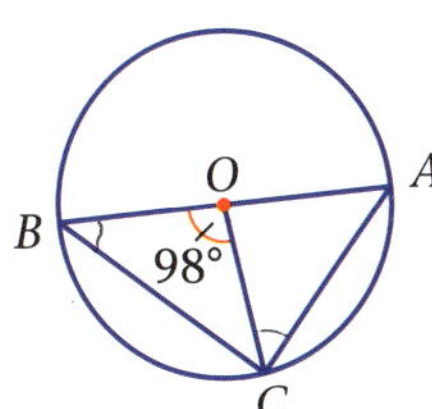

8 Calculate the radius of the circle and the length of the chord PQ.

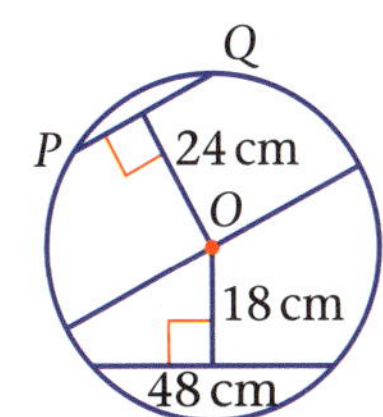

9 Triangle ABC is isosceles. Calculate the sizes of these angles:

(a) $B\hat{A}D$ (b) $A\hat{C}B$ (c) $A\hat{D}B$

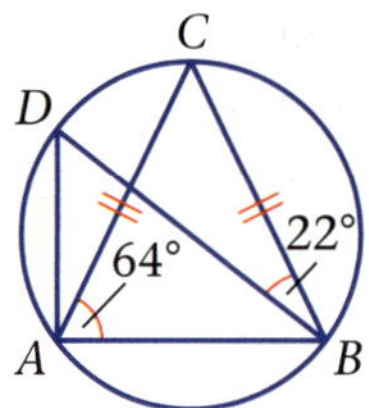

10 The straight lines PSX and PTY are tangents to the circle with centre O.

Given that the radius of the circle is r, calculate the length of PB in terms of r.

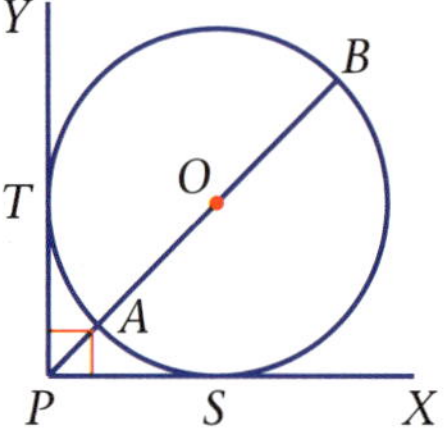

11 $PQRS$ is a cyclic quadrilateral.
PSB and QRB are straight lines. PQA and SRA are straight lines.
Calculate the values of x and y.

12 Triangle AOB is equilateral and DA is a tangent.
Calculate the sizes of these angles:

(a) $O\hat{A}B$ (b) $O\hat{A}D$ (c) $B\hat{D}A$

(d) $C\hat{A}B$ (e) $A\hat{C}B$

(f) Calculate the length of AC.

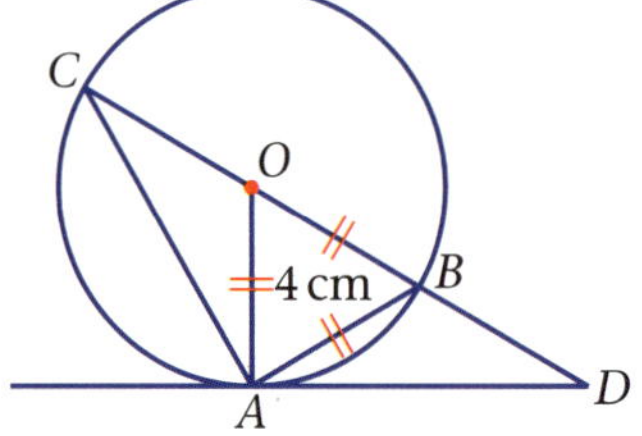

13 TA is a tangent to the circle, centre O.
DOB is a diameter of the circle.
Find the sizes of these angles:

(a) $D\hat{B}A$ (b) $B\hat{D}A$ (c) $C\hat{B}D$

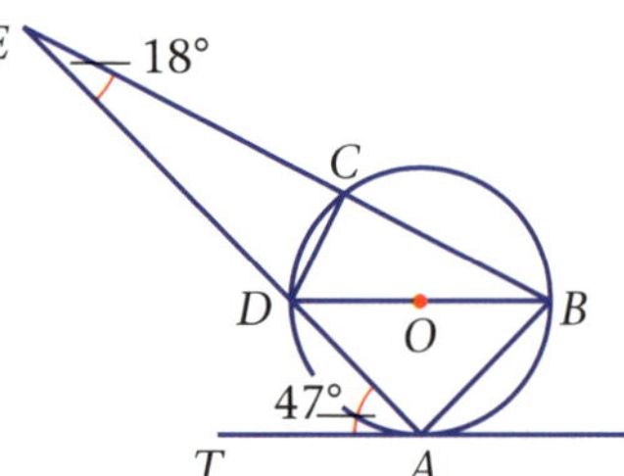

14 AB is a tangent to the circle. DOE is a diameter.
Find the sizes of these angles:

(a) $D\hat{O}B$ (b) $B\hat{E}D$

(c) Given that $AB = 5.8$ cm, calculate the radius.

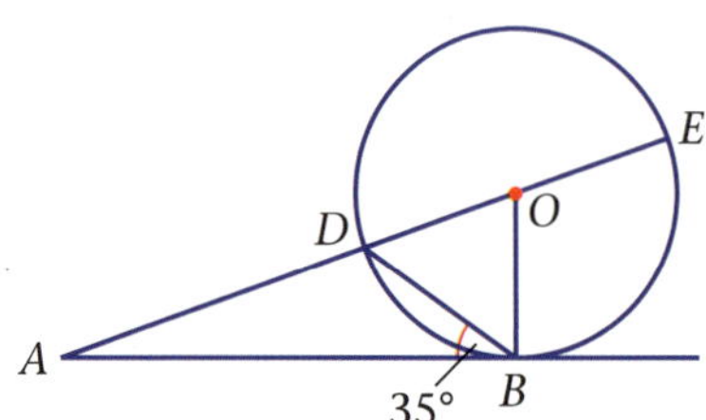

15 Prove that

(a) the tangent at A bisects the line XY

(b) angle $XAY = 90°$

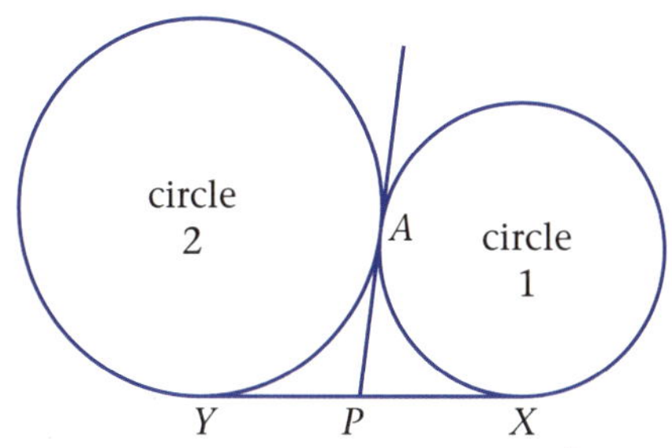

16 BCE and ADE are straight lines. AB and DC are parallel lines. Calculate the sizes of these angles:

(a) $A\hat{C}B$ (b) $D\hat{C}A$ (c) $C\hat{B}A$

(d) Show that triangle EBA is isosceles.

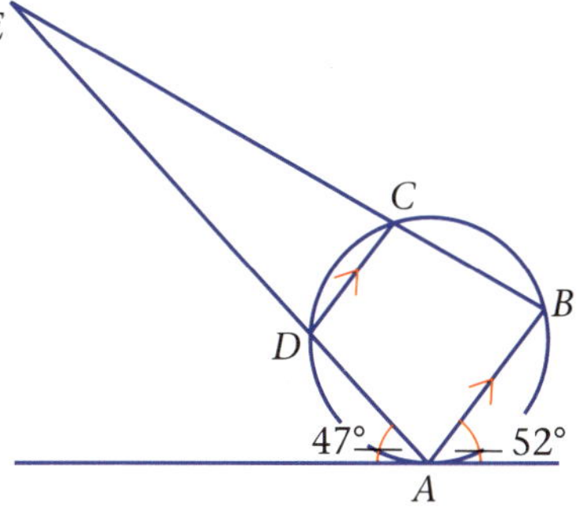

17 The circle, centre I, is the *inscribed* circle of triangle ABC. Calculate the size of angle EDF.

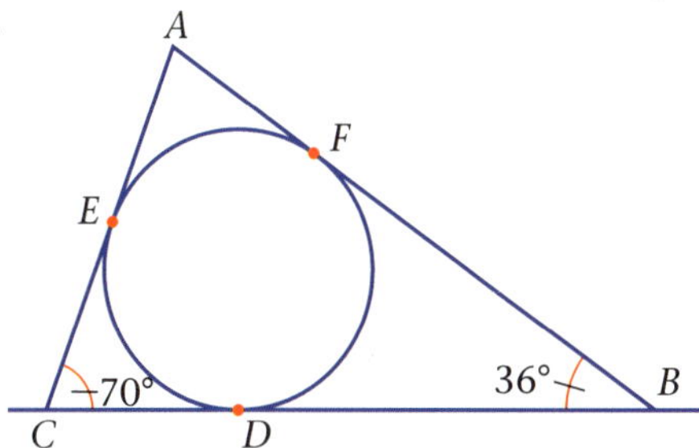

18 (a) Calculate the sizes of angles ACB and CBA. Give reasons for your answers.

(b) Prove that triangle ABC is isosceles.

(c) Prove that triangles PBR and ACR are similar.

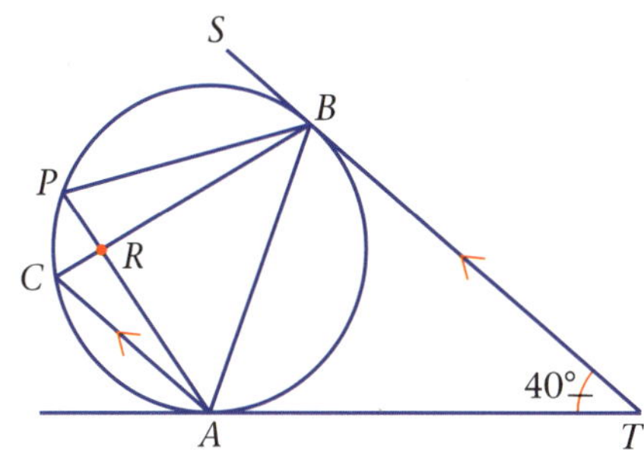

19 C is the centre of the large circle and O is the centre of the small circle. PT is a tangent to the small circle. $PCAO$ is a straight line. The small circle has radius 1 cm. Calculate the radius of the large circle.

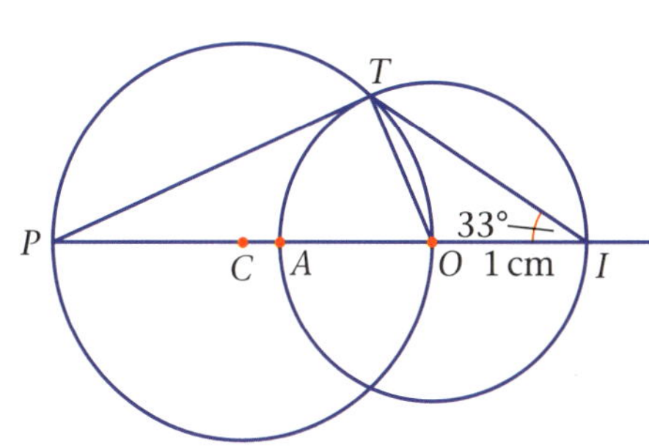

20 (a) Draw any acute-angled triangle. An **altitude** of a triangle is a straight line drawn from a corner to meet the opposite side at right angles. Draw the three altitudes of the triangle. Write what you notice.

(b) *AFB*, *AEC*, *BHE*, *AHD* and *FHC* are straight lines. *AOH* is a diameter. Find, in terms of x or y or both, the size of angle *BHD*. Prove that *FBCE* is a cyclic quadrilateral. Hence, prove that *AH* is perpendicular to *BC*.

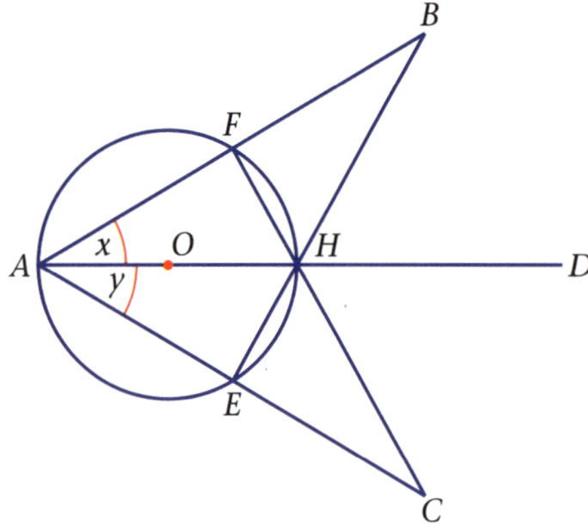

(c) What is the relationship between parts (a) and (b)?

Summary of key points

1. The angle between a tangent and a radius is 90°.
2. The lengths of the two tangents from a point to a circle are equal.
3. The perpendicular bisector from the centre of a circle to a chord bisects the chord.
4. The angle subtended at the centre of a circle is twice the angle at the circumference.
5. The angle in a semicircle is a right angle.
6. Angles in the same segment are equal.
7. Opposite angles of a cyclic quadrilateral are supplementary.
8. The angle between a tangent and a chord is equal to the angle in the alternate segment.

27 Vectors

In this chapter you will use vectors to represent translations and prove geometrical results.

27.1 Translations

A **translation** moves all the points on a shape the same distance and in the same direction. The shape is neither turned nor rotated.

For more on translations see Section 7.1 (in Book 1).

Translations can be described using **column vectors:** $\begin{pmatrix} x \\ y \end{pmatrix}$

$\begin{pmatrix} x \\ y \end{pmatrix}$ — x: displacement in the x-direction; y: displacement in the y-direction

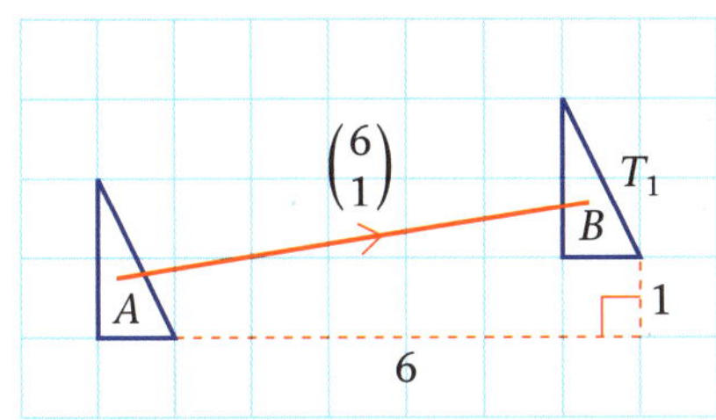

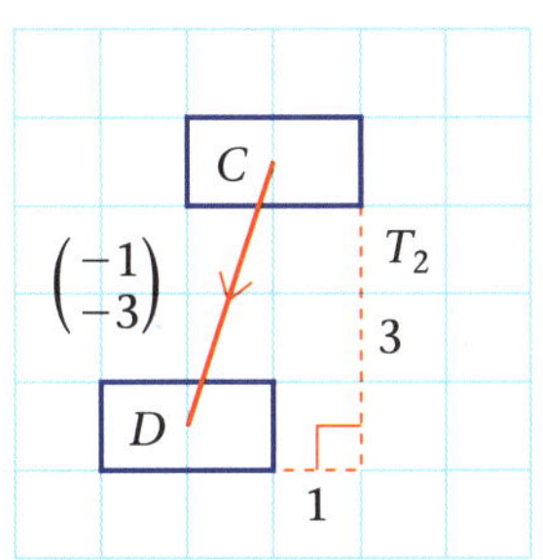

The translation T_1 is given by the column vector $\begin{pmatrix} 6 \\ 1 \end{pmatrix}$, meaning 6 units in the positive x-direction and 1 unit in the positive y-direction.

T_2 is given by $\begin{pmatrix} -1 \\ -3 \end{pmatrix}$, meaning 1 unit in the negative x-direction and 3 units in the negative y-direction.

The values of x and y in a column vector are called **components**.

The translation that takes A to B can be written as a translation vector $\overrightarrow{AB}$.

In the examples above,

$$\overrightarrow{AB} = \begin{pmatrix} 6 \\ 1 \end{pmatrix} \qquad \overrightarrow{CD} = \begin{pmatrix} -1 \\ -3 \end{pmatrix}$$

The arrow shows the direction of the translation:

A to $B = \overrightarrow{AB}$

B to $A = \overrightarrow{BA}$

Example 1

A is the point $(2, -3)$ and B is the point $(5, 2)$. $\overrightarrow{AC} = \begin{pmatrix} -1 \\ 3 \end{pmatrix}$

(a) Write the column vector $\overrightarrow{AB}$.

(b) Write the column vector $\overrightarrow{BA}$.

(c) Write the coordinates of C.

(a) $\overrightarrow{AB} = \begin{pmatrix} 3 \\ 5 \end{pmatrix}$

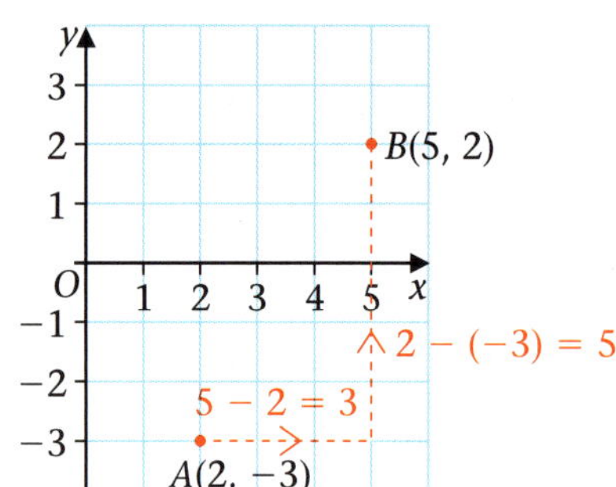

To get from A to B you move
3 in the positive x-direction
5 in the positive y-direction

(b) $\overrightarrow{BA} = \begin{pmatrix} -3 \\ -5 \end{pmatrix}$

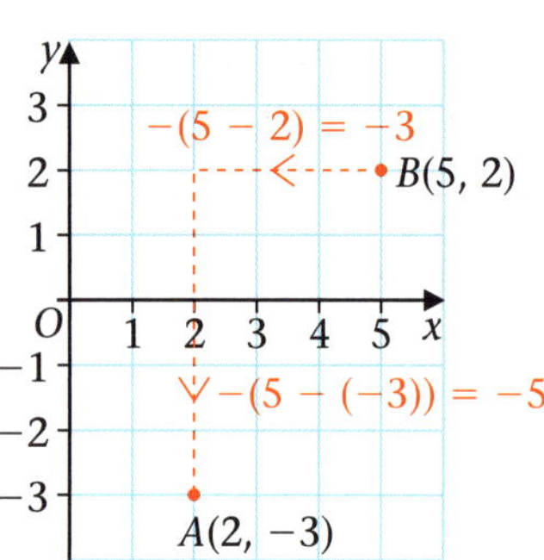

To get from B to A you move
3 in the negative x-direction
5 in the negative y-direction

(c) $\overrightarrow{AC} = \begin{pmatrix} -1 \\ 3 \end{pmatrix}$

So from A you move -1 unit in the x-direction and 3 units in the y-direction.
So C is at (1, 0).

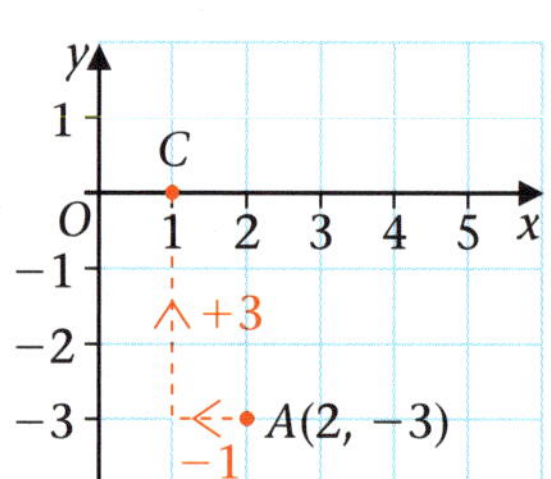

Example 2

$ABCD$ is a rectangle.

(a) Write down the column vectors for all sides.

(b) What do you notice about
(i) $\overrightarrow{BC}$ and $\overrightarrow{AD}$ (ii) $\overrightarrow{AB}$ and $\overrightarrow{DC}$?

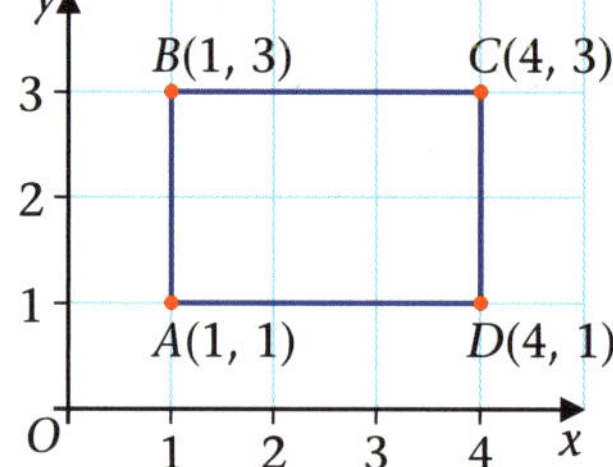

(a) $\overrightarrow{AB} = \begin{pmatrix} 0 \\ 2 \end{pmatrix}$ $\overrightarrow{BC} = \begin{pmatrix} 3 \\ 0 \end{pmatrix}$ $\overrightarrow{CD} = \begin{pmatrix} 0 \\ -2 \end{pmatrix}$ $\overrightarrow{AD} = \begin{pmatrix} 3 \\ 0 \end{pmatrix}$

(b) (i) $\overrightarrow{BC} = \begin{pmatrix} 3 \\ 0 \end{pmatrix} = \overrightarrow{AD}$

(ii) $\overrightarrow{AB} = \begin{pmatrix} 0 \\ 2 \end{pmatrix}$ $\overrightarrow{DC} = -\overrightarrow{CD} = \begin{pmatrix} 0 \\ 2 \end{pmatrix}$

$\overrightarrow{AB} = \overrightarrow{DC}$

If $\overrightarrow{AD} = \overrightarrow{BC}$, then AD and BC are parallel and have equal length.

Exercise 27A

1 A is the point (4, 6), B is the point (2, 5) and C is the point $(-1, 0)$. Write the column vectors

(a) $\overrightarrow{AB}$ (b) $\overrightarrow{BC}$ (c) $\overrightarrow{CA}$ (d) $\overrightarrow{AC}$

2 A is the point (2, 4), B is the point (3, 5) and C is the point (4, 2). The vector $\overrightarrow{CD}$ is parallel to the vector $\overrightarrow{BA}$. The point D lies on the y-axis. Find the coordinates of D.

3 (a) The point $A(0, 2)$ is reflected in the line $x = 3$ to give the point B. The point B is reflected in the line $x = 6$ to give C. Describe the single transformation that maps A to C.

(b) Generalise your result in the case where there are successive reflections in the lines $x = a$ and $x = b$, with $a < b$.

4 $A(2, 3)$, $B(5, 7)$ and $C(9, 5)$ are three points.

(a) Find the column vector $\overrightarrow{BC}$.

(b) $ABCD$ is a parallelogram with BC parallel to AD.
Use your answer to **(a)** to find the coordinates of D.

(c) Show that $\overrightarrow{AB}$ and $\overrightarrow{DC}$ have the same column vector.

27.2 Vectors

Another way of writing a translation is using bold type single letters such as **a** and **b**. By hand write them underlined.

Translations described in this way are called **vectors**. The vectors **a** and **b** are shown here. The lines with arrows are called **directed line segments** and show a unique **length** and **direction** for each of vectors **a** and **b**.

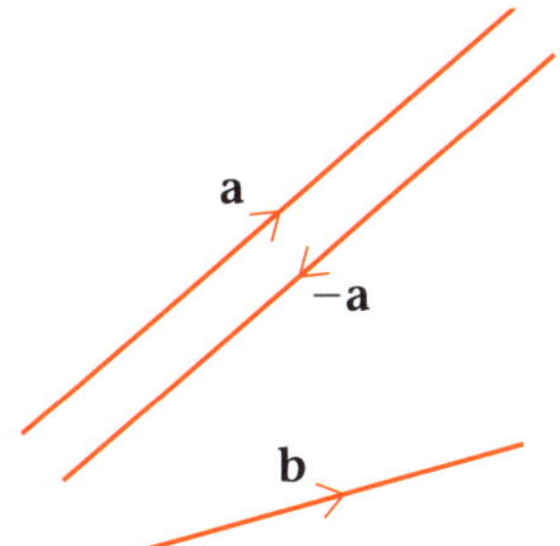

A **vector** defined as **a** has a unique length and direction.
The vector with the same length but opposite direction is $-\mathbf{a}$.

Addition of vectors

Look at the diagram below.

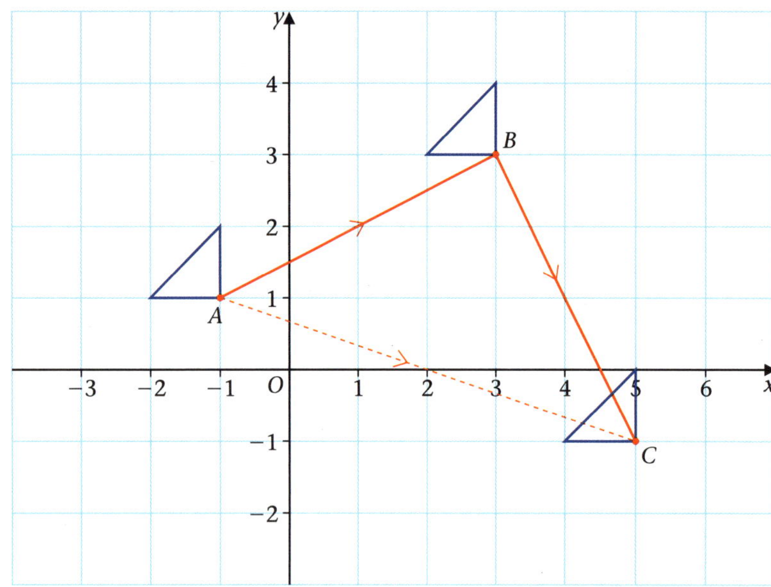

The vectors $\overrightarrow{AB}$ and $\overrightarrow{BC}$ can be written $\begin{pmatrix} 4 \\ 2 \end{pmatrix}$ and $\begin{pmatrix} 2 \\ -4 \end{pmatrix}$.

$\overrightarrow{AB} + \overrightarrow{BC}$ can be interpreted as the result of two successive translations, equivalent to $\overrightarrow{AC}$.

$$\begin{pmatrix} 4 \\ 2 \end{pmatrix} + \begin{pmatrix} 2 \\ -4 \end{pmatrix} = \begin{pmatrix} 4+2 \\ 2-4 \end{pmatrix} = \begin{pmatrix} 6 \\ -2 \end{pmatrix}$$

$$\overrightarrow{AB} + \overrightarrow{BC} = \overrightarrow{AC}$$

Here vectors $\overrightarrow{AB}$ and $\overrightarrow{BC}$ have been added to give the vector $\overrightarrow{AC}$.

For any two vectors **a** and **b** it is possible to add them by placing them 'nose to tail':

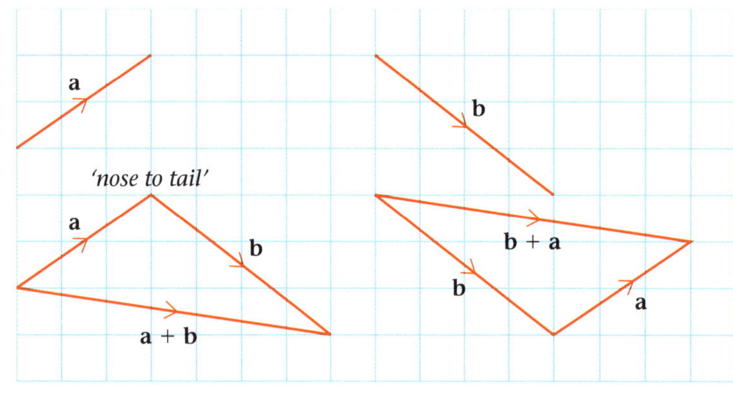

Note that
a + **b** = **b** + **a**
b + **a** gives a vector of the same length and direction as **a** + **b**.

This is called the **triangle law of addition**:

a + **b** = **b** + **a**

For example: $\begin{pmatrix} 3 \\ 2 \end{pmatrix} + \begin{pmatrix} 4 \\ -3 \end{pmatrix} = \begin{pmatrix} 4 \\ -3 \end{pmatrix} + \begin{pmatrix} 3 \\ 2 \end{pmatrix} = \begin{pmatrix} 7 \\ -1 \end{pmatrix}$

Subtraction of vectors

> The minus sign means a vector with the same length but opposite direction.

$\mathbf{p} - \mathbf{q}$ can be interpreted as $\mathbf{p} + (-\mathbf{q})$.

Then, using the triangle law of addition:

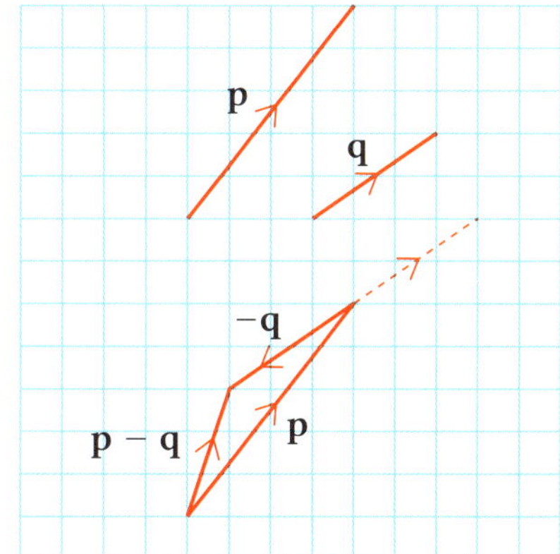

Using column vectors, this means:

$$\begin{pmatrix}4\\5\end{pmatrix} - \begin{pmatrix}3\\2\end{pmatrix} = \begin{pmatrix}4\\5\end{pmatrix} + \begin{pmatrix}-3\\-2\end{pmatrix} = \begin{pmatrix}4-3\\5-2\end{pmatrix} = \begin{pmatrix}1\\3\end{pmatrix}$$

Multiplication of vectors by scalars

Geometrically, the expression $2\overrightarrow{AB}$ means the directed line segment parallel to $\overrightarrow{AB}$, but twice the length. In other words, when vector $\overrightarrow{AB}$ is multiplied by 2 the result is $2\overrightarrow{AB}$.

> A scalar is a number, e.g. 3, 2, $\frac{1}{2}$...

If a vector **a** is multiplied by a scalar k then the vector $k\mathbf{a}$ is parallel to **a** and is equal to k times **a**.

For the column vector $\begin{pmatrix}p\\q\end{pmatrix}$, $\quad k \times \begin{pmatrix}p\\q\end{pmatrix} = \begin{pmatrix}kp\\kq\end{pmatrix}$

For example, $\quad 3\begin{pmatrix}2\\1\end{pmatrix} = \begin{pmatrix}3\times 2\\3\times 1\end{pmatrix} = \begin{pmatrix}6\\3\end{pmatrix}$

Exercise 27B

1 $\overrightarrow{AB} = \begin{pmatrix}3\\1\end{pmatrix}$

Write down the column vector for

(a) $3\overrightarrow{AB}$ (b) $5\overrightarrow{AB}$ (c) $-2\overrightarrow{AB}$ (d) $\overrightarrow{BA}$ (e) $k\overrightarrow{AB}$

2 In the diagram $\overrightarrow{OA} = \mathbf{a}$, $\overrightarrow{AM} = \mathbf{b}$.
M is the mid-point of AC.
Write down, in terms of **a** and **b**
(a) $\overrightarrow{AC}$ (b) $\overrightarrow{OM}$ (c) $\overrightarrow{OC}$

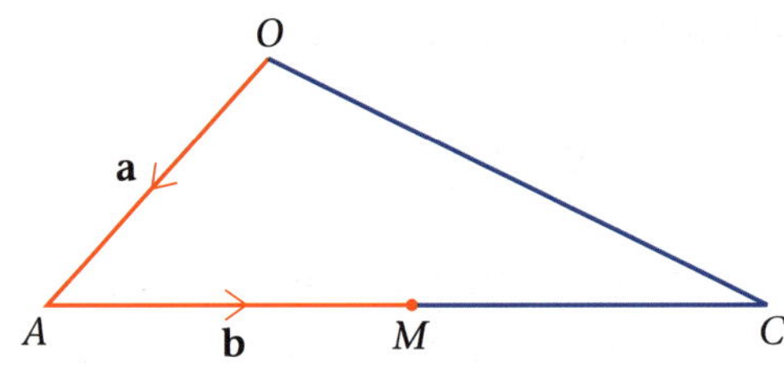

3 $\overrightarrow{AB}$ is the column vector $\begin{pmatrix} 4 \\ -3 \end{pmatrix}$. $\overrightarrow{BC}$ is the column vector $\begin{pmatrix} 2 \\ 4 \end{pmatrix}$.

Find the column vector $\overrightarrow{AC}$.
Draw a diagram to show your answer.

4 $\overrightarrow{AB} = \begin{pmatrix} 1 \\ 4 \end{pmatrix}$ $\overrightarrow{BC} = \begin{pmatrix} 2 \\ -3 \end{pmatrix}$ $\overrightarrow{CD} = \begin{pmatrix} -5 \\ 2 \end{pmatrix}$

(a) Find the column vector for $\overrightarrow{AD}$.
Draw a diagram to show this.

(b) Show that $\overrightarrow{AC} = \overrightarrow{DB}$.

5 M is the mid-point of OA.
$ON = \frac{1}{3}OC$
$\overrightarrow{OA} = \mathbf{a}$
$\overrightarrow{MN} = \mathbf{b}$
Find $\overrightarrow{OC}$ in terms of **a** and **b**.

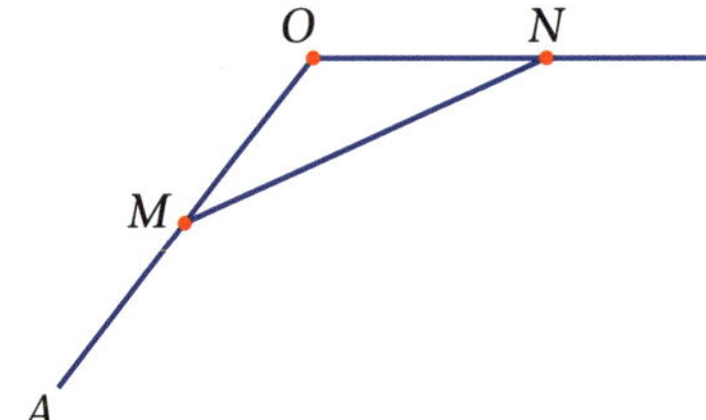

$\overrightarrow{MO} + \overrightarrow{ON} = \overrightarrow{MN}$
so $\overrightarrow{ON} = \overrightarrow{MN} - \overrightarrow{MO}$

27.3 Vector algebra

The rules of algebra that you already know can be applied to vectors, providing you do not multiply or divide one vector by another.

For any vectors **a**, **b** and **c** and any scalars p, q and k:
- $\mathbf{a} + \mathbf{b} = \mathbf{b} + \mathbf{a}$
- $\mathbf{a} + \mathbf{b} = \mathbf{c}$ can be written as $\mathbf{a} = \mathbf{c} - \mathbf{b}$
- $\mathbf{a} + (\mathbf{b} + \mathbf{c}) = (\mathbf{a} + \mathbf{b}) + \mathbf{c}$
- $k(\mathbf{a} + \mathbf{b}) = k\mathbf{a} + k\mathbf{b}$
- $(p + q)\mathbf{a} = p\mathbf{a} + q\mathbf{a}$

You can use these rules to solve vector equations. For example

$$2\mathbf{a} = \mathbf{b} \rightarrow \mathbf{a} = \frac{\mathbf{b}}{2}$$

Two column vectors are equal if they represent the same translation.

If $\begin{pmatrix} a \\ b \end{pmatrix} = \begin{pmatrix} c \\ d \end{pmatrix}$

then $a = c$ and $b = d$

If two vectors **a** and **b** are parallel, then $\mathbf{a} = k\mathbf{b}$ for some scalar k.

Example 3

$\mathbf{a} = \begin{pmatrix} 3 \\ -2 \end{pmatrix}$ and $\mathbf{b} = \begin{pmatrix} -1 \\ -3 \end{pmatrix}$

(a) Write as column vectors (i) $\mathbf{a} - \mathbf{b}$ (ii) $3\mathbf{a}$ (iii) $3\mathbf{a} - 2\mathbf{b}$

(b) Find the vector $\mathbf{x}$ such that $\mathbf{a} + 2\mathbf{x} = \mathbf{b}$

(c) Find a vector $\mathbf{c}$ such that $\mathbf{c} + 3\mathbf{a}$ is parallel to $\begin{pmatrix} 3 \\ -2 \end{pmatrix}$.

(a) (i) $\mathbf{a} - \mathbf{b} = \mathbf{a} + (-\mathbf{b}) = \begin{pmatrix} 3 \\ -2 \end{pmatrix} + -\begin{pmatrix} -1 \\ -3 \end{pmatrix} = \begin{pmatrix} 3 - -1 \\ -2 - -3 \end{pmatrix} = \begin{pmatrix} 4 \\ 1 \end{pmatrix}$

Remember:
$\mathbf{a} - \mathbf{b} = \mathbf{a} + (-\mathbf{b})$

(ii) $3\mathbf{a} = 3\begin{pmatrix} 3 \\ -2 \end{pmatrix} = \begin{pmatrix} 9 \\ -6 \end{pmatrix}$

(iii) $3\mathbf{a} - 2\mathbf{b} = \begin{pmatrix} 9 \\ -6 \end{pmatrix} - 2\begin{pmatrix} -1 \\ -3 \end{pmatrix} = \begin{pmatrix} 9 \\ -6 \end{pmatrix} - \begin{pmatrix} -2 \\ -6 \end{pmatrix} = \begin{pmatrix} 9 \\ -6 \end{pmatrix} + \begin{pmatrix} 2 \\ 6 \end{pmatrix} = \begin{pmatrix} 11 \\ 0 \end{pmatrix}$

(b) $\mathbf{a} + 2\mathbf{x} = \mathbf{b}$

So $2\mathbf{x} = \mathbf{b} - \mathbf{a}$

$\mathbf{x} = \dfrac{\mathbf{b} - \mathbf{a}}{2} = \dfrac{1}{2}\begin{pmatrix} -1 - 3 \\ -3 - -2 \end{pmatrix} = \dfrac{1}{2}\begin{pmatrix} -4 \\ -1 \end{pmatrix} = \begin{pmatrix} -2 \\ -\frac{1}{2} \end{pmatrix}$

(c) $\mathbf{c} + \begin{pmatrix} 9 \\ -6 \end{pmatrix} = \begin{pmatrix} 3 \\ -2 \end{pmatrix}$

Writing $\mathbf{c}$ as $\begin{pmatrix} p \\ q \end{pmatrix}$:

$\begin{pmatrix} p \\ q \end{pmatrix} + \begin{pmatrix} 9 \\ -6 \end{pmatrix} = \begin{pmatrix} 3 \\ -2 \end{pmatrix}$

So $p + 9 = 3 \rightarrow p = -6$

and $q - 6 = -2 \rightarrow q = 4$

So $\mathbf{c}$ is $\begin{pmatrix} -6 \\ 4 \end{pmatrix}$.

Exercise 27C

1 $\mathbf{a} = \begin{pmatrix} 2 \\ 1 \end{pmatrix}$ and $\mathbf{b} = \begin{pmatrix} -4 \\ 3 \end{pmatrix}$

Calculate (a) $\mathbf{a} + \mathbf{b}$ (b) $2\mathbf{a}$ (c) $2\mathbf{a} - 3\mathbf{b}$ (d) $2(\mathbf{a} - \mathbf{b})$

(e) Find a vector $\mathbf{c}$ such that $\mathbf{a} + \mathbf{c}$ is parallel to $\begin{pmatrix} 4 \\ 4 \end{pmatrix}$.

2 $\mathbf{a} = \begin{pmatrix} 3 \\ 1 \end{pmatrix}$ and $\mathbf{b} = \begin{pmatrix} 2 \\ 2 \end{pmatrix}$

Draw diagrams to show that

(a) $2(\mathbf{a} + \mathbf{b}) = 2\mathbf{a} + 2\mathbf{b}$ (b) $(2 + 3)\mathbf{a} = 2\mathbf{a} + 3\mathbf{a}$

3 P is the point (1, 3), Q is the point (2, 4) and R is the point (5, 4). S is the point such that $\overrightarrow{PQ} = \overrightarrow{SR}$. Find the coordinates of S.

4 $\mathbf{a} = \begin{pmatrix} -1 \\ 2 \end{pmatrix}$ and $\mathbf{b} = \begin{pmatrix} -3 \\ 4 \end{pmatrix}$

Calculate $\mathbf{x}$, given that $\mathbf{a} + \mathbf{x} = \mathbf{b}$

5 $\mathbf{c} = \begin{pmatrix} 2 \\ -1 \end{pmatrix}$ and $\mathbf{d} = \begin{pmatrix} 4 \\ -3 \end{pmatrix}$

Calculate $\mathbf{x}$ given that $2\mathbf{x} + \mathbf{c} = \mathbf{d}$

6 $\mathbf{e} = \begin{pmatrix} 4 \\ 1 \end{pmatrix}$ and $\mathbf{f} = \begin{pmatrix} -2 \\ 3 \end{pmatrix}$

Calculate $\mathbf{x}$ given that $2\mathbf{e} - \mathbf{x} = \mathbf{f}$

27.4 Finding the magnitude of a vector

The **magnitude** of a vector is the length of the directed line segment representing it.

If the vector is expressed in column form, you can use Pythagoras' theorem to find the magnitude.

Example 4

Find the magnitude of the vector $\overrightarrow{AB} = \begin{pmatrix} 6 \\ -8 \end{pmatrix}$.

Draw $\overrightarrow{AB}$ as the hypotenuse of a right-angled triangle:

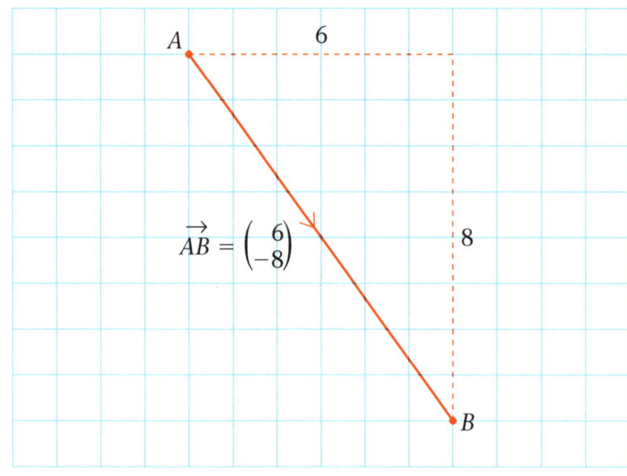

By Pythagoras' theorem, the length AB is given by

$$\begin{aligned} AB^2 &= 6^2 + 8^2 \\ &= 36 + 64 \\ &= 100 \\ AB &= 10 \end{aligned}$$

The magnitude of $\overrightarrow{AB}$ is 10 units.

In general, the magnitude of the vector $\begin{pmatrix} x \\ y \end{pmatrix}$ is $\sqrt{x^2 + y^2}$

Exercise 27D

1 Find the magnitude of each of these vectors:

(a) $\begin{pmatrix}-4\\3\end{pmatrix}$ (b) $\begin{pmatrix}7\\24\end{pmatrix}$ (c) $\begin{pmatrix}-6\\-8\end{pmatrix}$ (d) $\begin{pmatrix}7\\11\end{pmatrix}$

2 $\mathbf{a}=\begin{pmatrix}5\\9\end{pmatrix}$ and $\mathbf{b}=\begin{pmatrix}3\\3\end{pmatrix}$

Work out the magnitude of

(a) $\mathbf{a}$ (b) $\mathbf{b}$ (c) $\mathbf{a}+\mathbf{b}$ (d) $\mathbf{a}-\mathbf{b}$

3 $\mathbf{c}=\begin{pmatrix}2\\3\end{pmatrix}$ and $\mathbf{d}=\begin{pmatrix}-3\\4\end{pmatrix}$

Work out the magnitude of

(a) $\mathbf{c}$ (b) $2\mathbf{c}$ (c) $2\mathbf{d}$ (d) $\mathbf{c}-\mathbf{d}$

27.5 Linear combinations of vectors

One useful and important application of vectors is to produce special combinations of two given vectors.

Combinations of the vectors **a** and **b** of the form $p\mathbf{a}+q\mathbf{b}$, where p and q are scalars, are called **linear combinations** of the vectors **a** and **b**.

Generally, any two non-parallel vectors can be combined to give a single vector in a different direction.

Example 5

$\mathbf{a}=\begin{pmatrix}3\\2\end{pmatrix}$ and $\mathbf{b}=\begin{pmatrix}1\\3\end{pmatrix}$

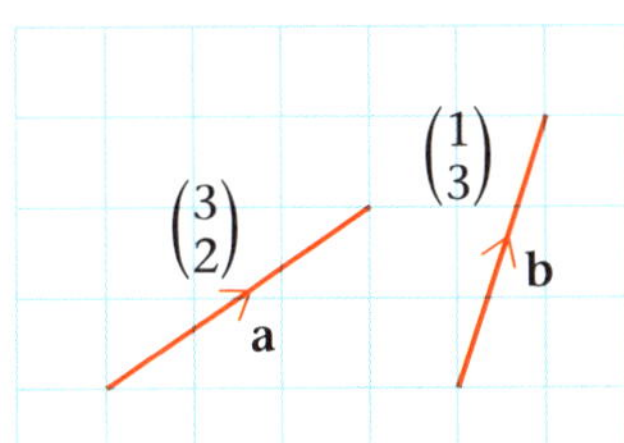

(a) Find scalars p and q such that $p\mathbf{a}+q\mathbf{b}$ is parallel to the x-axis.

Vectors parallel to the x-axis are of the form $\begin{pmatrix}x\\0\end{pmatrix}$.

(b) Find scalars r and s such that $r\mathbf{a}+s\mathbf{b}$ is parallel to the y-axis.

Vectors parallel to the y-axis are of the form $\begin{pmatrix}0\\y\end{pmatrix}$.

(a) $p\mathbf{a} + q\mathbf{b} = p\begin{pmatrix}3\\2\end{pmatrix} + q\begin{pmatrix}1\\3\end{pmatrix}$

The y-component of vector $p\mathbf{a} + q\mathbf{b}$ must be zero because the vector lies in the direction of the x-axis.

So $2p + 3q = 0$

Two possible values of p and q which satisfy the equation are

$p = 3, \quad q = -2$

$3\mathbf{a} - 2\mathbf{b}$ is parallel to the x-axis.

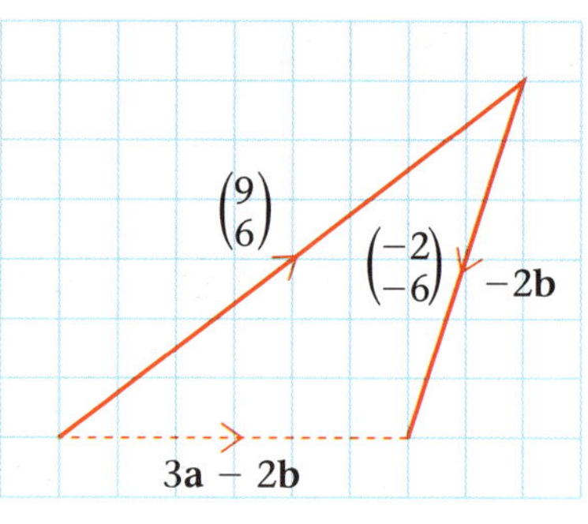

(b) $r\mathbf{a} + s\mathbf{b} = r\begin{pmatrix}3\\2\end{pmatrix} + s\begin{pmatrix}1\\3\end{pmatrix}$

The x-component must be zero because the vector is in the direction of the y-axis.

So $3r + s = 0$

Possible values of r and s are

$r = 1, \quad s = -3$

$\mathbf{a} - 3\mathbf{b}$ is parallel to the y-axis.

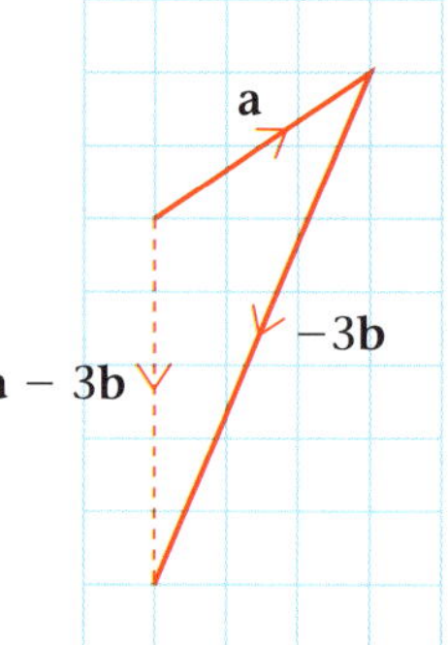

For any two vectors you can find a linear combination parallel to any required direction.

Example 6

Find a linear combination of vectors $\mathbf{a} = \begin{pmatrix}3\\2\end{pmatrix}$ and $\mathbf{b} = \begin{pmatrix}1\\3\end{pmatrix}$ which is equal to vector $\mathbf{c} = \begin{pmatrix}9\\13\end{pmatrix}$

$$p\mathbf{a} + q\mathbf{b} = \mathbf{c}$$

$$p\begin{pmatrix}3\\2\end{pmatrix} + q\begin{pmatrix}1\\3\end{pmatrix} = \begin{pmatrix}9\\13\end{pmatrix}$$

$$\begin{pmatrix}3p\\2p\end{pmatrix} + \begin{pmatrix}q\\3q\end{pmatrix} = \begin{pmatrix}9\\13\end{pmatrix}$$

Using simultaneous equations: $3p + q = 9$ (1)

$2p + 3q = 13$ (2)

Multiply equation (1) by 3: $9p + 3q = 27$ (3)

$2p + 3q = 13$ (2)

Subtract (2) from (3): $7p = 14$

$p = 2$

Substitute $p = 2$ in (1): $6 + q = 9$

$q = 3$

The linear combination is $2\mathbf{a} + 3\mathbf{b}$

Exercise 27E

1 $\mathbf{a} = \begin{pmatrix} 2 \\ -1 \end{pmatrix}$ and $\mathbf{b} = \begin{pmatrix} 1 \\ 1 \end{pmatrix}$

Given that $2\mathbf{a} + p\mathbf{b}$ is parallel to the x-axis, find the value of p.

2 $\mathbf{a} = \begin{pmatrix} 2 \\ -1 \end{pmatrix}$ and $\mathbf{b} = \begin{pmatrix} 1 \\ 1 \end{pmatrix}$

Given that $\mathbf{a} + q\mathbf{b}$ is parallel to the y-axis, find the value of q.

3 Find the values of x and y, given that $2\begin{pmatrix} 1 \\ y \end{pmatrix} + \begin{pmatrix} x \\ y \end{pmatrix} = \begin{pmatrix} 2 \\ -6 \end{pmatrix}$

4 Find the values of the scalars p and q, given that

$$p\begin{pmatrix} 2 \\ 1 \end{pmatrix} + q\begin{pmatrix} -1 \\ 2 \end{pmatrix} = \begin{pmatrix} 7 \\ -2 \end{pmatrix}$$

5 P is a variable point which moves so that the vector $\overrightarrow{OP}$ is given by

$$\overrightarrow{OP} = \begin{pmatrix} 2 \\ 6 \end{pmatrix} + t\begin{pmatrix} 1 \\ 1 \end{pmatrix}$$

Calculate the coordinates of P, for values of t from 0 to 5. Plot these coordinates.
What is the path of P as t varies? Give the equation of the path in the form $y = mx + c$.

6 A is the point (2, 1), B is the point (8, 4) and C is the point (6, 6).

(a) Calculate $\overrightarrow{AB}$.

(b) Write an expression in terms of k for $\overrightarrow{AB} + k\,\overrightarrow{BC}$.

(c) The line BC is extended to a point D where AD is parallel to the y-axis.
Find the value of k and the coordinates of D.

27.6 Position vectors

The column vector $\begin{pmatrix} x \\ y \end{pmatrix}$ denotes a translation.

There are an infinite number of points which are related by such a translation.

Look at the diagram, which shows several pairs of points linked by the same vector. The vector which translates O to P, $\overrightarrow{OP}$, is a special vector, called the **position vector** of P.

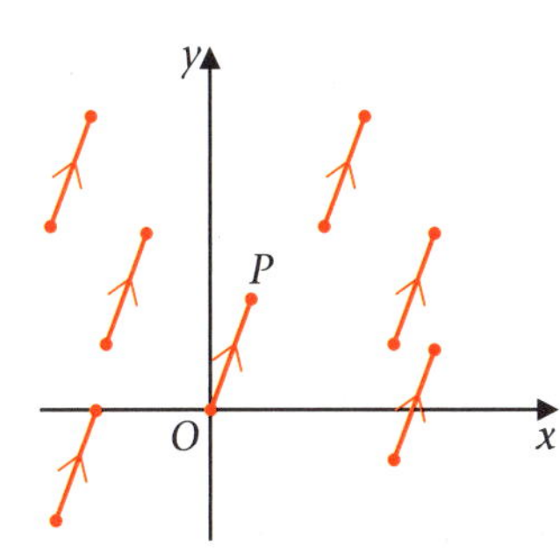

It is called this because it fixes the position of point P relative to a fixed reference point, which is usually the origin.

In this case, $\overrightarrow{OP} = \begin{pmatrix} x \\ y \end{pmatrix}$.

The **position vector** of a point P is $\overrightarrow{OP}$, where O is usually the origin.

Example 7

P is the point (2, 3). $\overrightarrow{PQ} = \begin{pmatrix} -1 \\ 2 \end{pmatrix}$.

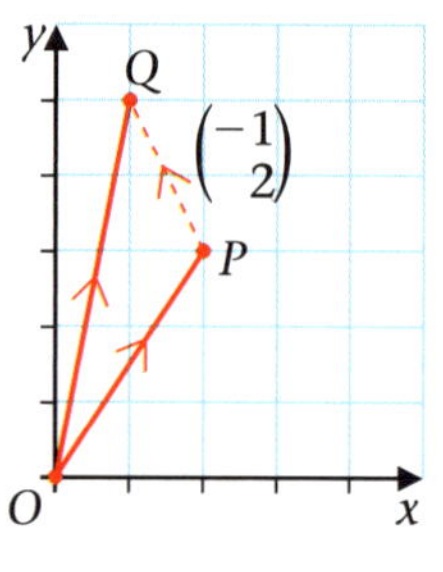

Find the position vector of Q.

The position vector of Q is

$$\overrightarrow{OQ} = \overrightarrow{OP} + \overrightarrow{PQ}$$

$$= \begin{pmatrix} 2 \\ 3 \end{pmatrix} + \begin{pmatrix} -1 \\ 2 \end{pmatrix}$$

$$= \begin{pmatrix} 1 \\ 5 \end{pmatrix}$$

Example 8

A is the point (3, 5) and B is the point (6, −1). C is the point on AB such that $AC = \frac{1}{2}CB$. Find the position vector of the point C.

The position vector of C is $\overrightarrow{OC}$. $\overrightarrow{OC} = \overrightarrow{OA} + \overrightarrow{AC}$

$$\overrightarrow{OA} = \begin{pmatrix} 3 \\ 5 \end{pmatrix}$$

$$\overrightarrow{AB} = \begin{pmatrix} 3 \\ -6 \end{pmatrix}$$

$$\overrightarrow{AC} = \tfrac{1}{3}\overrightarrow{AB}$$

$$= \tfrac{1}{3}\begin{pmatrix} 3 \\ -6 \end{pmatrix}$$

$$= \begin{pmatrix} 1 \\ -2 \end{pmatrix}$$

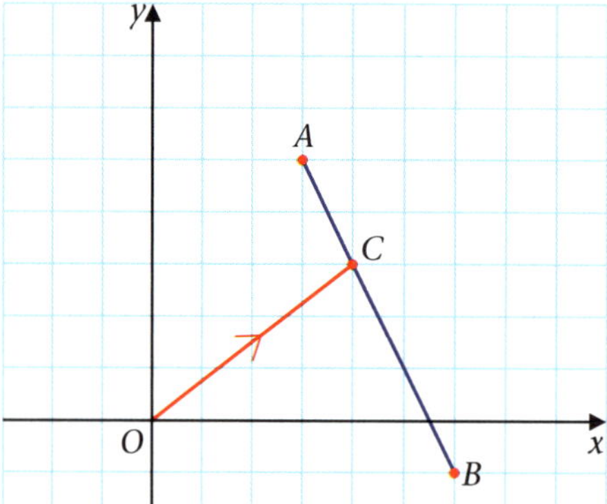

$$\overrightarrow{OC} = \overrightarrow{OA} + \overrightarrow{AC} = \begin{pmatrix} 3 \\ 5 \end{pmatrix} + \begin{pmatrix} 1 \\ -2 \end{pmatrix}$$

$$= \begin{pmatrix} 4 \\ 3 \end{pmatrix}$$

This problem is solved again in Example 9, using vector notation.

All the properties established for vectors earlier hold for position vectors.

Here are two very useful results.

If A and B have position vectors $\mathbf{a}$ and $\mathbf{b}$ respectively, then the vector

$\overrightarrow{AB} = \mathbf{b} - \mathbf{a}$ (Note the reversal of letters.)

From the diagram:

$$\overrightarrow{AB} = \overrightarrow{AO} + \overrightarrow{OB}$$
$$= -\overrightarrow{OA} + \overrightarrow{OB}$$
$$= -\mathbf{a} + \mathbf{b}$$
$$= \mathbf{b} - \mathbf{a}$$

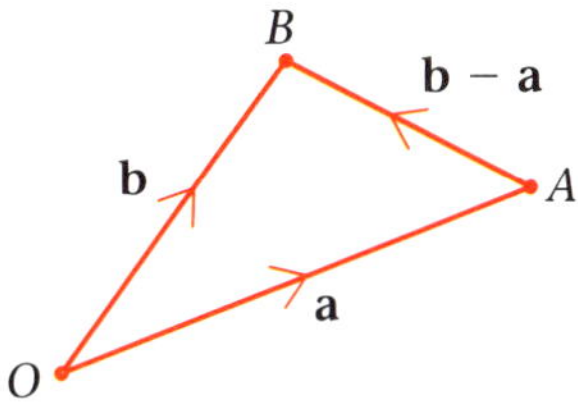

Example 9

If the position vector of A is $\mathbf{a}$ and the position vector of B is $\mathbf{b}$ find $\mathbf{c}$, the position vector of C, in terms of $\mathbf{a}$ and $\mathbf{b}$ so that $AC = \frac{1}{2}CB$.

$$\mathbf{c} = \overrightarrow{OC} = \overrightarrow{OA} + \overrightarrow{AC}$$
$$\overrightarrow{AB} = \mathbf{b} - \mathbf{a}$$
$$\overrightarrow{AC} = \tfrac{1}{3}(\mathbf{b} - \mathbf{a})$$
$$\mathbf{c} = \overrightarrow{OA} + \overrightarrow{AC} = \mathbf{a} + \tfrac{1}{3}(\mathbf{b} - \mathbf{a})$$
$$= \tfrac{2}{3}\mathbf{a} + \tfrac{1}{3}\mathbf{b}$$

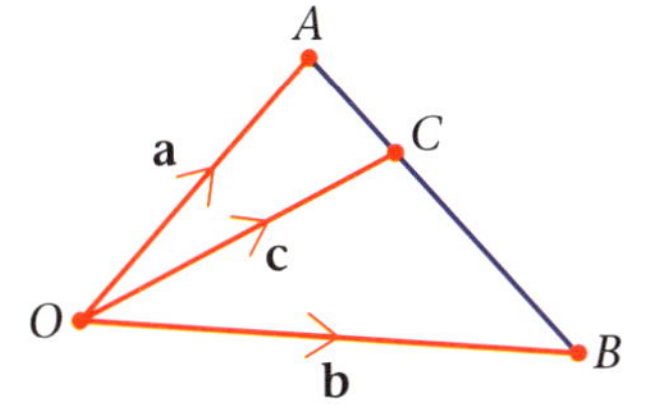

Check that this gives the same answer as Example 8.

If A and B have position vectors $\mathbf{a}$ and $\mathbf{b}$ respectively, then the position vector of the mid-point, M, of the line joining A to B is

$$\overrightarrow{OM} = \mathbf{m} = \tfrac{1}{2}(\mathbf{a} + \mathbf{b})$$

From the diagram:

$$\overrightarrow{AM} = \tfrac{1}{2}\overrightarrow{AB}$$
$$\overrightarrow{OM} = \overrightarrow{OA} + \overrightarrow{AM}$$
$$= \mathbf{a} + \tfrac{1}{2}(\mathbf{b} - \mathbf{a})$$
$$= \mathbf{a} + \tfrac{1}{2}\mathbf{b} - \tfrac{1}{2}\mathbf{a}$$
$$= \tfrac{1}{2}(\mathbf{a} + \mathbf{b})$$

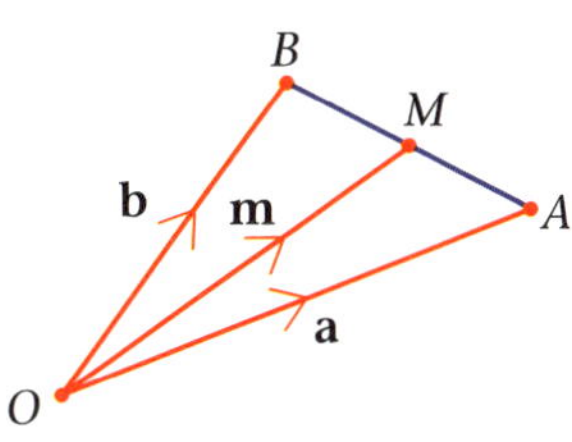

Exercise 27F

1 A is the point (1, 2) and B is the point (3, 6).
Write the position vector of the mid-point of AB.

2 C is the point (2, −2) and D is the point (8, 4). E lies on the line CD, such that $CE = \frac{1}{2}ED$.
Find the coordinates of E.

3 A is the point (2, 3) and B is the point (4, 7). C lies on the extension of the line AB, such that $BC = \frac{1}{2}AB$.
Find the coordinates of C.

4 $PQRS$ is a parallelogram, with $P = (1, 1)$, $Q = (5, 3)$ and $R = (7, 7)$.
Find the position vector of S and of the mid-point of PR.

27.7 Proving geometrical results

Example 10

A and *B* are the mid-points of the sides *OX* and *OY* of a triangle.
Prove that the line *XY* is parallel to the line *AB* and is twice the length of *AB*.

Use letters **a** and **b** for the position vectors of *A* and *B*, respectively.

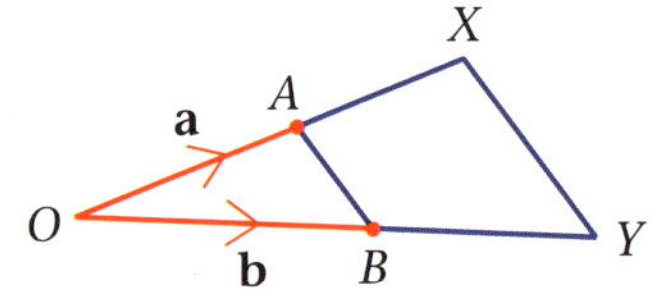

$\overrightarrow{OX} = 2\mathbf{a}$

$\overrightarrow{OY} = 2\mathbf{b}$

$\overrightarrow{XY} = \overrightarrow{OY} - \overrightarrow{OX}$

$= 2\mathbf{b} - 2\mathbf{a}$

$= 2(\mathbf{b} - \mathbf{a})$

But $\overrightarrow{AB} = \mathbf{b} - \mathbf{a}$

so $\overrightarrow{XY} = 2\overrightarrow{AB}$

So *XY* is twice the length of *AB* and *XY* is parallel to *AB*.

Example 11

Show that the diagonals of a parallelogram bisect one another.

In the parallelogram *OACB*, $\overrightarrow{OA} = \mathbf{a}$ and $\overrightarrow{OB} = \mathbf{b}$.

Opposite sides of a parallelogram are parallel and equal so $\overrightarrow{AC} = \mathbf{b}$.

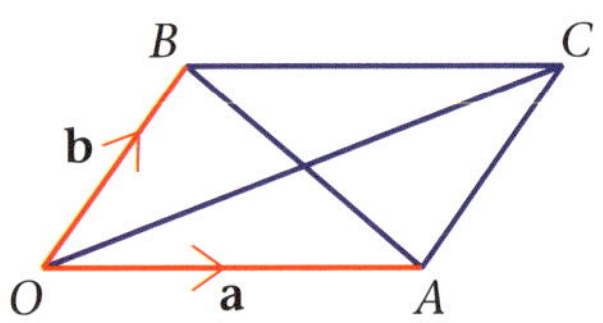

$\overrightarrow{OC} = \overrightarrow{OA} + \overrightarrow{AC}$

$= \mathbf{a} + \mathbf{b}$

If *D* is the mid-point of *OC*:

$\overrightarrow{OD} = \frac{1}{2}\overrightarrow{OC}$

$= \frac{1}{2}(\mathbf{a} + \mathbf{b})$

But $\frac{1}{2}(\mathbf{a} + \mathbf{b})$ is the position vector of the mid-point of *AB*.
So mid-point of *AB* = mid-point of *OC*, which means that *OC* bisects *AB*.

> Remember the result for two vectors **a** and **b**:
> the position vector of the mid-point of *AB* is $\frac{1}{2}(\mathbf{a} + \mathbf{b})$

Example 12

OABC is a quadrilateral, with $\overrightarrow{OA} = \mathbf{a}$, $\overrightarrow{OB} = \mathbf{b}$ and $\overrightarrow{OC} = \mathbf{c}$.
P, *Q*, *R* and *S* are the mid-points of sides *OA*, *AB*, *BC* and *CO*.
Show that *PQRS* is a parallelogram.

From the diagram,

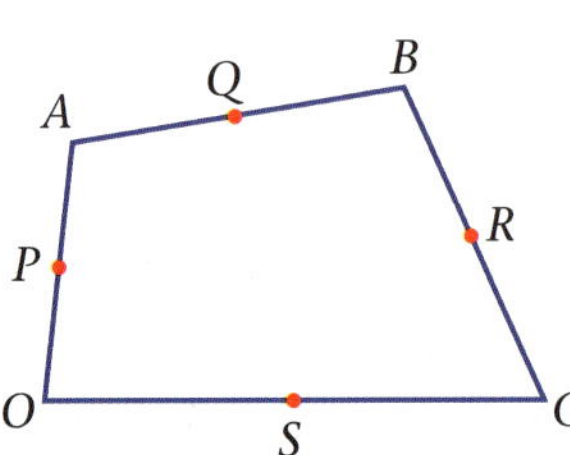

$\overrightarrow{OP} = \frac{1}{2}\mathbf{a}$ and $\overrightarrow{OS} = \frac{1}{2}\mathbf{c}$

$\overrightarrow{OQ} = \frac{1}{2}(\mathbf{a} + \mathbf{b})$ and $\overrightarrow{OR} = \frac{1}{2}(\mathbf{b} + \mathbf{c})$

Now $\overrightarrow{PQ} = \overrightarrow{OQ} - \overrightarrow{OP} = \frac{1}{2}\mathbf{b}$ and $\overrightarrow{SR} = \overrightarrow{OR} - \overrightarrow{OS} = \frac{1}{2}\mathbf{b}$

Thus *PQ* has equal length and is parallel to *SR*.
So *QR* is equal and parallel to *PS*, and *PQRS* is a parallelogram.

Exercise 27G

1 $\overrightarrow{OX} = \mathbf{x}$ and $\overrightarrow{OY} = \mathbf{y}$. X and and Y are $\frac{2}{3}$ of the way along OA and OB, respectively. Write the vector $\overrightarrow{XY}$ in terms of $\mathbf{x}$ and $\mathbf{y}$.
Write the geometrical relationship between the line XY and the line AB.

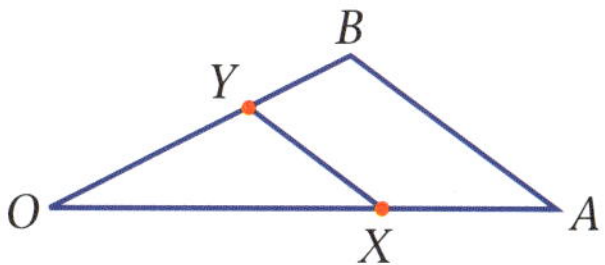

2 Express $\overrightarrow{AB}$ in terms of $\mathbf{a}$ and $\mathbf{b}$, where $\overrightarrow{OA} = \mathbf{a}$ and $\overrightarrow{OB} = \mathbf{b}$.
Given that $AC = 2OA$ and $BD = 2OB$, and that OAC and OBD are straight lines, express $\overrightarrow{CD}$ in terms of $\mathbf{a}$ and $\mathbf{b}$.
What is the geometrical relationship between AB and CD?

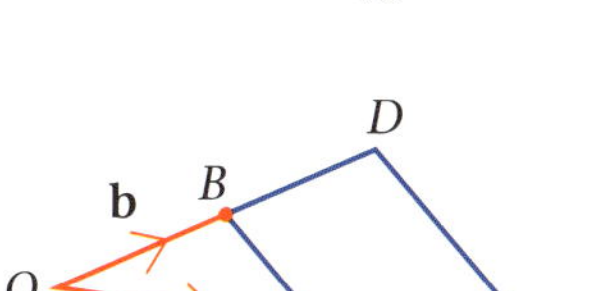

3 (a) X is the mid-point of AB and Y is the mid-point of OA. G is the point which is $\frac{2}{3}$ of the way along the line OX. Find the position vector of G.

(b) A point H is chosen to be $\frac{2}{3}$ of the way along the line BY. Find the position vector of H.
What geometrical fact can you conclude from your answers?

(c) The line AG, when extended, cuts the line OB at D. Find the position vector of D.

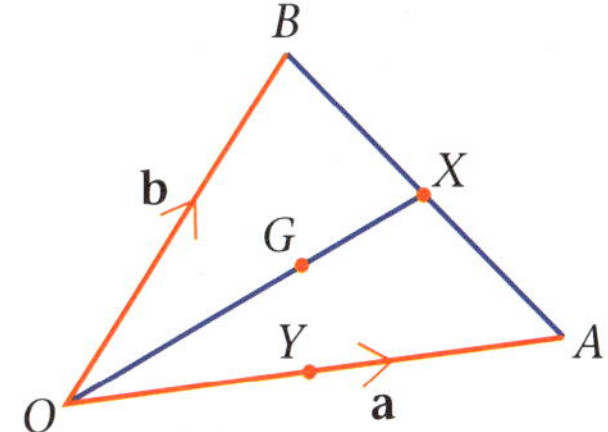

4 $OCDB$ is a trapezium, with OC parallel to BD. A is the mid-point of OC and E is the mid-point of BD. X is the point of intersection of AE and BC. $\overrightarrow{BD} = 4\mathbf{a}$.

(a) Show that $\overrightarrow{OX}$ can be written in the form $(1 + k)\mathbf{a} + k\mathbf{b}$, where k is a scalar.

(b) Show that $\overrightarrow{OX}$ can be written in the form $(2 - 2m)\mathbf{a} + m\mathbf{b}$, where m is a scalar.

(c) Find the values of k and m, and hence the position vector of X.

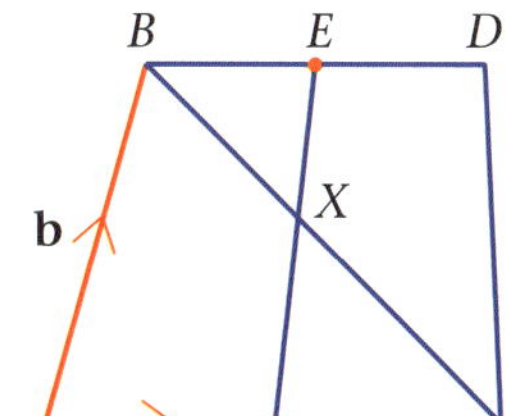

Diagram NOT accurately drawn

5 $OABC$ is a parallelogram. Points P, Q, R and S are taken $\frac{1}{3}$ of the way along each of the sides OA, AB, BC and CO, respectively.
Find whether or not $PQRS$ is a parallelogram. Justify your answer by using position vectors.
Are the conclusions you have drawn still valid when $OABC$ is a quadrilateral, but not a parallelogram?

6 Find, in terms of $\mathbf{a}$ and $\mathbf{b}$

(a) $\overrightarrow{AB}$ (b) $\overrightarrow{AF}$ (c) $\overrightarrow{AE}$

(d) The mid-points of each of the sides of the regular hexagon $ABCDEF$ are joined to give a second hexagon. Find the position vectors of each of the corners of this second hexagon. This process is repeated to produce a third hexagon. What is the relationship between the first and third hexagons? Justify your answer.

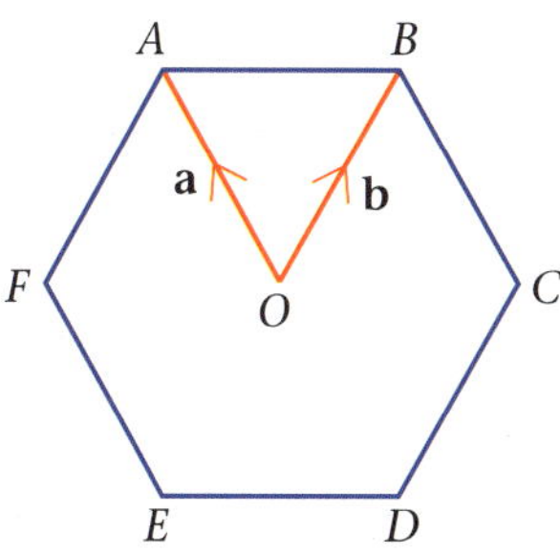

Mixed exercise 27

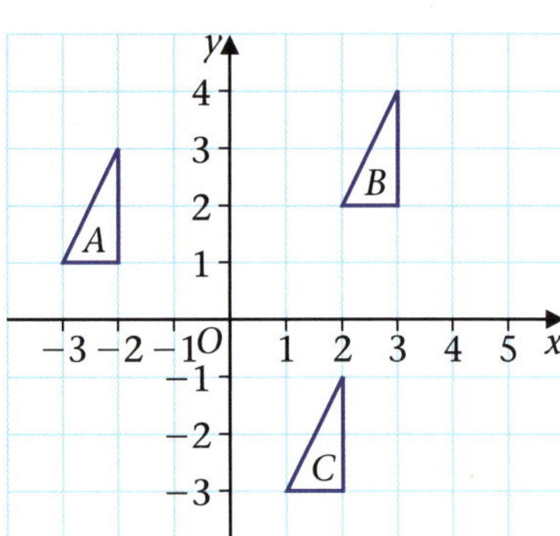

1 Give the column vector that describes the translation which maps

(a) A to B

(b) B to A

(c) B to C

(d) C to B

2 Write these as column vectors:

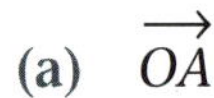

(a) $\overrightarrow{OA}$ (b) $\overrightarrow{OB}$

(c) $\overrightarrow{OA} + \overrightarrow{OB}$ (d) $\overrightarrow{OA} - \overrightarrow{OB}$

(e) $2\overrightarrow{OA}$ (f) $\overrightarrow{OB} + \overrightarrow{AO}$

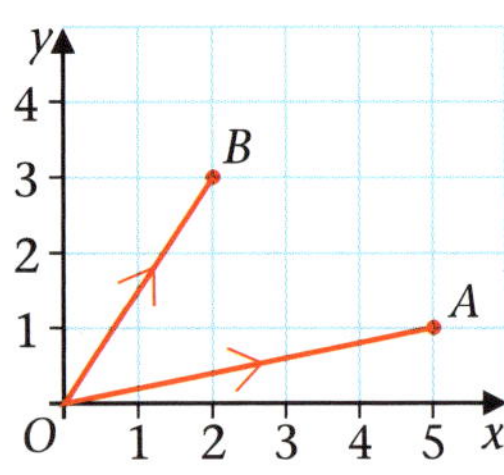

3 B is the point such that $OABC$ is a parallelogram. Copy the diagram and plot the point B.

Write the vector $\overrightarrow{OB}$.

Write the vector $\overrightarrow{OM}$ where M is the mid-point of OB.

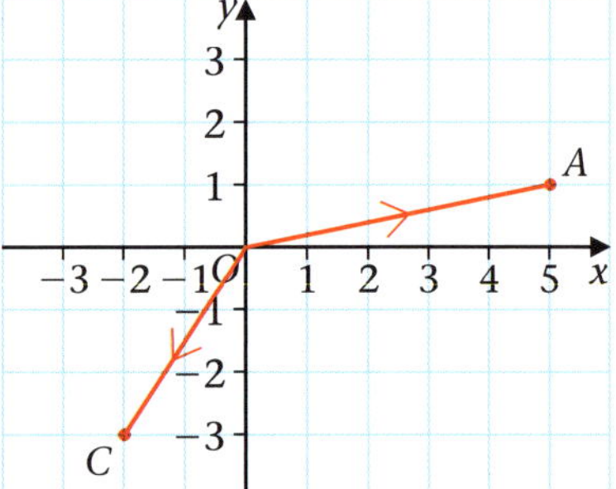

4 $\overrightarrow{OA} = \begin{pmatrix} 2 \\ 1 \end{pmatrix}$ and $\overrightarrow{OB} = \begin{pmatrix} 5 \\ 6 \end{pmatrix}$ Write down $\overrightarrow{AB}$.

5 $\overrightarrow{XY} = \begin{pmatrix} 2 \\ 3 \end{pmatrix}$ and $\overrightarrow{YO} = \begin{pmatrix} -1 \\ 4 \end{pmatrix}$ Write down $\overrightarrow{OX}$.

6 Simplify (a) $\begin{pmatrix} 2 \\ 1 \end{pmatrix} + \begin{pmatrix} 1 \\ -1 \end{pmatrix}$ (b) $\begin{pmatrix} 2 \\ 1 \end{pmatrix} - \begin{pmatrix} 1 \\ -1 \end{pmatrix}$

7 Simplify $3\begin{pmatrix} 2 \\ 1 \end{pmatrix} - 2\begin{pmatrix} -2 \\ 1 \end{pmatrix}$

8 Given that $\begin{pmatrix} 2 \\ x \end{pmatrix} + \begin{pmatrix} x \\ y \end{pmatrix} = \begin{pmatrix} 5 \\ 6 \end{pmatrix}$, find the values of x and y.

9 Solve the vector equation $\begin{pmatrix} a \\ 2 \end{pmatrix} - \begin{pmatrix} -3 \\ b \end{pmatrix} = \begin{pmatrix} 4 \\ b \end{pmatrix}$

10 $\mathbf{a} = \begin{pmatrix} 3 \\ 0 \end{pmatrix}$, $\mathbf{b} = \begin{pmatrix} 0 \\ 2 \end{pmatrix}$, $\mathbf{c} = \begin{pmatrix} 3 \\ 1 \end{pmatrix}$

Find the values of p and q such that $p\mathbf{a} + q\mathbf{b} = \mathbf{c}$

11 $ABCD$ is a parallelogram.
Express, in terms of **a** and **b**

(a) $\overrightarrow{AC}$ (b) $\overrightarrow{DA}$ (c) $\overrightarrow{DB}$

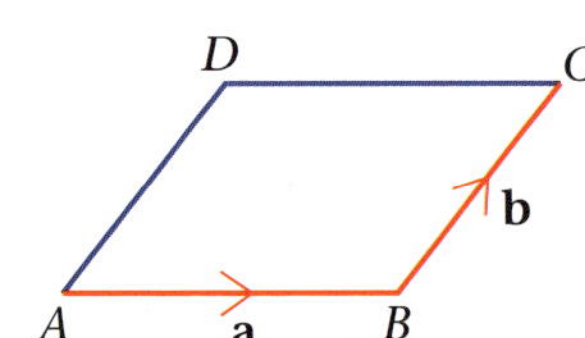

12 Given that $\overrightarrow{OC} = \frac{2}{5}\overrightarrow{OB}$, express, in terms of $\mathbf{a}$ and $\mathbf{b}$:

(a) $\overrightarrow{CB}$ (b) $\overrightarrow{BA}$

D is the point on BA so that $BD : DA = 3 : 2$

Express, in terms of $\mathbf{a}$ and $\mathbf{b}$

(c) $\overrightarrow{BD}$ (d) $\overrightarrow{CD}$

What can you conclude about CD and OA?

13 $OADEFC$ is a regular hexagon and B is the point of intersection of the diagonals.

$\overrightarrow{OA} = \mathbf{a}$, $\overrightarrow{OB} = \mathbf{b}$ and $\overrightarrow{OC} = \mathbf{c}$

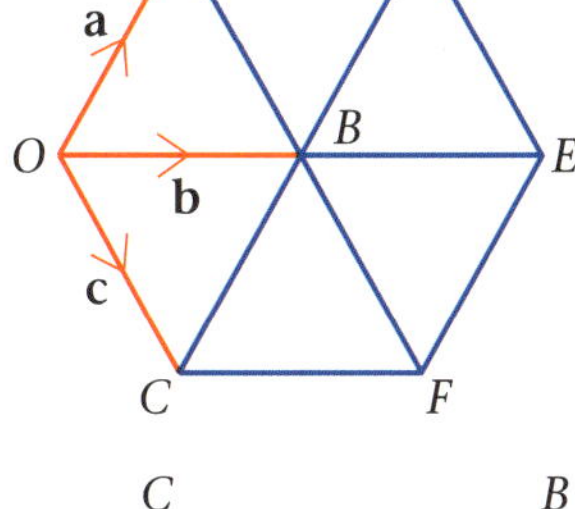

(a) Express, in terms of $\mathbf{a}$, $\mathbf{b}$ or $\mathbf{c}$ as appropriate, the vector $\overrightarrow{OD}$.

(b) Find two different expressions for the vector $\overrightarrow{OE}$.

(c) Write down an equality involving $\mathbf{a}$, $\mathbf{b}$ and $\mathbf{c}$.

14 $OABC$ is a parallelogram with $\overrightarrow{OA} = 4\mathbf{a}$ and $\overrightarrow{OB} = 4\mathbf{b}$.
The diagonals intersect at D.
P, Q, R and S are the mid-points of OD, AD, DB and DC respectively.
Show, using vector algebra, that $PQRS$ is a parallelogram.

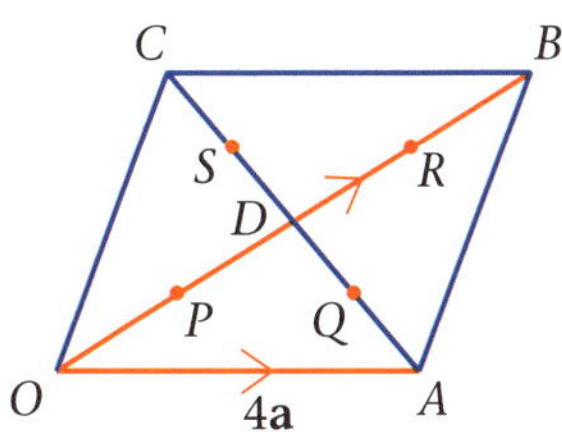

15 $\overrightarrow{OA} = \mathbf{a}$, $\overrightarrow{OB} = \mathbf{b}$ and $\overrightarrow{OC} = \mathbf{c}$. N is the mid-point of OB and M is the mid-point of AC. Express

(a) $\overrightarrow{AB}$ in terms of $\mathbf{a}$ and $\mathbf{b}$

(b) $\overrightarrow{ON}$ in terms of $\mathbf{b}$

(c) $\overrightarrow{AC}$ in terms of $\mathbf{a}$ and $\mathbf{c}$

(d) $\overrightarrow{AM}$ in terms of $\mathbf{a}$ and $\mathbf{c}$

(e) $\overrightarrow{OM}$ in terms of $\mathbf{a}$ and $\mathbf{c}$

(f) $\overrightarrow{NM}$ in terms of $\mathbf{a}$, $\mathbf{b}$ and $\mathbf{c}$.

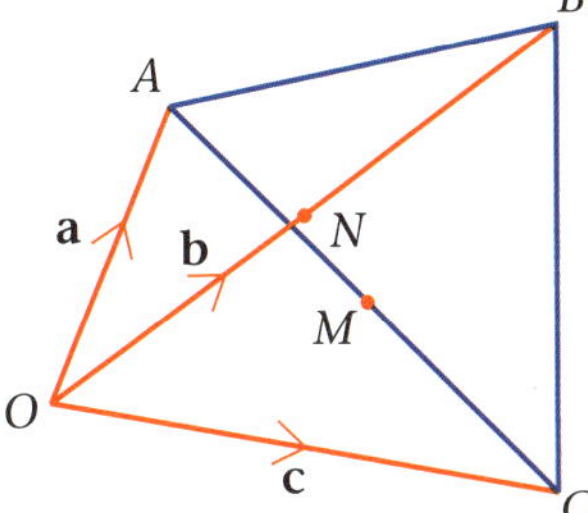

16 $\overrightarrow{OA} = \mathbf{a}$ and $\overrightarrow{OB} = \mathbf{b}$. X is the point such that $\overrightarrow{OX} = \frac{3}{2}\overrightarrow{OA}$ and Y is the point such that $\overrightarrow{OY} = 3\overrightarrow{OB}$.
Express, in terms of $\mathbf{a}$ and $\mathbf{b}$

(a) $\overrightarrow{OX}$ (b) $\overrightarrow{OY}$ (c) $\overrightarrow{YX}$

(d) The lines YX and BA are extended to meet at Z.
Explain why the position vector of any point on YX extended can be written as $3\mathbf{b} + p(\frac{3}{2}\mathbf{a} - 3\mathbf{b})$ and that the position vector of any point on BA extended can be written as $\mathbf{b} + q(\mathbf{a} - \mathbf{b})$.
Hence, or otherwise, find the position vector of Z.

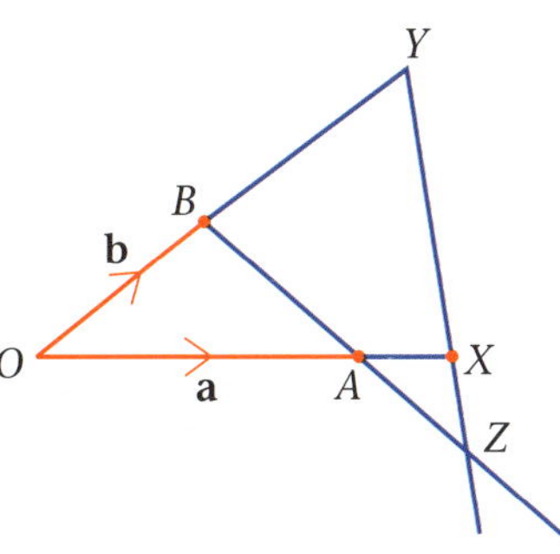

17 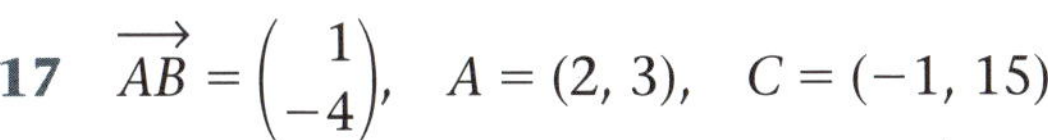
$\overrightarrow{AB} = \begin{pmatrix} 1 \\ -4 \end{pmatrix}$, $A = (2, 3)$, $C = (-1, 15)$

Find the values of x and y if $x\overrightarrow{OA} - y\overrightarrow{OB} = \overrightarrow{OC}$

Summary of key points

1 Translations can be described using **column vectors:** $\begin{pmatrix} x \\ y \end{pmatrix}$

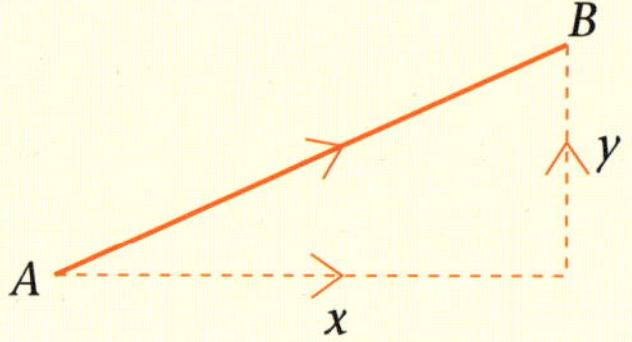

2 The values of x and y in a column vector are called **components**.

3 The translation that takes A to B can be written as a translation vector $\overrightarrow{AB}$.

4 If $\overrightarrow{AD} = \overrightarrow{BC}$, then AD and BC are parallel and have equal length.

5 A vector described as $\mathbf{a}$ has a unique length and direction. The vector with same length but opposite direction is $-\mathbf{a}$.

6 For any two vectors $\mathbf{a}$ and $\mathbf{b}$:
- $\mathbf{a} + \mathbf{b} = \mathbf{b} + \mathbf{a}$
- $\mathbf{a} - \mathbf{b} = \mathbf{a} + (-\mathbf{b})$

7 If a vector $\mathbf{a}$ is multiplied by a scalar k then the vector $k\mathbf{a}$ is parallel to $\mathbf{a}$ and is equal to k times $\mathbf{a}$.

8 For any vectors $\mathbf{a}$, $\mathbf{b}$ and $\mathbf{c}$ and any scalars p, q and k:
- $\mathbf{a} + \mathbf{b} = \mathbf{c}$ can be written as $\mathbf{a} = \mathbf{c} - \mathbf{b}$
- $k\mathbf{a} = k \times \mathbf{a}$
- $\mathbf{a} + (\mathbf{b} + \mathbf{c}) = (\mathbf{a} + \mathbf{b}) + \mathbf{c}$
- $k(\mathbf{a} + \mathbf{b}) = k\mathbf{a} + k\mathbf{b}$
- $(p + q)\mathbf{a} = p\mathbf{a} + q\mathbf{a}$

9 If two vectors $\mathbf{a}$ and $\mathbf{b}$ are parallel, then $\mathbf{a} = k\mathbf{b}$ for some scalar k.

10 The **magnitude** of a vector is the length of the directed line segment representing it.

11 In general, the magnitude of a vector $\begin{pmatrix} x \\ y \end{pmatrix}$ is $\sqrt{x^2 + y^2}$

12 Combinations of the vectors $\mathbf{a}$ and $\mathbf{b}$ of the form $p\mathbf{a} + q\mathbf{b}$, where p and q are scalars, are called **linear combinations** of the vectors $\mathbf{a}$ and $\mathbf{b}$.

13 For any two vectors you can find a linear combination parallel to any required direction.

14 The **position vector** of a point P is $\overrightarrow{OP}$, where O is usually the origin.

15 If A and B have position vectors $\mathbf{a}$ and $\mathbf{b}$ respectively, then the vector $\overrightarrow{AB} = \mathbf{b} - \mathbf{a}$.

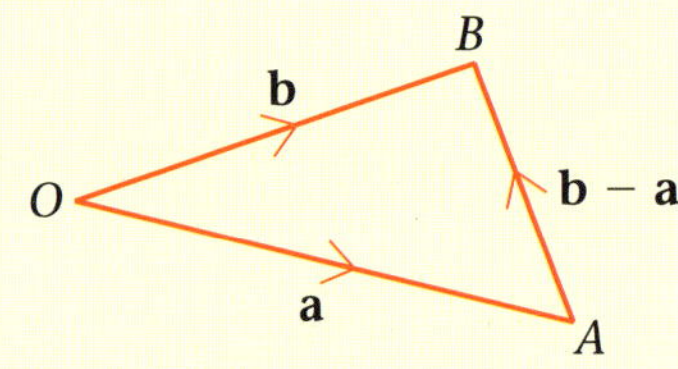

16 If A and B have position vectors $\mathbf{a}$ and $\mathbf{b}$ respectively, then the position vector of the mid-point, M, of the line joining A to B is $\overrightarrow{OM} = \mathbf{m} = \frac{1}{2}(\mathbf{a} + \mathbf{b})$.

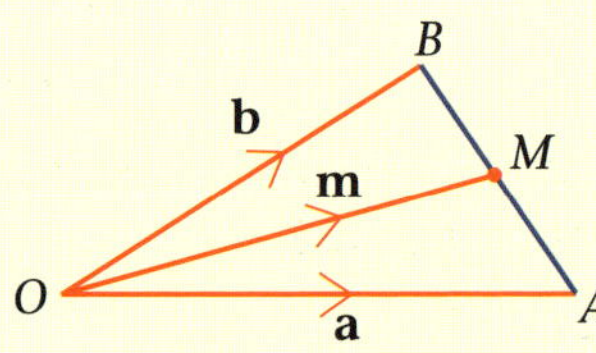

28 Introducing modelling

Simplifying a 'real-life' problem into a model which can be solved mathematically is called **mathematical modelling**. Estimating the height of a large waterfall using trigonometry is an example of mathematical modelling.

This chapter shows how exponential functions and trigonometric functions may be used in such models. It also shows how experimental data can be analysed to obtain relationships between two variables.

Mathematical model

55°

h

15 m

28.1 Modelling using exponential functions

2^x, $(0.5)^y$ and 3^{2t} are all examples of exponential functions.

> The function a^x, where a is a positive constant and x is a variable, is called an **exponential function**.

Example 1

Ben invests £2000 at Town Bank.
Town Bank pays 9% compound interest per annum, added yearly.
Ben does not intend to withdraw any interest.

(a) Find a formula which models this problem to give the value of the investment after t years.

(b) Use your formula to find when the investment is first worth more than £6000.

(a) Interest for the first year is $0.09 \times £2000$

Value of the investment after 1 year $= £2000 + 0.09 \times £2000$
$= (1 + 0.09) \times £2000$
$= 1.09 \times £2000$

9% = 0.09

Interest for the second year $= 0.09 \times (1.09 \times £2000)$

Value of the investment after 2 years $= (1.09 \times £2000) + 0.09 \times (1.09 \times £2000)$
$= (1 + 0.09)\,(1.09 \times £2000)$
$= 1.09 \times (1.09 \times £2000)$
$= (1.09)^2 \times £2000$

Similarly, the value of the investment after 3 years
$= (1.09)^3 \times £2000$

and the value of the investment after 4 years
$= (1.09)^4 \times £2000$

This is a sequence which gives the formua for the value, V, of the investment after t years as,

$$V = (1.09)^t \times £2000$$

(b) We need the smallest integer value of t such that $(1.09)^t \times £2000 > £6000$

so $(1.09)^t > 3$

Using the method of trial and improvement and a calculator, try:

$t = 12 \quad (1.09)^{12} = 2.8126\ldots$ — too small

$t = 13 \quad (1.09)^{13} = 3.0658\ldots$

So the value of the investment is over £6000 for the first time after 13 years.

The graph shows the value of the investment V after t years for Example 1.

This is an example of **exponential growth**.

The value of the investment is said to **grow exponentially** with a **multiplier** of 1.09

If $a > 1$ then a^x is an example of **exponential growth** with a multiplier of a.

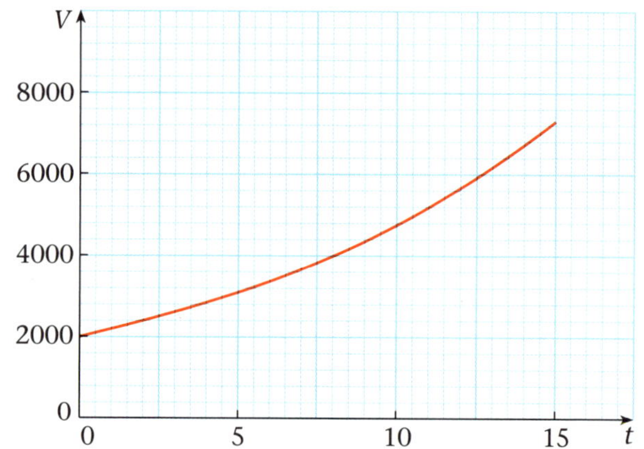

Example 2

A student published an article in which she reported that the number of birds of prey nesting in an area had been decreasing by 8% per year since 1990. There were 600 birds in 1990.

Assuming this same rate of decrease, find a formula for the number, N, of these birds of prey that will nest in the same area t years after 1990.

Decrease of birds during 1991 $= 0.08 \times 600$

Number of birds in 1991 $= 600 - 0.08 \times 600$

$= 0.92 \times 600$

Decrease of birds during 1992 $= 0.08 \times (0.92 \times 600)$

Number of birds in 1992 $= (0.92 \times 600) - 0.08 \times (0.92 \times 600)$

$= (1 - 0.08)\,(0.92 \times 600)$

$= (0.92)^2 \times 600$

Similarly, the number of birds 3 years after 1990 $= (0.92)^3 \times 600$

and the number of birds 4 years after 1990 $= (0.92)^4 \times 600$

So the number of birds t years after 1990 $= (0.92)^t \times 600$

$N = (0.92)^t \times 600$

The graph shows the number of nesting birds of prey, N, t years after 1990 for Example 2.

This is an example of **exponential decay**.

The number of birds is said to **decay exponentially** with a **multiplier** of 0.92.

If $0 < a < 1$ then a^x is an example of **exponential decay** with a multiplier of a.

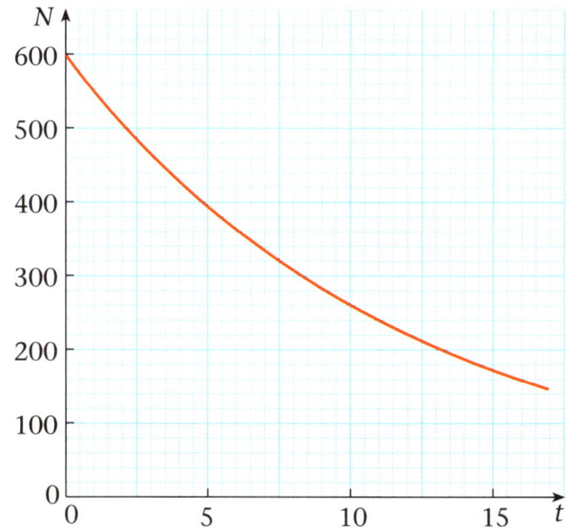

Exercise 28A

1 Rina invests £1500 at Shirebank. Shirebank pays 6% compound interest per annum, added yearly. Rina does not intend to withdraw any interest.

(a) Find a formula which models this problem to give the value of the investment after t years.

(b) Use your formula to find when the investment is first worth at least £3750.

2 A ball, dropped from a height x metres, rebounds to a height $0.6x$ metres. If the ball is dropped from a height of 8 metres, find

(a) a formula which models this problem to give the height of rebound after the nth bounce

(b) the total vertical distance the ball has travelled just before its third bounce.

3 The time taken for a mass of radioactive uranium to halve is 24 days. How long does it take for 40 mg to reduce to

(a) 10 mg

(b) 2.5 mg?

4 Winston's debt of £40 000 decreases by 20% per year.

(a) What is his debt after

(i) 1 year

(ii) 4 years

(iii) n years?

(b) After how many years will the debt first fall below £100?

28.2 Modelling using trigonometric functions

For the graphs of the sine and cosine functions, see Chapter 16.

For problems where the motion repeats itself after a certain time, the sine and cosine functions are the most appropriate.

Example 3

A travelling fair comes to a Cheshire town every May. The fair includes a big wheel which is constructed and tested. The diameter of the wheel is 20 m. Its centre is 12 m above the ground.

The wheel is first tested using one chair. The wheel rotates anticlockwise and is timed for each revolution once it reaches its working speed.

The timing starts as the chair moves upwards through the point level with the centre of the wheel.

The wheel rotates once every 36 seconds.

(a) Find the constants p and q so that $y = p + q\sin(10t)°$ is a suitable model for the height, y metres, of the chair above the ground t seconds after timing starts.

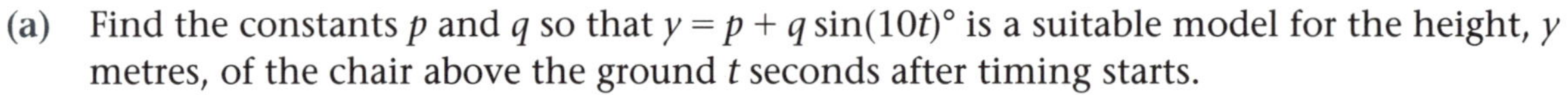

(b) Find the times during the first minute when the chair is 17 m above the ground.

(c) Sketch the graph of y against t for $0 \leqslant t \leqslant 54$.

(a) The diagram represents the big wheel, with A the position of the chair when the timing starts and B, the highest point reached by the chair shown.

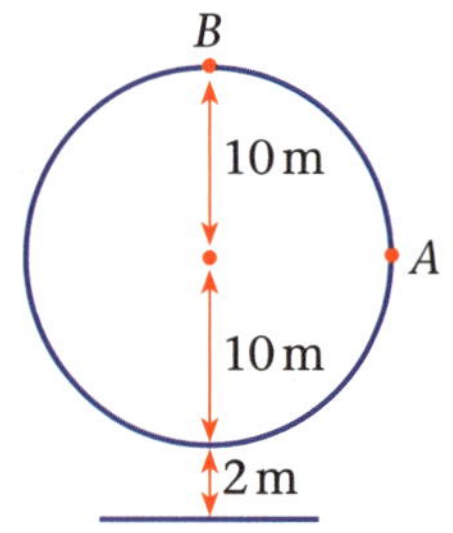

$$y = p + q\sin(10t)°$$

When $t = 0$, $y = 12$, giving $\quad 12 = p + q\sin 0°$

$$12 = p + q(0)$$

$$12 = p$$

The chair reaches B when the wheel completes a $\frac{1}{4}$ of a revolution. The time taken, t, is $\frac{1}{4} \times 36 = 9$ seconds.

$$y = p + q\sin(10t)°$$

When $t = 9$, $y = 22$, giving $\quad 22 = p + q\sin 90°$

$$22 = p + q(1)$$

But $p = 12$, so $\quad 22 = 12 + q$

$$10 = q$$

(b) Use $y = 12 + 10\sin(10t)°$ to find the value of t when $y = 17$:

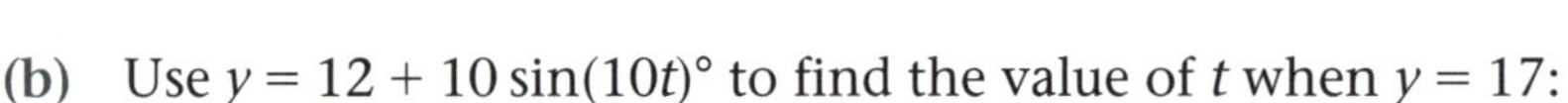

$$17 = 12 + 10\sin(10t)°$$

$$5 = 10\sin(10t)°$$

$$\sin(10t)° = 0.5$$

So $(10t)° = 30°, 180° - 30°, 360° + 30°, 540° - 30°, 720° + 30°, \ldots$

$$t = 3, 15, 39, 51, 75, \ldots$$

The required times are 3 s, 15 s, 39 s and 51 seconds.

(c)

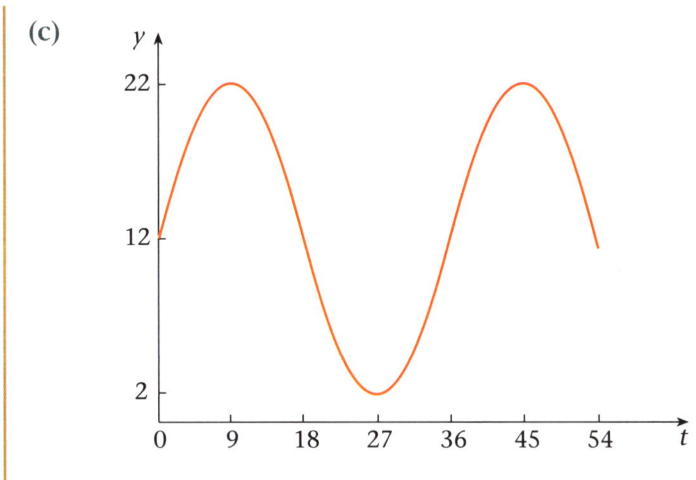

$y = 12 + 10\sin(10t)$ is the graph of $y = \sin t$

- stretched by 10 parallel to the y-axis
- stretched by $\frac{1}{10}$ parallel to the x-axis and
- translated 12 units parallel to the y-axis.

Check the formula for y:
when $t = 18$, $y = 12$
when $t = 27$, $y = 2$
when $t = 36$, $y = 12$.

In coastal areas the depth of the water depends on the time of day.

The depth of the water is greatest at high tide and least at low tide. Sailors need to know the times when these two extremes occur.

This situation can be modelled using trigonometric functions.

Example 4

Martin believes that the depth of water, d metres, at the end of a jetty t hours after low tide can be modelled by a formula of the form

$$d = a + b\cos(kt)°$$

where a, b and k are constants.

He measures the depth of water at low tide as 2 metres.

(a) Assuming that low tides occur every 12 hours, show that $k = 30$.

Martin also measures the depth of water at high tide as 6 metres.

(b) Calculate the values of a and b.

Martin needs at least 3 metres of water at the end of the jetty to sail his boat.

(c) Given that low tide on a particular day was at 09:00, find the earliest time that Martin could sail his boat.

(a) Low tide is when $t = 0$ and $t = 12$

$$d = a + b\cos(kt)°$$

When $t = 0, d = 2$ $\quad 2 = a + b\cos 0°$ $\quad$ so $2 = a + b$

When $t = 12, d = 2$ $\quad 2 = a + b\cos(12k)°$

This gives $\quad \cos(12k)° = 1$

$$12k = \cos^{-1} 1 = 0 \text{ or } 360$$

$$k = 30$$

$k \neq 0$ because the depth of water is not constant.

(b) High tide is when $t = 6$

$$d = a + b\cos(30t)°$$

When $t = 6$, $d = 6$ $\quad 6 = a + b\cos 180°$ $\quad$ so $6 = a - b$

But $2 = a + b$

$8 = 2a$

so $a = 4$ and $b = -2$

(c) Use $d = 4 - 2\cos(30t)°$ to find the value of t when $d = 3$:

$$d = 4 - 2\cos(30t)°$$

When $d = 3$ $\quad 3 = 4 - 2\cos(30t)°$

$$2\cos(30t)° = 1$$

$$\cos(30t)° = 0.5$$

$$30t = 60 \quad \text{so } t = 2$$

The **earliest** time that Martin can sail his boat is 11:00.

Exercise 28B

1 The depth, d metres, of water at the end of a jetty t hours after noon is modelled by the formula

$$d = 4 + 2.5\cos(30t)°$$

(a) Find the depth of water at
(i) noon (ii) 2 pm (iii) 3 pm (iv) 6 pm (v) midnight.

(b) Find the first time, correct to the nearest minute, when the depth of water is 6 metres.

(c) Sketch the graph of d against t for $0 \leqslant t \leqslant 12$.

2 One end of a spring is fixed to a wall at point P. A mass M, which lies on a table, is attached to the other end. PM is horizontal. Damien pushes the mass towards P and releases it. He models the distance, y cm, of the mass from P at time t seconds after releasing it by the formula

$$y = 15 - 5\cos(45t)°$$

(a) Find the distance of the mass from the wall when
(i) $t = 2$ (ii) $t = 4$ (iii) the mass is released.

(b) Sketch the graph of y against t for $0 \leqslant t \leqslant 8$.

3 t hours after midnight, the depth of water, d metres, at the entrance of a harbour is modelled by the formula

$$d = 6 + 3\sin(30t)°$$

(a) What is the depth of water at (i) 1 am (ii) noon?

(b) What is the depth of water at low tide?

(c) Find the times of high tide during a complete day.

(d) Sketch the graph of d against t for $0 \leqslant t \leqslant 24$.

4 The diameter of a big wheel is 16 m. Its centre is 9 m above the ground. The wheel rotates clockwise.
Mandy rides on the big wheel and starts to time it when her chair reaches its highest point. The wheel rotates once every 20 seconds.

(a) Find the constants p and q so that

$$y = p + q\cos(18t)°$$

is a suitable model for the height of the chair, y metres, above the ground t seconds after timing starts.

(b) Find the times during the first half minute when the chair is 13 m above the ground.

(c) Find the times during the first half minute when the chair is 5 m above the ground.

(d) Sketch the graph of y against t for $0 \leqslant t \leqslant 30$.

28.3 Using a line of best fit to obtain a relationship

Scientists frequently collect data from scientific experiments involving two quantities.

These experiments can be costly so the scientists try to use the data to obtain a relationship between the two quantities. They can then apply this relationship to other values of one of the variables and predict other results without having to carry out further experiments.

Experimental data is subject to errors in the measuring instruments so points are unlikely to lie exactly on a straight line when plotted.

For more on lines of best fit see Section 10.12 (in Book 1).

A **line of best fit** is used.

Example 5

This scatter diagram shows the results of a scientific experiment involving two variables x and y.

The scientist has drawn in the line of best fit.

(a) Find the equation of the line of best fit.

(b) Assuming that this line is valid for larger values of x, find the value of y when $x = 52$.

You cannot always assume that the results will be true for values outside the range of the data.

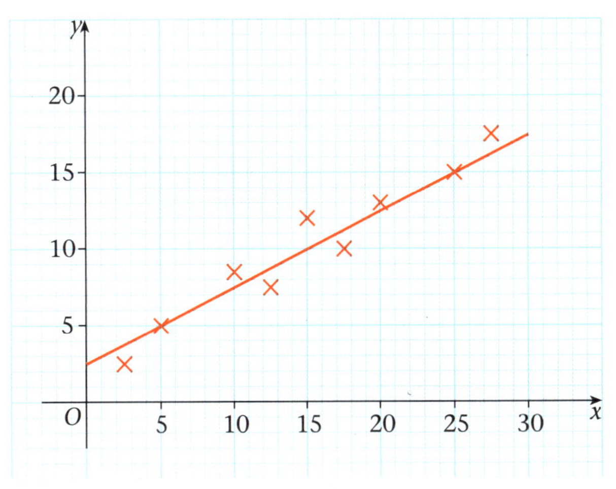

(a) The equation of a straight line is $y = mx + c$.
(25, 15) and (5, 5) are two points on the line of best fit.

You could use *any* two points on the line.

$$\text{Gradient } m = \frac{15 - 5}{25 - 5} = \frac{10}{20} = 0.5$$

The equation of the line will take the form $y = 0.5x + c$

The point (5, 5) lies on the line

so $5 = 0.5(5) + c \Rightarrow c = 2.5$

The equation of the line of best fit is $y = 0.5x + 2.5$

c could also have been read off from the graph as the y-intercept. In this example, reading off between squares may not be very accurate.

(b) $y = 0.5x + 2.5$

When $x = 52$, $y = 0.5(52) + 2.5 = 26 + 2.5$

So $y = 28.5$ when $x = 52$

To test the formula $y = px + q$, plot y against x.
If the points lie approximately on a straight line then p is the gradient of the line of best fit and q is the intercept on the vertical axis.

Exercise 28C

The scatter diagrams in questions **1–3** show the results of experiments involving two variables x and y. The line of best fit is drawn on each.

1 (a) Find the equation of the line of best fit.

(b) Assuming that this line is valid for larger values of x, find the value of y when $x = 48$.

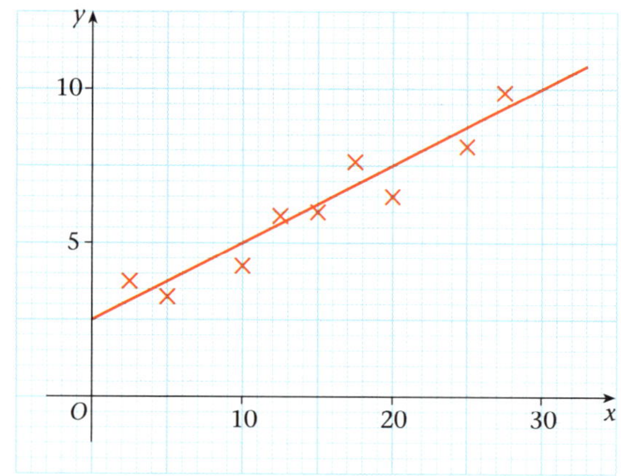

2 (a) Find the equation of the line of best fit.

(b) Assuming that this line is valid for larger values of x, find the value of y when $x = 18$.

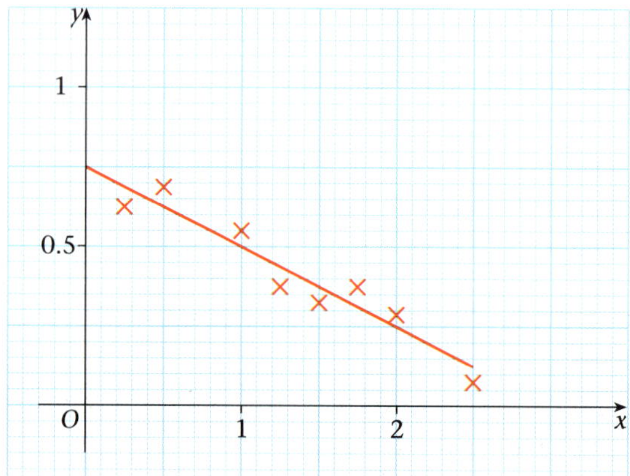

3 (a) Find the equation of the line of best fit.
(b) Assuming that this line is valid for larger values of x, find the value of y when $x = 75$.

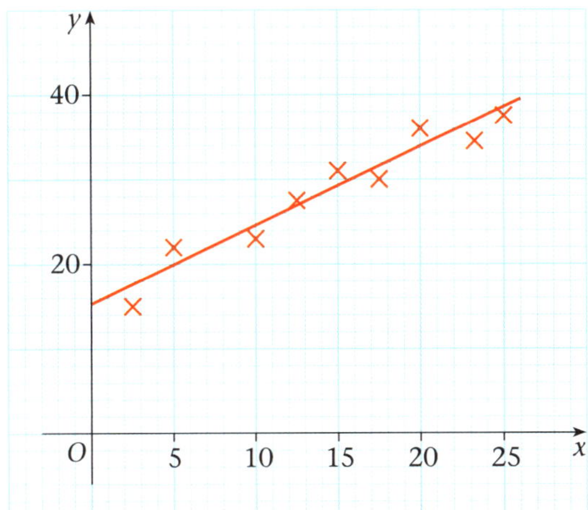

28.4 Reducing equations to linear form

Not all scientific data, when plotted as two variables, will lead to a straight line.

This section shows how to rewrite some relationships in a linear form. We shall use the general equation of a straight line as $Y = mX + c$, where Y and X are the two variables, m is the gradient of the line and c is the intercept on the y-axis.

We shall also use letters p and q to denote constants.

> Y and X are the variables transformed to form a linear relationship.

> Note: $Y = mX + c$ has three terms, two of which contain variables, that is Y and mX, and a third term, c, which does not contain a variable.

Equations of the form $y = px^2 + q$

Like $Y = mX + c$, $y = px^2 + q$ also has three terms, two with variables and one without.

Comparing the two

$$Y = mX + c$$
$$\downarrow \quad \downarrow\downarrow \quad \downarrow$$
$$y = px^2 + q$$

> If $Y = mX + c$ passes through the origin then $c = 0$.

To test the formula $y = px^2 + q$, plot y against x^2.
If the points lie approximately on a straight line then p is the gradient of the line of best fit and q is the intercept on the vertical axis.

The gradient of the line gives the value of p and the intercept on the y-axis gives the value of q.

Example 6

In an experiment these values of the variables V and R were obtained:

V	5	10	15	20	25
R	140	166	212	280	365

The variables V and R are thought to satisfy a relationship of the form $R = pV^2 + q$.

(a) Draw a graph to test this.

(b) Use your graph to estimate the values of the constants p and q.

(c) Use your relationship to find R when $V = 18$.

(a) Comparing $R = pV^2 + q$ to $Y = mX + c$

$$Y = mX + c$$
$$\downarrow \quad \downarrow\downarrow \quad \downarrow$$
$$R = pV^2 + q$$

Plotting R on the vertical axis and V^2 on the horizontal axis, should lead to an approximate straight line if $R = pV^2 + q$ is the correct relationship. The gradient of the line gives p and the intercept on the R-axis gives q.

V^2	25	100	225	400	625
R	140	166	212	280	365

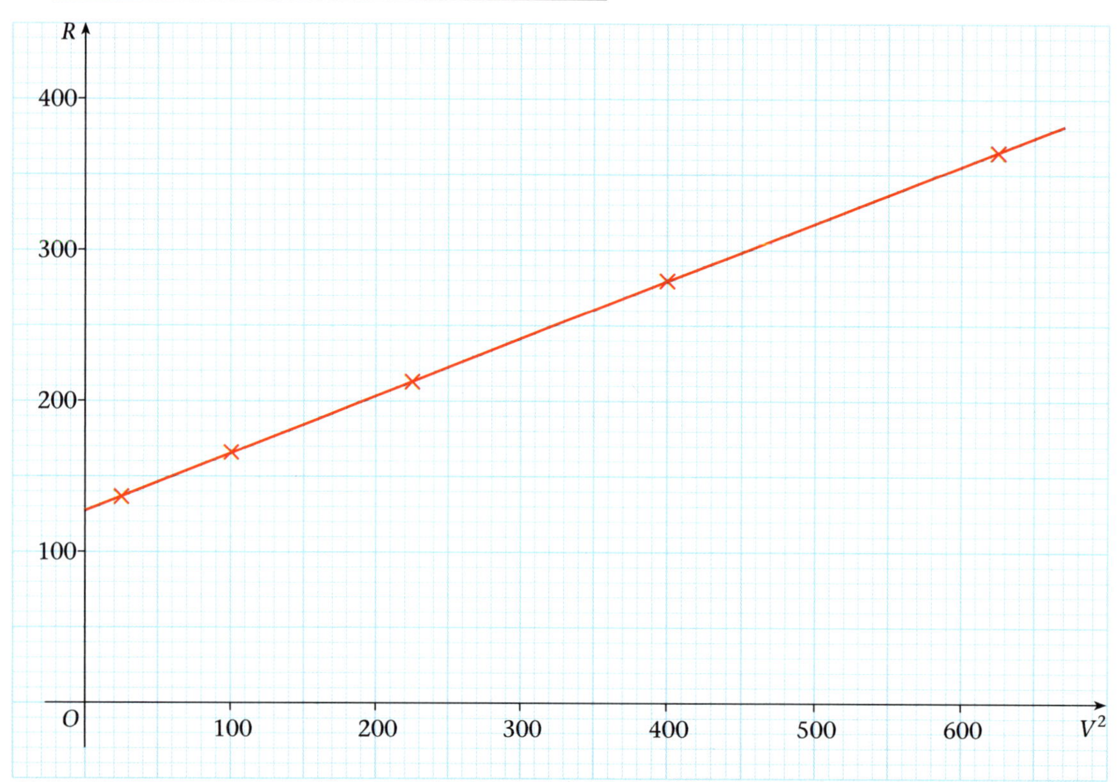

(b) Taking the points on the line as (100, 166) and (400, 280):

$$\text{the gradient, } m = p = \frac{280 - 166}{400 - 100} = \frac{114}{300} = 0.38$$

and the y-intercept $q = 128$

So $R = 0.38V^2 + 128$

You could take any two points **on the line**.

(c) When $V = 18$, $R = 0.38 \times 18^2 + 128$

$= 251.12$

$R = 251$ (to 3 s.f.)

Equations of the form $y = px^2 + qx$

In the equation $y = px^2 + qx$, all three terms contain variables so we cannot compare this with $Y = mX + c$ directly.

Dividing each term of $y = px^2 + qx$ by x gives $\frac{y}{x} = px + q$

$$y = px^2 + qx$$
$$\frac{y}{x} = \frac{px^2}{x} + \frac{qx}{x}$$
$$\frac{y}{x} = px + q$$

Comparing $\frac{y}{x} = px + q$ with $Y = mX + c$

$$Y = mX + c$$
$$\downarrow \quad \downarrow\downarrow \quad \downarrow$$
$$\frac{y}{x} = px^2 + q$$

To test the formula $y = px^2 + qx$, plot $\frac{y}{x}$ against x.
If the points lie approximately on a straight line then p is the gradient of the line of best fit and q is the intercept on the vertical axis.

The gradient of the line gives p and the intercept on the $\frac{y}{x}$-axis gives q.

Example 7

An object is fired vertically upwards and its height, h metres, above the firing point is recorded t seconds later. The table shows the results.

t	1	2	3	4	5
h	27	44	48	44	27

(a) Plot $\frac{h}{t}$ against t.

(b) Explain why your graph verifies that $h = pt^2 + qt$, and use your graph to estimate the values of the constants p and q.

(c) Use your relationship to find h when $t = 5.5$

(a)

t	1	2	3	4	5
$\frac{h}{t}$	27	22	16	11	5.4

(b) The graph of $\frac{h}{t}$ against t gives a straight line so $\frac{h}{t} = pt + q$, where p is the gradient and q is the intercept on the vertical axis. Multiplying both sides of the equation by t leads to $h = pt^2 + qt$.

$p = \text{gradient of the line} = \frac{-11}{2} = -5.5$

$q = \text{intercept on the vertical axis} = 33$

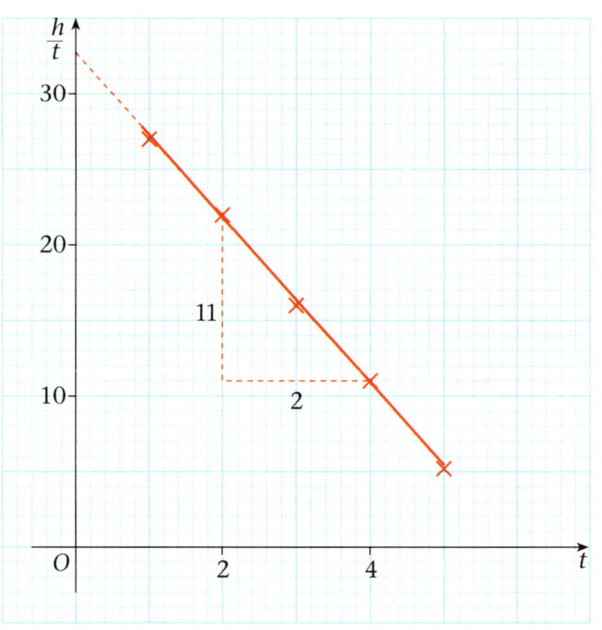

(c) $h = -5.5t^2 + 33t$

When $t = 5.5$,

$h = -5.5(5.5)^2 + 33(5.5)$

$= 15.125$ metres

Exercise 28D

1

x	11	20	27	36	45
y	8	10.2	12.4	15	17

The table shows corresponding values of the variables x and y.
Peter believes that they satisfy a relationship of the form $y = ax + b$.

(a) Draw a graph to test whether Peter is correct.

(b) Use your graph to estimate the values of the constants a and b.

2

x	1	2	3	4	5
y	3.5	9.3	19	33	52

y is approximately equal to $ax^2 + b$.
Plot y against x^2 and use the graph to estimate a and b.

3 Water is squirted horizontally from a hosepipe. The height of the water is y metres at a distance x metres from the hosepipe. Measurements of x and y are:

x	0	1	2	3	5	6
y	7.2	7.0	6.4	5.5	2.2	0.1

It is thought that the relationship between x and y is of the form $y = ax^2 + b$. Plot y against x^2 and use the graph to estimate a and b.

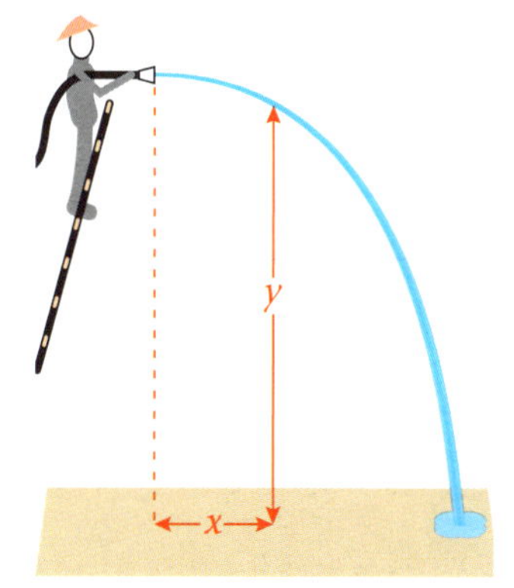

4

x	1	2	3	4	5
y	2.2	8.4	18.5	32.8	51.1

y is approximately equal to $ax^2 + bx$. Plot $\frac{y}{x}$ against x and use the graph to estimate a and b.

5

x	1	2	3	4	5
y	2.5	4.1	4.6	4.0	2.5

y is approximately equal to $ax^2 + bx$. Plot $\frac{y}{x}$ against x and use the graph to estimate a and b.

6

x	1	2	3	4	5
y	5.52	4.03	1.53	−1.96	−6.48

y is approximately equal to $ax^2 + b$. Use a graph to estimate a and b.

28.5 Finding the constants in an exponential relationship

To draw the graph of $y = 3^x$, you can complete a table of values of x by finding the corresponding values of y.

x	0	1	2	3
y	1	3	9	27

You can then plot these points and join them with a smooth curve.

The reverse process is also valid.

If a point lies on a curve then the coordinates of the point satisfy the equation of the curve.

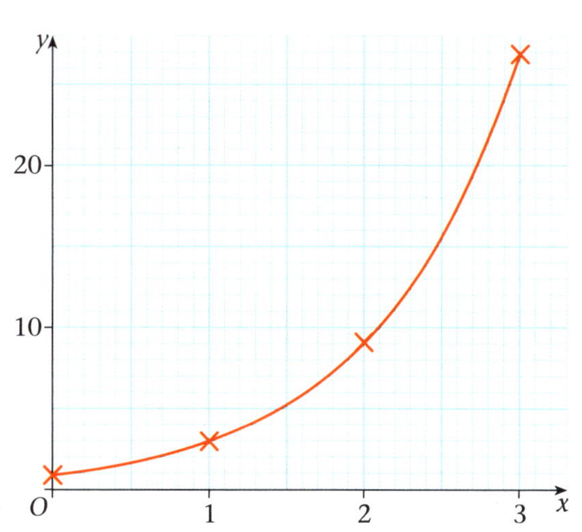

Example 8

This sketch shows part of the graph of $y = pq^x$.

It is known that the points (0, 5), (2, k) and (3, 40) lie on this curve.

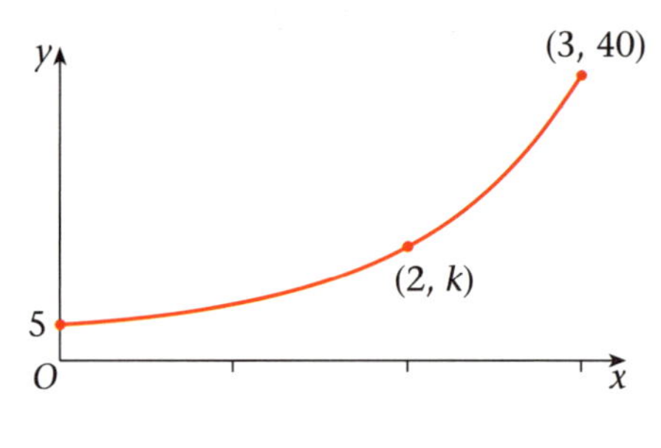

Use the sketch to find the values of p, q and k.

Point (0, 5) lies on the curve $y = pq^x$,

so $5 = pq^0$

$5 = p \times 1$ so $p = 5$

Point (3, 40) lies on the curve $y = 5q^x$,

so $40 = 5q^3$ so $q^3 = 8$

$q = 2$

So $y = 5 \times 2^x$

Point (2, k) lies on the curve $y = 5 \times 2^x$, so $k = 5 \times 2^2$

$k = 20$

Exercise 28E

1 This sketch shows part of the graph of $y = pq^x$.
Use the sketch to find the values of p, q and k.

2 The sketch below shows part of the graph of $y = pq^x$.
Use the sketch to find the values of p, q and k.

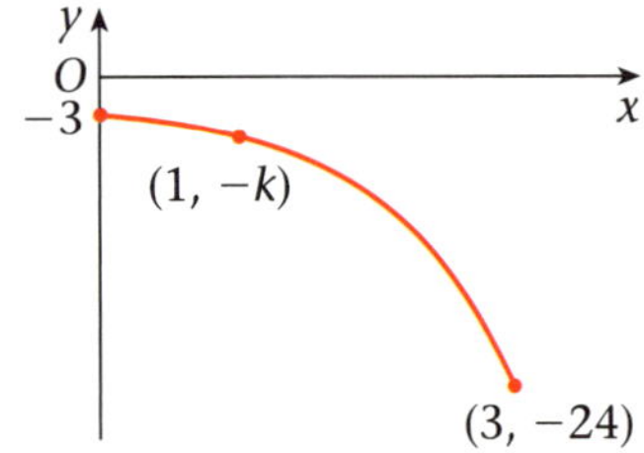

3 This sketch shows part of the graph of $y = a + b^x$.
Use the sketch to find the values of a, b and k.

4 The point (1, 3) lies on the curve $y = a^{-x}$.
Calculate the value of a.

5 The point $(2, 2\frac{1}{4})$ lies on the curve $y = a^{-x}$.
Calculate the two possible values of a.

6 The three points (0, 5), $(1, 4\frac{1}{3})$ and (2, k) lie on the curve $y = a + b^{-x}$.
Calculate the values of a, b and k.

7 The point (1, 8) lies on the curve $y = a^{-3x}$.
Calculate the value of a.

8 Challenge

The points (2, 32) and (5, 2048) both lie on the curve $y = pq^x$.

(a) Find the values of the constants p and q.

(b) Given also that the point $(k, 128)$ lies on this curve, find the value of k.

Summary of key points

1 The function a^x, where a is a positive constant and x is a variable, is called an **exponential function**.

2 • If $a > 1$ then a^x is an example of **exponential growth** with a multiplier of a.

• If $0 < a < 1$ then a^x is an example of **exponential decay** with a multiplier of a.

3 A point lies on a curve if the coordinates of the point satisfy the equation of the curve.

4 To test the formula $y = px + q$, plot y against x. If the points lie approximately on a straight line then p is the gradient of the line of best fit and q is the intercept on the vertical axis.

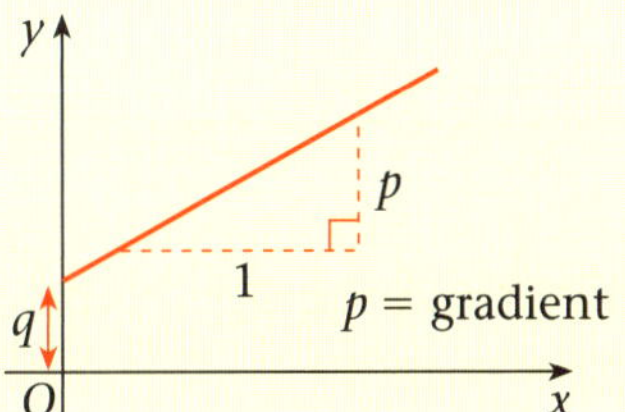

5 To test the formula $y = px^2 + q$, plot y against x^2. If the points lie approximately on a straight line then p is the gradient of the line of best fit and q is the intercept on the vertical axis.

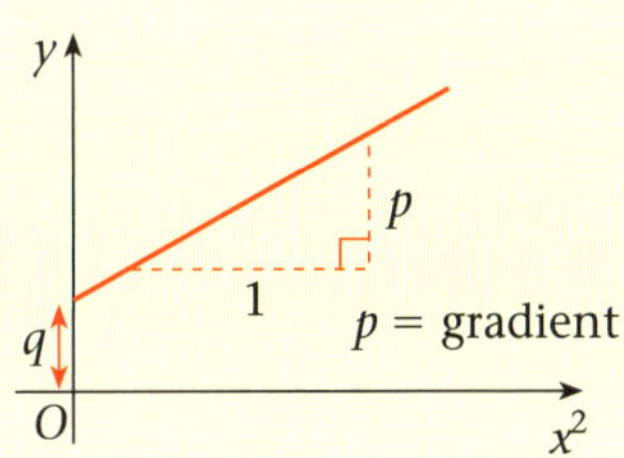

6 To test the formula $y = px^2 + qx$, plot $\frac{y}{x}$ against x. If the points lie approximately on a straight line then p is the gradient of the line of best fit and q is the intercept on the vertical axis.

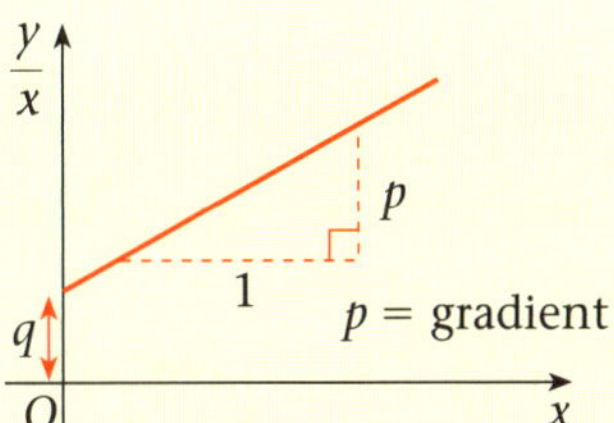

7 If a point lies on a curve then the coordinates of the point satisfy the equation of the curve.

29 Conditional probability

In this chapter you will find probabilities of events that are not independent.

29.1 Dependent and independent events

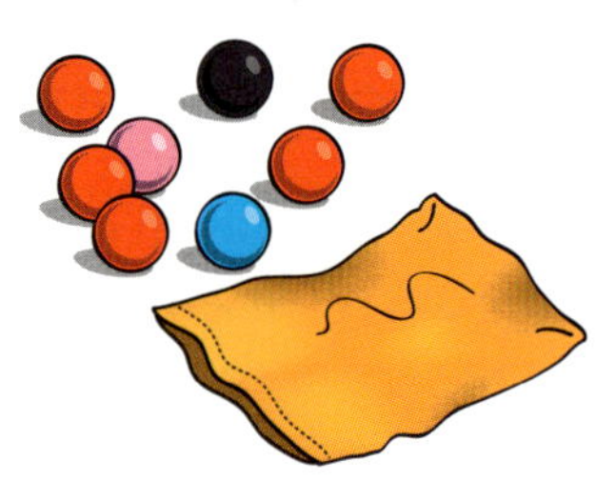

Imagine a bag containing eight snooker balls. Five are red and three are other colours (not red). If you pick two balls out of the bag at random, what is the probability that they will both be red?

The answer will depend on whether or not you put the first ball back in the bag before you pick the second ball out.

If you put the first ball back, there will be the same number of red balls to choose from second time round as there were first time. Then the probability of picking a second red ball *does not* depend on whether the first ball picked was red or not. It is **independent** of the colour of the first ball chosen.

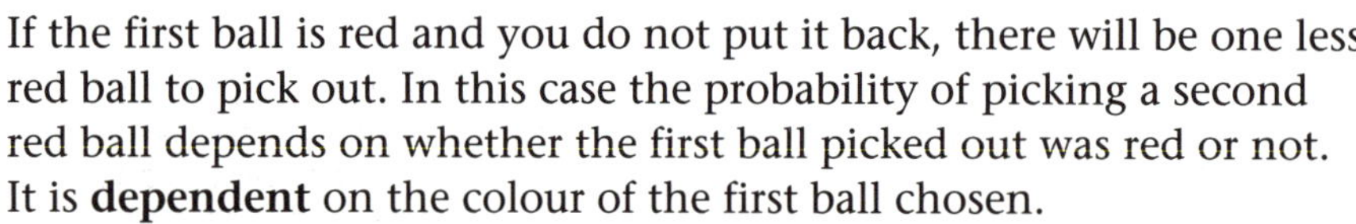

If the first ball is red and you do not put it back, there will be one less red ball to pick out. In this case the probability of picking a second red ball depends on whether the first ball picked out was red or not. It is **dependent** on the colour of the first ball chosen.

These tree diagrams show the probability of picking two red balls in these two different situations:

Independent events – first ball replaced before second ball picked

First choice **Second choice**

red $\frac{5}{8}$ → red $\frac{5}{8}$, not red $\frac{3}{8}$

not red $\frac{3}{8}$ → red $\frac{5}{8}$, not red $\frac{3}{8}$

Here the probability of picking two red balls is

$\frac{5}{8} \times \frac{5}{8} = \frac{25}{64}$

or

P(red) $\times$ P(red) = P(red and red)

Dependent events – first ball not replaced before second ball picked

First choice **Second choice**

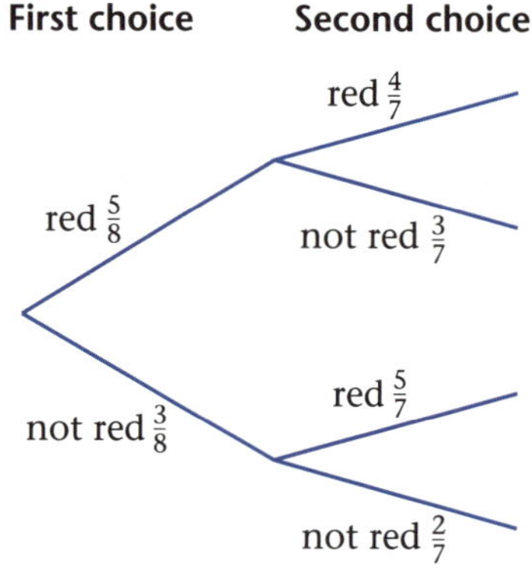

If a red ball is picked first and not replaced, there are only seven balls left to choose from. Only four of these are red, so for the second ball

P(red) = $\frac{4}{7}$ and P(not red) = $\frac{3}{7}$

If a 'not red' ball is picked first and not replaced, there are still seven balls left to choose from and five of these are red, so for the second ball

P(red) = $\frac{5}{7}$ and P(not red) = $\frac{2}{7}$

So when the first ball is not replaced, the probability of two reds being picked is

$\frac{5}{8} \times \frac{4}{7} = \frac{20}{56} = \frac{5}{14}$

Conditional probability is the name for the probability of an event that is dependent on a previous event. The probability depends on the conditions before the event.

Worked examination question

A box contains ten discs. Four of the discs are green and six are red. Two discs are removed at random from the box. By drawing a tree diagram, or otherwise, calculate the probability that both discs will be red.

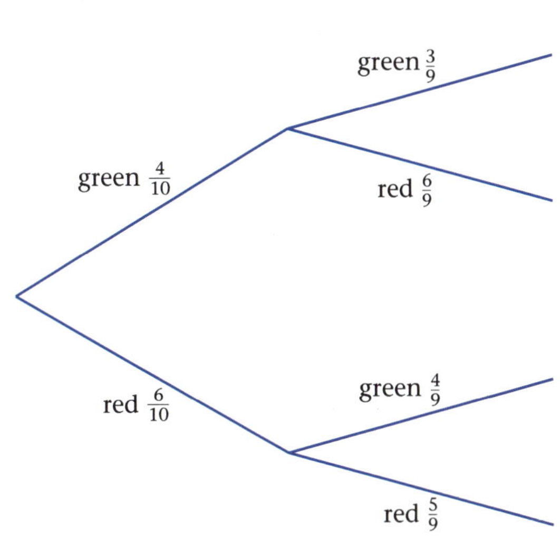

So the probability of both discs being red is:

$\frac{6}{10} \times \frac{5}{9} = \frac{30}{90} = \frac{1}{3}$

Any other exactly correct equivalent fraction, decimal or percentage would also gain full marks. Answers such as 0.3, 0.33, 0.333, 30% or 33% are not sufficiently accurate. The answer must be exact: $0.\dot{3}$, $\frac{1}{3}$ or $33\frac{1}{3}$%.

Exercise 29A

Read through the whole question before you start to draw the tree diagram because the choices to be made at each stage do not always become clear until the end.

1 Leo's cat has a litter of kittens: five female and two male. The vet examines them randomly one by one. Draw a tree diagram and use it to calculate the probability that the first three kittens examined

(a) will all be male

(b) will all be female

(c) will include at least one of each sex

(d) will include both males.

2 Nine playing cards numbered 2 to 10 are shuffled thoroughly. The top three cards are turned face up on a table. Draw a tree diagram and use it to calculate the probability that the numbers on the three cards

(a) will all be even

(b) will all be odd

(c) will have an even product.

3 Ten identical plastic counters numbered 1 to 10 are placed in a box. Meena picks three of them at random. She wins if the product of the numbers she picks is a multiple of 3.
Draw a tree diagram to illustrate the winning outcomes and their probabilities and use it to calculate the probability that Meena will win when she picks three counters.

4 One hundred raffle tickets numbered 1 to 100 are used in a tombola to decide who wins a prize. People who pick a ticket with a units digit of 0 win. The first person to try his luck picks two tickets.
By drawing a tree diagram, or otherwise, calculate the probability that he will win

(a) no prize

(b) at least one prize.

5 After a holiday abroad Janet has 10 coins in her purse. Five are €1 coins, three are €2 coins and two are £1 pieces. All the coins are similar sizes. Janet takes three coins at random from her purse. Calculate the probability that the three coins will

(a) all be €1 coins

(b) not include a €1 coin

(c) be one of each type.

29.2 Paths through tree diagrams

Large tree diagrams can take some time to draw.

You only need to draw paths through a tree diagram which are needed to solve the problem set. Make sure you include all the paths you need.

An incomplete tree showing only the relevant branches and leading to a correct answer is sufficient for full marks in the GCSE exam.

In the snooker ball problem at the start of Section 29.1, if you pick two balls at random, the probability that at least one of them is red includes every event except that of picking no reds at all. These two groups of events are **mutually exclusive** so

P(at least one red) = 1 − P(no reds at all)

For more about mutually exclusive events see Section 24.2.

It may be easier to find P(at least one red) by calculating 1 − P(no reds at all).

It may be quicker to calculate the probability of a mutually exclusive event than to draw a tree diagram.

Example 1

There are ten sweets in a box: three are orange, four are lime and three are lemon flavoured. Three sweets are taken randomly from the box and eaten.

Calculate the probability that those eaten are not all the same flavour.

P(not all the same flavour) = 1 − P(all the same flavour)

The paths through the tree for all three sweets the same flavour are:

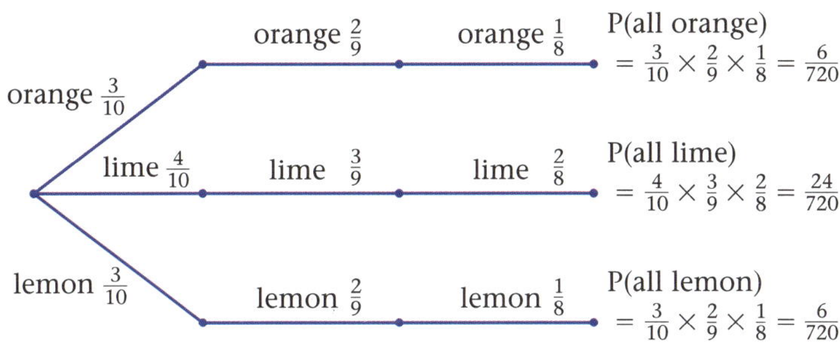

P(all the same flavour) $= \frac{6}{720} + \frac{24}{720} + \frac{6}{720} = \frac{36}{720} = \frac{1}{20}$

P(not all the same flavour) $= 1 - \frac{1}{20} = \frac{19}{20}$

Notice that when the products of the fractions were found they were not simplified straight away because they had to be added later. This usually saves time in an exam.

Exercise 29B

In this exercise try drawing only those parts of each tree diagram that you need to answer the questions.

1 Shelley has 15 full one-litre tins of paint. Six contain Sunset Red, five contain Sunflower Yellow and the other four contain Midnight Blue. Shelley selects three tins at random, opens them and empties them into a ten-litre bucket.
Calculate the probability that when she mixes the paint in the bucket the colour produced will not be exactly one of the original three colours.

2 Twenty-six tiles, each with one of the letters of the alphabet on, are placed on a table so that none of the letters shows. Winston picks four at random. Calculate the probability that:

(a) none of the letters picked will be a vowel (a, e, i, o, u)

(b) at least one of the letters picked will be a vowel.

3 Courtney has seven plastic letters: three As, two Rs and two Ts. She picks three at random and puts them on the table in a row, the first at the left and so on. Calculate the probability that

(a) the letters will spell (i) ART (ii) RAT (iii) TAR

(b) the three letters will all be different.

4 Helen has six pens in her pencil case. Three are blue, two are black and the other is red. She takes out three pens at random and puts them on her desk.
Calculate the probability that there will be one pen of each colour on the desk.

5 Under his sofa David has a pair of black shoes, a pair of brown shoes and an odd red shoe. He cannot see them and can only just reach them, so has to select them at random. He does not replace any shoe he pulls out.
Calculate the probability that:
(a) the first two shoes selected will form a pair
(b) David will obtain a pair of shoes by pulling out exactly three shoes, but not less than three
(c) David will obtain a pair after pulling out three shoes at most.

29.3 Probability and human behaviour

The probability that you will win a game can be affected by your previous success or failure.

For example, you might become demoralised by losing a game often and so be even more likely to lose. Or, if you fail a test or task the first time, you may be more likely to pass it the second time, as you may practise more. Tree diagrams can be used to represent situations like these as well.

Example 2

Steve is attempting to pass GCSE mathematics. The probability of him passing on his first attempt is 50%. If he fails on his first attempt then the probability of him passing on his second attempt will be 70%. Calculate the probability that he passes on his first or second attempt.

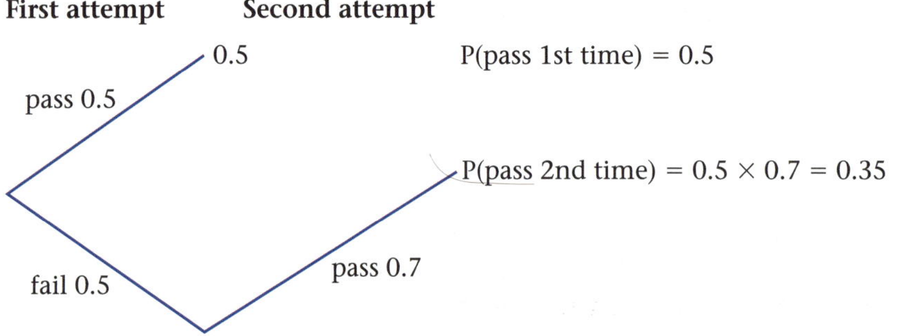

So the probability that Steve passes on his first or second attempt is $0.5 + 0.35 = 0.85$ or 85%.

Remember:
A probability can be written as a fraction, a percentage or a decimal.

For ease of calculation, convert the percentages to decimals before entering them on the probability tree. Draw only the relevant parts of the tree.

Exercise 29C

1 Rifat is playing darts. She is trying to score 180 points by throwing all three darts into the treble 20. The probability of her first dart landing in the treble 20 is 10%. If her first dart lands in the treble 20 then the probability of her second dart landing there as well is 5%. Having successfully thrown two darts into the treble 20, the probability of the third dart landing there as well is 3%.

(a) Calculate the probability that

(i) she will score 180 with her three darts

(ii) she will not score 180 with her three darts.

(b) Explain why it is impossible to calculate the probability of any two of her three darts landing in the treble 20 from the information given.

2 The probability of a letter posted first class on a Monday being delivered on Tuesday is 0.8. If it is not delivered on Tuesday the probability of it being delivered on Wednesday is 0.9. If it still has not been delivered then the probability of it being delivered on Thursday is 0.95.
Draw the relevant parts of a tree diagram to illustrate this situation and use it to calculate the probability that the letter will be delivered before Friday. Assume that the days mentioned all fall within the same week.

3 The probability that Mr Patel will have his free newspaper *The Advertiser* delivered to his house in any week is 0.8. If he gets *The Advertiser* the probability that he will also buy the local newspaper *The Herald* is 0.15. If he does not get *The Advertiser* the probability that he will buy *The Herald* is 0.55.
Draw a full tree diagram to illustrate the situation and use it to calculate the probability that he will only get one of the newspapers in any particular week.

4 When Ian and Bill go to buy ice-cream cornets, Ian always chooses first. The probability that Ian will choose a chocolate flavoured cornet is 70%. If Ian chooses chocolate the probability that Bill will choose chocolate as well is 80%. If Ian does not choose chocolate then the probability that Bill will not choose chocolate is 60%.
Draw a tree diagram and use it to calculate the probability that

(a) both boys choose to have chocolate flavoured cornets

(b) neither boy chooses a chocolate flavoured cornet

(c) the boys choose cornets of different flavours.

5 Majid goes to school by bus every day. The probability that the bus will be on time is 0.75. If the bus turns up on time the probability that Majid will get on it is 0.8, but if it is late the probability of him getting on falls to 0.65. The bus is never early.
Draw a tree diagram to illustrate this situation and include on it all the appropriate probabilities. Use the diagram to calculate the probability that on any particular school day Majid will get on the bus.

6 A box contains twelve discs. Five of the discs are green and seven are red. Two discs are removed at random from the box.

By drawing a tree diagram, or otherwise, calculate the probability that

(a) both discs will be red (b) at least one disc will be red.

7 When there are no darts in the 20 sector of the dartboard, a darts player estimates the probability of hitting the 20 sector as being 0.3. When she hits the 20 sector with one of her darts, her estimate of the probability of hitting the 20 sector changes to 0.15.

She throws three darts one after the other. Calculate an estimate of the probability that she will miss the 20 sector with her first dart, hit the 20 sector with her second dart and hit the 20 sector with her third dart.

Mixed exercise 29

1 Seven cards numbered 1 to 7 are shuffled thoroughly. The top two cards are turned face up on a table. Draw a probability tree diagram and use it to calculate the probability that the numbers will

(a) both be even (b) have an odd sum.

2 There are two red sweets and seven green sweets in a bag.
Two sweets are taken at random, one at a time, from the bag (the first sweet is not put back in the bag).
Find the probability that the sweets will be

(a) both red (b) of different colours (c) the same colour.

3 Arnold is throwing stones at a can. The probability that he will hit the can with his first throw is 0.4. If he hits the can with his first throw, the probability that he will hit the can with his second throw is 0.7. If he misses the can with his first throw, the probability that he will hit the can with his second throw is 0.5.
Arnold throws two stones, one at a time, at the can.
Calculate the probability that he will hit the can with

(a) both stones

(b) exactly one stone

(c) at least one stone.

4 The probability that it will rain today is $\frac{5}{8}$. If it does not rain today, the probability that it will rain tomorrow is $\frac{2}{9}$.
Calculate the probability that it will rain today or tomorrow.

5 In a group of 20 students, five do not have a mobile phone. If three students are selected at random from the group, work out the probability that exactly one of these three students does not have a mobile phone.

6 There are 15 plugs in a box, of which six are known to be faulty.
Three plugs are taken at random from the box.
Work out the probability that

(a) all three plugs are faulty

(b) none of the three plugs is faulty

(c) at least one of the three plugs is faulty.

7 80% of Dr Blunt's patients have a flu injection.
The probability of catching flu after having the injection is $\frac{1}{40}$.
The probability of catching flu after not having the injection is $\frac{13}{20}$.
Calculate the probability that any one of Dr Blunt's patients, selected at random, will catch flu.

8 A doctor diagnoses that a patient has a virus. She does not know which type of the virus, type A, B or C, the patient has. The probability of having each type of the virus is shown in the table.

Type A	Type B	Type C
$\frac{1}{2}$	$\frac{3}{8}$	$\frac{1}{8}$

The probabilities that the patient will recover from each of the types of the virus, A, B and C, are $\frac{1}{7}$, $\frac{4}{7}$ and $\frac{2}{7}$ respectively.
Work out the probability that the patient recovers from the virus.

9 A bag contains four strawberry, three orange and two lemon flavoured sweets.
Three sweets are taken at random from the bag.
Find the probability that they will be

(a) all strawberry flavoured (b) all the same flavour

(c) one of each flavour.

10 A school is divided into two parts, Upper school and Lower school.
Upper school has 300 boys and 200 girls.
Lower school has 400 boys and 300 girls.
A student is selected at random from the school.
If the first student comes from the Lower school, a second student is selected at random from the Upper school; if the first student comes from the Upper school, a second student is selected at random from the Lower school.
Find the probability that the second student will be a girl.

Summary of key points

1 **Conditional probability** is the name for the probability of an event that is dependent on a previous event. The probability depends on the conditions before the event.

2 You only need to draw paths through a tree diagram which are needed to solve the problem set. Make sure you include all the paths you need.

3 It may be quicker to calculate the probability of a mutually exclusive event than to draw a tree diagram.

Examination practice paper

Non-calculator

1 Four coins are made from an alloy using these materials:

60 g zinc, 30 g iron, 10 g copper

Work out how much of each material is needed to make six coins. **(3 marks)**

2 A television is advertised at £500 plus 17.5% VAT. Calculate the total cost of the television. **(3 marks)**

3 (a) Simplify $4p \times 3q$ **(1 mark)**

(b) Expand $y(y + 2)$ **(1 mark)**

(c) Factorise $x^2 - 5x$ **(2 marks)**

4 (a) £600 is divided between Amy and Beth in the ratio 1 : 4. How much does Beth receive? **(2 marks)**

(b) What percentage of the £600 is Beth's share? **(2 marks)**

5 Draw a plan, front elevation and side elevation of this solid.

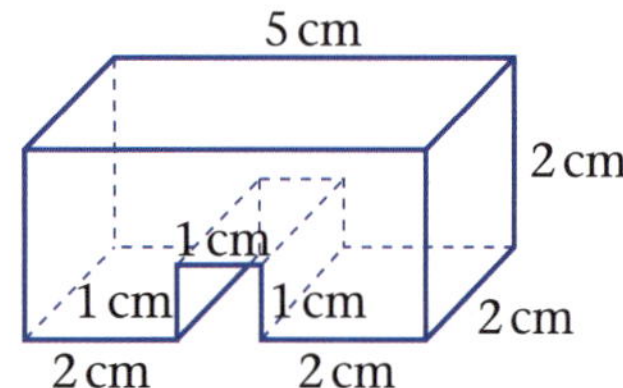

Show the hidden details. **(3 marks)**

6 (a) Copy the diagram and make the axes go up to 6 in each direction. Rotate **A** through 90° anticlockwise about (0, 0). Label the image **B**. **(2 marks)**

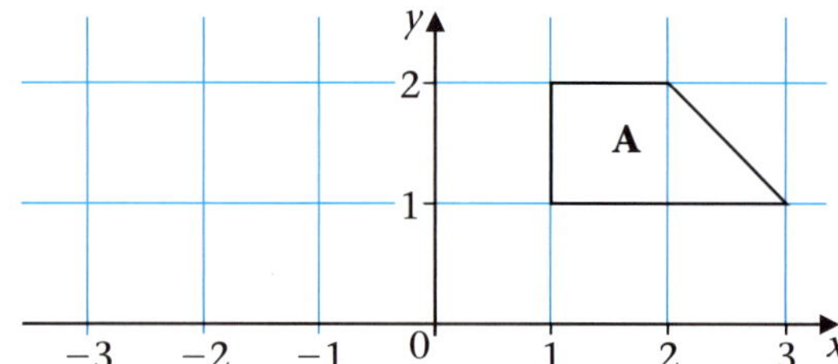

(b) Translate **A** by $\begin{pmatrix} 2 \\ 4 \end{pmatrix}$. Label the image **C**. **(1 mark)**

(c) Fully describe the transformation which maps **B** onto **C**. **(3 marks)**

7 (a) Construct a stem and leaf diagram for the data given.

Height of seedlings, in mm, after 3 weeks:

8, 12, 27, 11, 33, 19, 21, 10, 15, 24, 10, 12, 23, 16, 31,
7, 24, 19, 13, 32, 30, 26, 17, 20, 15, 11, 21, 10, 7, 21

(3 marks)

(b) What is the median value? **(1 mark)**

8 Two fair spinners can each score 1, 2, 3 or 4.
They are spun at the same time.
What is the probability that their sum will be 6? **(3 marks)**

9 (a) Solve the inequality $3(x + 2) \leqslant 7$. **(3 marks)**

(b) Write the value of the greatest integer which satisfies this inequality. **(1 mark)**

10 Work out an estimate for the value of $\dfrac{23.2 \times 57.6}{0.43}$ **(2 marks)**

11 The diagram shows a rectangle with length $x + 2$ and width $2x - 7$.

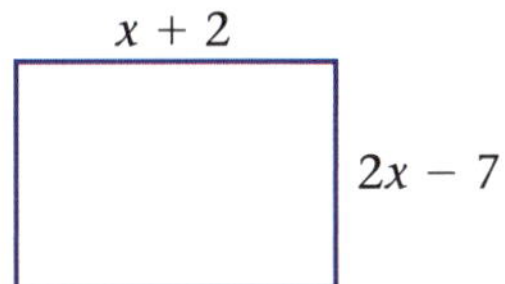

All measurements are given in centimetres.
The perimeter of the rectangle is 17 cm.
Find the value of x. **(3 marks)**

12 (a) Work out $\frac{5}{8} \div \frac{2}{3}$
Give your answer in its simplest form. **(2 marks)**

(b) Work out $3\frac{3}{4} \times 2\frac{2}{5}$
Give your answer in its simplest form. **(3 marks)**

13 A prism is 20 cm long. Its cross-section is a right-angled triangle ABC, in which $AB = 6$ cm and $AC = 10$ cm.

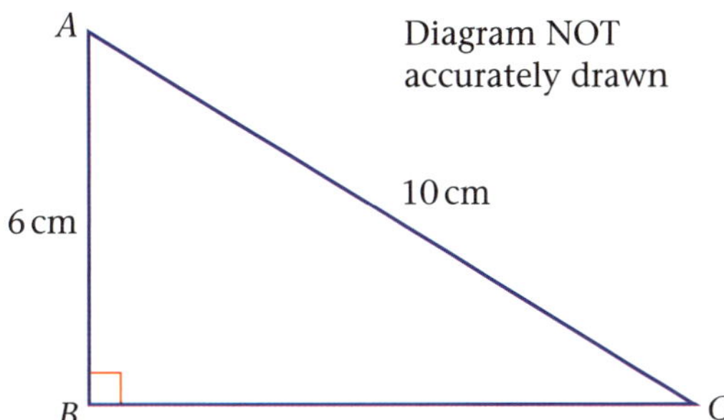

Calculate the total surface area of the prism. **(6 marks)**

14 The cumulative frequency graph gives information about the prices of 50 houses.

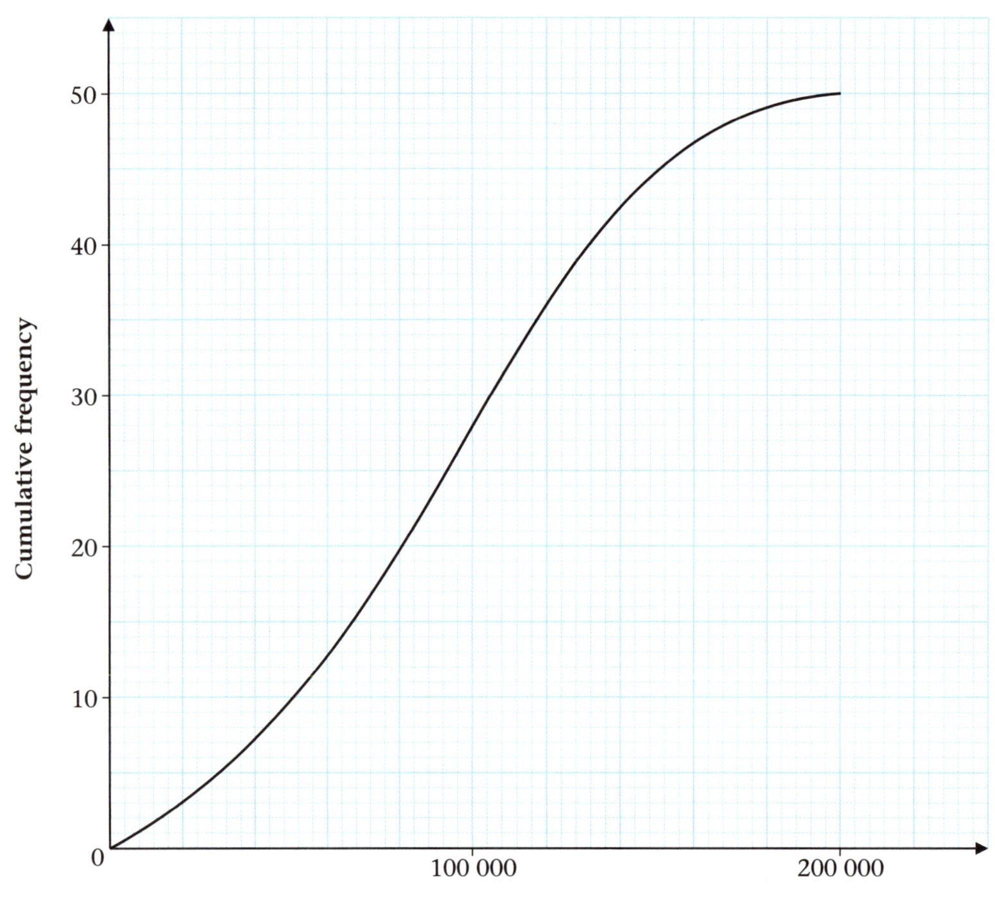

(a) Find the number of houses priced **below** £80 000. **(1 mark)**

(b) Find the median house price.
Show clearly how you found your answer. **(1 mark)**

(c) Find the interquartile range of the house prices. **(2 marks)**

15 A computer performs 400 million calculations per second.

(a) Write 400 million in standard form. **(1 mark)**

(b) Write out the number of calculations the computer performs in 10 minutes.
Give your answer in standard form. **(2 marks)**

16 The diagram shows five points A, B, C, D and E on the circumference of a circle.

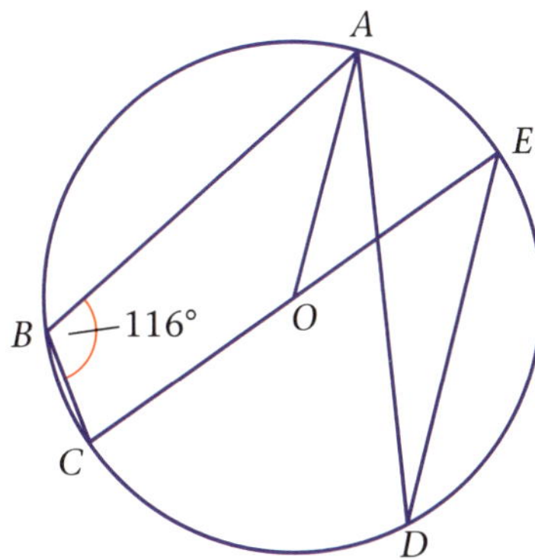

Diagram NOT accurately drawn

The centre of the circle is O.
CE is a diameter.
Angle $ABC = 116°$.

(a) State the size of angle CBE. Give a reason. **(2 marks)**

(b) Calculate the size of angle ADE. **(2 marks)**

(c) Calculate the size of angle AOE. **(2 marks)**

17 (a) Copy and complete the table of values for $y = x^3 - 2x^2 - 5x$.

x	−2	−1	0	1	2	3	4
y		2					

(2 marks)

(b) On graph paper plot the graph of $y = x^3 - 2x^2 - 5x$ for $-2 \leqslant x \leqslant 4$. **(2 marks)**

(c) Use your graph to solve the equation $x^3 - 2x^2 - 5x = 0$. Where necessary, give your answers correct to 1 decimal place. **(2 marks)**

18 (a) Evaluate

(i) 7^0

(ii) 4^{-3}

(iii) $64^{\frac{1}{3}}$ **(3 marks)**

(b) Express $\frac{6}{\sqrt{12}}$ in the form $a\sqrt{b}$, where a and b are integers. **(2 marks)**

19 100 car owners were asked the distances, in miles, their cars had travelled.
The unfinished histogram and table show this information.

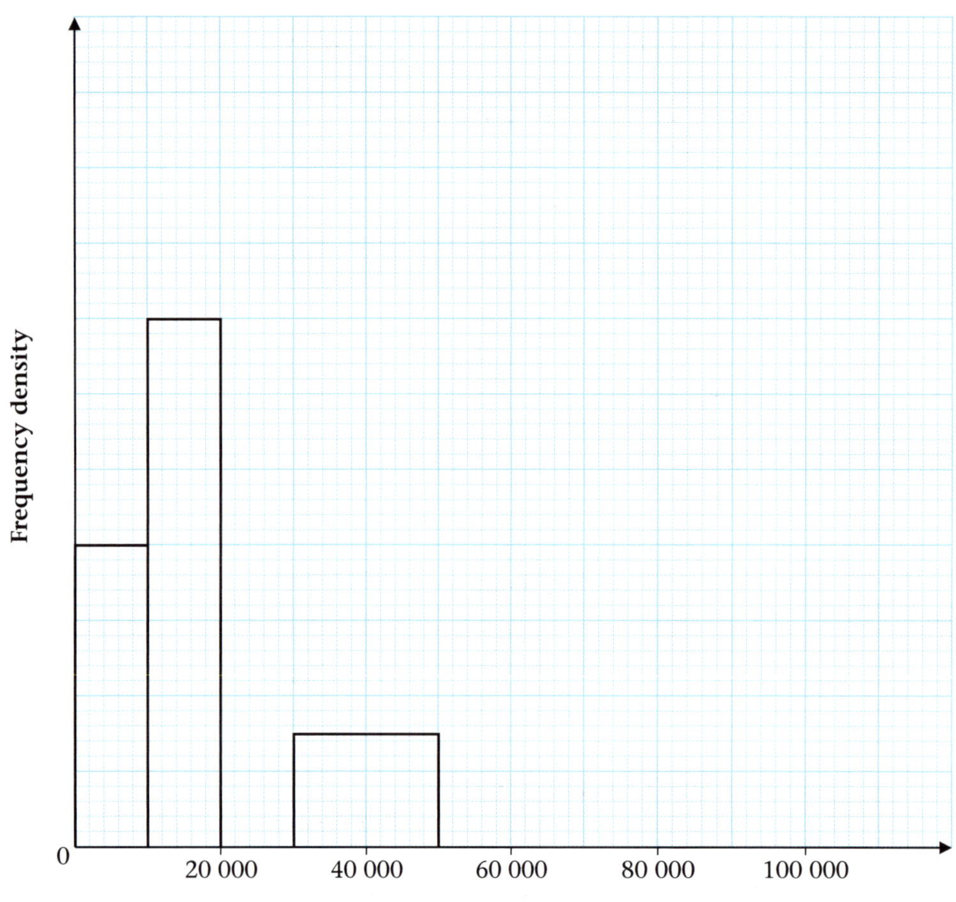

Distance (d) in miles	Frequency
$0 \leqslant d < 10\,000$	20
$10\,000 \leqslant d < 20\,000$	
$20\,000 \leqslant d < 30\,000$	25
$30\,000 \leqslant d < 50\,000$	
$50\,000 \leqslant d < 100\,000$	5

(a) Use the information in the histogram to complete the table. **(2 marks)**

(b) Make a copy of the histogram. Use the information in the table to complete it. **(2 marks)**

20 y is inversely proportional to the square of x. $y = 4$ when $x = 5$.

(a) Find a formula for y in terms of x. **(2 marks)**

(b) Find the value of x when $y = 400$. **(2 marks)**

21 A is the point with coordinates (2, 8) and B is the point with coordinates (14, 4).
A straight line L is perpendicular to the line AB and passes through A.
Find the equation of the straight line L. **(3 marks)**

22 Prove algebraically that the sum of two consecutive square numbers is always an odd number. **(3 marks)**

23 The diagram shows two squares $QRST$ and $PMLR$.
PS and LQ are straight lines.

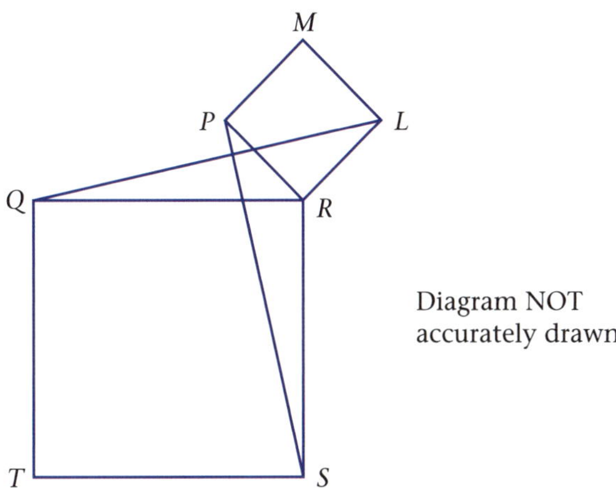

Diagram NOT accurately drawn

Prove that triangle QLR and triangle PRS are congruent.
(3 marks)

24 Rearrange $\frac{a}{x+b} = \frac{b}{x-a}$ to make x the subject. **(4 marks)**

25 The diagram shows the net of a cone.

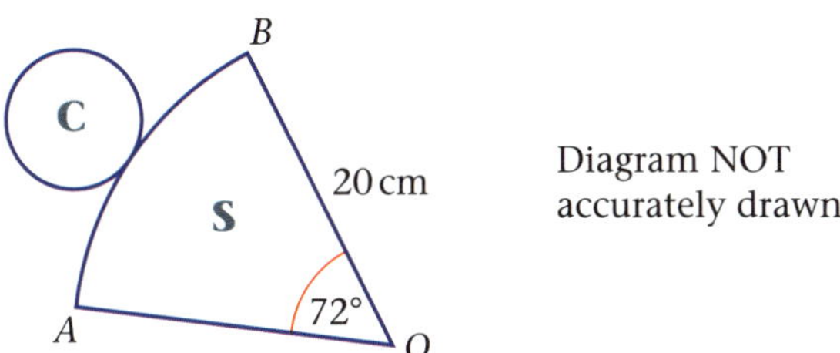

Diagram NOT accurately drawn

The net is made from a circle, **C**, and a sector, **S**, of a circle centre O.
Angle $AOB = 72°$.

(a) Find the length of the arc AB.
Give your answer as a multiple of π. **(2 marks)**

(b) The sector is folded to make a cone.
Find the total surface area of the cone.
Give your answer as a multiple of π. **(4 marks)**

Examination practice paper

Calculator

1 (a) Use your calculator to find the value of $\sqrt{\dfrac{3.21 \times 5.42}{1.41 \times 2.74}}$

Write down all the digits on your calculator display.

(3 marks)

2 A car tyre is advertised at £80. There is a discount of 15%.
Calculate the cost of buying **two** car tyres with this discount.

(2 marks)

3 The cost of 8 metres of wire fence is £3.28.
What is the cost of 5 metres of this wire fence? **(2 marks)**

4 (a) The velocity of a particle is given by the formula
$v^2 = u^2 + 2as$.
Calculate the velocity v when $u = 3$, $a = 0.8$ and $s = 4.35$.

(3 marks)

(b) Solve $3(2x - 5) = 30$. **(3 marks)**

5 Here are the first five numbers of an arithmetic sequence.

4 9 14 19 24

Write down, in terms of n, an expression for the nth term of the sequence. **(2 marks)**

6 The diagram shows the floor plan of a workshop.
Work out the area of the floor. **(3 marks)**

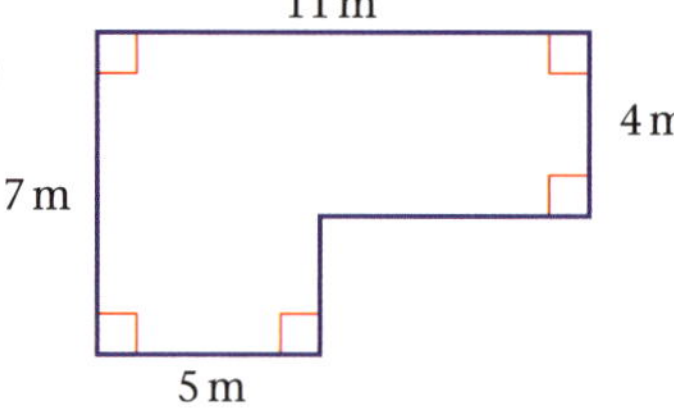

7 In the diagram BE is parallel to CD, angle $ABE = 105°$ and angle $BEC = 54°$.

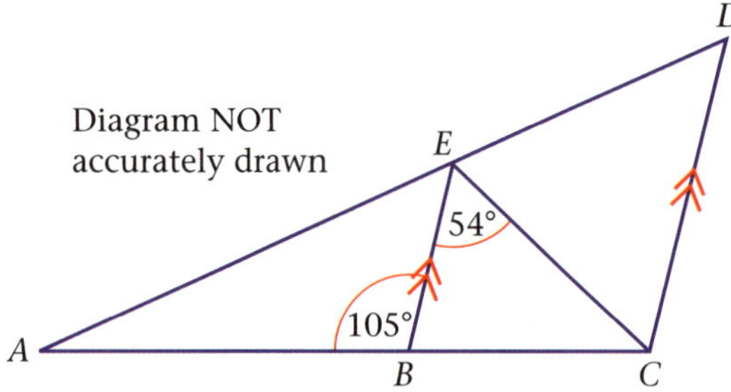

(a) Calculate the size of

(i) angle EBC (ii) angle ECD. **(3 marks)**

(b) Given that $AE = 10$ cm, $ED = 5$ cm and $CD = 6$ cm, calculate the length of EB. **(2 marks)**

8 In a bank account an amount of £500 appreciates at the rate of 5% compound interest per annum.
Calculate the amount of money that will be in the account at the end of three years. **(3 marks)**

9 Find the size of the angle x.

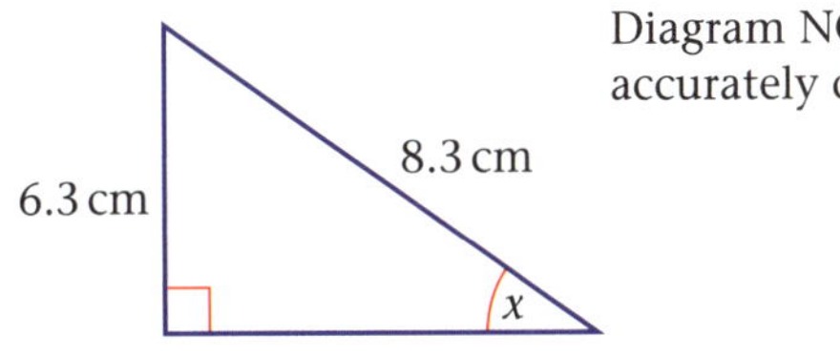

Diagram NOT accurately drawn

(3 marks)

10 The table and the scatter graph show the number of units of electricity used in heating a house on ten different days and the average temperature for each day.

Average temperature (°C)	6	2	0	6	3	5	10	8	9	12
Units of electricity used	30	39	41	34	33	31	22	25	23	22

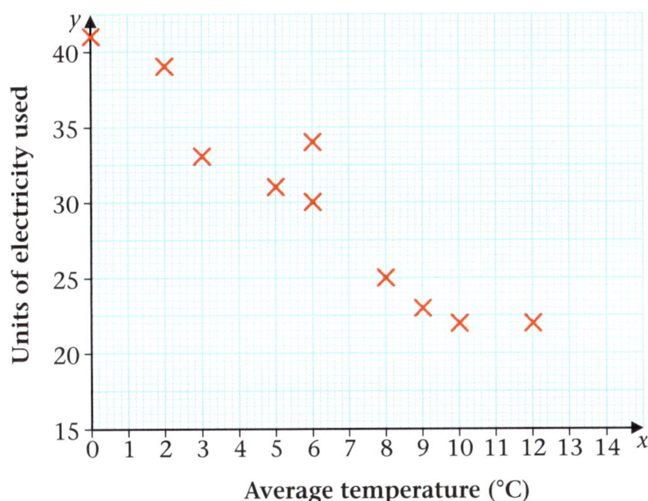

(a) Using the values in the table above, draw the scatter graph and mark on it a line of best fit. **(1 mark)**

(b) Use your line of best fit to estimate

(i) the average temperature when 35 units of electricity are used

(ii) the units of electricity used when the average temperature is 7° C. **(2 marks)**

11 The equation $x^3 - 7x = 81$ has a solution in the range $4 < x < 5$.
Use a method of trial and improvement to obtain this solution correct to two decimal places. **(4 marks)**

12 A year ago, Mrs Ford bought a new car. Its value has fallen by 12% since then. Its value now is £8624.

(a) Calculate the value of the car when it was new. **(2 marks)**

(b) The value of the car will continue to fall by 12% each year. Calculate the value of the car when it is five years old. **(3 marks)**

13 The grouped frequency table shows the distribution of weekly rainfall at Heathrow Airport in 2005.
Calculate an estimate for the mean weekly rainfall in 2005.
Give your answer correct to the nearest millimetre. **(4 marks)**

Weekly rainfall (r mm)	Frequency
$0 < r \leqslant 10$	32
$10 < r \leqslant 20$	13
$20 < r \leqslant 30$	4
$30 < r \leqslant 40$	1
$40 < r \leqslant 50$	1
$50 < r \leqslant 60$	0
$60 < r \leqslant 70$	1

14 A factory employs 100 people.
76 of these people are men. The other 24 are women.
The mean weekly wage of all 100 people is £407.
The mean weekly wage of the men is £395.
Work out the mean weekly wage of the 24 women. **(4 marks)**

15 (a) Solve $\dfrac{4}{y} - 3 = 7$ **(3 marks)**

(b) Express $\dfrac{2}{3x-1} + \dfrac{1}{x+6}$ as a single algebraic fraction. **(3 marks)**

(c) Factorise $2x^2 + 3x - 14$ **(3 marks)**

16 The diagram represents the cross-section of a church door.
The cross-section consists of a rectangle with a semicircular top.
The door has a uniform thickness of 6 cm.
The door is made of metal of density 7.2 g per cm^3.
Work out the mass of the door. **(6 marks)**

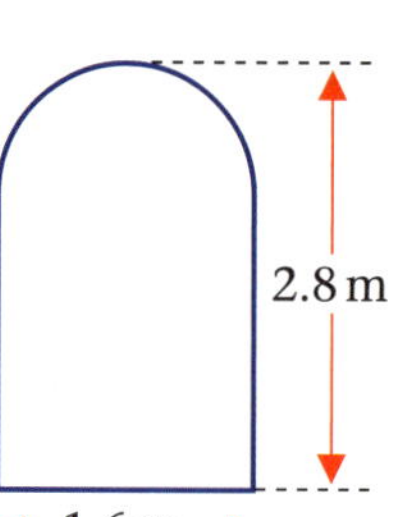

17 The diagram shows a square-based rectangular box.
Each side of its base is x cm long. The box has **no lid** and its height is h cm.

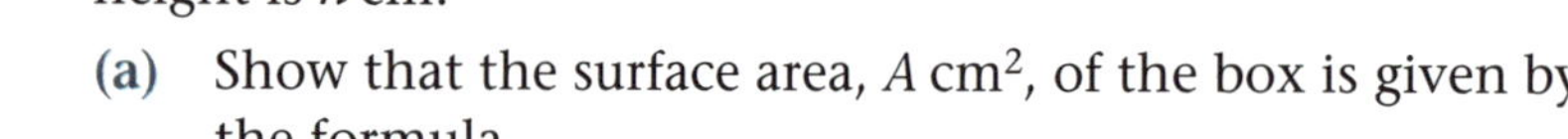

(a) Show that the surface area, A cm^2, of the box is given by the formula

$$A = x^2 + 4hx$$ **(2 marks)**

(b) Make h the subject of the formula. **(2 marks)**

(c) A lidless square-based box 2 cm high has a surface area of 48 cm^2. Find the length of the sides of its base. **(2 marks)**

(d) $A = 100$ and $h = 3$. Find the value of x.
Give your answer correct to 3 significant figures. **(2 marks)**

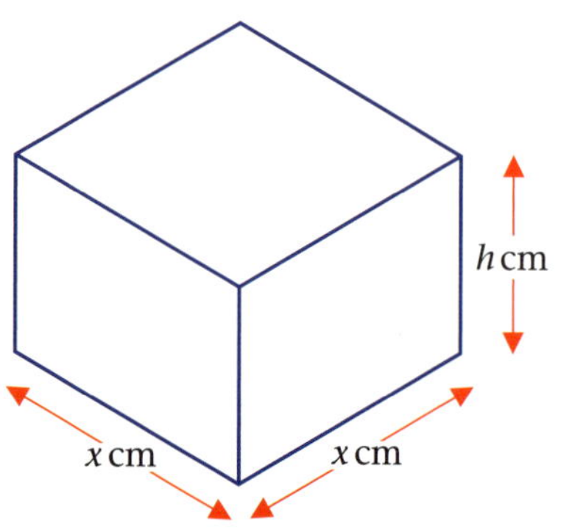

18 (a) Sketch graphs of
(i) $y = \cos x$ (ii) $y = \sin 3x$
for all values of x in the range $0° \leqslant x \leqslant 180°$. **(4 marks)**

(b) Solve the equation $\sin 3x = \frac{-2}{3}$
for all values of x in the range $0° \leqslant x \leqslant 180°$. **(3 marks)**

19 The diagram represents a side view of a cylindrical tin with three tennis balls in it. The diameter of each tennis ball is 6.5 cm. Calculate, correct to 2 significant figures:

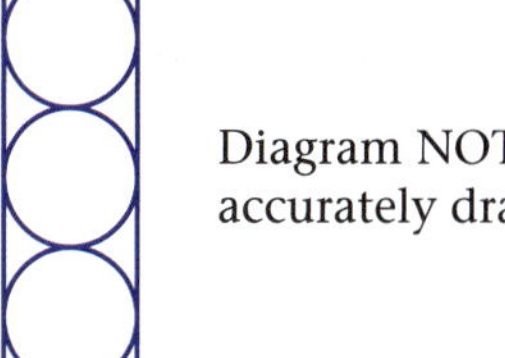

Diagram NOT accurately drawn

(a) the volume of the tin **(2 marks)**

(b) the curved surface area of the tin **(2 marks)**

(c) the total surface area of the three balls. **(2 marks)**

20 A rectangle is 68 cm long and 8.4 cm wide.
Each measurement is correct to 2 significant figures.
Calculate the greatest lower bound for the area of the rectangle, **giving with an explanation** your answer to an appropriate degree of accuracy. **(5 marks)**

21 The equation of a straight line is

$y = ax + b$, where a and b are constants.

The equation of a circle is:

$x^2 + y^2 = 64$

The straight line is a tangent to the circle.

Prove that $a^2 + 1 = \frac{b^2}{64}$ **(6 marks)**

22 A box contains three red pens, four blue pens and five black pens.
A pen is selected at random from the box, and is not replaced.
A second pen is then selected from the box.
Calculate the probability that the two pens selected will be the same colour. **(4 marks)**

Formulae sheet: Higher tier

Volume of a prism = area of cross section × length

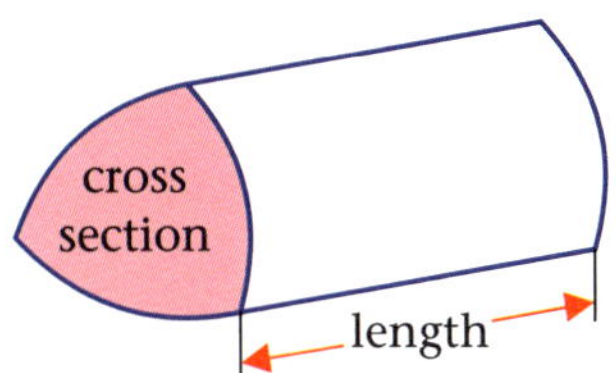

Volume of sphere $= \frac{4}{3}\pi r^3$

Surface of a sphere $= 4\pi r^2$

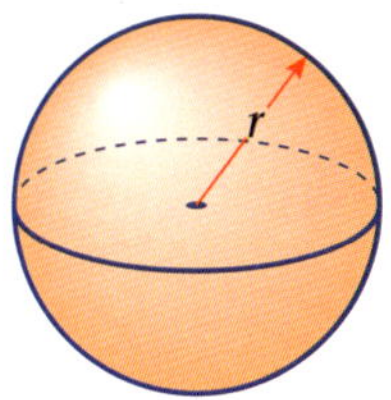

Volume of cone $= \frac{1}{3}\pi r^2 h$

Curved surface area of cone $= \pi r l$

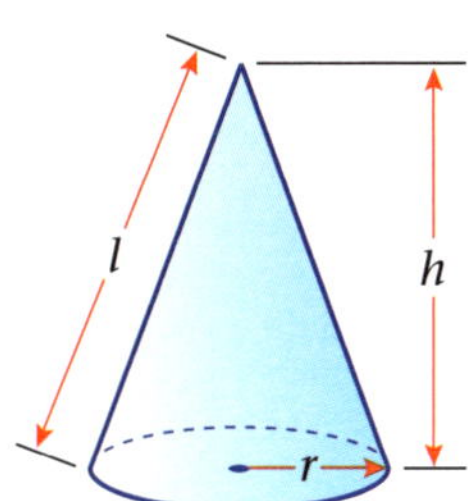

In any triangle ABC

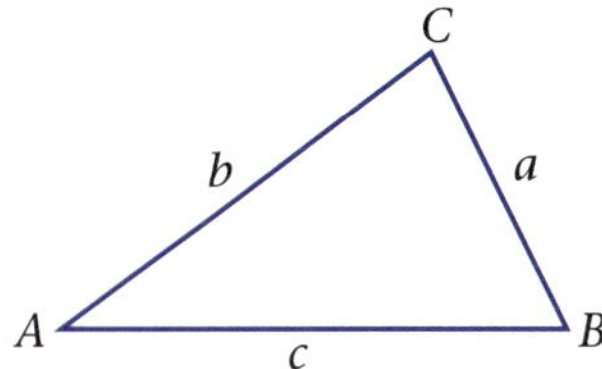

Sine rule $\dfrac{a}{\sin A} = \dfrac{b}{\sin B} = \dfrac{c}{\sin C}$

Cosine rule $a^2 = b^2 + c^2 - 2bc \cos A$

Area of a triangle $= \frac{1}{2} ab \sin C$

The quadratic equation

The solutions of $ax^2 + bx + c = 0$ where a = 0, are given by

$$x = \frac{-b \pm \sqrt{(b^2 - 4ac)}}{2a}$$

Answers

Chapter 16 Basic trigonometry

Exercise 16A

1 (a) cosine (b) cosine (c) tangent
(d) sine (e) sine (f) tangent
(g) sine (h) tangent (i) cosine

2 About 9.1 m

Exercise 16B

1 (a) 0.7314 (b) 0.5299 (c) 0.3839
(d) 8.1443 (e) 0.9063 (f) 0.8660
(g) −3.4874 (h) −0.0523 (i) 0.7431

2 (a) 20.6° (b) 82.2° (c) 54.7°
(d) 23.6° (e) 9.8° (f) 62.3°

Exercise 16C

1 44.4° **2** 38.7° **3** 48.2°
4 21.8° **5** 65.4° **6** 30°
7 18.4° **8** 24.3° **9** 52.4°

Exercise 16D

1 (a) 7.66 (b) 7.71 (c) 12.99
(d) 5.34 (e) 7.52 (f) 6.75
(g) 6.36 (h) 12.12 (i) 7.16

2 328° (to the nearest degree)

Exercise 16E

For example:

1 (b) $\sin 410° = \sin 50°$ (c) $\sin 50° = \sin 130°$

2 (a) $\cos 110° = -\cos 70°$ (b) $\cos(-85°) = \cos 85°$
(c) $\cos 405° = \cos 45°$

3 (a) $\tan(-45°) = -\tan 45°$ (b) $\tan 130° = -\tan 50°$
(c) $\tan 390° = \tan 30°$

Exercise 16F

3 (a)

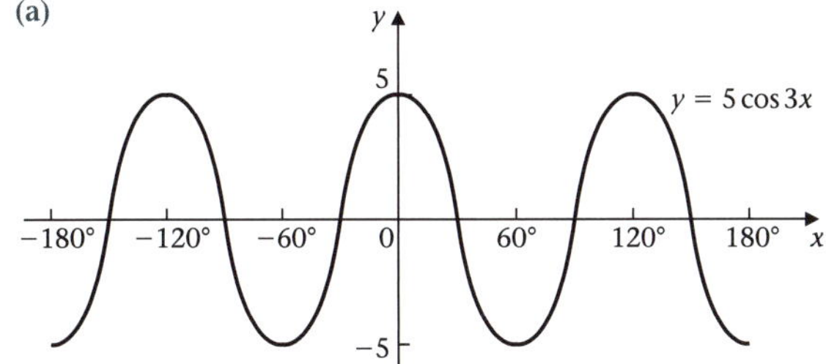

(b) 120° (c) Max of 5 at 0°, 120°, −120°
Min of −5 at 60°, −60°, 180°, −180°

4 (a) $y = 2\tan x$

(b) 180°

5 (a)

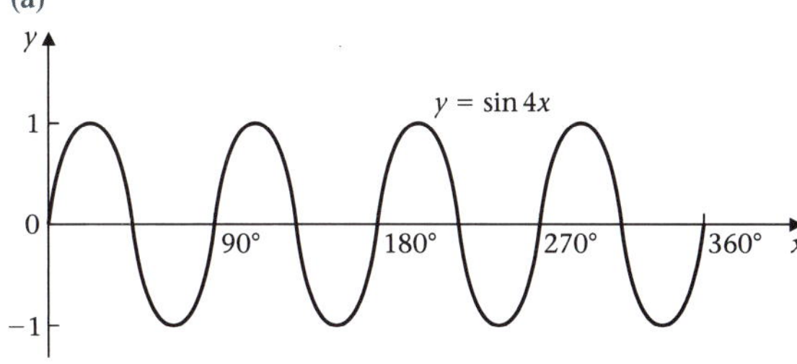

Period 90°

(b)

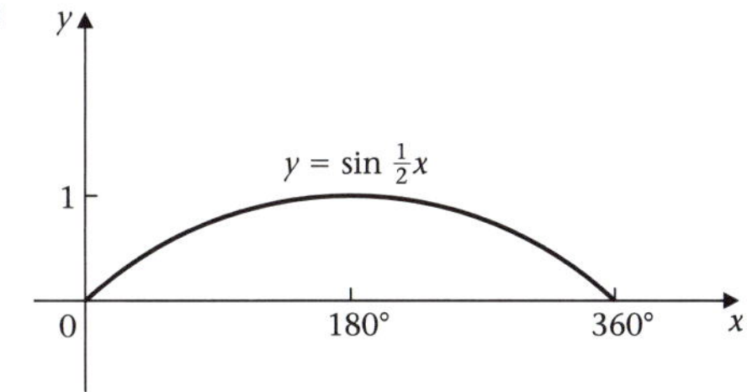

Period 720°

6 Period $\frac{360°}{B}$, maximum A, minimum $-A$

7 For sine and cosine functions, maximum is A, minimum is $-A$ and period is $\frac{360°}{B}$
For tangent, the period is $\frac{180°}{B}$

Exercise 16G

1 60°, −60°, 300°, −300°

2 (b) 23.6°, 156.4°, 383.6°, 516.4°

3 63.4°, −116.6°

4 (a) $y = 3\cos x$ (b) 70.5°, 289.5°

5 (b) 17.71°, 42.29°, 137.71°, 162.29°, −102.29°, −77.71°

6 (a) $y = 2\cos\theta$ (b) $y = 10\cos\theta$
(c) $y = 3\sin\frac{1}{2}\theta$ (d) $y = 3\sin 2\theta$

Mixed exercise 16

1 (a) 12.37 m (b) 72.1°

2 (a) 8.15 m (b) 38.7°

3 7.71 m **4** 021.6° **5** $\sin 35° \neq 0.7$

6 (a) $h = 1247.47$ m (b) 5868.89 m

7 (a) 26.4° (b) 125.9 m

8 (a) (b) 120°, 240°

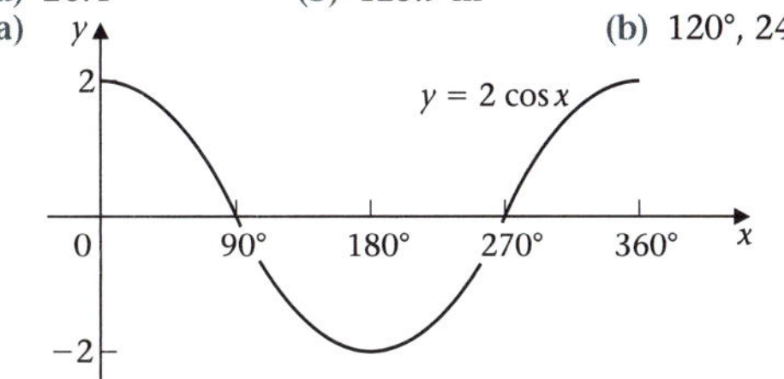

9 (a) 13 m (b) 11.1 hours

10 (a) 41.8°, 138.2° (b) 113.6°, 246.4° (c) 70.5°, 289.5°

Chapter 17 Graphs and equations

Exercise 17A

1

x	−4	−3	−2	−1	0	1	2	3	4
y	21	14	9	6	5	6	9	14	21

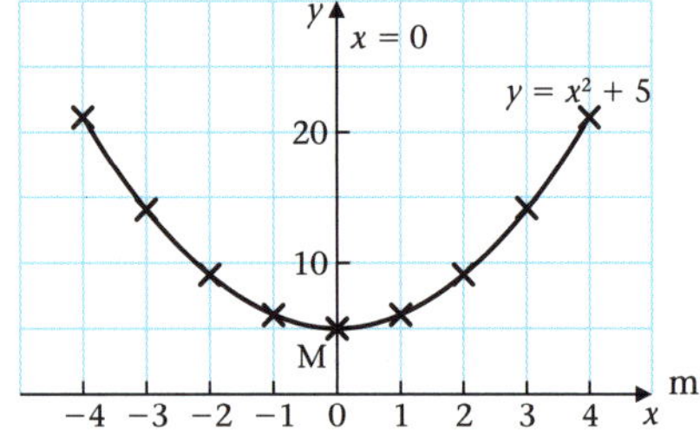

minimum (0, 5)

2

x	−4	−3	−2	−1	0	1	2	3	4
y	6	−1	−6	−9	−10	−9	−6	−1	6

$x = 0$, minimum $(0, -10)$

3

x	−4	−3	−2	−1	0	1	2	3	4
y	48	27	12	3	0	3	12	27	48

$x = 0$, minimum $(0, 0)$

4

x	−4	−3	−2	−1	0	1	2	3	4
y	8	4.5	2	0.5	0	0.5	2	4.5	8

$x = 0$, minimum $(0, 0)$

5

x	−4	−3	−2	−1	0	1	2	3	4
y	−16	−9	−4	−1	0	−1	−4	−9	−16

$x = 0$, maximum $(0, 0)$

6

x	−4	−3	−2	−1	0	1	2	3	4
y	−32	−18	−8	−2	0	−2	−8	−18	−32

$x = 0$, maximum $(0, 0)$

7

x	−4	−3	−2	−1	0	1	2	3	4
y	8	3	0	−1	0	3	8	15	24

$x = -1$, minimum $(-1, -1)$

8

x	−4	−3	−2	−1	0	1	2	3	4
y	4	0	−2	−2	0	4	10	18	28

$x = -1\frac{1}{2}$, minimum $(-1\frac{1}{2}, -2\frac{1}{4})$

9

x	−4	−3	−2	−1	0	1	2	3	4
y	9	4	1	0	1	4	9	16	25

$x = -1$, minimum $(-1, 0)$

10

x	−4	−3	−2	−1	0	1	2	3	4
y	36	25	16	9	4	1	0	1	4

$x = 2$, minimum $(2, 0)$

11

x	−4	−3	−2	−1	0	1	2	3	4
y	31	20	11	4	−1	−4	−5	−4	−1

$x = 2$, minimum $(2, -5)$

12

x	−4	−3	−2	−1	0	1	2	3	4
y	23	13	5	−1	−5	−7	−7	−5	−1

$x = 1\frac{1}{2}$, minimum $(1\frac{1}{2}, -7\frac{1}{4})$

13

x	−4	−3	−2	−1	0	1	2	3	4
y	24	16	10	6	4	4	6	10	16

$x = \frac{1}{2}$, minimum $(\frac{1}{2}, 3\frac{3}{4})$

14

x	−4	−3	−2	−1	0	1	2	3	4
y	15	4	−3	−6	−5	0	9	22	39

$x = -\frac{3}{4}$, minimum $(-\frac{3}{4}, -6\frac{1}{8})$

15

x	−4	−3	−2	−1	0	1	2	3	4
y	66	41	22	9	2	1	6	17	34

$x = \frac{2}{3}$, minimum $(\frac{2}{3}, \frac{2}{3})$

Exercise 17B

1

x	−3	−2	−1	0	1	2	3
y	−22	−3	4	5	6	13	32

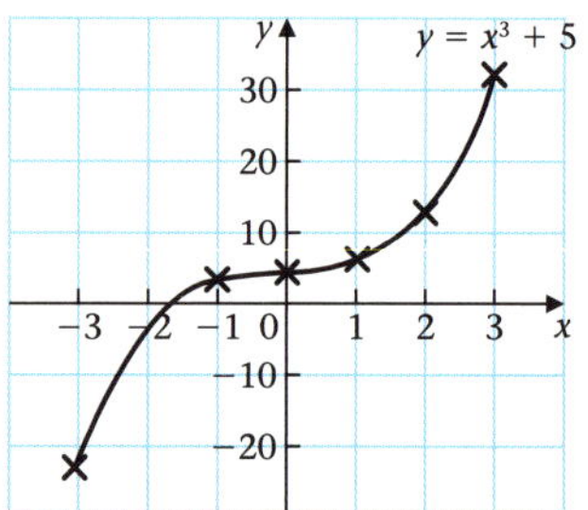

2

x	−3	−2	−1	0	1	2	3
y	−37	−18	−11	−10	−9	−2	17

3

x	−3	−2	−1	0	1	2	3
y	−54	−16	−2	0	2	16	54

4

x	−3	−2	−1	0	1	2	3
y	−13.5	−4	−0.5	0	0.5	4	13.5

5

x	−3	−2	−1	0	1	2	3
y	27	8	1	0	−1	−8	−27

6

x	−3	−2	−1	0	1	2	3
y	54	16	2	0	−2	−16	−54

7

x	−3	−2	−1	0	1	2	3
y	−125	−64	−27	−8	−1	0	1

8

x	−3	−2	−1	0	1	2	3
y	−8	−1	0	1	8	27	64

9

x	−3	−2	−1	0	1	2	3
y	−45	−16	−3	0	−1	0	9

10

x	−3	−2	−1	0	1	2	3
y	−18	−4	0	0	2	12	36

11

x	−3	−2	−1	0	1	2	3
y	−42	−18	−6	0	6	18	42

12

x	−3	−2	−1	0	1	2	3
y	−12	2	4	0	−4	−2	12

13

x	−3	−2	−1	0	1	2	3
y	6	12	8	0	−6	−4	12

14

x	−3	−2	−1	0	1	2	3
y	−38	−16	−6	−2	2	12	34

15

x	−3	−2	−1	0	1	2	3
y	−43	−14	−1	2	1	2	11

Exercise 17C

1

x	−3	−2	−1	−0.5	−0.2	0.2	0.5	1	2	3
y	−0.7	−1	−2	−4	−10	10	4	2	1	0.7

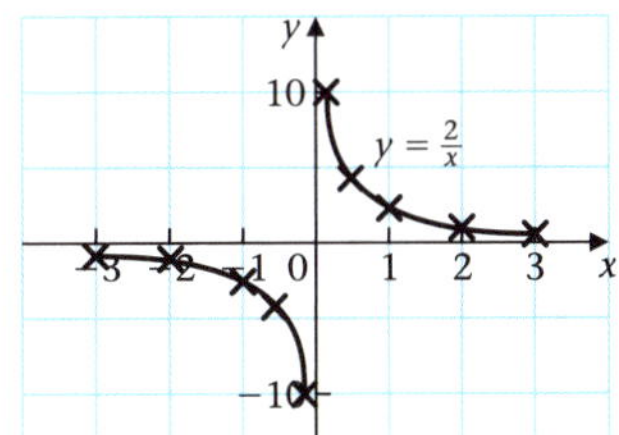

Asymptotes: $x = 0$
$y = 0$

2

x	−3	−2	−1	−0.5	−0.2	0.2	0.5	1	2	3
y	0.3	0.5	1	2	5	−5	−2	−1	−0.5	−0.3

Asymptotes: $x = 0$, $y = 0$

3

x	−3	−2	−1	−0.5	−0.2	0.2	0.5	1	2	3
y	1	1.5	3	6	15	−15	−6	−3	−1.5	−1

Asymptotes: $x = 0$, $y = 0$

4

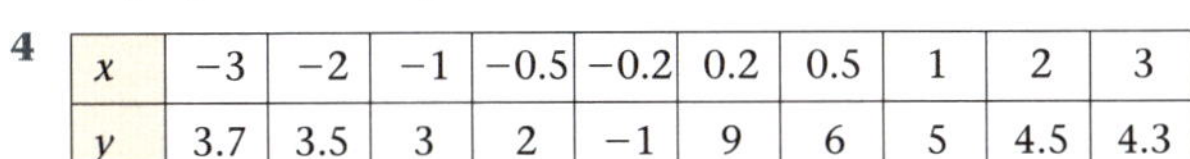

x	−3	−2	−1	−0.5	−0.2	0.2	0.5	1	2	3
y	3.7	3.5	3	2	−1	9	6	5	4.5	4.3

Asymptotes: $x = 0$, $y = 4$

5

x	−3	−2	−1	−0.5	−0.2	0.2	0.5	1	2	3
y	6.3	7	9	13	25	−15	−3	1	3	3.7

Asymptotes: $x = 0$, $y = 5$

6

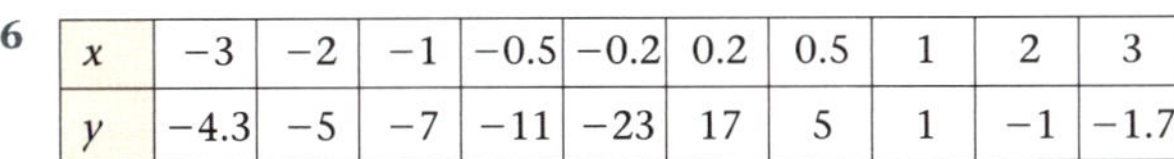

x	−3	−2	−1	−0.5	−0.2	0.2	0.5	1	2	3
y	−4.3	−5	−7	−11	−23	17	5	1	−1	−1.7

Asymptotes: $x = 0$, $y = −3$

Exercise 17D

1

x	−1	0	1	2	3	4
y	6	1	−2	−3	−2	1

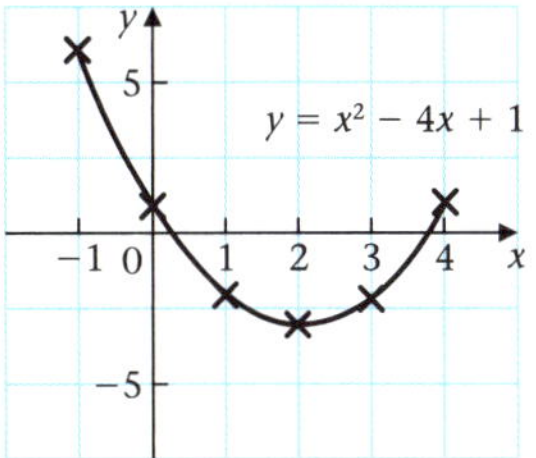

2

x	−3	−2	−1	0	1	2
y	−12	−3	−2	−3	0	13

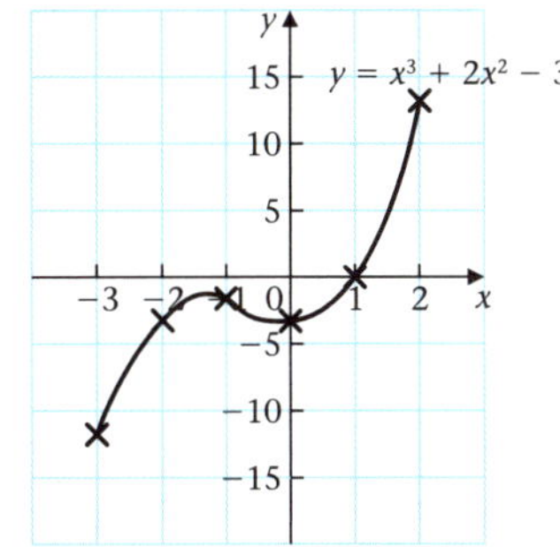

3

x	−2	−1	0	1	2	3
y	−8	0	0	−2	0	12

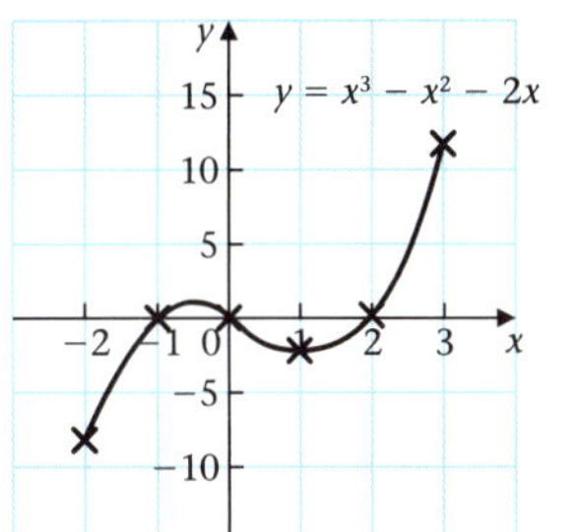

4

x	−3	−2	−1	0	1	2	3
y	−10	4	6	2	−2	0	14

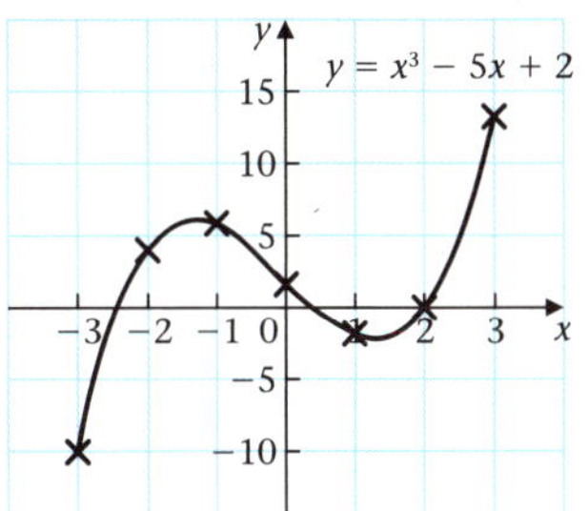

5

x	−2	−1	0	1	2	3	4
y	−7	−2	1	2	1	−2	−7

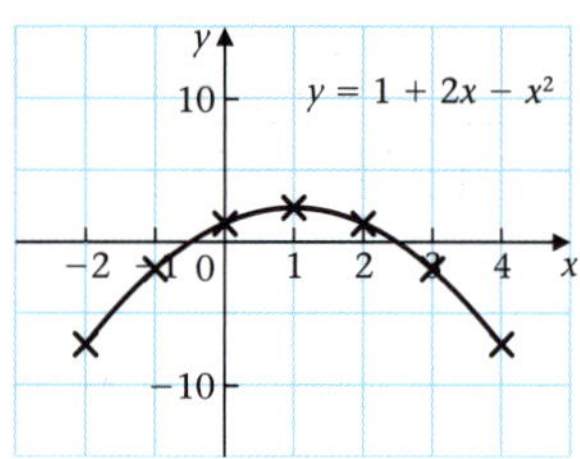

6

x	−3	−2	−1	−0.5	−0.2	0.2	0.5	1	2	3
y	−6.3	−4.5	−3	−3	−5.4	5.4	3	3	4.5	6.3

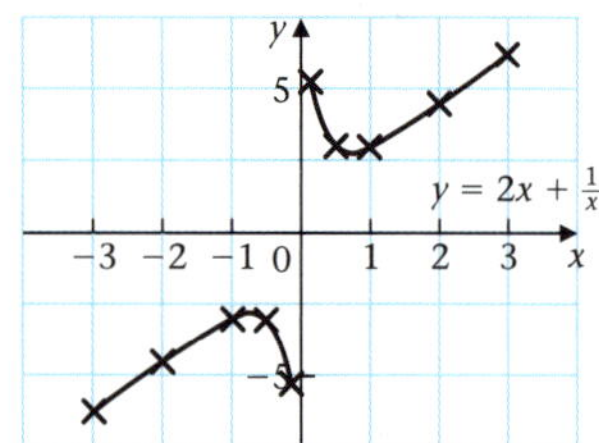

7

x	−3	−2	−1	−0.5	−0.2	0.2	0.5	1	2	3
y	9.3	4.5	2	2.3	5.0	−5.0	−1.8	0	3.5	8.7

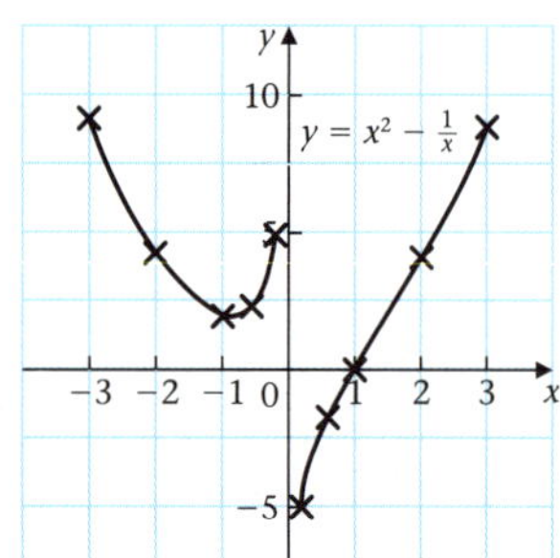

8

x	0.1	0.2	0.5	1	2	3	4	5
y	22.1	12.2	6.5	5	5	5.7	6.5	7.4

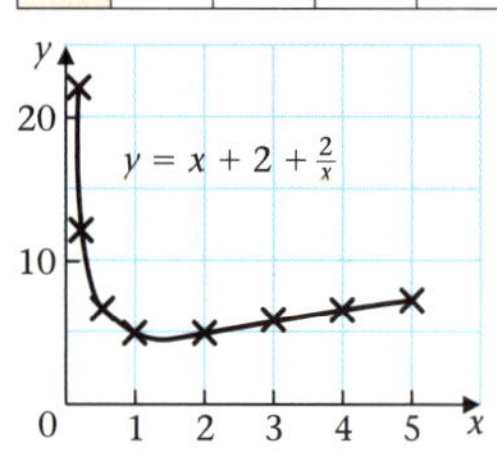

9

x	0.2	0.5	1	2	3
y	−5.0	−1.9	0	7.5	26.7

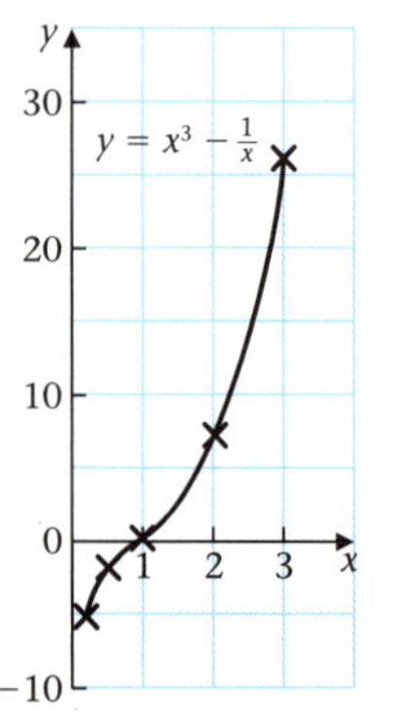

10

x	−3	−2	−1	−0.5	−0.2	0.2	0.5	1	2	3
y	11.3	5	0	−3.3	−9.8	9.8	3.8	2	3	6.7

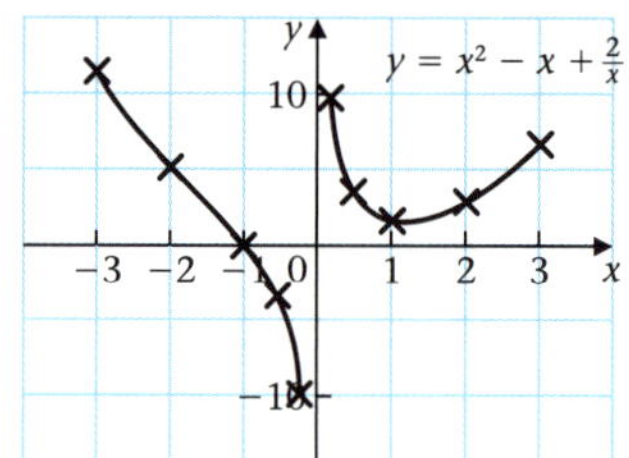

Exercise 17E

1 5.6 or 1.4 **2** 2.3 or −1.3 **3** 2.8 or −1.3
4 1.3 or 0.3 **5** −2.1, 0.3 or 1.9 **6** −2.3, 0 or 1.3
7 2.2 **8** 0 or 2 **9** 2.2
10 0.7 or 2.9

Exercise 17F

1 1.3 **2** 2.1 **3** 2.1 **4** 2.47 **5** 6.6
6 8.56 **7** 5.6 **8** 6.89 **9** 4.35 **10** 2.4

Exercise 17G

1 4.64 cm **2** 2.89 cm **3** 71.6°F

Exercise 17H

1 (a) Sharon.
(b) Tracey overtakes Sharon.
(c) Pass each other travelling in opposite directions.

2

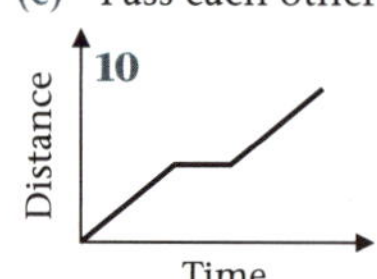

3 (a) 11:00 (b) 12:30 (c) 2 hrs (d) 60 mph

4

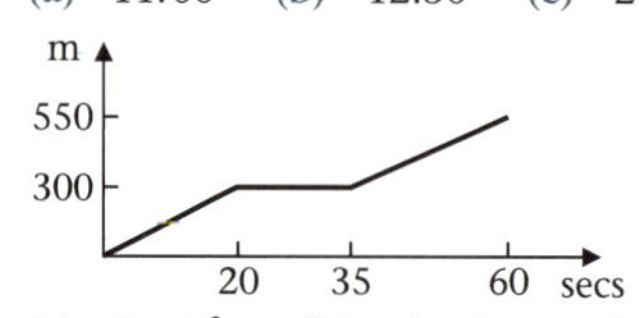

5 (a) 7 m/s² (b) steady speed of 36 m/s
(c) −9 m/s² (d) 274 m

6 (a) (b) 486 m

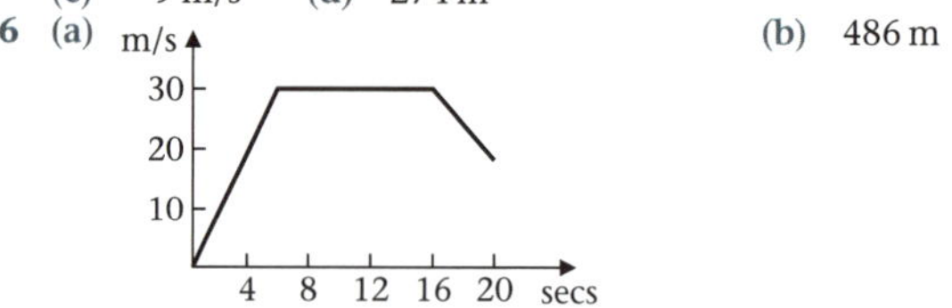

7 (a) E (b) A (c) B (d) C

8 (a) (b) (c) (d)

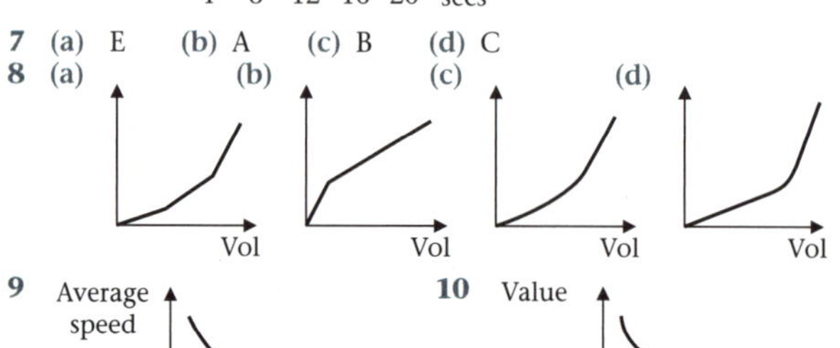

9 **10**

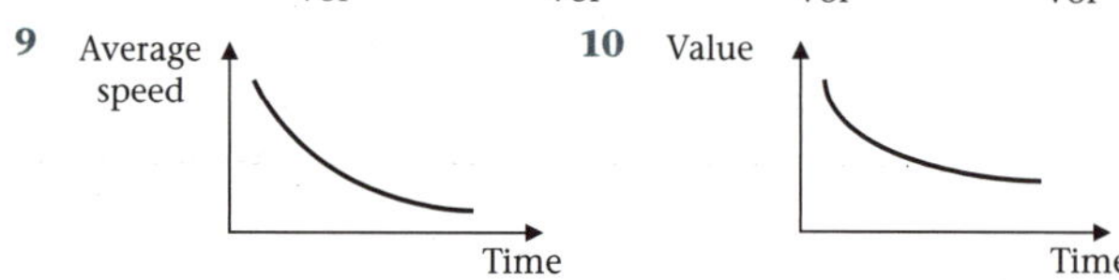

11 (a) Starts slowly then speeds up. Has a break. Continues at a steady speed more slowly than before.
(b) (i) 09:00 (ii) Post Office closed

12 (a) B (b) D

Mixed exercise 17

1 4.4

2 4.2

3

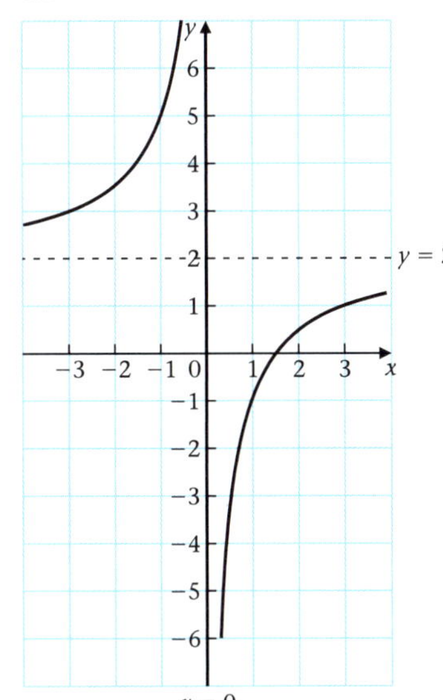

4

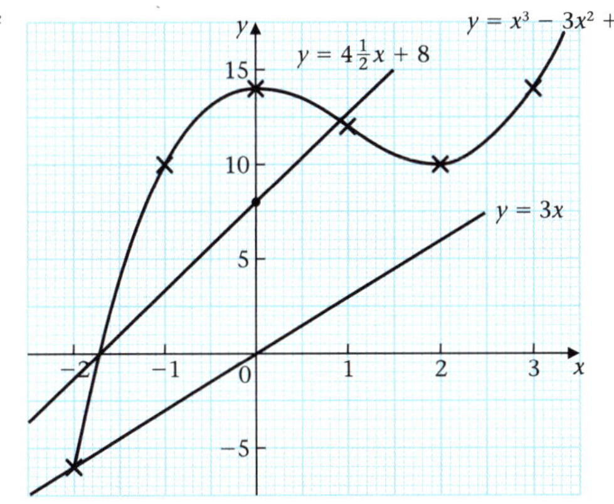

(a) −1.7 (b) −1, 2 (c) −2 (d) 0.9, −1.7

5 (a)

x	0	1	2	3	4	5	6
y	10	5	2	1	2	5	10

(b)

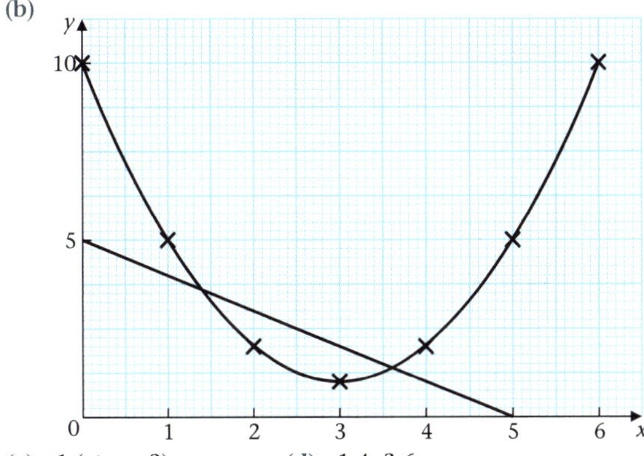

(c) 1 (at $x = 3$) (d) 1.4, 3.6

6 A

7 (a)

x	−2	−1	0	1	2	3	4
y	−18	−2	2	0	−2	2	18

(b)

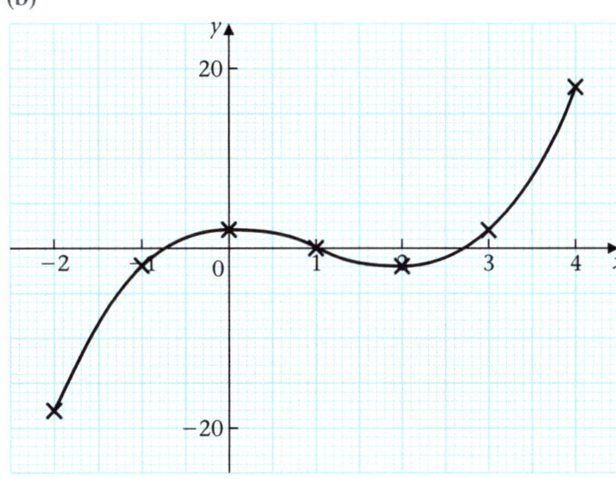

(c) (i) −0.7, 1, 2.7 (ii) 3.4

8 (a) About 6 m/s^2 (b) About 100 m

Chapter 18 Proportion

Exercise 18A

1 (a) Yes (b) Yes (c) No
(d) Yes (e) Yes (f) No

2 (a) 12 (b) 4

3 (a) 24 (b) $2\frac{1}{2}$

4 (a) 12 (b) 54

Exercise 18B

1 (a)

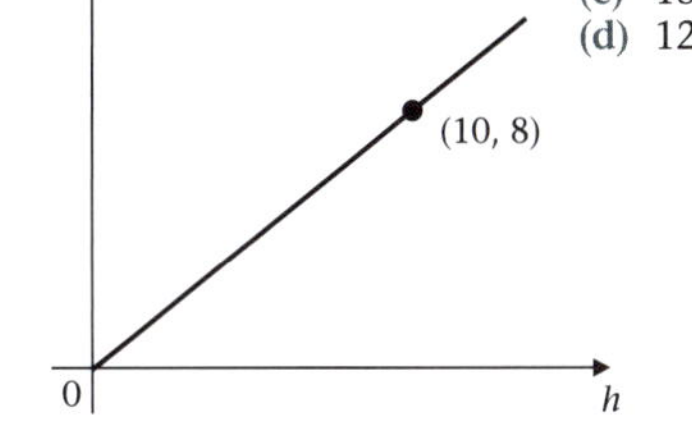

(b) $l = 0.8h$
(c) 15.625 = 15.63 (2 d.p.)
(d) 12

2 C

3 (a)

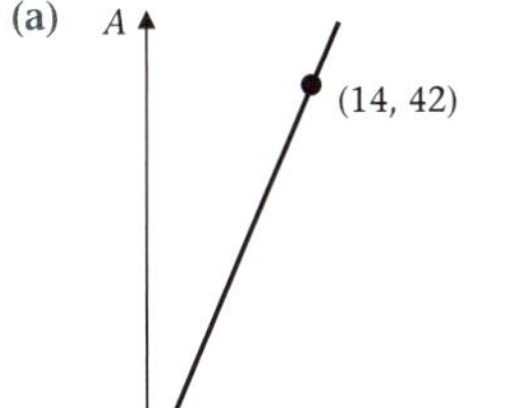

(b) $A = 3l$
(c) 97.2 cm^2
(d) 8.2

4 (a)

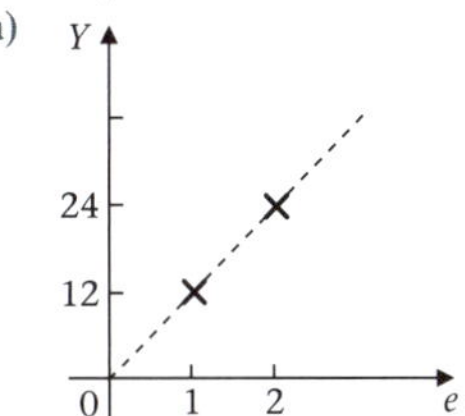

(b) Student's explanation is 2 → 24 so 1 → 12 etc.
(c) 84 ÷ 12 = 7

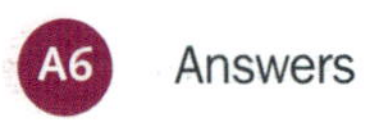

Exercise 18C

1 (a) (i) $w = 1.05\,h$ (ii) 12.6 (b) (i) $s = \frac{41}{24}h$ (ii) 28.7
(c) (i) $p = \frac{39}{34}l$ (ii) 31.7 (d) (i) $p = \frac{9}{4}a$ (ii) 248.4
2 (a) 9.36 volts, 5.2 amps (b) $V = \frac{9}{5}I$
(c) 6.4 amps (d) 4.428 volts
3 (b) 4.6 should be 5.6 (c) $V = 2.8\,I$
(d) 9.8 (e) 7.321
4 (a) 1.67 (b) 16.53
5 (a) $C = 3.6A$ (b) 360p or £3.60
6 (a) $d = 38\,t$ (b) 190 miles (c) 11 hours

Exercise 18D

1 $12\frac{1}{3}$, $86\frac{1}{3}$ **2** $\frac{2}{3}$, $4\frac{2}{3}$ **3** $z = kx$, 8.4 **4** $z = kw$, 4725
5 (a) 15 (b) 39 (c) $3\frac{1}{3}$
6 (a) 225 (b) 1250 (c) 72
7 $y = 2.8$, $p = 1.43$ (2 d.p.) **8** 5.71 cm^3 (2 d.p.) **9** 40%
10 (a) $h = 7.5d$
(b) 187.5 cm
(c) $42\frac{2}{3}$ cm

Exercise 18E

1 5, 80
2 (a) 6.25 (b) 156.25 (c) 1.265
3 (a) 2 (b) 128 (c) 4
4 (a) $l = km^3$ (b) (i) 25.6 (ii) 0.952
5 25 000 N
6 (a) 45 (b) 101.25
7 $p = 0.75$, $q = 3$ **8** 0.002
9 (a) 1 m (b) 1.5625 m
10 4 **11** $z = 2$, $w = 1.5$ **12** 125% **13** 4.14 m

Exercise 18F

1 (a) 72 (b) 7.2
2 (a) 4.8 (b) 9.6
3 (a) 512 (b) 128
4 (a) 2.5 (b) 40
5 (a) 233 lines (b) 291lines
6 (a) $l \propto \frac{1}{w}$, $l = \frac{k}{w}$ (b) area of the rectangle
7 4 units
8 $f = \frac{33\,024}{w}$ (b) 384 hertz (c) 96 cm

Mixed exercise 18

1 9.6 units
2 5.56 kg
3 28 800 km
4 (a) $h = \frac{35}{64}s^2$ (b) 315 m
5 18
6 (a) 31.25 m (b) 45 m
7 1 hour 48 minutes
8 0.576 units
9 50
10 (a) $S = \frac{8000}{f^2}$ (b) 500
11 (a) D (b) A (c) B (d) C

Chapter 19 Quadratic equations

Exercise 19A

1 (a) −2, 1 (b) 0, 3 (c) $-\frac{1}{2}$, 4 (d) 0, $1\frac{1}{2}$
(e) $\frac{1}{2}$, $1\frac{1}{3}$ (f) 2, 5
2 (a) 0, 3 (b) ±4 (c) −1, 4 (d) −7, −4
(e) −3, $\frac{1}{2}$ (f) $-\frac{3}{4}$, $1\frac{1}{3}$ (g) $\frac{3}{4}$, 2 (h) 0, 9
(i) $-\frac{1}{2}$, $2\frac{1}{3}$
3 (a) ±5 (b) 0, $\frac{1}{3}$ (c) −2, $\frac{1}{3}$ (d) ±2
(e) 0, $2\frac{1}{2}$ (f) −7, 5 (g) −3, 4 (h) 1, 3
(i) $-2\frac{1}{3}$, $\frac{1}{2}$ (j) $\frac{1}{2}$, 1
4 Both sides have been divided by $6y$, and $y = 0$ is a solution.
$y = 0$, $y = 2$

Exercise 19B

1 (a) $(x + 2)^2 - 4$ (b) $(x - 7)^2 - 49$ (c) $(x + \frac{3}{2})^2 - \frac{9}{4}$
(d) $(x + \frac{1}{2})^2 - \frac{1}{4}$ (e) $(x - \frac{1}{2})^2 - \frac{1}{4}$ (f) $(x - 2)^2 - 4$
(g) $(x + 3.5)^2 - 12.25$ (h) $(x - 5)^2 - 25$
2 (a) $2(x + 4)^2 - 32$ (b) $3(x - 2)^2 - 12$ (c) $2(x + \frac{1}{4})^2 - \frac{1}{8}$
(d) $5(x - \frac{3}{2})^2 - \frac{45}{4}$ (e) $2(x + \frac{1}{4})^2 - \frac{1}{2}$ (f) $4(x - 1)^2 - 4$
(g) $3(x - 2.5)^2 - 18.75$ (h) $7(x - 2)^2 - 28$

Exercise 19C

1 (a) $-5 \pm \sqrt{22}$ (b) $4 \pm \sqrt{18}$ (c) $\frac{-9 \pm \sqrt{69}}{2}$
(d) $1 \pm \sqrt{\frac{2}{3}}$ (e) $\frac{3 \pm \sqrt{41}}{4}$ (f) $1 \pm \sqrt{\frac{9}{2}}$
(g) $\frac{-5 \pm \sqrt{61}}{6}$ (h) $\frac{7 \pm \sqrt{65}}{4}$ (i) $\frac{4 \pm \sqrt{19}}{3}$
2 (a) −0.65, 4.65 (b) 0.35, 5.65 (c) −3.12, 1.12
(d) −0.69, 2.19 (e) −0.15, 2.15 (f) −1.29, 1.54
(g) −0.65, 4.65 (h) −0.84, 0.24 (i) −0.47, 2.14

Exercise 19D

1 (a) 5 (b) 8 (c) 44 (d) 288
(e) 41 (f) 28
2 (a) −2.62, −0.38 (b) −0.41, 2.41 (c) −3.16, 0.16
(d) ±1.06 (e) −2.35, 0.85 (f) −0.82, 1.82
3 (a) 0.27, 3.73 (b) 0.21, 4.79 (c) −2.13, −0.12
(d) −0.65, 1.15 (e) 0.13, 7.87 (f) −5.65, −0.35
4 $9 - \sqrt{60}$ and $9 + \sqrt{60}$
5 $3 + \sqrt{24}$ and $-3 + \sqrt{24}$

Exercise 19E

1 $-\frac{4}{7}$, 3 **2** 0.22, 2.28 **3** $-\frac{2}{3}$, 2
4 −0.11, 1.11 **5** −7, 4 **6** −1.30, 2.30

Exercise 19F

1 4, 5 **2** 5 **3** −8, 3 **4** 2.47 m, 247 cm
5 (a) £$\frac{400}{x}$ (c) £50
6 4.7
7 (a) $\frac{84}{x}$ km/h (c) 7

Exercise 19G

1 (a) $x = 4$, $y = 16$; $x = -4$, $y = 16$
(b) $x = 6$, $y = 36$
(c) $x = 7$, $y = 49$; $x = -5$, $y = 25$
(d) $x = 9$, $y = 81$; $x = -2$, $y = 4$
(e) $x = \frac{3}{2}$, $y = \frac{9}{2}$; $x = -1$, $y = 2$
(f) $x = -\frac{2}{3}$, $y = \frac{4}{3}$; $x = 3$, $y = 27$
(g) $x = 2$, $y = -2$; $x = -3$, $y = -7$
(h) $x = \frac{3}{4}$, $y = \frac{7}{4}$; $x = -\frac{4}{3}$; $y = \frac{49}{3}$
2 (a) (1, 1), (−3, 9) (b) (2, 16), $(-\frac{5}{4}, \frac{25}{4})$
(c) (5, 10), (−2, 3) (d) (0, 7), $(-\frac{1}{2}, 5\frac{1}{2})$

3 (a) none
(b) one: (5, 25)
(c) two: (−1, 2) and $(\frac{7}{2}, \frac{49}{2})$
(d) none
(e) two: (3, 45) and $(-\frac{1}{5}, \frac{1}{5})$
(f) two: (3, 36) and $(-\frac{1}{2}, 1)$
(g) one: (2, 2)
(h) two: $(\frac{5}{4}, \frac{25}{2})$ and $(-\frac{1}{3}, 3)$

Exercise 19H

1 (a) $x = 4, y = 3;\ x = -4, y = 3$ meet in 2 points
(b) $x = 0, y = 5;\ x = -5, y = 0$ meet in 2 points
(c) $x = -3, y = 4;\ x = -\frac{24}{5}, y = -\frac{7}{5}$ meet in 2 points
(d) $x = 3, y = -4; x = -4, y = 3$ meet in 2 points
(e) $x = 5, y = -5$ meet in 1 point, line is a tangent
(f) $x = 1, y = -7; x = -\frac{49}{65}, y = \frac{457}{65}$ meet in 2 points
(g) $x = 3, y = -1$ meet in 1 point, line is a tangent
(h) $x = 2, y = 1$ meet in 1 point, line is a tangent
(i) $x = -\frac{7}{5}, y = -\frac{1}{5}$ meet in 1 point, line is a tangent
(j) $x = 0, y = 2; x = \frac{48}{25}, y = -\frac{14}{25}$ meet in 2 points

3 (a) $y = x + 4$ touches circle at $x = -2$ only
(b) (i) $y = x - 4$; (2, −2)
(ii) $4\sqrt{2}$ or $2\sqrt{8}$
(c) $2r$

Exercise 19I

1 (a) (b)

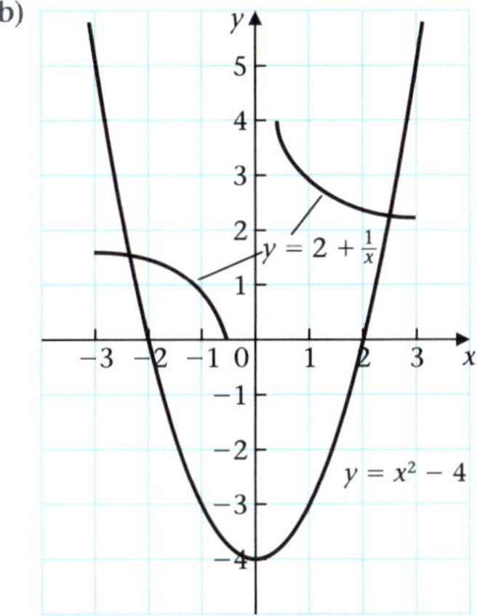

(c) (i) −1.4, 1.4 (ii) −0.8 (iii) −2.4, 2.5

2 (a) (i) $y = 1$ (ii) $y = -2$ (iii) $y = 2x + 1$
(iv) $y = -2x + 4$
(b) $x^3 - 2x = 4$ ($y = 4 - 2x$ meets the curve in only one point, (2, 0))
(c) $x^4 - 4x^2 = 1$

3 (a)

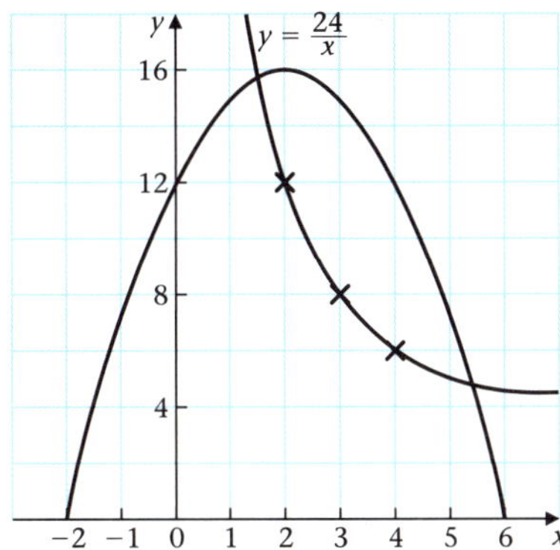

(b) 1.5 m, 5.4 m

4 (a)

x	−3	−2	−1	0	1	2
y	−8	5	6	1	−4	−3

(b) (c) (i)

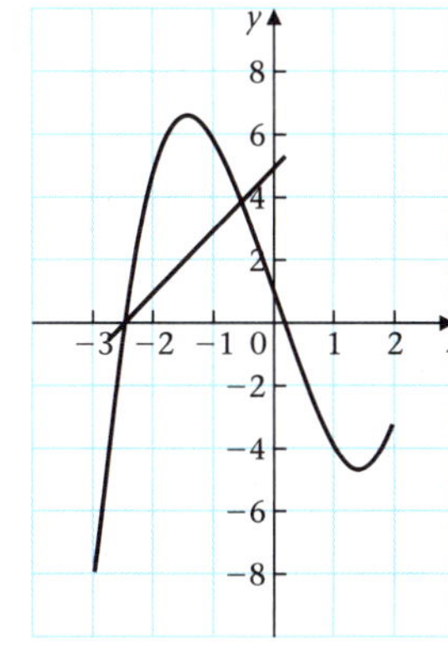

(ii) −2.5, −0.5
(d) $x^3 - 8x - 4 = 0$ (e) $y = 2x + 1$ (f) $0, \pm\sqrt{8}$

Mixed exercise 19

1 2 cm
2 $4\frac{1}{2}$
3 $2 + \sqrt{13}$
4 $-3 \pm \sqrt{13}$
5 (a) $(2x - 7)(x - 14)$ (b) $x = 3.5, 14$
6 $x = 2, y = 5; x = -5, y = -2$
7 (a) 1.30, −2.30
(b) Untrue for $x = 11$, as 11 is a factor
8 (a) Simplified from Pythagoras: $(x + 8)^2 = x^2 + (x + 5)^2$
(b) 9.93 cm
9 (a)

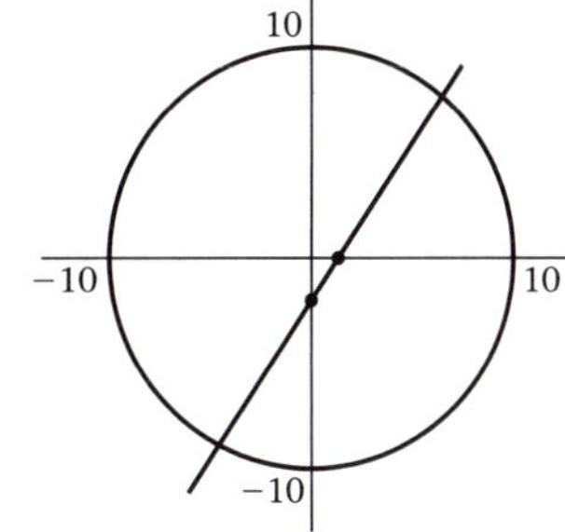

(b) (6.4, 7.7), (−4.6, −8.9)
(c) 9
(d) $x = 3, y = 10$

Chapter 20 Presenting and analysing data 2

Exercise 20A

1 (a)

Time watching TV (hours)	Cumulative frequency
$0 \leqslant t < 3.5$	3
$0 \leqslant t < 7.5$	8
$0 \leqslant t < 11.5$	16
$0 \leqslant t < 15.5$	19
$0 \leqslant t < 18.5$	20

(b)

Number on bus	Cumulative frequency
0–5	8
0–10	15
0–15	24
0–20	31
0–25	40

(c)

Age (years)	Cumulative frequency
$16 \leqslant a < 20.5$	3
$16 \leqslant a < 25.5$	9
$16 \leqslant a < 30.5$	26
$16 \leqslant a < 35.5$	52
$16 \leqslant a < 40.5$	63
$16 \leqslant a < 50.5$	65

(d)

Temperature (°C)	Cumulative frequency
$-10 \leqslant t < 0$	12
$-10 \leqslant t < 10$	98
$-10 \leqslant t < 20$	283
$-10 \leqslant t < 30$	362
$-10 \leqslant t < 40$	365

2

Weight of baby (kg)	Frequency
$1 \leqslant w < 2$	5
$2 \leqslant w < 3$	12
$3 \leqslant w < 4$	24
$4 \leqslant w < 5$	8
$5 \leqslant w < 6$	1

Exercise 20B

1 (a)

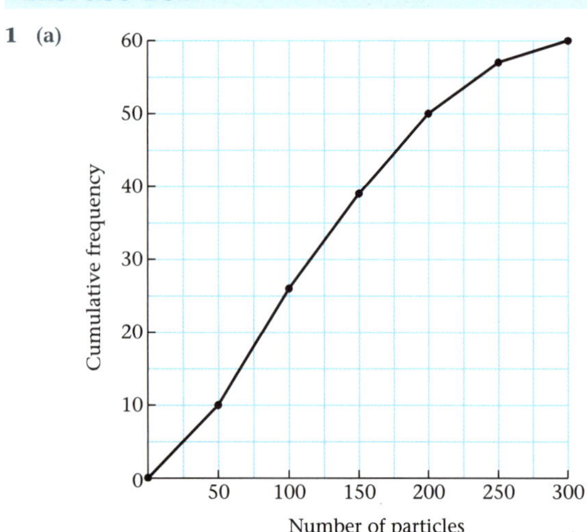

(b) (i) 115 (ii) 66 (iii) 177 (iv) 111

2 (a)

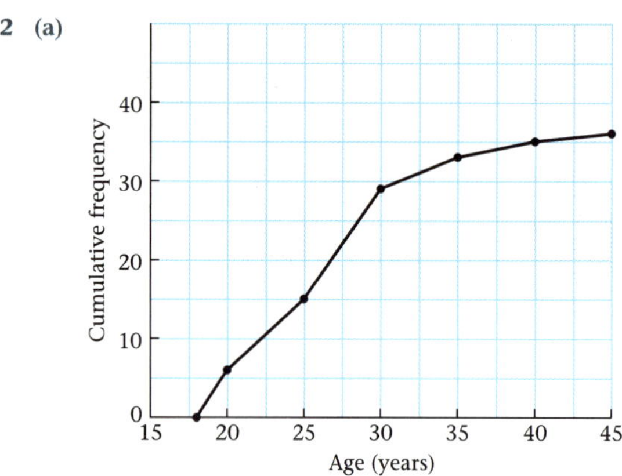

(b) (i) 26 years (ii) 8 years

3 (a) 36.75°C (b) 0.65°C (c) 86 people

Exercise 20C

1 (a)

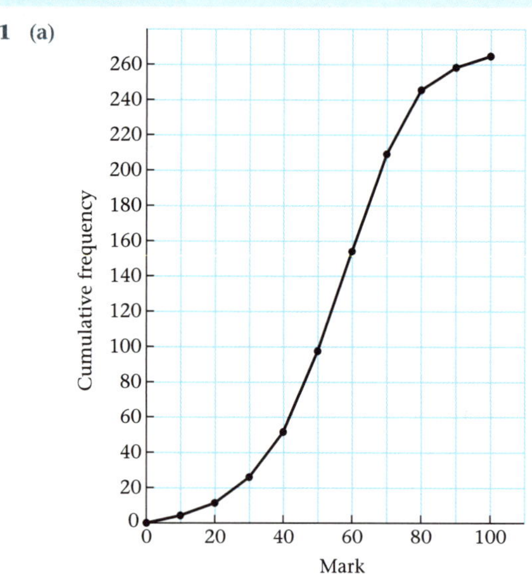

(b) 70 (c) 52

2 (a)

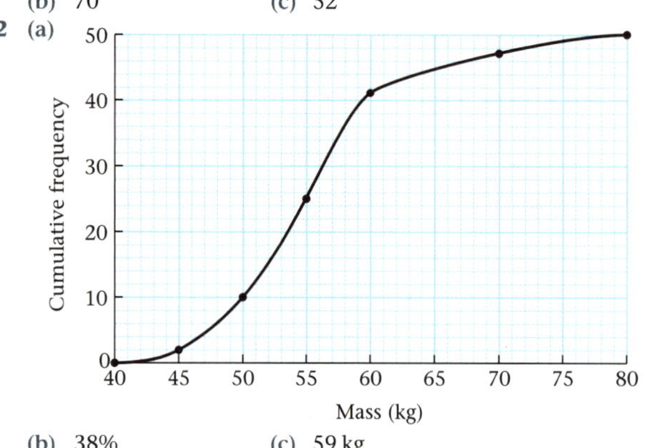

(b) 38% (c) 59 kg

3 (a)

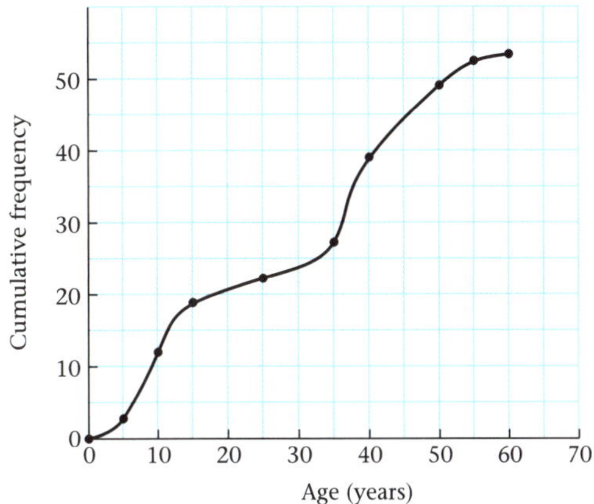

(b) 34 years
(c) 4

Exercise 20D

1

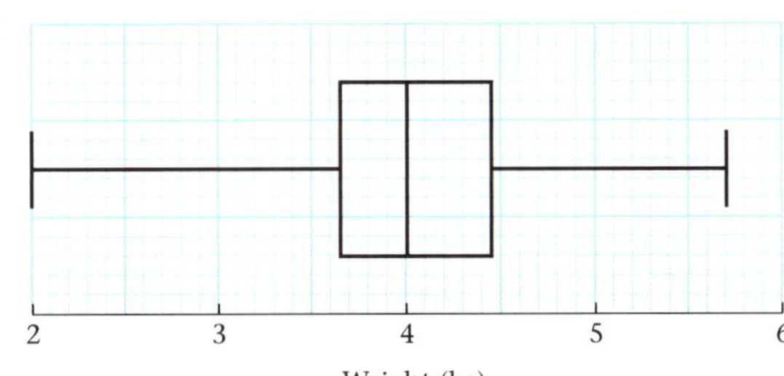

2

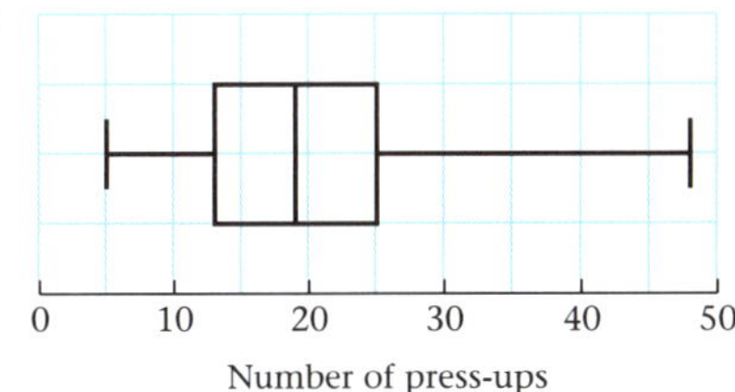

Exercise 20E

1 Class B had a slightly higher median but their results were spread over a wider range. Class A was more consistent.

2 (a)

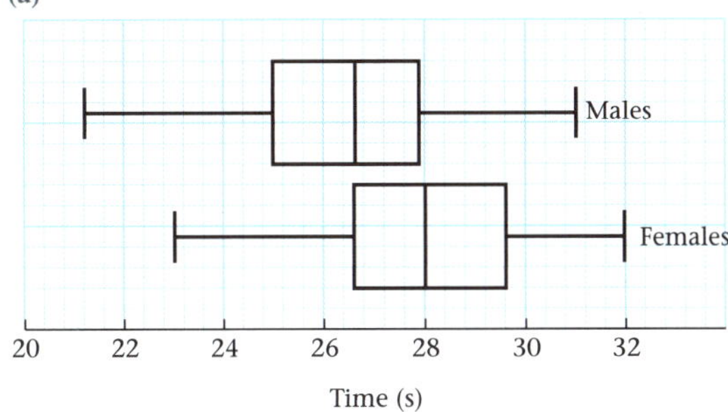

(b) The male median time was lower. The box plots are alike with the male times lower than the female times.

Exercise 20F

1

Class widths (s)	Frequency density
30	1
30	3
20	5
10	8
10	6
50	2.4

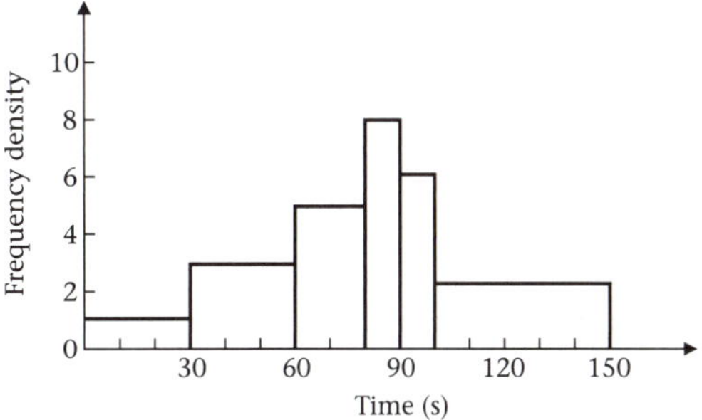

2

Class widths (g)	Frequency density
30	2.5
15	7
15	11
15	8
30	4.5

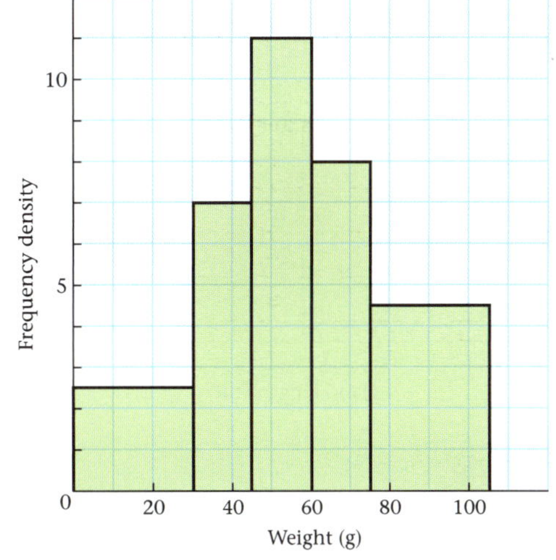

3

Distance (m)	Frequency density
0–9	18 ÷ 9.5 = 1.9
10–14	14 ÷ 5 = 2.8
15–19	16 ÷ 5 = 3.2
20–24	15 ÷ 5 = 3
25–34	17 ÷ 10 = 1.7
35–50	10 ÷ 16 = 0.6

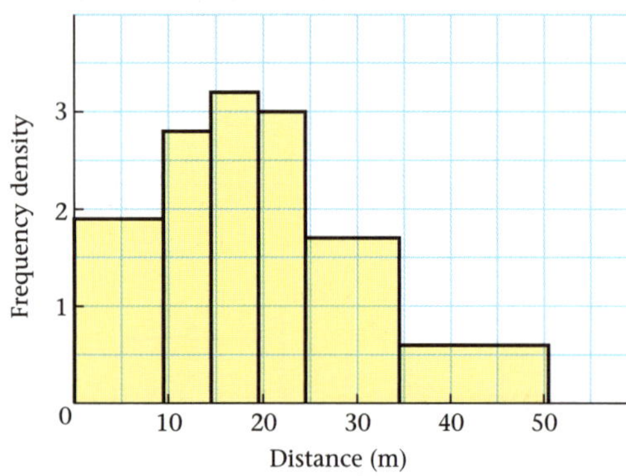

4 (a)

Hand length (cm)	Frequency	Frequency density
$12.5 \leqslant h < 17.5$	5	1
$17.5 \leqslant h < 19.5$	12	6
$19.5 \leqslant h < 21.5$	10	5
$21.5 \leqslant h < 25.5$	15	3.75

(b)

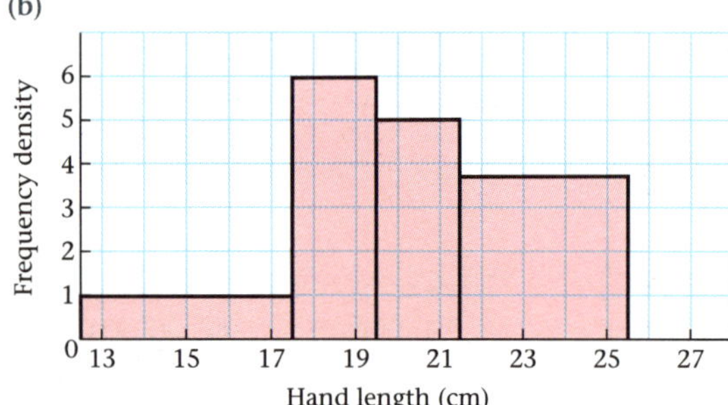

Exercise 20G

1

Estimated length (cm)	Frequency
$10 < l \leqslant 20$	14
$20 < l \leqslant 24$	12
$24 < l \leqslant 28$	20
$28 < l \leqslant 32$	16
$32 < l \leqslant 36$	12
$36 < l \leqslant 50$	7

2

Lifetime (hours)	Frequency
$100 < t \leqslant 400$	30
$400 < t \leqslant 600$	32
$600 < t \leqslant 700$	36
$700 < t \leqslant 900$	108
$900 < t \leqslant 400$	36

3 (a)

Weight (grams)	Frequency
$8 \leqslant w < 24$	24
$24 \leqslant w < 32$	41
$32 \leqslant w < 40$	32
$40 \leqslant w < 56$	30
$56 \leqslant w < 72$	18
$72 \leqslant w < 112$	15

(b) 160 letters
(c) 39.4%

4 (a)

Time (minutes)	Frequency
$10 \leqslant t < 25$	15
$25 \leqslant t < 35$	30
$35 \leqslant t < 40$	20
$40 \leqslant t < 45$	40
$45 \leqslant t < 60$	75

(b) 45 operations

Mixed exercise 20

1

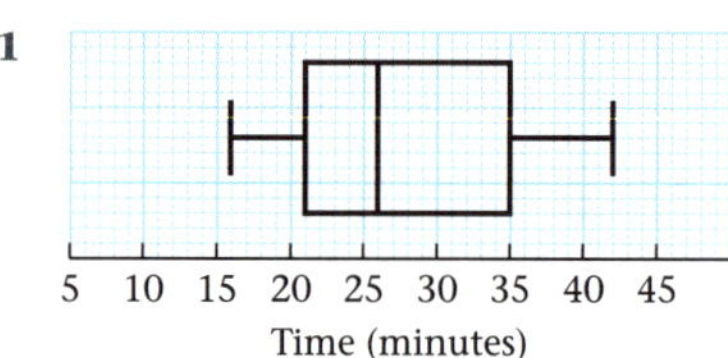

2 (a)

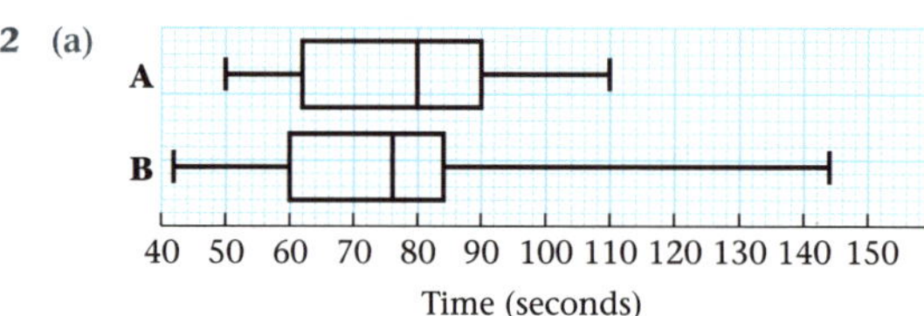

(b) 142 is an extreme value – minimum, lower quartile, median, upper quartile are all less than Assistant A's values.

3 (a) 5, 23, 35, 39, 40

(b)

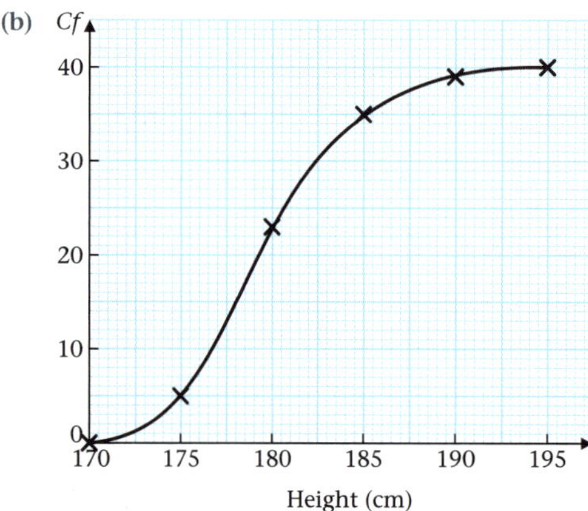

(c) 179 cm

4 (a) 32 seconds

(b)

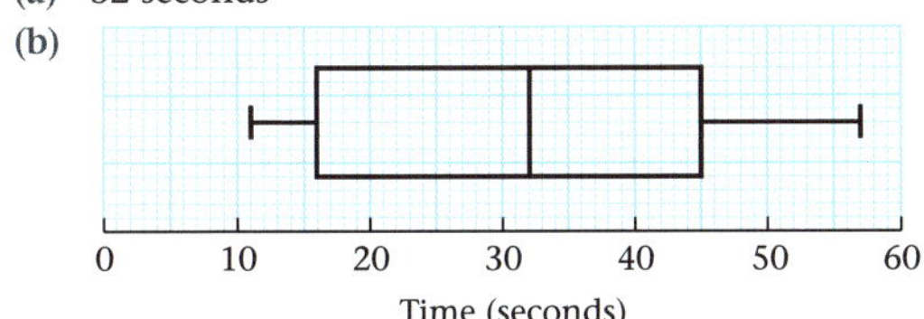

(c) Boys have: bigger median, wider range, wider interquartile range, bigger maximum value, smaller minimum value.

5 (a) 60, 40

(b)

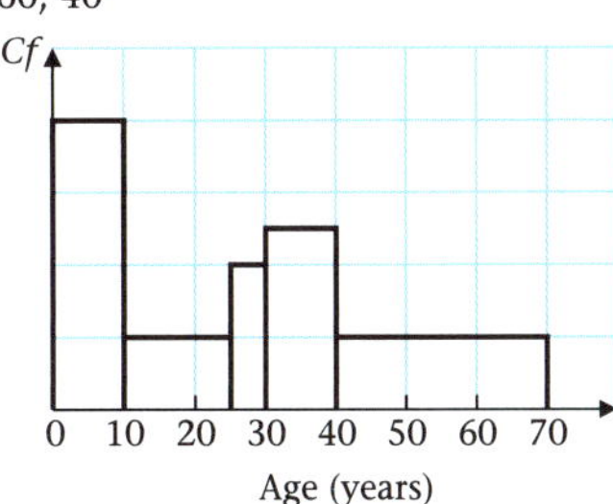

6 20, 18, 45, 52

7 (a)

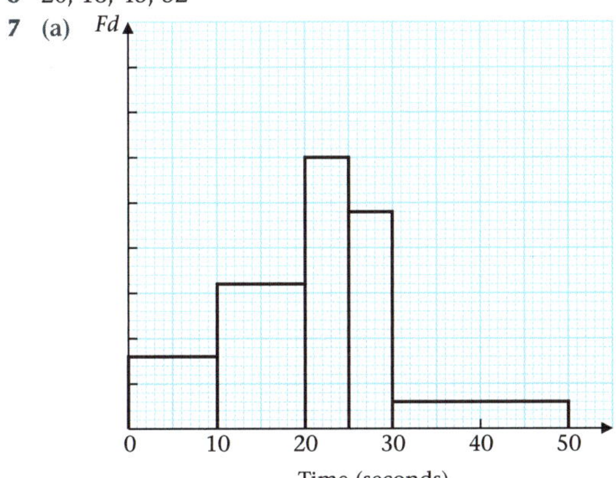

(b) 10, 18, 14, 10, 8

8 (a)

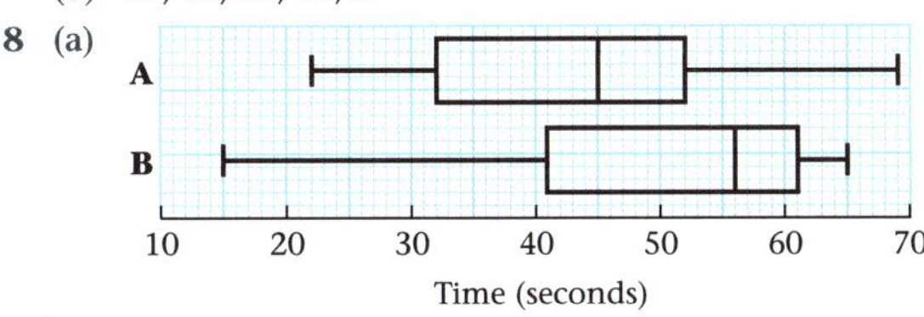

(b) Forest A has the oldest tree but generally the trees in forest B are older.

Chapter 21 Advanced trigonometry

(All answers correct to 2 d.p.)

Exercise 21A

1 (a) $17.32\,\text{cm}^2$ (b) $29.60\,\text{cm}^2$ (c) $76.31\,\text{cm}^2$
(d) $32.14\,\text{cm}^2$ (e) $40.26\,\text{cm}^2$ (f) $111.54\,\text{cm}^2$

2 $492.61\,\text{m}^2$ **3** $73.54\,\text{cm}^2$ **4** 53.13° **5** 123.56°

Exercise 21C

1 (a) 9.92 cm (b) 11.43 cm (c) 14.95 cm
(d) 8.28 cm (e) 13.32 cm (f) 6.24 cm

2 (a) 33.27° (b) 23.71° (c) 13.72°

3 (a) 61.90 km (b) 37.82 km

Exercise 21D

$P\hat{Q}R = 63.73°$ or $P\hat{Q}R = 20.27°$

Exercise 21E

1 (a) 6.22 cm (b) 6.25 cm (c) 11.53 cm (d) 24.70 cm

2 (a) 36.34° (b) 101.54° (c) 100.95° (d) 98.25°

3 146.46 m

4 145.26 km

Exercise 21F

1 (a) 13 cm (b) 23.85 cm (c) 23.32 cm
(d) 22.62° (e) 12.10° (f) 17.75°

2 (a) 14.14 cm (b) 14.35 cm (c) 63.77°
(d) 26.23°

3 (b) (i) 38.42 cm (ii) 30.81 cm
(c) 6.72 cm (d) 77.37°

Mixed exercise 21

1 (a) $15.76\,\text{cm}^2$ (b) 6.30 cm (c) 38.71°

2 (a) $56.4\,\text{cm}^2$ (b) 7.84 cm

3 18.3 cm

4 (a) 183.97 km (b) 320.64° (c) 28.54 km

5 (a) 9.94 km (b) 151.18° (c) 3.19 km

6 (a) 17.4 cm (b) 17.9 cm (c) 54.47°

Chapter 22 Advanced mensuration

(All answers correct to 2 d.p. for Exercises 22A to 22D.)

Exercise 22A

1 (a) 9.77 cm (b) 10.47 cm (c) 7.38 cm
(d) 39.10 cm (e) 47.12 cm (f) 60.21 cm

2 (a) 50.13° (b) 80.21° (c) 47.75°
(d) 222.82° (e) 73.52° (f) 39.14°

Exercise 22B

1 (a) $22.34\,\text{cm}^2$ (b) $61.09\,\text{cm}^2$ (c) $30.54\,\text{cm}^2$
(d) $45.95\,\text{cm}^2$ (e) $139.63\,\text{cm}^2$ (f) $279.25\,\text{cm}^2$

2 72.15° **3** 10.06 cm

Exercise 22C

1 (a) $9.06\,\text{cm}^2$ (b) $10.98\,\text{cm}^2$ (c) $0.51\,\text{cm}^2$
(d) $3.22\,\text{cm}^2$ (e) $308.83\,\text{cm}^2$ (f) $192.04\,\text{cm}^2$

Exercise 22D

1 (a) 68.75° (b) $135\,\text{cm}^2$

2 (a) 82.08 m (b) 83.78 m (c) $5026.54\,\text{m}^2$
(d) $398.38\,\text{m}^2$

3 (a) 7.16 m (b) $2.99\,\text{m}^2$

Exercise 22E

1 $314\,\text{cm}^3$, $283\,\text{cm}^2$ **2** $156\,\text{cm}^3$, $211\,\text{cm}^2$

3 $0.942\,\text{m}^3$ **4** $11\,972\,\text{cm}^3$

5 (a) $8311\,\text{cm}^3$
(b) $2354\,\text{cm}^2$

Exercise 22F

1 $960\,\text{cm}^3$ **2** $140\,\text{cm}^3$ **3** 6.18 cm

4 (a) $301.59\,\text{cm}^3$ (b) 6.71

5 7.08

Exercise 22G

1 (a) 2144.7 cm^3, 804.25 cm^2 (b) 1563.5 cm^3, 651.4 cm^2
(c) 3591.4 cm^3, 1134.1 cm^2 (d) $\frac{1}{6}\pi x^3$, πx^2
2 10.61 cm
3 9.67

Exercise 22H

1 23.4 cm
2 $\left(\frac{12.5}{12}\right)^3 = 1.13$ i.e. 13% increase
3 (a) 4:9 (b) 8 : 27 **4** $\frac{1}{50^3} = \frac{1}{125000}$
5 (a) 12.60 cm (b) 1 : 1.31

Exercise 22I

1 $618.\dot{6}\text{ cm}^3$ **2** 112.72 cm^3
3 496.37 cm^3 **4** 45389.33 cm^3

Mixed exercise 22

1 (a) 6.76 cm (b) 6.98 cm (c) 27.93 cm^2 (d) 3.41 cm^2
2 9048 cm^3, 2413 cm^2
3 268.08 cm^3
4 $\frac{4}{3}\pi r^3 = r$, $r^2 = \frac{3}{4\pi}$, $r = \sqrt{\frac{3}{4\pi}}$
5 1120 cm^3
6 9366.4 cm^3
7 26.66 cm
8 2165.60 cm^3
9 3200 cm^3
8 270 cm^3

Chapter 23 Exploring numbers 2

Exercise 23A

1 0.75, 0.6, 0.428 571…, 0.375, 0.3, 0.2727…
$\frac{3}{7}$ and $\frac{3}{11}$ are recurring decimals
2 $\frac{5}{8}$, $\frac{5}{16}$ are terminating decimals because the denominators divide exactly into powers of 10. The others are recurring.
3 0.142 857…, 0.285 714…, 0.428 571…, 0.571 428…, 0.714 285…, 0.857 142…
Same digits in the same order.
4 16
5 $\frac{1}{13}$, $\frac{3}{13}$, $\frac{4}{13}$, $\frac{9}{13}$, $\frac{10}{13}$, $\frac{12}{13}$ use the same digits in the same order
$\frac{2}{13}$, $\frac{5}{13}$, $\frac{6}{13}$, $\frac{7}{13}$, $\frac{8}{13}$, $\frac{11}{13}$ use the same digits in the same order.
Doubling the decimal form of the first set of fractions gives the pattern of recurring digits in the second set.
6 (a) Decimal recurs because 17 does not divide exactly into any power of 10.
(b) When dividing by 17 there can only be 16 different remainders and 16 different subtractions.

Exercise 23B

1 (a) $\frac{2}{3}$ (b) $\frac{7}{9}$ (c) $\frac{34}{99}$ (d) $\frac{91}{99}$
(e) $\frac{2}{11}$ (f) $\frac{125}{999}$ (g) $\frac{19}{37}$ (h) $\frac{91}{909}$
(i) $\frac{1279}{9999}$ (j) $\frac{9}{101}$ (k) $1\frac{31}{75}$ (l) $4\frac{119}{165}$
(m) $2\frac{19}{55}$ (m) $5\frac{69}{110}$
2 1; there is no number between 0.9999… and 1.

Exercise 23C

1 $\pm\sqrt{30}$
2 $\sqrt{40} = 2\sqrt{10}$ cm
3 (a) Perimeter = 12 units
(b) Area = 4 (units)^2
4 (a) $\frac{\sqrt{7}}{7}$ (b) $\frac{3\sqrt{5}}{5}$ (c) $\frac{\sqrt{17}}{17}$
(d) $\frac{\sqrt{11}}{11}$ (e) 4 (f) $\frac{3\sqrt{5}-5}{4}$
(g) $-\frac{2\sqrt{7}+7}{3}$ (h) $-2\sqrt{3}+3$ (i) $-\frac{7\sqrt{11}+11}{38}$
5 (a) $x = 3 \pm \sqrt{7}$ (b) $x = -5 \pm \sqrt{11}$
7 $\sqrt{11}$ units
8 (a) $\frac{3}{2}$ (units)^2 (b) $\sqrt{22}$ units
9 $\frac{\sqrt{6}}{2}$

Exercise 23D

1 3.5, 4.5; 13.5, 14.5; 103.5, 104.5; 9.5, 10.5; 99.5, 100.5
2 25, 35; 45, 55; 175, 185; 3015, 3025; 5, 15; 95, 105
3 4.65, 4.75; 2.85, 2.95; 13.55, 13.65; 0.25, 0.35; 157.45, 157.55; 9.95, 10.05; 99.95, 100.05
4 36.5, 37.5; 49.5, 50.5; 175, 185; 3.15, 3.25; 9.45, 9.55; 9350, 9450; 9.5, 10.5; 95, 105
5 4.25, 4.75; 7.25, 7.75; 16.25, 16.75; 2.75, 3.25; 15.25, 15.75; 9.75, 10.25; 99.75, 100.25
6 3.3, 3.5; 3.1, 3.3; 3.9, 4.1; 9.3, 9.5; 12.1, 12.3; 24.5, 24.7; 9.9, 10.1; 99.9, 100.1
7 3.625, 3.875; 3.375, 3.625; 4.125, 4.375; 5.875, 6.125; 15.375, 15.625; 9.875, 10.125; 99.875, 100.125
8 (a) 7.5 m, 6.5 m; 6.5 m, 5.5 m
(b) 735 cm, 725 cm; 595 cm, 585 cm
(c) 7.325 m, 7.315 m; 5.945 m, 5.935 m
(d) Yes, the range of (a) contains the range of (b) which contains the range of (c).
9 (a) 74.365 s, 74.355 s
(b) It is not necessarily the fastest lap time.

Exercise 23E

Answers are either exact or given to 4 s.f.
1 55.25 cm^2, 41.25 cm^2 **2** 30 cm, 26 cm
3 57.0025 cm^2, 55.5025 cm^2 **4** 30.2 cm, 29.8 cm
5 38.48 cm^2, 19.63 cm^2 **6** 2.168 m, 2.105 m
7 5411 mm^2, 5153 mm^2 **8** 27.625 cm^2, 20.625 cm^2
9 24.35 cm^2, 23.65 cm^2 **10** 161.5 cm^2, 127.5 cm^2
11 6.297 cm^2, 4.984 cm^2 **12** 23.56 cm, 20.42 cm
13 (a) $22\,450\text{ cm}^3$, 8181 cm^3 (b) $15\,599\text{ cm}^3$, $12\,770\text{ cm}^3$
(c) $14\,279\text{ cm}^3$, $13\,996\text{ cm}^3$

Exercise 23F

Answers are either exact or given to 4 s.f.
1 1 cm, 0.8 cm **2** 4 min, 2 min **3** 20.5 cm, 9.5 cm
4 (a) 6.826 m/s, 6.780 m/s (b) 6.860 m/s, 6.746 m/s
5 (a) 9.571 miles/l, 8.784 miles/l (b) 43.45 mpg, 39.88 mpg
6 26.10 cm, 23.68 cm **7** 3.857 g/cm^3, 2.778 g/cm^3
8 54.77°, 39.59°

Mixed exercise 23

1 (a) 0.875 T (b) $0.\dot{7}$ R (c) 0.7 T
(d) $0.\dot{6}\dot{3}$ R (e) $0.58\dot{3}$ R (f) $0.\dot{5}3846\dot{1}$ R
2 (a) $13\frac{74}{99}$ (b) $6\frac{25\,082}{33\,300}$
3 (a) $\frac{\sqrt{5}}{5}$ (b) $\frac{5\sqrt{7}}{7}$ (c) $\frac{\sqrt{29}}{29}$
(d) 3 (e) $2\sqrt{6}$ (f) $2\sqrt{2}$
4 (a) 255 000, 245 000 miles (b) 6.5×10^6, 5.5×10^6 cm
5 4 cm is correct to nearest cm
4.0 cm is correct to 1 d.p.
4.00 cm is correct to 2 d.p.
6 75.398 cm^2, 25.133 cm^2 **7** 3.81 mm, 3.79 mm
8 (a) 4 (b) $4\sqrt{10}$ (c) 83.3%
9 (a) 9.719, 11.710 (b) 10 to 1 s.f.

Chapter 24 Probability

(Any correct fraction, decimal or percentage equivalents are acceptable unless otherwise stated.)

Exercise 24A

1 (a) $\frac{4}{9}$ (b) $\frac{2}{9}$
2 (a) $\frac{3}{10}$ (b) $\frac{8}{10}$
3 (a) $\frac{1}{6}$ (b) $\frac{3}{6}$ (c) $\frac{3}{6}$ (d) $\frac{5}{6}$
4 (a) $\frac{3}{8}$ (b) $\frac{2}{8}$ (c) $\frac{5}{8}$
5 (a) $\frac{6}{20}$ (b) $\frac{10}{20}$ (c) $\frac{16}{20}$ (d) $\frac{16}{20}$
(e) Add the answers to (a) and (b)
(c) Subtract p from 1

Exercise 24B

1 (a)

+	1	3	5	7
2	3	5	7	9
4	5	7	9	11
6	7	9	11	13
8	9	11	13	15

(b) $\frac{3}{16}$

2 (Only correct fraction equivalents are acceptable.)
(a) $\frac{1}{6}$ (b) $\frac{9}{36}$ (c) $\frac{6}{36}$ (d) $\frac{15}{36}$

3

H	H	H	H	T	H	H	H	T	T	T	H	T	T	T	T
H	H	H	T	H	H	T	T	H	H	T	T	H	T	T	T
H	H	T	H	H	T	H	T	H	T	H	T	T	H	T	T
H	T	H	H	H	T	T	H	T	H	H	T	T	T	H	T

(a) $\frac{1}{16}$ (b) $\frac{6}{16}$ (c) $\frac{15}{16}$

4

Red	Red	Red	Red	Red	Red	Red	Red	Red
Bro	Bro	Bro	Gre	Gre	Gre	Yel	Yel	Yel
Blu	Pin	Bla	Blu	Pin	Bla	Blu	Pin	Bla
Whi	Whi	Whi	Whi	Whi	Whi	Whi	Whi	Whi
Bro	Bro	Bro	Gre	Gre	Gre	Yel	Yel	Yel
Blu	Pin	Bla	Blu	Pin	Bla	Blu	Pin	Bla

$\frac{3}{18}$

5 (a) $\frac{15}{36}$ (b) $\frac{18}{36}$ (c) $\frac{27}{36}$ (d) $\frac{22}{36}$
6 (a) $\frac{1}{6}$ (b) $\frac{1}{8}$ (c) $\frac{4}{48}$ (d) $\frac{6}{48}$
(e) $\frac{6}{48}$ (f) $\frac{3}{48}$

Exercise 24D

1 (a) $\frac{1}{12}$ (b) $\frac{1}{10}$ (c) $\frac{26}{120}$
2 (a) $\frac{1}{5}$ (b) (i) $\frac{1}{25}$ (ii) $\frac{1}{5}$

Exercise 24E

1 (a) $\frac{1}{60}$ (b) $\frac{24}{60}$ (c) $\frac{9}{60}$ (d) $\frac{10}{60}$
2 (a) $\frac{2}{60}$ (b) $\frac{13}{60}$ (c) $\frac{45}{60}$

Mixed exercise 24

1 (H, H, H, H), (H, H, H, T), (H, H, T, H), (H, T, H, H), (T, H, H, H), (H, T, H, T), (T, H, T, H), (H, T, T, H), (T, H, H, T), (H, H, T, T), (T, T, H, H), (H, T, T, T), (T, H, T, T), (T, T, H, T), (T, T, T, H), (T, T, T, T)
(a) $\frac{6}{16}$ (b) $\frac{5}{16}$
2 (a) $\frac{1}{13}$ (b) $\frac{3}{13}$ (c) $\frac{5}{13}$
3 120
4 (a) $\frac{x}{8}$ (b) $1-\frac{x}{8}$ (c) 2 **5** $\frac{140}{360}$

6

+	1	2	3	4
1	2	3	4	5
2	3	4	5	6
3	4	5	6	7

(a) $\frac{3}{12}$
(b) $\frac{3}{12}$
(c) $\frac{6}{12}$

7 $\frac{10}{24}$
8 (a) $\frac{4}{9}$ (b) $\frac{34}{63}$
9 $\frac{1}{72}$ **10** $\frac{32}{100}$
11 (a) $\frac{11}{17}$ (b) No, he may improve with practice.
12 (a) (i) $\frac{165}{340}$ (ii) $\frac{32}{340}$ (b) $\frac{137}{165}$
13 (a)

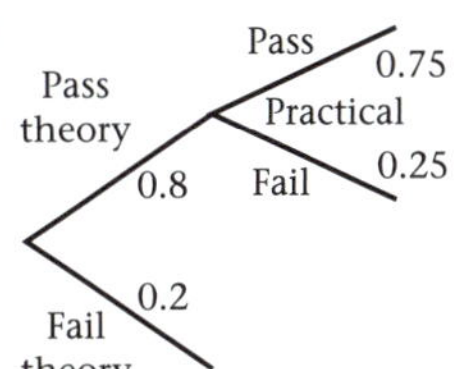

(b) 0.6 **14** $\frac{\pi}{4}$

Chapter 25 Transformations of graphs

Exercise 25A

1 (a) 2 (b) 14 (c) −2 (d) −1
(e) 7 (f) $-1\frac{15}{16}$
2 (a) x^2 (b) $9x^2$ (c) x^2+4x+4
(d) x^2+2x+4 (e) $\frac{1}{4}x^2-x-3$ (f) $5-4x^2$
(g) $k^2x^2+2akx+a^2+b$
3 (a) (i) 5 (ii) −3 (iii) −4 (iv) −3 (b) −2, 2

Exercise 25B

1 $y=x^2-4$
2 $y=x^2+k$ for any three values of k between 0 and 8
3 $-15<k<0$

Exercise 25C

1 (a) A: 4 units vertically in the negative y-direction.
B: 4 units vertically in the positive y-direction.
C: 6 units vertically in the positive y-direction.
(b) A: 5 units vertically in the positive y-direction.
B: 12 units vertically in the positive y-direction
C: 8 units vertically in the negative y-direction.
(c) A: 10 units vertically in the negative y-direction.
B: 2.5 units vertically in the positive y-direction.
C: 6 units vertically in the positive y-direction.
(d) A: 2 units vertically in the positive y-direction.
(e) A: 3 units vertically in the negative y-direction.
2 (c) Translation 2 units vertically in the positive y-direction.

Exercise 25D

1 $y=(x-1)^2$
2 (a)

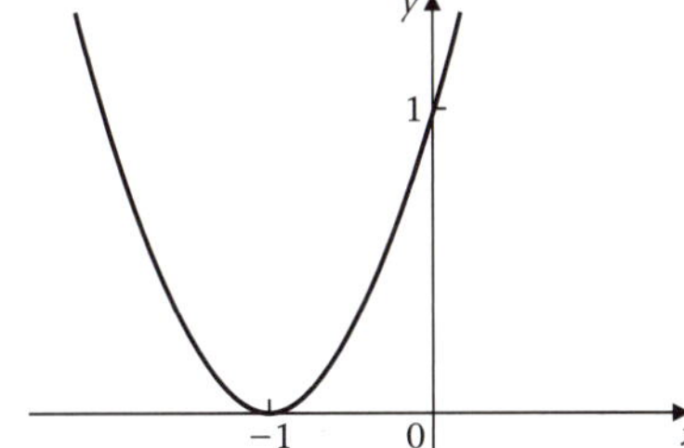

(b)

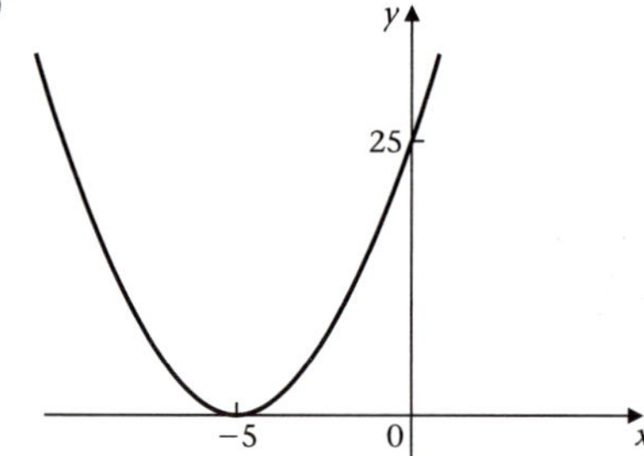

3

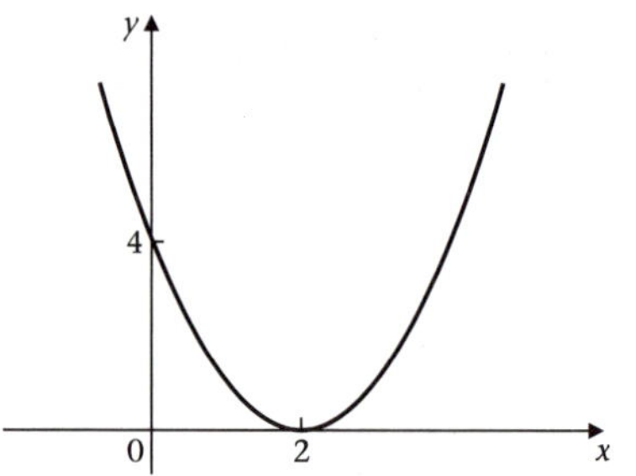

Exercise 25E

1 A horizontal translation of 1 unit in the positive x-direction.
2 A horizontal translation of 1 unit in the positive x-direction.
3 A vertical translation of 7 units in the positive y-direction.
4 $y = x^3 + 2$
5 $y = (x - 4)(x - 5)(x + 1)$

Exercise 25F

1 (a)

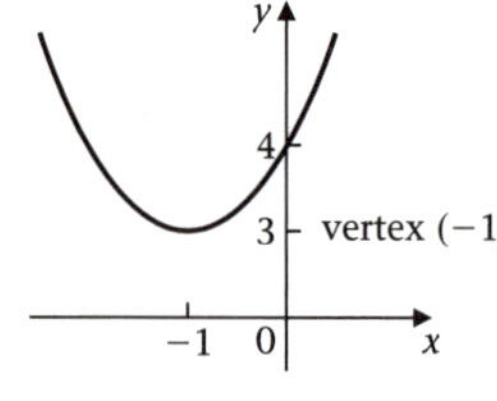

(b)

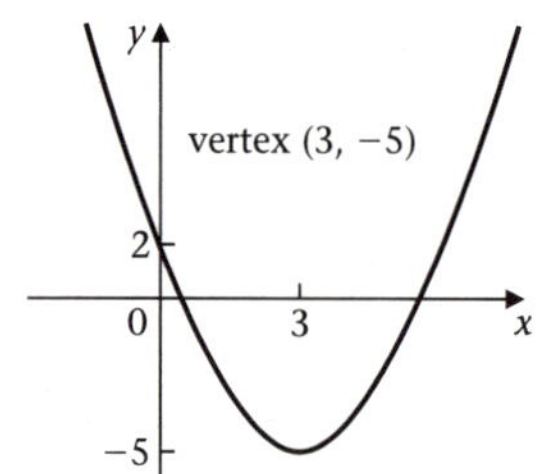

(c)

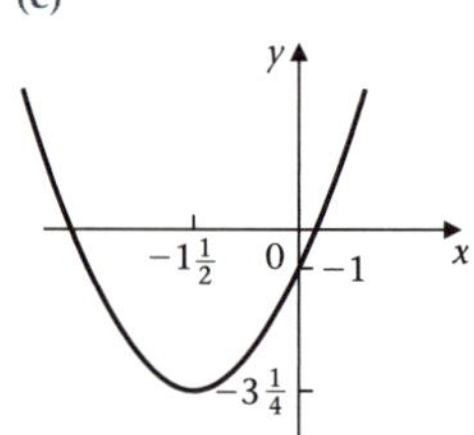

vertex $(-1\frac{1}{2}, -3\frac{1}{4})$

(d)

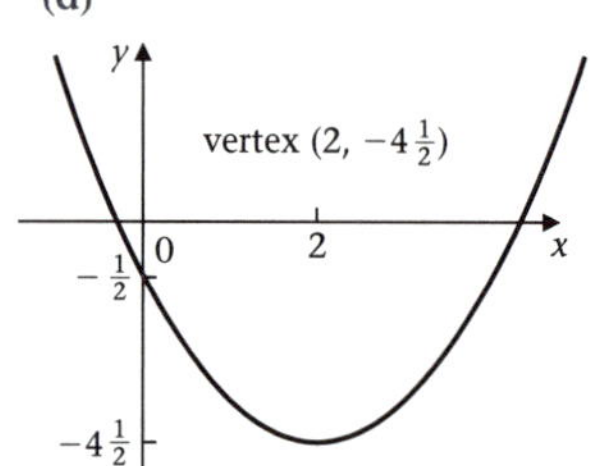

2 (a) A horizontal translation of 6 units in the negative x-direction.
(b) A horizontal translation of 4 units in the positive x-direction followed by a vertical translation of 4 units in the negative y-direction.

3 (a) (b)

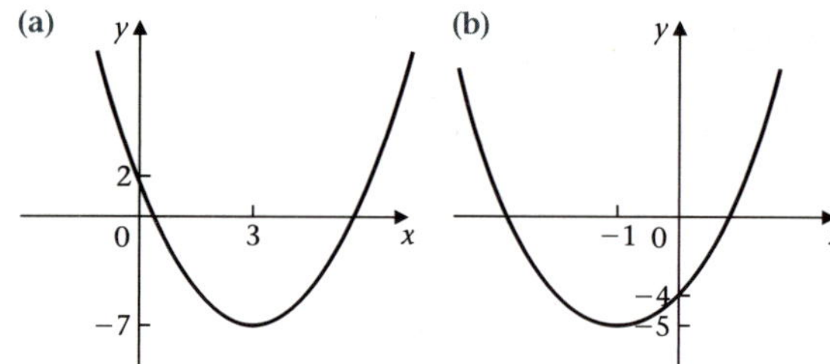

A horizontal translation of 4 units in the negative x-direction followed by a vertical translation of 2 units in the positive y-direction.

4 $y = x^2 - 18x + 14$

5

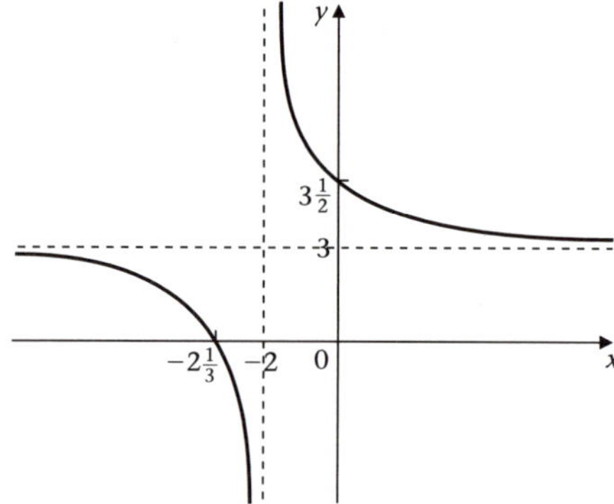

Exercise 25G

1 (a) $f(-x) = x^2 + 2x$
(b)

(c)

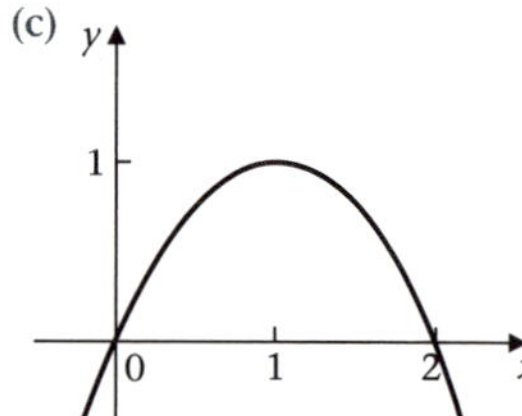

(d) (1,1)

2 (a) $y = -x^3 - 2x^2$
(b) $y = -x^3 + 2x^2$

3 (b)

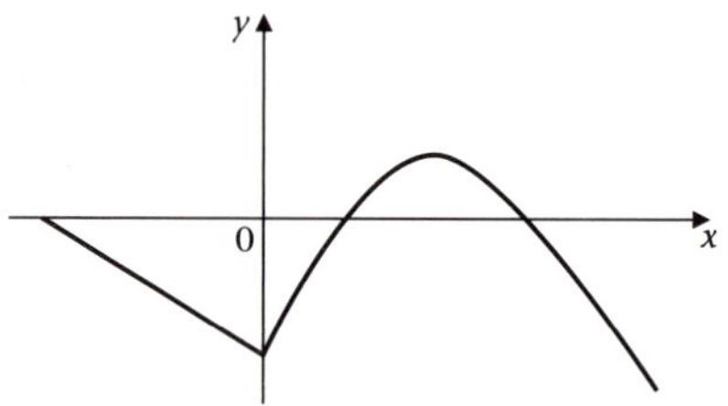

(c) Reflection in the x-axis.

4 (b)

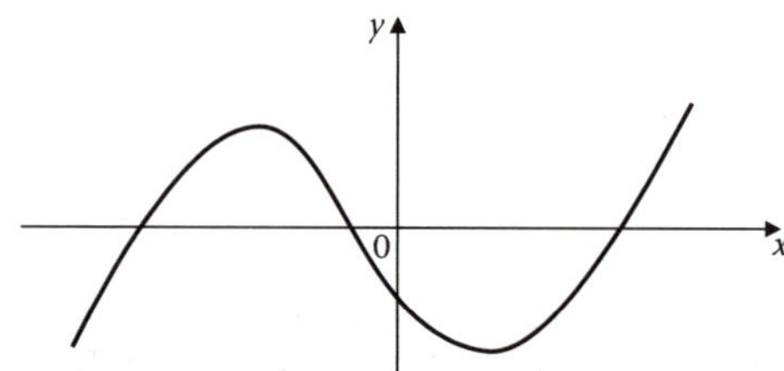

(c) Reflection in the y-axis.

Exercise 25H

1 (a) Reflection in x-axis then a vertical translation of 6 units in the positive y-direction.

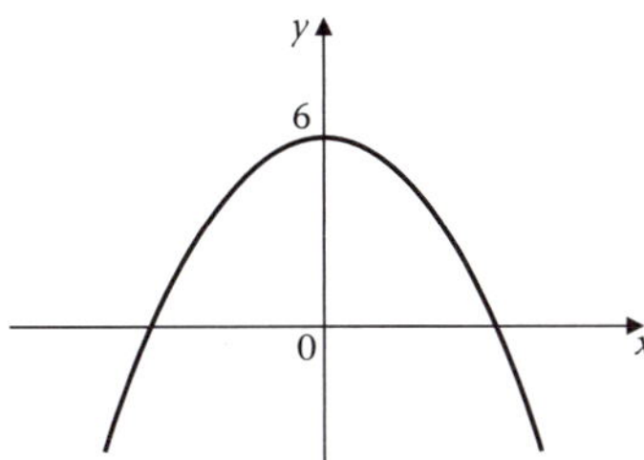

(b) Horizontal translation of 4 units in the positive x-direction then a vertical translation of 2 units in the positive y-direction.

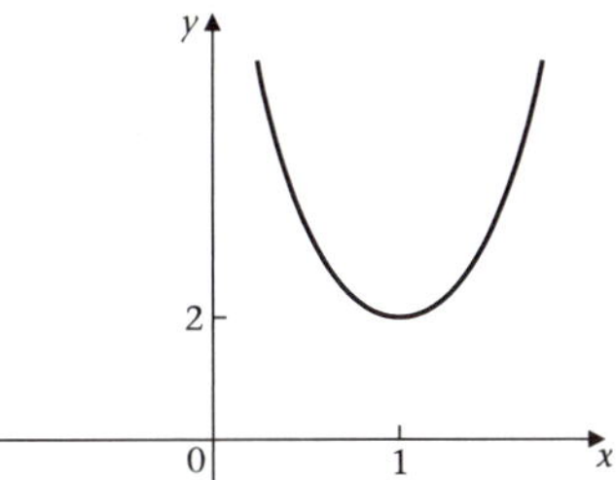

(c) Horizontal translation of 2 units in the positive x-direction then a reflection in x-axis then a vertical translation of 1 unit in the positive y-direction.

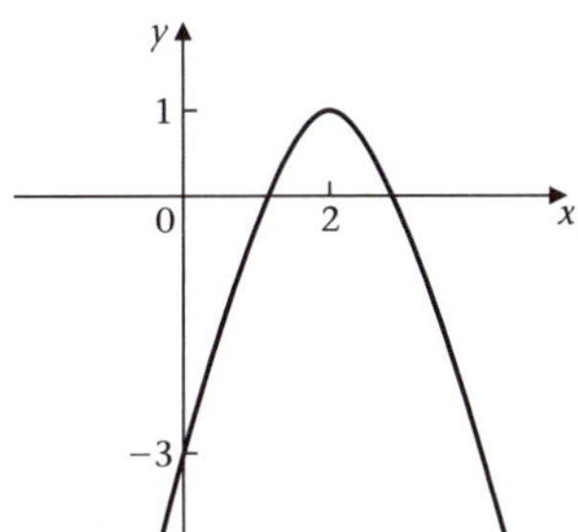

Exercise 25I

1 (a) Horizontal translation of 1 unit in the negative x-direction then a stretch scale factor 2 parallel to the y-axis then a vertical translation of 3 units in the negative y-direction.

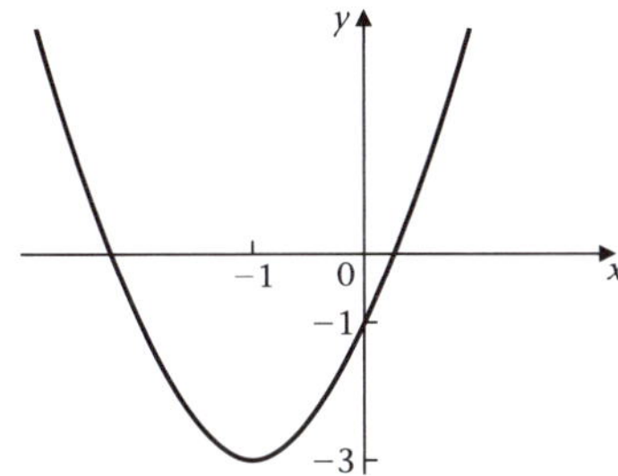

(b) Horizontal translation of 2 units in the positive x-direction then a stretch scale factor 3 parallel to the y-axis then a vertical translation of 10 units in the negative y-direction.

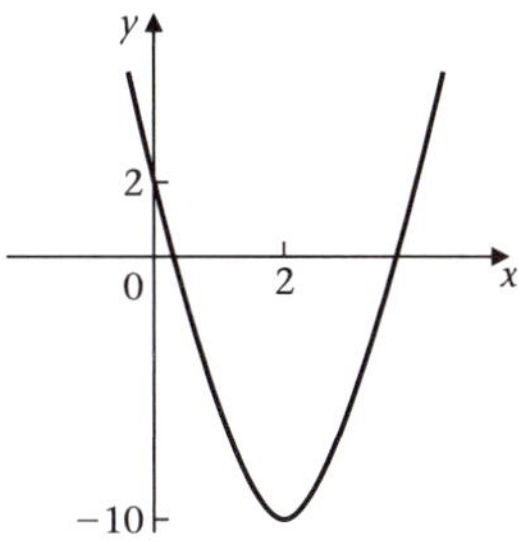

(c) Horizontal translation of 2 units in the positive x-direction then a vertical translation of 2 units in the negative y-direction

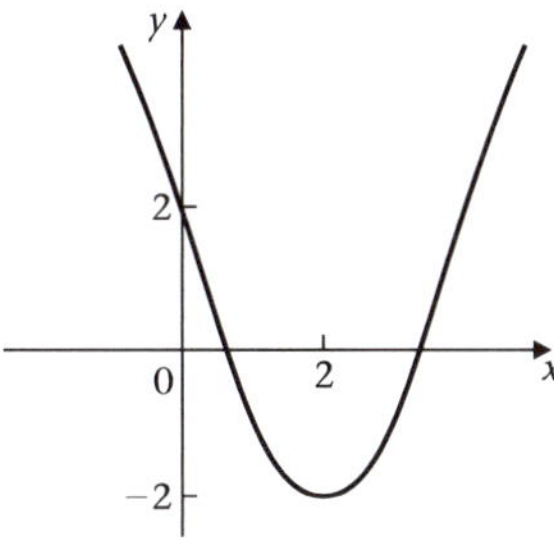

2 (a) Horizontal translation of 2 units in the negative x-direction then a stretch scale factor 4 parallel to the y-axis.

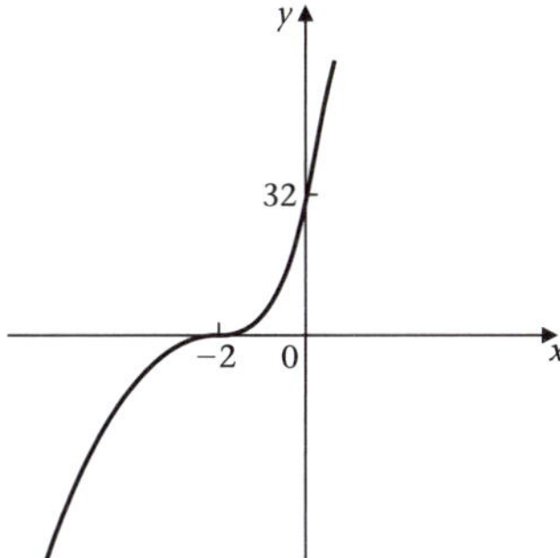

(b) Reflection in the x-axis then a vertical translation of 8 units in the positive y-direction.

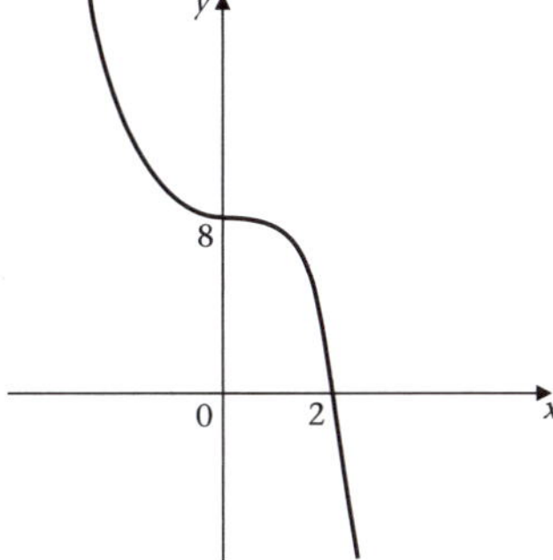

(c) Horizontal translation of 1 unit in the positive x-direction then a vertical translation of 5 units in the positive y-direction.

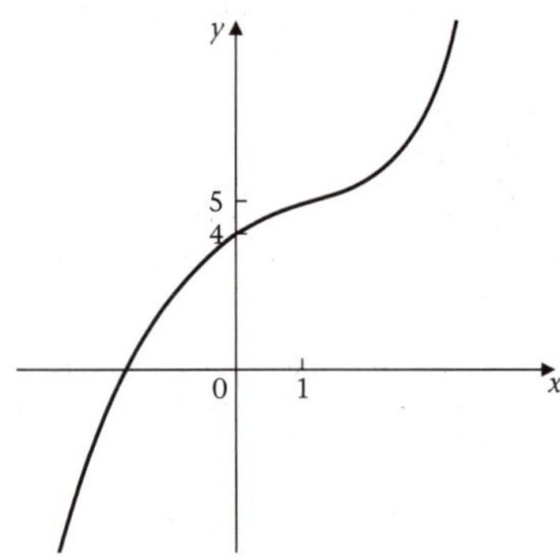

(d) Stretch scale factor 0.5 parallel to the x-axis then a vertical translation of 8 units in the negative y-direction.

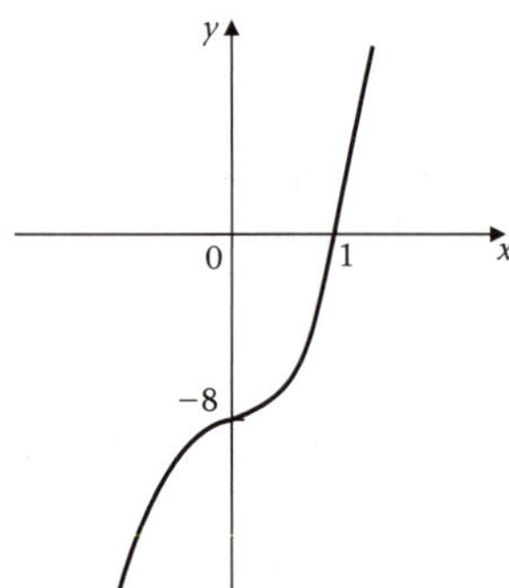

3 (a) Horizontal translation of 1 unit in the negative x-direction.
(b) Horizontal translation of 4 units in the negative x-direction, or a reflection in the y-axis.
(c) Reflection in the x-axis then a vertical translation of 2 units in the positive y-direction.

Exercise 25J

1 $\sin(x + 90°) = \cos x$
2 (a) Stretch scale factor 0.5 parallel to the x-axis.
(b)

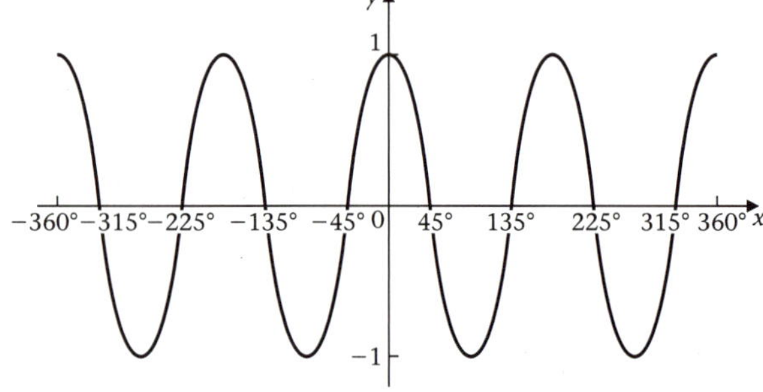

(c) 8
3 (a) Stretch scale factor 2 parallel to the y-axis.
(b)

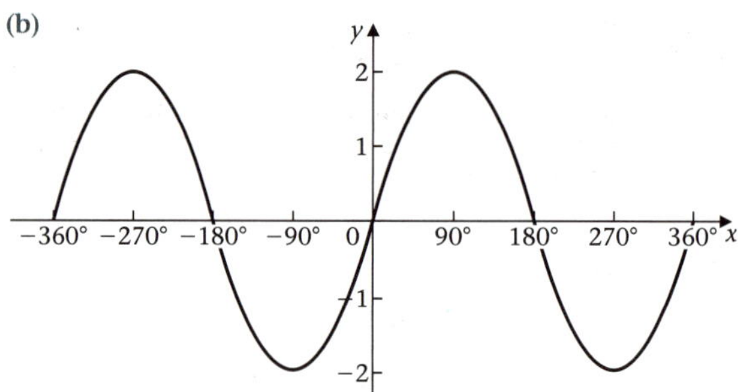

(c) 4
(d) 8
4 (a)

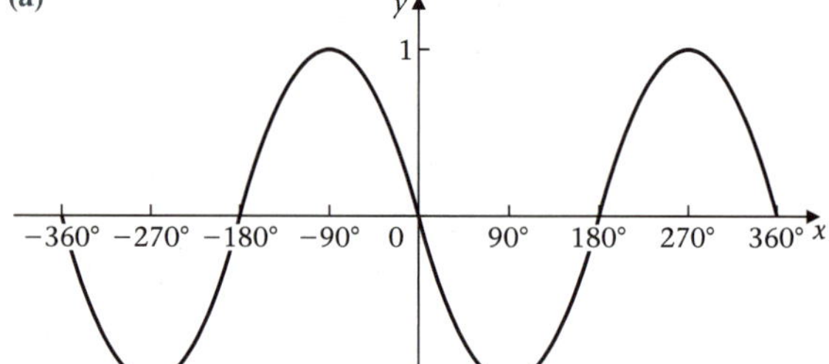

(b) Same graph for both $y = f(-x)$ and $y = -f(x)$.
5 (a) greatest: 5, lowest: −5
(b) greatest: 1, lowest: −1
(c) greatest: 1, lowest: −1
(d) greatest: 2, lowest: −2
(e) greatest: 9, lowest: 3

Mixed exercise 25

1 (a) (i) $y = \sin x + 1$ (ii) $y = 2\sin x$
(b) Horizontal stretch with scale factor $\frac{1}{2}$, vertical stretch with scale factor 3
2 (a) $a = 2, b = -1$
(b) 0°, 233°, 360°, 593°, 720°
(c) 3
3 (a) (i) (5, −4) (ii) (2, −9) (iii) (2, 4) (iv) (1, −4)
(b) $f(x) = x^2 - 4x$
4 (a) (1, 6) (b) (3, 10) (c) (3, −6)
5 (a) (i) (4, − 25) (ii) (2, − 3) (iii) (1, − 25)
(b) $a = 1, b = 9$

Chapter 26 Circle theorems

Exercise 26A

1 38°
2 (a) 66° (b) 24°
3 (a) 34° (b) 17°

Exercise 26B

1 (a) 56° (b) 34°
2 (a) 34° (b) 56° (c) 68° (d) 68° (e) 22°
3 (a) $a = 36°, b = 36°, c = 108°, d = 36°$
4 (a) $P\hat{Q}R = 90°$ (b) $Q\hat{R}P = 47°$
5 (a) $A\hat{D}E = 78°$ (b) $A\hat{B}C = 78°$
(c) $D\hat{C}B = 78°$ (d) $B\hat{A}D = 102°$
6 25°, 27°
7 8.49 cm, 4.24 cm
8 82°, 8°
9 8 cm, 120 cm^2
10 32°
11 112°, 22°
12 (a) $90° - x°$ (b) $x°$
13 24 cm^2

14 70°, 70°, 40°
15 128°, 29°
16 10.6 cm
17 40°
18 6.5 m
19 The sides are chords of the circle. So, the perpendicular bisectors pass through the centre. Hence, their point of intersection is the centre.

Exercise 26C

1 angle TCB = angle OAB (alternate segment)
angle OBA = angle OAB (isosceles triangle)
angle TBC = angle TCB (equal tangents)
Since two angles are equal then the third must also be equal.
Hence triangles AOB, BTC are similar.

2 (a) P lies on the perpendicular bisector of RY
$\therefore PR = PY$ and triangle PRY is isosceles
$\therefore$ angle YPX = angle XPR.
But angle XPR = angle XSQ (angles in the same segment)
$\therefore$ angle YPX = angle XSQ
(b) angle XSZ + angle XSQ = 180° (angles on a straight line)
angle XSZ + angle YPX = 180° (from part (a))
$\therefore$ angle PZS = 360° − 180° − angle PXS = 90°

3 (a) angle BAD = angle ADC (alternate angles)
angle ABC = angle ADC (angles in the same segment)
Hence, triangle ABE is isosceles.
$\therefore$ angle AEB = 180° − 2 × angle ABE
Also, angle AEB = 180° − angle AEC (angles on a straight line)
$\therefore$ angle AEC = 2 × angle ABC
(b) Since triangle ABE is isosceles, $AE = BE$

4 Let angle $CXE = x°$ = angle AXE and angle $XCD = y°$
The angle CFX = 180° − $x°$ − $y°$ (angle sum of a triangle)
angle DFE = 180° − $x°$ − $y°$ (vertically opposite angles)
angle $XAB = y°$ (cyclic quadrilateral)
In triangle AXE, angle XEA = 180° − $x°$ − $y°$ (angle sum of a triangle)
$\therefore$ angle DFE = angle FEA

5 angle ADC = 180° – angle DAB (interior angles of parallel lines)
angle BCD = 180° – angle DAB (opposite angles of a cyclic quadrilateral)
$\therefore$ angle ADC = angle BCD

6 Join D to B and A to C.
Triangle ABD is isosceles $\therefore$ angle ABD = angle ADB
angle ABD = angle ACD (angles in the same segment)
angle ADB = angle ACB (angles in the same segment)
$\therefore$ angle ACD = angle ACB
$\therefore AC$ bisects angle BCD.

7 Join A to E
angle AEC + angle ABC = 180° (cyclic quadrilateral)
angle AEC + angle AED = 180° (angles on a straight line)
$\therefore$ angle ABC = angle AED.
But angle ABC = angle ADC (opposite angles of a parallelogram)
$\therefore$ angle ADC = angle AED
$\therefore AE = AD$ (isosceles triangle)

8 Let angle CDF = angle $FDE = x°$
angle CBF = angle $CDF = x°$ (angles in the same segment)
angle CBA = 180° – angle CDA (cyclic quadrilateral)
angle CDE = 180° – angle CDA (straight line)
$\therefore$ angle $CBA = 2x°$
$\therefore FB$ bisects angle ABC

9 Join F to D. Let angle DAF = angle $FAB = x°$
Then angle AED = angle $EAB = x°$ (alternate angles)
angle AFD = 90° (angle in a semi-circle)
Hence FD is a line symmetry of triangle AED $\therefore AF = FE$

10 angle COA = 2 × angle CBA (angle at the centre)
= 4 × angle TBA
But angle TBA = angle ATP (alternate segment)
$\therefore$ angle COA = 4 × angle ATP

Mixed exercise 26

1 (a) 8 cm (b) 10.4 cm
2 $A\hat{D}C$, $B\hat{C}D$, $D\hat{A}B$
3 103°
4 (a) 90° (b) 35° (c) 125°
5 (a) 21° (b) 53° (c) 68°
6 26°
7 41°, 49°
8 30 cm, 36 cm
9 (a) 86° (b) 52° (c) 52°
10 $(1 + \sqrt{2})r$
11 101°, 63°
12 (a) 60° (b) 90° (c) 30° (d) 90°
(e) 30° AC = 6.93 cm
13 (a) 47° (b) 43° (c) 25°
14 (a) 70° (b) 35° (c) 2.11 cm
15 (a) Two tangents from the same point are equal, so $PY = PA$ and $PX = PA$. So $PY = PX$, meaning that P is the midpoint of XY and PA is a bisector.
(b) As PX, PY and PA are all equal, they are all radii of a circle centre P. XY is a diameter of this circle, so angle XAY must equal 90°.
16 (a) 52° (b) 47° (c) 81°
(d) $D\hat{A}B$ = 180° − 47° − 52° (angles on a straight line)
= 81°
$\therefore D\hat{A}B = C\hat{B}A$ and EAB is isosceles
$\therefore EA = EB$
17 53°
18 (a) 70°, 40° (b) $B\hat{A}C = B\hat{C}A$ = 70°
(c) In $\triangle PBR$ and $\triangle ACR$
$P\hat{B}R = C\hat{A}R$ (angles in same segment)
$B\hat{P}R = R\hat{C}A$ (angles in same segment)
$P\hat{R}B = C\hat{R}A$ (vertically opposite)
$\triangle PBR$ is similar to $\triangle CAR$
19 1.23 cm
20 (a) The altitudes meet at a point.
(b) Angle $BHD = 90° - y$. Join B to C so that BC cuts AD at K. BC subtends 90° at F and at E, so is the diameter of a circle through $FBCE$.
Angle $EFC = y$ (angles in the same segment: EH)
Angle $EBC = y$ (angles in the same segment: EC)
From $\triangle BHK$:
Angle BKH = 180° − angle BHD − angle HBK
= 180° − (90° − y) − y
= 90°
(c) BE, CF are altitudes of ABC, meeting at H.
AK also goes through H so is the third altitude.
So AK is perpendicular to BC.

Chapter 27 Vectors

Exercise 27A

1 (a) $\begin{pmatrix}-2\\-1\end{pmatrix}$ (b) $\begin{pmatrix}-3\\-5\end{pmatrix}$ (c) $\begin{pmatrix}5\\6\end{pmatrix}$ (d) $\begin{pmatrix}-5\\-6\end{pmatrix}$
2 (0, −2)
3 (a) Translation by $\begin{pmatrix}6\\0\end{pmatrix}$ (b) Translation by $\begin{pmatrix}2b-2a\\0\end{pmatrix}$
4 (a) $\begin{pmatrix}4\\-2\end{pmatrix}$ (b) (6, 1)
(c) $\overrightarrow{AB} = \begin{pmatrix}5-2\\7-3\end{pmatrix} = \begin{pmatrix}3\\4\end{pmatrix}$ $\overrightarrow{DC} = \begin{pmatrix}9-6\\5-1\end{pmatrix} = \begin{pmatrix}3\\4\end{pmatrix}$

Exercise 27B

1 (a) $\begin{pmatrix}9\\3\end{pmatrix}$ (b) $\begin{pmatrix}15\\5\end{pmatrix}$ (c) $\begin{pmatrix}-6\\-2\end{pmatrix}$ (d) $\begin{pmatrix}-3\\-1\end{pmatrix}$ (e) $\begin{pmatrix}3k\\k\end{pmatrix}$
2 (a) $\mathbf{2b}$ (b) $\mathbf{a + b}$ (c) $\mathbf{a + 2b}$
3 $\overrightarrow{AC} = \begin{pmatrix}6\\1\end{pmatrix}$

4 (a) $\overrightarrow{AD} = \begin{pmatrix}-2\\3\end{pmatrix}$

(b) $\overrightarrow{AC} = \begin{pmatrix}1+2\\4-3\end{pmatrix} = \begin{pmatrix}3\\1\end{pmatrix}$

$\overrightarrow{DB} = \begin{pmatrix}--2+1\\-3+4\end{pmatrix} = \begin{pmatrix}3\\1\end{pmatrix}$

5 $\frac{3}{2}\mathbf{a} + 3\mathbf{b}$

Exercise 27C

1 (a) $\begin{pmatrix}-2\\4\end{pmatrix}$ (b) $\begin{pmatrix}4\\2\end{pmatrix}$ (c) $\begin{pmatrix}16\\-7\end{pmatrix}$ (d) $\begin{pmatrix}12\\-4\end{pmatrix}$

(e) For example, $\mathbf{c} = \begin{pmatrix}2\\3\end{pmatrix}$ or $\begin{pmatrix}-1\\0\end{pmatrix}$

3 (4, 3)

4 $\begin{pmatrix}-2\\2\end{pmatrix}$ 5 $\begin{pmatrix}1\\-1\end{pmatrix}$ 6 $\begin{pmatrix}10\\-1\end{pmatrix}$

Exercise 27D

1 (a) 5 (b) 25 (c) 10 (d) $\sqrt{170} = 13.0$

2 (a) $\sqrt{106} = 10.3$ (b) $\sqrt{18} = 4.24$

(c) $\sqrt{208} = 14.4$ (d) $\sqrt{40} = 6.32$

3 (a) $\sqrt{13} = 3.61$ (b) $2\sqrt{13} = 7.21$

(c) 10 (d) $\sqrt{26} = 5.10$

Exercise 27E

1 $p = 2$
2 $q = -2$
3 $x = 0, y = -2$
4 $p = 2.4, q = -2.2$
5 (2, 6), (3, 7), (4, 8), (5, 9) (6, 10) (7, 11). A straight line, $y = x + 4$.

6 (a) $\begin{pmatrix}6\\3\end{pmatrix}$ (b) $\begin{pmatrix}6\\3\end{pmatrix} + k\begin{pmatrix}-2\\2\end{pmatrix} = \begin{pmatrix}6-2k\\3+2k\end{pmatrix}$

(c) $k = 3$, $D = (2, 10)$

Exercise 27F

1 $\begin{pmatrix}2\\4\end{pmatrix}$ 2 (4, 0)

3 (5, 9) 4 $\begin{pmatrix}3\\5\end{pmatrix}$, $\begin{pmatrix}4\\4\end{pmatrix}$

Exercise 27G

1 $\mathbf{y} - \mathbf{x}$. XY is parallel to AB and $\frac{2}{3}$ of the length of AB.
2 $\mathbf{b} - \mathbf{a}$. $3\mathbf{b} - 3\mathbf{a}$. CD is parallel to AB and 3 times the length of AB.
3 (a) $\frac{1}{3}(\mathbf{a} + \mathbf{b})$ (b) $\frac{1}{3}(\mathbf{a} + \mathbf{b})$. G and H are the same point.
(c) $\frac{1}{2}\mathbf{b}$
4 (c) $k = \frac{1}{3}$, $m = \frac{1}{3}$, $\frac{4}{3}\mathbf{a} + \frac{1}{3}\mathbf{b}$
5 e.g. $\overrightarrow{OA} = 3\mathbf{a}$, $\overrightarrow{OC} = 3\mathbf{b}$. $\overrightarrow{PQ} = 2\mathbf{a} + \mathbf{b}$, $\overrightarrow{SR} = \mathbf{b} + 2\mathbf{a}$. $PQRS$ is a parallelogram. No longer true.
6 (a) $\mathbf{b} - \mathbf{a}$ (b) $-\mathbf{b}$ (c) $-\mathbf{b} - \mathbf{a}$
(b) Midpoints are $\frac{1}{2}(\mathbf{a} + \mathbf{b})$, $\frac{1}{2}(2\mathbf{a} - \mathbf{b})$, $\frac{1}{2}(\mathbf{a} - 2\mathbf{b})$, $-\frac{1}{2}(\mathbf{a} + \mathbf{b})$, $\frac{1}{2}(\mathbf{b} - 2\mathbf{a})$, $\frac{1}{2}(2\mathbf{b} - \mathbf{a})$
The third hexagon is an enlargement, scale factor 0.75, centre O, of the first hexagon.

Mixed exercise 27

1 (a) $\begin{pmatrix}5\\1\end{pmatrix}$ (b) $\begin{pmatrix}-5\\-1\end{pmatrix}$ (c) $\begin{pmatrix}-1\\-5\end{pmatrix}$ (d) $\begin{pmatrix}1\\5\end{pmatrix}$

2 (a) $\begin{pmatrix}5\\1\end{pmatrix}$ (b) $\begin{pmatrix}2\\3\end{pmatrix}$ (c) $\begin{pmatrix}7\\4\end{pmatrix}$

(d) $\begin{pmatrix}3\\-2\end{pmatrix}$ (e) $\begin{pmatrix}10\\2\end{pmatrix}$ (f) $\begin{pmatrix}-3\\2\end{pmatrix}$

3 $\begin{pmatrix}3\\-2\end{pmatrix}$, $\begin{pmatrix}1.5\\-1\end{pmatrix}$ 4 $\begin{pmatrix}3\\5\end{pmatrix}$ 5 $\begin{pmatrix}-1\\-7\end{pmatrix}$

6 (a) $\begin{pmatrix}3\\0\end{pmatrix}$ (b) $\begin{pmatrix}1\\2\end{pmatrix}$

7 $\begin{pmatrix}10\\1\end{pmatrix}$ 8 $x = 3$ $y = 3$

9 $a = 1, b = 1$ 10 $p = 1, q = \frac{1}{2}$
11 (a) $\mathbf{a} + \mathbf{b}$ (b) $-\mathbf{b}$ (c) $\mathbf{a} - \mathbf{b}$
12 (a) $\frac{3}{5}\mathbf{b}$ (b) $a - \mathbf{b}$ (c) $\frac{3}{5}\mathbf{a} - \frac{3}{5}\mathbf{b}$ (d) $\frac{3}{5}\mathbf{a}$
CD is parallel to OA and $\frac{3}{5}$ of the length of OA.
13 (a) $\mathbf{a} + \mathbf{b}$ (b) $2\mathbf{b}$, $\mathbf{a} + \mathbf{b} + \mathbf{c}$ (c) $\mathbf{a} + \mathbf{c} = \mathbf{b}$
14 $\overrightarrow{DA} = 4\mathbf{a} - 2\mathbf{b}$
$\overrightarrow{PQ} = -\mathbf{a} + 2\mathbf{b} - (2\mathbf{a} - \mathbf{b}) = 2\mathbf{a}$
$\overrightarrow{SR} = 2\mathbf{a} - \mathbf{b} + \mathbf{b} = 2\mathbf{a}$
Thus PQ has equal length and is parallel to SR and $PQRS$ is a parallelogram.
15 (a) $\mathbf{b} - \mathbf{a}$ (b) $\frac{1}{2}\mathbf{b}$ (c) $\mathbf{c} - \mathbf{a}$
(d) $\frac{1}{2}(\mathbf{c} - \mathbf{a})$ (e) $\frac{1}{2}(\mathbf{a} + \mathbf{c})$ (f) $\frac{1}{2}(\mathbf{a} + \mathbf{c}) - \frac{1}{2}\mathbf{b}$
16 (a) $\frac{3}{2}\mathbf{a}$ (b) $3\mathbf{b}$ (c) $\frac{3}{2}\mathbf{a} - 3\mathbf{b}$
(d) $\overrightarrow{OZ} = \overrightarrow{OY} + p\overrightarrow{YX} = 3\mathbf{b} + p(\frac{3}{2}\mathbf{a} - 3\mathbf{b})$
$\overrightarrow{OZ} = \overrightarrow{OB} + q\overrightarrow{BA} = \mathbf{b} + q(\mathbf{a} - \mathbf{b})$
$\overrightarrow{OZ} = 2\mathbf{a} - \mathbf{b}$
17 $x = 4, y = -3$

Chapter 28 Introducing modelling

Exercise 28A

1 (a) £$1500(1.06)^t$ (b) 16 years
2 (a) $8(0.6)^n$ metres (b) 23.36 metres
3 (a) 48 days (b) 96 days
4 (a) (i) £32 000 (ii) £16 384 (iii) £$40000(0.8)^n$
(b) 27 years

Exercise 28B

1 (a) (i) 6.5 m (ii) 5.25 m (iii) 4 m (iv) 1.5 m
(v) 6.5 m
(b) 1.14 pm (c)

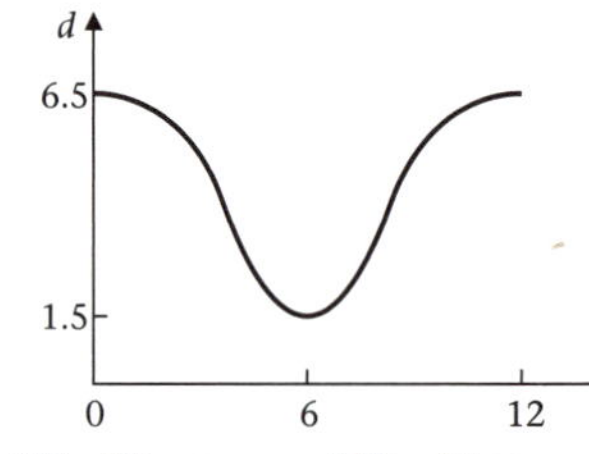

2 (a) (i) 15 cm (ii) 20 cm (iii) 10 cm
(b)

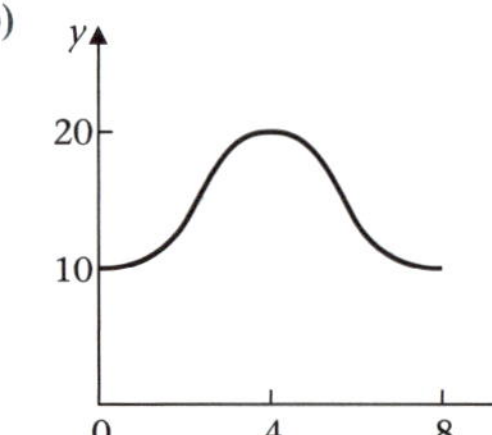

3 (a) (i) 7.5 m (ii) 6 m
(b) 3 m (c) 3 am, 3 pm
(d)

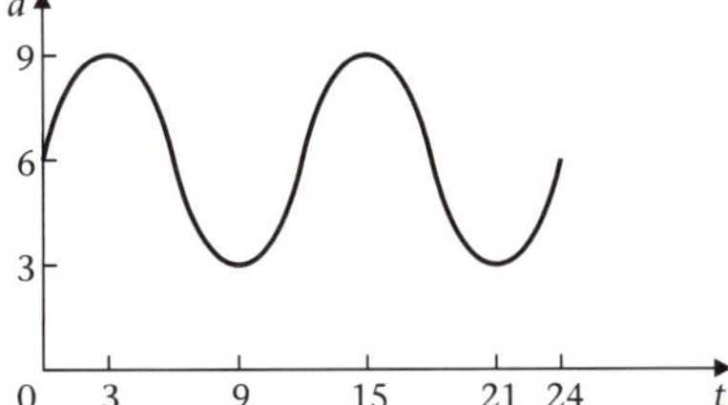

4 (a) $p = 9, q = 8$
(b) $3\frac{1}{3}$ sec, $16\frac{2}{3}$ sec, $23\frac{1}{3}$ sec
(c) $6\frac{2}{3}$ sec, $13\frac{1}{3}$ sec, $26\frac{2}{3}$ sec
(d)

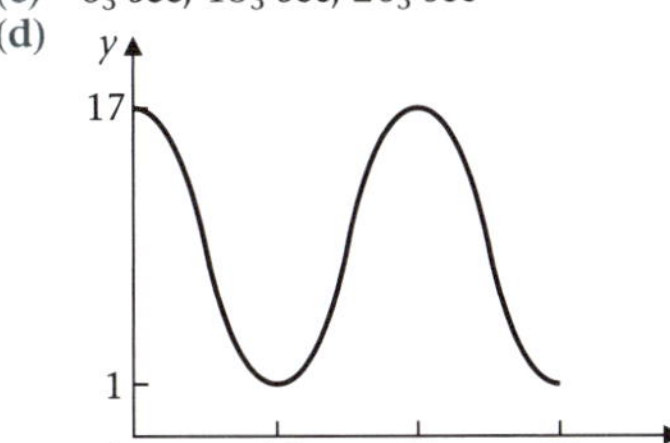

Exercise 28C

1 (a) $y = 0.25x + 2.5$ (b) 14.5
2 (a) $y = -0.25x + 0.75$ (b) -3.75
3 (a) $y = \frac{14}{15}x + \frac{46}{3}$ (b) $85\frac{1}{3}$

Exercise 28D

(The following answers are estimates from a line of best fit. Your answers may therefore differ slightly and still be correct.)

1 $a = 0.28, b = 5$
2 $a = 2, b = 1$
3 $a = -0.2, b = 7.2$
4 $a = 2, b = 0.2$
5 $a = -0.5, b = 3$
6 $a = -0.5, b = 6$

Exercise 28E

1 $p = 2, q = 4, k = 32$
2 $p = -3, q = 2, k = 6$
3 $a = 3, b = 4, k = 67$
4 $\frac{1}{3}$
5 $\frac{2}{3}$ and $-\frac{2}{3}$
6 $a = 4, b = 3, k = \frac{37}{9}$
7 $\frac{1}{2}$
8 (a) $p = 2, q = 4$
(b) 3

Chapter 29 Conditional probability

Exercise 29A

1 (a) 0 (b) $\frac{2}{7}$ (c) $\frac{5}{7}$ (d) $\frac{1}{7}$
2 (a) $\frac{5}{42}$ (b) $\frac{1}{21}$ (c) $\frac{20}{21}$
3 $\frac{17}{24}$
4 (a) $\frac{89}{110}$ (b) $\frac{21}{110}$
5 (a) $\frac{1}{12}$ (b) $\frac{1}{12}$ (c) $\frac{1}{4}$

Exercise 29B

1 $\frac{421}{455}$
2 (a) $\frac{1197}{2990}$ (b) $\frac{1793}{2990}$
3 (a) (i) $\frac{2}{35}$ (ii) $\frac{2}{35}$ (iii) $\frac{2}{35}$ (b) $\frac{12}{35}$
4 $\frac{3}{10}$
5 (a) $\frac{1}{5}$ (b) $\frac{2}{5}$ (c) $\frac{3}{5}$

Exercise 29C

1 (a) (i) 0.00015 (ii) 0.99985
(b) The probabilities of a dart landing in treble 20 when the first or second miss are unknown.
2 0.999 3 0.79
4 (a) 0.56 (b) 0.18 (c) 0.26
5 0.7625
6 (a) $\frac{7}{22}$ (b) $\frac{28}{33}$
7 0.0315

Mixed exercise 29

1 (a) $\frac{1}{7}$ (b) $\frac{4}{7}$
2 (a) $\frac{1}{36}$ (b) $\frac{7}{18}$ (c) $\frac{11}{18}$
3 (a) 0.28 (b) 0.42 (c) 0.7
4 $\frac{17}{24}$
5 $\frac{35}{76}$
6 (a) $\frac{4}{91}$ (b) $\frac{12}{65}$ (c) $\frac{53}{65}$
7 $\frac{3}{20}$
8 $\frac{9}{28}$
9 (a) $\frac{1}{21}$ (b) $\frac{5}{84}$ (c) $\frac{1}{7}$
10 $\frac{173}{420}$

Examination practice paper: Non-calculator

1 90 g zinc, 45 g iron, 15 g copper
2 £587.50
3 (a) $12pq$ (b) $y^2 + 2y$ (c) $x(x - 5)$
4 (a) £480 (b) 80%
5
6 (a)
(b)

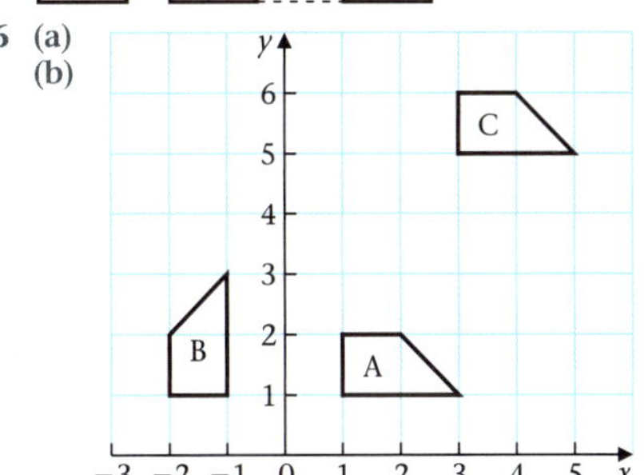

(c) Rotation, 90° clockwise about (3, 1)

7 (a)

0	7, 7, 8
1	0, 0, 0, 1, 1, 2, 2, 3, 5, 5, 6, 7, 9, 9
2	0, 1, 1, 1, 3, 4, 4, 6, 7
3	0, 1, 2, 3

Key: 2 | 1 means 21

(b) 18 marks

8 $\frac{3}{16}$

9 (a) $x \leqslant \frac{1}{3}$ (b) 0
10 e.g. $\frac{20 \times 60}{0.5} = 2400$
11 4.5
12 (a) $\frac{15}{16}$ (b) 9
13 528 cm^2
14 (a) 19 (b) £93 000 (c) £65 000
15 (a) 4×10^8 (b) 2.4×10^{11}
16 (a) 90° (b) 26° (c) 52°
17 (a) $y = -6, 0, -6, -10, -6, 12$
(b)

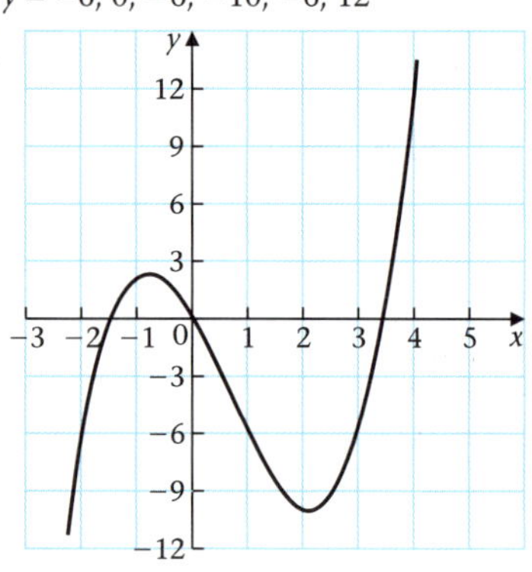

(c) −1.5, 0, 3.5
18 (a) (i) 1 (ii) $\frac{1}{64}$ (iii) 4
(b) $\sqrt{3}$
19 (a) Frequency: 20, 35, 25, 15, 5
(b)

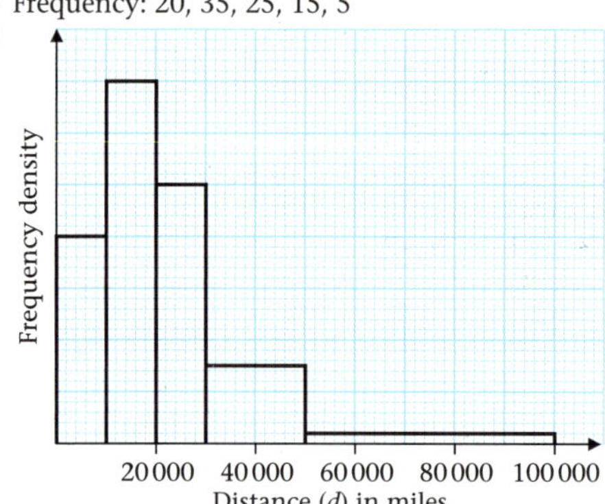

20 (a) $y = \frac{100}{x^2}$ (b) $\frac{1}{2}$
21 $y = 3x + 2$
22 $x^2 + (x+1)^2 = x^2 + x^2 + 2x + 1$
$= 2(x^2 + x) + 1$
1 more than an even number is an odd number.
23 $LR = PR$ (sides of a square)
$QR = SR$ (sides of a square)
$L\hat{R}Q = 90° + P\hat{R}Q$
$P\hat{R}S = 90° + P\hat{R}Q = L\hat{R}Q$
LQR and PRS are congruent (SAS)
24 $x = \frac{a^2 + b^2}{a - b}$
25 (a) 8π cm (b) 96π cm^2

Examination practice paper: Calculator

1 2.122 107 214
2 £136
3 £2.05
4 (a) 3.995 (b) 7.5
5 $5n - 1$
6 59 m^2
7 (a) (i) 75° (ii) 54° (b) 4 cm
8 £578.81
9 49.38°
10 (a)

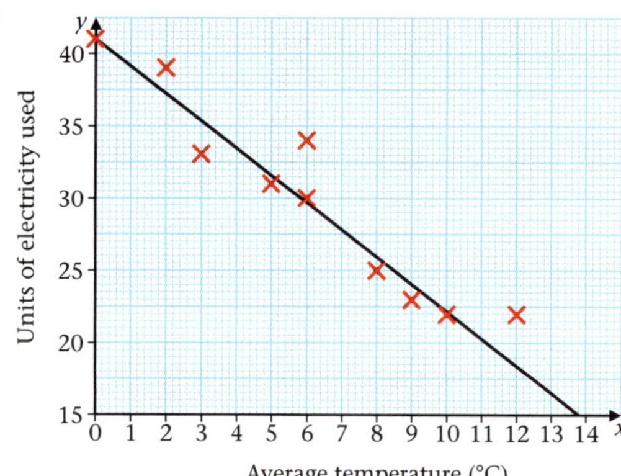

(b) (i) 3°C (ii) 27.5 units
11 4.86
12 (a) £9800
(b) £5171.77
13 12 mm
14 £445
15 (a) $y = 0.4$ (b) $\frac{5x + 11}{(3x - 1)(x + 6)}$
(c) $(2x + 7)(x - 2)$
16 1817 kg or 1.817 tonnes
17 (a) A = area of base + area of 4 sides
$= x^2 + 4hx$
(b) $h = \frac{A - x^2}{4x}$
(c) 4 cm
(d) 5.66
18 (a) (i)

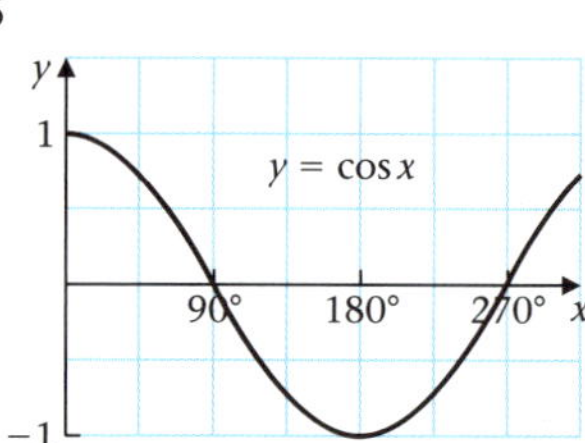

(ii)

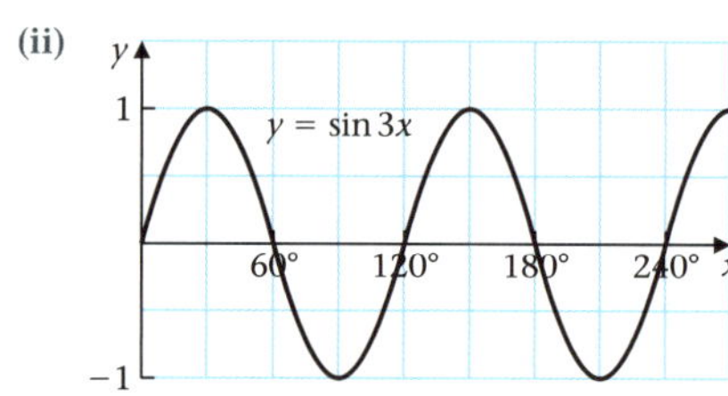

(b) $x = 80°$ or $x = 100°$
19 (a) 650 cm^3 (b) 400 cm^2 (c) 400 cm^2
20 The lower bound for the length is 67.5 cm and for the width is 8.35 cm
So the lower bound for the area is 67.5×8.35 cm^2
$= 563.625$ cm^2
21 If $y = ax + b$ is a tangent to the circle, then $x^2 + (ax + b)^2 = 64$ has only one solution, so is a perfect square.
$(a^2 + 1)x^2 + 2abx + (b^2 - 64) = 0$ is a perfect square
So $\sqrt{(a^2 + 1)} \times \sqrt{(b^2 - 64)} = ab$
$\therefore (a^2 + 1)(b^2 - 64) = a^2 b^2$
$a^2 b^2 - 64a^2 + b^2 - 64 = a^2 b^2$
Rearranging gives $b^2 = 64(a^2 + 1)$
$a^2 + 1 = \frac{b^2}{64}$
22 $\frac{19}{66}$

Index to Books 1 and 2

You can find pages 1–290 in Book 1.